Digital Elevation Model Technologies and Applications: The DEM Users Manual, 2nd Edition

Edited by David F. Maune, PhD, CP

The American Society for Photogrammetry and Remote Sensing
Bethesda, Maryland

asprs

THE IMAGING & GEOSPATIAL INFORMATION SOCIETY

FOREWORD

The 1st edition of this manual, published in 2001, answered such fundamental questions as "What's a DEM? What's a TIN? What's the difference between a DEM, DTM and DSM? What is a hydro-enforced DEM? What DEM technology is best for my needs? How do I know what to ask for to ensure these needs are satisfied? How do I determine that I received the quality data I paid for? Why can't we just refer to *contour intervals* like we used to? Why isn't there a simple checklist – like a DEM *menu* – for me to choose what I need? How can I understand the acronyms, terminology, and accuracy standards that seem so confusing?"

The 1st edition answered all such questions and many more, but this 2nd edition is much better, not only updating the original chapters, but adding new chapters, new subjects, and digital datasets on a DVD for users and students to visualize and "play with" actual data on their own computers.

As Editor and principal author of many chapters in both editions, I am thrilled with the enthusiastic response from readers, and by the willingness of authors to volunteer their time to update this manual as a labor of love. The following summarizes the major focus of each chapter and major changes between the 1st and 2nd editions:

- Chapter 1 (Introduction) explains DEM terminology, presents a tutorial on 3-D surface concepts, and provides an introduction to tides. It is important for DEM users to understand the concepts of mass points and breaklines, triangulated irregular networks (TINs), how uniformly-spaced DEMs are produced from mass points and breaklines (or from TINs), and the impact of tides on DEM data in coastal areas. It is also important for DEM users to understand the differences between digital surface models (DSMs) and digital terrain models (DTMs). Whereas DEMs are often synonymous with DTMs, the "DEM umbrella" includes bathymetric DEMs and irregularly spaced mass points and breaklines, TINs, digital contours, and other forms of digital elevation data. This 2nd edition has improved information on breaklines, contours, hydrologic enforcement and hydrologic conditioning, and the latest 18.6-year National Tidal Datum Epoch (NTDE) from 1983-2001.

- Chapter 2 (Vertical Datums) explains why there are so many vertical datums used in the United States and why the "official" North American Vertical Datum of 1988 (NAVD 88) is normally the only one that ought to be used for topographic applications. It also explains the different tidal datums and how they are used. It is essential that DEM users understand what the *geoid* is, the difference between ellipsoid heights and orthometric heights, and reasons why DEM users should not combine data sets that are referenced to different datums.

- Chapter 3 (Accuracy Standards and Guidelines) explains the National Standard for Spatial Data Accuracy (NSSDA) and compares it with the traditional National Map Accuracy Standard (NMAS) published in 1947, as well as the ASPRS Standard for Large Scale Maps published in 1990 (ASPRS 90), both of which were replaced by the NSSDA. Chapter 3 also explains the relevant standards for hydrographic surveys. This 2nd edition includes the new National Ocean Service "Hydrographic Surveys Specifications and Deliverables;" the new Appendix A, *Aerial Mapping and*

Surveying, to FEMA's "Guidelines and Specifications for Flood Hazard Mapping Partners;" the National Digital Elevation Program (NDEP) "Guidelines for Digital Elevation Data;" and the "ASPRS Guidelines, Vertical Accuracy Reporting for Lidar Data." If you don't know the meanings of Fundamental Vertical Accuracy (FVA), Consolidated Vertical Accuracy (CVA) and Supplemental Vertical Accuracy (SVA), Chapter 3 explains what you need to know.

- Chapter 4 (National Elevation Dataset) explains the NED which includes the best available standard DEMs produced and/or distributed nationwide by USGS, comprising the elevation layer of *The National Map*. NED data are available to the public at minimal cost, and all users are encouraged to share their data sets with the NED which places DEM data in the public domain. This 2nd edition does a better job explaining the three NED resolution layers available, and how such data can be obtained by the public. Samples of NED data are provided on the DVD included with this 2nd edition.

- Chapter 5 (Photogrammetry) has been rewritten to incorporate the latest information from the Fifth Edition of the *Manual of Photogrammetry* published by ASPRS. In addition to film cameras, it addresses the latest airborne digital systems and satellite imagery. For production of digital elevation data, it addresses planning considerations, georeferencing and aerotriangulation, photogrammetric data collection methods, post processing, quality control, data deliverables, supporting technologies, calibration procedures, capabilities and limitations compared with competing/complementary technologies, user applications, cost considerations, and technological advancements for the future.

- Chapter 6 (IFSAR) explains the capabilities and limitations of Interferometric Synthetic Aperture Radar, both airborne and spaceborne. This technology sees through clouds and is less weather dependent that others, and it also acquires elevation data sets of large areas at relatively low costs. It is important that DEM users understand that elevations derived from x-band IFSAR are initially the elevations of top surfaces (treetops and rooftops) and not the bare-earth terrain, so if you need DSMs of large areas, this technology may be best for you. DTMs can be produced from IFSAR DSMs, and a sample IFSAR data set, including an orthorectified radar image, is included on the DVD accompanying this 2nd edition.

- Chapter 7 (Topographic and Terrestrial Lidar) is improved significantly from the 1st edition, especially in describing different laser systems and how they work, modern sensors with very high pulse repetition rates, and explaining what a lidar *point cloud* is. This 2nd edition includes entirely new sections on lidargrammetry and ground-based lidar (terrestrial laser scanning) for which there are nearly 2000 systems in use world wide today, providing high resolution scanned images of infrastructure so detailed that every pixel has its own 3-D coordinate. Sample lidar datasets are provided on the DVD included with this 2nd edition, including topographic and terrestrial lidar fly-throughs.

- Chapter 8 (Airborne Lidar Bathymetry) documents in detail how this rapidly emerging technology is complementary to both sonar and topographic lidar. ALB systems are able to survey the terrain above and below the water surface down to a depth limited by the clarity of the water. ALB is ideal for operations in clear water to depths of 50 meters and near the land/shore interface for a wide range of near-shore surveying and engineering applications where sonar may be limited and/or inefficient. The 2nd edition includes a considerable number of updates from the 1st edition.

- Chapter 9 (Sonar) explains the basic principles of sonar systems and compares the various kinds of sonars in use today, including vertical beam, multibeam, interferometric, and side scan sonar. It compares these technologies with competing and complementary technologies. The 2nd edition has much better graphics than the 1st

edition of this manual, helping the topographic mapping community to better understand the bathymetric and hydrographic surveying community, including their similarities and differences. The DVD accompanying this 2nd edition includes interesting examples of multibeam and side scan sonar and ancillary data.

- Chapter 10 (Enabling Technologies) supports all the technologies described in Chapters 5 through 9 and answers the question of how such high geopositioning accuracies are achievable. This chapter includes updated sections on precise Global Positioning System (GPS) positioning on rapidly-moving platforms; GPS-aided inertial navigation systems; direct georeferencing systems for airborne remote sensing; and motion sensing systems for multibeam sonar bathymetry.

- Chapter 11 (DEM User Applications) provides detailed explanations, plus numerous graphic examples, of how digital elevation data are used in innovative ways for general and coastal mapping applications; transportation applications (land, air and sea); underwater and other technical applications; military, commercial and individual applications. The 2nd edition includes a new section on coastal mapping applications (shoreline delineation, sea level rise, coastal management, coastal engineering, coastal inundation) and a new section on geological applications of digital elevation data. The DVD accompanying this 2nd edition includes an interesting 3D fly-through of a virtual city (Detroit, MI) produced from elevation data and oblique aerial imagery of that city.

- Chapter 12 (DEM Quality Assessment) has been largely re-written to address new accuracy standards and guidelines published by FEMA, NDEP and ASPRS since the 1st edition. This chapter addresses Quality Assurance/Quality Control (QA/QC) goals and definitions; quantitative procedures (with example statistics and graphics for a lidar dataset) for assessing digital elevation data accuracy in accordance with FEMA, NDEP and ASPRS guidelines and accuracy reporting consistent with NSSDA requirements; different procedures used for qualitative assessments of digital topographic data at macro and micro levels (with issues and examples); and procedures used by NOAA for quality assessment of digital hydrographic data.

- Chapter 13 (DEM User Requirements) updates the popular *User Requirements Menu* with explanations of menu choices, further explains the new accuracy standards (FVA, CVA and SVA), and provides example Statements of Work (SOWs) for users who need help in documenting requirements for digital elevation data that also satisfy requirements of FEMA Appendix A. By popular demand, the User Requirements Menu and two example SOWs are included digitally (as Word documents) on the DVD accompanying this 2nd edition.

- Chapter 14 (Lidar Processing and Software), a new chapter in the 2nd edition, explains lidar software requirements and process flow, to include data collection, raw data calibration and QA, data production of classified data, and high-level analysis of discrete features, including automated feature extraction. This chapter peers into the future with regard to lidar software and processing.

- Chapter 15 (Sample Elevation Datasets), also a new chapter, is the most exciting addition to the 2nd edition. It explains the viewer software and sample datasets on the attached DVD. Readers with a computer and DVD reader should explore the contents of the DVD and view the impressive array of sample data, including: NED data (Chapter 4), photogrammetric data (Chapter 5), IFSAR data (Chapter 6), topographic lidar data (Chapter 7), terrestrial laser scan data (Chapter 7), bathymetric lidar data (Chapter 8), and sonar data (Chapter 9). It also includes avi video fly-throughs of elevation data from multiple sources, including Pictometry imagery, topographic and terrestrial lidar. The software and various datasets on the DVD are all explained in this exciting new chapter.

It has long been my goal that this DVD be instrumental to the development of an exciting academic curriculum in which DEM technologies and applications are taught to our future industry leaders. Professors and students will not be disappointed.

I wish to thank all the chapter authors and individual contributors for their professional input and for volunteering their time to help me and ASPRS publish this important manual. I wish to thank Kim Tilley, Rae Kelley, and Matthew Austin at ASPRS headquarters for their publishing support. Individual contributors were too numerous to have all their names acknowledged for each chapter; but I thank them for their input. My wife, Mary Ellen, was a true angel in never complaining when I worked 80 hours per week, or more, to get this manual published. We have been married for 45 years, and Mary Ellen has lovingly supported my volunteer work with ASPRS since the 1960s when I first became a member. I truly believe that membership and active involvement with ASPRS is vital for anyone's career in the imaging and geospatial information profession. Mine has been long and rewarding - enhanced by my active involvement with ASPRS.

Lastly, I again want to thank the Federal Emergency Management Agency (FEMA) for giving me the opportunity, through my job at Dewberry & Davis, to serve in a leadership role for exploitation of new DEM technologies. Those who perform flood risk analyses must utilize the best elevation data possible and they must have efficient means for rapid update of hydrologic and hydraulic models used to map ever-changing flood risks. Virtually every chapter in this manual is relevant to floodmap modernization in one way or another, and I know that the geospatial community as a whole has largely benefited from initiatives taken by FEMA during the past decade.

Lastly, to students and potential DEM users who read this manual and dream of the possibilities of DEM technologies and applications - *may all your DEMs come true*!

David F. Maune, PhD., CP, Editor
January 2007

———

This 2nd edition is dedicated to the memory of two friends and colleagues, Ken Osborn and Bob Fowler, who contributed so much to the world's understanding of DEM technologies and applications. Ken was the principal author of Chapter 4, National Digital Elevation Program (NDEP), in the 1st edition of this manual; Ken passed away in March of 2004. Bob was the principal author of Chapter 7, Topographic Lidar, in the 1st edition of this manual, as well as Chapter 7, Topographic and Terrestrial Lidar, in this 2nd edition. Among Bob's final emails, before passing away in July of 2006, was his approval of the final manuscript to Chapter 7.

———

Table of Contents

Digital Elevation Model Technologies and Applications: The DEM Users Manual, 2nd Edition

Edited by David F. Maune, PhD, CP

Chapter 1

Introduction

David F. Maune, Stephen M. Kopp, Clayton A. Crawford, and Chris E. Zervas

DIGITAL ELEVATION MODELS (DEM'S)

This chapter has three basic goals:

- To explain the basic terminology used in this *DEM Users Manual* and simple DEM concepts. See also Appendix A (Acronyms) and Appendix B (Definitions).
- To explain 3-D surface modeling, especially the importance of breaklines, how elevation data are "hydrologically enforced," and explanations of ways in which gridded elevation data (uniformly-spaced) are interpolated from irregularly-spaced elevation data.
- To introduce the concept of tides as relevant to digital bathymetric/hydrographic data which are now being merged with digital topographic data.

DEM Definitions

Although Digital Elevation Data (DED) would be a more generic term for use in the title of this book, few recognize the acronym "DED," whereas many recognize and use the acronym "DEM," even though they may have different understandings of the meaning of this popular term. The term *Digital Elevation Model (DEM)* has several different meanings:

- As used in the title of this *DEM Users Manual*, DEM is a generic term for digital topographic and/or bathymetric data, in all its various forms. It is called a "model" because computers can use such data to model and automatically analyze the earth's topography in 3-dimensions, minimizing the need for labor-intensive human interpretation. Unless specifically referenced as a Digital Surface Model (DSM), the generic DEM normally implies elevations of the terrain (bare earth z-values) void of vegetation and manmade features. This bare-earth DEM is generally synonymous with a Digital Terrain Model (DTM). DEM elevations of lakes and rivers normally imply the water surface. Bathymetry refers to depths below the water surface, and hydrography is bathymetry applied to nautical charting of oceans, lakes and rivers, especially with reference to their navigational and commercial uses. All such elevations are referenced to a horizontal and vertical datum. Because of the importance of vertical datums to DEM users, Chapter 2 covers vertical datums in detail, including initiatives to link datasets compiled to different topographic and tidal datums.
- As used by the U.S. Geological Survey (USGS), a DEM is the digital cartographic representation of the elevation of the terrain at regularly spaced intervals in x and y directions, using z-values referenced to a common vertical datum. As described in Chapter 4 of this manual, there are several types of standard USGS DEMs archived in the National Elevation Dataset (NED) with uniform Universal Transverse Mercator (UTM) grid spacing (e.g., 10-by 10-meters or 30- by 30-meters) or arc second grid spacing in geographic coordinates (e.g., one elevation point every 1-arc-second in latitude and longitude). This definition is similar to that of Digital Terrain Elevation Data (DTED) produced by the National Geospatial-Intelligence Agency (NGA).
- As used by others in the U.S. and elsewhere, a DEM has bare earth z-values at regularly spaced intervals in x (Eastings) and y (Northings); however, grid spacing, datum, coordinate systems, data formats, and other characteristics may vary widely, but normally follow

alternative specifications, with narrow grid spacing and State Plane coordinates for example. Whereas UTM coordinates are commonly used for Federal mapping programs that cross state boundaries, State Plane coordinates are normally preferred for state, county, and community mapping programs. State Plane scale factor errors, caused by forcing a spherical earth to map as though the world is locally flat, are smaller than scale factor errors from UTM coordinates, and most local surveys are performed using the State Plane Coordinate System (SPCS) which is tailored to each state.

Related Definitions

Other related terms are defined as follows:

- A *Digital Terrain Model (DTM)* also has multiple definitions. In some countries, DTMs are synonymous with DEMs, representing the bare earth terrain with uniformly spaced z-values. As used herein, DTMs may be similar to DEMs, but they frequently incorporate the elevation of significant topographic features on the land, plus mass points and breaklines that are irregularly spaced so as to better characterize the true shape of the bare earth terrain. The net result of DTMs is that the distinctive terrain features are more clearly defined and precisely located, and contours generated from DTMs more closely approximate the real shape of the terrain. Whereas DTMs are normally more expensive and time consuming to produce than uniformly spaced (gridded) DEMs because breaklines are ill suited for automated collection, such DTMs are technically superior to gridded DEMs for many applications.

- A *Digital Surface Model (DSM)* is similar to a DEM or DTM, except that a DSM depicts the elevations of the top (reflective) surfaces of buildings, trees, towers, and other features elevated above the bare earth. DSMs are especially relevant for telecommunications management, forest management, air safety, and 3-D simulation and fly-throughs.

- A *Triangulated Irregular Network (TIN)* is a set of adjacent, non-overlapping triangles computed from irregularly spaced points with x/y coordinates and z-values. The TIN's vector data structure is based on irregularly-spaced point, line, and polygon data interpreted as mass points and breaklines and stores the topological relationship between triangles and their adjacent neighbors. See Figure 1.1a, below, for mass points and breaklines, and Figure 1.1b for the resulting TIN. TINs are excellent for calculation of slope, aspect, surface area and length; volumetric and cut-fill analysis; generation of contours; and interpolation of surface z-values. The TIN model is preferable to a DEM when it is critical to preserve the precise location of narrow or small surface features such as ditches or stream centerlines, levees, isolated peaks or pits in the data model.

- A *breakline* is a linear feature that describes a change in the smoothness or continuity of a surface. A *soft breakline* ensures that known z-values along a linear feature are maintained (e.g., elevations along a pipeline or road centerline), and ensures that linear features and polygon edges are maintained in a TIN surface model, by enforcing the breaklines as TIN edges; but a soft breakline does not define interruptions in surface smoothness. Soft breaklines are generally synonymous with 3-D breaklines because they are depicted with series of x/y/z coordinates. A *hard breakline* defines interruptions in surface smoothness. A hard breakline is used to define streams, shorelines, dams, ridges, building footprints, and other locations with abrupt surface changes. Although some hard breaklines are 3-D breaklines, they are often depicted as 2-D breaklines because features such as shorelines and building footprints are normally depicted with series of x/y coordinates only, e.g., shorelines digitized with x/y coordinates from digital orthophotos that include no elevation data.

- *Mass points* are irregularly spaced points, each with an x/y location and a z-value, typically (but not always) used to form a TIN. They are normally generated by automated methods, e.g., by lidar or IFSAR scanners or photogrammetric auto-correlation techniques. When generated by automated methods, mass point spacing and pattern depend on characteristics of the technologies used to acquire the data.

- *Spot heights* are individual points, each with an x/y location and a z-value. They are normally generated manually and deliberately placed to depict elevations of prominent features representing highest or lowest elevations in an area, or elevations of prominent features, e.g., dams, levees and road intersections. They may also be chosen to depict the most significant variations in the slope or aspect of TIN triangles. According to National Map Accuracy Standards (Bureau of the Budget, 1947) and ASPRS Accuracy Standards for Large-Scale Maps (ASPRS, 1990), spot heights are twice as accurate as mass points and contours. See Chapter 3 for details.
- *Contour lines* are isolines connecting points of equal elevation. See the section on Contour Representation below for greater detail.

3-D SURFACE MODELING

A uniformly-spaced DEM grid can be compiled directly with photogrammetric procedures that automatically drive the photogrammetric operator or stereo instrument to precalculated x/y UTM or State Plane coordinates (e.g., every 10 meters in Eastings and Northings) and then determine the elevations at each of those points using stereo photogrammetric procedures as explained in Chapter 5. However, with most DEM technologies, it is more common to first acquire a series of irregularly-spaced elevation points from which uniformly-spaced elevation points are interpolated. This will be demonstrated below.

Assume Figure 1.1a represents a small island in the ocean, and the island includes hills and one interior lake with a small stream running through the hillside from the lake to the ocean. A scattered array of elevation points is shown on the island, as well as several types of breaklines. These few elevation points could have been carefully compiled by a photogrammetrist to reflect key spot heights, for example. Alternatively, one can imagine hundreds or thousands of similar mass points randomly acquired by a lidar or IFSAR sensor, for example.

Figure 1.1a shows three breaklines. The island's shoreline with the ocean is a breakline, as is the shoreline of the interior lake; and the centerline of the stream is a third breakline. When elevation points are selected randomly (e.g., by photogrammetric image correlation, IFSAR, topographic or bathymetric lidar, or sonar, as explained in Chapters 5 through 9 of this manual), none of these three breaklines would be accurately delineated. The problem would be even worst if engineers needed a hydraulic model of the stream and had to know the breaklines at the tops and bottoms of these stream banks. The lesson here is that there are lots of ways to generate low-resolution or high-resolution mass point elevations, but photogrammetry is still the best way to delineate breaklines. Procedures for generation of accurate breaklines from randomly-spaced mass points are still evolving, although some such procedures yield reasonable approximations of those breaklines. Nevertheless, it usually takes a human operator to recognize when drainage patterns pass under the visible surface because of bridges and culverts.

As stated previously, the TIN data structure is based on irregularly-spaced point, line, and polygon data interpreted as mass points and breaklines. Figure 1.1b shows how the mass points and breaklines from Figure 1.1a are converted into a TIN. All of the breaklines along the ocean and lake shorelines and the stream centerline are edges of the TIN triangles. This TIN data structure will be described in greater detail below.

Once we have mass points and breaklines, or a TIN derived therefrom, a DEM can be produced by interpolating the elevations at the exact x/y coordinates computed for the DEM grid. This interpolation process yields a DEM surface that is less accurate than the dataset used for the interpolation, however, the DEM is normally easier to store in a GIS database. Whenever elevations are estimated by interpolation from surrounding points, the interpolated elevations are less certain. This section on 3-D surface modeling explains the rationale for using different forms of interpolation so as to reduce those uncertainties. Explanations of inverse distance weighted interpolation, natural neighbor interpolation, splines and kriging, for example, may appear to be far-fetched, but those are valuable concepts for understanding the processes used in interpolation of DEM elevation values.

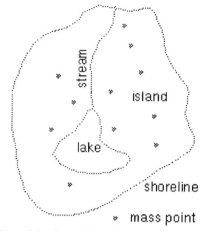

Figure 1.1a Example breaklines and mass points.

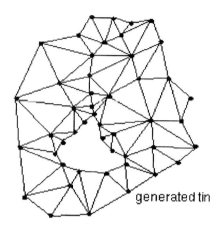

Figure 1.1b TIN derived from mass points and breaklines.

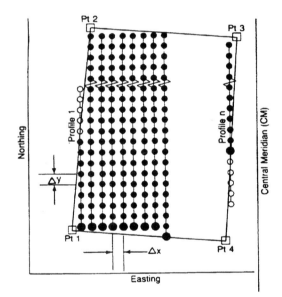

Figure 1.1c DEM interpolated from nearest TIN triangle corners.

Figure 1.1

1.1a: Mass points and breaklines where: mass points are irregularly spaced and breaklines follow linear surface edges

1.1b: Triangulated Irregular Network (TIN) derived from the mass points and breaklines in 1.1a

1.1c: Digital Elevation Model (DEM) where Δx and Δy represent the uniform spacing between DEM elevation "posts." DEM z-values are interpolated from surrounding z-values at TIN triangle corners

Topographic Surface Modeling

The topographic surface can be considered to be a mathematically continuous surface. No matter how small an area, an infinite number of points may be selected to represent the topography. In practice, only a sample can be utilized. Interpolation is used to construct a digital model of the surface by estimating heights at any location based on sample elevations.

A digital model used to represent a topographic surface should contain adequate elevation and planimetric measurements compatible in number and distribution with the terrain being modeled, so that the elevation of any location can be interpolated accurately for any given application (Ayeni, 1982). "All the major difficulties with computer interpolation are caused by insufficient data and observational error" (Watson, 1992). Emphasis is therefore placed on data capture and storage techniques. The initial data capture for building elevation models is traditionally very expensive and time consuming. New technologies have emerged recently that have made it easier and less costly to collect larger amounts of accurate sample data. The techniques for collecting data are discussed in chapters 5 through 10.

Commonly, surface data are collected to represent the bare earth, without tree canopy or buildings. Linear features like roads may possibly be included. As explained above, surfaces such as these are often referred to as digital terrain models (DTMs). Surfaces that include tree canopy or buildings are called digital surface models (DSMs).

There are three data structures commonly used to store elevation surfaces; Triangulated Irregular Networks (TINs), sampling at regularly spaced grids (DEMs/DTMs/DSMs), and lines of equal elevation (contours).

Triangulated Irregular Networks

A TIN is a digital terrain model that is based on an irregular array of points which form a sheet of non-overlapping contiguous triangle facets (Peuker, et al, 1978) as in Figure 1.2a. It is a vector model that supports the incorporation of point, line, and area based features to capture and represent surface morphology, Figure 1.2 b.

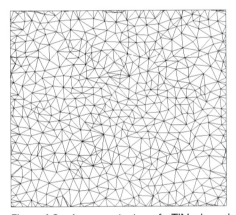

Figure 1.2a A geometric view of a TIN where the terrain sample points are connected into a set of non-overlapping triangles.

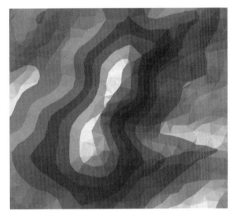

Figure 1.2b A surface view of a TIN where the triangles are hillshaded and colored by elevation. See color plate in Appendix C.

The points used to construct a TIN come from individually sampled locations or from the vertices of linear features. Ideally, these represent a set of critical locations on the surface which define breaks in slope such as peaks, pits, ridges, valleys, and passes. Sometimes additional points are included to ensure completeness of coverage and control for interpolation. Point samples are generally referred to as *spot heights* or *mass* points. Linear features are referred to as *structure lines* or *breaklines*. Spot heights are generally lower density, but higher accuracy, as when measured manually from stereo photogrammetry. Mass points are generally higher density (but lower accuracy than spot heights) as when measured automatically from automated stereo correlation or lidar.

Input data locations and height values are preserved in the model. No transformation to an intermediate data structure takes place. Analysis is performed on these source locations with the neighborhood relationships, the topology, being calculated and used where necessary to optimize certain operations.

An accurate, well-designed TIN maintains consistency with the degree of variation in surface heights found in the terrain. As the terrain becomes more complex the density of the TIN should increase accordingly. In computations such as spot height estimation, elevation values are interpolated for a given location based on the triangle in which it falls or a neighborhood relative to that triangle. Because triangles in the TIN are more densely packed in rough terrain, and the original data values are used as triangle nodes, relatively precise interpolations can be performed.

The simplest interpretation of the model, in terms of defining a continuous surface, is a linear approach and is based on the principal that a flat plane can be fit to any three (3) non-collinear points (Carter, 1988). Thus, areas of consistent slope and aspect are represented in the TIN by individual triangles. Areas can be considered uniform if changes in slope or aspect are within a given tolerance level. A tolerance allowing for high levels of error will result in a generalized model of the surface. Slope and aspect can be computed rapidly because only individual triangles need to be examined, rather than the relationships between them.

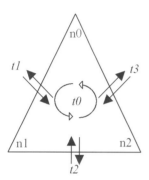

Figure 1.3 Representation of topology for a TIN triangle. Nodes and edges are oriented clockwise or counter-clockwise (depending on system). A reference is made to each adjacent triangle, each of which also has a reference pointing back.

A topological structure is another important characteristic of the TIN. Once the topology of the TIN has been defined, the neighborhood of a sample point can be reconstructed without resorting to searching (Peuker, et al, 1978). Various approaches to topology exist. For example, a triangle record contained in a TIN may maintain explicit reference to the three nodes that define it and the three associated triangles that share its borders. Alternately, a triangle edge may refer to its two nodes and the triangles on either side of it, as in Figure 1.3. Regardless of implementation, topology is extremely useful for certain functions such as spatial searching. The amount of information associated with topology can get quite large. To minimize storage and I/O costs, different systems choose to save various degrees of topology, only building that which is necessary at runtime. With the advent of the very large point databases now becoming readily available through such sources as lidar, research is focussing on implicit triangulations that store no topology but information that permits rapid retrieval of points with all topology being constructed on-the-fly (Kidner et al. 2000).

TIN based surface models have several advantages over other surface representations. One advantage is that TIN models adapt to the variable complexity of terrain. Where there is little variation in the surface only a small amount of data is stored, and where there is much variation, more data is stored. The vector based structure supports the incorporation of point, line, and polygon based features. This enables the original source measurements to be embedded directly in the triangulation. Therefore, resulting analysis honors the source data exactly. TINs are also the native structure used for 3D graphics rendering, and therefore can be used to improve performance of interactive 3D visualization.

TINs have several disadvantages. Good quality data used for their construction, typically photogrammetric- or lidar-based, can be expensive to obtain. Additionally, there aren't as many tools to process TINs as with gridded surfaces, and some operations aren't as efficient because the data structure is more complex.

Breaklines

Usually, mass points are the predominant input to a TIN and form the overall shape of the surface. Breaklines can then augment this information. Breaklines are linear features, or the boundaries of areal features, which represent important natural or artificial discontinuities in slope contained in the landscape. Examples of natural features are ridges, channels, geological faults, and lakes. Examples of artificial features are roads and canals. See Figures 1.4a and 1.4b. The incorporation of breaklines into a TIN is achieved by enforcing them as edges in the triangulation (Chen, 1988).

The enforcement of lines may require the addition of software generated densification points along the breaklines if the triangulation is to remain Delaunay (See Appendix B, Definitions). These densification points can increase the model size but maintain the desirable properties of generating equiangular triangles from nodes that are in close proximity. *Constrained* Delaunay triangulations relax conditions along breaklines so densification points need not be added. This is useful when there is a need to keep the model as small as possible.

Figure 1.4a A set of sample points and breaklines collected to create a TIN. See color plate in Appendix C.

Figure 1.4b The resulting surface model. See color plate in Appendix C.

Breaklines play an important role in defining the structure of a surface. Without them, abrupt changes in slope that occur along linear features and boundary lines can't be modeled properly. They're needed to keep roads smooth, lakes flat, and to maintain the downhill flow of rivers. Smooth interpolators, in particular, can produce dramatically different results depending on whether or not breaklines are present. These interpolators are often used in the process of creating gridded surfaces from TINs. See Figures 1.5a and 1.5b.

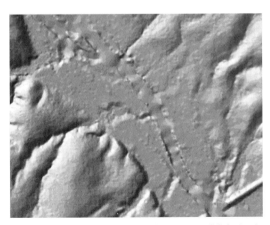
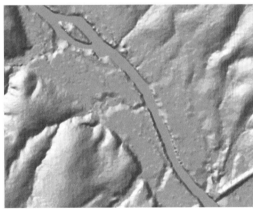

Figure 1.5a Hillshaded raster elevation model derived from a lidar TIN without breaklines.

Figure 1.5b A 2nd version of the model where breaklines for the river shoreline were included.

The TIN model, with its support for variable sample density and breaklines, is a good candidate for capturing terrain information that includes buildings and other man-made features. These DSMs are increasingly being used in urban areas and are especially important for applications such as the siting of high frequency digital communications where line-of-sight is required between rooftop transmitters. While a TIN, like other single valued surfaces, cannot represent truly vertical features like walls, the use of dense point sampling or breaklines enables an acceptable approximation for most applications. For example, lidar can capture both the building and ground detail with a dense carpet of points, as with Figure 1.6a generated from a lidar TIN with 1-meter post spacing. For efficient representation in a TIN, points within areas of constant slope may be removed while those along the tops and bottoms of building perimeters and their rooflines are kept. The TIN at Figure 1.6b was produced by another process (ADS40 surface model) with breaklines on rooflines of the tallest structures collected photogrammetrically from ADS40 stereo pairs to supplement the surface model generated by autocorrelation using the ISTAR® software suite. This image shows how breaklines can give sharp edges to rooflines.

Figure 1.6a Lidar TIN of Los Angeles   **Figure 1.6b** ADS40 TIN with breaklines

Figures (also shown on front cover of this manual in color) courtesy of EarthData.

Gridded Surfaces (DEMs, DTMs, DSMs)

A grid is a rectangular array of cells, each of which stores a value. In the case of uniformly-spaced DEMs, DTMs or DSMs, each cell stores the elevation value for the centroid of the cell. The cell is a uniform unit that represents a defined area of the earth, such as a square meter or square mile. For most terrain models, grid cells are usually square, having the same resolution in width and height (easting and northing), and organized in rows and columns of data as in Figure 1.7.

The cells of a grid can be interpreted in two ways. When used to represent surfaces, the grid cell value represents the surface value at the centroid of each cell. The area between cell centers is assumed to be a value between that of adjacent cells (Figure 1.8a). A grid cell can also be viewed as representing an area. In this interpretation the entire cell is assumed to be of the same value, and changes in value only occur at the border of cells. This interpretation is referred to as discrete, because changes in value occur at *discrete* boundaries. It is used for categorical data such as landcover or soil type, and also digital imagery, such as a satellite image or digital orthophoto. The elements of a 2-dimensional grid are called "pixels" (Figure 1.7), and the elements of a 3-dimensional grid are called "voxels" (Figure 1.8b).

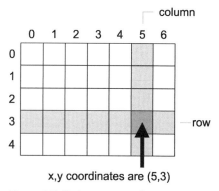

Figure 1.7 Basic structure of a grid.

The resolution of the grid — the width and height of the cells — determines the precision of the grid representation. The size of a grid cell depends upon the data resolution required for the most detailed analysis and level of detail of the input data used to create the grid. The cell must be small enough to capture the required detail, but large enough so that computer storage and analysis can be performed efficiently. For example, if you are interested in drainage features that may be 10 meters wide, you would not want to use a 30 meter grid. At a minimum, you should use a grid whose spatial resolution is half the size of the smallest feature of interest. If the smallest feature of interest is 10 meters, you would want to use a grid with a cell size of 5 meters or less. Conversely, if the application requires only 30 meter resolution data, creating or using 5 meter data would be very costly and inefficient. Keep in mind that to create a finer resolution grid, a larger number of sample points with higher accuracy should be used.

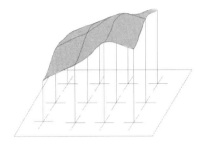

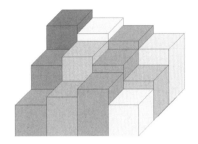

Figure 1.8a Surface interpretation of a grid.

Figure 1.8b Discrete interpretation of a grid. The 3-dimensional cells are called "voxels."

Discrete grids (Figure 1.8b) are the most common representation of terrain surfaces because elevation data are widely available in this form at low cost. An example of grid surface data are the DEMs produced by the United States Geological Survey, described in Chapter 4.

Gridded terrain models are appropriate for small-scale mapping applications where absolute positional accuracy is not paramount and where surface features do not need to be characterized exactly. The grid format is a fast and efficient data structure for analysis algorithms and the primary surface representation for analysis. There are more analysis tools for grids than for the other data structures used to represent surfaces.

The disadvantages of the grid representation are that surface discontinuities such as ridges and stream centerlines are not well represented, and precise locations for features such as peaks are lost in the sampling of the grid. For these same reasons, grids are not good for representing man-made objects such as road cuts, buildings, etc, but are good for bare earth terrain models. Grids can be an inefficient storage method in cases where there is little change in value over an area. A grid will store a value at every location, even if all adjacent cells have the same or nearly the same value, whereas TINs and contours will not. However there are compression techniques, such as run-length encoding, that can be applied to gridded data to minimize storage space when adjacent cells have the same value.

Creating Gridded Surfaces (Interpolation Methods)

Creating a gridded surface from sample data requires the estimation of values for location based on sample data. There are many techniques for creating gridded surface from sample data, generally referred to as interpolation. As this manual is focused on terrain, the discussion of interpolation will focus on the basics, and on methods most appropriate for terrain interpolation. The reason for many techniques is because the input sample data and the surface being modeled may have many different characteristics. As a result, no single interpolation technique is the best for all situations.

A basic principle shared by all interpolation methods is that things that are closer together tend to be more alike than things that are farther apart. When trying to build a terrain surface, you can assume that the sample values closest to the prediction location will be similar. As you move further away from the prediction location, the influence of the points will decrease. All interpolation methods apply weights to the influence of a sample point based on its proximity to the location being predicted.

There are two classes of interpolation, deterministic and probabalistic. Deterministic methods are based directly on the surrounding measured values and/or mathematical formulas applied to those values. Geostatistical methods are probabalistic statistical models that include autocorrelation, which is the strength of similarity between measured samples accounting for distance and direction. The goal of geostatistical interpolation techniques, such as kriging, is to create a surface while minimizing the error between the predicted values and the statistical model of the surface. All the interpolation techniques discussed here are deterministic techniques, except for kriging.

Inverse Distance Weighted Interpolation

Inverse distance weighted interpolation (IDW) determines new cell values using a linearly weighted combination of values from nearby points. The weight is a function of inverse distance. Most implementations provide a weighting factor the user can specify to control the significance of input points based upon their distance from the location being interpolated. This method is one of the simplest methods of interpolation and is presented here only as an introduction to interpolation. IDW interpolation is useful when

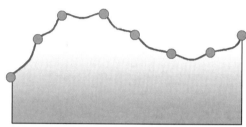

Figure 1.9 Cross section of inverse distance weighted interpolation.

the variable being interpolated decreases in influence with distance from the sample location, such as consumer purchasing power. This assumption is not true for terrain data, and IDW should not be used for terrain. The cross section in Figure 1.9 illustrates this effect.

This effect can also be seen in the contours in Figure 1.10. The surface has a dimpled effect at the sample point locations.

Figure 1.10a Input sample points (mass points).

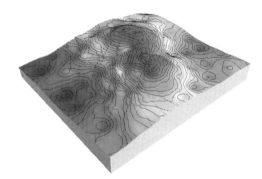

Figure 1.10b IDW interpolated surface. See color plate in Appendix C.

Natural Neighbor Interpolation

Natural neighbor interpolation, also known as Sibson or "area-stealing" interpolation, finds the closest subset of input samples to a query point and applies weights to them based on proportionate areas in order to interpolate a value (Sibson, 1981). It works equally well with regular or irregularly distributed data, produces a smooth yet conservative surface, and completes in a time proportional to the size of the input data (Watson, 1992).

As the name implies, its key strength is in finding appropriate input samples (neighbors) to use when interpolating a height for a given point. Based on the Delaunay triangulation and its dual, the voronoi (Thiessen) diagram, this algorithm finds the closest points in all directions. It does so by determining a query point's voronoi neighbors (see Figure 1.11). These are the samples the query point would form triangle edges with if inserted into the Delaunay triangulation of the samples. It therefore provides good representation from the samples in both proximity and direction, with the interpolated value depending only on a local subset of data. Since the neighborhood automatically adjusts itself to fit the local data configuration, there is no need for parameters like search radius or sample quotas that have drawbacks when the input data distribution is unevenly sampled or clustered.

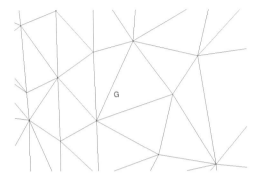

Figure 1.11a The location of a query point that needs an interpolated height relative to the position of TIN elements.

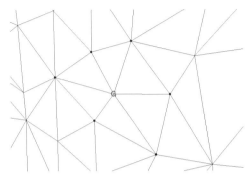

Figure 1.11b The interpolant has found the closest surrounding nodes in all directions to the query point (the natural neighbors) and establishes a relationship to them for use in height estimation.

Another important aspect of this interpolant is its weighting scheme. Weights are not based on distance but on the amount of area that would be 'stolen' from the voronoi (Thiessen) polygons representing input samples if the query point were inserted into the diagram. As shown at Figure 1.12, this scheme exhibits the important property that the weight of each neighbor drops to zero by the time it ceases to be part of the neighborhood (Gold, 1989). This form of interpolation is considered linear if the area based weights are applied against only the data heights. If gradients, estimated for samples based on their neighbors, are included it's a non-linear interpolation scheme.

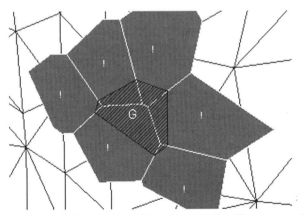

Figure 1.12 The weighting scheme used by natural neighbor interpolation. The point symbolized by a cross in the center is a query point requiring height estimation. The hatched polygon represents its voronoi region if it were to be inserted in the triangulation. The other solid fill polygons are the voronoi regions for the surrounding nodes in the triangulation. The weight of each node is based relative to the area of overlap between its voronoi region, the query point's region, and the areas of overlap for the other nodes. In this example, the natural neighbor to the southwest will be given the most weight. See color plate in Appendix C.

The linear based natural neighbor surface is smooth everywhere except at the data locations (see Figure 1.13). The surface is similar to triangle based linear interpolation but there is no break in slope along triangle edges. The non-linear natural neighbor surface, based on blended gradients, is smooth everywhere including the data locations (see Figure 1.14).

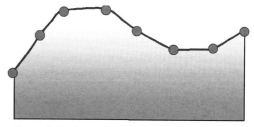

Figure 1.13 Cross section of linear natural neighbors interpolated surface.

The linear natural neighbors interpolator is a conservative interpolator that will not manufacture data. The resultant surface is a true representation of just the input data. It will honor the input data points and be constrained to the input data range. Therefore peaks and valleys must be included in the input sample data to appear in the surface.

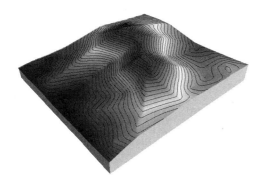

Figure 1.14a Natural neighbor linear interpolation

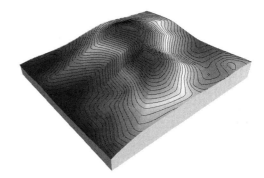

Figure 1.14b Natural neighbor interpolation with blended gradients.

See color plate in Appendix C.

Spline

Splines are a general class of interpolation techniques that use a mathematical formula to create a surface that minimizes the overall surface curvatures, resulting in a smooth surface that passes through the input points.

Conceptually a spline is like bending a sheet of rubber through a set of points. It fits a mathematical function to a specified number of neighboring input points to determine the value at each location. There are different types of

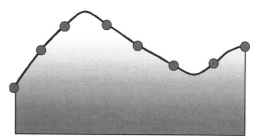

Figure 1.15 Spline

splines and parameters to specify for them that make the surface more tightly conform to the input points or perform more smoothing (Mitas and Mitasova 1988; Franke, 1982).

This method is very useful for creating elevation models of areas with gently varying terrain with smooth slope transitions. It is very sensitive to, and not suitable for sharp changes in value over short distances such as steep cliffs or man-made features. In such situations it has a tendency to over-exaggerate the value of neighboring cells.

Splines will honor the input points and extrapolate beyond the input data range so that unsampled peaks or valleys can be represented as in Figure 1.15.

Splined surfaces, because of their smoother characteristic, are often the preferred interpolation method when the end goal is to create cartographic quality contours. Notice the smoothness of the contours in Figure 1.16.

Geostatistical Techniques (Kriging)

Kriging is a geostatistical interpolation technique, similar to deterministic interpolation techniques in that it weights the surrounding measured values to derive a prediction for each location. However, the weights are based not only on the distance between the measured points and the prediction location but also on

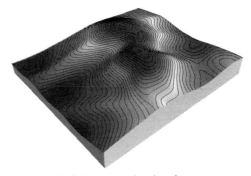

Figure 1.16 Spline interpolated surface. See color plate in Appendix C.

the strength of the overall correlation among the measured points. With kriging, the data are used to define the spatial correlation model to determine the weights for neighboring samples that are used to fit a surface to the points. Whereas with deterministic techniques the model is based only on user defined input.

These weights are derived through an examination of the data and fitting of a model. The data is examined as a semivariogram, a graph of differences in z-value (variance) versus map distance and direction between sample point pairs as in Figure 1.17. This builds off the previous assumption that things close together are more alike than things farther apart, only now distance *and* direction are used. Fitting the model involves selecting the appropriate parameters that fit the best line through the semivariogram. There is more to this process than can be sufficiently explained in this text.

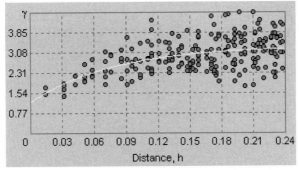

Figure 1.17 Semivariogram model. Each point in the graph represents a pair of points, their location in the graph is based upon their difference in z-value and map distance and direction away from each other. The line represents the fit model.

A specific type of kriging known as *ordinary kriging* is most appropriate for interpolation of terrain data. Ordinary kriging recalculates a local mean for each location to be estimated. For further discussion of variogram modeling and different kriging options refer to (Issaks and Srivastava, 1989).

In most cases kriging is used as an exact interpolator, the surface being created passes exactly through the input points. However there are situations in which data accuracy may be questionable or there is a known measurement error, such as a measurement device thats known accuracy is 1 foot. In these cases kriging provides an ability to pay more attention to the local trend of the surface than to a single value. Figure 1.18a shows a cross section of a kriging surface. Figure 1.18b shows a similar surface with an erroneous data point. Notice that the surface maintains its general shape even with the value of one point changed.

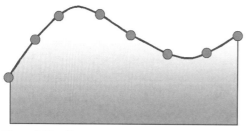

Figure 1.18a Cross section of a surface from kriging.

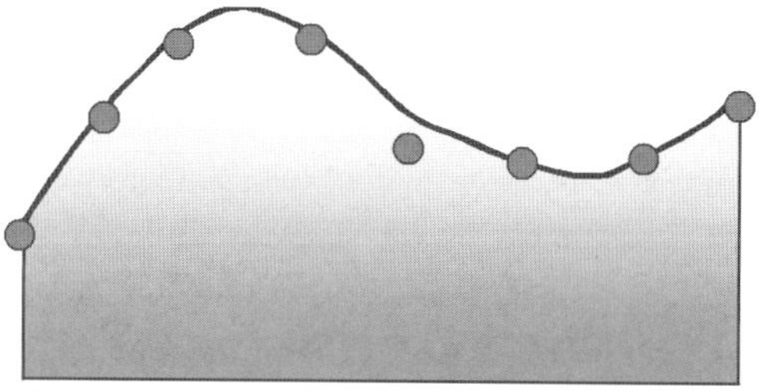

Figure 1.18b Cross section of the same surface with one of the data points changed illustrating the model can create a surface that does not exactly conform to the data points.

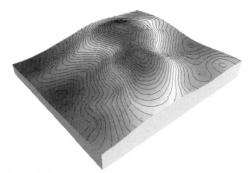

Figure 1.19 Interpolation result from kriging. See color plate in Appendix C.

Because kriging uses the value and distribution of input data to determine weights, it is sensitive to the homogeneity of the surface being interpolated. The more homogeneous the terrain of the input sample points the better the model that can be fitted and the better the resulting surface will be (see Figure 1.19). For example, if you had a point dataset for the entire United States and fit a model, it would be much different than the model for the state of Kansas.

Specialized Terrain Interpolation

A variation on the spline technique is an interpolator specially designed for the interpolation of elevation data known as ANUDEM (Hutchinson, 1989). This interpolator is optimized for the creation of hydrologically correct terrain models. It is unique in both its inputs and technique for building good terrain models.

Most interpolators use only point data as input. This interpolator uses not only point data, but also lines in the form of contours for elevation, streams and ridges for drainage, and polygons as lake boundaries. It works intelligently with contour data by recognizing the critical points in areas of highest contour line curvature.

ANUDEM also has an option for hydro-enforcement, discussed above. This option will create a network of valleys and ridges, then use a spline interpolator to build a surface while maintaining consistent flow downslope.

General Interpolation Issues

When creating surfaces using any of the previously described techniques, there are some issues that are common to all of them.

The number, distribution, and location of sample points is key to building a good representative surface model. If building a TIN or using an interpolator such as IDW or linear natural neighbors, where the output surface values are constrained to the range of the input values, it is important that the high and low areas are adequately represented in the sample data. Having more sample points is always better, assuming they are accurate. Generally it is best if these points are well distributed spatially, not all clumped in small areas, but this distribution should vary with surface roughness. The number necessary to create a good representative surface will vary with the character of the original surface. If the elevation samples are relatively evenly distributed and the surface characteristics do not change across the landscape, a smaller number of points may be needed. If however the surface is quite varied such as in a mountainous area, more sample points should be used. If it is mixed, mountains and plains, the mountainous area should be more densely sampled than the plain. There are at least two known exceptions to this policy for civilian and military applications:

- For hydrologic and hydraulic (H&H) modeling of flood hazards, the hydrologic modeling of the mountains and hills that drain into the floodplain do not require high-accuracy, high-resolution elevation data to determine the direction in which water will flow into the floodplain; whereas the hydraulic modeling of the relatively flat floodplain requires high-accuracy, high-resolution elevation data to model the subtleties of the terrain to determine where flood waters will encroach. In other words, better elevation data are needed of the relatively flat floodplains than are needed of the surrounding hills that drain into the floodplains. See the section below on hydrologic conditioning.
- For military terrain analyses, it is easy to perform intervisibility and cover and concealment modeling, for example, in rugged terrain where elevation errors of several meters have little impact on the result; but it is difficult to perform such modeling in relatively flat terrain where differences of a few inches can impact whether or not one can see between points A and B on the terrain. Similarly, for automated terrain correlation guidance for smart weapons, it is easy to correlate the terrain when it is rugged, but it is far more complex with sand dunes and subtle variations in the terrain where there are not clearly defined terrain features on which to base the automated terrain correlation algorithms.

Related to the distribution of sample points, it is important to note that the interpolation at the edge of a study area should include sample data from all directions, not just inside the study area. The same principal holds true for interpolation of surfaces that fit into a map series with finite boundaries. Additional data from neighboring maps should be included so areas along the edge can be accurately portrayed.

Contour lines are a special kind of input for interpolation. They are generally not considered to be a good input dataset to an interpolator because of the high density of sample points along the contour and the sparse sampling of data between the contours. Surfaces created from contours are often biased to the contour interval values. In the worst cases a terraced or stair-step effect may be noticeable. In almost all cases, a histogram of the grid values will show spikes of high frequency at the contour interval. This phenomena is minimized in the ANUDEM interpolator mentioned above because it has been optimized to work intelligently with contour input.

All interpolators except natural neighbors and TINs have parameters for specifying which nearby sample points will be used in the prediction of a value for a cell. These neighborhoods are often specified as a fixed number of points (e.g., use the eight nearest sample points to predict a value) or as a radius (e.g., use all points within 50 meters). It is most common to use between six and 12 points. Some software also allows the neighborhood to be divided into sections of four or eight and a sample is taken from each quadrant. This has an effect similar to the input point selection for natural neighbors, and minimize effects of contour biasing.

In addition to the sample points to be used, most interpolators have other parameters to specify. Because the characteristics of a surface change through space, what is a good set of parameters in one area may not be good in another area. In the case of terrain interpolation, changes in geomorphology will often mean changes in parameters. A coastal plain will require different parameters than mountains. If you have two very different landscapes to interpolate it may be better to separate them into two different points sets and interpolate them independently using the best parameters for each, then merge the surfaces back together.

There are many types of errors that can occur in a surface model, some significant, others minor depending upon the application. Contour biasing of a surface, mentioned previously, can be a significant source of error when creating slope or curvature maps, but may not be noticeable when used for visualization. Previous photomechanical methods of creating DEMs sometimes resulted in striping patterns that can still be found in older data (see Figure 1.25a in the visualization section below).

If a DEM will be used for water resources applications, it should be *hydrologically correct*. A hydrologically correct or hydro-enforced DEM is one that can effectively route the flow of water downslope. To do this, most DEMs need some further processing to identify areas that do not drain downslope, often referred to as sinks, pits, or puddles. If there is no basis for draining these puddles, they are sometimes filled to the point they can continue to route flow downslope. The ANUDEM interpolator discussed above does this as part of the interpolation process. When building a database of terrain data it is important to know if the data are intended for hydrologic and hydraulic modeling purposes or not. This will determine how features such as bridges are modeled. If the DEM will be used for hydraulic modeling, the bridge must be removed from the DEM or it will act as a dam, preventing the downstream modeling of the water. If the surface is to be used for transportation modeling or visualization then bridge elevations can be included.

There are some quick and easy techniques to find errors in DEM data. The first is to look at the minimum and maximum values to see if they are within a realistic data range. A histogram of the data distribution can also be helpful. There should be no values that occur much more frequently than nearby values. In other words, the elevation 625 should occur with roughly the same frequency as 623, 624, and 626. An interactive fly-through of the data, discussed later, is also a good technique for finding significant errors. The analysis tools discussed later in this chapter can also be quite useful, particularly hillshade or shading. Using a low-angle hillshade makes it very easy to pick out striping or patterns in the data as well as other errors that may be in error by only a few feet. Creating slope maps can also be useful, by checking for an appropriate range of slope values, and also when analyzed visually.

Because there are so many ways to create a gridded surface from point data, it is useful to evaluate how well different methods or parameters for a method perform at creating a good surface. In this case, a good surface is described as one that most closely matches the input data. The techniques used to do this are known as validation and cross validation. The simpler approach is validation, when some percentage of the known input data is withheld from the interpolation, and the value at each withheld sample location is compared to the interpolated surface value and a statistical measure such as a root-mean-square-error (RMSE) is calculated. Cross validation is very similar, except that each point is removed individually and the interpolated value at each location recalculated one at a time.

Contour Representation

Contour lines are lines of equal elevation on a surface. Contours are primarily used for human interpretation of the 3-D terrain surface, whereas mass points, breaklines, TINs, DEMs, DTMs and DSMs are better for computer display and analyses of the 3-D surface. Contours are an excellent way to represent the heights and variations of a surface on a two-dimensional map because they provide precise location of elevations and have very high visual information content. With a little training, a map reader can recognize many things from contours such as ridges, valleys, peaks, relative slope, aspect, stream direction, and other characteristics that can not be easily interpreted from a TIN or grid.

Historically, contours were created by manual interpretation of spot heights and drawn by hand, but more recently they were derived through photogrammetric compilation. Today, most contours are derived from a TIN or grid which is first created using techniques like those described in the previous section.

When creating contours from a surface, producers and users must consider the purpose of the contours, accuracy of the source surface, and intended map scale (Robinson 1995). These factors will guide producers and users in selecting an appropriate contour interval, and type of contour. There are two types of contours commonly referred to as engineering contours and cartographic contours. Engineering contours are a direct, accurate representation of the TIN or grid they were derived from, they have little or no smoothing or generalization, and as a result they can appear unnaturally jagged and angular. Engineering contours are desirable if users intend to do further visual or computer analysis of the contours, or if they are an archival form of the surface to be used for unspecified future purposes. Cartographic contours are what users are accustomed to seeing on a map. They are smoother, with few sharp angles, and may even be modified to properly point upstream in a valley or appropriately model a bridge overpass or road cut in more detail than the source surface would allow. Traditionally these were drawn by hand, and the cartographer would use his/her knowledge and artistry to create a smoother, more representational line for the appropriate map scale. Cartographic contours should be used exclusively for mapping purposes where humans will analyze the contours; for their increased costs, cartographic contours have little additional value for computer analyses of the surface.

To provide additional information to the map reader, it is common to add spot heights and color in addition to the contours. The spot heights are most often used to mark the height of prominent hills or peaks. Figure 1.20 is an example of cartographic contours with 2-foot contour interval. This example includes a spot height (marked by an "x" with annotation of 689 ft for the elevation of this prominent hilltop, and it also includes index contours (shown here with 10-ft intervals), intermediate contours (2-ft intervals), and depression contours (surrounded by terrain of higher elevation).

Since contours are most often derived from a TIN or grid surface, any analysis should be performed on the original surface; therefore there are few analytical tools that use contours. The only common use of contour data for analysis is the creation of profiles and cross sections which can also be calculated from TIN or grid models. Some softwares also allow the calculation of areas between contour ranges, which can also be performed on a grid model. When using contour data as input to analysis or input to surface creation, it is important to understand the origin of the data. If the contours were generated from a grid or TIN, the contours will be no more accurate, and likely less accurate, than the surface they were created from.

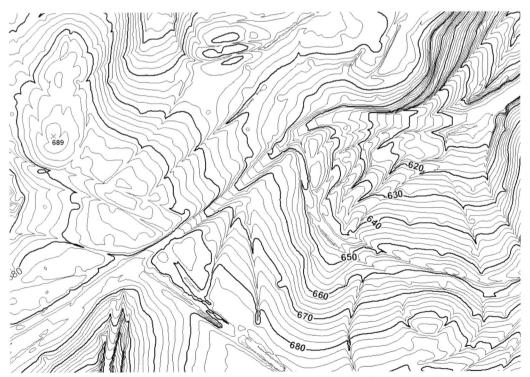

Figure 1.20 Example of 2-ft contours that depict a road and drainage features. Image provided as a courtesy by Dewberry.

It is critically important that producers and users of contours understand the meaning and importance of the contour interval. Using standard GIS software, contours can be generated from a grid or TIN with any contour interval selected. However it is a violation of professional ethics to produce maps for public use that have a contour interval smaller than warranted by the underlying accuracy of the grid or TIN data from which the contours are generated. For example, elevation data equivalent to 2-ft contours means that 90% of vertical test points must be accurate within 1-ft in order to satisfy National Map Accuracy Standards for paper maps with 2-ft contours; or the vertical accuracy should test to 1.2-ft at the 95% confidence level in order to satisfy equivalent National Standard for Spatial Data Accuracy test criteria for 2-ft contours. Statistically, the vertical root-mean-square-error ($RMSE_z$) must be 0.6-ft or less in order to be accurate enough to support 2-ft contours. If one had a digital elevation dataset that tested with $RMSE_z$ of 1-ft, for example, GIS software could easily enable maps to be drawn with 2-ft contours, but it would be unprofessional to do so because such accuracy would only support a contour interval between 3 and 4 feet. These accuracy relationships are explained in greater detail in Chapter 13. See Table 13.2 for a quick reference.

Hydrologic Enforcement

Especially with lidar, which captures every irregular feature along a shoreline, it is very possible for shorelines to undulate up and down. Lake shoreline elevations do not appear to be level and stream shoreline elevations do not appear to flow smoothly downstream. It is also very possible that uniformly-spaced DEM points will "jump" across a stream and fail to show that a stream passes through. Thus, the absence of breaklines in a DEM, by definition, makes them less accurate in depicting the true 3-D shape of the terrain, especially drainage features used for hydrologic and hydraulic (H&H) modeling. For this reason, a new form of *hydro-enforced* DEM is now being produced by the Federal Emergency Management Agency (FEMA) and others who need drainage features to be reflected in DEMs and DTMs and where it is necessary for the elevation data to depict the downward flow of water. In most cases, it is necessary for breaklines to be used to enforce the desired depiction of drainage features and water bodies.

An excellent example of hydro-enforcement of lidar data is shown in Figures 1.21 through 1.23. The initial lidar dataset (i.e., mass points) is irregularly spaced and may become even more irregular after post-processing to remove points that do not represent the bare earth terrain. An example of lidar mass points is shown in Figure 1.21. The mass points are shown in red; those outside the stream's floodplain were omitted for simplicity. Areas covered by water create natural voids in lidar datasets (identified by green lines). Other voids (areas within white lines) were created during post-processing where lidar failed to penetrate dense vegetation. Points shown in yellow represent bare earth elevations, near shorelines, that are higher than surrounding points; these points are depicted to highlight how lidar data along streams may not accurately reflect decreasing shoreline elevations in the downstream direction.

Figure 1.22 shows the TIN when only the lidar mass points are used to create the 3-D surface model. The natural undulations along the shorelines make this TIN appear as though water will not flow through areas that are modeled with higher elevations shown in yellow, orange, and red.

Figure 1.23 shows how this TIN changes when breaklines are added for the shorelines and assumed stream centerline. These breaklines were originally 2-D breaklines where x/y coordinates were digitized from digital orthophotos. These breaklines were then converted to 3-D breaklines by assigning z-values to the upstream and downstream ends of the 2-D breaklines using elevation data from field surveyed cross sections at upstream and downstream bridges, then interpolating remaining z-values between upstream and downstream values to make the stream flow downstream.

Lakes and reservoirs are routinely hydro-enforced by digitizing shorelines in 2-D and then adding a single z-value for an assumed water surface elevation for the entire breakline.

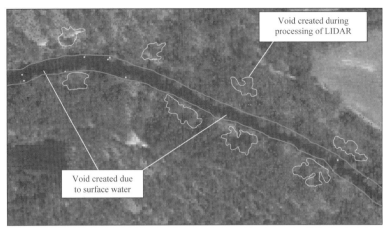

Figure 1.21 Post-processed bare-earth lidar mass points along a North Carolina stream. See color plate in Appendix C.

Figure 1.22 Geometric view of a TIN, hillshaded by elevation, created without breaklines. See color plate in Appendix C.

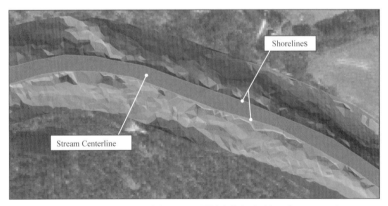

Figure 1.23 Geometric view of the same TIN, hillshaded by elevation, after breaklines are added. See color plate in Appendix C.

Figures 1.21 through 1.23 were all provided as a courtesy by the North Carolina Floodplain Mapping Program (NCFMP) which has an excellent website at www.ncfloodmaps.com.

Bridges and major culverts also need to be hydro-enforced. Elevations on the tops of bridges and culverts will appear identical to a dam, so a hydraulic model would erroneously indicate that water can't pass through this dam. A hydro-enforced DEM or DTM ensures that visible surfaces of bridges and culverts are cut by stream breaklines so that H&H computer models will accurately represent stream flow.

Figure 1.24 demonstrates this concept with contour lines. Even though no deliberate attempt was made to hydro-enforce the bridge in the northwest corner of Figure 1.24, the lidar post-processing algorithm (processing west-east with surrounding points) apparently discarded some high points on the bridge when jumping from low elevations near the shoreline up to the top of the bridge. The net result is that the contours almost were automatically hydro-enforced, but not quite because the "cut" through the bridge is incomplete.

The bridge in the southeast corner of Figure 1.24 shows no similar "cut." Here the automated west-east processing apparently passed smoothly on the top of the bridge, so the contours passed over the river on top of the bridge. This bridge now looks like a dam.

Hydro-enforcement almost always requires human intervention to "cut" breaklines through bridges so that all contours are parallel with the shoreline under the bridge, and so that computer models will allow the water to flow under the bridge, rather than appearing to be dammed by the bridge when not hydro-enforced. This concept of hydro-enforcement applies, whether dealing with contours, TINs or DEMs.

Figure 1.24 The dots on this image show lidar "hits" on the ground. The contour lines were produced by automated post-processing procedures, prior to manual clean-up. The bridge in the southeast corner shows contours crossing over the bridge, making the bridge appear as a dam in a hydraulic model. The bridge in the northwest corner shows contours that are almost hydro-enforced. To be fully hydro-enforced, a human analyst would "cut" a breakline through the bridge, with the breakline having an elevation at or slightly below the elevation of the water level; then, the contour lines on either side of the river would be separated by the breakline, and the hydraulic model would accommodate water passing beneath the bridge. Image provided as a courtesy by Dewberry. See color plate in Appendix C.

TINs should normally be hydro-enforced with ditch and stream centerlines serving as drainage system breaklines, forming triangle edges in the TIN data structure. The importance of breaklines cannot be overemphasized in the explanation of 3-D surface concepts.

Hydrologic Conditioning

Whereas *hydro enforcement* is relevant to drainage features and water bodies that are generally mapped, *hydro conditioning* is relevant to the entire land surface and is done so that water flow is continuous across the surface, whether that flow is in a stream channel or not. The purpose for continuous flow is so that relationships/links among drainage basins can be known for large areas. This term is specifically used when describing Elevation Derivatives for National Applications (EDNA) (see Chapter 4), the dataset of NED derivatives made specifically for hydrologic modeling applications.

Hydrologic conditioning is the processing of a DEM or TIN so that the flow of water is continuous across the entire terrain surface, including the removal of all spurious sinks. The only sinks that are retained are the real ones on the landscape.

Suppose that mass points from photogrammetry, IFSAR or lidar accurately recorded the elevations of the terrain in the vicinity of a small creek with steep or moderate banks on either side, and with an adjoining complex network of natural shallow ditches leading to the creek. With 10- or 30-meter DEM grid spacing, it is very common for DEM point elevations to "jump" the creek or ditches. It is common for hundreds, even thousands of artificial sinks (also called pits or puddles) to be formed by the DEM interpolation process, where these sinks are DEM points that are surrounded by other DEM points of higher elevation. (With a 5-meter DEM grid for example, this problem is reduced, but the file size quadruples compared with a 10-meter grid.) The physical terrain includes intricate drainage patterns, but the DEM interpolation process creates these artificial sinks.

Hydro-conditioning could either fill the sinks, or preferably drain them by using other available information to determine drain paths, e.g., small culverts beneath roads in order to drain a sink on one side of the road to an outlet on the other side of the road. Without hydro-conditioning, water appears to flow into these sinks with no apparent outlet. It is very quick and inexpensive to fill sinks, but it is time-consuming and expensive to drain them.

Terrain Visualization

While digital terrain models provide the benefit of computer based analysis, they also offer the equally important ability to provide an intuitively comprehensible visual display of the terrain characteristics. Computers offer a dizzying array of options when it comes to viewing surface models and the data derived from them. Uses include analysis, mapping, simulation, and entertainment. See Figures 1.25 and 1.26. Also see Chapter 13 of this manual for explanations of how terrain visualization is used for DEM quality assessment.

The human visual system is the most powerful information-processing mechanism known. Through our sight we can identify patterns and relationships between features and their attributes. Computers enable us to render terrain using both realistic and highly abstract, symbolized, methods. Symbolized representations make it easy for us to focus on a particular aspect of the terrain and not hide the patterns we're searching for behind unrelated noise. On the other hand, certain applications benefit from a high degree of realism.

In addition to analysis, visualization of terrain data offers benefits in the form of presentation and communication. People who aren't trained to read maps may have an easier time understanding them if terrain information is included. For example, this can by accomplished by compositing a hillshade image of the surface with relevant thematic information for display on a map. Alternatively, a 3-D perspective with data overlain on top of a terrain model can improve peoples' understanding of the problem. Such as interpreting geology in Figure 1.27a or seeing patterns of visibility from a transmission tower in Figure 1.27b. Hillshades are also used extensively for quality control purposes (see Chapters 11 and 12 for examples).

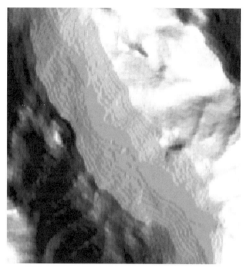

Figure 1.25a and **1.25b** Visualization used to reveal anomalies. Horizontal strips in Figure 1.25a and contour plateaus in Figure 1.25b show artifacts present in the terrain models.

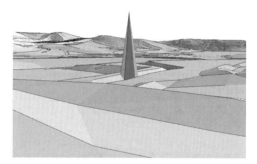

Figures 1.26a. and **1.26b** A planimetric view of terrain in Figure 1.26a doesn't reveal a data error that stands out in obvious fashion in the perspective view in Figure 1.26b.

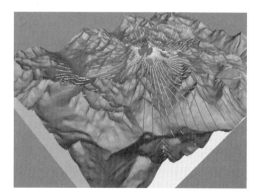

Figure 1.27a Composite display between soils and hillshaded terrain model. The composite makes it easier for those familiar with the area to orient themselves and shows some correlation between soil type and terrain. See color plate in Appendix C.

Figure 1.27b Multiple lines of sight generated radially around an individual observation point. Green portion of lines are visible, red are not. These are draped on a terrain model in perspective to increase information content. See color plate in Appendix C.

The simulation and video game industries have long been using terrain models as a necessary component of their products. Flight simulators also require this information in order to create realistic views of the world. A satellite or ortho-image draped on top of terrain surface with sky, fog, and haze added for effect goes a long way, as in Figure 1.28 below. For military applications, computer simulations of the potential battlefield terrain for mission rehearsals and "fly-throughs" are vital for saving lives in actual combat.

Figure 1.28 Landsat Thematic Mapper satellite imagery draped on a terrain model. Sky, haze, and fog are added to provide a sense of realism. See color plate in Appendix C.

Terrain Analysis

In addition to visualization, terrain data are very useful when performing spatial analysis. Most information derived from analysis of terrain data is created as input to site selection models in a geographic information system (GIS). Whether the problem is to find the best location to build a new road, tower, or housing development, or identify the best place to find a particular animal or plant species, the analysis of terrain data will almost always be a key ingredient.

Hillshade

Hillshade is a function to create an illuminated representation of the surface to show the terrain and topography. It does this by setting a position for a hypothetical light source and calculating the illumination values of each location. It can greatly enhance the visualization of a surface for analysis or graphical display, and it is a very common cartographic technique. Figure 1.29 shows an example of a DEM illuminated from the northwest. Both chapters 11 and 12 provide examples of how hillshaded DTMs are superior for quality control purposes.

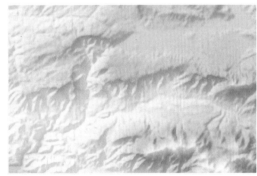

Figure 1.29 Hillshade elevation model. See color plate in Appendix C.

Slope

Slope is a calculation of the maximum rate of change across the surface, either from cell to cell in a gridded surface or of a triangle in a TIN. Every cell in an output grid or triangle in a TIN has a slope value. The lower the slope value, the flatter the terrain; the higher the slope value, the steeper the terrain. Slope is often calculated as either percent slope or degree of slope.

Slope calculations on terrain models are used in applications such as site selection models to find areas suitable for development or as input to forest fire spread models. Figure 1.30 shows a slope map, where light green represents low to moderate slope and dark red is high slope, based on the same DEM used in Figure 1.29.

Figure 1.30 Slope calculated from an elevation model. Red is high slope, green is low slope. See color plate in Appendix C.

Aspect

Aspect identifies the steepest downslope direction on a surface. It can be thought of as slope direction or the compass direction a hill faces.

It is usually measured clockwise in degrees from 0 (due north) to 360 (again due north, coming full circle). The value of each location in an aspect dataset indicates the direction the surface slope faces.

The aspect of a hillside says a lot about what can grow or live somewhere because it determines how much solar energy it receives. This is useful information when planning of

Figure 1.31 Aspect calculation from elevation model. See color plate in Appendix C.

development or recreation sites, and also agriculture and forestry depending on the latitude and climate. Figure 1.31 shows an aspect map where warm colors are northerly aspects and cool colors (blue and green) are southerly aspects, based on the same DEM used in Figure 1.29.

Intervisibility/Viewshed/Line-of-Sight

Viewshed identifies the observation points that can be seen from each cell in the input raster. Each cell in the output grid receives a value that indicates whether or not a location is visible from the observer point. Some softwares allow users to input multiple observation points and return a map showing how many points and which ones are visible.

Viewshed is helpful when users want to know how visible objects might be — for example, "From which locations on the landscape will the landfill be visible if it is placed in this location?" or "What will the view be like from this road if we build this building or log this hillside?" In Figure 1.32, areas shaded green are visible and red are not visible.

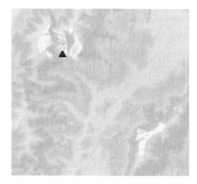

Figure 1.32 Viewshed calculation from an elevation model showing areas visible from the triangle. See color plate in Appendix C.

Terrain analysis has a significantly different meaning for the military services for which there are terrain analyst military occupational specialties that support battlefield intelligence. U.S. Army and Marine Corps combat units have specialized terrain analysts, equipped with computers and GIS software, to perform military terrain analyses of intervisibility, slope, aspect, cover and concealment, and cross country movement, for example, often based on digital terrain elevation data (DTED) from the National Geospatial-Intelligence Agency (NGA). The intent is to achieve superior use of the battlefield terrain itself in order to effect mission accomplishment and save lives.

Hydrologic Analysis

Elevation models are the key input to performing hydrologic analysis. The elevation provides the input data for calculating flow direction across the terrain which is subsequently used for the creation of stream networks and watersheds (Jenson and Domingue, 1988; Tarboton, 1997). See Figure 1.33. Using these tools it is possible to find the upslope contributing area and downslope flow path for any location. These derived data are then used to estimate rainfall runoff, predict flood levels, and manage water resources.

Figure 1.33 Watersheds and stream networks delineated from an elevation model. Hillshading has been added to show the underlying terrain. See color plate in Appendix C.

TIDES

Characteristics of the Tides

The word "tide" is a generic term used to define the alternating rise and fall of the oceans with respect to the land, produced by differential variations in the gravitational attraction of the moon and sun. Non-astronomical factors such as configuration of the coastline, local depth of the water, ocean-floor topography, and other hydrographic and meteorological influences play an important role in determining the range of tide, delay times of the tide, and the time interval between high and low waters.

There are three basic types of tides (Figure 1.34): semidiurnal (semi-daily), mixed, and diurnal (daily). The semidiurnal tide has two high waters (high tides) and two low waters (low tides) each tidal day. A tidal day is the time of rotation of the Earth with respect to the Moon, and its mean value is approximately equal to 24.84 hours. The two high waters and the two low waters for each tidal day are almost equal in height. In Figure 1.35, semidiurnal tides occur at Boston, New York, Hampton Roads, and Savannah. The mixed tide is similar to the semidiurnal tide except that the two high waters and the two low waters of each tidal day have marked differences in their heights. The two high waters are designated as higher high water and lower high water; the two low waters are designated as higher low water and lower low water. In Figures 1.35 and 1.36, mixed tides occur at Key West, San Francisco, Seattle, Ketchikan, and Dutch Harbor. The diurnal tide has one high water and one low water each tidal day. In Figure 1.35, Pensacola illustrates a diurnal tide.

The most important modulations of the tides are associated with the phases of the moon relative to the sun. Spring tides occur at the time of the new and full moon. These are the tides of greatest amplitude, meaning that the highest and lowest waters are recorded at these times. Neap tides occur approximately midway between the times of the new and full moon. The neap tidal range is usually 10 to 30 percent less than the mean tidal range. In addition to spring and neap tides, there are lesser, but significant, monthly modulations due to the elliptical orbit of the moon about the earth (perigee and apogee) and yearly modulations due to the elliptical orbit of the earth about the sun (perihelion and aphelion). Modulations in mixed and diurnal tides are especially sensitive to the monthly north and south declination of the moon relative to the earth's equator (tropic and equatorial tides) and to the yearly north and south declination of the sun relative to the earth's equator (solstices and equinoxes). The equinoxes are the two times of the year, March 21 and September 23, when the sun's apparent path crosses the earth's equator.

Although the astronomical influences of the moon and sun upon the earth would seem to imply a uniformity in the tide, the type of tide can vary both with time at a single location and in distance along the coast (Figures 1.35 and 1.36). The transition from one type to another is usually gradual either temporally or spatially, resulting in hybrid or transition tides. A good example in Figure 1.35 is Galveston, which transitions from diurnal to semidiurnal to mixed. Key West (Figure 1.35) transitions from mixed to semidiurnal to mixed. Dutch Harbor (Figure 1.36) shows similar transitions. There are gradual spatial transitions from mixed to diurnal to mixed and back to diurnal in the Gulf of Mexico. It is important to know the location of these transition zones because they limit how far tidal datum computation procedures can be applied successfully.

There is another important modulation in the amplitude of the tide due to orbital paths of the earth and moon. The path the sun appears to take among the stars, due to the annual revolution of the earth in its orbit, is called the ecliptic (Bowditch, 1995). This path may be represented on a globe of the earth by drawing a great circle about the Earth which makes an angle of 23° 27' with the earth's equator. Likewise, the path of the moon about the earth may be referenced to the ecliptic, such that the moon's orbit makes an angle of 5° with respect to the ecliptic. When the moon's ascending node corresponds to the vernal (spring) equinox, the angle of the moon's orbit about the earth's equator is about 28.5° (Schureman, 1941). When the moon's descending node corresponds to the vernal equinox, the angle of the moon's orbit about the earth's equator is about 18.5°.

This variation in the path of the moon about the sun has a period of about 18.6 years, and is called the regression of the moon's nodes. The regression of the nodes introduces an important variation into the amplitude of the monthly and annual mean range of the tide, as may be seen in Figure 1.36 for Seattle, WA. The regression of the moon's nodes forms the basis for the definition of the National Tidal Datum Epoch (NTDE) by the National Ocean Service (NOS), a component of the National Oceanic and Atmospheric Administration (NOAA). Because the monthly variability of the mean range is larger than the regression of the nodes, the NTDE is defined as an even 19-year period so as not to bias the estimate of the tidal datum. Data from continuously operating water level stations in the National Water Level Observation Network (NWLON) provide the basis for maintaining and updating the NTDE.

Some of the basic references for tides are Hicks, 1985; Hicks, 1989; International Oceanographic Commission, 2000; Marmer, 1951; Mero, 1998; National Ocean Service, 1999; Schultz and Scherer, 1999; Swanson, 1974; and U.S. Department of Commerce, 1970.

Nontidal Water Level Variations

Tides are not the only factor causing the sea surface height to change. Additional factors include waves and wave setup; ocean and river currents; ocean eddies; temperature and salinity variation of the ocean water; wind; barometric pressure; seiches; and relative sea level change. All of these factors are location dependent, and contribute various amounts to the height of the sea surface. Typical values are: wind setup - up to about 1 meter (~3.2 feet); ocean eddies - up to about 25 centimeters (~0.8 foot); upper ocean water temperature - up to about 35 centimeters (~1.1 foot); ocean currents or ocean circulation - about 1 meter; and relative sea level rise - around 0.3 meter (1 foot) per century.

It is NOS procedure not to separate other sea level fluctuations from the tides for computation of tidal datums. No mathematical or statistical filters are applied to the data before processing. Therefore, tidal tabulations will include, for instance, the effects of storm surge; however, NWLON water level gauges use a combination mechanical/numerical filter to remove the unwanted effects of high frequency wind waves and currents. The filter is part of the physical design of the sensor and the data collection algorithm of the data collection platform (Scherer, 1986).

The National Tidal Datum Epoch

As mentioned above, a specific nineteen-year period named a NTDE is used to compute tidal datums because it is the closest full year to the 18.6-year nodal cycle of the moon, the period

DISTRIBUTION OF TIDAL PHASE

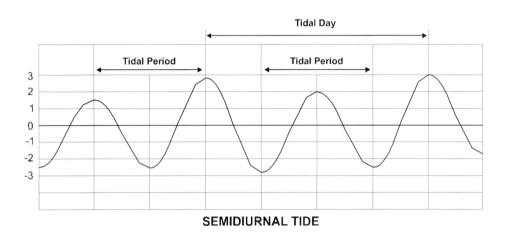

SEMIDIURNAL TIDE

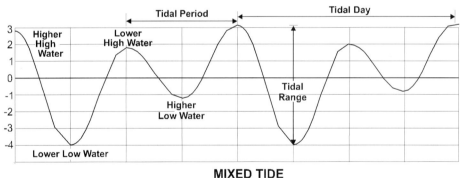

MIXED TIDE

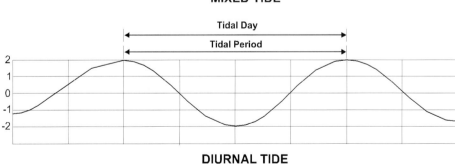

DIURNAL TIDE

Figure 1.34 A depiction of the three primary kinds of tides. From the top panel downward they are semidiurnal, mixed, and diurnal. Standard tidal terminology is used to describe the various aspects of the tides. The zero on these graphs illustrates the relationship of the tides to Mean Sea Level (MSL).

TYPICAL TIDE CURVES FOR UNITED STATES PORTS

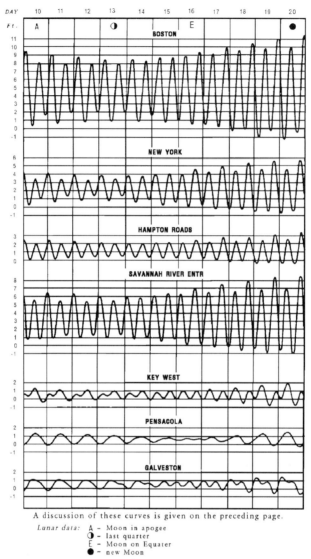

Figure 1.35 Characteristic tide curves near port facilities along the U.S. East and Gulf Coasts. The tides depicted are primarily semidiurnal along the East Coast. The tides at Pensacola are primarily diurnal. The effects of the phases of the moon are also illustrated. The elevations in feet of the tide are referenced to the tidal datum Mean Lower Low Water (MLLW).

required for the regression of the moon's nodes (Schureman, 1941). The NTDE is defined as the standard period of time for the determination of tidal datums because it includes all significant tidal periods, is long enough to average out local meteorological effects on sea level, and, by specifying the NTDE, a uniform approach is applied to all the tidal datums. For example, the average of all the observed higher high waters for a nineteen year period is defined as the Mean Higher High Water (MHHW) tidal datum. MHHW will have a specific height, which is not necessarily equal to any higher high water observed during a given tidal day. The same is true for the other tidal datums. The averaging technique defines a reference plane, from which all sea level fluctuations discussed here, except for relative sea level change, are considered to have been removed. These reference planes are necessary for determining marine boundaries, estimating

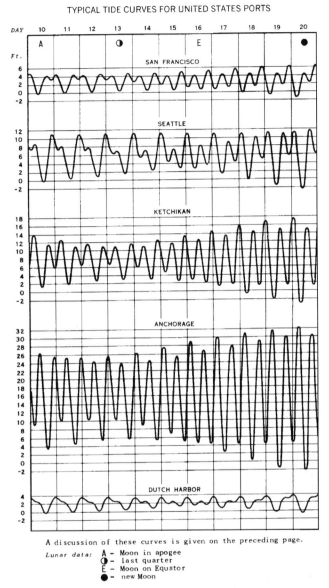

TYPICAL TIDE CURVES FOR UNITED STATES PORTS

A discussion of these curves is given on the preceding page.

Lunar data: A – Moon in apogee
☽ – last quarter
E – Moon on Equator
● – new Moon

Figure 1.36 Characteristic tide curves for the West Coast. The tides depicted are primarily mixed. The tidal range at Anchorage is quite large. The effects of the phases of the moon are also illustrated. The elevations in feet of the tide are referenced to the tidal datum Mean Lower Low Water (MLLW).

heights or depths relative to the reference plane, and for a wide variety of other scientific and practical engineering applications.

The relative sea level change, as well as the variability of the change by geographic region, is readily seen when yearly mean sea level is plotted against time. Because of the relative sea level change, tidal datums become out of date for navigational purposes as the years pass. Thus, a new National Tidal Datum Epoch must be considered periodically (Figure 1.38). The policy of NOS is to consider defining a new NTDE every 25 years to appropriately update tidal datums for global sea level rise and any long-term vertical adjustment of the local landmass due to, for example, subsidence or glacial rebound (Gill et al, 1998). Estimated relative sea level trends compiled from observations at U.S. water level stations are listed in Zervas, C. E., 2001.

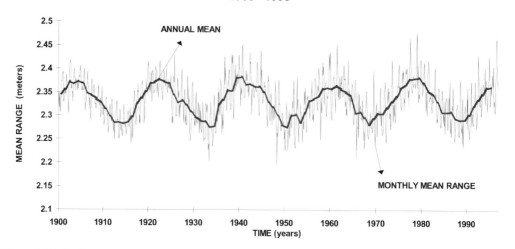

Figure 1.37 An illustration of the effect of the regression of the moon's nodes on the water level range at Seattle, WA. The heavy black curve is the annual mean range, or the difference in height between mean high water and mean low water. The time elapsed between peaks is the period of oscillation of the regression and is about 18.6 years. The more rapidly varying curve is the monthly mean range. Changes in the monthly mean range are due to astronomical, meteorological, and oceanographic conditions.

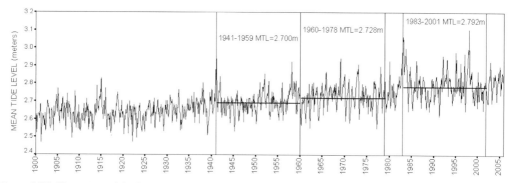

Figure 1.38 Illustration of the long term change in sea level causing the need to repeatedly update such tidal datums as the mean tide level (MTL) for San Francisco, CA from 1941-1959, 1960-1978 and 1983-2001. Measurements are relative to the station datum, an arbitrary zero level which is tied to the local tidal bench mark network and maintained by annual leveling.

Tide Station Networks

The various tidal datums are defined in Chapter 2, Vertical Datums, of this DEM Users Manual.

The NOS provides unique water level and ancillary data sets and information to users in support of a wide variety of critical activities. A priority is to provide the basic data for the vertical, tidal datum control for the nation. The instrumentation consists of the NWLON water level stations, and any additional short-term stations operating for special projects such as hydrographic surveys, photogrammetry, and United States Army Corps of Engineers dredging activities. The NWLON is composed of approximately 175 long-term stations distributed around the country and the world.

Except for the water level stations in the Great Lakes, most of the stations in the NWLON are in coastal areas that come under the influence of the tide to a significant degree and are referred to as control tide stations. Although the NWLON is designed to provide the fundamental tidal datum control network, most applications require tidal datum knowledge at a higher resolution than the network spacing. Depending on the application, networks of shorter-term stations are established. The NWLON stations have accepted tidal datums computed either over the NDTE or, at least, over multiple years. They provide direct datum control for a nearby area and control for short-term stations over a larger geographic area. The extent of datum control depends upon the complexity of the coastal zone in terms of changes in tidal characteristics, localized effects of river runoff and wind, and differences in long-term sea level trends.

The locations of tide stations are organized into a hierarchy. Control (or primary) tide stations sometimes have open ocean exposure, or are within the mouth of a bay or estuary, secondary stations are also within the mouth of a bay or estuary, and tertiary stations are usually further within an estuary.

Control tide stations are generally those that have been operated for 19 or more years, are expected to continue to operate in the future, and are used to obtain a continuous record of the water levels in a locality. Control tide stations are sited to provide datum control for national applications, and located in as many places as needed for datum control. As the records from such a station constitute basic water level data for present and future use, during the installation and maintenance of the station, the aim is to obtain the highest degree of reliability and precision that is practical. The essential equipment of a control tide station includes an automatic water level sensor, protective well, shelter, back-up water level sensor, a system of bench marks, and possibly ancillary geophysical instruments.

Secondary water level stations are those that are operated for less than 19 years but more than 1 year, and have a planned finite lifetime. Secondary stations provide control in bays and estuaries where localized tidal effects are not realized at the nearest control station. Observations at a secondary station are not usually sufficient for a precise independent determination of tidal datums, but when reduced by comparison with simultaneous observations at a suitable control tide station, very accurate results are obtained. Secondary tide stations also provide data for the reduction of soundings in connection with hydrographic surveys.

Tertiary water level stations are those that are operated for more than a month but less than one year. Short-term water level measurement stations (secondary, tertiary, and seasonal) may have their data reduced to equivalent 19-year tidal datums through mathematical simultaneous comparison with a nearby control station. Short-term data, often at several locations, are collected routinely to support hydrographic surveying. In the Great Lakes, seasonal data are simultaneously compared to adjacent stations for datum determination in harbors.

The station site selection criteria include spatial coverage of significant changes in tidal characteristics such as tide type, range of tide, time of tide, daily mean sea level, and long-term mean sea level trends. Other criteria include coverage of critical navigation areas and transitional zones, historical station sites, proximity to the geodetic network, and the availability of existing structures, such as piers suitable for the location of the scientific equipment.

For tidal datum applications, it is important for gauge sensors to be carefully calibrated with either frequent calibration checks or cycled swaps of calibrated sensors for long-term installations. The sensor "zero" must be precisely related to either a tide staff and/or the bench marks through staff/gauge comparisons or direct leveling between the sensor and the bench marks. Vertical stability of the sensor "zero", both physically and internally, must be monitored and any movement taken into account in the data reduction and datum computation.

Bench Marks and Differential Leveling

A network of bench marks is an integral part of every water level measurement station. A bench mark is a fixed physical object or mark used as a reference for a vertical datum. For example, a tidal bench mark is a mark near a tide station to which the tidal datums are referenced. Since gauge measurements are referenced to the bench marks, it follows that the overall quality of tidal datums is partially dependent on both the quality of the bench mark installation and the quality of the leveling between the bench marks and the gauge.

Bench marks have site selection considerations much like the tide stations they support. The first consideration is longevity; bench marks are sited to minimize susceptibility to damage or destruction. Bench marks are sited to ease future recovery (locating and leveling to the mark) and to ensure accessibility (open, overhead clearance). Bench marks must also be placed in the most stable structure for the locality. Preference should be given to disks set in bedrock, in large man made structures with deep foundations, or installation of stainless steel rods driven to substantial resistance.

Since bench marks are vulnerable to natural disturbances, such as geologic and soil activity, in addition to damage inflicted by man, more bench marks are installed around stations with longer term data series. At primary control stations, where 19 years of observations have been conducted or are planned, a network of at least ten bench marks is installed in the vicinity of the station. Five bench marks are installed at secondary and tertiary stations. At least three bench marks are installed at shorter-term (less than 30 days) stations.

Differential leveling is used to check the elevation differences between bench marks, to extend vertical control, and to monitor the stability of the water level measurement gauge. Bench marks are leveled whenever a new tide station is established, or when data collection is discontinued at a tide station. Bench marks are also leveled before and after maintenance is performed at a station, and at least annually to perform stability checks. In addition, whenever new bench marks are installed, the existing bench marks are re-leveled. The quality of leveling is a function of the procedures used, the sensitivity of the leveling instruments, the precision and accuracy of the rod, the attention given by surveyors, and the refinement of the computations.

The *User's Guide for the Installation of Bench Marks and Leveling Requirements for Water Level Stations* (Hicks et al, 1987) and NOAA Manual NOS N.S. 1 (Floyd, 1978) provide detailed guidelines for bench mark installations and leveling.

The National Tidal Bench Mark System (NTBMS) provides datum information for previously and currently occupied tidal measurement locations. The number of stations in the NTBMS is approximately 6000. There are approximately 3000 along the U.S. East Coast, 500 on the Gulf Coast, 1000 along the West Coast, 1200 in Alaska, 150 in the Pacific Islands; and 177 around the Great Lakes. In many cases, bench marks in the NTBMS have not been re-leveled in many years, resulting in some uncertainty in their validity. Bench marks may become invalid due to crustal movement or by changes in local tidal characteristics due to dredging, erosion, or accretion. At present, about 2000 stations have bench marks with valid published elevations. Information on geodetic or tidal datum elevations and bench marks are available from NOS web sites at www.co-ops.nos.noaa.gov and www.ngs.noaa.gov.

Tide Zoning

An important aspect of hydrographic surveys of the nation's harbors, bays, and estuaries is to accurately account for the varying height of the water at the time and location of each depth measurement (or sounding). NOS computes the tide corrections (or tide reducers) that adjust depth soundings taken during hydrographic survey operations to the NOS chart datum, Mean Lower Low Water (MLLW). Since tidal characteristics (time of tide, range of tide, shape of the tide curve) vary spatially, the data observed at water level stations are not representative of the water levels throughout an entire hydrographic survey area. Therefore, discrete tidal zoning enables the extrapolation of observed tide curves from a water level station to an area of the survey which lacks observations. The tide reducers are derived either directly from observations at a primary (or control) tide station or indirectly through discrete tidal zoning. Hydrographic project requirements must specify water level station locations and provide discrete tidal zoning schemes.

In tide zoning methodology, the estuaries and embayments are described by a set of discrete geographical areas or zones of similar tidal characteristics. Each zone is assigned a time corrector (phase shift) and a range ratio (amplitude correction) that are used to adjust the observed tide from a nearby water level station in order to reduce the soundings taken in a particular zone to

MLLW. Co-tidal maps consisting of co-range and co-phase lines describe the tidal characteristics of an area. The shape and orientation of the co-tidal lines are determined using historical tide station data, numerical and theoretical tide models, and offshore measurements. NOS develops discrete tide zones as polygons generated from the co-tidal lines using MapInfo GIS software. The shape and number of the polygons are determined by the changes in tidal characteristics of the area. The minimum requirement is for a new zone for every 0.06 m change in mean range of tide and every 0.3 hour progression in time of tide.

Discrete tidal zoning is used in conjunction with the appropriate number and location of water level stations so that the total error budget is met. Errors in the tide adjustments to soundings are maximum at the edge of each zone where there will be a discrete shift or jump in the range and time of tide. Discrete tidal zoning becomes problematic in areas where the tides are hydrodynamically complex such that extrapolation of tidal characteristics from a location with observed tides to locations where the tides are not understood becomes uncertain.

AUTHOR BIOGRAPHIES

David F. Maune is a geodesist, photogrammetrist, Associate and Senior Project Manager for Mapping and Remote Sensing at Dewberry in Fairfax, Virginia. He is an ASPRS Fellow, Certified Photogrammetrist, and Certified Floodplain Manager. He is also a licensed Geodetic Land Surveyor and Photogrammetric Surveyor. For the Federal Emergency Management Agency (FEMA), he authored the aerial mapping and surveying guidelines and specifications (Appendix A) which includes lidar guidelines widely used nationwide. He manages Dewberry's contracts with the U.S. Geological Survey (USGS), National Oceanic and Atmospheric Administration (NOAA), and U.S. Department of Agriculture (USDA) that entail production of DEMs and related products from photogrammetry, lidar, IFSAR, and sonar. He was previously an active duty Army Colonel, retiring after 30 years with the U.S. Army Corps of Engineers where he served as Director, U.S. Army Topographic Engineering Center (TEC); Director, Defense Mapping School (DMS); and Inspector General, Defense Mapping Agency (DMA) — now the National Geospatial-Intelligence Agency (NGA). He is a remote sensing consultant to federal, state and local governments, specializing in independent quality assurance/quality control (QA/QC) of lidar data, contours and digital orthophotos. He received his BS degree in Mechanical Engineering in 1961 from the University of Missouri, Rolla, and in 1970 and 1973 he received his MS and PhD degrees in geodetic science and photogrammetry from The Ohio State University.

Stephen M. Kopp currently leads the Raster/Modeling Product Development teams at the Environmental Systems Research Institute, Inc. During his 16 years at ESRI, he focused primarily on development of the ArcInfo GRID and ArcView Spatial Analyst products. He received his MA degree in Geography from Indiana State University, Terre Haute, Indiana, in 1990.

Clayton A. Crawford is currently the Product Lead for the 3D Development Team at ESRI. He received his M.S. degree in Geography from the University of Tennessee, Knoxville, in 1990.

Chris E. Zervas is an oceanographer for the Products and Services Division of the Center for Operational Oceanographic Products and Services of the National Ocean Service. He has worked for the National Oceanic and Atmospheric Administration for the past 10 years. He has a BA in physics from Johns Hopkins University (1979), an MS in geophysics from the University of Washington (1984), and a PhD in geophysics from the University of Washington (1988). He also worked for the David Taylor Ship Research and Development Center, Bethesda, Maryland for three years in the field of acoustics.

ACKNOWLEDGMENTS

Appreciation is also expressed to Eric Constance of USGS' Mid-Continent Mapping Center, who provided many of the definitions in Appendix B.

REFERENCES

ASPRS, 1990. ASPRS accuracy standards for large-scale maps, *Photogrammetric Engineering and Remote Sensing*, 56(7): 1068-1070.

Ayeni, O.O., 1982. Optimum sampling for digital terrain models: A trend towards automation, *Photogrammetric Engineering and Remote Sensing*, 48(11): 1687-1694.

Bowditch, N., 1995. *The American Practical Navigator, An Epitome of Navigation*, Defense Mapping Agency Hydrographic/Topographic Center, Bethesda, MD, pp. 873.

Bureau of the Budget, 1947. *National Map Accuracy Standards*, Office of Management and Budget, Washington, D.C.

Carter, J.R., 1988. Digital representations of topographic surfaces, *Photogrammetric Engineering and Remote Sensing*, 54(11): 1577-1580.

Chen, Zi-Tan, 1988. Break lines on terrain surfaces, *Proceedings, GIS/LIS '88*, Falls Church, VA, American Society for Photogrammetry and Remote Sensing, pp. 781-790.

Franke, R., 1982. Smooth interpolation of scattered data by local thin plate splines, *Comp. & Maths. with Appls.*, 8(4). Great Britain.

Floyd, R.P., 1978. Geodetic bench marks, *NOAA Manual* NOS NGS 1, U.S. Department of Commerce, NOAA, National Ocean Survey, Rockville, MD, pp.51.

Gill, S.K., J.R. Hubbard, and W.D. Scherer, 1998. Updating the national tidal datum epoch for the United States, *Proceedings Ocean Community Conference*, November 16-19, 1998, Marine Technology Society Annual Conference, 1040-1043.

Gold, Christopher, 1989. Surface interpolation, spatial adjacency and GIS, *Three Dimensional Applications in Geographic Information Systems*, Jonathan Raper ed., Taylor and Francis, pp. 21-35.

Hicks, S.D., 1989. *Tide and Current Glossary*, NOAA National Ocean Service, Silver Spring, MD.

Hicks, S.D., 1985. Tidal datums and their uses - A summary, *Shore and Beach*, 27-33.

Hicks, S.D., P.C. Morris, H.A. Lippincott, and M.C. O'Hargan, 1987. *User's Guide for the Installation of Bench Marks and Leveling Requirements for Water Levels*, NOAA National Ocean Service, Silver Spring, MD, pp. 73.

Hutchinson, M.F., 1989. A new procedure for gridding elevation and stream line data with automatic removal of spurious pits, *Journal of Hydrology*, 106, 211-232.

International Oceanographic Commission (IOC), 2000. Manual on sea level measurement and interpretation, Volume 3 - Reappraisals and recommendations as of the year 2000, *Manuals and Guides*, 14, UNESCO.

Issaks, E.H. and R.M. Srivastava, 1989. *An Introduction to Applied Geostatistics*, Oxford University Press, New York.

Jenson, S.K. and J.O. Domingue. 1988. Extracting topographic structure from digital elevation data for geographic information system analysis, *Photogrammetric Engineering and Remote Sensing*, 54(11): 1593-1600.

Kidner, David B., A.J. Sparkes, M.J. Ware, and C.B. Jones, 2000. Multiscale terrain and topographic modeling with the implicit TIN, *Transactions in GIS*, 4(4), 379-408.

Marmer, H.A., revised 1951. *Tidal Datum Planes*, NOAA National Ocean Service, Special Publication No. 135, U.S. Coast and Geodetic Survey, U.S. Govt. Printing Office.

Mero, T.N., 1998. NOAA/National Ocean Service application of real-time water levels, *Proceedings, Volume 2, Ocean Community Conference*, The Marine Technology Society Annual Conference, November 16-19, 1998, 1036-1039.

Mitas, L., and H. Mitasova, 1988. General variational approach to the interpolation problem, *Comput. Math. Applic.*, 16(12), Great Britain.

National Geodetic Survey, 1997. Guidelines for establishing GPS-derived ellipsoid heights (Standards: 2cm and 5cm) Version 4.3, *NOAA Technical Memorandum* NOS NGS-58.

National Ocean Service, 1999. *NOS Hydrographic Surveys Specifications and Deliverables*, NOAA National Ocean Service, Silver Spring, MD, pp. 91.

Peucker, T.K., R.J. Fowler, J.J. Little, and D.M. Mark, 1978. The triangulated irregular network, *Proceedings of the Digital Terrain Models (DTM) Symposium*, St. Louis, American Society of Photogrammetry, 516-540.

Robinson, A.H., J.L. Morrison, P.C. Muehrcke, A.J. Kimmerling, and S.C. Guptill, 1995. *Elements of Cartography, Sixth Edition*, John Wiley & Sons.

Scherer, W.D., 1986. *National Ocean Service's Next Generation Water Level Measurement System*, Vol. 4, International Congress of Surveying, Toronto, Ontario, Canada, pp 232-243.

Schultz, J.R. and W.D. Scherer, 1999. Tidal datums and their applications, *NOAA Technical Report* NOS CO-OPS 1, Center For Operational Oceanographic Products and Services, Silver Spring, MD.

Schureman, P., revised 1941. Manual of harmonic analysis and prediction of tides, *Special Publication No. 98* (1940), U.S. Coast and Geodetic Survey, U.S. Govt. Printing Office.

Sibson, R., 1981. A brief description of natural neighbor interpolation, *Interpolating Multivariate Data*, John Wiley & Sons, New York, pp. 21-36.

Swanson, R.L., 1974. Variability of tidal datums and accuracy in setermining satums from short series of observations, *NOAA Tech. Rep.* NOS 64, Silver Spring, MD, pp. 41.

Tarboton, D.G, 1997. A new method for the determination of flow directions and contributing areas in grid digital elevation models, *Water Resources Research*, 33(2): 309-319.

U.S. Department of Commerce, 1970. *Demarcating and Mapping Tidal Boundaries*, Environmental Science Services Administration, Coast & Geodetic Survey.

Watson, D., 1992. *Contouring: A Guide to the Analysis and Display of Spatial Data*, Pergamon Press, England.

Zervas, C.E., 2001. Sea level variations of the United States 1954-1999, *NOAA Technical Report* NOS CO-OPS 36, U.S. Department of Commerce, National Oceanic and Atmospheric Administration, National Ocean Service, Silver Spring, MD.

Chapter 2

Vertical Datums

David B. Zilkoski

INTRODUCTION

The word "elevation" in the term Digital Elevation Model (DEM) is usually misunderstood, and its true meaning is not readily agreed upon by its users. Technically, the correct meaning is "height." There are several types of heights — ellipsoid, geodetic, geoid, orthometric, Helmert Orthometric, dynamic, etc. — and they generally refer to different reference surfaces. The definitions of these various types of heights are explained in Appendix B, Definitions, of this manual. Unless explicitly stated, the word "elevation" in DEM refers to orthometric heights, referenced to a vertical datum; however, there are a variety of different vertical datums explained in this chapter.

What is a vertical datum? Vertical datum is defined as the set of constants defining a height system. The realization of a vertical datum is the set of constants, the coordinate system, and points that have been consistently determined by observations, corrections, and computation. There have been numerous national vertical datums and hundreds of local vertical datums established in the United States during the past century. Users of vertical datums should understand and know the differences between the national and local varieties of each. It is important that users know which datum their data are referred to. Differences between datums can exceed tens of meters; therefore, combining or mixing vertical data products, not referenced to the same datum, can result in large errors in new products and cause problems for their users — chiefly modelers and planners. In addition, with the advent of technologies like Global Positioning Systems (GPS), Light Detection and Ranging (lidar), and Synthetic Aperture Radar (SAR) to generate heights and height products, users should also fully understand the differences between ellipsoid and orthometric heights, in addition to a base knowledge of the history of vertical datums in the United States. This chapter will address these, and related issues. For further information, please visit NGS' web site at http://www.ngs.noaa.gov.

HISTORY OF U.S. NATIONAL VERTICAL DATUMS

The first leveling route (considered to be of geodetic quality) in the United States was established in 1856-57, under the direction of G.B. Vose of the U.S. Coast Survey. The U.S. Coast Survey was the predecessor of the U.S. Coast and Geodetic Survey and, later, the National Ocean Service. The first leveling survey was needed to support current and tide studies in the New York Bay and Hudson River areas. The first leveling line, officially designated as "geodesic leveling" by the Coast and Geodetic Survey, followed an arc of triangulation along the 39th parallel. This 1887 survey began at bench mark A in Hagerstown, Maryland.

By 1900, the vertical control network had grown to 21,095 km of geodetic leveling. A reference surface was determined in 1900 by holding elevations referenced to local mean sea level (LMSL), fixed at five tide stations. Data from two other tide stations indirectly influenced the determination of the reference surface. Subsequent readjustments of the leveling network were performed by the Coast and Geodetic Survey in 1903, 1907, and 1912 (Berry, 1976).

The next general adjustment of the vertical control network, accomplished in 1929, was the National Geodetic Vertical Datum of 1929 (NGVD 29). By 1929, the international nature of geodetic networks was well understood, and Canada provided data for its first-order vertical network to combine with the U.S. network. The two networks were connected at 24 locations through vertical control points (bench marks), from Maine/New Brunswick to Washington/British Columbia. Although Canada did not adopt the "Sea Level Datum of 1929," determined by the United States, Canadian-U.S. cooperation in the general adjustment greatly strengthened the 1929 network. Table 2.1 lists the kilometers of leveling involved in the readjustments and the number of tide stations used to establish the datums. Figure 2.1 depicts the U.S. portion of the primary network used in the 1929 readjustment.

Table 2.1 Amount of leveling and number of tide stations involved in previous readjustments.

Year of Adjustment	Kilometers of Leveling	Number of Tide Stations
1900	21,095	5
1903	31,789	8
1907	38,359	8
1912	46,468	9
1929	75,159 (U.S.)	21 (U.S.)
	31,565 (Canada)	5 (Canada)

The most recent general adjustment of the U.S. vertical control network, which is known as the North American Vertical Datum of 1988 (NAVD 88), was completed in June 1991 (Zilkoski et al., 1992). Approximately 625,000 km of leveling has been added to the National Spatial Reference System (NSRS) since NGVD 29 was created (See Figure 2.2). In the intervening years, discussions were held periodically to determine the proper time for the inevitable new general adjustment. In the early 1970s, the National Geodetic Survey (NGS) conducted an extensive inventory of the vertical control network. The search identified thousands of bench marks that had been destroyed, due primarily to post-World War II highway construction, as well as other causes. Many existing bench marks were affected by crustal motion associated with earthquake activity, postglacial rebound (uplift), and subsidence resulting from the withdrawal of underground liquids. Some observed changes, amounting to as much as 9m, are discussed in published reports (Zilkoski et al., 1989; Zilkoski, 1986; Zilkoski and Young, 1985).

An important feature of the NAVD 88 program was the releveling of much of the first order NGS vertical control network in the United States. The dynamic nature of the network requires a framework of newly observed height differences to obtain realistic, contemporary height values from the readjustment. To accomplish this, NGS identified 81,500 km (50,600 miles) for releveling. Replacement of disturbed and destroyed monuments preceded the actual leveling. This effort also included the establishment of stable "deep-rod" bench marks, which are now providing reference points for new GPS-derived orthometric height projects as well as for traditional leveling projects.

The general adjustment of NAVD 88 consisted of 709,000 unknowns (approximately 505,000 permanently monumented bench marks and 204,000 temporary bench marks) and approximately 1.2 million observations.

For the general adjustment of NAVD 88 and the International Great Lakes Datum of 1985 (IGLD 85), a minimum-constraint adjustment of Canadian-Mexican-U.S. leveling observations was performed. The height of the primary tidal bench mark at Father Point/Rimouski, Quebec, Canada, was held fixed as the constraint (Figures 2.3 and 2.4). Therefore, IGLD 85 and NAVD 88 are one and the same. Father Point/Rimouski is an IGLD water-level station located at the mouth of the St. Lawrence River and is the reference station used for IGLD 85. This constraint satisfied the

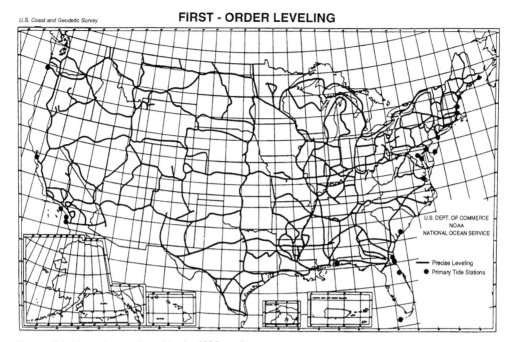

Figure 2.1 Vertical control used in the 1929 readjustment.

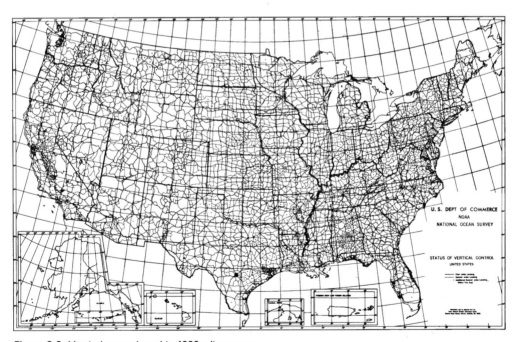

Figure 2.2 Vertical control used in 1988 adjustment.

requirements of shifting the datum vertically, to minimize the impact of NAVD 88 on U.S. Geological Survey (USGS) mapping products, and provides the datum point desired by the IGLD Coordinating Committee for IGLD 85. The only difference between IGLD 85 and NAVD 88 is that IGLD 85 bench mark values are given in dynamic height units, and NAVD 88 values are given in Helmert orthometric height units.

Geopotential numbers for individual bench marks are the same in both systems. IGLD 85 and different types of heights will be discussed in more detail later in the chapter. Differences between IGLD 85 and the previous International Great Lakes Datum of 1955 (IGLD 55) have also been compiled (Figure 2.4).

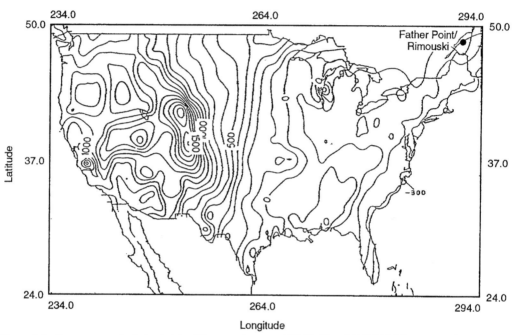

Figure 2.3 Contour map depicting height differences between NAVD 88 and NGVD 29 (units = mm).

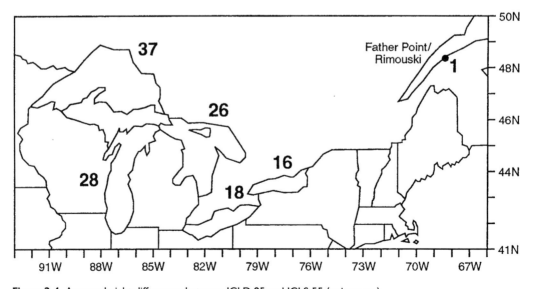

Figure 2.4 Average height differences between IGLD 85 and IGLS 55 (units = cm).

NATIONAL GEODETIC VERTICAL DATUM OF 1929 (NGVD 29)

Many users of vertical data ask the question, why did NGVD 29 need to be readjusted? Or why is NGVD 29 now obsolete? This section provides a brief explanation. As mentioned in the previous section, there were general adjustments performed every few years in the early 1900s, i.e., in 1903, 1907, and 1912. Then, 17 years elapsed before the next adjustment in 1929. To understand why NGVD 29 is obsolete, the reader must first understand how NGVD 29 was derived. The following excerpt from Berry's 1976 report does an excellent job of explaining how NGVD 29 was established.

"The net had become much more extensive and complex and had more sea level connections. An innovation introduced was the inclusion of the Canadian first order network in the adjustment computation.

The composition of the network by agencies is not determined, but the lengths included 75,159 km. of U.S. lines and 31,565 km. of Canadian lines for a total of 106,724 km. of leveling included in the adjustment. The U.S. and Canadian networks were connected at 24 points, extending from Calais, Me./ Brunswick, N.B., to Blaine, Wash./Colebrook, B.C. There were 693 'links' in the network (including 19 long water-level transfers in the Great Lakes), 253 in Canada, 416 in the United States, and 24 international, which were combined to make 246 closed circuits and 25 sea-level circuits. The adjustment provided elevations for 450 junction points.

"Mean sea level was held fixed at 26 gauge sites, 21 in the United States and five in Canada at the following locations:

Father Point Que.	St. Augustine, Fla.
Halifax. N.S.	Cedar Keys, Fla.
Yarmouth, N.S.	Pensacola, Fla.
Portland. Me.	Biloxi, Miss.
Boston, Mass.	Galveston, Tex.
Perth Amboy, N.J.	San Diego, Calif.
Atlantic City, N.J.	San Pedro, Calif.
Baltimore, Md.	San Francisco, Calif.
Annapolis, Md.	Fort Stevens, Md.
Old Point Comfort, Va.	Seattle, Wash.
Norfolk, Va.	Anacortes, Wash.
Brunswick, Ga.	Vancouver, B.C.
Fernandina, Fla.	Prince Rupert, B.C.

"The elevations of junction points and of intermediate bench marks on 'links' connecting the junction points define a datum to which the elevations of all bench marks in the U.S. vertical control network are referred. This datum is defined by the observed heights of mean sea level at the 26 tide gauges listed above and the set of elevations of all the bench marks resulting from the adjustment of the network to these specific sea level determinations.

"It should be further noted that, while the extensive Canadian first order net was used to strengthen the 1929 adjustment, the datum was not adopted in Canada because an independent adjustment of the separate Canadian network had been accomplished in 1928, and the resulting elevations published in a series of official books. Consequently, since the 1928 adjustment defined the official datum for elevations in Canada, which is still in use today, differing elevations are published by the United States and Canada for the set of bench marks which constitute the junction points between the U.S. network and the Canadian network.

"Shortly after accomplishment of the 1929 adjustment, the resulting datum was designated as the 'Sea Level Datum of 1929,' because of its dependence on a series of mean sea level determinations. "It was known at the time of the adjustment that, because of currents, prevailing winds and barometric pressures, water temperature and salinity differentials, topographic configuration of the bottom in the area of the gauge site, and other physical causes, a series of discrete mean sea level determinations, based on tide gauge observations, would not define a single equipotential surface (having a constant potential value). The result of this situation is, in actuality, no two determinations of mean sea level at different localities will be on the same level surface; they will, therefore, have different elevations as determined by the differential leveling process.

"In spite of these known variations in the elevations of local mean sea level, it was concluded (1) that these variations were probably of about the same order of magnitude as the observational errors in the leveling network, and (2) that confusion would be caused in the operations of the engineering community if the published elevations of bench marks near the coast would not be compatible with the local mean sea level as determined by tidal observations. Accordingly, in the 1929 adjustment, the network was constrained to hold fixed the observed local mean sea level at each of the 26 gauge sites listed above.

"It is now known that this constraint resulted in some deformations in the level net as defined by the leveling observations alone. Furthermore, since the elevations of mean sea level at different sites do not vary linearly along the coast line segments that connect them, it follows that elevations of mean sea level as defined by tidal observations at intermediate points between the 26 points held fixed in the adjustment will not agree precisely with the 'zero' elevations at the same points as defined by leveling adjusted to conform to the 1929 adjustment (the 'Mean Sea Level Datum of 1929').

"This has resulted in considerable confusion and misunderstanding, especially in these times when substantial emphasis is being applied to the precise determination of coastal boundary lines and offshore jurisdictional limits. These lines and limits are almost universally defined by reference to some line (mean low water, 'ordinary high water line,' etc.) defined by the rise and fall of the tide. It is a probable cause for considerable error to assume that these lines can be fixed by reference to the 'zero' line as defined by leveling from bench marks whose elevations are referred to the geodetic datum for elevations.

"To eliminate some of the confusion caused by the original name of the current geodetic datum for elevations ('Sea Level Datum of 1929'), the name of the datum has been changed to 'National Geodetic Vertical Datum of 1929,' eliminating all reference to 'sea level' in the title. This is a change in name only; the mathematical and physical definitions of the datum established in 1929 have not been changed in any way."

In support of NAVD 88, NGS converted the historic height difference links involved in the 1929 general adjustment to computer-readable form. The 1929 general adjustment was reconstructed by constraining the heights of the original 26 coastal stations. Free-adjustment results were then compared with the general adjustment constrained results (Zilkoski et al., 1992). Several differences exceeded 50 cm. A large relative difference, 86 cm, existed between St. Augustine, Florida, and Fort Stevens, Oregon. This is indicative of the amount of distortion present in the 1929 general adjustment (Figure 2.5). Other problems (distortions in the network) were caused by forcing the 625,000 km of leveling to fit previously determined NGVD 29 height values.

In addition, as previously mentioned, many existing bench marks were affected by crustal motion associated with earthquake activity, postglacial rebound (uplift), and subsidence resulting from the withdrawal of underground liquids. These are some of the reasons why NGVD 29 needed to be readjusted.

NORTH AMERICAN VERTICAL DATUM OF 1988 (NAVD 88)

Analyses indicate that the overall differences for the conterminous United States between orthometric heights referred to NAVD 88 and to NGVD 29 range from –49 cm to +158 cm. In Alaska, the differences range from approximately +94 cm to +240 cm. However, in most "stable" areas, relative height changes between adjacent bench marks appear to be less than 1 cm. In many areas, a single bias factor, describing the difference between NGVD 29 and NAVD 88, can be estimated and used for most mapping applications (NGS has developed a program called VERTCON to convert from NGVD 29 to NAVD 88 to support mapping applications (more will be said about this later in this chapter). The overall differences between dynamic heights referred to IGLD 85 and to IGLD 55 range from 1 cm to 37 cm (See Figure 2.4).

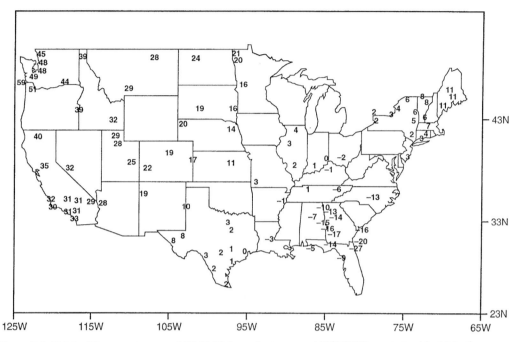

Figure 2.5 Height differences between NGVD 29 free adjustment and NGVD 29 constrained (published) adjustment (units = cm).

Comparison of NAVD 88 with NGVD 29 Published Heights

As mentioned previously and shown in Figure 2.6 below, the overall difference for the contermi-nous United States between orthometric heights referred to NAVD 88 and NGVD 29 range from –49 cm to +158 cm. It is difficult to separate the overall change in bench mark heights into individual components, such as the effects of systematic errors, crustal motion, and datum distortions. Comparison of adjusted heights, with or without corrections applied, indicates that, except for the magnetic correction, the adjusted heights are not changed significantly in a global sense, but in some regions they do have a large local effect (Zilkoski et al., 1989). Figure 2.6 provides examples of differences between NAVD 88 heights and NGVD 29 published height values due to local effects.

Along the U.S. coastlines, the differences between NAVD 88 and NGVD 29 are very large. These are due mostly to constraints imposed in 1929 (i.e., 26 tidal stations were constrained in NGVD 29, and only one was constrained in NAVD 88). Figure 2.5 depicts some of these effects on NGVD 29 caused by the constraints (e.g., in northern Florida, 22 cm were forced into NGVD 29 between the Atlantic Ocean and the Gulf Coast).

As shown in Figure 2.6, there is more than a 1-meter difference between the two datums, from Minnesota to Washington. This is due mostly to a large distribution correction (89 cm) applied in the 1929 adjustment (Zilkoski et al., 1989).

Inconsistent adjustments in the years prior to 1991 caused the large relative differences of closely spaced bench marks shown in the panhandle of Florida and in southern Illinois (i.e., for number pairs 6 and -14 in Florida, and 9 and -10 in Illinois, as shown at Figure 2.6).

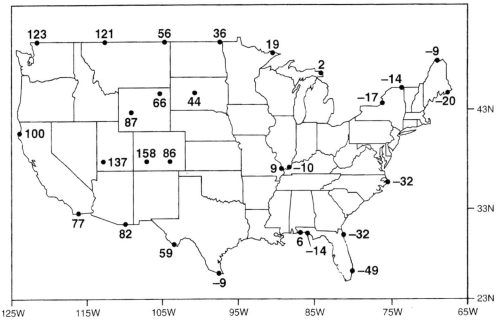

Figure 2.6 NAVD 88 minus NGVD 29 (units = cm).

The difference between adjusted Helmert orthometric heights (computed using geopotential differences based on observed gravity) and adjusted normal orthometric heights (computed using the normal gravity formula) is another component of the differences shown in Figure 2.6. This is the dominant effect in the Rocky Mountain states.

In Alaska, the differences between NAVD 88 heights and NGVD 29 published height values are much larger, due to local effects in Alaska. In Fairbanks, there is a 65 cm relative difference between closely spaced bench marks due to inconsistent adjustment constraints in NGVD 29. Other differences are due to effects of crustal movement, constraints imposed in NGVD 29, and Helmert orthometric heights versus normal orthometric heights. Some examples of differences between NAVD 88 and NGVD 29 for major cities in Alaska are Prudhoe Bay (110 cm), Fairbanks (160 cm), Anchorage (190 cm), Valdez (205 cm), and Homer (175 cm).

INTERNATIONAL GREAT LAKES DATUM OF 1985 (IGLD 85)

There are several different height systems used by the surveying and mapping community. Two of these height systems are relevant to IGLD 85: orthometric heights and dynamic heights. Geopotential numbers relate these two systems to each other.

The geopotential number (C) of a bench mark is the difference in potential measured from the reference geopotential surface to the equipotential surface passing through the survey mark. It is the amount of work required to raise a unit mass of 1 kg against gravity through the orthometric height to the mark. Geopotential differences are differences in potential which indicate hydraulic head, i.e., the direction water flows.

The orthometric height of a mark is the distance from the reference surface to the mark, measured along the line perpendicular to every equipotential surface in between. A series of equipotential surfaces can be used to represent the gravity field. These surfaces defined by the gravity field are not equally spaced because of the rotation of the Earth and gravity anomalies in the gravity field. Two points, therefore, could have the same potential but may have two different orthometric heights. The value of the orthometric height at a point depends on all the equipotential surfaces beneath that point. The orthometric height (H) and the geopotential number (C) are related through the following equation: C = G x H, where G is the gravity value estimated for a particular system. Height systems are called different names depending on the C and G selected. When G is computed using the Helmert height reduction formula (Helmert, 1890), which is what was used in NAVD 88, the heights are called Helmert orthometric heights; when G is computed using the International formula for normal gravity, the heights are called normal orthometric heights; and when G is equal to normal gravity at 45 degrees latitude, the heights are called normal dynamic heights, which is what was used in IGLD 85.

It should be noted that dynamic heights are just geopotential numbers scaled by a constant, using normal gravity at 45 degrees latitude equal to 980.6199 gals. Therefore dynamic heights are also an estimate of hydraulic head. In other words, points that have the same geopotential number will have the same dynamic height. The primary users of dynamic heights use the heights for measuring water-level heights and/or height differences on large bodies of water, i.e., the Great Lakes, because they are interested in knowing the hydraulic head. The IGLD 85 heights were established because they are used to regulate water levels on the Great Lakes system and the dynamic heights are needed to describe hydraulic head.

Some vertical datums were established for a single purpose or because it would cost too much to connect the local project to the National network. Some older local networks were established as the network grew. That is, many local leveling networks were established between 1912 and 1929, and then the 1929 general adjustment eventually connected them all. Most users will, if they have a reasonable option, connect their local project to the National network even though they only require local height differences from an arbitrary starting monument.

TIDAL DATUMS

Principal Tidal Datums

A vertical datum is called a tidal datum when it is defined by a certain phase of the tide. Tidal datums are local datums and are referenced to nearby monuments. Since a tidal datum is defined by a certain phase of the tide, there are many different types of tidal datums. This section will discuss the principal tidal datums that are typically used by Federal, state, and local government agencies: Mean Higher High Water (MHHW), Mean High Water (MHW), Mean Sea Level (MSL), Mean Low Water (MLW), and Mean Lower Low Water (MLLW), as shown below in Figure 2.7.

As explained in Chapter 1, a determination of the principal tidal datums in the United States is based on the average of observations over an 19-year period, e.g., 1960-78, or 1983-2001. A specific 19-year Metonic cycle is denoted as a National Tidal Datum Epoch (NTDE). NOAA's National Ocean Service (NOS) Center for Operational Oceanographic Products and Services (CO-OPS) publishes the official United States local mean sea level values. Users need to know to which NTDE their data refers. Relative sea level trends measured by tide gauges are a combination of any local or regional vertical land movement as well as any regional or global sea level change (Zervas, C. 2001). Users can refer to the following data link to the CO-OPS web site which addresses this issue <http://tidesandcurrents.noaa.gov>. Figure 2.8 illustrates the tidal datums defined below.

Mean Higher High Water (MHHW)

MHHW is defined as the arithmetic mean of the higher high water heights of the tide observed over a specific 19-year Metonic cycle denoted as the NTDE. Only the higher high water of each pair of high waters of a tidal day is included in the mean. For stations with shorter series, a comparison of simultaneous observations is made with a primary control tide station in order to derive the equivalent of the 19-year value (Marmer, 1951).

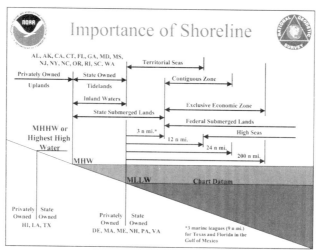

Figure 2.7 Local sea level boundaries. See color plate in Appendix C.

Mean High Water (MHW)

MHW is defined as the arithmetic mean of the high water heights observed over a specific 19-year Metonic cycle. For stations with shorter series, a computation of simultaneous observations is made with a primary control station in order to derive the equivalent of a 19-year value (Marmer, 1951).

Mean Sea Level (MSL)

MSL is defined as the arithmetic mean of hourly heights observed over a specific 19-year Metonic cycle. Shorter series are specified in the name, like monthly mean sea level or yearly mean sea level (Marmer, 1951; Hicks, 1985).

Mean Lower Low Water (MLLW)

MLLW is defined as the arithmetic mean of the lower low water heights of the tide observed over a specific 19-year Metonic cycle. Only the lower low water of each pair of low waters of a tidal day is included in the mean. For stations with shorter series, a comparison of simultaneous observations is made with a primary control tide station in order to derive the equivalent of a 19-year value (Marmer, 1951).

Other Tidal Values

Other tidal values typically computed include the Mean Tide Level (MTL), Diurnal Tide Level (DTL), Mean Range (Mn), Diurnal High Water Inequality (DHQ), Diurnal Low Water Inequality (DLQ), and Great Diurnal Range (Gt).

Mean Tide Level (MTL)

MTL is a tidal datum which is the average of Mean High Water and Mean Low Water.

Diurnal Tide Level (DTL)

DTL is a tidal datum which is the average of Mean Higher High Water and Mean Lower Low Water.

Mean Range (Mn)

Mn is the difference between Mean High Water and Mean Low Water.

Diurnal High Water Inequality (DHQ)

DHQ is the difference between Mean Higher High Water and Mean High Water.

Diurnal Low Water Inequality (DLQ)
DLQ is the difference between Mean Low Water and Mean Lower Low Water.

Great Diurnal Range (Gt)
Gt is the difference between Mean Higher High Water and Mean Lower Low Water. All of these tidal datums and differences have users that need a specific datum or difference for their particular use (See Figure 2.8 below).

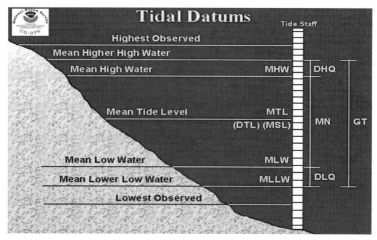

Figure 2.8 Tidal datums.

The important point for users is to know which tidal datum their data are referenced to. Like geodetic vertical datums, local tidal datums are all different from one another, but they can be related to each other.

Figure 2.7 was created by Mike Aslaksen of NGS, based on two figures from Hicks, 1985. The relationship of a local tidal datum (941 4290, San Francisco, California) to geodetic datums is illustrated by the example below:

PBM 180 1946	——	5.794m (the Primary Bench Mark)
Highest Water Level	——	4.462m
MHHW	——	3.536m
MHW	——	3.353m
MTL	——	2.728m
MSL	——	2.713m
DTL	——	2.646m
NGVD 1929	——	2.624m
MLW	——	2.103m
NAVD 88	——	1.802m
MLLW	——	1.759m
Lowest Water Level	——	0.945m

Station Datum
9/1/87 tide staff: 0.000m

Please note that in this example, NAVD 88 heights, which are the official National geodetic vertical control values, and LMSL heights, which are the official National local mean sea level values, at the San Francisco tidal station differ by almost 1 meter. Therefore, if a user obtained a set of heights relative to the local mean sea level and a second set referenced to NAVD 88, the two sets would disagree by about 1 meter due to the datum difference. In addition, the difference between MHW and MLLW is more than 1.5m (5 feet). Due to regulations and laws, some users relate their data to MHW, while others relate their data to MLLW (See Figure 2.7).

As long as a user knows which datum the data are referenced to, the data can be converted to a common reference and the data sets can be combined.

This is an important point because many digital products that users are combining have been referenced to different datums, i.e., USGS topographic maps are referenced to NGVD 29, FEMA flood plain maps are related to NGVD 29 or NAVD 88, and NOAA nautical charts are referenced to MLLW. Both the USGS map and the NOAA chart depict a shoreline, but these may be derived from different elevation data sets at different scales and use different datums. In addition, newer maps are being generated using the latest technology such as GPS-positioned lidar systems. Again, it is important that users know to which datum the heights derived from these systems are referring.

COMPARISON OF NAVD 88 HEIGHTS WITH LOCAL MEAN SEA LEVEL

Figure 2.9 gives the differences between adjusted heights from the NAVD 88 general adjustment and the heights of tidal bench marks above LMSL (epoch 1960-78). There is no apparent systematic difference along the East Coast of the United States. There are some large relative tilts between closely spaced tidal-station pairs. There is a large tilt along both coasts of Florida. In addition, there is an apparent tilt between the Atlantic Ocean and the Gulf of Mexico.

NAVD 88 minus LMSL (1960-78)
(units = cm)

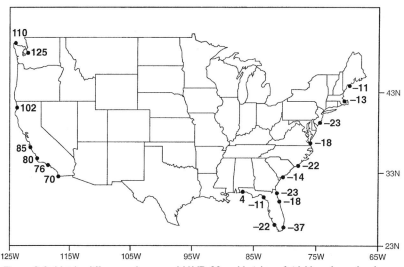

Figure 2.9 Height differences between NAVD 88 and heights of tidal bench marks above LMSL (1960-78 NDTE).

There is also an apparent tilt between NAVD 88 heights and LMSL (NTDE 1960-78) along the West Coast of the United States. The difference from southern California to northern Washington is 40 cm (a distance of about 1,500 km). The difference, however, from southern to northern California is 32 cm, while from northern California to northern Washington it is only 8 cm. These differences could be caused by remaining systematic errors in the leveling data. A possible error source in the leveling data could be network design in mountainous areas. There are long north-south leveling lines through the valleys, and only a few east-west lines that cross the mountains to create loops to help control and check accumulation of errors.

Another possible error source could be a small, systematic gravity effect in leveling height differences, because a large, denser mass (the Rocky Mountain range) is always on the east-side of the north-south leveling lines, with relatively less dense mass (the Pacific Ocean) on the west side.

It must be emphasized, in looking at Figure 2.9, that LMSL determined by tidal data at different sites does not lie on the same equipotential surface. The difference between measured LMSLs and a global equipotential surface, coincident with LMSL at one point, is due to the effects of sea surface topography (SST).

In 1986, NGS provided a small grant to a group of investigators to estimate SST effects at five tidal stations in the northeastern United States using a technique documented by Merry and Vanicek (1983). The results indicated much additional work would be required, and it was decided that estimating SST effects at primary stations in support of NAVD 88 would not be cost-effective. SST effects should be pursued in the future. With the release of the updated National Tidal Datum Epoch for 1983-2001, the relationship between NAVD 88 and Local Mean Sea Level has changed at each tide station. Table 2.2 shows how the water levels have changed, and it gives an indication of the change in the relationship between these datums.

Table 2.2 NAVD 88 LMSL (created by Stephen Gill of NOAA/CO-OPS).

Station Names	MSL-NAVD 88 1960-78 (meters)	MSL-NAVD 88 1983-2001 (meters)	Change between NTDE's (cm)	Lat	Lon
Portland, Maine	-0.111	-0.095	1.600	43 39.4	70 14.8
Boston, Boston Harbor	-0.131	-0.092	3.900	42 21.3	71 3.1
Atlantic City, Atlantic Ocean	-0.226	-0.122	10.400	39 21.3	74 25.1
Sewells Point, Hampton Roads	-0.194	-0.089	10.500	36 56.8	76 19.8
Oregon Inlet Marina, North Carolina	-0.104	-0.026	7.800	35 47.7	75 32.9
Charleston, Cooper River Entrance	-0.142	-0.067	7.500	32 46.9	79 55.5
Fernandina Beach, Florida	-0.226	-0.161	6.500	30 40.3	81 27.9
Lakeworth Pier, Florida	-0.340	-0.279	6.100	26 36.7	80 2.0
Virginia Key, Florida	-0.331	-0.0267	6.400	25 43.9	80 9.7
Naples, Gulf of Mexico	-0.230	-0.0194	3.600	26 7.8	81 48.4
Cedar Key, Gulf of Mexico	-0.109	-0.066	4.300	29 8.1	83 1.9
Pensacola, Pensacola Bay	0.046	0.090	4.400	30 24.2	87 12.7
San Diego, San Diego Bay	0.700	0.765	6.500	32 42.8	117 10.4
San Pedro, Los Angeles Outer Harbor	0.761	0.799	3.800	33 43.2	118 16.3
Port San Luis, Pacific Ocean	0.801	0.829	2.800	35 10.6	120 45.6
Monterey, Monterey Harbor	0.846	0.905	5.900	36 36.3	121 53.3
Crescent City, Pacific Ocean	1.019	1.014	-0.500	41 44.7	124 11.0
Neah Bay, Strait of Juan De Fuca	1.100	1.059	-4.100	48 22.1	124 37.0
Seattle, Puget Sound	1.255	1.309	5.400	47 36.3	122 20.3

Looking at Figure 2.9, it should be obvious that without removing the SST effects at tidal stations, it would be incorrect to constrain the heights of tidal bench marks in NAVD 88. The next best thing would be to include the heights as weighted observations. However, a priori estimates of standard errors for tidal stations where SST effects were not removed would be too large, relative to the precise leveling differences to contribute anything to the final adjusted heights.

It is certainly correct, but not practical, to implement at the time of the readjustment. As estimates of SST improve, tidal height observations corrected for SST will be incorporated into NAVD 88 and future vertical adjustments. What this means to users is that some LMSL values and NAVD 88 heights differ by more than 1 meter on the West Coast. As users demand higher levels of accuracies in their height-related products such as DEMs, these differences will become more important.

NATIONAL HEIGHT MODERNIZATION STUDY

In 1998, the U.S. Congress directed the National Geodetic Survey, the nation's positioning agency and an office within the National Oceanic and Atmospheric Administration (NOAA), Department of Commerce, to conduct a National Height Modernization Study. The purpose of the study was to determine the effectiveness of height modernization in California and North Carolina and its potential benefits to the nation. Prior to the study, there were many indications that considerable time and funding costs could be reduced by using the Global Positioning System (GPS) technology in surveying, and in particular, in measuring heights.

The study not only proved this, but projected, in some cases, a 90 percent cost savings over conventional surveying methods. Moreover, the study indicated the emergence of many height modernization applications ranging from improvements to air and marine navigational safety, to precision farming and mining; also high-accuracy flood mitigation and mapping, to real-time monitoring of gravity and aquifer-based water systems.

These findings caught the attention of Congress and the Administration. Recently, over the past six years, more than $18 million has been appropriated, with 90 percent going to participating states, to initiate the implementation of the study nationwide. Today, state and local governments spend tens of millions of dollars each year correcting engineering projects that are continually affected by changing land surfaces due to subsidence, crustal plate movements of the earth, floods, earthquakes, and other natural phenomena.

For example, the Northridge, California, earthquake in 1994 required more than $1 million in federal government expenditures for extensive resurveying that had to be done as a result of the earthquake. The indirect costs associated with the inability to adjust for elevation change may result in even greater costs. Through the use of the GPS, a constellation of 24, high-altitude (11,000 miles) NAVSTAR satellites operated by the U.S. military, and originally designed for use as an advanced weapon delivery system first deployed in the 1980's, pinpoint positioning accuracies can be provided 24 hours a day.

The combination of an improved national height system (NAVD 88) first adopted by the federal government in 1993, along with the positioning technology of GPS, offers the nation and its governments, for the first time, the ability to obtain precise vertical measurements in real-time.

Integrating the horizontal, vertical, and gravity control networks into a unified national positioning system, joined and maintained by GPS, and administered by the National Geodetic Survey, sets the stage for many advances. A state-of-the-art National Spatial Reference System, with NAVD 88 as its elevation reference, can make available to the nation a common, consistent set of real-time geographical coordinates, or reference points.

The applications of this break-through national positioning system can provide the following: improved aircraft navigational aids, and safer approach and landing procedures; advanced surface transportation control and monitoring; highly efficient fertilizer and pesticide spreading, resulting in reduced run-off water pollution; more accurate modeling of storm surge and pollution trajectories; increased accuracy for improved resource management decision making; significant time savings in field surveying; and improved disaster preparedness and earthquake detection (See Illustrations in Figure 2.10). In addition, when elevation references are related directly to local water level data, other applications are supported, such as coastal habitat restoration, storm surge modeling and monitoring of sea level changes. See Figure 2.10.

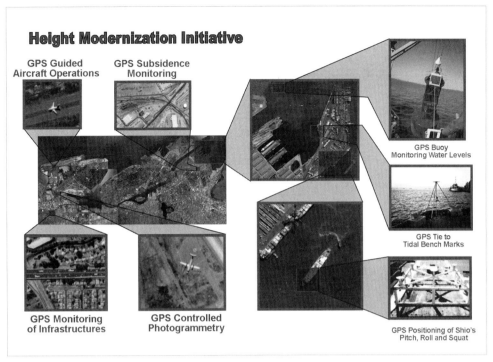

Figure 2.10 Pictorial representation of Height Modernization Initiative. See color plate in Appendix C.

DIFFERENCES BETWEEN ELLIPSOID HEIGHTS AND ORTHOMETRIC HEIGHTS

Since 1983, NGS has performed control survey projects in the United States using GPS satellites. Analysis of GPS survey data has shown that GPS can be used to establish precise relative positions in a three-dimensional Earth-centered coordinate system, either as rectangular (X, Y, Z) coordinates or converted to geodetic (latitude, longitude, ellipsoidal height) coordinates using an Earth-centered ellipsoid. GPS carrier phase measurements are used to determine vector base lines in space, where the components of the base line are expressed in terms of Cartesian coordinate differences. These vector base lines can be converted to distance, azimuth, and ellipsoidal height differences (dh) relative to a defined reference ellipsoid.

Over the past decade, GPS surveying techniques have proven to be so efficient and accurate; they are now routinely used in place of classical line-of-sight surveying methods for establishing horizontal control.

Understandably, interest has been growing in using GPS techniques to establish accurate vertical control as well. Progress in the past had been hampered due to difficulties in obtaining sufficiently accurate geoid height differences to convert GPS-derived ellipsoid height differences to accurate orthometric height differences.

These factors have recently coalesced, making GPS-derived orthometric heights a viable alternative to classical line-of-sight leveling techniques for many applications:

- completion of the general adjustment of NAVD 88;
- development of NGS guidelines for establishing GPS-derived ellipsoid heights to meet 2- and 5-cm standards (Zilkoski et al., 1997), generally known as "NGS-58" (visit <http://www.ngs.noaa.gov/PUBS_LIB/NGS-58.pdf> to access the guide-lines); and
- computation of an accurate, nationwide, high-resolution geoid model, GEOID03.

It is important to have a clear understanding of the basic concepts of establishing GPS-derived orthometric heights, otherwise water (or something worse) may not flow "down hill."

Basic Concepts of GPS-Derived Heights

There are three types of heights involved in determining GPS-derived orthometric heights – orthometric, ellipsoid, and geoid. These heights are significantly different in value and meaning; and, if used incorrectly, could cause errors resulting in costly repairs. Figure 2.11 depicts the relationship between the three types of heights.

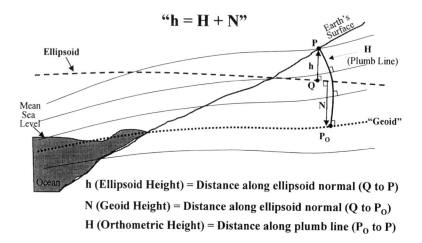

$$\text{``}h = H + N\text{''}$$

h (Ellipsoid Height) = Distance along ellipsoid normal (Q to P)

N (Geoid Height) = Distance along ellipsoid normal (Q to P_0)

H (Orthometric Height) = Distance along plumb line (P_0 to P)

Figure 2.11 Relationships between ellipsoid, geoid, and orthometric heights. See color plate in Appendix C.

Orthometric Heights

Orthometric heights (H) are referenced to an equipotential reference surface, e.g., the geoid. The orthometric height of a point on the Earth's surface is the distance from the geoidal reference surface to the point, measured along the plumb line normal to the geoid. These are the heights most surveyors have worked with in the past and are often called "mean sea level" heights. Recall that local mean sea level heights and NAVD 88 are not the same.

It should be noted that the terms elevation and height are frequently used as synonyms for height. In geodesy, height also refers to the distance above an ellipsoid, i.e., ellipsoid height, as well as the difference between ellipsoid heights and orthometric heights, i.e., geoid height.

Ellipsoid Heights

Ellipsoid heights (h) are referenced to a reference ellipsoid. The ellipsoid height of a point on the Earth's surface is the distance from the reference ellipsoid to the point, measured along the line which is normal to the ellipsoid. The term ellipsoid height may be a new concept to many traditional surveyors and has become prevalent because ellipsoid heights are readily derived from GPS measurements, including airborne GPS derived heights from lidar, for example.

Geoid Heights

At the same point on the earth's surface, the difference between an ellipsoid height and an orthometric height is defined as the geoid height (N). (See N in Figure 2.11 or geoid undulation in Figure 2.12) The geoid is a specified equipotential surface which best fits, in a least squares sense, global mean sea level. Least squares adjustments are used because one of their inherent properties is that they provide unbiased estimates (smallest standard deviations) of the unknowns. For equally-weighted observations that have normally distributed errors, these values are also the most probable. The most probable value of a quantity is the specific value for which the sum of the squares of the errors (or corrections) is a minimum, i.e., best fits in a least squares sense.

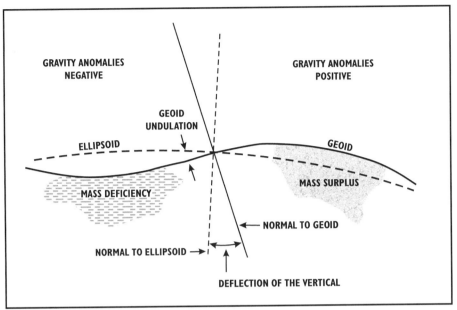

Figure 2.12 The effect of mass anomalies on the geoid. (From "Geodesy for the Layman," Defense Mapping Agency).

The basic thesis is that an equipotential surface surrounds earth in all three dimensions and represents an undulating surface where the potential of gravitation is the same everywhere. One could consider this similar in concept to an isoline on a topographic map where the contour line represents a series of points that are all at the same height. In other words, no matter where you are on the line in terms of latitude and longitude, you are always at the same height. Similarly, no matter where you are situated with respect to earth's center of mass (geocenter), the potential of gravity is the same everywhere on such an equipotential surface.

Using the previous example, equate the contour line with the potential of gravitation. On a topographic map, closely spaced contour lines demonstrate a region of high slope such as a cliff face, while broadly spaced contours indicate a region that is very flat. Similarly, closely spaced equipotential surfaces indicate regions of stronger gravitation while broader spacing between equipotential surfaces indicates regions of lower gravitation.

So, what causes these different regions of gravitation? Earth's mass is irregularly distributed throughout the core, mantle and crust. These differences can be thought of in terms of mass anomalies. A standard model is selected and then deviations of earth's true mass distribution from the standard distribution are these anomalies. Since mass creates gravitation, the positive anomalies will cause higher local potentials of gravitation while mass deficiencies will cause lower local potentials. Since an equipotential surface is defined by having a constant potential value, this surface will undulate, i.e., higher over mass excesses and lower over mass deficiencies, as depicted in Figure 2.12.

These approximations of earth's potentials of gravitation are termed geopotential surfaces (geops for short). A specific geop, selected such that it will pass through the average sea surface for earth, is called the geoid. The differences between the geoid and the selected ellipsoid are a function of the mass anomalies and are called geoid heights or undulations. The geoid reacts to the presence of mountains and deep ocean basins while the ellipsoid does not.

As previously stated, due to sea surface topography effects, such as atmospheric pressure, temperature, prevailing winds and currents, and salinity variations, local mean sea level can depart from an equipotential surface by 1 meter or more. Therefore, National and regional vertical datums around the world, which are typically referenced to local mean sea level, can differ by more than 1 meter from one another when considered on a global basis.

The geoid can vary by up to 100 meters in height from a geocentric ellipsoid. Geoid height models provide a means of transforming from a specific ellipsoidal datum to a specific-geoid or orthometric datum. Several models exist for the United States in two basic types: gravimetric and "hybrid." A gravimetric geoid is derived entirely from gravity field information including Earth Gravitational Models (EGMs), observed gravity data (airborne, terrestrial and ship borne), satellite-altimeter implied gravity, and terrain models. A hybrid geoid then uses control data, usually GPS-derived ellipsoidal heights on leveled bench marks (GPSBMs), to fit a gravimetric geoid to different ellipsoidal and orthometric datums. For the Conterminous United States, the most recent such models are USGG 2003 and GEOID 03. USGG 2003 references different ellipsoidal and orthometric datums than GEOID 03. The USGG 2003 ellipsoidal reference datum is of a GRS-80 ellipsoid centered in the International Earth Rotation Service Terrestrial Reference Frame (ITRF) reference frame, while GEOID 03 uses the same GRS-80 ellipsoid but centered on the NAD 83 reference frame.

Transformation between ITRF 00 and NAD 83 is easily accomplished using NGS' Horizontal Time-Dependent Positioning software. The orthometric datums are more complicated. USGG 2003 refers to the same geopotential surface as the EGM 96 model. It is enhanced by shorter wave-length gravity field information and corrected for some long wavelength errors, but these changes do not alter the geop selected as the geoid. GEOID 03 refers to the NAVD 88 vertical datum instead. The relationship between the EGM 96 and NAVD 88 datums is complicated by the non-linear relationship between them and a possible bias and trend. This is exactly why the GPSBMs are required to map this difference using least squares collocation. Spatial distribution and quality will impact the reliability of the conversion surface that is derived, but this surface can be used to warp the USGG 2003 model to fit the NAD 83 and NAVD 88 datums.

GEOID 03 is about optimal, more so than its predecessor the GEOID 99 model. It uses more data and models even shorter wavelength signal. However, the GEOID 03 remains only a datum conversion tool and does not necessarily relate to the actual geopotential surfaces. This is problematic when oceanographic phenomena impact the shore regions (i.e., storm surge, tsuna-mis, or coastal wetland management). Recall that the intent of a vertical datum is to relate to heights above mean sea level. A better approach would be to improve the fit of the gravimetric geoid model to the ocean surface.

This can be accomplished by using an EGM that has only centimeter-level commission errors and a consistent and seamless set of gravity observations and terrain models. Such a model could be validated at the shoreline against the models of sea surface topography (or mean dynamic topography) and observations of the actual ocean surface. If the topography is consistently accounted for at the shoreline, then the remaining ocean signal must derive from the geoid.

With the advent of dedicated satellite gravity missions, e.g. the Gravity Recovery and Climate Experiment (GRACE) and the Gravity Field and Steady-State Ocean Circulation Explorer (GOCE), EGMs are already available that nearly meet the cm-level accuracy requirement. A seamless terrain data set is already currently available with even more refined models impending. Acquisition of a seamless gravity field from coast to coast would provide the missing piece to complete a cm-level accurate gravimetric geoid model. Such a model would be consistent with similarly generated models for other countries assuming they used the same EGM. In this manner, the meter level inconsistencies observed between the vertical datums of various nations would be eliminated or at least reduced to decimeter to centimeter levels. Such a model could be used in conjunction with cm-level accurate GPS-derived ellipsoidal heights to directly infer cm-level accurate GPS-orthometric heights. Future research and models at NGS will be dedicated to achieving this end. Likewise, gravimetric and hybrid geoid models will be generated for outlying U.S. states and territories to ensure equity.

GPS-DERIVED ORTHOMETRIC HEIGHTS

Several error sources that affect the accuracy of the orthometric, ellipsoid, and geoid height values are generally common to nearby points on the Earth's surface. Because these error sources are in common, the uncertainty of height differences between nearby points is significantly smaller than the uncertainty of the absolute heights of each point. This is the key to establishing accurate orthometric heights using GPS.

Orthometric height differences (dH) can then be obtained from ellipsoid height differences (dh) by subtracting the geoid height differences (dN): dH = dh - dN.

Adhering to NGS guidelines, ellipsoid height differences (dh) over short base lines, i.e., less than 10 km, can now be determined from GPS carrier-phase measurements with 2-sigma uncertainties that are typically better than +/- 2 cm. This is now possible because of the availability of a greater number of satellites, more accurate satellite orbits, full-wavelength dual-frequency carrier-phase data, improved antenna designs, and improved data processing techniques. The requirement that each base line must be repeated and agree to within 2 cm of each other, and they must be repeated on two separate days, during different times of the day, should provide a final GPS-derived ellipsoid height better than 2 cm at the 2-sigma (95% confidence) level. It should also be noted that the GPS-derived ellipsoid height guidelines documented by NGS (Zilkoski et al., 1997) were intentionally designed to produce ellipsoid heights slightly better than 2 cm (i.e., about 1.4 cm) so they could also be used when generating 2-cm GPS-derived orthometric heights. The requirement that spacing between local network stations cannot exceed 10 km helps to keep the relative error in geoid height small, i.e., typically less than 0.5 cm. Adding in the small error for the uncertainty of the geoid height difference and controlling the remaining systematic differences between the three height systems will produce a GPS-derived orthometric height with 2-sigma uncertainties that are typically +/- 2 cm. Therefore, it is possible to establish GPS-derived orthometric heights to meet certain standards, not millimeter standards, but 2-cm (95%) standards are routinely met now using GPS.

In many areas of the United States, geoid height differences can be determined with uncertainties that are typically better than 1 cm for distances of as much as 20 km and less than 2 to 3 cm for distances from 20 to 50 km. The small values for the differential geoid height uncertainties have been demonstrated in tests in several regions of the United States. Larger uncertainties can be expected in other areas, depending on the density of the observed gravity network and uncertainties in the determination of observed and interpolated gravity anomalies.

When high accuracy field procedures are used, orthometric height differences can be computed from measurements of precise geodetic leveling with an uncertainty of less than 1 cm over a 50-kilometer distance. Less accurate results are achieved when third order leveling methods are employed. Depending on the accuracy requirements, GPS surveys and present high-resolution geoid models can be employed as an alternative to classical leveling methods. In the past, the primary limiting factor was the accuracy of estimating geoid height differences. With the computation of the latest National high-resolution geoid model, GEOID 03, and the development of the 2- and 5-cm guidelines for estimating GPS-derived ellipsoid heights, the limiting factor is ensuring that the NAVD 88 orthometric height values used to control the project are valid. Strategically occupying bench marks with GPS that have valid NAVD 88 height values is critical to detecting, reducing, and/or eliminating blunders and systematic errors between the three height systems.

When users follow the appropriate guidelines, i.e., Zilkoski, et al. (2005), the GPS-derived orthometric heights should meet the standards desired. However, users still must be careful that they aren't mixing datums or the results won't be comparable. An error made by users that aren't familiar with datum issues, is mixing ellipsoid heights, i.e., ITRF ellipsoid heights with NAD 83 ellipsoid heights. These heights are not in the same reference frame even though they are both ellipsoid heights and the differences can easily exceed 1 meter. So, if one user publishes heights using ITRF ellipsoid heights and another uses NAD 83, the differences can exceed 1 meter.

ITRF coordinates can be transformed into NAD 83 coordinates and vice versa using simple transformation programs provided by NGS, as well as others. Converting vertical datums to a common datum will be discussed in the next section of this chapter. Once again, users must always know which datum their heights are referenced to. If two individual products state that their results are based on GPS-derived orthometric heights and they are determined using NGS guidelines, then the two products can be compared to each other. If not, the user must ensure the two products are referenced to the same datum so they can be compared and/or combined.

RELATING VERTICAL DATUMS TO ONE ANOTHER

If users need to combine or mix DEM values that are referenced to different datums, then one or both DEMs must be converted to a common datum. This is not a difficult task, but there are different ways of performing the task. This section provides some examples of methods employed to transform one set of values referenced to one datum to another datum.

NOAA/NGS' NGVD 29 TO NAVD 88 VERTICAL CONVERSION PROGRAM VERTCON

One of the first tasks that NGS undertook after computing the heights for NAVD 88 bench marks was to create a program called VERTCON that converted NGVD 29 heights values to the new NAVD 88 datum. The first version of the program was distributed about one year after the completion of NAVD 88. NGS continued to improve the program by adding models for removing effects due to systematic errors. The program is suitable for mapping and charting purposes. The following is an excerpt from the VERTCON documentation:

"Program VERTCON computes the modeled difference in orthometric height between the North American Vertical Datum of 1988 (NAVD 88) and the National Geodetic Vertical Datum of 1929 (NGVD 29) for a given location specified by latitude and longitude.

"The VERTCON 2.0 model was computed on May 5, 1994, using 381,833 datum difference values. A key part of the computation procedure was the development of the predictable, physical components of the differences between the NAVD 88 and NGVD 29 datums. This included models of refraction effects on geodetic leveling, and gravity and elevation influences on the new NAVD 88 datum. Tests of the predictive capability of the physical model show a 2.0 cm RMS agreement at our 381,833 data points. For this reason, the VERTCON 2.0 model can be considered accurate at the 2 cm (one sigma) level. Since 381,833 data values were used to develop the corrections to the physical model, VERTCON 2.0 will display even better overall accuracy than that displayed by the uncorrected physical model. This higher accuracy will be particularly noticeable in the eastern United States.

"It should be emphasized that VERTCON 2.0 is a datum transformation model, and can not maintain the full vertical control accuracy of geodetic leveling. Ideally, one should process level data using the latest reduction software and adjust it to established NAVD 88 control. However, VERTCON 2.0 accuracy is suitable for a variety of mapping and charting purposes.

"Most horizontal positions of the bench marks used to generate VERTCON were scaled from USGS topographic maps. The estimated uncertainty of the scaled positions, 6", is greater than the differences between NAD27 and NAD83. Therefore, the latitude and longitude provided to VERTCON can be on either the NAD27 or NAD83 datum.

"The VERTCON 2.0 model expresses datum differences between NAVD 88 and NGVD 29 due to removal of distortions in the level data, as well as due to the physical differences in the height systems. In some rare cases, these local NGVD 29 distortions could be 20 cm or more. If both ends of your old vertical survey were tied to one of these 'problem' lines, then the datum difference of the problem line is appropriate to use to transform the survey data. If both ends of a vertical survey are tied to 'undistorted lines,' then it is appropriate to use a slightly distant point to compute the transformation, no matter how close your survey data may approach a given problem line. The possible presence of a problem NGVD 29 line in the vicinity of your survey will become evident if dramatically different datum transformation values are computed within a small area."

The U.S. Army Corp of Engineers created a program called CORPSCON that incorporates NGS program VERTCON to convert NGVD 29 heights to NAVD 88 height values. The following is an excerpt from the CORPSCON documentation:

"CORPSCON, Version 6.0, is a MS-Windows-based program which allows the user to convert coordinates between Geographic, State Plane, Universal Transverse Mercator (UTM) and US National Grid systems on the North American Datum of 1927 (NAD 27), the North American Datum of 1983 (NAD 83) and High Accuracy Reference Networks (HARNs). CORPSCON uses the National Geodetic Survey (NGS) program NADCON to convert between NAD 27, NAD 83 and HARNs. CORPSCON, Version 6.0, performs vertical conversions to and from the National Geodetic Vertical Datum of 1929 (NGVD 29) and the North American Vertical Datum of 1988 (NAVD 88). Vertical conversions are based on the NGS program VERTCON and can be performed for the continental U.S. only. CORPSCON, Version 6.0, will also calculate geoid-ellipsoid separations based on the NGS program GeoidXX (XX = 90, 93, 96, 99, and 03). Geoid-ellipsoid separations can be calculated for the Continental U.S., Alaska, Hawaii and Puerto Rico/U.S. Virgin Islands."

Local Datums

As previously stated, there are hundreds of vertical datums that have been used throughout the United States during the past century. NGS does not have the resources to investigate vertical datums differences other than those differences between NGVD 29 and NAVD 88. If users can convert their data to NGVD 29, they can use VERTCON to convert values to NAVD 88. However, anyone can write to NGS and formally request information on differences between any and all datums. These requests will be answered based on available resources, and a nominal fee may be charged, depending on the extent of the research required. In addition to NGS, some State agencies provide publications describing the differences between many National and local vertical datums. In the past, in order to perform their tasks, State agencies' surveying departments prepared documents describing differences between datums. A good example is a 1949 State of Illinois Department of Public Works and Buildings, Division of Waterways publication which lists differences between NGVD 29 and various vertical datums (State of Illinois, 1949).

It was prepared by the Department of Public Works and Buildings, to meet their surveying operational requirements. The datum descriptions from the document are listed below to show readers the variety of datums that surveyors, engineers, and mappers employ, depending on the activity they are performing. It also points out that historic information may already be available; the user, however, will probably have to do some research to find these types of documents. The following is taken from the State of Illinois 1949 publication:

"MEAN TIDE NEW YORK (1935 ADJUSTMENT) AT CHICAGO
AS USED BY UNITED STATES LAKE SURVEY

Mean Tide New York is a name adopted by the Lake Survey to differentiate their datum from that of the Coast and Geodetic Survey. It is an arbitrary datum which assumes that the surfaces of each of the Great Lakes are level surfaces. This datum is 0.40 feet below Mean Sea Level (1929 - 5th General Adjustment) at Chicago, Illinois.

"PEORIA CITY DATUM

A chart showing datum planes prepared by the Illinois Valley Department of the Sanitary District of Chicago gives the value of 413.10 feet above Memphis Datum (north of Cairo) for the Peoria City Datum. By subtracting 7.430 feet, a value extracted from a table prepared by the United States Engineer Office, Chicago District, we are able to reduce Memphis Datum to Mean Sea Level 1929. Therefore, the Peoria City Datum is 405.670 feet above Mean Sea Level (1929).

"LASALLE CITY DATUM

A chart showing datum planes prepared by the Illinois Valley Department of the Sanitary District of Chicago, gives the value of 455.38 feet above Memphis Datum (north of Cairo) for the LaSalle City Datum. By subtracting 7.456 feet, a value extracted from a table prepared by the United States Engineer Office, Chicago District, we are able to reduce Memphis Datum to Mean Sea Level (1929). Therefore, the LaSalle City Datum is 447.924 feet above Mean Sea Level (1929 Adjustment).

"OTTAWA CITY DATUM

A chart showing datum planes prepared by the Illinois Valley Department of the Sanitary District of Chicago gives the value of 440.38 feet above Memphis Datum (north of Cairo) for the Ottawa City Datum. By subtracting 7.455 feet, a value extracted from a table prepared by the United States Engineer Office, Chicago District, we are able to reduce Memphis Datum to Mean Sea Level (1929). Therefore, the Ottawa City Datum is 432.925 feet above Mean Sea Level (1929 Adjustment).

"CHICAGO CITY DATUM AS USED BY (COOK COUNTY HIGHWAY DEPARTMENT)

Mr. Charles W. Greengard of the Cook County Highway Department has established the Chicago City Datum to be 579.31 feet above Mean Sea Level (1929). This elevation was obtained by a comparison between published elevations of several Bureau of Sewers bench marks and preliminary fixed elevations of the same bench marks as determined by the U.S. Coast and Geodetic Survey in 1947.

"CHICAGO CITY DATUM AS USED BY
(BUREAU OF SEWERS & DEPARTMENT OF THE ARMY)

The Chicago City Datum has been established at 579.48 feet above Mean Sea Level (1929) by the Bureau of Sewers, the Great Lakes Division, and the Upper Mississippi Valley Division of the U.S. Corps of Engineers.

"CHICAGO CITY DATUM BY CITY ORDINANCE

The Chicago City Datum has been established by the City Ordinance, and the United States Geological Survey to be 579.480 feet above Mean Sea Level (1929 Adjustment).

"CHICAGO CITY DATUM AS USED BY SANITARY DISTRICT OF CHICAGO

The Sanitary District of Chicago considers the zero of the Chicago City Datum to be 579.94 Mean Tide New York. By subtracting 0.40 feet, you obtain 579.54 feet above Mean Sea Level 1929."

Puerto Rico Vertical Datum

At least three different geodetic vertical datums have developed in Puerto Rico; all defined as "Mean Sea Level" (MSL). USGS established the first datum during 1928 – 1941, to provide vertical control for the USGS topographic mapping program, commonly referred to as "7.5-minute topo quads."

These surveys were performed to third-order accuracy (the lowest order of geodetic accuracy) and consisted of approximately 709 permanent bench marks (BMs) across the island of Puerto Rico and 21 on the nearby island of Vieques. Other than tide gauging stations to support the productions of nautical charts, there does not appear to have ever been any geodetic vertical control surveys conducted on the nearby islands of Culebra or Mona.

Mixing Bathymetric and Topographic DEMs

This chapter has discussed different types of vertical heights and datums and mentioned several times the importance of not combining or mixing data sets that are referenced to different datums without converting them to a common datum. The NOS has undertaken a pilot project with USGS to demonstrate how to mix topographic and bathymetric products, which are referenced to different datums, to obtain a quality product. A report titled "A Tampa Bay Bathymetric/Topographic Digital Elevation Model With Internally Consistent Shorelines for Various Datums" by Bruce Parker, Dennis Milbert, Robert Wilson, Kurt Hess, Jon Bailey, and Cindy Fowler — NOS, NOAA, and Dean Gesch and Russell Berry — National Mapping Division, USGS, presented at Hydro 2001. The 12th Biennial Conference of the Hydrographic Society held at the University of East Anglia, Norwich, United Kingdom, does an excellent job of explaining what's required when mixing products that were not originally referenced to the same datum. The abstract of the report and a summary of the sections related to vertical datums are listed below.

"Abstract: In a joint demonstration project for the Tampa Bay region, the National Oceanic and Atmospheric Administration (NOAA) and the U.S. Geological Survey (USGS) have blended their bathymetric and topographic data sets (respectively) into a digital elevation model (DEM) with all data initially referenced to the ellipsoid. A datum transformation tool allows easy transformation of elevations with respect to any of 26 orthometric, 3-D, or tidal datums. The geographic distribution of particular tidal datums (relative to mean sea level) was produced using a calibrated and verified numerical hydrodynamic model of Tampa Bay. This datum transformation tool was used to transform all bathymetric data from a mean lower low water datum (or from a mean low water datum for older data) to the ellipsoid. For areas where low water and high water shorelines are significantly different, an ultimate objective will be to incorporate a higher-resolution "shoreline zone" into the DEM, so that various internally consistent "shorelines" can be generated by moving the water level in the DEM to the desired tidal datum heights. The bathymetric/topographic DEM will not only solve the problem of inconsistency between NOAA and USGS shorelines that have caused difficulty for a variety of mariners and coastal managers, but it will also provide a standard DEM on which other third-party bathymetric and topographic data can be appended, as well as a great variety of geospatial data layers. The applications benefiting from the bathy/topo DEM range from electronic nautical charts to improved storm surge modeling to better sea grass (and other habitat) restoration projects."

Joint NOAA-USGS Tampa Bay Demonstration Project

To demonstrate blending bathymetric and topographic data sets into a bathymetric/topographic DEM in the Tampa Bay region of Florida, NOAA's NOS and the USGS's National Mapping Division (NMD) have undertaken a joint demonstration project. All data sets were transformed to a common vertical datum using a newly developed Vertical Datum Transformation Tool. This tool, called VDatum, allows transformations of 26 vertical datums and is being provided as a user-friendly tool to the coastal user community. In support of the demonstration project, a fully calibrated hydrodynamic model of Tampa Bay was used to determine the geographic distribution of the tidal datums. A great variety of other types of marine and terrestrial geospatial data can be added to the bathymetric/topographic DEM using the datum transformation tool. In the Tampa Bay project, third-party bathymetric and topographic data are being incorporated into the DEM using VDatum.

Vertical Datum Transformation Tool (VDatum)

VDatum is a software tool developed jointly by NOAA's Office of Coast Survey and National Geodetic Survey. VDatum is designed to transform coastal elevations between 28 different vertical datums consisting of tidal, orthometric, and ellipsoidal (3-D, three dimensional) datums (See Table 2.3). Software such as VDatum becomes crucial for developing the geospatial infrastructure of the U.S. coastal zone. The coastal land-water interface depends on how water levels change in both space and time. To combine or compare coastal elevations (heights and depths) from diverse sources, they must be referenced to the same vertical datum as a common framework. Using inconsistent datums can cause artificial discontinuities that become acutely problematic when producing maps at the accuracy that is critically needed by Federal, state, and local authorities to make informed decisions. VDatum for several coastal regions is now available for many important applications and technologies, such as: storm surge models, tsunami inundation maps, coastal change analysis, shoreline demarcation, bathymetric standardization, referencing of hydrographic surveys with kinematic GPS, lidar data collection, sea level rise prediction, ecosystem resource management, navigation services, and disaster mitigation planning. VDatum version 1.06 transformation software, geographic boundaries, and documentation for each project area are available for download as a zipped (.zip) file. General software documentation accompanies each VDatum software bundle.

Disclaimer: Although many of the vertical datum transformations between NAVD 88 and local mean sea level, and between local mean sea level and the other tidal datums, are based on tidal values from the present National Tidal Datum Epoch (NTDE, 1983 to 2001), some are based on data from older tidal epochs. The National Ocean Service is in the process of updating the data in VDatum to conform to the latest NTDE. In the meantime, care should be used when applying these transformations.

Table 2.3 The 28 different vertical datums included in VDatum.

Orthometric Datums
NAVD 88	North American Vertical Datum 1988
NGVD 29	National Geodetic Vertical Datum 1929

Tidal Datums
MLLW	Mean Lower Low Water
MLW	Mean Low Water
LMSL	Local Mean Sea Level
MTL	Mean Tide Level
DTL	Diurnal Tide Level
MHW	Mean High Water
MHHW	Mean Higher High Water

3-D Datums
NAD 83 (86)	North American Datum 1983 (1986)
WGS 84 (G1150)	World Geodetic System 1984 (G1150)
WGS 84 (G873)	World Geodetic System 1984 (G873)
WGS 84 (G730)	World Geodetic System 1984 (G730)
WGS 84 (orig)	World Geodetic System 1984 (original system — 1984)
WGS 72	World Geodetic System 1972
ITRF 00	International Terrestrial Reference Frame 2000
ITRF 97	International Terrestrial Reference Frame 1997
ITRF 96	International Terrestrial Reference Frame 1996
ITRF 94	International Terrestrial Reference Frame 1994
ITRF 93	International Terrestrial Reference Frame 1993
ITRF 92	International Terrestrial Reference Frame 1992
ITRF 91	International Terrestrial Reference Frame 1991
ITRF 90	International Terrestrial Reference Frame 1990
ITRF 89	International Terrestrial Reference Frame 1989
ITRF 88	International Terrestrial Reference Frame 1988
SIO/MIT 92	Scripps Institution of Oceanography/ Massachusetts Inst. of Tech. 1992
NEOS 90	National Earth Orientation Service 1990
PNEOS 90	Preliminary National Earth Orientation Service 1990

For Additional Information:

Tidal Modeling
Edward Myers, Ph.D.
Edward.Myers@noaa.gov
Coast Survey Development Laboratory
NOAA National Ocean Service

Bathymetry
Michael Brown
Mike.Brown@noaa.gov
Coast Survey Development Laboratory
NOAA National Ocean Service

Geoid and VDatum Tool
Jason Woolard
Jason.Woolard@noaa.gov
National Geodetic Survey
NOAA National Ocean Service

Topography and Merged Data
Stephen White
Stephen.A.White@noaa.gov
National Geodetic Survey
NOAA National Ocean Service

VDatum Reference Site: http://nauticalcharts.noaa.gov/csd/Vdatum.htm

As previously mentioned, VDatum was initially developed for the Tampa Bay Demonstration Project, conducted by NOAA and USGS. For this pilot project, VDatum was applied to transform coastal elevations to a common vertical datum to integrate bathymetry and land topography into a digital elevation model useful for coastal managers and decision makers (Millbert and Hess, 2001; Parker, 2002). Subsequent VDatum software development for other coastal regions marks the steady expansion toward national VDatum coverage (Hess et al. 2005; Myers, 2005 (7 pages, pdf); Myers et al. 2005).

In addition to those completed above, VDatum projects are well underway for the Strait of Juan de Fuca (Spargo et al. in prep.), Southern California (Myers et al. in prep.), the Pensacola Bay (Spargo et al. in prep., Feyen et al. in prep.), the Chesapeake Bay (Myers et al. in prep.), the Delaware Bay (Yang et al. in prep.), New Jersey - New York Harbor -Long Island Sound to the Narragansett Bay (Yang et al. in prep.), and the Gulf of Maine (Yang et al. in prep.). uAs regional projects begin to overlap, a seamless National VDatum will emerge to cover all of the U.S. coastal areas, from estuaries out to 25 nautical miles (463 km) from land.

EXCERPT FROM VDATUM'S SOFTWARE DOCUMENTATION

"The VDatum transformation software (Milbert, 2002) encodes a four-step traversal path along a minimal spanning tree whose nodes represent the vertical datums categorized as tidal datums, orthometric datums, and ellipsoidal (3-D) datums. Transformations between the three main categories rely on datum conversions to the primary datum of each category: Local Mean Sea Level for the tidal datums, North American Vertical Datum of 1988 (NAVD 88) for the orthometric datums, and North American Datum of 1983 (1986) for the ellipsoidal datums. Currently, 28 different vertical datums are incorporated into the VDatum software. Conversions between the ellipsoidal datums apply the seven-parameter Helmert transformation that ascribes the 3-D distance, rotation, and scale changes. To account for coastal land-water boundaries, the tidal datums within VDatum are computed from calibrated numerical hydrodynamic models, or by spatially interpolating water levels computed from tide gauge measurements (Hess et al. 1999; Hess, 2002, 2003).

"Sea surface topography, which relates the NAVD 88 orthometric heights to Local Mean Sea Level, is regionally interpolated from water depth measurements taken at leveled tidal benchmarks in each area. Based upon geopotential fields from the Earth Gravity Model of 1996, the GEOID99 height model (html) relates the NAVD 88 orthometric heights with the North American Datum of 1983 (1986) ellipsoid heights (Smith and Roman, 2000; Smith and Roman, 2001 (html)). Future software upgrade to VDatum (upon completion of beta testing) will also permit use of the GEOID03 height model, which will substantially increase spatial resolution and reduce interpolation errors (Roman et al. 2004).

SUMMARY OF THINGS TO REMEMBER

- There are a large number of vertical datums used in the United States.
- There can be large differences between these various datums, i.e., as much as tens of meters.
- Users must know which datum their products are referenced to.
- Users should not combine data sets that are referenced to different datums.
- Published local mean sea level heights, i.e., LMSL and published National vertical heights, i.e., NAVD 88, are not the same.
- New technology heights may not be compatible with old published heights.

Users should reference their products to the latest National Vertical Datum, i.e., NAVD 88, because of traceability and the likelihood of being able to transfer from one datum to another.

AUTHOR BIOGRAPHY

David B. Zilkoski is a geodesist and is currently the director of the National Geodetic Survey (NGS). NGS is a program office in the National Ocean Service (NOS) which is part of the National Oceanic and Atmospheric Administration (NOAA). Zilkoski has been employed by NGS since 1974. From 1974 to 1981, as a member of the Horizontal Network Branch, he participated in the new adjustment of the North American Datum. In 1981, Zilkoski transferred to the Vertical Network Branch, where he served as chief of the Vertical Analysis Section, and project manager for the New Adjustment of the North American Vertical Datum of 1988 (NAVD 88).

In February 1998, he was named chief of the NGS' Geosciences Research Division; and in February 2000, he was selected as deputy director of NGS and acting director in October 2005. In February 2006, he was selected as the director of NGS.

Under the auspices of the Federal Geodetic Control Subcommittee, he evaluates new leveling instrumentation, e.g., the Leica Wild NA3000 digital, bar-code leveling system. Based on instrument testing, he develops and verifies new specifications and procedures to estimate classically-derived, as well as GPS-derived, orthometric heights. He has written numerous technical reports in the geodetic surveying and mapping field. He's also an instructor for the NGS Vertical Control Workshop, and the NAVD 88 and Leveling-Derived Heights & GPS-Derived Heights Seminars. Zilkoski received his BS degree in Forest Engineering from the College of Environmental Science and Forestry at Syracuse University in 1974; and a MS degree in Geodetic Science from Ohio State University in 1979.

ACKNOWLEDGEMENTS

The assistance of several NOAA staff is gratefully acknowledged for input, revisions, and editing this chapter; in addition to providing numerous suggestions and material for improvements and updates.

REFERENCES

Berry, R.M., 1976. History of geodetic leveling in the United States, *Surveying and Mapping*, 36(2): 137-153.

Helmert, F.R. 1890. Die Schwerkraft im Hochgebirge, Insbesondere in den Tyroler Alpen. Veroff. Konigl. Preuss., *Geod. Inst.*, No. 1.

Hicks, S.D., 1985. *Tide Datums and Their Uses - A Summary, Shore and Beach*, 27-33.

Hess, K.W., 2003. Water level simulation in bays by spatial interpolation of tidal constituents, residual water levels, and datums, *Continental Shelf Research*, Vol. 23: 395-414.

Hess, K.W., 2002. Spatial interpolation of tidal data in irregularly-shaped coastal regions by numerical solution of Laplace's equation, *Estuarine, Coastal and Shelf Science*, Vol. 54: 175-192.

Hess, K.W., 2001. Generation of tidal datum fields for Tampa Bay and the New York Bight. U.S. Department of Commerce, National Oceanic and Atmospheric Administration, Silver Spring, Maryland, *NOAA Technical Report* NOS CS 11, 43 p.

Hess, K.W., E. Myers, A. Wong, S. White, E. Spargo, J. Feyen, Z. Yang, P. Richardson, C. Auer, J. Sellars, J. Woolard, D. Roman, S. Gill, C. Zervas, and K. Tronvig, 2005. Development of a National VDatum, and its Application to Sea Level Rise in North Carolina (presentation). U.S. Hydrographic Conference, San Diego, California, March 28-31, 2005.

Hess, K.W., E.A. Spargo, A. Wong, S.A. White, and S.K. Gill, 2005. VDatum for coastal North Carolina: tidal datums, marine grids, and sea surface topography, U.S. Department of Commerce, National Oceanic and Atmospheric Administration, Silver Spring, Maryland, *NOAA Technical Report* NOS CS xx, in review.

Hess, K.W., and S.A. White, 2004. VDatum for Puget Sound: Generation of the grid and population with tidal datums and sea surface topography, U.S. Department of Commerce, National Oceanic and Atmospheric Administration, Silver Spring, Maryland, *NOAA Technical Memorandum* NOS CS 4, 27 p.

Hess, K.W., S.A. White, J. Sellars, E.A. Spargo, A. Wong, S.K Gill, and C. Zervas, 2004. North Carolina sea level rise project: Interim technical report, U.S. Department of Commerce, National Oceanic and Atmospheric Administration, Silver Spring, Maryland, *NOAA Technical Memorandum* NOS CS 5, 25 p.

Hess, K.W., R. Wilson, D. Roman, and D. Milbert, 2004. Final Report on NOAA's Work on the Southern Louisiana Coastal Topographic/Bathymetric Project, unpublished manuscript.

Hess, K.W., and S.K. Gill, 2003. Puget Sound tidal datums by spatial interpolation, *Proceedings, Fifth Conference on Coastal Atmospheric and Oceanic Prediction and Processes*, August 6-8, Seattle, Washington, (American Meteorological Society), Paper 6.1, pp. 108-112.

Hess, K.W., D.G. Milbert, S.K. Gill, D.R. Roman, 2003. Vertical datum transformations for kinematic GPS hydrographic surveys (pdf), U.S. Hydrographic Conference, Biloxi, Mississippi, March 24-27.

Hess, K.W., R.A. Schmalz, C. Zervas and W.C. Collier, 1999. Tidal constituent and residual interpolation (TCARI): A new method for the tidal correction of bathymetric data, U.S. Department of Commerce, National Oceanic and Atmospheric Administration, Silver Spring, Maryland, *NOAA Technical Report* NOS CS 4, 99 p.

Hess, K., 1994. Tampa Bay oceanography project: Development and application of the numerical circulation model, *NOAA Technical Report*, NOS OES 005, National Ocean Service, NOAA, 90 pages.

Marmer, H.A., 1951. Tidal datum planes, NOAA National Ocean Service, *Special Publication No. 135*, U.S. Coast and Gedoetic Survey, U.S. Government Printing Office, revised ed.

Merry, C., and P. Vanicek, 1983. Investigation of local variations of sea surface topography, *Marine Geodesy*, 7(1-4): 101-126.

Milbert, Dennis G., 2002. Documentation for VDatum and a Datum Tutorial: Vertical Datum Transformation Software, Version 1.06 (pdf).

Milbert, D.G. and K.W. Hess, 2001. Combination of topography and bathymetry through application of calibrated vertical datum transformations in the Tampa Bay region (pdf), *Proceedings of the Second Biennial Coastal GeoTools Conference*, January 8-11, 2001, Charleston, South Carolina.

Myers, E.P., 2005. Review of progress on VDatum, a vertical datum transformation tool (7 pages, pdf), *Marine Technology Society/IEEE OCEANS Conference*, September 19-23, 2005, Washington, D.C.

Myers, E.P., A. Wong, K. Hess, S. White, E. Spargo, J. Feyen, Z. Yang, P. Richardson, C. Auer, J. Sellars, J. Woolard, D. Roman, S. Gill, C. Zervas, and K. Tronvig, 2005. Development of a national VDatum, and its application to sea level rise in North Carolina (pdf), *U.S. Hydrographic Conference*, March 28-31, 2005, San Diego, California.

Myers, E.P., *Modeling of Tidal Datum Fields in Support of VDatum Development along the North and Central Coasts of California*, unpublished manuscript.

National Research Council, 2004. *A Geospatial Framework for the Coastal Zone: National Needs For Coastal Mapping and Charting*, National Academies Press, Washington, D.C., 148 p. Report in Brief (4 pages, pdf).

Parker, B., 2003. The difficulties in measuring a consistently defined shoreline – The problem of vertical referencing, *Journal of Coastal Research*, 38: 44-56.

Parker, B., 2002. The integration of bathymetry, topography, and shoreline and the vertical datum transformations behind it, *International Hydrographic Review*, 3(3), November: 35-47.

Parker, B., 2001. Where is the shoreline?, *Hydro International*, July/August: 6-9.

Parker, B., K.W. Hess, D.G. Milbert, and S. Gill, 2003. A national vertical datum transformation tool, *Sea Technology*, 44(9): 10-15.

Parker, B., K.W. Hess, D.G. Milbert, and S. Gill, 2003. National VDatum - The implementation of a national vertical datum transformation database (pdf), U.S. Hydrographic Conference, March 24-27, 2003, Biloxi, Mississippi.

Parker B., D. Milbert, R. Wilson, K. Hess, J. Bailey, C. Fowler, D. Gesch and R. Berry, (in Press). A Tampa Bay bathymetric/topographic digital elevation model with internally consistent shorelines for various datums, presented at Hydro 2001, The 12th Biennial Conference of the Hydrographic Society held at the University of East Anglia, Norwich, United Kingdom.

Roman, D.R., Y.M. Wang, W. Henning, and J. Hamilton, 2004. Assessment of the new national geoid height nodel, GEOID03 (pdf), *Proceedings of the American Congress on Surveying and Mapping*, April 16-21, 2004, Nashville, Tennessee.

Smith, D.A., and D.R.Roman, 2001. GEOID99 and G99SSS: One arc-minute models for the United States (html), *Journal of Geodesy*, 75: 469-490.

Spargo, E.A., and J.W. Woolard, 2005. VDatum for the Calcasieu River from Lake Charles to the Gulf of Mexico, Louisiana: Tidal datum modeling and population of the grid, U.S. Department of Commerce, National Oceanic and Atmospheric Administration, Silver Spring, Maryland, *NOAA Technical Report* NOS CS 19, 26 p.

State of Illinois, 1949. Preliminary report - Relation of various datum planes to mean sea level (1929 - 5th General Adjustment), State of Illinois, Department of Public Works and Buildings, Division of Waterways, Unpublished Technical Report.

Zilkoski, D.B. 1986. The North American vertical datum of 1988 (NAVD 88): Tasks, impacts, and benefits, *Proceedings of the Symposium on Height Determination and Recent Vertical Crustal Movements in Western Europe*, Hannover, Germany.

Zilkoski, D.B., and G.M. Young. 1985. North American vertical datum (NAVD) update, *Proceedings of the U.S. Army Corps of Engineers 1985 Survey Conference*, Jacksonville, Florida. Vicksburg, Mississippi, U.S. Army Corps of Engineers.

Zilkoski, D.B., E.I. Balazs, and J.M. Bengston, 1989. NAVD 88 Datum Definition Study, Unpublished NGS technical report.

Zilkoski, D., J. Richards, and G. Young, 1992. Results of the general adjustment of the North American vertical datum of 1988, *Surveying and Land Information Systems*, 52(3): 133-149.

Zilkoski, D., J.D. D'Onofrio, and S. Frakes, 1997. Guidelines for establishing GPS-derived ellipsoid heights (Standards: 2 cm and 5 cm), Version 4.3, *NOAA Technical Memorandum* NOS NGS-58, National Geodetic Survey Information Center, Silver Spring, MD 20910.

Zilkoski, D., E. Carlson, and C. Smith, 2005. A Guide for establishing GPS-derived orthometric heights (Standards: 2 cm and 5 cm), Version 1.4, *NOAA Technical Memorandum* (Draft).

Zervas, C. 2001. Sea level variations of the United States 1854 - 1999, *NOAA Technical Report* NOS CO-OPS. 36, U.S. Dept. of Commerce, NOAA, National Ocean Service, 185 pp., July 2001.

Chapter 3

Accuracy Standards & Guidelines

David F. Maune, Julie Binder Maitra, and Edward J. McKay

ACCURACY VS. PRECISION

As referenced to the vertical datum, the *accuracy* of a single measured elevation point is the closeness of its estimated elevation (as surveyed or computed) to a standard or accepted correct value. The accuracy is commonly referred to as "high" or "low" depending on the size of the differences between the estimated and the standard value. Sometimes, correct or true elevations are known, as with NGS's Continuously Operating Reference Stations (CORS), but often the true elevations are unknown.

When errors follow a normal error distribution, as is common with photogrammetric data, the vertical accuracy of a set of elevation points (as in a DEM or TIN) may first be determined by its root-mean-square error (RMSE), the square root of the average of the set of squared differences between dataset coordinate values and coordinate values from an independent source of higher accuracy for identical points. The vertical RMSE is then converted into vertical accuracy at an established confidence level, normally 95%. This process is explained below in the section for the National Standard for Spatial Data Accuracy (NSSDA).

When errors do not follow a normal error distribution, as is common with lidar bare-earth data, the 95th percentile method is used to determine vertical accuracy at the 95% confidence level. This process is explained below in the section for the National Digital Elevation Program (NDEP), *Guidelines for Digital Elevation Data*, and in the section for the *ASPRS Guidelines, Vertical Accuracy Reporting for Lidar Data*.

Often confused with accuracy, *precision* is a measure of the tendency of a set of values to cluster about a number determined by the set. The usual measure of precision is the standard deviation or the standard error. Precision is distinguished from accuracy by the fact that accuracy is a measure of the tendency to cluster about a number not determined by the data set but specified in some other manner. Precision may also be considered as a measure of consistency among repeat measurements. Note, however, that measurements may be consistent, but they may be consistently inaccurate.

If a surveying system is out of calibration, it may yield systematic errors in elevations so that the precision may be high while the accuracy is low. In other words, a precise system may consistently yield inaccurate measurements. A good example is a GPS elevation survey, whereby a GPS surveyor may survey 3-D coordinates for 90 minutes on Monday morning, and for another 90 minutes on Tuesday afternoon, for example. If the two elevations agree within 1 or 2 cm, the surveyor may erroneously conclude that the average of the two elevations is accurate within 0.5 or 1 cm. However, the average elevation might be in error by several centimeters for the following reasons:

- If the surveyor had surveyed for 120 minutes on Monday morning and 120 minutes on Tuesday afternoon, the elevations would undoubtedly have been different because standard GPS software typically applies tropospheric corrections for sessions of 2 hours or more, and tropospheric corrections normally cause elevations to vary by a centimeter or more. Furthermore, regardless of tropospheric corrections, longer observation times are almost always more accurate than shorter observation times.

- If the surveyor had used a lower accuracy benchmark as the GPS base station, any elevations derived therefrom would have poorer accuracy than if a higher accuracy benchmark had been used. If the base station is in error by several centimeters, elevations derived therefrom will also be in error by several centimeters.

For either of these reasons, the surveyor might have received precise elevations (and could even have obtained identical results from repeat surveys) and could have erroneously assumed that the elevations were accurate also. But he/she would have been consistently wrong because of either or both of these systematic errors. It is far easier to be precise (consistent) than to be accurate.

INTRODUCTION TO GEODETIC CONTROL STANDARDS

With conventional land surveys (differential leveling or trigonometric leveling), traditional accuracy standards were actually measures of precision; they identified the consistency with which relative accuracy could be determined between directly connected points or benchmarks, and the referenced benchmark itself normally had questionable accuracy relative to the vertical datum. If the true accuracy of the reference monument or benchmark is questionable, then all elevations derived therefrom will also have questionable accuracy.

Traditional orders and classes of vertical control surveys are computed as a function of the distance surveyed between the referenced benchmark and new points to be surveyed. Furthermore, different routes used to survey between points A and B could yield different elevations because the magnitude and direction of gravity may vary along different survey routes between A and B. For decades, vertical accuracy was assumed to be synonymous with relative vertical accuracy because, normally, no one knew the absolute elevations of control points relative to the vertical datum. Per FGCC, 1984, the Federal Geodetic Control Committee (FGCC) classified conventional vertical control surveys as shown at Table 3.1.

Table 3.1 Accuracy Standards for Conventional Vertical Control Surveys.

Order	Class	Relative Accuracy Between Directly Connected Points or Benchmarks
First	I	Standard Error = 0.5 mm $\sqrt{K}$
First	II	Standard Error = 0.7 mm $\sqrt{K}$
Second	I	Standard Error = 1.0 mm $\sqrt{K}$
Second	II	Standard Error = 1.3 mm $\sqrt{K}$
Third	N/A	Standard Error = 2.0 mm $\sqrt{K}$
Where K is the distance in kilometers between the directly connected points surveyed		

When GPS surveys became commonplace for measuring the differences in ellipsoid heights between two points, the FGCC developed accuracy standards for using GPS relative positioning techniques (FGCC, 1988) that also varied as a function of the distance between the points surveyed. Table 3.2 provides examples for different order/class (OC) codes at common distances. The first character of the OC code indicates the order and the second character the class, in accordance with (NOAA, 2006) NGS *Blue Book* standards for classifying ellipsoid height determinations.

As shown at Table 3.3, the FGCC (FGCC, 1988) also specified geometric relative positioning accuracy standards for three-dimensional (3-D) surveys using space system techniques, and the three highest accuracy orders are called AA, A and B, respectively, surveyed relative to NGS' CORS.

Table 3.2 Standard Errors of GPS Ellipsoid Height Differences at Common Distances.

OC Codes	11	12	21	22	31	32	41	42	51	52
Distance = 1 Km	0.5 mm	0.7 mm	1.0 mm	1.3 mm	2.0 mm	3.0 mm	6.0 mm	15 mm	30 mm	60 mm
Distance = 5 Km	1.1 mm	1.6 mm	2.2 mm	2.9 mm	4.5 mm	6.7 mm	13 mm	34 mm	67 mm	134 mm
Distance = 10 Km	1.6 mm	2.2 mm	3.2 mm	4.1 mm	6.3 mm	9.5 mm	19 mm	47 mm	95 mm	190 mm
Distance = 25 Km	2.5 mm	3.5 mm	5.0 mm	6.5 mm	10 mm	15 mm	30 mm	75 mm	150 mm	300 mm
Distance = 50 Km	3.5 mm	4.9 mm	7.1 mm	9.2 mm	14 mm	21 mm	42 mm	106 mm	212 mm	424 mm
Distance = 75 Km	4.3 mm	6.1 mm	8.7 mm	11 mm	17 mm	26 mm	52 mm	130 mm	260 mm	520 mm
Distance = 100 Km	5.0 mm	7.0 mm	10 mm	13 mm	20 mm	30 mm	60 mm	150 mm	300 mm	600 mm

Table 3.3 Geometric Relative Positioning Accuracy Standards for Three-Dimensional Surveys using Space System Techniques.

Survey categories	Order	(95 percent confidence level) Minimum geometric Accuracy standard		
		Base error e (cm)	Line-length Dependent error p (ppm)	a (1:a)
Global-regional geodynamics; deformation measurements	AA	0.3	0.01	1:100,000,000
National Geodetic Reference System, "primary" networks; regional-local geodynamics; deformation measurements	A	0.5	0.1	1:10,000,000
National Geodetic Reference System, "secondary networks; connections to the "primary" NGRS network; local geodynamics; deformation measurements; high-precision engineering surveys	B	0.8	1	1:1,000,000
National Geodetic Reference System (Terrestrial based); dependent control surveys to meet mapping, land information, property, and engineering requirements	(C) 1 2-I 2-II 3	1.0 2.0 3.0 5.0	10 20 50 100	1:100,000 1:50,000 1:20,000 1:10,000
Note: For ease of computation and understanding, it is assumed that the accuracy for each component of a vector base line measurement is equal to the linear accuracy standard for a single-dimensional measurement at the 95 percent confidence level. Thus, the linear one-standard deviation (s) is computed by: $s = \pm[\, e^2 + (0.1d \cdot p)^2]/1.96$ where d is the length of the baseline in kilometers			

This formula makes correct use of the term "±." However, others often erroneously use the term "±" to indicate the approximate accuracy of a coordinate (e.g., "the vertical accuracy is ± 15-cm"), but "±" is the most abused accuracy reference of all time, having a different perceived meaning to everyone who speaks or hears the term. By the early 1990s, the FGCS recognized a need for a *local accuracy* standard as well as a *network accuracy* standard, both stated as numeric quantities (centimeters or millimeters) at the 95% confidence level, and NOT used as a distance dependent expression. Local accuracy would represent an average of observation accuracy relative to directly connected points, and network accuracy would be relative to CORS sites where horizontal and vertical coordinates are assumed to be exactly known relative to the official horizontal and vertical datums (NAD 83 and NAVD 88). *Local accuracy* is very similar to what has previously been called *relative accuracy*, and *network accuracy* is very similar to what has previously been called *absolute accuracy*. Vertical accuracy defines the one-dimensional (vertical) linear error at the 95% confidence level, and horizontal accuracy defines the two-dimensional (radial) circular error at the 95% confidence level. This vision came to fruition in the Geospatial Positioning Accuracy Standards (FGDC, 1998b), described below, published by the Federal Geographic Data Committee (FGDC).

INTRODUCTION TO MAPPING STANDARDS

With traditional photogrammetric mapping with film cameras, the flying height of the aerial photography used as the primary source material and mapping camera characteristics more or less dictate the vertical accuracy of printed topographic maps, i.e., the interval of topographic contours. For example, if a client needs 2' contours, a typical flying height for acquisition of aerial photography is 4,000' above mean terrain (amt) when using a mapping camera with a 6" focal length; if a client needs 5' contours, a typical flying height is 10,000' amt, etc. Today, the imaging and geospatial information community represented by ASPRS has numerous alternative technologies available for DEM production that are less dependent, or nearly totally independent, of flying height to determine the vertical accuracy of the data. IFSAR, lidar, and sonar, which will be discussed in subsequent chapters, are leading examples of these technologies. These technologies are quite different from technologies used to generate planimetric GIS data such as vector base maps and digital orthophotos. Furthermore, satellites are delivering both horizontal and vertical spatial data with accuracies previously considered unthinkable for high-altitude remote sensing.

In 1947, prior to the advent of DEMs, the U.S. Bureau of the Budget (Bureau of the Budget, 1947) published the National Map Accuracy Standards (NMAS) that defined the vertical map accuracy standard for contour maps at all publication scales. In 1990, ASPRS published the ASPRS Accuracy Standards for Large-Scale Maps (ASPRS, 1990), with the expectation that these standards would form the basis for revision of the NMAS. A major feature of the ASPRS standards is that they indicate limiting root-mean-square (rms) vertical errors at ground scale as a function of the contour interval. In 1998, the FGDC endorsed and published Geospatial Positioning Accuracy Standards that include the National Standard for Spatial Data Accuracy (NSSDA). The NSSDA was developed to evaluate and report the accuracy of digital geospatial data, including DEMs. The draft Content Standard for Framework Land Elevation Data, which did not reach FGDC endorsement, includes NSSDA-based procedures for evaluating DEMs from multiple sources.

The objective of this chapter is to help DEM users understand FGDC standards as they apply to digital elevation data in general and DEMs in particular. This chapter includes a review of the NMAS and ASPRS Accuracy Standards for Large-Scale Maps, designed for printed maps with a published map scale and contour interval, and the new FGDC standards designed for geographic information systems (GIS) and digital geospatial data that are not constrained by scale and contours.

In 2005, FGDC published the Geospatial Positioning Accuracy Standards, Part 5: Standards for Nautical Charting Hydrographic Surveys (FGDC, 2005). This FGDC standard is based upon the International Hydrographic Organization (IHO) Standards for Hydrographic Surveys, Special Publication No. 44 (IHO, 1998).

Ultimately, DEM users must identify acceptable accuracies for their diverse applications. Therefore, this chapter establishes the framework for user-defined DEM quality assessment to be explained in Chapter 12. Those quality assessments are based partly on additional guidelines, summarized below, published for diverse technologies and applications:

- *NOS Hydrographic Surveys Specifications and Deliverables,* published by the National Oceanic and Atmospheric Administration (NOAA), National Ocean Service (NOS), Office of Coast Survey (OCS), March, 2003 (NOAA, 2003).
- *Guidance for Aerial Mapping and Surveying*, Appendix A, to "Guidelines and Specifications for Flood Hazard Mapping Partners," published by the Federal Emergency Management Agency (FEMA), April, 2003 (FEMA, 2003).
- *Guidelines for Digital Elevation Data,* version 1.0, published by the National Digital Elevation Program (NDEP), May 10, 2004 (NDEP, 2004).
- *ASPRS Guidelines, Vertical Accuracy Reporting for Lidar Data,* published by the American Society for Photogrammetry and Remote Sensing, May 24, 2004 (ASPRS, 2004).

NATIONAL MAP ACCURACY STANDARDS (NMAS), 1947

The NMAS (Bureau of the Budget, 1947) indicates that the vertical accuracy of published maps may be a function of the horizontal accuracy. Therefore the NMAS definitions of horizontal and vertical accuracy, also called the Circular Map Accuracy Standard (CMAS) and Vertical Map Accuracy Standard (CMAS), are both quoted below:

Circular Map Accuracy Standard (CMAS)

"*Horizontal accuracy.* For maps on publication scales larger than 1:20,000, not more than 10 percent of the points tested shall be in error by more than 1/30 inch, measured on the publication scale; for maps on publication scales of 1:20,000 or smaller, 1/50 inch. These limits of accuracy shall apply in all cases to positions of well-defined points only. 'Well defined' points are those that are easily visible or recoverable on the ground, such as the following: monuments or markers, such as bench marks, property boundary monuments; intersections of roads, railroads, etc.; corners of large buildings or structures (or center points of small buildings), etc. In general what is 'well defined' will also be determined by what is plottable on the scale of the map within 1/100 inch. Thus while the intersection of two roads or property lines meeting at right angles would come within a sensible interpretation, identification of the intersection of such lines meeting at an acute angle would obviously not be practicable within 1/100 inch. Similarly, features not identifiable upon the ground within close limits are not to be considered as test points within the limits quoted, even though their positions may be scaled closely upon the map. In this class would come timber lines, soil boundaries, etc."

Vertical Map Accuracy Standard (VMAS)

"*Vertical accuracy,* as applied to contour maps on all publication scales, shall be such that not more than 10 percent of the elevations tested shall be in error more than one-half the contour interval. In checking elevations taken from the map, the apparent vertical error may be decreased by assuming a horizontal displacement within the permissible horizontal error for a map of that scale."

Major Points in Understanding the NMAS

The most significant points to understand about the NMAS are as follows:
- The NMAS pertains to graphic contour maps with a published scale and contour interval.
- The NMAS predated the introduction of DEMs.
- Apparent vertical errors can be offset by permissible horizontal errors
- Test points must be well defined

Therefore, it is advisable not to use the NMAS for evaluating and reporting the vertical accuracy of DEM's.

SPECIFICATIONS FOR AERIAL SURVEYS AND MAPPING BY PHOTOGRAMMETRIC METHODS FOR HIGHWAYS

In 1968, the Photogrammetry for Highways Committee of the U.S. Department of Transportation, published the "Reference Guide Outline: Specifications for Aerial Surveys and Mapping by Photogrammetric Methods for Highways" (Photogrammetry for Highways Committee, 1968). This is essentially a modification to the NMAS, and both versions of these accuracy statements have been widely used over the years in specifications for hardcopy mapping projects.

A. *Contours* — Ninety (90) percent of the elevations determined from the solid-line con tours of the topographic maps shall have an accuracy with respect to true elevation of one-half (1/2) contour interval or better and the remaining ten (10) percent of such elevations shall not be in error by more than one contour interval. This accuracy shall apply only to the contours which are on each map. Thus, in each particular area where the intermediate contours have had to be omitted because of the steepness of the ground slopes and only the index contours are delineated on the maps, the accuracy stipulations apply to contour interval of the index contours. Wherever the intermediate contours are not omitted, of course, the accuracies are applicable to the contour interval specified for the topographic maps. In densely wooded areas where heavy brush or tree cover fully obscures the ground and the contours are shown as dashed lines, they shall be plotted as accurately as possible from the stereoscopic model, while making full use of spot elevations obtained during ground-control surveys and all spot elevations measured photogrammetrically in places where the ground is visible.

B. *Coordinate Grid Lines* — The plotted position of each plane coordinate grid line shall not vary by more than one one-hundredth (1/100) of an inch from true grid value on each map manuscript.

C. *Horizontal Control* — Each horizontal control point shall be plotted on the map manuscript within the coordinate grid in which it should lie to an accuracy of one one-hundredth (1/100) of an inch of its true position as expressed by the plane coordinates computed for the point.

D. *Planimetric Features* — Ninety (90) percent of all planimetric features which are well-defined on the photographs shall be plotted so that their position on the finished maps shall be accurate to within at least one-fortieth (1/40) of an inch of their true coordinate position, as determined by the test surveys, and none of the features tested shall be misplaced on the finished map by more than one-twentieth (1/20) of an inch from their true coordinate position. The true coordinate position shall be determined by making accurate measurements originating and closing on station markers of the project basic control survey, which shall have a closure accuracy conforming with the requirements for the basic control.

E. *Special Requirements* — When stipulated in special provisions that all specified features (planimetry and contours) shall be delineated on the maps, regardless of whether they can or cannot be seen on the aerial photographs and on stereoscopic models formed therefrom, the consultant shall complete compilation of the required maps by field surveys on the ground so as to comply with all accuracy and completeness stipulations.

F. *Spot Elevations* — Ninety (90) percent of all spot elevations placed on the maps shall have an accuracy of at least one-fourth (1/4) the contour interval, and the remaining ten (10) percent shall be not in error by more than one-half (1/2) the contour interval.

ASPRS ACCURACY STANDARDS FOR LARGE-SCALE MAPS, 1990

ASPRS Accuracy Standards for Large-Scale Maps (ASPRS, 1990), like the NMAS, indicate that vertical accuracy may be a function of horizontal accuracy. Therefore, explanations of both horizontal and vertical accuracy are provided below:

Horizontal Accuracy

"Horizontal map accuracy is defined as the (root-mean-square) rms error in terms of the project's planimetric survey coordinates (X,Y) for checked points as determined at full (ground) scale of the map. The rms error is the cumulative result of all errors including those introduced by the processes of ground control surveys, map compilation and final extraction of ground dimensions from the map. The limiting rms errors are the maximum permissible rms errors established by this standard. These limiting rms errors for Class 1 maps are tabulated [in attached tables] … along with typical map scales associated with the limiting errors. These limits of accuracy apply to tests made on well-defined points only."

Vertical Accuracy

"Vertical map accuracy is defined as the rms error in elevation in terms of the project's elevation datum for well-defined points only. For Class 1 maps the limiting rms error in elevation is set by the standard at *one-third* the indicated contour interval for well-defined points only. Spot heights shall be shown on the map within a limiting rms error of *one-sixth* of the contour interval."

Map Classes

"Map accuracies can also be defined at lower spatial accuracy standards. Maps compiled within limiting rms errors of twice or three times those allowed for a Class 1 map shall be designated Class 2 or Class 3 maps respectively. A map may be compiled that complies with one class of accuracy in elevation and another in plan. Multiple accuracies on the same map are allowed provided a diagram is included which clearly relates segments of the map with the appropriate map accuracy class." The NSSDA subsequently chose to get rid of Classes that might create subjective interpretations of the quality of geospatial data and chose instead to rely on the estimated accuracy value.

Accuracy Testing

"Tests for compliance of a map sheet are optional. Testing for horizontal accuracy compliance is done by comparing the planimetric (X and Y) coordinates of well-defined ground points to the coordinates of the same points as determined by a horizontal check survey of higher accuracy."

"Testing for vertical accuracy compliance shall be accomplished by comparing the elevations of well-defined points as determined from the map to corresponding elevations determined by a survey of higher accuracy. For purposes of checking elevations, the map position of the ground point may be shifted in any direction by an amount equal to twice the limiting rms error in position. The vertical check survey should be designed to produce rms errors in elevation differences at check point locations no larger than *1/20ᵗʰ of the contour interval*."

"Discrepancies between the X, Y, or Z coordinates of the ground point, as determined from the map and by the check survey, that exceed *three* times the limiting rms error shall be interpreted as blunders and will be corrected before the map is considered to meet this standard."

"A minimum of 20 check points shall be established throughout the area covered by the map and shall be distributed in a manner agreed upon by the contracting parties."

"Maps produced according to this spatial accuracy standard shall include the following statement in the title block: THIS MAP WAS COMPILED TO MEET THE ASPRS STANDARD FOR CLASS 1 MAP ACCURACY."

Major Points in Understanding ASPRS 90 Standards

The most significant points to understand about the ASPRS 1990 standards are:
- They postdate the introduction of DEMs, but they still pertain to graphic contour maps with a published scale and contour interval.
- They classify maps as Class 1, Class 2, or Class 3, according to accuracy.
- They establish limiting rms errors for both horizontal and vertical accuracy.
- The limiting rms errors are ground distances (feet or meters) as opposed to map distances (fractions of an inch) used by the NMAS.
- Apparent vertical errors can be offset by permissible horizontal errors.
- Test points must be well defined.

Therefore, it is advisable not to apply ASPRS Accuracy Standards for Large-Scale Maps for evaluating and reporting vertical accuracy of DEM's.

FGDC GEOSPATIAL POSITIONING ACCURACY STANDARDS, 1998

In 1998, the FGDC published new Geospatial Positioning Accuracy Standards in support of the National Spatial Data Infrastructure (NSDI). These standards have three parts that are relevant to DEMs:
- Part 1, Reporting Methodology, FGDC-STD-007.1-1998 (FGDC, 1998a) provides guidance on how to report the accuracy of horizontal and vertical coordinates.
- Part 2, Standards for Geodetic Networks, FGDC-STD-007.2-1998 (FGDC, 1998b) provides guidance on how to utilize and supplement the National Spatial Reference System (NSRS) maintained by the National Geodetic Survey (NGS) to establish network accuracy of spatial data.
- Part 3, National Standard for Spatial Data Accuracy (NSSDA), FGDC-STD-007.3- 1998 (FGDC, 1998c) provides guidance on how to implement a testing and statistical methodology for positional accuracy of digital geospatial data.

Part 1: Reporting Methodology

Part 1 (FGDC, 1998a) "provides a common methodology for reporting the accuracy of horizontal coordinate values and vertical coordinate values for clearly defined features where the location is represented by a single point coordinate: examples are survey monuments, such as brass disks and rod marks; prominent landmarks, such as church spires, standpipes, radio towers, tall chimneys, and mountain peaks; and targeted photogrammetric control points. It provides a means to directly compare the accuracy of coordinate values obtained by one method (e.g., a cartographically-derived value) with that obtained by another method (e.g., a Global Positioning System (GPS) geodetic network survey) for the same point. It is increasingly important for users to not only know the coordinate values, but also the accuracy of those coordinate values, so users can decide which coordinate values represent the best estimate of the true value for their applications." Part 1 also provides a reporting standard for Parts 2 & 3:

- "The reporting standard in the horizontal component is the radius of a circle of uncertainty, such that the true or theoretical location of the point falls within that circle 95-percent of the time." (This is called Accuracy$_r$ in Part 3.)
- "The reporting standard in the vertical component is a linear uncertainty value, such that the true or theoretical location of the point falls within ± of that linear uncertainty value 95-percent of the time." (This is called Accuracy$_z$ in Part 3.)

Part 2: Standards for Geodetic Networks

Part 2 (FGDC, 1998b) "provides a common methodology for determining and reporting the accuracy of horizontal coordinate values and vertical coordinate values for geodetic control points represented by survey monuments, such as brass disks and rod marks. It provides a means to directly compare the accuracy of coordinate values obtained by one method (e.g., a classical line-of-sight traverse) with the accuracy of coordinate values obtained by another method (e.g., a Global Positioning System (GPS) geodetic network survey) for the same point." Other relevant quotes from Part 2 are as follows:

- "Geodetic control surveys are usually performed to establish a basic control network (framework) from which supplemental surveying and mapping work, covered in other parts of this document, is performed. Geodetic network surveys are distinguished by use of redundant, interconnected permanently monumented control points that comprise the framework for the National Spatial Reference System (NSRS) or are often incorporated into the NSRS. These surveys must be performed to far more rigorous accuracy and quality assurance standards than those for control surveys for general engineering, construction, or topographic mapping purposes."
- "It is not necessary to directly connect to a CORS to compute the network accuracy of a control point. However, it is necessary that the survey be properly connected to existing NSRS control points with established network accuracy values."
- "By supporting both local accuracy and network accuracy[1], the diverse requirements of NSRS users can be met. Local accuracy is best adapted to check relations between nearby control points. For example, a surveyor checking closure between two NSRS points is mostly interested in a local accuracy measure. On the other hand, someone constructing a Geographic or Land Information System (GIS/LIS) will often need some type of positional tolerance associated with a set of coordinates. Network accuracy measures how well coordinates approach an ideal, error-free datum."

Part 3: National Standard for Spatial Data Accuracy (NSSDA)

Part 3 (FGDC, 1998c), The National Standard for Spatial Data Accuracy (NSSDA), "implements a statistical and testing methodology for estimating the positional accuracy of points on maps and in digital geospatial data, with respect to georeferenced ground positions of higher accuracy."

---

[1]Appendix 1-A, Glossary of Terms (FGDC, 1998a) defines local accuracy and network accuracy as follows: "The local accuracy or a control point is a value that represents the uncertainty in the coordinates of the control point relative to the coordinates of other directly connected, adjacent control points at the 95-percent confidence level. The reported local accuracy is an approximate average of the individual local accuracy values between this control point and other observed control points used to establish the coordinates of the control point. The network accuracy of a control point is a value that represents the uncertainty in the coordinates of the control point with respect to the geodetic datum at the 95-percent confidence level. For NSRS network accuracy classification, the datum is considered to be best expressed by the geodetic values at the Continuously Operating Reference Stations (CORS) supported by NGS. By this definition, the local and network accuracy values at CORS sites are considered to be infinitesimal, i.e., to approach zero."

The scope of Part 3 (FGDC, 1998c) is as follows: "The NSSDA applies to fully georeferenced maps and digital geospatial data in either raster, point, or vector format, derived from sources such as aerial photographs, satellite imagery, and ground surveys. It provides a common language for reporting accuracy to facilitate the identification of spatial data for geographic applications. This standard does not define threshold accuracy values. Agencies are encouraged to establish thresholds for their product specifications and applications and for contracting purposes. Ultimately, users identify acceptable accuracies for their applications. Data and map producers must determine what accuracy exists or is achievable for their data and report it according to NSSDA." Other relevant quotes from Part 3 are as follows:

"Applicability. Use the NSSDA to evaluate and report the positional accuracy of maps and geospatial data produced, revised, or disseminated by or for the Federal Government. According to Executive Order 12906, Coordinating Geographic Data Acquisition and Access: the National Spatial Data Infrastructure (Clinton, 1994, Sec. 4. Data Standards Activities, item d), 'Federal agencies collecting or producing geospatial data, either directly or indirectly (e.g., through grants, partnerships, or contracts with other entities), shall ensure prior to obligating funds for such activities, that data will be collected in a manner that meets all relevant standards adopted through the FGDC process.' Accuracy of new or revised spatial data will be reported according to the NSSDA. Accuracy of existing or legacy spatial data and maps may be reported, as specified, according to the NSSDA or the accuracy standard by which they were evaluated."

"Testing Methodology and Reporting Requirements. Spatial Accuracy. The NSSDA uses root-mean-square error (RMSE) to estimate positional accuracy. RMSE is the square root of the average of the set of squared differences between dataset coordinate values and coordinate values from an independent source of higher accuracy for identical points. Accuracy is reported in ground distances at the 95% confidence level. Accuracy reported at the 95% confidence level means that 95% of the positions in the dataset will have an error with respect to true ground position that is equal to or smaller than the reported accuracy value. The reported accuracy value reflects all uncertainties, including those introduced by geodetic control coordinates, compilation, and final computation of ground coordinate values in the product."

"Accuracy Test Guidelines. According to the Spatial Data Transfer Standard (SDTS) (ANSI-NCITS, 1998), accuracy testing by an independent source of higher accuracy is the preferred test for positional accuracy. Consequently, the NSSDA presents guidelines for accuracy testing by an independent source of higher accuracy. The independent source of higher accuracy shall be the highest accuracy feasible and practicable to evaluate the accuracy of the dataset.[2] The data producer shall determine the geographic extent of testing. Horizontal accuracy shall be tested by comparing the planimetric coordinates of well-defined points[3] in the dataset with coordinates of the same points from an independent source of higher accuracy. Vertical accuracy shall be tested by comparing the elevations in the dataset with elevations of the same points as determined from an independent source of higher accuracy. A minimum of 20 check points shall be tested, distributed to reflect the geographic area of interest and the distribution of error in the dataset.[4] When 20 points are tested, the 95% confidence level allows one point to fail the threshold given in product specifications."

---

[2] Appendix 3-C, section 2 (FGDC, 1998c) states: "The independent source of higher accuracy shall be acquired separately from data used in the aerotriangulation solution or other production procedures. The independent source of higher accuracy shall be of the highest accuracy feasible and practicable to evaluate the accuracy of the dataset. Although guidelines given here are for geodetic ground surveys, the geodetic survey is only one of many possible ways to acquire data for the independent source of higher accuracy. Other possible sources for higher accuracy information are Global Positioning System (GPS) ground surveys, photogrammetric methods, and data bases of high accuracy point coordinates." *footnotes continued on next page*

Accuracy Reporting

"Accuracy Reporting. Spatial data may be compiled to comply with one accuracy value for the vertical component and another for the horizontal component. If a dataset does not contain elevation data, label for horizontal accuracy only. Conversely, when a dataset, e.g., a gridded digital elevation dataset or elevation contour dataset, does not contain well-defined points, label for vertical accuracy only. Report accuracy at the 95% confidence level for data *tested* for both horizontal and vertical accuracy as:

"Tested _____ (meters, feet) horizontal accuracy at 95% confidence level
_____ (meters, feet) vertical accuracy at 95% confidence level

"Use the 'compiled to meet' statement below when the above guidelines for testing by an independent source of higher accuracy cannot be followed and an alternative means is used to evaluate accuracy. Report accuracy at the 95% confidence level for data *produced according to procedures that have been demonstrated to produce data with particular horizontal and vertical accuracy values* as:

"Compiled to meet _____ (meters, feet) horizontal accuracy at 95% confidence level
_____ (meters, feet) vertical accuracy at 95% confidence level"

For digital geospatial data, report the accuracy value in digital geospatial metadata as described in the FGDC Content Standard for Digital Geospatial Metadata (CSDGM) Version 2 (FGDC, 1998d).

Appendix 3-A (FGDC, 1998c) provides the following accuracy statistics for computation of Accuracy$_r$ and Accuracy$_z$:

Horizontal Accuracy

"Horizontal Accuracy. Let:

"$RMSE_x = sqrt[\Sigma(x_{data\,I} - x_{check\,I})^2/n$

"$RMSE_y = sqrt[\Sigma(y_{data\,I} - y_{check\,I})^2/n]$ where:

"$x_{data\,I}, y_{data\,I}$ are the coordinates of the Ith check point in the dataset

"$x_{check\,I}, y_{check\,I}$ are the coordinates of the Ith check point in the independent source of higher accuracy

"n is the number of check points tested

"I is an integer ranging from 1 to n

---

[3] Appendix 3-C, section 1 (FGDC, 1998c) states: "A well-defined point represents a feature for which the horizontal position is known to a high degree of accuracy and position with respect to the geodetic datum. For the purpose of accuracy testing, well-defined points must be easily visible or recoverable on the ground, on the independent source of higher accuracy, and on the product itself. Graphic contour data and digital hypsographic data may not contain well-defined points. The selected points will differ depending on the type of dataset and output scale of the dataset. For graphic maps and vector data, suitable well-defined points represent right-angle intersections of roads, railroads, or other linear mapped features, such as canals, ditches, trails, fence lines, and pipelines. For orthoimagery, suitable well-defined points may represent features such as small isolated shrubs or bushes, in addition to right-angle intersections of linear features. For map products at scales of 1:5,000 or larger, such as engineering plats or property maps, suitable well-defined points may represent additional features such as utility access covers and intersections of side-walks, curbs, or gutters."

[4]Appendix 3-C, section 3 (FGDC, 1998c) states: "Due to the diversity of user requirements for digital geospatial data and maps, it is not realistic to include statements in this standard that specify the spatial distribution of check points. Data and/or map producers must determine checkpoint locations. This section provides guidelines for distributing the checkpoint locations. Checkpoints may be distributed more densely in the vicinity of important features and more sparsely in areas that are of little or no interest. When data exist for only a portion of the dataset, confine test points to that area. When the distribution of error is likely to be nonrandom, it may be desirable to locate check points to correspond to the error distribution."

"Horizontal error at point I is defined as:

$$\sqrt{[(x_{data\ I} - x_{check\ I})2 + (y_{data\ I} - y_{check\ I})^2]}$$

"Horizontal RMSE is:

$$RMSE_r = \sqrt{[\Sigma((x_{data\ I} - x_{check\ I})^2 + (y_{data\ I} - y_{check\ I})^2)/n]}$$
$$= \sqrt{[RMSE_x^2 + RMSE_y^2]}$$

"Computing Accuracy According to the NSSDA when $RMSE_x = RMSE_y$

$$RMSE_r = \sqrt{(2 * RMSE_x^2)} = \sqrt{(2 * RMSE_y^2)}$$
$$= 1.4142 * RMSE_x = 1.4142 * RMSE_y$$

"It is assumed that systematic errors have been eliminated as best as possible. If error is normally distributed and independent in each the x- and y-component and error for the x-component is equal to and independent of error for the y-component, the factor 2.4477 is used to compute horizontal accuracy at the 95% confidence level (Greenwalt and Schultz, 1968). When the preceding conditions apply, $Accuracy_r$, the accuracy value according to NSSDA, shall be computed by the formula:

$$Accuracy_r = 2.4477 * RMSE_x = 2.4477 * RMSE_y = 2.4477 * RMSE_r/1.4142$$
$$Accuracy_r = 1.7308 * RMSE_r"$$

Vertical Accuracy

"Vertical Accuracy. Let:

"$RMSE_z = \sqrt{[\Sigma(z_{data\ I} - z_{check\ I})^2/n]}$ where

"$z_{data\ I}$ is the vertical coordinate of the Ith check point in the dataset

"$z_{check\ I}$ is the vertical coordinate of the Ith check point in the independent source of higher accuracy

"n = the number of points being checked

"I is an integer from 1 to n

"It is assumed that systematic errors have been eliminated as best as possible. If vertical error is normally distributed, the factor 1.9600 is applied to compute linear error at the 95% confidence level (Greenwalt and Schultz, 1968). Therefore, vertical accuracy, $Accuracy_z$, reported according to the NSSDA shall be computed by the following formula:

$$Accuracy_z = 1.9600 * RMSE_z"$$

Comparison of NSSDA and NMAS

Per Appendix 3-D (FGDC, 1998c), the relationship between NSSDA and NMAS are defined as follows:

"Relationship between NSSDA and NMAS (horizontal) ... $CMAS = 2.1460 * RMSE_x = 2.1460 * RMSE_y = 2.1460 * RMSE_r/1.4142 = 1.5175 * RMSE_r$

"$Accuracy_r = 2.4477/2.1460 * CMAS = 1.1406 * CMAS$

"Relationship between NSSDA and NMAS (vertical) ... $VMAS = 1.6449 * RMSE_z$

"The VMAS can be converted to $Accuracy_z$ accuracy reported according to the NSSDA using equations from Appendix 3-A, Section 2:

"$Accuracy_z = 1.9600/1.6449 * VMAS = 1.1916 * VMAS$

"Therefore, vertical accuracy reported according to the NSSDA is $(1.1916)/2 * CI = 0.5958 * CI$, where CI is the contour interval."

Rearranging these equations, $CI = Accuracy_z/.5958 = (1.9600 * RMSE_z)/.5958 = 3.2898 * RMSE_z$.

Major Points in Understanding the NSSDA

The most significant points to understand about the NSSDA are:
- They postdate the introduction of DEMs and they replace the NMAS for digital geospatial data, including DEMs.

- DEMs are evaluated by computing $RMSE_z$ and $Accuracy_z$ values. Graphic contour data and digital hypsographic data do not normally contain well-defined points. Thus the reporting methodology for DEMs shall include $Accuracy_z$ determinations, but exclude $Accuracy_r$ determinations, if there are no well-defined points.
- Both $RMSE_z$ and $Accuracy_z$ are computed in terms of ground distances (feet or meters) as opposed to map distances (fractions of an inch) used by the NMAS.
- Accuracy is reported in ground distances at the 95% confidence level.
- When comparing the vertical relationship between NSSDA and NMAS, the equivalent contour interval per the NMAS = $3.2898 * RMSE_z$ when the vertical error has a normal distribution.
- The reported accuracy value reflects all uncertainties, including those introduced by geodetic control coordinates, compilation, and final computation of ground coordinate values in the product. Apparent vertical errors in DEMs are not offset by permissible horizontal errors as allowed by the NMAS and ASPRS 90 standards.
- The NSSDA does not define threshold accuracy values. Ultimately, users identify acceptable accuracies for their applications. Data and map producers must determine what accuracy exists or is achievable for their data and report it according to the NSSDA. For example, the Federal Emergency Management Agency (FEMA) has published lidar standards (FEMA, 2000) that specifies DEMs with 5-meter post spacing, and vertical RMSE of 18.5-cm, evaluated separately for all (normally 3-5) land cover categories representative of the floodplain being mapped.

PART 5: STANDARDS FOR NAUTICAL CHARTING HYDROGRAPHIC SURVEYS

In 2005, the FGDC published this standard, based upon the International Hydrographic Organization Standard for Hydrographic Surveys as contained in the Special Publication No. 44 (SP-44). It provides minimum standards for the horizontal and vertical accuracy of features associated with hydrographic surveys that support nautical charting. Such features include, but are not limited to, water depths, objects on the seafloor, navigational aids, and shoreline. Significant paragraphs are quoted below.

"For the purposes of this Standard, hydrographic surveys are defined as those surveys conducted to determine the configuration of the bottom of water bodies and to identify and locate all features, natural and man-made, that may affect navigation. Nautical charts are compilations of data from numerous sources, principally hydrographic surveys, designed specifically to meet the requirements of marine navigation. The scope of these standards includes the coastal waters of the U.S. and its territories.

"These standards are intended to be used by federal agencies and their contractors for conducting hydrographic surveys that will be used for updating nautical charts. They do not apply to hydrographic surveys for river and harbor navigation projects or surveys for project construction which are covered by Part 4 of the FGDC Geospatial Positioning Accuracy Standards. Local authorities may also prescribe these standards for high quality surveys for other purposes.

"These standards may be used in conjunction with, or independent of, other Parts of the overall Geospatial Positioning Accuracy Standard. Part 1 (Reporting Methodology) applies directly to this part with the exception that vertical coordinate values should be referenced to the applicable chart datum and not one of the geodetic vertical datums (NAVD 88 or NGVD 29).

"There may be occasions where geodetic control points need to be established to support hydrographic surveys. In such instances, the specifications in Part 2 (Standards for Geodetic Networks) should be referenced. The accuracy testing described in Part 3 (National Standard for Spatial Data Accuracy) is generally inapplicable to this Part 5 since the referenced features are not repeatedly measured. Part 4 (Standards for Architecture, Engineering, Construction (A/E/C) and Facility Management) provide accuracy standards for other categories of hydrographic surveys (Contract Payment, Project Condition and Reconnaissance) that are not explicitly conducted to support nautical charts.

"As defined in Part 1, horizontal spatial accuracy is the two-dimensional circular error of a data set's horizontal coordinates at the 95% confidence level. Vertical spatial accuracy is defined by the one-dimensional linear error of depths at the 95% confidence level."

Hydrographic Reference Datums

"The horizontal reference datum should be the North American Datum of 1983 (NAD 83). If other datums or coordinate systems are used, their relationship to NAD 83 should be documented. Vertical coordinate values should be referenced to the applicable chart datum and not one of the geodetic vertical datums (NAVD 88 or NGVD 29). The Mean Lower Low Water (MLLW) datum is used for Atlantic, Pacific and Gulf coast charts. The nautical chart vertical datum for each of the Great Lakes is referenced to the International Great Lakes Datum (1985). Other water level-based datums are used on lakes and rivers."

Classification of Hydrographic Surveys

"To accommodate in a systematic manner different accuracy requirements for areas to be surveyed, four orders of survey are defined. These are described below, with specific details provided in [Table 3.4].

Special Order

"Special Order hydrographic surveys approach engineering standards and their use is intended to be restricted to specific critical areas with minimum underkeel clearance and where bottom characteristics are potentially hazardous to vessels. These areas must be explicitly designated by the agency responsible for survey quality. Examples are harbors, berthing areas, and associated critical channels. All error sources must be minimized. Special Order requires the use of closely spaced lines in conjunction with side scan sonar, multitransducer arrays or high resolution multibeam echosounders to obtain 100% bottom search. It must be ensured that cubic features greater than 1 meter can be discerned by the sounding equipment. The use of side scan sonar in conjunction with a multibeam echosounder may be necessary in areas where thin and dangerous obstacles may be encountered. Side scan sonar should not be used for depth determination but to define areas requiring more detailed and accurate investigation."

Order 1

"Order 1 hydrographic surveys are intended for harbors, harbor approach channels, recommended tracks, inland navigation channels, and coastal areas of high commercial traffic density where underkeel clearance is less critical and the geophysical properties of the seafloor are less hazardous to vessels (e.g. soft silt or sand bottom). Order 1 surveys should be limited to areas with less than 100 m water depth. Although the requirement for seafloor search is less stringent than for Special Order, full bottom search is required in selected areas where the bottom characteristics and the risk of obstructions are potentially hazardous to vessels. For these areas searched, it must be ensured that cubic features greater than 2 m up to 40 m water depth or greater than 10% of the depth in areas deeper than 40 m can be discerned by the sounding equipment. In some areas the detection of 1-meter cubic features may be specified."

Order 2

"Order 2 hydrographic surveys are intended for areas with depths less than 200 m not covered by Special Order and Order 1 and where a general description of the bathymetry is sufficient to ensure there are no obstructions on the seafloor that will endanger the type of vessel expected to transit or work the area. It is the criteria for a variety of maritime uses for which higher order hydrographic surveys cannot be justified. Full bottom search may be required in selected areas where the bottom characteristics and the risk of obstructions may be potentially hazardous to vessels."

Table 3.4 Summary of Minimum Standards for Hydrographic Surveys.

ORDER	Special	1	2	3
Examples of Typical Areas	Harbors, berthing areas, and associated critical channels with minimum underkeel clearances	Harbors, harbor approach channels, recommended tracks and some coastal areas with depths up to 100 m	Areas not described in Special Order and Order 1, or areas up to 200 m water depth	Offshore areas not described in Special Order, and Orders 1 and 2
Horizontal Accuracy (95% Confidence Level)	2 m	5 m + 5% of depth	20 m + 5% of depth	150 m + 5% of depth
Depth Accuracy for [1] **Reduced Depths (95% Confidence Level)** [2]	a = 0.25 m b = 0.0075	a = 0.5 m b = 0.013	a = 1.0 m b = 0.023	Same as Order 2
100% Bottom Search [3]	Compulsory	Required in selected areas	May be required in selected areas	Not applicable
System Detection Capability	Cubic features > 1 m	Cubic features > 2 m in depths up to 40 m; 10% of depth beyond 40 m	Same as Order 1	Not applicable
Maximum Line Spacing [4]	Not applicable, as 100% search compulsory	3 x average depth or 25 m, whichever is greater	3-4 x average depth or 200 m, whichever is greater	4 x average depth

[1] To calculate the error limits for depth accuracy the corresponding values of a and b listed in Table 3.4 should be introduced into:

$$\pm \sqrt{[a^2 + (b*d)^2]}$$

where:

a is a constant depth error, i.e. the sum of all constant errors, b*d is the depth dependent error, i.e. the sum of all depth dependent errors where b is a factor of depth dependent error, and d is depth.

[2] The confidence level percentage is the probability that an error will not exceed the specified maximum value.

[3] A method of exploring the seabed which attempts to provide complete coverage of an area for the purpose of detecting all features addressed in this publication.

[4] The line spacing can be expanded if procedures for ensuring an adequate sounding density are used

The rows of Table 3.4 are explained as follows:

Row 1 "Examples of Typical Areas" gives examples of areas to which an order of survey might typically be applied.

Row 2 "Horizontal Accuracy" lists positioning accuracies to be achieved to meet each order of survey.

Row 3 "Depth Accuracy" specifies parameters to be used to calculate accuracies of reduced depths to be achieved to meet each order of survey.

Row 4 "100% Bottom Search" specifies occasions when full bottom search should be conducted.

Row 5 "System Detection Capability" specifies the detection capabilities of systems used for bottom search.

Row 6 "Maximum Line Spacing" is to be interpreted as either (1) spacing of sounding lines for single beam sounders or (2) distance between the outer limits of swaths for swath sounding systems.

Order 3

"Order 3 hydrographic surveys are intended for all areas not covered by Special Order, and Orders 1 and 2 in water depths in excess of 200 m."

Positioning

"The horizontal accuracy, as specified in [Table 3.4], is the accuracy of the position of soundings, dangers, and all other significant submerged features with respect to a geodetic reference frame, specifically NAD 83. The exceptions to this are Order 2 and Order 3 surveys using single-beam echo sounders where it is the positional accuracy of the sounding system sensor. In such cases, the agency responsible for the survey quality should determine the accuracy of the positions of soundings on the seafloor.

"If the accuracy of a position is affected by different parameters, the contributions of all parameters to the total position error should be accounted for. A statistical method, combining different error sources, for determining positioning accuracy should be adopted. The position error, at 95% confidence level, should be recorded together with the survey data. Although this should preferably be done for each individual sounding, the error estimate may also be derived for a number of soundings or even for an area, provided differences between error estimates can be safely expected to be negligible.

"It is strongly recommended that whenever positions are determined by terrestrial systems, redundant lines of position should be observed. Standard calibration techniques should be completed prior to and after the acquisition of data. Satellite systems should be capable of tracking at least five satellites simultaneously; integrity monitoring for Special Order and Order 1 surveys is recommended.

"Primary shore control points should be located by ground survey methods to a relative accuracy of 1 part in 100,000. When geodetic satellite positioning methods are used to establish such points, the error should not exceed 10 cm at 95% confidence level. Secondary stations for local positioning, which will not be used for extending the control, should be located such that the error does not exceed 1 part in 10,000 for ground survey techniques or 50 cm using geodetic satellite positioning.

"The horizontal positions of navigation aids and other important features should be determined to the accuracy stated in [Table 3.5], at 95% confidence level.

Table 3.5 Summary of Minimum Standards for Positioning of Navigation Aids and Important Features.

	Special Order surveys	Order 1 surveys	Order 2 and 3 surveys
Fixed aids to navigation and features significant to navigation	2m	2m	5m
Natural Coastline	10m	20m	20m
Mean position of floating aids to navigation	10m	10m	20m
Topographical features	10m	20m	20m

Depths

"The navigation of commercial vessels requires increasingly accurate and reliable knowledge of the water depth in order to exploit safely the maximum cargo capabilities. It is imperative that depth accuracy standards in critical areas, particularly in areas of marginal underkeel clearance and where the possibility of obstructions exists, be more stringent than those established in the past and that the issue of adequate bottom coverage be addressed.

"In determining the depth accuracy of the reduced depths, the sources of individual errors should be quantified and combined to obtain a Total Propagated Error (TPE) at the 95% confidence level. Among others these errors include:

a) measurement system and sound velocity errors
b) tidal measurement and modeling errors, and
c) data processing errors.

"A statistical method for determining depth accuracy by combining all known errors should be adopted and checked. Recognizing that both constant and depth dependent errors affect the accuracy of depths, the formula under [Table 3.4] is to be used to compute the allowable depth errors at 95% confidence level by using the values from row 3 for a and b. As an additional check on data quality, an analysis of redundant depths observed at crossline intersections should be made.

"For wrecks and obstructions which may have less than 40 m clearance above them and may be dangerous to normal surface navigation, the least depth over them should be determined either by high definition sonar examination or physical examination (diving). Mechanical sweeping may be used when guaranteeing a minimum safe clearance depth.

"All anomalous features previously reported in the survey area and those detected during the survey should be examined in greater detail and, if confirmed, their least depth should be determined. The agency responsible for survey quality may define a depth limit beyond which a detailed seafloor investigation, and thus an examination of anomalous features, is not required.

"Measured depths should be reduced to chart or survey datum, by the application of tidal or water level height. Tidal reductions should not be applied to depths greater than 200 m, except when tides contribute significantly to the TPE."

Sounding Density

"In planning the density of soundings, both the nature of the seabed in the area and the requirements of the users have to be taken into account to ensure adequate bottom coverage. It should be noted that no method, not even 100% search, guarantees by itself the reliability of a survey nor can it disprove with certainty the existence of hazards to navigation, such as isolated natural hazards or man made objects such as wrecks, between survey lines.

"Line spacing for the various orders of hydrographic surveys is proposed in [Table 3.4]. The results of a survey should be assessed using procedures developed by the agency responsible for the survey quality. Based on these procedures the adequacy of the sounding density should be determined and the line spacing reduced if warranted."

Bottom Sampling

"The nature of the seabed should be determined by sampling or may be inferred from other sensors (e.g. single beam echo sounders, side scan sonar, sub-bottom profiler, video, etc.) up to the depth required by local anchoring or trawling conditions. Under normal circumstances sampling is not required in depths greater than 200 meters. Samples should be spaced according to the seabed geology, but should normally be 10 times that of the main scheme line spacing. In areas intended for anchorages, density of sampling should be increased. Any inference technique should be substantiated by physical sampling."

Tidal Observations

"Tidal height observations should be made throughout the course of a survey for the purpose of providing tidal reductions for soundings, and providing data for tidal analysis and subsequent prediction. Observations should extend over the longest possible period, and if possible, for not less than 29 days. Tidal heights should be observed so that the total measurement error at the tide gauge, including timing error, does not exceed +/- 5 cm at 95% for Special Order surveys. For other surveys +/- 10 cm should not be exceeded."

Metadata

"To allow a comprehensive assessment of the quality of survey data it is necessary to record or document certain information together with the survey data. Such information is important to allow exploitation of survey data by a variety of users with different requirements, especially as requirements may not be known when survey data is collected. The information describing the data is called metadata. Examples of metadata include overall quality, data set title, source, positional accuracy and copyright. Metadata is data implicitly attached to a collection of data.

"Metadata should comprise at least the following information:
• The survey in general (e.g. date, area, equipment used, name of survey platform).
• The horizontal and vertical datum.
• Calibration procedures and results.
• Sound velocity for corrections to echo soundings.
• Tidal datum and reduction procedures.
• Accuracies achieved and the respective confidence levels.

"Metadata should preferably be in digital form in compliance with the FGDC-endorsed Content Standard for Digital Geospatial Metadata (version 2.0), FGDC-STD-001-1998, and an integral part of the survey record. Shoreline metadata should comply with the Metadata Profile for Shoreline Data. If this is not feasible, similar information should be included in the documentation of a survey. It is recommended that agencies responsible for the survey quality systematically develop and document a list of metadata used for their survey data.

"It is understood that each sensor (i.e. positioning, depth, heave, pitch, roll, heading, seabed characteristic sensors, water column parameter sensors, tidal reduction sensor, data reduction models etc.) possesses unique error characteristics. Each survey system should be uniquely analyzed to determine appropriate procedure(s) to obtain the required spatial statistics. These analysis procedure(s) should be documented or referenced in the survey record."

Elimination of Doubtful Data

"To improve the safety of navigation it is desirable to eliminate doubtful data, i.e. data which are usually denoted on charts by PA (Position Approximate), PD (Position Doubtful), ED (Existence Doubtful), SD (Sounding Doubtful) or as "reported danger". To confirm or disprove the existence of such data it is necessary to carefully define the area to be searched and subsequently survey that area according to the standards outlined in this publication.

"No empirical formula for defining the search area can suit all situations. For this reason, it is recommended that the search radius should be 3 times the estimated position error of the reported hazard at the 95% confidence level as determined by a thorough investigation of the report on the doubtful data by a qualified hydrographic surveyor. If such report is incomplete or does not exist at all, the position error must be estimated by other means as, for example, a more general assessment of positioning and depth measurement errors during the era when the data in question was collected.

"The methodology for conducting the search should be based on the area in which the doubtful data is reported and the estimated danger of the hazard to navigation. Once this has been established, the search procedure should be that of conducting a hydrographic survey of the extent defined in the preceding paragraph, to the standards established in this publication. If not detected, the agency responsible for the survey quality shall decide whether to retain the hazard as charted or to expunge it."

Quality Control

"To ensure that the required accuracies are achieved it is necessary to check and monitor performance. Establishing quality control procedures which ensure that data or products meet certain standards and specifications should be a high priority for hydrographic authorities. This section provides guidelines for the implementation of such procedures.

"Quality control for positioning ideally involves observing redundant lines of position and/or monitor stations which are then analyzed to obtain a position error estimate. If the positioning system offers no redundancy or other means of monitoring system performance, rigorous and frequent calibration is the only means of ensuring quality.

"A standard quality control procedure should be to check the validity of soundings by conducting additional depth measurements. Differences should be statistically tested to ensure compliance of the survey with the standards given in [Table 3.4]. Anomalous differences should be further examined with a systematic analysis of contributing error sources. All discrepancies should be resolved, either by analysis or re-survey during progression of the survey task.

"Crosslines intersecting the principal sounding lines should always be run to confirm the accuracy of positioning, sounding, and tidal reductions. Crosslines should be spaced so that an efficient and comprehensive control of the principal sounding lines can be effected. As a guide it may be assumed that the interval between crosslines should normally be no more than 15 times that of the selected sounding lines.

"The proposed line spacing from [Table 3.4] may be altered depending on the configuration of the seafloor and the likelihood of dangers to navigation. In addition, if side scan sonar is used in conjunction with single beam or multibeam sonar systems, the specified line spacing may be increased. Multibeam sonar systems have great potential for accurate seafloor coverage if used with proper survey and calibration procedures. An appropriate assessment of the accuracy of measurements with each beam is necessary for use in areas surveyed to Special Order and Order 1 standards. If any of the outer beams have unacceptable errors, the related data may be used for reconnaissance but the depths should be otherwise excluded from the final data set. All swaths should be intersected, at least once, by a crossline to confirm the accuracy of positioning, depth measurements and depth reductions."

NOS HYDROGRAPHIC SURVEYS SPECIFICATIONS

The National Ocean Service *Hydrographic Surveys Specifications and Deliverables* (NOAA, 2003) provide technical specifications that detail the requirements for hydrographic surveys to be undertaken either by National Oceanic and Atmospheric Administration (NOAA) field units or by organizations under contract to the Director, Office of Coast Survey (OCS), National Ocean Service (NOS), NOAA, U.S. Department of Commerce. These specifications are based in part on the International Hydrographic Organization's Standards for Hydrographic Surveys, Special Publication 44, Fourth Edition, April 1998, specifically for Order 1 surveys. Hydrographic surveys classified as Order 1 are intended for harbors, harbor approach channels, recommended track, inland navigation channels, coastal areas of high commercial traffic density, and are usually in shallower areas lower than 100 meters in water depth. These specifications can be viewed and downloaded at http://nauticalcharts.noaa.gov/hsd/specs/specs.htm. Highlights of major sections are extracted as follows:

Section 2, Datums:

"All positions will be referenced to the North American Datum of 1983 (NAD 83). This datum must be used throughout a survey project for everything that has a geographic position or for which a position is to be determined. Those documents used for comparisons, such as charts, junctional surveys, and prior surveys, must be referenced or adjusted to NAD 83. In addition, all software used on a survey must contain the correct datum parameters. All sounding data will be reduced to Mean Lower Low Water (MLLW). Heights of bridges and overhead cables will be referenced to Mean High Water (MHW). Coordinated Universal Time (UTC) will be used for all time records."

Section 3, Hydrographic Position Control:

"The hydrographer will conduct a 24-hour certification of all non-USCG differential reference stations prior to use for positioning control. The purpose of this certification is to ensure that no multipath or other site specific problems exist. Once the differential station is set up at the site and configured for survey operations, differential corrections will be broadcast and received at a remote site. This remote site may be within 2 meters of the differential reference station control point or over an existing control point (third order or better). The remote site will receive correctors, compute a final position at a rate of not less than once per second, and compare that position to the control point position. A position plot will be constructed comparing the known position and the differentially computed position. An analysis of the data must prove that the position accuracy requirements of Section 3.1 are met. Certification for any non-USCG differential station is valid for one year only. All related position accuracy plots will be included in the Vertical and Horizontal Control Report for each project."

Section 4, Tides and Water Levels Requirements:

"The present NOAA Nautical Chart Reference Datum for tidal waters is Mean Lower Low Water (MLLW) based on the NOAA National Tidal Datum Epoch (NTDE) of 1983-2001 as defined in the Tide and Current Glossary. All tidal datum computations and water level reductions shall be referenced to this datum. In non-tidal areas, including the Great Lakes, special low water datums have been defined for specific areas and are used as chart datum in these locations. In some cases where historical sites are re-occupied, site datum shall be zeroed to a pre-established MLLW datum held on a bench mark. In that case, data can be acquired relative to MLLW for immediate application during the survey. At present, in Great Lakes areas, a special Low Water Datum relative to IGLD 85 is the reference datum."

Section 5, Depth Soundings and Accuracy Standards:

"Depths shall be recorded in meters, with a precision of at least tenths of meters … NOAA standards for the accuracy of measured depths in hydrographic surveys apply to the systematic measurement of general water depths and to the least depths determined over wrecks and obstructions. By extension, they also apply to the elevations of rocks or other features which uncover at low water and to the measurement of overhead clearances. These standards apply regardless of the method of determination; whether by single beam echosounder, Multibeam echosounder, lead line or diver investigation. The total sounding error in a measured depth at the 95 percent confidence level, after systematic and system specific errors have been removed, shall not exceed: $\pm\sqrt{[a^2+(b*d)^2]}$ where in depths less than 100 meters, a = 0.5 meters and represents the sum of all constant errors, (b*d) represents the sum of all depth dependent errors, b = 0.013 and is a factor of depth dependent error, and d is depth (in meters)(IHO S-44, Order 1). In depths greater than 100 meters, a = 1.0, b = 0.023, d = depth (IHO S-44, Order 2). The maximum allowable error in measured depth includes all inaccuracies due to residual systematic and system specific instrument errors; the velocity of sound in water; static vessel draft; dynamic vessel draft; heave, roll, and pitch; and any other sources of error in the actual measurement process, including the errors associated with water level (tide) variations (both tidal measurement and zoning errors). For Multibeam echosounders, the total sounding error is applicable to swath widths of at least two times the water depth (i.e., 45° to both sides of nadir). However, swath widths greater than two times the water depth may be used if the depth accuracy criteria stated above is met."

Subsection 5.2.2, Multibeam Resolution Standards:

"The hydrographer shall maintain and operate the Multibeam sonar system, from data acquisition to processing, such that it detects shoals that measure 2 meters x 2 meters horizontally and 1 meter vertically in depths of 40 meters or less. For depths greater than 40 meters, the minimum size of detectable targets shall be 10 percent of the depth for horizontal dimensions and 5 percent of the depth for vertical dimensions. Depths shall be determined and recorded with a vertical resolution no coarser than 10 centimeters. The hydrographer shall ensure that vessel speed is adjusted so that no less than 3.2 beam footprints, center-to-center, fall within 3 m, or a distance equal to 10 percent of the depth, whichever is greater, in the along track direction. Total swath width shall be no less than twice the water depth (i.e., 45° to both sides of nadir). The portions of the swath widths greater than twice the water depth that do not meet these resolution requirements and the accuracy requirements in Section 5.2.1 shall not be depicted on the preliminary smooth sheet or included in the digital file for the preliminary smooth sheet. Sounding tracklines shall generally be parallel. Sinuous lines and data acquired during turns shall not be included in the final processed data, and shall not be used to meet coverage requirements.

Subsection 5.4, Corrections to Echo Soundings:

"To meet the accuracy and resolution standards for measured depths specified in Section 5.2, observed echosounder depths must be corrected for all departures from true depths attributable to the method of sounding or to faults in the measurement apparatus. In recognition of the possibility that some discrepancies in sounding may not be detected until the post-processing phase of the survey, the determination and application of corrections to echo soundings must be accomplished and documented in a systematic manner. In addition, all corrections shall be applied in such a way that the on-line values may be removed and replaced with a revised set of correctors in post- processing. Corrections to echo soundings are divided into five categories, and listed below in the sequence in which they are applied:

- *"Instrument error corrections* account for sources of error related to the sounding equipment itself.
- *"Draft corrections* shall be added to the observed soundings to account for the depth of the echosounder transducer below the water surface.
- *"Appropriate corrections for settlement and squat* shall be applied to soundings to correct the vertical displacement of the transducer, relative to its position at rest, when a vessel is underway.
- *"Velocity of sound correctors* shall be applied to soundings to compensate for the fact that echosounders may only display depths based on an assumed sound velocity profile while the true velocity may vary in time and space.
- *"Heave, roll, pitch, heading, and navigation timing error (latency) corrections* shall be applied to Multibeam soundings to correct the effect of vessel motion caused by waves and swells (heave, roll, pitch), the error in the vessel's heading, and the time delay from the moment the position is measured until the data is received by the data collection system (navigation timing error)."

Subsection 5.5.3, Crosslines:

"The regular system of sounding lines shall be supplemented by a series of crosslines for verifying and evaluating the accuracy and reliability of surveyed depths and plotted locations. Crosslines shall be run across all planned sounding lines at angles of 45° to 90°. The preferred area in which to run crosslines is in an area of gently sloping bottom … The lineal nautical miles of crosslines for single-beam surveys shall be at least 8 percent of the lineal nautical miles of all planned sounding lines … The lineal nautical miles of crosslines for Multibeam surveys shall be at least 5 percent of the lineal nautical miles of all planned sounding lines."

Subsection 5.5.4, Multibeam Sun-Illuminated Digital Terrain Model (DTM) Images:

"Regardless of the Multibeam coverage technique used, the hydrographer shall create two sun-illuminated DTM images. These sun-illuminated DTM images are the preferred method for detection of depth artifacts associated with errors in bottom detection algorithms, vessel motion compensation, navigation timing, water level correctors and false bottom detections.

Each image shall depict data illuminated from orthogonal directions, using a light source with an elevation no greater than 45 degrees. At a minimum, an 8 bit color depth shall be used for compilation of the sun-illuminated images. The two sun-illuminated images shall be created from fully corrected data that meet accuracy and resolution specifications (see Section 5, Depth Soundings) are cleaned of all anomalous soundings, and serve as the source for all smooth sheet soundings. Data shall be binned, line by line, using shoal biased filtering at a bin size not to exceed 5 meters + 5 percent of the depth. The submitted digital image file shall be in a standard geo-referenced image format."

Section 8, Deliverables, documents requirements for Field Reports (Progress Report, Danger to Navigation Report, Descriptive Report), Preliminary Smooth Sheet Specifications (Cartographic Specifications and Conventions), Shallow-Water Multibeam Sonar Swath Coverage Plot, Side Scan Sonar Coverage Plot and Sonargrams, and Digital Data Files.

Subsection 8.5.3, Shallow-Water Multibeam Data:

"The hydrographer's Multibeam data format shall provide complete traceability for all positions, soundings, and correctors including sensor offsets, biases, dynamic attitude, sound velocity, position, sensor position, date and time, vertical datum reducers, and sounding data from acquisition through post-processing. Data quality and edit flags must be traceable.

"Raw Multibeam Data. The hydrographer shall submit full resolution Multibeam data in a format readable by CARIS HIPS (Version 5.3, by CARIS). Full resolution multibeam data shall be delivered fully corrected for tides, sound velocity, vessel offsets, draft and settlement and squat. These corrections may be made within CARIS, with data submitted as a complete CARIS project (including HDCS files, sound velocity files, Vessel Configuration, CARIS tide files, etc.). Or the data may be submitted fully corrected, such that it will be read in CARIS HIPS using a "zeroed' Vessel Configuration file (.vcf) and a 'zero' tide file (.tid), etc. Full resolution data are defined as all data acquired and logged during normal survey operations.

"Edited Multibeam Data. The hydrographer shall submit an edited Multibeam data set in ASCII text format. Edited data are defined as fully corrected data that meet accuracy and resolution specifications (see Section 5, Depth Sounding) are cleaned of all anomalous soundings, and serve as the source for all preliminary smooth sheet soundings and sun-illuminated DTMs (see Section 5.5.4). Edited data sets shall contain XYZ, z' (tide corrector), date/time stamp, and a unique identifier which indicates whether the sounding is depicted on the smooth sheet. Coordinates (XY) shall be latitude/longitude NAD 83 (decimal degrees to eight decimal places), and depth (Z) shall be in meters to nearest centimeter (fully corrected for tide (MLLW datum), sound velocity, dynamic and static craft, and all vessel offsets). Tide corrector (z') shall be in meters to the nearest centimeter. Time shall be UTC to the nearest second. Data shall be binned, line by line, at a bin size not less than 5 m + 5 percent of the depth, using shoal biased filtering. All depths shall retain their survey position and shall not represent the binned area centroid or other abstract position (i.e., binned, not gridded data)."

Major Points in Understanding the NOS Specifications

- All horizontal positions are referenced to NAD 83.
- All sounding data are reduced to Mean Lower Low Water (MLLW).
- Heights of bridges and overhead cables are referenced to Mean High Water (MHW).
- Hydrographic survey data is focused on safety of marine navigation.
- Hydrographic surveys with Multibeam echosounders have many similarities to topographic surveys with lidar sensors. They both rely upon differential GPS to position sensors relative to known control points. They both collect swaths of elevation data points, either as raw lidar data or raw Multibeam data. They both perform extensive post-processing to generate edited terrain surfaces, above and below water levels. They both use crosslines and sun-illuminated DTM images for QA/QC purposes.

- One major difference is that all depths must retain their survey position and not represent the binned area centroid or other abstract position, whereas heights (elevations) from airborne sensors are frequently altered and depicted as uniformly-gridded DEMs.
- Multibeam sonar data depicts dangers to marine navigation (e.g., depths of rocks, shoals, wrecks, and underwater obstructions) much like photogrammetric, IfSAR or lidar digital surface models (DSMs) depict dangers to aviation (heights of buildings, towers, trees, and other elevated obstructions).

FEMA GUIDELINES

The Federal Emergency Management Agency (FEMA) has published *Guidance for Aerial Mapping and Surveying,* Appendix A, to its "Guidelines and Specifications for Flood Hazard Mapping Partners" (FEMA, 2003). See http://www.fema.gov/plan/prevent/fhm/gs_main.shtm. Appendix A includes horizontal and vertical accuracy guidelines that pertain to all technologies, to include digital elevation data equivalent to 2-foot contours for flat terrain (Accuracy$_z$ = 1.2 ft at the 95-percent confidence level) and 4-foot contours for rolling to hilly terrain (Accuracy$_z$ = 2.4 ft at the 95-percent confidence level). Appendix A also describes requirements for topographic mapping, cross sections, and hydraulic structure surveys; datums, projections, coordinate systems, and data formats; hydrologically enforced elevation data; ground control and ground surveys; photogrammetric surveys; and lidar surveys.

Appendix A, Section A.8 on lidar surveys, has caused these FEMA guidelines to become the lidar industry's *de facto* standard for many years because the National Flood Insurance Program, administered by FEMA, has the most demanding requirement for lidar data. As such, most states and counties advertise for acquisition of lidar data to satisfy these FEMA guidelines to ensure their data satisfies FEMA requirements when entering into a Cooperating Technical Partner (CTP) agreement for FEMA's Map Modernization funding. The major provisions are summarized as follows:

- For the majority of floodplains that are essentially flat, hydro-enforced DEMs or TINs are required with nominal point spacing of 2 meters and vertical accuracy of 1.2 feet at the 95-percent confidence level (Accuracy$_z$) equivalent to 2-foot contours. For floodplains that are in rolling to hilly terrain, hydro-enforced DEMs or TINs are required with nominal point spacing of 4 meters and vertical accuracy of 2.4 feet at the 95-percent confidence level (Accuracy$_z$) equivalent to 4-foot contours. Nominal point spacing should never be greater than 5 meters. When errors follow a normal distribution, Accuracy$_z$ = RMSE$_z$ x 1.9600. Therefore, either Accuracy$_z$ or RMSE$_z$ values can be established for accuracy testing.
- Lidar data at the established level of accuracy is required for the projected 500-year (0.2% annual chance) floodplain, with data of lesser accuracy acceptable for the remainder of the watershed outside this floodplain. However, for other non-FEMA requirements, a consistent level of accuracy is required throughout the county or watershed being studied.
- Daily in-situ calibration checks are recommended, to include repetitive overflights of terrain features of known and documented size and elevation using flight paths similar to those that will be used in the flood insurance study area.
- For hydraulic modeling, high-resolution, high-accuracy, bare-earth ground elevation data is needed, requiring the removal of elevation points on vegetation, bridges, buildings, and other structures.
- Supplemental breaklines are needed for all shorelines and for tops and bottoms of major stream banks. These breaklines are preferably compiled from stereo photogrammetry. Other breaklines specified in FEMA's Appendix A are desirable but not mandatory.

- The accuracy of the bare-earth DEM or TIN must be evaluated and reported separately for each of the major land cover categories representative of the flood plains being modeled. The five most-common land cover categories are: (a) bare-earth and low grass, including plowed fields, lawns, golf courses, sand, and rocks; (b) high grass, weeds, and crops, including hay, corn and wheat fields; (c) brush lands, bushes and low trees, including chaparrals and mesquite; (d) forested areas fully covered by trees, including hardwoods, evergreens and mixed forests; and (e) urban areas, normally with high, dense manmade structures and large impervious surface areas. Other areas might include sawgrass or mangrove swamps, for example. These definitions may be further subdivided and expanded to better accommodate the predominant vegetation types in the study area.
- For accuracy testing, a minimum of 20 test points (checkpoints) must be selected for each major land cover category representative of the floodplain. Therefore, a minimum of 60 test points must be selected for three (minimum) major land cover categories, 80 test points for four major categories, and so on. Confidence in the calculated RMSE values increases with the number of test points and is a function of sample size. By specifying a minimum of 60 checkpoints, FEMA is specifying that 60 points are the minimum necessary for a practical level of confidence in the calculated RMSE statistic, but recognizing that a higher number of checkpoints (if affordable) will provide higher confidence that performance standards have been achieved for major land cover categories in which hydraulic modeling will be performed.
- Test points should be selected in terrain that is flat or uniformly sloped within 5 meters in all directions. The uniform slope must not exceed 20 percent. The test points must never be located near to breaklines, such as bridges or embankments. Test points on sloping or irregular terrain would be unreasonably affected by the linear interpolation of test points from surrounding TIN points and, therefore, must not be selected.
- Error histograms are prepared for each land cover category, and mean error, maximum and minimum errors, standard deviations and skew are evaluated to identify systematic errors for correction.
- Whereas it is relatively easy to determine the magnitude of systematic errors and adjust all data accordingly, such errors must not be "corrected" until the error source is clearly identified and documented. The Mapping Partner must report systematic errors to the FEMA Lead for review before systematic reprocessing of data that initially failed to pass the accuracy criteria.
- All artifacts do not need to be removed for hydraulic modeling, so long as representative cross sections are not cut through artifact areas. Whereas it is common to say that flood-plains should be 90% or 95% clean, for example, there is no practical way to measure such percentages. Although FEMA does not need for all artifacts to be removed, other users may have more-demanding requirements for artifact removal.

Whereas the FEMA guidelines as of April 2003 are based on RMSE calculations described above, these guidelines are expected to be modified in the future to accommodate 95th percentile calculations endorsed by the NDEP and ASPRS. RMSE procedures are only valid when errors follow a normal distribution. It is now widely known that errors from the lidar sensor itself follow a normal distribution; but errors resulting from bare-earth processing, to remove lidar points on vegetation and man-made structures, do not follow a normal distribution.

Major Points in Understanding the FEMA Guidelines
- For hydraulic modeling of floodplains, hydro-enforced DEMs or TINs equivalent to 2ft contours are required, accurate to 1.2 ft at the 95% confidence level, for flood plains that are essentially flat.
- The vertical accuracy is to be tested individually in each of the major land cover categories representative of the floodplain being studied, with a minimum of three categories.

- A minimum of 20 high-accuracy checkpoints are required for each of the land cover categories, i.e., 60 or more checkpoints total since there are a minimum of three categories.
- Checkpoints must be located on uniformly sloping terrain for at least 5 meters in all directions, and not be near to breaklines, such as bridges or embankments, where linear interpolation would cause errors in determining the true accuracy of the surface being tested.
- Supplemental breaklines are required for all shorelines, and for tops and bottoms of major stream banks, normally obtained from stereo photogrammetry.

NDEP GUIDELINES

The National Digital Elevation Program (NDEP) published its "Guidelines for Digital Elevation Data, Version 1.0," on May 10, 2004 (NDEP, 2004).

See http://www.ndep.gov/NDEP_Elevation_Guidelines_Ver1_10May2004.pdf.

The NDEP guidelines were developed by representatives of the U.S. Geological Survey (USGS), National Geospatial-Intelligence Agency (NGA), U.S. Army Corps of Engineers (USACE), National Oceanic and Atmospheric Administration (NOAA), Bureau of Land Management (BLM), National States Geographic Information Council (NSGIC), National Aeronautics and Space Administration (NASA), Natural Resources Conservation Service (NRCS), U.S. Forest Service (USFS), Federal Emergency Management Agency (FEMA), and U.S. Census Bureau. Because FEMA had the best base of experience, FEMA requirements were used to draft the initial NDEP guidelines — subsequently expanded to address the needs of the other organizations represented as well as the perceived needs of counties and local communities for digital elevation data. The NDEP guidelines also drew heavily from case studies, user requirements guidance, and accuracy assessment procedures documented in the first edition of this ASPRS manual: *Digital Elevation Model Technologies and Applications: The DEM Users Manual* (ASPRS 2001). In turn, this 2nd Edition, especially Chapter 12, DEM Quality Assessment, and Chapter 13, DEM User Requirements, draws heavily upon the NDEP guidelines.

Vertical Accuracy

The following paragraphs are quoted from section 1.5.1.1 of the NDEP guidelines:

"The NDEP recommends that users attempt to assess vertical accuracy requirements in terms of potential harm that could be done to the public health and safety in the event that the digital elevation data fail to satisfy the specified vertical accuracy. Many states have regulations that require digital elevation data to be produced by licensed individuals to protect the public from any harm that an incompetent data producer may cause. Licensing is generally linked to experience in proving that products are delivered in accordance with the National Map Accuracy Standards, or equivalent.

"It is important to specify the vertical accuracy expected for all final products being delivered. For example, when contours or gridded DEMs are specified as deliverables from photogrammetric or LIDAR-generated mass points, a TIN may first be produced from which a DEM or contours are derived. If done properly, error introduced during the TIN to contour/ DEM process should be minimal; however, some degree of error will be introduced. Accuracy should not be specified and tested for the TIN with the expectation that derivatives will meet the same accuracy. Derivatives may exhibit greater error, especially when generalization or surface smoothing has been applied to the final product. Specifying accuracy of the final product(s) requires the data producer to ensure that error is kept within necessary limits during all production steps.

"The vertical accuracy of elevation models is also a function of horizontal resolution … An understanding of the basic principles of [NMAS and NSSDA] standards will be helpful for understanding the following guidance for determining vertical and horizontal accuracy requirements.

"With the NSSDA, the $RMSE_z$ is defined in terms of feet or meters at ground scale, rather than in terms of the published map's contour interval. Because the NSSDA does not address the suitability of data for any particular product, map scale, contour interval, or other application, no error thresholds are established by the standard. However, it is often helpful to use familiar NMAS thresholds for determining reasonable NSSDA accuracy requirements for various types of terrain and relief. The $Accuracy_z$ values shown in [Table 3.6] are NSSDA equivalents to the NMAS error thresholds for common contour intervals.

Table 3.6 Comparison of NMAS/NSSDA Vertical Accuracy.

NMAS Equivalent Contour Interval	NMAS VMAS, 90 percent confidence level	NSSDA $RMSE_z$	NSSDA $Accuracy_z$, 95 percent confidence level
1 ft	0.5 ft	0.30 ft or 9.25 cm	0.60 ft or 18.2 cm
2 ft	1 ft	0.61 ft or 18.5 cm	1.19 ft or 36.3 cm
4 ft	2 ft	1.22 ft or 37.0 cm	2.38 ft or 72.6 cm
5 ft	2.5 ft	1.52 ft or 46.3 cm	2.98 ft or 90.8 cm
10 ft	5 ft	3.04 ft or 92.7 cm	5.96 ft or 1.816 m
20 ft	10 ft	6.08 ft or 1.853 m	11.92 ft or 3.632 m
40 ft	20 ft	12.16 ft or 3.706 m	23.83 ft or 7.264 m
80 ft	40 ft	24.32 ft or 7.412 m	47.66 ft or 14.528 m

"In completing the User Requirements Menu [Table 13.1 in this *DEM Users Manual*], the required vertical accuracy should be specified in terms of $Accuracy_z$, which may be uniquely derived for a particular application or extracted from the right column of [Table 3.6] above. Testing of elevation data over various ground cover categories has revealed that magnitude and distribution of errors often vary between different cover types. For NDEP purposes, the dataset's "fundamental" vertical accuracy (accuracy required over open terrain) must be specified. If specific accuracy is to be met within other ground cover categories, "supplemental" accuracies should be stated for individual or multiple categories. It may be preferable to specify a different vertical accuracy in forested areas, for example, than in tall grass. Supplemental accuracy requirements should be explained in attached documentation."

Horizontal Accuracy

The following paragraphs are quoted from section 1.5.1.2 of the NDEP guidelines:

"Horizontal accuracy is another important characteristic of elevation data; however, it is largely controlled by the vertical accuracy requirement. If a very high vertical accuracy is required then it will be essential for the data producer to maintain a very high horizontal accuracy. This is because horizontal errors in elevation data normally (but not always) contribute significantly to the error detected in vertical accuracy tests.

"Horizontal error is more difficult than vertical error to assess in the final elevation product. This is because the land surface often lacks distinct (well defined) topographic features necessary for such tests or because the resolution of the elevation data is too coarse for precisely locating distinct surface features. For these reasons, the NDEP does not require horizontal accuracy testing of elevation products. Instead, the NDEP requires data producers to report the expected horizontal accuracy of elevation products as determined from system studies or other methods.

"With the NSSDA, the $RMSE_r$ is defined in terms of feet or meters at ground scale, rather than in terms of the published map's scale. No error thresholds are established for horizontal accuracy by NSSDA. As a general guide, $Accuracy_r$ values shown in Table 3.7 are the NSSDA equivalents to horizontal error thresholds established by NMAS for common map scales.

Table 3.7 Comparison of NMAS/NSSDA Horizontal Accuracy.

NMAS Map Scale	NMAS CMAS 90 percent confidence level	NSSDA $RMSE_r$	NSSDA $Accuracy_r$ 95 percent confidence level
1" = 100' or 1:1,200	3.33 ft	2.20 ft or 67.0 cm	3.80 ft or 1.159 m
1 " = 200' or 1:2,400	6.67 ft	4.39 ft or 1.339 m	7.60 ft or 2.318 m
1" = 400' or 1:4,800	13.33 ft	8.79 ft or 2.678 m	15.21 ft or 4.635 m
1" = 500' or 1:6,000	16.67 ft	10.98 ft or 3.348 m	19.01 ft or 5.794 m
1" = 1000' or 1:12,000	33.33 ft	21.97 ft or 6.695 m	38.02 ft or 11.588 m
1" = 2000' or 1:24,000 *	40.00 ft	26.36 ft or 8.035 m	45.62 ft or 13.906 m

* The 1:24,000- and 1:25,000-scales of USGS 7.5-minute quadrangles are smaller than 1:20,000; therefore, the NMAS horizontal accuracy test for well-defined test points is based on 1/50 inch, rather than 1/30 inch for maps with scales larger than 1:20,000.

"[Table 3.7] is primarily relevant to photogrammetric data for which both planimetric and elevation data are compiled and for which the mapped features are visible on the imagery. However, it is also important to specify some minimum expectation of horizontal accuracy for elevation data acquired through non-photogrammetric means. A horizontal accuracy specification requires the data producer to ensure that an appropriate technology and horizontal control structure is applied during the collection and processing of the elevation data.

"In completing the User Requirements Menu [Table 13.1 in Chapter 13], the required horizontal accuracy should be specified in terms of $Accuracy_r$ which may be uniquely derived for a particular application or extracted from the right column of [Table 3.7] above."

Calculating and Reporting Vertical Accuracy – NDEP Requirements
The following paragraphs are quoted from section 1.5.3 of the NDEP guidelines:

Fundamental Vertical Accuracy
"The *fundamental vertical accuracy* of a dataset must be determined with check points located only in open terrain, where there is a very high probability that the sensor will have detected the ground surface. The fundamental accuracy is the value by which vertical accuracy can be equitably assessed and compared among datasets. *Fundamental accuracy is calculated at the 95-percent confidence level as a function of vertical RMSE.*

Supplemental and Consolidated Vertical Accuracies
"In addition to the fundamental accuracy, *supplemental or consolidated accuracy* values may be calculated for other ground cover categories or for combinations of ground cover categories. Because elevation errors often vary with the height and density of ground cover, a normal distribution of error cannot be assumed and, therefore, RMSE cannot be used to calculate the 95-percent accuracy value. *Consequently a nonparametric testing method (95th Percentile) is employed for supplemental and consolidated accuracy tests.*

95th Percentile
"For supplemental and consolidated accuracy tests, the 95th percentile method shall be employed to determine accuracy. The 95th percentile method may be used regardless of whether or not the errors follow a normal distribution and whether or not errors qualify as

outliers. Computed by a simple spreadsheet command, a "percentile" is the interpolated absolute value in a dataset of errors dividing the distribution of the individual errors in the dataset into one hundred groups of equal frequency. The 95th percentile indicates that 95 percent of the errors in the dataset will have absolute values of equal or lesser value and 5 percent of the errors will be of larger value. With this method, Accuracy$_z$ is directly equated to the 95th percentile, where 95 percent of the errors have absolute values that are equal to or smaller than the specified amount.

Major Points in Understanding the NDEP Guidelines

- The NDEP guidelines supplement the NSSDA standards, specifically with regards to lidar and IFSAR bare-earth elevation errors that typically do not have a normal distribution (bell curve) above and below the true elevations.
- True elevations for quality control (QC) checkpoints are determined by an independent source of higher accuracy that should be at least three times more accurate than the dataset being tested whenever possible. For example, when testing elevations that should be equivalent to 2 ft contours, i.e., accurate to 1.2 ft (36.6 cm) at the 95% confidence level, checkpoints should be surveyed to 0.4 ft (12.2 cm) accuracy or better at the 95% confidence level, preferably following NGS-58 procedures documented in (NOAA, 1997) or equivalent.
- QC checkpoints should be selected on flat terrain, or on uniformly sloping terrain for x-meters in all directions from each checkpoint, where "x" is the nominal spacing of the DEM or mass points evaluated. Wherever possible, terrain slope should not be steeper than a 20 percent grade because horizontal errors will unduly influence the vertical RMSE calculations. Furthermore, checkpoints should never be selected near severe breaks in slope (such as bridge abutments or edges of roads) where subsequent interpolation might be performed with inappropriate TIN or DEM points on the wrong sides of the breaklines.
- The NDEP recommends following the current industry standard of utilizing a minimum of 20 checkpoints in each of the major land cover categories representative of the project area for which digital elevation modeling is to be performed. This helps to identify systematic errors in an elevation dataset. Thus, if five major land cover categories are determined to be applicable, then a minimum of 100 total checkpoints are required.
- Because vegetation and manmade structures can limit ground detection, causing greater elevation errors than unobstructed terrain, the NDEP requires open terrain to be tested separately from other ground cover types. DEM accuracy testing in open terrain results in the reporting of *Fundamental Vertical Accuracy* (FVA). The FVA is calculated at the 95-percent confidence level as a function of vertical RMSE, i.e., Accuracy$_z$ = RMSE$_z$ x 1.9600. Report Accuracy$_z$ as "Tested ___ (meters, feet) fundamental vertical accuracy at 95 percent confidence level in open terrain using RMSE$_z$ x 1.9600."
- Testing over any other ground cover category is required only if that category constitutes a significant portion of the project area deemed critical to the customer. DEM accuracy testing in obstructed terrain (e.g., weeds and crops, forests, built-up areas) results in the reporting of *Supplemental Vertical Accuracy* (SVA) in each of the individual land cover categories. The SVA is calculated at the 95-percent confidence level for each supplemental land cover category and equals the 95th percentile error for each category. Report as "Tested ___ (meters, feet) supplemental vertical accuracy at 95th percentile in (specify land cover category)." Repeat for other individual land cover categories.
- When 40 or more checkpoints are consolidated for two or more of the major land cover categories, representing both the open terrain and other land cover categories, *Consolidated Vertical Accuracy* (CVA) is reported as the 95th percentile error for open terrain and other land cover categories combined. Report as "Tested ___ (meters, feet) consolidated vertical accuracy at 95th percentile in: open terrain, (specify all other categories tested)."

- For both SVA and CVA, the metadata should document the errors larger than the 95th percentile. For a small number of errors above the 95th percentile, report x/y coordinates and z-error for each QC checkpoint error larger than the 95th percentile. For large QC checkpoint datasets with a large number of errors above the 95th percentile, report only the quantity and range of values. This is known as the NDEP's "truth in advertising" provision for letting users know the number and size of "outliers" larger than the 95th percentile.
- When mass points are specified as a deliverable, a TIN derived from the mass points provides a surface from which elevations can be directly interpolated at the horizontal location of each checkpoint. When a gridded DEM is specified as a deliverable, it must be tested to ensure it meets required accuracies even when a TIN (tested to meet accuracy) is used as the DEM source; this is because generalization or smoothing processes employed during DEM interpolation may degrade the elevation surface. Contours should be tested when specified as a deliverable whether they were directly compiled or derived from another data model, even if the source model meets required accuracies; this is because the accuracy of any derived product can be degraded by interpolation, generalization, or smoothing.
- When testing by an independent source of higher accuracy cannot be followed, report accuracy at the 95 percent confidence level for data produced according to procedures that have been demonstrated to produce data with particular vertical accuracy values as: "Compiled to meet ___ (meters, feet) fundamental vertical accuracy at 95 percent confidence level in open terrain" or "Compiled to meet ___ (meters, feet) consolidated vertical accuracy at 95th percentile in all land cover categories." This is typical for photogrammetric data because photogrammetric procedures are mature and consistently yield desired accuracies when manual stereo compilation techniques are employed.

ASPRS LIDAR GUIDELINES

ASPRS adopted its *ASPRS Guidelines, Vertical Accuracy Reporting for Lidar Data*, Version 1.0, on May 24, 2004 (ASPRS, 2004). See http://www.asprs.org/society/committees/lidar/downloads/Vertical_Accuracy_Reporting_for_Lidar_Data.pdf. This is the first in a series of guidelines to be published by ASPRS covering the emerging technology of lidar and its use in the mapping sciences. Created by the ASPRS Lidar Committee's Working Group on lidar guidelines and standards, the guidelines have undergone a public review process and represent the best practices and reporting methods endorsed by ASPRS when working with lidar-derived elevation data.

ASPRS recommends that all mapping professionals adhere to and follow these guidelines when generating or contracting for mapping products derived from lidar data. As part of the Lidar Committee's Working Group efforts, the ASPRS guidelines were harmonized with the relevant sections of the Guidelines for Digital Elevation Data (Version 1.0) released by the National Digital Elevation Program (NDEP) as described above.

The ASPRS Guidelines cover the recommended methods for measuring and reporting the vertical accuracy of elevation data recorded by airborne lidar mapping instruments. Essentially, they outline necessary steps to analyze the vertical accuracy of elevation data generated using airborne lidar technology. In addition, the Guidelines cover determining what level of accuracy can be associated with a mapping product, such as a contour map, that is generated from a given lidar dataset (or conversely, what level of accuracy is required in the lidar data to support a given contour interval map). Finally, they also include recommendations for the proper planning and implementation of appropriate ground checkpoints to support a lidar data set, including how to handle different land cover classes across a project site.

Other lider guidelines currently under development by ASPRS include "Horizontal Accuracy Reporting," "Sensor Calibration," and "Laser Eye Safety."

ASPRS Accuracy Requirements

Most of the Accuracy Requirements section of the ASPRS Guideline are identical to the NDEP Guidelines and will not be repeated. This includes ASPRS requirements for testing and reporting of fundamental, supplemental, and consolidated vertical accuracy, to include requirements for errors larger than the 95th percentile to be reported in the metadata. ASPRS guidelines that differ (albeit slightly) from NDEP Guidelines are quoted below. None of these differences are substantial.

"With the NSSDA, the vertical accuracy of a data set (Accuracy$_{(z)}$) is defined by the root mean square error (RMSE$_{(z)}$) of the elevation data in terms of feet or meters at ground scale, rather than in terms of the published map's contour interval. Because the NSSDA does not address the suitability of data for any particular product, map scale, contour interval, or other application, no error thresholds are established by the standard. However, it is often helpful to use familiar NMAS thresholds for determining reasonable NSSDA accuracy requirements for various types of terrain and relief. This relationship can be shown to be:

[1] NMAS CI = 3.2898*RMSE$_{(z)}$
[2] NMAS CI = Accuracy$_{(z)}$/0.5958
     where
[3] Accuracy$_{(z)}$ = 1.9600*RMSE$_{(z)}$ (Normally Distributed Error)" and
[4] CI = Contour Interval.

"Note that for error that is not normally distributed, ASPRS recommends Accuracy$_{(z)}$ be determined by 95th percentile testing, not by the use of Equation [3]. A normal distribution can be tested for by calculating the skewness of the dataset. If the skew exceeds ±0.5 this is a strong indicator of asymmetry in the data and further investigation should be completed to determine the cause. Based on this relationship, the Accuracy$_{(z)}$ values shown in Table [3.8] below are NSSDA equivalents to the NMAS error thresholds for common contour intervals and should be taken as the recommended ASPRS vertical accuracy requirements for lidar data to support mapping products that meet the corresponding NMAS standard.

Table 3.8 Comparison of NMAS/NSSDA Vertical Accuracy.

NMAS Equivalent Contour Interval (ft)	NSSDA RMSE$_{(z)}$	NSSDA Accuracy$_{(z)}$	Required Accuracy for Reference Data for "Tested to Meet"
0.5	0.15 ft or 4.60 cm	0.30 ft or 9.1 cm	0.10 ft
1	0.30 ft or 9.25 cm	0.60 ft or 18.2 cm	0.20 ft
2	0.61 ft or 18.5 cm	1.19 ft or 36.3 cm	0.40 ft
4	1.22 ft or 37.0 cm	2.38 ft or 72.6 cm	0.79 ft
5	1.52 ft or 46.3 cm	2.98 ft or 90.8 cm	0.99 ft
10	3.04 ft or 92.7 cm	5.96 ft or 1.816 m	1.98 ft

Note: the right column of Table 3.8 indicates that the vertical accuracy of the checkpoints should be three times more accurate than the required accuracy of the lidar dataset being evaluated.

"In contracting for lidar data production, the required vertical accuracy should be specified in terms of Accuracy$_{(z)}$, rather than NMAS CI, the correct value for which may be calculated from Equation [2] above for any given NMAS CI, extracted from the third column of Table [3.8] or uniquely derived for a particular application. Consistent use of the User Requirements Menu when contracting/specifying lidar-derived elevation data is highly recommended by ASPRS. Details of the User Requirements Menu can be found in the NDEP Guidelines or the DEM (Users) Manual …" (ASPRS, 2001) and Table 13.1 of this 2nd Edition of the *DEM Users Manual*.

"However, it should be noted that stating a single vertical accuracy requirement without providing additional clarification and details of the intended purpose of the lidar-derived elevation dataset may not be sufficient information to allow for proper planning and implementation of the field data collection by the data provider. Testing of lidar-derived elevation data over various ground cover categories has revealed that the magnitude and distribution of errors often vary between different land cover types. To account for this, ASPRS recommends the following:

1. "For ASPRS purposes, the lidar dataset's required 'fundamental vertical accuracy,' which is the vertical accuracy in open terrain tested to 95% confidence (normally distributed error), shall be specified, tested and reported. If no distinction is made when a document references 'vertical accuracy,' it shall be assumed to be 'fundamental' (best case) vertical accuracy.

2. "If information is required on the vertical accuracy achieved within other ground cover categories outside open terrain, either to meet the same specification as the fundamental vertical accuracy or a more relaxed specification, then 'supplemental' vertical accuracies, that is vertical accuracy tested using the 95th percentile method (not necessarily normally distributed) shall be specified, tested and reported for each land cover class of interest.

3. "If contour maps or similar derivative products are to be generated across an entire project area, the project-wide vertical accuracy requirement shall be the same as calculated by Equation [1] or listed in [Table 3.8] across all land cover classes. For ASPRS purposes this means that vertical accuracy in such cases shall be specified, tested and reported for each land cover class, reporting a fundamental vertical accuracy in open terrain and a supplemental vertical accuracy in each unique land cover class, each of which must independently meet the requirements for the desired contour interval.

4. "Contour maps or similar derivative products that cover several different land cover classes in a project shall only be reported as 'Tested' or 'Compiled to Meet' … a given accuracy in accordance with the worst vertical accuracy, fundamental or supplemental, of any of the land cover classes to be included in the mapping product.

5. "In some circumstances, it may be preferable to specify a different vertical accuracy in different land cover classes, specifying a relaxed vertical accuracy in forested areas, for example, than in tall grass. Such situations shall be explicitly stated in the project specifications.

6. "It is commonly accepted that vertical accuracy testing in very irregular or steep sloping terrain is inappropriate due to the high probability that the error in the testing process is a significant contributor to the final error statistic and thus biases the results. For example a small but acceptable horizontal shift in the data may reflect in an unacceptable vertical error measurement. Because of this concern, ASPRS recommends that vertical accuracy testing always be done in areas where the terrain is as level and consistent as possible. In mountainous areas, level areas may not be easy to access, but attempts should be made to keep test points in reasonably low slope and smooth terrain as possible.

"Note that for the specific case of contour mapping, ASPRS does not support extrapolating a fundamental vertical accuracy across different land cover classes with the assumption the vertical accuracy will meet the stated mapping standard. For example, if a dataset is reported with a fundamental vertical accuracy that just meets the vertical accuracy requirement listed in [Table 3.8] for the desired contour interval, it is probable that it will not meet that mapping standard outside of open terrain. Supplemental vertical accuracy reporting shall always be requested and provided for every land cover class for which it is intended to generate contour maps and care should be taken to verify that the required vertical accuracy for the given contour interval is met in each and every land cover class.

"For legacy datasets for which only 'vertical accuracy' was reported with no indication if this is fundamental, supplemental or consolidated accuracy, ASPRS recommends assuming this is a fundamental (best-case) vertical accuracy and recommends caution when working with the dataset in different land cover classes. If possible, review the QA/QC data and retest the data to measure supplemental vertical accuracies (95th percentile testing) in areas outside open terrain."

AUTHOR BIOGRAPHIES

The principal authors for this chapter are David Maune, Geographic Information Services Division, Dewberry, 8401 Arlington Blvd., Fairfax, Virginia 22031-4666; Julie Binder Maitra, FGDC Standards Secretariat, c/o U.S. Geological Survey, 590 National Center, Reston, VA 22092; and Edward J. McKay, NOAA, NGS (retired).

Maune is Senior Project Manager for Dewberry where he manages DEM and other map production contracts with the U.S. Geological Survey, National Oceanic and Atmospheric Administration, Federal Emergency Management Agency, Natural Resources Conservation Service, and numerous state and local clients. He also manages independent QA/QC contracts nationwide. He was a principal author of the FEMA and NDEP guidelines which formed the basis for the ASPRS Guidelines, all summarized in Chapter 3 of this manual. He is an ASPRS Fellow and Certified Photogrammetrist. He teaches ASPRS workshops on *QA/QC of Lidar Data* and *Fundamentals of Mapping and Geospatial Technologies*. Both of these workshops include explanations and case studies on FGDC accuracy standards. He has over 40 years of experience in the mapping profession, including 30 years as an Army officer (Topographic Engineer) in the U.S. Army Corps of Engineers. Maune earned his BS in Mechanical Engineering in 1961 from the University of Missouri-Rolla, and his MS (1970) and PhD (1973) degrees in Geodetic Science and Photogrammetry from the Ohio State University. Prior to joining Dewberry in 1992, he served as Commander and Director of the U.S. Army Topographic Engineering Center (TEC); Director, Defense Mapping School (DMS); and Inspector General, Defense Mapping Agency (DMA), now the National Geospatial-Intelligence Agency (NGA).

Julie Binder Maitra is the Standards Program Coordinator for the Federal Geographic Data Committee (FGDC). In this capacity, she chairs the FGDC Standards Working Group and provides guidance to other FGDC Subcommittees and Working Groups that are developing standards. She is the FGDC representative to the National Committee for Information Technology Standards (NCITS) Technical Committee L1 on Geographic Information Systems, which is a standards development organization accredited by the American National Standards Institute (ANSI). Ms. Maitra received a BS in Chemical Engineering in 1980 from Washington University in St. Louis, Missouri, and MS in Engineering Management in 1992 from the University of Missouri-Rolla. She began her career at the Defense Mapping Agency in 1984 and joined the U.S. Geological Survey in 1987. She joined the USGS headquarters in 1993 where she developed data standards for the National Mapping Program and began participation in ISO standards activities. She was named the FGDC Standards Program Coordinator in 1999.

Prior to his retirement in 2005, Edward J. McKay served as chief, Spatial Reference System Division, National Geodetic Survey, NOAA, and he also served as chair, Methodology Work Group, Federal Geodetic Control Subcommittee which is responsible for developing standards and specifications for geodetic control surveys. He received a BS degree in Mathematics in 1964 from Lebanon Valley College, Pennsylvania, and a MS degree in Geodetic Science in 1973 from the Ohio State University. He began his career in surveying and mapping with the U.S. Coast and Geodetic Survey in 1966. He is a Fellow member and past president of the American Congress on Surveying and Mapping (ACSM) and past president of the American Association for Geodetic Surveying (AAGS).

REFERENCES

ASPRS, 1990. ASPRS accuracy standards for large-scale maps, *Photogrammetric Engineering and Remote Sensing*, 56(7): 1068-1070.

ASPRS, 2001. *Digital Elevation Model Technologies and Applications: The DEM Users Manual,* American Society for Photogrammetry and Remote Sensing, October, 2001.

ASPRS, 2004. *ASPRS Guidelines, Vertical Accuracy Reporting for Lidar Data*, American Society for Photogrammetry and Remote Sensing, May 24, 2004, http://www.asprs.org/society/committees/lidar/downloads/Vertical_Accuracy_Reporting_for_Lidar_Data.pdf.

Bureau of the Budget, 1947. *National Map Accuracy Standards*, Office of Management and Budget, Washington, D.C.

FEMA, 2003. Appendix A, Guidance for aerial mapping and surveying, *Guidelines and Specifications for Flood Hazard Mapping Partners*, Federal Emergency Management Agency.

FGCC, 1984. *Standards and Specifications for Geodetic Control Networks,* Federal Geodetic Control Committee, Rockville, MD, reprinted August 1993.

FGCC, 1988. *Geometric Geodetic Accuracy Standards and Specifications for Using GPS Relative Positioning Techniques,* Federal Geodetic Control Committee, Silver Spring, MD, reprinted with corrections, August, 1989.

FGDC, 1998a. *Geospatial Positioning Accuracy Standards, Part 1: Reporting Methodology*, Federal Geographic Data Committee, c/o USGS, Reston, VA, http://www.fgdc.gov/standards/standards_publications/.

FGDC, 1998b. *Geospatial Positioning Accuracy Standards, Part 2: Standards for Geodetic Networks*, Federal Geographic Data Committee, c/o USGS, Reston, VA, http://www.fgdc.gov/standards/standards_publications/.

FGDC, 1998c, *Geospatial Positioning Accuracy Standards, Part 3: National Standard for Spatial Data Accuracy*, Federal Geographic Data Committee, c/o USGS, Reston, VA, http://www.fgdc.gov/standards/standards_publications/.

FGDC, 1998d. *Content Standard for Digital Geospatial Metadata (CSDGM)*, Federal Geographic Data Committee, c/o USGS, Reston, VA, www.fgdc.gov/metadata/contstan.html.

FGDC, 1999. *Content Standards for Framework Land Elevation Data* (final draft), Federal Geographic Data Committee, c/o USGS, Reston, VA. http://www.fgdc.gov/standards/projects/FGDC-standards-projects/elevation/elev_199.pdf.

FGDC, 2005. *Geospatial Positioning Accuracy Standards, Part 5: Standards for Nautical Charting Hydrographic Surveys*, Federal Geographic Data Committee, c/o USGS, Reston, VA, http://www.fgdc.gov/standards/standards_publications/.

Greenwalt, C.E. and M.E. Schultz, 1968. Principles and error theory and cartographic applications, *ACIC Technical Report* No. 96, St. Louis, MO, Aeronautical Chart and Information Center, U.S. Air Force, 89p.

IHO, 1998. International Hydrographic Organization, April 1998, IHO standards for hydrographic surveys, *Special Publication* No. 44, 4th Edition, 23p.

NDEP, 2004, *Guidelines for Digital Elevation Data*, Version 1.0, National Digital Elevation Program (NDEP), May 10, 2004, http://www.ndep.gov/NDEP_Elevation_Guidelines_Ver1_10May2004.pdf.

NOAA, 1997. Guidelines for establishing GPS-derived ellipsoid heights (standards: 2 cm and 5 cm), *NOAA Technical Memorandum* NOS NGS-58, November, 1997.

NOAA, 2003. *NOS Hydrographic Surveys Specifications and Deliverables,* March, 2003, http://nauticalcharts.noaa.gov/hsd/specs/specs.htm.

NOAA, 2006. *NGS Blue Book*, www.ngs.noaa.gov, Products & Services, Publications, NGS Blue Book, Annex G, Ellipsoid Height Order and Class Codes.

Photogrammetry for Highways Committee, 1968. *Reference Guide Outline: Specifications for Aerial Surveys and Mapping by Photogrammetric Methods for Highways*, U.S. Department of Transportation, Washington, D.C.

Chapter 4

The National Elevation Dataset

Dean B. Gesch

INTRODUCTION

The National Elevation Dataset (NED) is the primary elevation data product produced and distributed by the U.S. Geological Survey (USGS). Since its inception, the USGS has compiled and published topographic information in many forms, and the NED is the latest development in this long line of products that describe the land surface. The NED provides seamless raster elevation data of the conterminous United States, Alaska, Hawaii, and the island territories. The NED is derived from diverse source data sets that are processed to a specification with a consistent resolution, coordinate system, elevation units, and horizontal and vertical datums. The NED is the logical result of the maturation of the long-standing USGS elevation program, which for many years concentrated on production of map quadrangle-based digital elevation models (DEM). The NED serves as the elevation layer of the *The National Map* (Kelmelis *et al.*, 2003), and it provides basic elevation information for earth science studies and mapping applications in the United States.

Background, Rationale, and History

The history of USGS DEM production is detailed in Osborn *et al.* (2001). The production of 7.5-minute quadrangle-based DEMs began in the mid-1970s, and once-over coverage of the conterminous United States at a post spacing of 30 meters or better was completed in 1999. Production of 10-meter resolution DEMs continues today where the USGS and its partners have the requirement of upgrading the basic 30-meter resolution elevation data coverage. The geospatial data community has made extensive use of these quadrangle-based DEMs; however, a significant amount of pre-processing is required to assemble multiple DEMs into a seamless data set suitable for application. Gesch *et al.* (2002) describe the steps required for production of an elevation layer, including projection transformation and resampling, datum conversions, mosaicking, edge-matching, sliver filling, filtering for artifact removal, and elevation unit conversion. The consistent, seamless structure of the NED removes the requirement for users to handle and individually process multiple input files. Instead, the NED provides application-ready data and allows users to focus on analysis rather than data preparation.

The NED is designed to address the requirement for large-area coverage of the "best available" elevation data. This approach fulfills the *framework* data concept as promoted by the National Spatial Data Infrastructure (NSDI) (Federal Geographic Data Committee, 1995) in which the most commonly needed geographic data themes are integrated into coherent data sets based upon source data from multiple public and private entities. The USGS has been designated as the agency having the lead responsibility for national elevation data (Office of Management and Budget, 2002). As such, the USGS has assembled the NED as an implementation of the framework data concept.

The USGS began the development of seamless elevation data sets in the early 1990s, first working on continental and global data sets at a resolution of 1 kilometer (Gesch *et al.*, 1999). The experience gained in assembling multi-source, multi-resolution elevation data into a global seamless data set proved to be valuable, as the methods were adapted, refined, and further developed for use in producing regional U.S. elevation framework prototypes in 1996. The first complete seamless coverage of the conterminous United States was finished in 1997 and was based on 10-meter, 30-meter, 2-arc-second, and 3-arc-second resolution DEM source data. In 1999, for the first time, the NED was assembled completely (for the conterminous United States) from 7.5-minute DEM source data (10-meter and 30-meter data). The bimonthly update cycle for the NED began in June 2000 and continues to the present.

SPECIFICATIONS AND PRODUCTION

To maintain seamlessness in its national coverage, the NED uses a raster data model cast in a geographic coordinate system (horizontal locations are referenced in decimal degrees of latitude and longitude). The NED employs a multi-resolution structure, with national coverage at a grid spacing of 1-arc-second (approximately 30 meters). The exception is Alaska where lower resolution source data warrant the use of a 2-arc-second spacing. Where higher resolution source data exist, the NED also contains a layer at a post spacing of 1/3-arc-second (approximately 10 meters). Some areas are also available at a 1/9-arc-second (approximately 3 meters) post spacing, where very high-resolution source data exist. The NED production approach ensures that georeferencing of the layers results in properly nested and coincident data across the three resolutions. In the context of the raster data model used for the NED, the area represented by one elevation post in the 1-arc-second layer is represented by nine elevation posts in the 1/3-arc-second layer, and by eighty-one elevation posts in the 1/9-arc-second layer (Figure 4.1). Where all three resolution layers can be produced, each layer is constructed independently from the same high-resolution source data using an aggregation method appropriate to the grid spacing being produced.

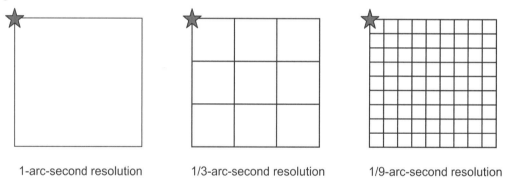

1-arc-second resolution   1/3-arc-second resolution   1/9-arc-second resolution

Figure 4.1 NED nested multi-resolution raster elevation layers. The area represented by one elevation post (or cell) in the 1-arc-second layer is represented by nine elevation posts in the 1/3-arc-second layer and by eighty-one elevation posts in the 1/9-arc-second layer.

In all three NED resolution layers, the elevation units are standardized to decimal meters. The horizontal datum for the NED is the North American Datum of 1983 (NAD 83), and the vertical datum is the North American Vertical Datum of 1988 (NAVD 88). Federal Geographic Data Committee (FGDC) compliant metadata are provided for efficient documentation. Additionally, spatially referenced metadata are supplied as an attributed geospatial data layer that captures all metadata from the source DEMs and NED processing steps on a polygonal footprint basis (Figure 4.2).

The NED is a logically seamless data set, as computer-processing considerations require that the data be assembled on a tiled basis, and the tiles collectively form the virtual national mosaic. Currently, NED production uses a 1- by 1-degree tile as the unit for assembly and processing of the 1-arc-second and 1/3-arc-second layers. Adjacent tiles are edge matched to ensure the seamless nature of the data set. In its entirety, the NED comprises nearly 1,400 1- by 1-degree tiles, with more than 900 tiles covering the conterminous United States, more than 400 covering Alaska, and the remainder covering Hawaii and the island territories.

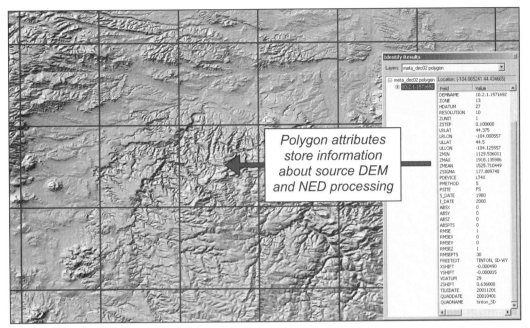

Figure 4.2 NED spatially referenced metadata layer. See color plate in Appendix C.

When a NED tile is assembled, the best available source data are selected according to the following criteria (ordered from first to last): high-resolution elevation data (usually derived from lidar or aerial photogrammetry), USGS 10-meter DEM, USGS 30-meter Level 2 DEM, USGS 30-meter Level 1 DEM, and USGS 2-arc-second DEM (see Osborn *et al.*, 2001 for an explanation of DEM level designations). The goal is to continuously upgrade the NED, thus the emphasis on high-resolution lidar and photogrammetric source data, and 10-meter DEMs, as the primary and secondary sources, respectively. For the conterminous United States, the area covered by high-resolution elevation data and 10-m DEMs is increasing continuously, so the percentage of the 1-arc-second NED layer derived from 30-meter DEMs has been decreasing correspondingly. Figure 4.3 shows the composition of the NED source data by DEM type for the first five-and-a-half years of NED bimonthly updates. As of January 2006, more than 60 percent of the conterminous United States had been covered by source data with a resolution of 10 meters or better. Figure 4.4 shows the geographic distribution of source data resolution across the conterminous United States.

The NED is assembled from approximately 59,000 files of source elevation data. As source data for NED production, more than 55,000 DEM files are used for the conterminous United States and nearly 4,000 DEM files for Alaska, Hawaii, and the island territories. Production of 7.5-minute DEMs at the 10-meter (or 1/3-arc-second) post spacing is an ongoing activity at the USGS, so the NED is updated on a regular basis to incorporate all new USGS DEM production, thus retaining the "best available data" framework concept. A new version of the NED is released every two months, containing updated areas for which new source DEMs became available since the previous release. The new source data may come from USGS production or from newly available high-resolution data acquisitions. On average, approximately 8 percent of the total number of 1-by 1-degree tiles are updated at each release. An update is required for a tile if even one new DEM file is available, as edge matching must be done to ensure the seamless quality of the NED. The spatially referenced metadata provided with each NED release indicate the specific areas where new source DEMs have been incorporated since the previous release.

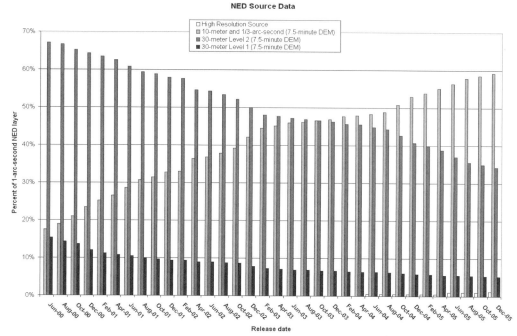

Figure 4.3 Source data by DEM type for each NED release.

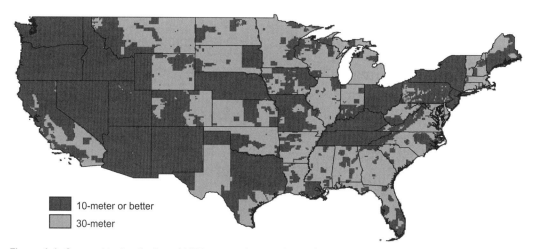

Figure 4.4 Geographic distribution of NED source data resolution (as of January 2006).

NED Production Steps

NED assembly and updating are accomplished with a highly automated production process that was developed specifically for this seamless elevation data set. The main steps in the process are outlined in Figure 4.5. The selection of source data is accomplished by an automated query of a database of USGS and partner-supplied DEMs. The "best available" data criteria outlined above are applied to select specific file-based DEMs from the database. The headers of the selected DEMs are read to create an index, which controls production and triggers subsequent processing steps. Industry standard tools from the National Geodetic Survey (NGS), NADCON and VERTCON, are used to perform horizontal and vertical datum transformations, respectively.

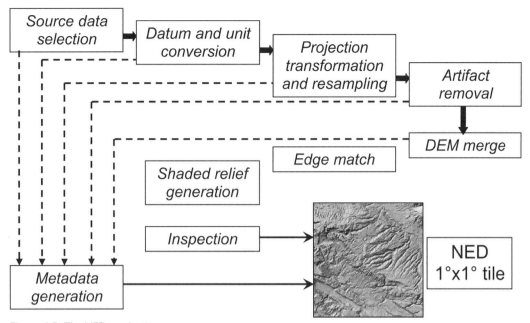

Figure 4.5 The NED production process.

The source DEMs are projected from their native coordinate system to a geographic coordinate system (decimal degrees of latitude and longitude) using standard cartographic transformation software. Resampling of the original elevation values is done with an implementation of cubic convolution that is optimized for elevation data by maintaining the integrity of shorelines and water bodies. Artifact removal is performed on the older USGS Level 1 DEMs that were produced with photogrammetric methods. The "mean profile filter" (Oimoen, 2000) was specifically designed to process these 7.5-minute DEMs. The filter process uses a series of directional filters to isolate the high-frequency artifacts, which are then subtracted from the DEM. The magnitude of these artifacts is small, typically less than 1 meter, so the change to the DEM is negligible, but the removal results in significant improvements in derivative elevation products, such as shaded relief, slope, and aspect.

The final steps in the production process include paneling the DEMs to fill the 1- by 1-degree tile, filling slivers of missing data along DEM boundaries as necessary by interpolating adjacent values, and edge matching the seams along the DEM boundaries and tile edges. The edge match algorithm uses a feathering approach that maintains local slope continuity across the seam. Figure 4.6 shows the results of the artifact filtering, sliver filling, and edge matching operations for an area derived from USGS Level 1 DEMs. Finally, a shaded-relief image of the tile is generated for inspection by an analyst to verify successful processing, especially artifact filtering and edge matching. In some cases, DEM header information, which automatically triggers certain processing options, is incorrect, and the result is data that are not acceptable for inclusion into the NED. These cases are detected in the visual inspection step, the DEM header is corrected, and the tile is submitted for reprocessing. Tiles passing inspection are transferred to the next release version, and the spatially referenced metadata are updated accordingly.

An interactive map server (Figure 4.7) on the NED home page (http://ned.usgs.gov/) allows a user to display the NED data source index, which indicates the date of the most recent update, the resolution of the source data, and the production method of the source data for specific areas. The user can also query the spatially referenced metadata to examine additional information about each file-based DEM used to assemble the NED. The NED Web site also contains documentation on the NED assembly process, accuracy, metadata, standards, data distribution, and release notes.

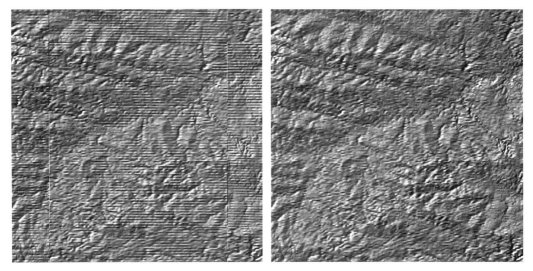

Figure 4.6 Source DEMs without artifact filtering, sliver filling, and edge matching are shown on the left. NED data produced with artifact filtering, sliver filling, and edge matching operations are shown on the right.

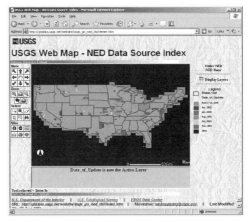

Figure 4.7 Data source index, available on the NED home page (http://ned.usgs.gov/), displays the most recently updated areas in the NED. See color plate in Appendix C.

Data Distribution

In keeping with the framework concept of easily accessible data, NED products are available in several common formats through a Web-based seamless data distribution system (http://seamless.usgs.gov/) linked to the NED home page. The system uses interactive map server technology to provide users the capability for viewing shaded relief images derived from the NED. The map server also includes numerous reference layers to help users define their study areas. The system incorporates a geographic names capability whereby users can automatically pan and zoom to specific feature locations. Orders for products resulting in network-compatible file sizes can be downloaded interactively at no cost to the user. Products covering very large areas, including the entire data set, are available on hard media (Figure 4.8).

ACCURACY ASSESSMENT

The accuracy of the NED varies spatially because of the variable quality of the source DEMs. As such, the NED inherits the accuracy of the source DEMs. Some accuracy statistics are available in the header records of the USGS DEM source files, and this information is captured in the spatially referenced metadata. Many times, this accuracy information has limited usefulness because it is a relative measure of how well the DEM fits the source material from which it was generated. In an effort to provide more information to users on the vertical accuracy of the NED, the data set has been tested by comparing it with an independent reference source of very high accuracy. The reference data are the geodetic control points that NGS uses for gravity and geoid modeling (Smith and Roman, 2001; National Geodetic Survey, 2003). The distribution of this set of more than 13,000 high-precision survey points across the conterminous United States is shown in Figure 4.9.

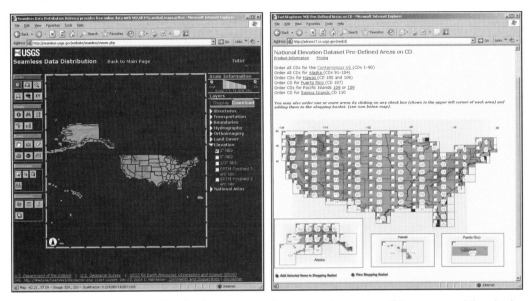

Figure 4.8 Web-based seamless data distribution system (http://seamless.usgs.gov/) for viewing and downloading of NED products (left). Large area coverage of NED products available on hard media (right). See color plate in Appendix C.

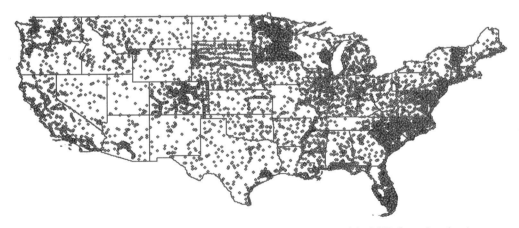

Figure 4.9 Reference control point data set used for accuracy assessment of the NED. See color plate in Appendix C.

Absolute Vertical Accuracy

To complete the accuracy assessment, the NED value at each of the NGS control point locations was derived through bilinear interpolation, and error statistics were calculated (Table 4.1). The overall absolute vertical accuracy expressed as the root mean square error (RMSE) is 2.44 meters. Table 4.1 also contains the accuracy expressed in terms of the National Map Accuracy Standards (NMAS), which use a 90 percent confidence interval, and in terms of the National Standard for Spatial Data Accuracy (NSSDA), which uses a 95 percent confidence interval. The methods described in Maune *et al.* (2001) were used to convert the measured vertical RMSE to equivalent NMAS and NSSDA expressions.

Table 4.1 Error statistics (in meters) of the NED vs. 13,305 reference geodetic control points.

Minimum	Maximum	Mean	Standard Deviation	RMSE	NMAS (90%)	NSSDA (95%)
−42.64	18.74	−0.32	2.42	2.44	3.99	4.75

An advantage of the 2.44-meter RMSE as an accuracy report is that it is an actual measured quantity, in contrast to the often quoted RMSE of 7 meters for USGS DEMs, from which most of NED is derived. The 7-meter RMSE, often cited as the accuracy of USGS 7.5-minute DEMs, is a production goal described in the USGS Data Users Guide 5—Digital Elevation Models, last published in 1993 and traditionally known by many users as the "blue book" (see also U.S. Geological Survey, 1997). Note that the version of the NED that was tested by comparison with the Global Positioning System (GPS) points was the 1-arc-second layer released in June 2003, which was the last version assembled completely from USGS 10-meter and 30-meter 7.5-minute DEMs. Since that time, some areas have been updated based on high-resolution lidar or photo-grammetric data, which may have even better accuracy than the quadrangle-based USGS DEMs.

Accuracy assessments were conducted on earlier versions of the NED using a smaller set of control points from the NGS known as the High Accuracy Reference Network (HARN). Approximately 5,800 points were used to measure the absolute vertical accuracy of the 1-arc-second layer of the NED for the conterminous United States as it existed in September 1999, October 2001, and October 2002. Table 4.2 shows the improvement in overall vertical accuracy of the NED, as the more recent versions have incorporated better source data. Most of the HARN points used for the earlier assessments were also included in the larger GPS benchmarks data set, which was used for the most recent assessment of the June 2003 version of the NED.

Table 4.2 Results of accuracy assessments of the NED vs. reference geodetic control points (all numbers are in meters).

Version Date of the NED	RMSE	NMAS (90%)	NSSDA (95%)
September 1999	3.74	6.15	7.34
October 2001	3.13	5.15	6.14
October 2002	2.70	4.44	5.29
June 2003	2.44	3.99	4.75

Use of the NED spatially referenced metadata also allows for the calculation of accuracy statistics segmented by source DEM characteristics. Because the NED is derived from source DEMs that were produced with several different methods, it may be important for a user to know what levels of accuracy can be expected for areas based on DEMs produced with the various methods. The four primary production methods used for USGS 7.5-minute DEMs include electronic image correlation (Gestalt Photo Mapper (GPM) instrument), manual profiling (MP) on stereoplotters, contour-to-grid interpolation (CTOG), and an improved contour-to-grid interpolation known as "LineTrace+" (LT4X). Details for each production method are given in Osborn *et al.* (2001). To calculate the accuracy of DEMs resulting from each production method, the reference control point data set was partitioned into subsets according to the production method of the quadrangle on which each point was located. Table 4.3 shows the error statistics for the areas of the NED derived from DEMs produced with each of the four production methods. Note that the DEMs derived from photogrammetric methods (GPM and MP) are less accurate than those derived from 1:24,000-scale contours. This is not surprising, given that the photogrammetric DEMs were compiled from 1:80,000-scale aerial photography and were a by-product of the orthophoto generation process.

Table 4.3 Error statistics (in meters) of the NED for areas derived from USGS 7.5-minute DEMs produced with each of the four primary production methods.

Production Method	Number of Reference GPS Points	Minimum	Maximum	Mean	Standard Deviation	RMSE
GPM	809	−11.98	17.44	2.00	4.21	4.66
M P	465	−15.31	14.34	0.05	3.63	3.63
CTOG	1,537	−20.83	9.18	−0.60	1.94	2.03
LT4X	10,476	−42.64	18.74	−0.47	2.12	2.17

Land surface characteristics derived directly from the NED, including slope, aspect, and local relief, allow for examining accuracy as a function of specific terrain conditions. Figure 4.10 shows the NED error at each GPS control point plotted against elevation, slope, aspect, and local relief (relief within approximately one square mile centered on the point location). The NED errors appear to be truly random, as there is no discernible correlation or relationship with any of the terrain parameters. This is evident in the distribution of data points in the scatterplots; in each case, the values are uniformly distributed around the zero error axis. Thus, in general, NED users can expect a consistent level of accuracy across the data set regardless of varying terrain conditions.

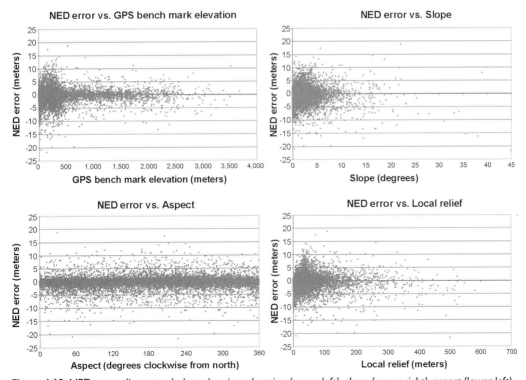

Figure 4.10 NED errors (in meters) plotted against elevation (upper left), slope (upper right), aspect (lower left), and local relief (lower right).

Relative Vertical Accuracy

For some applications of elevation data, the relative, or point-to-point, vertical accuracy is more important than the absolute vertical accuracy. Whereas absolute accuracy accounts for the combined effects of systematic and random errors, relative accuracy is a measure of just random errors. The relative vertical accuracy of a data set is especially important for derivative products that make use of the local differences among adjacent elevation values, such as slope and aspect calculations. To characterize the relative vertical accuracy of the NED, the same set of reference geodetic control points used in the assessment of absolute vertical accuracy was processed and analyzed. As with the test of absolute accuracy, the NED 1-arc-second layer released in June 2003 was tested. Each point in the reference control point data set was processed to identify its closest neighboring point, and this resulted in 9,187 unique point pairs for which the NED elevation at each point location and the distance between the points were recorded. The relative vertical accuracy, RV, was calculated for each point pair with the following formula (National Digital Elevation Program, 2004):

$$RV = |\Delta ref - \Delta NED|$$

where $\Delta ref = |\text{reference elevation difference}|$
$\Delta NED = |\text{NED elevation difference}|$

Averaged over all 9,187 point pairs, the relative vertical accuracy is 1.64 meters (other summary statistics are shown in Table 4.4). The separation distance for points in a pair ranges from a few meters to more than 118 kilometers, with the average distance slightly greater than 7,000 meters and the median distance slightly less than 2,200 meters. Assessing relative accuracy across very long distances can have the effect of averaging random errors, thereby reducing the overall error. As stated, the pairs of reference points used here have a wide range of distances. At the lower end of the range is a subset of 109 point pairs that have a distance of 90 meters or less, which is about three times the nominal post spacing of the 1-arc-second NED layer. For this subset of 109 point pairs, the average relative vertical accuracy is 0.78 meters, so the very closely spaced points that were tested show a very high degree of relative accuracy.

Table 4.4 Relative vertical accuracy statistics for the NED based on 9,187 unique pairs of reference geodetic points (all numbers are in meters).

Minimum	Maximum	Mean	Standard Deviation	Median
0.00	22.07	1.64	2.08	0.89

One use of relative accuracy information is to estimate the uncertainty of slope calculated from raster elevation data such as the NED. Slope is often calculated from DEMs by assigning a slope value to each grid cell based on the maximum elevation change across its eight adjacent neighbors (a 3-by-3 window). To illustrate how relative vertical accuracy of a DEM affects slope accuracy, assume that an area of the land surface represented by a 3-by-3 window of elevation cells is flat. Thus, all nine elevation values should be the same and the derived slope should be zero. However, because of random errors inherent in elevation data, assume that the maximum elevation difference among the cells surrounding the center cell of the window is 1.64 meters. The minimum measurement baseline for slope within the window occurs when the maximum elevation difference is between two cells that are either immediately above and below, or left and right, of the center cell. In this case, if the post spacing of the DEM is 30 meters, the measurement baseline, or run, for slope calculation is 60 meters. Given the elevation difference (rise) of 1.64

meters and the baseline (run) of 60 meters, the calculated slope (rise/run x 100) is 2.73 percent (1.57 degrees). Thus, using the relative vertical accuracy figure of 1.64 meters results in an average accuracy of 2.73 percent for slope derived from the 1-arc-second NED layer. Figure 4.11 depicts in graphic form how this estimate of slope accuracy is calculated.

3-by-3 window of raster elevation data:

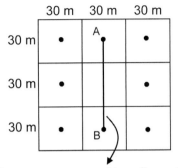

Relative vertical accuracy (rise) between
point A and point B = 1.64 meters

Baseline (run) = 60 meters

Percent slope = (rise/run) x 100

= (1.64/60) x 100

= 2.73%

Minimum measurement baseline = 60 meters

Figure 4.11 Calculation of accuracy of slope derived from 30-meter resolution elevation data. Assume that the area covered by the window is flat, and thus all elevation posts within the window should be the same. However, random error in the elevation data causes a difference of 1.64 meters in elevation between point A and point B. If the elevation data were free of error, a slope of zero would be assigned to the center cell, but in this case a slope of 2.73% is calculated, and it represents the slope accuracy.

One caveat to note about the accuracy assessment presented here is that even though the reference control point data set is large, the number of quadrangle-based USGS DEMs on which the points are located is relatively small. Approximately 11 percent of the source DEMs have at least one point located within. Thus, if users have a need for very specific accuracy information for the NED for a local area, a separate assessment should be done with suitable reference data just for that area. In addition, even though the reference control points are located broadly across the conterminous United States, the distribution of elevations and terrain conditions within the data set is not completely representative of the nation's topography. This stands to reason, as surveyed benchmarks are generally located in open, accessible areas. Thus, high elevation, steep slope locations are under-represented in the reference data set. Despite this limitation with the reference data, the overall vertical accuracy reported here is useful for applications that need to factor in the quality of the NED over large areas. Also, prior to the accuracy assessment reported here, there were no actual measured absolute or relative error statistics for USGS DEMs as a whole, so for the first time the user community now has a useful quantitative estimate of quality. As the NED is continually upgraded based on new acquisitions of high-resolution data, the overall vertical accuracy should improve. In many cases, the source data sets will have comprehensive error reports supplied with them, and these statistics will be captured and preserved in the NED metadata.

APPLICATIONS
As a primary source of basic topographic information for the United States, the NED is used in numerous applications that require elevation as an input. Elevation data are critically important for many hydrologic studies, and these studies are one of the main uses of the NED and associated derived products. The USGS data set known as the Elevation Derivatives for National Applications (EDNA) is based on the 1-arc-second NED and offers a multi-layered hydrologically conditioned database that was developed specifically for large-area hydrologic modeling applica-

tions (Verdin, 2000; Franken, 2004). Hydrologic conditioning results in elevation data with improved hydrologic flow representation and allows for derivation of multiple raster and vector layers optimized for hydrologic modeling, including flow direction, flow accumulation, streamlines, catchments, slope, and aspect. A primary use of the EDNA layers has been for drainage basin delineation and characterization (Kost and Kelly, 2001). Interactive basin delineation based on the EDNA data set is available through Web-enabled tools linked to the EDNA Web site (Verdin *et al.*, 2004) (Figure 4.12). These tools allow for delineation of the watershed above any point on the landscape, not just at stream junctions or other pre-defined points. Watershed characteristics, including the calculated mean annual stream flow at the basin outlet point, can be displayed, and the watershed delineation can be downloaded. The EDNA database has also been used for flash flood modeling and prediction (Arthur *et al.*, 2005), national assessment of hydroelectric power potential (Carroll *et al.*, 2004; Hall *et al.*, 2004), and watershed-based sampling design for water quality monitoring sites (Detenbeck *et al.*, 2005). Current EDNA development includes taking advantage of the higher resolution layers of the NED for improved flow routing.

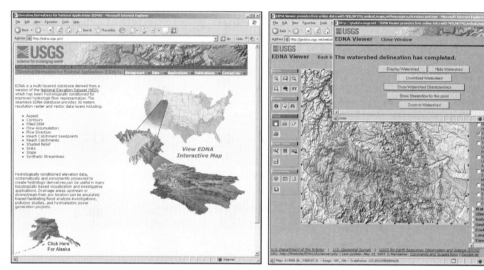

Figure 4.12 EDNA Web site (http://edna.usgs.gov/), on the left, and the Web-based interactive drainage basin delineation tool available on the EDNA data viewer, on the right. See color plate in Appendix C.

Data from the NED have been merged with bathymetry data to facilitate applications at the land/water interface. Many applications of geospatial data in coastal environments require knowledge of the near-shore topography and bathymetry. However, because existing topographic and bathymetric data have been collected independently for different purposes, it has been difficult to use them together. A tool developed by the National Oceanic and Atmospheric Administration (NOAA), VDatum (Parker *et al.*, 2003; Myers, 2005), is used to transform disparate data sets into a common vertical datum, which then facilitates development of merged seamless elevation models across the land/water interface. The USGS and NOAA are working collaboratively to produce such merged coastal topographic/bathymetric data sets (Gesch and Wilson, 2002). Figure 4.13 shows a merged elevation model for Tampa Bay, Florida, in which the topographic data came from the 1-arc-second NED layer and the bathymetric data came from NOAA's hydrographic survey database. This hybrid model has been used for improved storm surge simulations for Tampa Bay (Weisberg and Zheng, 2005). As the quality of the NED 1/3-arc-second and 1/9-arc-second layers improves through integration of recent, high-resolution data acquisitions, the quality of merged topographic/bathymetric elevation models made from those layers will improve accordingly.

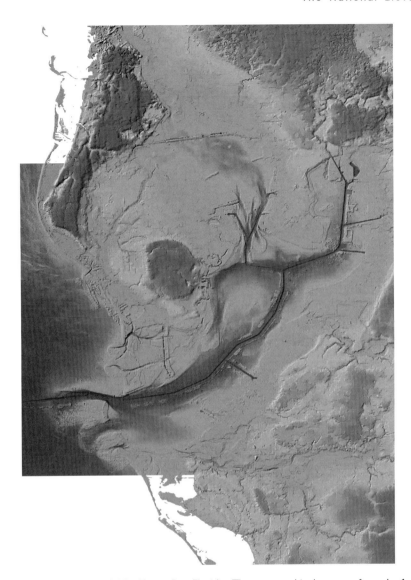

Figure 4.13 Merged elevation model for Tampa Bay, Florida. The topographic data came from the 1-arc-second NED layer and the bathymetric data came from NOAA's hydrographic survey database. See color plate in Appendix C.

Because topographic information is a fundamental requirement for so many earth science studies and operational geospatial applications, the NED has gained wide acceptance and attained broad usage by the user community. Among the characteristics of the NED that support its broad applicability are its national coverage, multi-resolution design, and regular update cycle. Some of the applications that have benefited from these advantages are large-area land cover mapping (Homer *et al.*, 2004), regional soil erosion vulnerability modeling (Das *et al.*, 2004), climate data analysis (Gallo, 2005), vegetation height estimation (Kellndorfer *et al.*, 2004), and wildland fire fuel mapping (see http://www.landfire.gov/). Current applications research at the USGS includes use of the NED as the historical component for topographic change detection and monitoring across the United States and development of a Web-based tool for generation of contours from the NED for use in producing updated topographic map products.

CURRENT DEVELOPMENT AND FUTURE DIRECTIONS

From the beginning of development of the NED and continuing to the present, the goal has always been to provide the best publicly available elevation data for the nation. Many sources of elevation data are available that could potentially be used for the NED; however, the focus has been, and will continue to be, on integrating the highest resolution, highest accuracy data that are free from licensing or other redistribution restrictions. The NED is a public domain resource, and it must remain so to fulfill the requirements of being a national framework geospatial data theme. To make sure that the NED fully meets the intent of the NSDI framework approach, the USGS elevation program is taking the direction that the primary source for updating the NED is recent collections of high-resolution data acquired through partnerships with other organizations. When necessary, the USGS still produces DEM data from quadrangle-based hypsography data, but only when there is no clear alternative for data to upgrade the NED.

In contrast to the situation several decades ago, there are many elevation data producers in addition to the USGS. Numerous federal, state, local, and tribal agencies either produce or contract for elevation data. Much of the data are actually generated by private sector mapping and engineering companies. For the NED to truly reflect the best publicly available data, elevation data from all these entities must be considered as potential information sources. The USGS has a cadre of liaisons to states and federal agencies that are dedicated to developing and implementing partnerships that benefit both parties by improving USGS geospatial data production, integration, and distribution. Much of the newer, high-resolution elevation data that have been integrated into the NED are the result of partnering arrangements led by the liaison staff.

Another entity that fosters collaboration on elevation data development is the National Digital Elevation Program (NDEP), which is a consortium of federal agencies working together to satisfy multiple elevation data requirements. The states also have a voice in the NDEP through a representative from the National States Geographic Information Council. Details on the background and operations of the NDEP are given in Osborn *et al.* (2001). The NDEP has produced a best practices document titled "Guidelines for Digital Elevation Data" (National Digital Elevation Program, 2004) to help member agencies as they acquire high-resolution elevation data. Data collected with the characteristics discussed in the guidelines meet the requirements of multiple federal agencies, and thus make efficient use of federal funds available for new geospatial data collection. The NDEP also operates a project tracking system whereby information on proposed, planned, in-work, or completed elevation projects is posted and shared (Figure 4.14). The project tracking tool is useful for agencies that are seeking partners to acquire data over a specific area. The NED benefits from NDEP activities in that it becomes the repository for bare earth elevation data as projects are completed. In this way, the benefits of data acquired by one agency are extended to other agencies, and eventually to the general user community, through the NED.

A new USGS activity, the Center for Lidar Information Coordination and Knowledge (CLICK), is another forum for information exchange and topographic data discovery that benefits the NED. CLICK is a virtual Web-based center (Figure 4.15) with the goal of providing a clearinghouse for lidar information and point cloud data. The CLICK Web site (http://lidar.cr.usgs.gov) provides a bulletin board with numerous topics related to lidar data for discussion among the community, including topics on bare earth data and NDEP. The site also includes a tool for viewing the coverage of available data and downloading point cloud data, in addition to an extensive list of lidar-related Web sites and references. Data acquired for distribution through the CLICK are also used as a source of high-resolution bare earth elevation data to enhance the coverage of the NED 1/9-arc-second layer. In addition, through the CLICK, users have access to the full-return point cloud form of lidar data that is included in the NED as bare earth gridded elevation data.

The NED will continue to be upgraded as new high-resolution source data become available. Ideally, source data that support the 1/9-arc-second posting will be acquired and used to update all three NED layers. In most cases, these source data will come from lidar or photogrammetric data, such as mass points and breaklines compiled from very large-scale stereo photography. To

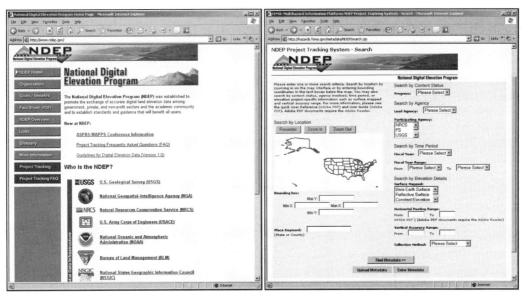

Figure 4.14 The NDEP Web site (http://www.ndep.gov/), shown on the left, includes a link to the NDEP project tracking system, shown on the right. See color plate in Appendix C.

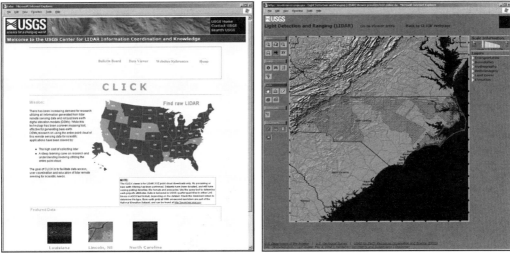

Figure 4.15 The USGS Center for LIDAR Information Coordination and Knowledge (CLICK) is a Web-based (http://lidar.cr.usgs.gov) virtual center that serves as a clearinghouse for lidar information exchange and point cloud data distribution. See color plate in Appendix C.

date, airborne interferometric synthetic aperture radar (IFSAR) data have not been used as a source for the NED, but as bare earth processing algorithms improve, or as coverage over suitable land cover such as Alaskan tundra increases, then these data will become a viable source for updating the NED.

As the primary USGS elevation data product, the NED is at the center of much of the topographic research and development conducted throughout the USGS. Driven by customer requirements and technology considerations, the goal of the USGS elevation program for many years was the production of 7.5-minute DEMs. These DEMs will still be produced for areas where it is unlikely that high-resolution, high-accuracy lidar or photogrammetric data will be available in the near future. In these cases, 10-meter DEMs in the standard Universal Transverse Mercator projection with a fully populated header record will be produced only when a funding partner requires it. Otherwise, data will be produced in a geographic coordinate system at a posting of 1/3-arc-second, which facilitates direct integration into the NED with minimal processing. Because the NED is the primary elevation data set produced and distributed by the USGS, distribution of the 7.5-minute DEMs was discontinued as of early 2006. By directing all users to the NED instead of supplying the older tiled data, they are assured of receiving the highest quality, most up-to-date elevation layer for the nation.

As more high-resolution, high-accuracy source data become available, it is anticipated that the areal coverage of the NED 1/9-arc-second layer will increase significantly. When new areas are covered by 1/9-arc-second data, the corresponding portions of the 1/3-arc-second and 1-arc-second layers are also upgraded. A current development activity at the USGS involves investigation of approaches to provide raster elevation data with a user-specified resolution, projection, units, and file format. If such a system could be implemented efficiently, then the NED architecture could be modified to hold only properly prepared source data, and distributable products could be generated to customer specifications on the fly. However, for the foreseeable future, the NED will continue to be provided in the three layers of differing resolution, which allows a user to access elevation data at the resolution that best matches the application and other input data layers. The continuing goal for the NED is to provide quality controlled, well documented elevation data that are useful for many geospatial applications.

EXAMPLE DATA

To help geospatial data users explore the use of the multi-resolution NED, examples are provided here as graphics and as digital data sets on the media accompanying this volume. The example areas include portions of the NED derived from different types of source data.

Figure 4.16 shows data from the three NED layers for an area in southern West Virginia. The source data for this area were derived through photogrammetric compilation of mass points and breaklines (MPBL) and subsequent surface generation. Figure 4.17 shows how the integration of the high-resolution photogrammetric data is reflected in the source data polygons in the NED spatially referenced metadata. The NED spatially referenced metadata are included with the elevation data for each example area.

Figure 4.18 shows data from the three NED layers for an area in southern Louisiana. The source data for this area are lidar-derived elevation grids.

Figure 4.19 shows data from two NED layers for an area in western Montana. The source data for this area are USGS 7.5-minute DEMs that were derived from 1:24,000-scale hypsography and hydrography through contour-to-grid interpolation.

AUTHOR BIOGRAPHY

Dean Gesch is employed by the U.S. Geological Survey (USGS) as a research physical scientist at the Center for Earth Resources Observation and Science (EROS) in Sioux Falls, South Dakota. His work is focused on research, development, and applications related to digital topographic data, including the investigation of newer remote sensing sources of elevation data, development of national and global seamless elevation data sets, accuracy assessment, topographic change detection and monitoring, and analysis of the risk of sea level rise based on high-resolution coastal mapping data sets. His previous experience includes work at NASA's Goddard Space Flight Center investigating remote sensing applications and work in terrain analysis at the Defense Mapping Agency. His educational background includes a bachelor's degree in geography from Carroll College, Waukesha, Wisconsin (1982), and a master's degree in geosciences from Murray State University, Murray, Kentucky (1984). He is currently a PhD candidate (ABD) in the geospatial science and engineering program at South Dakota State University, Brookings, South Dakota.

Figure 4.16 Multi-resolution NED layers for an area in West Virginia (1-arc-second data on the left; 1/3-arc-second data in the center; 1/9-arc-second data on the right). These data are derived from photogrametrically compiled mass points and breaklines. The digital data for this example area are provided on the media accompanying this book.

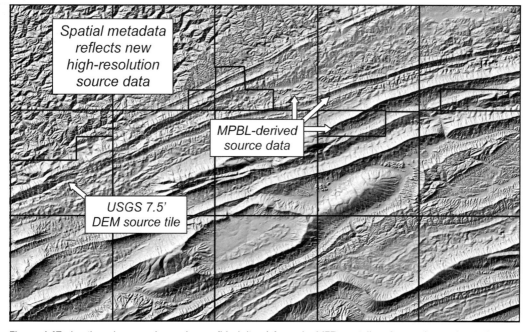

Figure 4.17 Attributed source data polygons (black lines) from the NED spatially referenced metadata indicate where new high-resolution source data have been used to produce the NED.

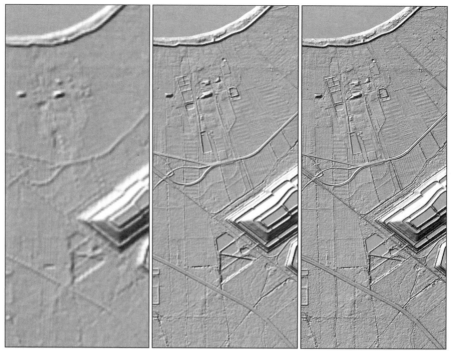

Figure 4.18 Multi-resolution NED layers for an area in Louisiana (1-arc-second data on the left; 1/3-arc-second data in the center; 1/9-arc-second data on the right). The source data for this area are lidar-derived elevation grids. The digital data for this example area are provided on the media accompanying this book.

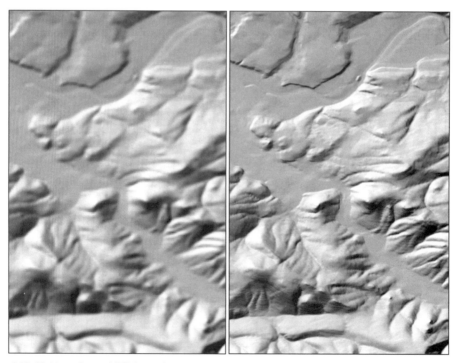

Figure 4.19 Multi-resolution NED layers for an area in western Montana (1-arc-second data on the left; 1/3-arc-second data on the right). The source data for this area are USGS 7.5-minute DEMs that were derived from 1:24,000-scale hypsography and hydrography through contour-to-grid interpolation. The digital data for this example area are provided on the media accompanying this book.

REFERENCES

Arthur, A.T., G.M. Cox, N.R. Kuhnert, D.L. Slater, and K.W. Howard, 2005. The national basin delineation project, *Bulletin of the American Meteorological Society*, 86(10): 1443–1452.

Carroll, G., K. Reeves, R. Lee, and S. Cherry, 2004. Evaluation of potential hydropower sites throughout the United States, *Proceedings of the Environmental Systems Research Institute, Inc. Twenty-Fourth Annual ESRI International User Conference*, August 9-13, 2004, San Diego, California, URL: http://gis.esri.com/library/userconf/proc04/docs/pap2010.pdf (last date accessed: 25 January 2006).

Das, C., W.J. Capehart, H.V. Mott, P.R. Zimmerman, and T.E. Schumacher, 2004. Assessing regional impacts of conservation reserve program-type grass buffer strips on sediment load reduction from cultivated lands, *Journal of Soil and Water Conservation*, 59(4): 134–142.

Detenbeck, N.E., D. Cincotta, J.M. Denver, S.K. Greenlee, A.R. Olsen, and A.M. Pitchford, 2005. Watershed-based survey designs, *Environmental Monitoring and Assessment*, 103(1–3): 59–81.

Federal Geographic Data Committee, 1995. Development of a national digital geospatial framework, URL: http://www.fgdc.gov/framework/framdev.html (last date accessed: 17 January 2006).

Franken, S., 2004. USGS EROS Data Center produces seamless hydrologic derivatives with GIS, *ArcNews*, Fall 2004, Environmental Systems Research Institute, Inc., URL: http://www.esri.com/news/arcnews/fall04articles/usgs-eros.html (last date accessed: 25 January 2006).

Gallo, K.P., 2005. Evaluation of temperature differences for paired stations of the U.S. Climate Reference Network, *Journal of Climate*, 18(10): 1629–1636.

Gesch, D., M. Oimoen, S. Greenlee, C. Nelson, M. Steuck, and D. Tyler, 2002. The national elevation dataset, *Photogrammetric Engineering & Remote Sensing*, 68(1): 5–11.

Gesch, D.B., K.L. Verdin, and S.K. Greenlee, 1999. New land surface digital elevation model covers the earth: Eos, *Transactions*, American Geophysical Union, 80(6): 69–70.

Gesch, D., and R. Wilson, 2002. Development of a seamless multisource topographic/ bathymetric elevation model of Tampa Bay, *Marine Technology Society Journal*, 35(4): 58–64.

Hall, D.G., S.J. Cherry, K.S. Reeves, R.D. Lee, G.R. Carroll, G.L. Sommers, and K.L. Verdin, 2004. Water energy resources of the United States with emphasis on low head/low power resources, DOE/ID-11111, U.S. Department of Energy, Idaho Operations Office, 52 p., URL: http://hydropower.inl.gov/resourceassessment/pdfs/03-11111.pdf (last date accessed: 25 January 2006).

Homer, C., C. Huang, L. Yang, B. Wylie, and M. Coan, 2004. Development of a 2001 national land-cover database for the United States, *Photogrammetric Engineering & Remote Sensing*, 70(7): 829–840.

Kellndorfer, J., W. Walker, L. Pierce, C. Dobson, J. Fites, C. Hunsaker, J. Vona, and M. Clutter, 2004. Vegetation height estimation from Shuttle Radar Topography Mission and National Elevation Datasets, *Remote Sensing of the Environment*, 93(3): 339–358.

Kelmelis, J.A., M.L. DeMulder, C.E. Ogrosky, N.J. Van Driel, and B.J. Ryan, 2003. The National Map—From geography to mapping and back again, *Photogrammetric Engineering & Remote Sensing*, 69(10): 1109–1118.

Kost, J., and G. Kelly, 2001. Watershed delineation using the National Elevation Dataset and semiautomated techniques, *Proceedings of the Environmental Systems Research Institute, Inc. Twenty-First Annual ESRI International User Conference*, July 9–13, 2001, San Diego, California (CD-ROM).

Maune, D.F., J.B. Maitra, and E.J. McKay, 2001. Accuracy standards, in *Digital Elevation Model Technologies and Applications: The DEM Users Manual* (D.F. Maune, editor), American Society for Photogrammetry and Remote Sensing, Bethesda, MD, pp. 61–82.

Myers, E.P., 2005. Review of progress on VDatum, a vertical datum transformation tool, presented at MTS/IEEE Oceans 2005 Conference, Washington, D.C., September 18–23, 2005, 7 p., URL: http://nauticalcharts.noaa.gov/csdl/Vdatum_pubs/myersOceans05.pdf (last date accessed: 25 January 2006).

National Digital Elevation Program, 2004. Guidelines for digital elevation data—Version 1, 93 p., URL: http://www.ndep.gov/NDEP_Elevation_Guidelines_Ver1_10May2004.pdf (last date accessed: 23 January 2006).

National Geodetic Survey, 2003. GPS on bench marks for GEOID03, URL: http://www.ngs.noaa.gov/GEOID/GPSonBM03/index.html (last date accessed: 26 April 2004).

Office of Management and Budget, 2002. Circular No. A-16 Revised—Coordination of geographic information and related spatial data activities, URL: http://www.whitehouse.gov/omb/circulars/a016/a016_rev.html (last date accessed: 17 January 2006).

Oimoen, M.J., 2000. An effective filter for removal of production artifacts in U.S. Geological Survey 7.5-minute digital elevation models, *Proceedings of the Fourteenth International Conference on Applied Geologic Remote Sensing*, November 6–8, 2000, Las Vegas, Nevada, Ann Arbor, Michigan, Veridian ERIM International, p. 311–319.

Osborn, K., J. List, D. Gesch, J. Crowe, G. Merrill, E. Constance, J. Mauck, C. Lund, V. Caruso, and J. Kosovich, 2001. National digital elevation program (NDEP), *Digital Elevation Model Technologies and Applications: The DEM Users Manual* (D.F. Maune, editor) American Society for Photogrammetry and Remote Sensing, Bethesda, MD, p. 83–120.

Parker, B., K. Hess, D. Milbert, and S. Gill, 2003. A national vertical datum transformation tool, *Sea Technology*, 44(9): 10–15.

Smith, D.A., and D.R. Roman, 2001. GEOID99 and G99SSS: 1-arc-minute geoid models for the United States, *Journal of Geodesy*, 75(9–10): 469–490.

U.S. Geological Survey, 1997. Part 1: General—Standards for digital elevation models, 11 p., URL: http://rockyweb.cr.usgs.gov/nmpstds/acrodocs/dem/1DEM0897.PDF (last date accessed: 20 January 2006).

Verdin, K., 2000. Development of the National Elevation Dataset-Hydrologic Derivatives (NED-H), *Proceedings of the Environmental Systems Research Institute, Inc. Twentieth Annual ESRI International User Conference*, July 10–14, 2000, San Diego, California (CD-ROM).

Verdin, K., M. Cast, and S. Greenlee, 2004. Web-based tools for watershed delineation and characterization using EDNA, *Proceedings of the Environmental Systems Research Institute, Inc. Twentieth Annual ESRI International User Conference*, August 9–13, 2004, URL: http://gis.esri.com/library/userconf/proc04/abstracts/a1584.html (last date accessed: 25 January 2006).

Weisberg, R.H., and L. Zheng, 2005. Hurricane storm surge simulations for Tampa Bay, 42 p., URL: http://ocgweb.marine.usf.edu/Products/StormSurge/TB_stormsurge.pdf (last date accessed: 25 January 2006).

Chapter 5

Photogrammetry

J. Chris McGlone

TECHNOLOGY OVERVIEW

The photogrammetric production of DEMs has a long history, dating from the earliest days of photogrammetry, and involves a chain of technologies under continuous development. It has been transformed in recent years by the adoption of digital image acquisition, storage, and processing technologies, as well as Airborne Global Positioning System (ABGPS) and Inertial Measurement Unit (IMU) developments.

The photogrammetric process includes:
1. Project planning: selecting data acquisition parameters to ensure a satisfactory product;
2. Data acquisition: Obtaining the imagery and any ground control or other auxiliary information required;
3. Image georeferencing: Determining the position and orientation of all images, to allow their use for mapping;
4. Data collection: Extracting the required products from the imagery;
5. Post-processing and quality control: Preparation of the products for delivery.

This chapter covers the process and considerations in its use for the generation of digital elevation data.

SENSOR TYPES

Three types of sensors are currently used for photogrammetric mapping: airborne film cameras and airborne or satellite digital sensors. Aerial film photography remains the choice for the majority of projects, due to the large installed base and cost-effectiveness, but airborne digital systems are becoming more widely available and cost-effective, especially when used as the first component of fully digital workflows. While originally suitable only for small-scale mapping, the increasing resolution of satellite sensors has made their use feasible for larger scale applications.

Film Cameras

Film mapping cameras have been in use for decades. Continuous improvements in lenses, film, and construction have resulted in a mature technology producing micrometer-level accuracy. Current high-resolution mapping lenses have negligible distortions and precise color correction, taking full advantage of the film resolution. Image motion compensation removes the blur due to aircraft motion.

The standard film mapping camera has a 6-inch focal length lens and a 9 by 9-inch format. Its 90° field of view provides strong ray intersection geometry and therefore high accuracy for mapping. Focal lengths of 8.25 or 12 inches are generally used only to acquire imagery for digital orthoimage production, since using a longer focal length reduces image relief displacement and less effort is required to accurately mosaic overlapping orthoimages in urban areas. However, the longer focal lengths are not suitable for most topographic contouring or planimetric work, due to a proportionately lower accuracy in the vertical coordinate.

Aerial film is usually scanned with pixel sizes ranging from 10-30 micrometers, with 15 micrometers/pixel being typical. This is equivalent to roughly 1,700 dots per inch (dpi), although most image scanners support resolutions as high as 8 micrometers/pixel (3,000 dpi). This is a compromise between ensuring capture of image resolution and keeping storage manageable. At 1,700 dpi, a 9" x 9" format will result in roughly 15,000 x 15,000 pixels or 225MB for a black-and-white image (675MB for a color image). In situations where softcopy aerotriangulation is performed, it is not uncommon to scan at 3,000 dpi and either re-scan at 1,700 dpi or down-sample the images to a more manageable size for product generation. Moderate image compression may be used to reduce the image storage by 2-4X for panchromatic and 4-10X for color images.

There is no development work on film cameras at this point and they are leaving production, since their use can be expected to decline as the capital costs of airborne digital sensors decrease and fully-digital workflows become more common.

Satellite Imagery

High-resolution satellite imagery, 1m or less, is now available from a number of commercial remote sensing satellites (Table 5.1). The highest ground sample distance (GSD) currently available is 0.6 meters/pixel, with 0.4-0.5 meter GSD sensors planned for the near future. Satellite imagery is typically used for smaller-scale mapping, with 1m imagery usually specified for 1:24000 scale and smaller.

Table 5.1 Some current and planned commercial high-resolution satellites [Stoney, 2006].

Satellite	Company	Resolution (m)
Orbview 3	GeoEye (formerly Orbimage)	1.0
Ikonos 2	GeoEye (formerly SpaceImaging)	1.0
Quickbird 2	DigitalGlobe	0.6
Worldview 1 (planned 2007)	DigitalGlobe	0.5
GeoEye-1 (planned 2007)	GeoEye	0.41

Most current high-resolution commercial satellites employ a linear pushbroom imaging geometry in which the single-line image sensor is effectively a straight line perpendicular to the satellite track and scans a linear swath along the orbital track. The pointing direction of the sensor is steerable to either side of the orbital track and also fore and aft along the orbit. This capability increases the number of opportunities to cover any point on the ground, since a given area may be imaged from more than one orbit, and also allows stereo imaging. Satellite images have 11-12 bits of dynamic range and can also collect multispectral imagery, albeit at a four-times lower GSD than the panchromatic images.

Exploitation of satellite sensors is more complex than for frame cameras because of the dynamic acquisition geometry. Due to the complexity of the full physical model and the proprietary design information it reveals, the physical sensor models are usually not distributed or implemented; instead, a replacement or generic sensor model which is simpler to implement and use is derived from the original physical model. The generic sensor model takes the form of a set of rational polynomials which express the image coordinates in terms of latitude, longitude and elevation.

Stereo imagery can be collected in two modes, same-orbit and different-orbit. For same-orbit stereo the sensor must look forward and then pivot to look backwards at the same area on the ground. This provides the best stereo viewing, since the two images are nearly simultaneous, but the area which can be covered is limited by the maximum forward and backward look angles and the amount of time required to change the pointing angle. Different-orbit stereo provides the most flexibility in terms of acquisition, but the differing acquisition times may result in changes in the scene or atmospheric conditions.

Satellite imagery may be supplied as uncorrected imagery, as geo-rectified images corrected to a uniform elevation, orthorectified images corrected to an elevation model, or as stereo pairs ready to exploit. Some commercial triangulation packages support the block adjustment of multiple satellite images, possibly in conjunction with images of other sensors.

As with aerial imagery, the amount of cloud cover must be taken into account when acquiring satellite imagery. However, since satellites have less flexibility in timing overflights, it can be harder to obtain cloud-free stereo scenes. The ability to image from multiple orbits mitigates this somewhat, but it still can be an issue.

Airborne Digital Systems

An all-digital workflow has a number of advantages, both economic and practical. The elimination of film handling, processing, duplication and scanning greatly reduces production timelines and material expenses. Digital sensors can capture a broader dynamic range of scene intensities, allowing data collection from scenes collected with less than ideal lighting, shadows or highlights. In addition, many current sensors have the ability to collect both color and near-infrared, increasing the potential applications of the imagery. The main obstacle to adoption of airborne digital sensors up to now has been the inability to build an affordable sensor with enough pixels to give sufficient coverage and resolution for mapping applications. Advances in chip technology have now made large-format digital sensors possible.

While current chip technology is well established for area arrays of about 4Kx4K pixels, with some up to 9Kx9K, this is not a sufficient number of pixels for mapping purposes. Two main design approaches are therefore in use for airborne digital sensors: mosaiced area arrays and linear pushbroom sensors.

The mosaiced area array approach uses a number of area imagers with overlapping fields of view, arranged so that the combined image is equivalent to a single frame image. Two current examples are the Z/I Imaging DMC [Figure 5.1] and the Microsoft Vexcel UltraCam [Figure 5.2]. The DMC uses four panchromatic area arrays, along with four multispectral sensors and provides 12-bit radiometric resolution. Electronic image motion compensation and radiometric calibrations are applied to the final image, producing an ideal pinhole geometry. The Vexcel camera uses nine panchromatic sensors and four multispectral sensors, with electronic motion compensation and real-time tie point generation to ensure registration between the images. The final image is 11500 by 7500 pixels, with a 100mm focal length and 9 micrometer pixel size, giving 55° and 37° field of view in the cross-track and along-track directions, respectively. For both systems, once the final image has been formed (panchromatic, color, or false-color, or pan-sharpened) the frame geometry allows the use of standard photogrammetric software.

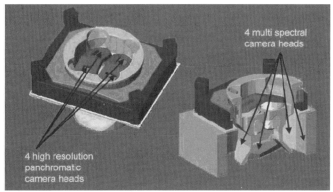

Figure 5.1 Optical configuration of the Z/I Imaging DMC camera. See color plate in Appendix C.

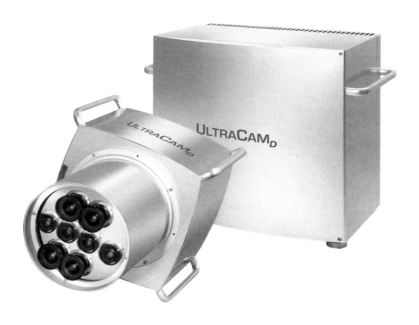

Figure 5.2 Microsoft Vexcel UltraCam large-format digital camera.

The Leica ADS40 is an example of a pushbroom aerial sensor. Multiple linear arrays, facing forward, down and aft, enable along-track stereo coverage as well as color and multispectral imaging [Figure 5.3]. Three separate stereo viewing combinations are available, due to the three panchromatic arrays. GSDs down to 15cm are obtained in standard operation, with 5cm possible in some circumstances. The exploitation of pushbroom imagery requires special sensor models and continuous GPS/IMU information.

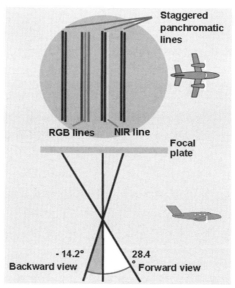

Figure 5.3 Focal plane of the Leica ADS40 showing the layout of the sensors. See color plate in Appendix C.

PLANNING CONSIDERATIONS

Planning for photogrammetric data acquisition must include considerations such as:
- Image resolution (scale) versus product scales.
- Leaf-on/leaf-off acquisition.
- The number and distribution of ground control points and/or checkpoints.
- GPS satellite constellation geometry.
- Atmospheric conditions and sun angle.

Project planning using traditional film cameras is well understood and parameterized, with most of the same considerations applying to digital airborne sensors. Planning for projects using satellite imagery is performed using vendor guidelines to identify the acquisition parameters that will produce the desired results.

Project planning has been made easier by in-flight control systems using GPS navigation which can now maintain very precise flightlines and trigger each exposure at pre-planned points to optimize coverage, overlap, or viewpoint. This reduces the necessity of adding extra frames or overlap to allow for possible navigation errors.

Image Resolution

The image resolution required is determined by the required product types and accuracies. In the case of film systems, various classes of accuracy for each product type are tied to photographic scale via ASPRS or user specifications. For satellites or digital airborne cameras, the concept of scale is replaced with the concept of ground sample distance (GSD), or image resolution. Thus, comparing film and digital systems is most easily done by comparing the GSD of each.

The GSD of an image is the size of a pixel projected to the ground surface and is reported as linear units/pixel, such as 1 meter/pixel, 1 foot/pixel, etc. For digital systems, it is a function of the focal length, altitude (or range from sensor to ground), and the size of a CCD element. In the case of film cameras, it is a function of the digitized image scanning resolution and the photographic scale.

Experience has shown that scanning resolutions of around 10 to 20 micrometers is sufficient in nearly all cases for DEM and planimetric extraction – both in terms of product accuracy and interpretation. Using the photographic scale and the scanning resolution, the GSD of a film system can be computed as:

GSD = (photographic scale) * (1 / dpi)

where photographic scale is expressed in feet/inch and the scanning resolution is in dots per inch. For example, a scanning resolution of 1,700 dpi at a photographic scale of 1" = 660' results in a GSD of 0.39 foot/pixel.

This same relationship can be used to determine the equivalent photographic scale of a satellite or digital airborne system if the GSD is known and the effective size of a CCD element is known. For example, assuming the CCD element to be 12 micrometers (2,117 dpi) and the GSD known to be 0.8 meters (2.6 feet), the equivalent photographic scale is 1" = 5,500 feet.

The GSD should not be confused with interpretive resolution. While it is true the GSD represents the ground footprint of a pixel, interpretation (identification) of linear features is often better than the GSD. Conversely, poor imaging conditions or low-contrast targets may mean that the effective resolution is less than the GSD.

Leaf-On/Leaf-Off Acquisition

Particularly at larger map scales, nearly all image acquisition must be performed during leaf-off periods to allow collection of bare-earth elevations. At smaller map scales, average tree crown heights may be used to reduce data to bare earth. If the elevation data is used only for digital orthoimage production, the leaf-off requirement may be dropped.

Ground Control Points

The number and distribution of ground control points is primarily based on the presence of bodies of water within the project and whether ABGPS/IMU data acquisition is employed. If ABGPS and IMU data are available, aerotriangulation can even be forgone for some projects and the control points will serve as quality control checkpoints.

ABGPS data dramatically diminishes the number of ground control points required for all types of projects since it essentially serves as additional control points during the aerotriangulation. Although the cost of aerotriangulation is generally less than 10% of the total cost of a project, obtaining ground control points can be a cost and logistics driver. It is often difficult to measure and panel control points, especially in dense urban areas. Paneling, if required, presents a logistics problem since it must be synchronized with flight missions.

The presence of large and/or numerous bodies of water may require additional cross-strips that help span the bodies of water or provide control up to the boundaries of the water. If complete stereomodels are not possible over water, additional control points will be required either side of the area.

Ground control points are generally marked with panels prior to flying. However, this can be time-consuming and costly. In some cases, photo-identifiable points can be used as control provided they can be easily identified and accurately measured at all required photographic scales for the project.

ABGPS Considerations

Flight planning with ABGPS in mind will alter the overall imagery coverage plan. Traditional cross-strips which maintain the rigor of the block are not generally required with ABGPS, only for irregularly shaped areas and/or included bodies of water. Time of day must be considered to ensure an adequate geometric configuration of GPS satellites. Current flight planning packages contain models of GPS satellite orbits and availability to ensure an adequate constellation.

Periods of solar flare activity, which interfere with GPS signals, must also be avoided.

Atmospheric Conditions and Sun Angle

While atmospheric conditions cannot be accurately predicted, they must be monitored as the data acquisition proceeds. Cloud-free days are required and, preferably, low haze conditions. For DEM generation, acquisition of imagery below the clouds can sometimes be considered provided illumination is still adequate to measure and interpret in low-contrast areas. Cloud coverage must be no more than 10% for most satellite applications. As noted earlier, this is perhaps the most limiting factor for satellite imagery in many areas of the world.

The sun should be at least 30° above the horizon to avoid long shadows within the scene which affect interpretability and image appearance, if orthoimagery is to be produced. The sun angle varies with the latitude of the project and time of year and can be calculated using flight planning software.

GEOREFERENCING AND AEROTRIANGULATION

Georeferenced images are defined as those in which 3D ground coordinates can be mathematically projected into the 2D image space, and vice-versa. No mapping of any type can begin until all acquired imagery is accurately tied to the ground reference frame. In most cases this requires aerotriangulation, but can sometimes be accomplished with the collection of Airborne GPS (ABGPS) and Inertial Measurement Unit (IMU) data.

Georeferenced images require a geometric sensor model that accurately models a number of components:
- Interior orientation.
- Transformation from film to digitized images for film cameras.

- Exterior orientation.
- Atmospheric affects
- Earth curvature or coordinate system compensation

Interior orientation establishes the internal geometry of the camera and includes such information as the camera's focal length, the location of the principal point in the image, the orientation of the image coordinate axes, and optical or film distortions. The principal point is defined as the intersection of the optical axis of the camera with the image and serves as the origin of the image coordinate system. Film cameras use fiducial marks in calibrated positions at the corners and sides of the format that are imaged onto the film. These marks define the origin and orientation of the image coordinate system and are also used to correct for film distortion. Lens distortion includes both radial and tangential components, although current lens designs reduce distortions to nearly-negligible levels. For digital imaging systems, both airborne and space-borne, the image coordinate system is defined by the lines and samples of the digital image itself.

In a softcopy environment, film photography is digitized using high-precision photogrammetric scanners. In this case, the fiducials must be measured in the digital image and the transformation from the pixels to the image coordinates defined. An affine (linear) transformation is generally used, but some types of scanners may require higher-order polynomial transformation or finite element modeling. In analytical stereoplotters, operators measure the fiducial coordinates and the instrument calculates the transformation tying the instrument coordinate system to the image coordinate system. Most softcopy workstations now have automated routines which recognize and measure fiducial marks without operator inputs.

The exterior orientation of an image refers to the position of the exposure station (camera lens center, or nodal point) and the angular attitude of the image coordinate system with respect to the ground coordinate frame. For a frame sensor, the exterior orientation is valid for the whole image, while in linear pushbroom or other dynamic acquisition geometries, the exposure station position and orientation change with each image line. The exterior orientation must therefore be modeled as a function of time, based on inputs from GPS and IMU measurements. Since GPS measurements occur at finite intervals, common approaches are to use splines, polynomials, or other interpolation methods to model the behavior of the exterior orientation between the discrete readings. When triangulating dynamic imagery, the parameters of the interpolation model are solved instead of the parameters themselves.

Atmospheric refraction alters the image coordinates of a ground object since the light ray bends as it moves through the atmosphere. Thus, image points need corrections to determine their actual (non-refracted) position. Standard atmospheric models and correction formulae are available [McGlone, 2004] and are applied by the triangulation program.

There are a number of choices for the project coordinate system, including latitude-longitude or various projected coordinate systems, such as UTM or state plane. If the coordinate system is a projection and the project covers a large area, earth curvature effects will be present. These are caused by representing the Z coordinate relative to a plane tangent to the earth's curved surface, instead of modeling Z relative to the ellipsoid or geoid. Some triangulation packages do their computations in geocentric or local tangent coordinates to avoid this problem; otherwise, an earth curvature correction must be applied.

ABGPS and IMU data can be combined to define the exterior orientation of images as long as the camera boresighting and antenna offsets are well calibrated and the ground coordinate and datum transformations are well-understood. If the ABGPS and IMU data are not sufficiently accurate to georeference the images involved in the project, then the aerotriangulation process will be required.

Aerotriangulation determines consistent orientation parameters for a block of imagery, minimizing errors between images which would lead to unacceptable parallax in the stereomodels and accurately relating the entire block to the world coordinate system using the minimum amount of control information possible. When ABGPS/IMU data is available, aerotriangulation may still be used to refine the relative orientation of the imagery, as a check on the ABGPS/IMU data, and to relate the navigation information to the world coordinate system datum.

Imagery to be triangulated is acquired in strips along flight lines and the strips aggregated into a block of imagery covering the project area. Imagery is overlapped along each strip, with at least 60% overlap required for stereo viewing. The strips, in turn, are flown parallel to one another and generally overlap adjoining strips by about 30% of the image width. With digital sensors, where acquiring additional images does not incur additional costs, many blocks are flown with 80-90% overlap in both directions. The additional redundant images enable automated matching methods to work better and allow a choice of images from different viewpoints for viewing particular points on the ground and for orthoimage production.

As input to the triangulation solution, a number of points are measured on the overlapping imagery:

- Control points with known horizontal, known vertical, or both horizontal and vertical positions.
- Pass points between photos in a strip.
- Tie points between photos in overlapping strips.

Most manual procedures focus on measuring pass points at the center, left center edge, and right center edge of each image along the direction of flight. This results in nearly all points falling in triple-overlap areas if the forward overlap is at least 60%. Tie points are measured at the tops and bottom edges of each image where strips overlap and thus many of these will appear on 4-6 images. The points will then appear as a 3 by 3 array on each image.

Most current triangulation packages incorporate automated tie point measurement techniques, where the software identifies well-defined points in the overlap areas and uses the approximate image orientations and image correlation to match the points between images. Large numbers of tie points can be produced, allowing bad matches to be removed while giving a very accurate triangulation solution.

Control points are accurately ground surveyed or located by GPS, and either chosen as well-defined photo-identifiable points, such as sidewalk corners, or are paneled prior to flying. In some cases, the panels are truly wood or plastic material, or if the point is on a street or parking lot, may be painted. Many different patterns are used to signalize ground control points, including crosses and discs. Control points must be chosen to be in localized flat areas, free of obstructions (such as overhanging trees or nearby structures), easily identified, and sized to be accurately measured based on the image scale.

Aerotriangulation packages simultaneously determine the ground coordinates of all measured points and exterior orientation elements using the method of least squares adjustment and the sensor's geometric model. This process yields a "best fit" of all parameters (ground coordinates, image measurements, and exterior orientation) and the statistical basis of the least squares approach yields estimation of accuracies of parameters at completion. All parameters generally include estimates of precision, which are used to evaluate the stability and rigor of the solution through the least squares process. The input parameters typically include:

- Ground control point coordinates.
- Image coordinate readings and their estimated precision.
- Estimates of exposure station position, such as from ABGPS.
- Modeling of ABGPS drift parameters and their estimated precision.
- Estimates of attitude, such as from IMU data.

The use of GPS for exterior orientation significantly strengthens the aerotriangulation results, particularly for smaller scale projects. Since the GPS positions effectively act as additional control points, blocks using GPS require fewer ground control points. Incorporation of IMU information, which measures the attitude of the sensor, results in somewhat more strength in the adjustment. Ground control point distribution throughout the block of images is generally focused on a number of horizontal/vertical control points along the edges of the block and a lesser number of points scattered in the center of the block. It is not unusual for only 10-12 control points to control a block of hundreds of images when ABGPS is employed.

Aerotriangulation software packages also support self-calibration, in which some of the sensor interior orientation parameters, the sensor boresight parameters, and the ABGPS/IMU drift parameters are determined as part of the solution. This models any changes between the calibrated parameters and the actual in-flight conditions.

With the ever-increasing reliance upon ABGPS/IMU instrumentation, automatic triangulation provides cost-efficient quality control for the navigation data by checking the results prior to production. At a minimum, this capability can be used to assess the relative orientation of images to one another before detailed operator inspection of suspect areas is required. At its fullest, it stands to decrease triangulation timeframes and cost if they are required.

PHOTOGRAMMETRIC DATA COLLECTION METHODS

Both manual and automated methods are used for photogrammetric collection of digital elevation models. In practice, collection tends to be a combination of both, with the exact proportions determined by the project scale, the characteristics of the scene, and the available production facilities.

In the past, DEM production was primarily focused on producing topographic contours. However, the increasing emphasis on digital orthoimage production over the past decade, as well as GIS and other applications which utilize digital terrain data, have made elevation rasters the most common product.

Orthoimage DEMs require significantly less time and cost to produce as compared to DEMs generated to support contour generation. Since many projects involve both feature (planimetric) data production in addition to general elevation data and digital orthoimages, it is difficult to determine the cost of the DEM generation itself. Many production techniques will use planimetric collection to initialize the DEM generation by extracting elevations from the planimetric data, which is generally collected in 3D with feature coding useful in determination of usable "bare earth" points.

Digital correlation techniques have been employed in production for at least a decade, but are not in heavy use as yet for projects at larger map scales. However, hybrid approaches to projects can be both cost-effective and expedient. An example is the use of digital correlation to produce DEMs for digital orthoimages at the smaller scales required by such projects. These DEMs can be collected quickly and accurately over some types of terrain and allow production of the smaller scale digital orthoimages far in advance of the planimetric, topographic, and digital orthoimages at the larger scales.

Analytical Stereoplotters

A significant amount of current-day stereoscopic compilation still uses film viewed in analytical stereoplotters. A large body of experience with these systems and their products keeps them in production. From an economic standpoint, the capital costs have long been amortized, with the main cost drivers now being the maintenance costs of the hardware and electronics and the productivity penalty of not fitting easily into an all-digital workflow, in terms of data handling and lack of automation.

Softcopy Stereoplotters

Softcopy systems were first introduced into the commercial production environment in the early 1990's and at this point have replaced most analytical instruments. The advantages of softcopy workstations over analytical stereoplotters are:
- Stereoscopic graphics superimposition of all types of geospatial data over the imagery.
- Ability to use either digitized film imagery or digitally acquired imagery.

- Ability to easily perform collection of feature data from digital orthoimages or utilize digital orthoimages as a backdrop to collection activity.
- Ability to be used in common office environments, though subdued lighting is still preferred or even required in some cases.
- No requirement to use model setup or index points.
- Ease of hardware and/or software upgrading to keep up with progress in technology.
- Relatively free sitting and head position for the user as compared to analytical systems.

The disadvantages of softcopy are:

- Transition by trained compilers familiar with analytical instruments.
- Arguably less stereo viewing quality than film-viewing systems.
- Film scanning is required for projects flown with film cameras.

The greatest advantage of softcopy workstations is perhaps their ability to overlay graphics data in a stereoscopic environment. In the context of DEM generation, this means that all elevation points and even contours can be superimposed for review against the actual ground form. The ability to review existing, new, and changed data is easier if all can be selectively reviewed in the same stereoscopic display [Figure 5.4].

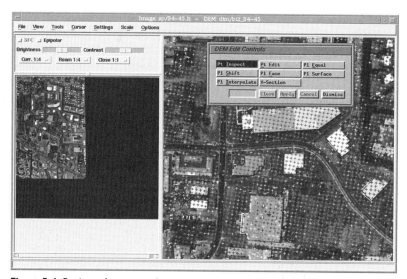

Figure 5.4 Review of automated terrain extraction by superimposing color-coded crosses to show post accuracies (Courtesy of Boeing). See color plate in Appendix C.

Softcopy workstations are now moving toward integration with GIS or CAD packages. Collecting and editing data directly within the final application package has the advantage of avoiding errors and effort in data translation. Workstation costs have decreased as functionality has become more specialized. Early softcopy workstations often included all triangulation, collection, and editing functions; the current approach is to provide lower-cost workstations optimized only for collection, supported by a smaller number of general purpose workstations or by specialized triangulation, editing, or management stations.

The all-digital workflow has enabled new efficiencies, but managing the massive volume of image and product data has led to its own set of problems. The requirements of distributing imagery to the various workstations, then collecting, merging, and editing the extracted data products, while tracking the progress of the project through the system, has motivated the development of digital data and project management systems.

Data management systems include large amounts of data storage, often with terabyte capacities, and a database system which maintains the metadata. This metadata includes the acquisition parameters, sensor and GPS data, as well as versioning and processing history for the imagery itself. Due to the critical nature of the data and the impact on production should the server have problems, the systems are often configured with redundant disk storage to cope with the failure of any one component. Project management software allows the manager to assign specific images or areas to each operator, to monitor progress, and to generate cost and time estimates for completion of the project.

Manual Elevation Compilation

There are several standard approaches to collecting elevation data:

- Capturing spot elevations and breaklines.
- A digital elevation matrix is collected, augmented with breaklines and spot elevations.
- If planimetric compilation is also being performed, the elevation data may be initialized from the planimetric data, with spot elevations and breaklines added as needed to finalize the DEM.

If planimetric data are not part of the overall project, or if it is scheduled at a later date, most mapping firms will use skilled operators to focus on the collection of breaklines and spot elevations. A breakline is defined as a polyline that defines a slope reversal along its extent and may include both naturally-occurring and man-made features. Common examples of breaklines include ridges, valleys, edges of embankments, edges of rivers, curbs/gutters, etc. Breaklines are augmented by spot elevations in areas devoid of natural or man-made breaks in the terrain surface. A number of spot elevations are collected at identifiable points for later checking and are also collected at local maxima and minima that are not represented by a contour line. The advantage of this approach is that the minimum amount of points required to describe the terrain is collected. The fewer points collected, the more quickly editing can be performed and finishing completed. If a digital workstation is used, it is common to periodically produce the contours in the stereoscopic view to ensure that sufficient points and breaklines have been collected.

Some mapping firms use a grid or profile approach to the collection of elevation data, augmenting as needed with breaklines and spot elevations. This is most common in very smooth areas where it is difficult to ensure that subtle changes in the terrain elevation are captured. It is also the most common approach and final format for smaller map scales.

If planimetric data are part of the overall project, in addition to a DEM and/or contours, then it is common to first collect the attributed feature data and then derive the elevation points by filtering feature codes for appropriate data. Since most planimetric features are collected at the ground level, their codes can be used to extract elevations and even breaklines (such as along a river edge or road edge). Generally only a small number of additional breaklines are collected. However, a relatively large amount of spot elevations may be added, sometimes using a rough grid to ensure the terrain form is captured.

Automated Elevation Collection

Automatic collection of DEMs by means of digital image correlation has been a topic of research and implementation for over 40 years. As more powerful desktop computers have become available, more robust and intensive algorithms have been implemented. Automated collection has mostly been applied to smaller-scale projects, with wider applicability as users gain experience.

Many issues dealing with the management and editing of automatically-collected elevation data are similar to those with the processing of data derived from lidar systems. Both approaches yield a large number of elevation points, including erroneous values and noise, which may tax standard terrain elevation modeling packages tailored to traditional compilation approaches. Advances in thinning large numbers of points and reducing elevations on man-made structures to "bare earth" in both disciplines will inevitably pay off for both.

Automatically deriving elevations by digital correlation amounts to directly comparing pixel patches on conjugate images or indirectly comparing features derived from the digital images.

Direct comparison techniques were the first to be researched, with increasing work done in comparing derived information, such as edge features in the images. Edge/feature collection techniques tend to be superior in large scale projects, with area-based techniques more common for smaller scale projects. Newer techniques employ hybrid approaches that attempt to take advantage of the best of each.

Successfully employing automated approaches in day-to-day production requires an understanding of the strengths and weaknesses of the technology as a whole. General strengths include:

- Ability to generate a very dense array of elevation points in short periods of time in an unattended mode.
- Generally good capture of the overall surface of a ground scene.
- Generally high quality results at high accuracies.
- Very good results at smaller map scales (lower resolutions).

General statements on weaknesses are:

- The need to edit large amounts of data that does not necessarily reflect what would be captured interactively by a human stereocompiler. Skilled stereocompilers collect mass points and breaklines that model the terrain with essentially a minimal set of data. Digitally correlated data produces a sampling of elevations without regard to breaklines, etc.
- Even small percentages of false or erroneous data can yield editing times in excess of the time required to interactively capture the data.
- Necessity to "tune" various collection parameters for specific areas of a project or the project as a whole.
- Difficulty in effectively using data for larger product scales.

Strengths and weaknesses can be parlayed into a number of practical usages in a production system:

- Generation of elevation models for large areas at smaller product scales (generally 1:20,000 and smaller), where less effort is required to reduce elevations to a "bare earth" model. This also applies to extreme flat or smooth areas.
- Capture of digital surface models (DSMs), as opposed to bare earth digital terrain models (DTMs), for visualization database generation.
- Generation of DSMs adequate for fast production of interim digital orthoimages at most scales.
- Automatic assessment of changes in surfaces over periods of time – such as for production planning efforts or elevation model updates.

Area-based techniques tend to focus on the extraction of elevations on a roughly gridded basis in ground space, while feature-based techniques tend to produce data at discrete objects and along linear or area features.

Digital correlation is often used to quickly develop a surface over large areas, leaving final editing to softcopy workstations. This approach supports interim or expedited delivery of digital orthoimages, with the softcopy compilation used to develop breakline information required for topographic contours. For smaller map scales, this approach can be very effective. At larger map scales, the approach becomes marginally effective since extensive editing of the digital correlation data may exceed the time to perform softcopy compilation from the beginning.

POST-PROCESSING AND QUALITY CONTROL

Post-processing of photogrammetrically-derived DEMs may be required for several reasons:
- Editing of elevation data generated by digital correlation.
- Generation of contours from elevation data.
- Conversion between elevation data formats.

The amount of interactive editing required in the case of digital correlation becomes the limiting factor on this automated approach. Typical problem areas include:
- Reduction of elevations to bare earth in urban areas or heavily vegetated areas.
- Editing of error-prone areas, such as those containing minimal contrast and extensive localized variations in elevation that produce "noisy" contours. This is especially true for very small contour intervals.
- Failure to capture sufficient detail around natural and/or man-made breaklines.
- False correlations (erroneous elevations) in low-contrast and low-content areas.
- Failure to provide a sufficiently detailed boundary between land and bodies of water.

Most digital correlation applications have correlation parameters which can be tuned to optimize the processing for particular types of projects, or even areas within projects. For instance, elevation capture in urban areas with many vertical areas uses different slope tolerances than for areas with rolling terrain. In addition, familiarization with the characteristics of each digital correlation algorithm and package yields editing procedures that focus in on known problems. Bulk editing functions such as correcting water body boundaries and reducing elevations from the treetops in a forest to bare earth are often developed and tailored to the digital correlation approach.

Generation of contours from elevation data is mostly automated but still involves significant manual editing to produce contours which are aesthetically pleasing (smoothed) and conform to cartographic representation principles, such as:
- Ensuring that contours cross breaklines at correct angles and are "pointed" toward higher elevations.
- Ensuring that contours do not cross or overlap in rugged terrain.
- Placement of intermediate contours in slowly-varying terrain for better representation.
- Placement of spot elevations to mark local minima and maxima and to serve as reference elevations at periodic intervals.

Depending upon the end-user requirements, native DEM forms and formats may require conversion or translation. For example, mapping at larger scales nearly always requires breaklines and spot elevations to ensure proper contour generation, which generally involves some type of TIN (Triangulated Irregular Network) format. Some deliverables, however, require a gridded elevation data set which must be extracted from the TIN data.

Quality control of photogrammetrically-produced DEMs requires both statistical and visual procedures:
- Statistical sampling of elevations measured at checkpoints and/or control points.
- Inspection of contours and/or TIN surfaces graphically and/or overlayed on stereo imagery.

In most cases, control and/or checkpoints are provided by the mapping service customer and are checked by the mapping firm and/or the customer. If aerotriangulation is utilized, most mapping firms also select photo-identifiable tie and pass points to be carried along in the production process as quality control points. These points are then used to check compilation measurements, as elevation check values against those interpolated from the DEM model, and as horizontal check points on digital orthoimages.

Proper behavior of contours also present a quick visual check against the quality of the DEM itself. A number of software packages also provide the capability to visualize the TIN surface (triangle sides) to determine conformance to the ground surface.

DATA DELIVERABLES

Data deliverables are a function of the end-user's requirements. A DEM may itself be a deliverable or may be delivered as supporting data, e.g., as part of an orthoimage project. Standard DEM formats include:

- Gridded (raster) elevation data, including elevation profiles.
- TIN (triangulated irregular network) data.
- Mass point and breakline data.

DEMs are defined as "bare earth," in which case they are usually referred to as digital terrain models (DTMs), or "surface," referred to as digital surface models (DSMs) and including treetops and rooftops. Topographic contouring requires elevations on the bare earth, whereas DEMs for digital orthoimages do not necessarily require this in all areas. The term "surface model" is often used for DEMs in which the tops of all surface features are captured as opposed to bare earth; this is common for raw lidar and digitally correlated data sets. For digital orthoimage generation, it is entirely acceptable to use elevations on the top of forest canopies at smaller scales (as opposed to lowering elevations to the underlying bare earth) if the required planimetric (horizontal) accuracy of the resulting digital orthoimage can still be achieved. Large man-made features such as buildings and bridges require special treatment so that "smearing" or "fracturing" of the features on overlapping orthoimages does not occur. During the orthoimage generation process, any point on the ground can be mapped to multiple pixels in the input image due to obscurations along the line-of-sight defined by an image point and the elevation surface. The degree to which smearing or fracturing occurs depends both upon the robustness of the elevation model and the exact process used to generate the orthoimage. The digital orthoimage process inevitably requires some massaging of the DEM to ensure no smearing or fracturing occurs. Depending on the complexity required, the localized DEMs may or may not be retained in the final DEM data set. Bridges on orthoimages often have an erroneous "hourglass" shape when draped over a bare earth DTM, requiring breaklines at the edges of the bridge deck to correct the distortion, as shown in Figures 5.5 and 5.6.

Figure 5.5 Digital orthophoto showing bridge distorted by use of bare earth DTM only (Courtesy of Dewberry). **Figure 5.6** Digital orthophoto showing bridge corrected by use of DTM with breaklines (Courtesy of Dewberry).

See color plates in Appendix C.

Gridded models are often used for smaller map scale projects, particularly state, province and national mapping programs at scales of 1:20,000 or smaller. These are easy to use (simple indexing) and to convert from one file format to another. However, they are not always appropriate for contour generation, which requires breaklines of some type. If contours are required, or if breaklines are required around bridges and large structures, the gridded data is augmented with at least localized TIN information.

Mass points are generally intermediate products and are relatively easy to convert from one specific data file format to another. However, they are more difficult to deal with in terms of indexing. They are often imported into or exported from TIN packages for use and are not commonly delivered unless accompanied by breaklines.

TIN models are the best way to represent terrain for contouring and are also most suitable for digital orthoimages at larger map scales. A TIN represents the terrain surface as a set of triangles; the stored data consists of the triangle vertices and the links between them. TINs are a very efficient terrain representation, but TIN data file formats are more difficult to convert to/from since they tend to be software package-specific. The large amount of points generated by digital correlation and lidar systems may overwhelm the capacity of standard TIN packages.

SUPPORTING TECHNOLOGIES

A discussion of photogrammetric approaches requires a review of the supporting technologies that impact production processes: image scanners and ABGPS/IMU instrumentation.

Image Scanners

With accurate, high-quality, and high-speed systems now available, production companies can continue to utilize both hardcopy and softcopy compilation to meet project cost and schedules requirements and to extend the useful life of existing film cameras. Image scanning systems have progressed in the following critical areas over the last decade:

- Scanning speed has increased from roughly 30 minutes per image to only 3-5 minutes for high-resolution color and black-and-white imagery.
- Automated roll-feeders allow completely unattended operation, approaching 24x7 operation.
- Accuracies on the order of 0.2 pixel or better are common. In a softcopy environment, this is sufficient to support both aerotriangulation and product generation.
- Advances in digital sensor subsystems are ensuring the capture of film information of at least 8 bits/pixel. In addition, 10+ bits/pixel are offered by most vendors.
- Cost-efficiency and reliability are continuously increasing.

A single image scanner is now capable of nearly keeping up with film collection rates. At a capture speed of 4 minutes per image, 200+ images can be scanned in a 24-hour period with minimal operator intervention. Scanning speed is also now on a par with network transfer speeds, ensuring readiness for use in aerotriangulation.

Older scanners were often very sensitive to capture settings and yielded substandard results unless extreme care was exercised. In addition, older digital camera technology, that introduced noise into the digital image, has been replaced with improved technology that has dramatically increased the signal-to-noise ratio. With increased dynamic range and quality, settings are less critical and results are more consistent.

The increased dynamic range allows for activities such as "digital dodging" and reduces dependence upon capture settings. Sun illumination angles and atmospheric haze combine to produce brightness and contrast trends across the images. This interferes with the mosaicking of digital orthoimages and also hampers digital correlation and stereoscopic compilation. With the increased dynamic range, dodging can be performed with more computational latitude, and more effective digital dodging can be performed.

ABGPS/IMU Instrumentation

Photogrammetrists first began using ABGPS to augment aerotriangulation roughly a decade ago to record accurate positions for all exposure stations. With ABGPS, fewer ground control points are necessary because exposure stations can effectively function as control points in the aerotriangulation process. Though this reduced the amount of ground control necessary, lack of known camera attitude still prevented attainment of the final goal: elimination of the aerotriangulation step. Advanced IMU systems can now provide attitudes accurate to 0.2-0.4 arc-minutes. Combining this with the better than 0.5 foot GPS accuracy, aerotriangulation can be eliminated for larger map scales for some applications. For example, for 1"=660' photographic scale, IMU measurements will provide an angular pointing and positioning accuracy of roughly 0.4' on the ground, satisfying requirements for 2' contour generation.

At a minimum, integrated ABGPS/IMU can provide sufficient accuracy, without aerotriangulation, to meet nearly all ASPRS Class II and most Class I specifications [ASPRS, 1990] for some products, including DEMs. In addition, aerotriangulation based on ABGPS/IMU instrumentation would require only minimal control points to attain Class I for all projects. This technology is also extremely critical to the proper execution of lidar and digital airborne imaging systems. When using ABGPS/IMU systems, care must be taken to achieve reliable results. Atmospheric disturbances, poor GPS satellite constellation geometry during data collection, or other system discrepancies can lead to poor results.

CALIBRATION PROCEDURES

Calibration generally applies to the instrumentation used to obtain the imagery and its supporting data. Procurers of mapping services must determine whether complete system calibration is required or whether a component-level calibration approach is to be taken. Unfortunately, when taking into consideration all available types of imaging systems, a common component-level calibration approach is essentially impossible. Approaches to system calibration include utilizing more check points in the project or focusing on a pilot area and scrutinizing product results.

Calibration of data capture systems, such as analytical and softcopy compilation workstations, amounts to first certifying that the mathematical parameterizations in these workstations reflects perfectly the acquisition system and any aerotriangulation results. Secondarily, procedures to convert captured data to the final DEM format should be reviewed and approved.

Film Systems

The U.S. calibration standard for film cameras is laboratory calibration by the U.S. Geological Survey. Calibration certificates for film cameras include:
- Calibrated focal length.
- Offset of the intersection of the optical (collimated) axis with the nominal center of the film format.
- Fiducial mark coordinates.
- Radial and tangential lens distortion.

Certifications of the camera system are done regularly, often annually, and reporting formats from a variety of international agencies and private groups are standard and convertible from one to another. Current cameras are now of such high metric quality that lens distortions amount to no more than a few micrometers.

If ABGPS and IMU instrumentation is to be used with a camera system, the relationship between these and the aircraft and cameras must also be considered, including:
- Surveying of GPS antenna positions and IMU device relative to the camera in the aircraft reference frame.
- Calibration, or boresighting, of the IMU with respect to the camera's optical axis.

In normal practice, the GPS antenna positions and IMU positions are surveyed relative to the aircraft reference frame by land survey techniques, easily yielding offset accuracies on the order of 0.1 foot or less. Boresighting, on the other hand, requires a procedure involving a well-controlled range and multiple overflights on a periodic basis. The angular resolution of the IMU, on the order of 0.1 arc-minute or better, is impossible to calibrate in other than an *in situ* manner. The result of boresighting is a set of angular offsets of the IMU reference axes relative to the camera's image coordinate system.

Boresighting is accomplished by flying a controlled range (an area containing a large number of control points) using forward and reverse strips and multiple cross strips. The imagery is then triangulated and the angular alignment differences computed by comparing the orientations from the IMU and the triangulation. The triangulation process must use the most stringent of approaches and often involves some level of self-calibration, including parameters such as antenna and IMU positional offsets to the aircraft reference frame.

Depending on the exact mounting of the IMU device, boresighting may have to be carried out both at a local range and also prior to, or following, missions over project areas. If the IMU device is mounted in a position and manner that precludes inadvertent contact, it will be stable for long periods of time and generally is only boresighted every few months. If, on the other hand, it is mounted in an open area susceptible to being bumped or interfered with, it may require boresighting for every project or flight.

Digital Airborne Systems

Frame digital systems, in which all pixels are captured in a manner analogous to a film camera exposure, use calibration procedures analogous to those of film cameras [Kröpfl, et al, 2004]. However, as with satellites, airborne linear pushbroom systems require the sensor to be in motion before they can form an image. This makes complete laboratory calibration impossible, so test-range calibration is the method of choice. Most digital airborne systems depend upon ABGPS/IMU instrumentation and require the same boresighting calibration as film systems.

Satellite Systems

Satellite imaging systems are calibrated on-orbit by imaging test ranges at periodic intervals [Mulawa, 2004]. The calibration includes orbital parameters as well as geometric and radiometric parameters, allowing long-term monitoring and characterization of sensor performance. Due to the proprietary nature of the sensor-specific physical parameters and the complex nature of the sensor models, this calibration is performed only by the imagery provider. End-users must use statistical sampling of checkpoints to ensure overall adherence to accuracy specifications, or perform pilot projects to prove system accuracy.

CAPABILITIES AND LIMITATIONS

If bare earth elevations are required, DEM generation by photogrammetric means is generally only hampered or cost-constrained by dense vegetative coverage. In the case of seasonal tree coverage, such as from deciduous trees, leaf-off conditions are required. Even with leaf-off conditions, however, obtaining sufficient measurements through the trees will be time-consuming and costly.

The primary advantages of the photogrammetric approach are:
- The imagery can be re-used for other purposes, such as planimetric data extraction.
- The imagery can always be used to correct errors of commission and omission at a later time.
- Steps such as editing and finishing can always rely upon a stereomodel to resolve discrepancies and correct errors to the highest accuracy the system provides.
- A proven and well-understood approach.

COMPARISONS WITH COMPETING/COMPLEMENTARY TECHNOLOGIES

Ground surveying is generally less cost-effective than photogrammetric mapping and has largely been abandoned for all but the smallest projects. The main alternative to photogrammetric mapping is therefore lidar data capture or some combination of the two [Baltsavias, 1999].

Lidar instrumentation and processing has moved from infancy to maturity over the last few years. This technology is another tool for use by mapping companies and has advantages and disadvantages for virtually every project relative to the photogrammetric approach. As time and experience with lidar collection has progressed, it is common to see both it and photogrammetric means utilized in the same project to optimize schedule and cost.

Advantages of lidar include:
- Fast capture of large amounts of elevation data
- Capture of high amounts of detail
- Smaller field of view yielding less problems with obscuration (from buildings, rugged terrain, etc.)
- Direct digital capture of data
- Ability to "see through" the trees substantially better than photogrammetric approaches
- Adequate accuracy for all but the very largest scales
- More leeway on flight conditions (under cloud cover, day/night, etc.)

Lidar's disadvantages, relative to the photogrammetric approach are:
- Processing large amounts of data – generally hundreds of times more information than collected with photogrammetric means. This means more editing time and more specialized software. Editing of data can become extensive enough that it exceeds that of photogrammetric capture using skilled operators.
- Most elevations are at the surface of man-made features (such as tops of buildings) and must be reduced to "bare earth" for use in topographic mapping and for DEM generation in general. Though some automated techniques have been developed for filtering data down to bare earth, this increases editing times in areas that can be quickly collected by skilled operators – vegetation-free areas and urban areas specifically.
- The narrow field of view requires more flight time. This is countered, however, by the day/night and somewhat all-weather collection capability of lidar.
- Accuracy is acceptable for nearly all products, but high accuracies at large scales are still problematical – such as 1 foot contours. This is partly due to smoothing of the data to an accurate, but representative surface, and also the fact that lidar elevations are an average over a finite spot size on the ground. If the spot size is too large relative to the vertical accuracy requirement, especially in rugged areas, the product specification may not be met.
- Contours generated by lidar automated processes generally lack the smooth appearance of contours compiled manually by photogrammetrists who follow principles of cartographic representation. This is especially true for lidar-generated contours along shorelines of rivers and the manner in which contour lines cross over river surfaces to the other side.
- Lidar requires high-quality ABGPS and IMU data. Balky equipment, atmospheric conditions, or poor ABGPS results can invalidate a flight and require re-collection. Photogrammetric approaches often use IMU data as an enhancement to processing, whereas lidar requires it to project range data to ground coordinates. Re-collection may not be required by photogrammetric approaches provided sufficient ground control is available for aerotriangulation.
- Without imagery, the checking of data and resolving of elevation ambiguities becomes problematical. Photogrammetric mapping provides a fall-back to re-collecting elevation data at a later time. For this reason, many lidar systems utilize companion digital cameras, or overlapping film coverage.

Lidar's ability to see through trees is one of the primary reasons it may be selected over photogrammetric means. By inspecting the multiple returns associated with each point, the ground surface can often be determined as opposed to the elevations at the top of the trees. Dense broad-leaf trees in leaf-off condition will likely be amenable to lidar whereas a leaf-on condition may preclude the sensor seeing the ground. Densely populated areas of evergreens generally hamper the use of both lidar and photogrammetry.

USER APPLICATIONS

Uses of photogrammetrically-derived DEMs generally fall into several classes:

- Topographic mapping.
- GIS applications.
- Generation of digital orthoimages.
- Engineering requirements.

Contours are either delivered in digital form (as polylines and spot elevations) or in topographic line map form, which is the most common. Other than smaller map scales, contours are nearly always derived from TIN data models.

GIS applications of photogrammetrically-derived DEMs have become widespread, for uses such as slope and runoff analysis and viewshed delineation. Digital orthoimages have become popular for use as base layers in GIS systems, since they provide visual context for the other data layers and allow additional planimetric detail to be derived as required. Accurate digital orthoimage databases can be used to derive reasonably accurate planimetric data in an expedient manner

Some projects call for the generation of "true orthoimages," where building lean is removed and the building sides are not visible. To produce a true orthoimage, building models are added to the terrain surface. This allows the displacement of buildings due to their height to be removed, since the roof is modeled at its correct elevation. Occluded and shadowed areas are filled in using imagery from other viewpoints.

Engineering efforts at larger scales nearly always require the delivery of a TIN-like dataset, minimally as a set of breaklines and spot elevations. At smaller scales, generally for planning, gridded elevation data sets are used. Some engineering projects also require the delivery of elevation profiles, which may be derived from TIN data. In some cases, such as highway projects requiring profiles along planned centerlines or perpendicular to the centerlines, data is sometimes directly compiled as profiles. In this case, elevations are measured along programmed azimuths in stereocompilation equipment at each break in the terrain.

COST CONSIDERATIONS

Costs for photogrammetrically-derived elevation models are mainly determined by scale requirements and the area covered, with additional expense added by the amount of dense urban areas and vegetative cover within a project. Dense urban areas present major challenges to DEM generation and may rule out automated correlation techniques, although recent work with highly-overlapping imagery and well-tuned correlation parameters may allow some success. However, skilled compilers are often required to make urban collection cost-effective. If planimetric compilation is part of the overall project, feature codes are used to determine elevations and breakline information from previously collected planimetric data. In this case, the incremental cost to producing DEMs supporting contouring is relatively low.

Dense vegetative cover or trees will always increase the cost of elevation model extraction but leaf-off imagery exploited by experienced compilers can reduce the additional cost.

TECHNOLOGICAL ADVANCEMENTS

It is safe to predict that all-digital workflows will be adopted at an increasing pace, as the initial capital costs of digital sensors decrease, and that processing and storage costs will also continue their steady decline. Optimization of airborne and satellite image acquisition will leave the most potential for improvement in the areas of automated data extraction, systems for the management of large volumes of data and the associated workflows, and in data distribution systems.

Effective digital imaging systems designed for mapping, both airborne and satellite, will diminish the exploitation timeline for mapping firms by eliminating the film scanning step and enabling a fully-digital workflow. The replacement of film cameras by digital sensors has already begun, and can be expected to accelerate as initial capital costs for digital sensors decrease and associated productivity gains increase.

Advances in automated data extraction will provide cost and time savings as productivity improvements are incorporated into the photogrammetric process. Automation thus far has been most successful for ancillary operations, such as fiducial mark and tie point measurement, with automated elevation extraction effective for some, but not all, scenes. Continuing algorithm refinement, probably based on new image acquisition techniques made possible by digital sensors, will improve performance across a wider variety of scenes. Increased operational experience will allow users to apply automated techniques more effectively and productively.

At the current time, much of the DEM and planimetric data collection is "stereomodel-centric" within a production flow. Most production entities collect data in stereomodels, merge models into areas representing mapsheets, and then merge mapsheets into total project data models. As elevation and feature data models become more sophisticated and as data handling becomes more sophisticated, operation in a seamless environment will become more viable. Seamless data storage and access, coupled with transactional concepts such as automated merging, will make data generation more efficient and cost-effective. Finishing steps can be better integrated into the collection step to catch and resolve errors of commission and omission immediately, while data collected in previous stereomodels can be quickly brought into new stereomodels to be reviewed and extended.

AUTHOR BIOGRAPHY

Chris McGlone received a PhD in Photogrammetry from Purdue University in 1980 and since then has focused his career on the integration of photogrammetry and computer vision techniques. His employers have included H. Dell Foster Associates, Loral Fairchild, Carnegie Mellon University, and currently SAIC. He was a co-founder of TerraSim, Inc., a producer of visual simulation database construction software. McGlone was Editor-in-Chief of the Fifth Edition of the *Manual of Photogrammetry*, published by the American Society for Photogrammetry and Remote Sensing, and a co-author of the textbook *Introduction to Modern Photogrammetry*. He was the 2004 recipient of the ASPRS Photogrammetric Award (Fairchild).

ACKNOWLEDGMENTS

The author wishes to acknowledge the contributions of Craig Molander of Surdex Corporation who authored the Photogrammetry chapter in the 1st edition of this manual, portions of which have been reused and updated for this 2nd edition.

REFERENCES

ASPRS, 1990. ASPRS accuracy standards for large-scale maps, *Photogrammetric Engineering and Remote Sensing*, 56(7): 1068-1070.

ASPRS, 2000. *Camera Calibration Panel Report,* American Society for Photogrammetry and Remote Sensing, Bethesda, MD, 2000.

Baltsavias, E.M., 1999. A comparison between photogrammetry and laser scanning, *ISPRS Journal of Photogrammetry and Remote Sensing,* 54:83-94.

Bureau of the Budget, 1947. *National Map Accuracy Standards*, Office of Management and Budget, Washington, D.C.

DOD, 2000. *Performance Specification Digital Terrain Elevation Data (DTED)*, MIL-PRF-89020B, U.S. Department of Defense, Washington, D.C., 23 May, 2000.

Kröpfl, M. et al, 2004. Geometric calibration of the digital large format aerial camera Ultracam, *International Archives of Photogrammetry and Remote Sensing* XXXV-B1:42-44, 2004.

McGlone, J.C., 2004. *Manual of Photogrammetry*, Fifth Edition (J.C. McGlone, editor), American Society for Photogrammetry and Remote Sensing, Bethesda, MD, 2004.

Mulawa, D., 2004. On-orbit geometric calibration of the Orbview-3 high resolution imaging satellite, *International Archives of Photogrammetry and Remote Sensing* XXXV-B1:1-6.

Pacey, Roger, M. Scheidt, A.S. Walker, 1999. Calibration of analog and digital airborne sensors at LH Systems, Paper presented at 1999 ASPRS Annual Conference, Portland, Oregon.

Stoney, W.E., 2006. *Guide to Land Imaging Satellites,* American Society for Photogrammetry and Remote Sensing, http://www.asprs.org/news/satellites/ (accessed 27 July 2006).

U.S. Army Corps of Engineers, 1993. U.S. Army Corps of Engineers (USACE) Engineer Manual 1110-1-1000, *Photogrammetric Mapping*.

USGS, 1998. *Standards for Digital Elevation Models*, U.S. Department of the Interior, U.S. Geological Survey, National Mapping Division, Washington, D.C., January, 1998. URL: http://rockyweb.cr.usgs.gov/nmpstds/demstds.html (accessed 27 July, 2006).

Chapter 6

Interferometric Synthetic Aperture Radar (IFSAR)

Scott Hensley, Riadh Munjy, and Paul Rosen

TECHNOLOGY OVERVIEW

The last two decades has seen the development from initial concept to commercial systems of a mapping technology based on interferometric synthetic aperture radar (SAR). Conventional SAR has been used extensively since its inception in the late 1950's for fine resolution mapping and remote sensing applications [Elachi, 1988]. Operating at microwave frequencies (3-40,000 MHz) these systems are used to generate imagery that provides a unique look at the electromagnetic and structural properties of the surface being imaged, at day or night and in nearly all weather conditions. Conventional SAR systems typically measure only two image coordinates. One coordinate is measured along an axis oriented parallel to the flight direction while the other coordinate is the range (or distance) from the SAR to the point being imaged. By augmenting a conventional SAR system to have two spatially separated antennas in the cross-track plane it is possible to measure the three dimensional location of imaged points to a high degree of accuracy. Measurement of the third coordinate is based on an interferometric technique developed in the radio astronomy community over several decades for fine angular measurements. Combining of SAR and interferometry techniques into a single system is called interferometric synthetic aperture radar (IFSAR or sometimes referred to as InSAR or ISAR).

The main objectives of this chapter are to provide DEM users with an overview of how SAR and IFSAR systems work, what are the advantages and disadvantages of such systems, and to give users practical information regarding the collection, processing and quality assessment of data collected using IFSAR systems. Because many DEM users are not very familiar with SAR and IFSAR systems, this chapter includes a general overview of such systems in slightly greater detail than that found in other chapters. This overview will concentrate on the geometric aspects of SAR data collection and processing that are necessary for understanding IFSAR fundamentals. Readers interested in more of the hardware, system engineering or signal processing aspects of SAR are recommended to consult [Kovaly, 1976], [Curlander and McDonough, 1991].

Basic Concept

As with many surveying or mapping techniques IFSAR determines the location of a point in three dimensions by solving for an unknown component of a triangle associated to the observation geometry. The observation triangle in standard stereoscopic observations for determining topography is formed from two spatially separated viewing positions and a common point imaged from both vantages. Traditional stereoscopic measurement of the 'parallax' or relative displacement that an object has from two stereo images is proportional to the height of the object and to the separation between the two imaging points [Leberl, 1990]. For SAR systems the parallax is the range difference from a point to the two observing antennas. Useful topography measurements are possible when the observed parallax is measurable for height variations of interest. IFSAR allows measurements of parallax and consequent solution of the observation triangle for geometric conditions that would normally be considered degenerate.

The key to extending the range of useful stereoscopic observations is that parallax measurements are obtained by measuring the phase difference between signals received by the two IFSAR antennas. Distance measurements are related to phase measurements by converting the distance to units of wavelength and recalling each wavelength corresponds to 2π radians or $360°$ of phase. Explicitly, if $\Delta\rho$ is the distance, and λ is the wavelength of the microwave radiation, then the phase, ϕ, is given by

$$\phi = \underbrace{2\pi}_{\text{Radians per wavelength}}\ \underbrace{\frac{\Delta\rho}{\lambda}}_{\text{Number of wavelengths}} \tag{6.1}$$

which is illustrated in Figure 6.1. Phase measurements in interferometric systems can be made with degree level accuracy, and with typical wavelengths in the range of 3-20 cm, corresponds to parallax measurements having millimeter to centimeter accuracy. This is in sharp contrast to the standard stereoscopic approach where the accuracy of the parallax measurement is usually on the order of the resolution of the imagery (several meters or more).

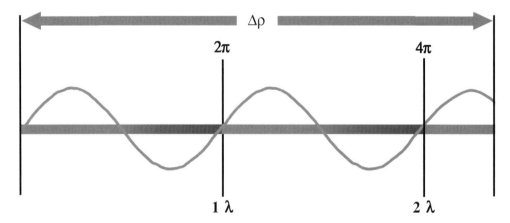

Figure 6.1 Figure illustrating the relationship between phase, distance and wavelength. See color plate in Appendix C.

Introduction to SAR

Before proceeding directly to IFSAR concepts and systems, a brief introduction to SAR systems and terminology is provided. Synthetic aperture radar can be used to produce high resolution imagery from either airborne or spaceborne platforms [Raney, 1999]. Unlike optical sensors operating at wavelengths between 3nm-30µm, such as photogrammetric or hyperspectral systems that form images from reflected solar radiation, SAR systems transmit their own radiation and record the signals reflected from the terrain. With optical systems images are generally formed instantaneously[1] whereas for SAR, data collected from multiple points along the flight path are required in order to achieve useful resolution in the along track, or azimuth, direction. Rather sophisticated image processing is required to form recognizable images from the raw data. The resolution and quality of the imagery depends on a number of system parameters as well as how the data are collected and processed.

---

[1] Exceptions include scanning optical systems such as Landsat where the optics are scanned and the image is generated one line (or pixel) at a time. This is not a fundamental sensor constraint, that is if adequate lenses and optical recording technology are available then a full two dimensional image could be made instantaneously.

SAR takes advantage of the motion of the platform to synthesize a large antenna that may be many hundreds of meters in length to achieve fine along track resolution. Figure 6.2 shows the typical SAR imaging geometry with the SAR platform moving along in flight. The radar antenna points in a direction perpendicular to the flight path called the range or cross track direction imaging the terrain below. At approximately regular intervals along the flight path the radar transmits a signal called a pulse and then records the returned echo.

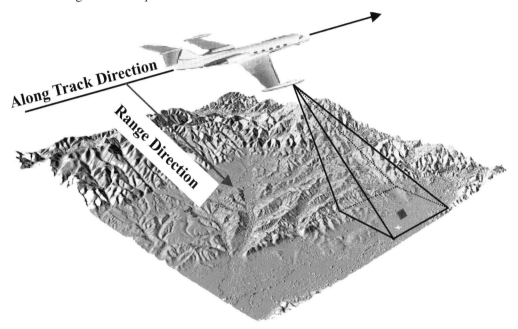

Figure 6.2 A typical SAR imaging geometry has a platform containing a radar instrument moving in the along track direction and imaging the terrain to one side of the flight path. The SAR transmits a series of pulses at regular intervals along track that simultaneously illuminates an area in the along track direction much greater than the desired azimuth resolution. By recording the returned echo from each pulse and using signal processing techniques to "synthesize" a larger antenna, fine resolution in azimuth is achieved. The blue square in the center of beam shows the size of a resolution element compared with the illuminated area from a single pulse indicated in green. See color plate in Appendix C.

Range or cross track resolution is achieved by finely gating the received echo in time. Nominally, range resolution is limited by the width of the transmitted pulse because energy returned from any point of a pulse cannot be distinguished from another point within the pulse. For systems that transmit ultra-narrow pulses, no additional processing in range is required. Many operational systems find it impractical to transmit such narrow pulses due to peak power limitations or other hardware considerations. In order to reduce the peak power in a transmitted pulse yet maintain the same average power, it is desirable to have longer pulses without somehow sacrificing range resolution. This is achieved by encoding the transmitted pulse in such a way as to be able to distinguish where within a pulse the returned energy originated. The method used by many airborne platforms is chirp encoding where the frequency is linearly changed across the pulse as illustrated in Figure 6.3. The amount of frequency variation across a pulse is called the range bandwidth. Range resolution is inversely proportional to the bandwidth. For coded pulses the desired range resolution is achieved only after a signal processing step called range compression. Table 6.1 shows the conversion between range resolution and bandwidth for a wide range of currently operational SAR systems.

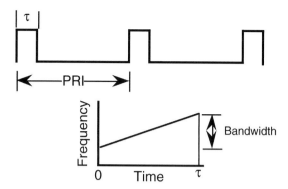

Figure 6.3 The radar emits a sequence of pulses separated in time. The time duration between pulses is called the interpulse period (IPP) and the associated pulse frequency is called the pulse repetition frequency (PRF=1/ IPP). The pulse duration, τ, is called the pulse length. For many radars, each pulse is frequency encoded with a linear frequency ramp across the pulse known as a chirp.

Table 6.1 Bandwidth to resolution table.

Bandwidth (MHz)	Resolution (m)
400	.37
300	.5
160	.95
80	1.9
40	3.7
20	7.5
10	15.0

Azimuth resolution is achieved by synthesizing a large antenna from the echoes received from a sequence of pulses illuminating a target. Without signal processing the intrinsic azimuth resolution from a single transmitted pulse would be the azimuth angular width of the antenna beam times the range, that is the width the antenna footprint on the ground. By combining the echoes using appropriate signal processing algorithms from all the pulses imaging a point, the azimuth resolution is dramatically improved. Azimuth resolution after processing is determined by the size of the synthetic aperture (or antenna), which is the length of flight track over which a fixed point stays within the azimuth antenna beamwidth. The beamwidth of an antenna, θ_{bw}, is given by

$$\theta_{bw} = k \frac{\lambda}{L} \tag{6.2}$$

where λ is the wavelength, L is the physical antenna length, and k is a constant that depends on the antenna (typically between .8 and 1.5). The size of the antenna footprint on the ground in the azimuth direction is approximately given by

$$l_{az} = \rho\theta_{bw} = \rho\frac{\lambda}{L} \tag{6.3}$$

where ρ is the range to a point in the footprint as is depicted in Figure 6.4. This is the synthetic aperture length.

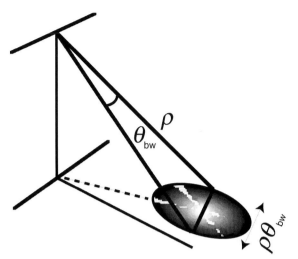

Figure 6.4 Figure showing the antenna footprint size in the azimuth direction depends on the range and the antenna beamwidth in the azimuth direction.

Since the length of the synthetic aperture is much longer than the actual antenna mounted on the SAR platform, Equation 6.2 indicates that if we were to replace the actual antenna length with the synthetic aperture length we should achieve a much narrower beamwidth, and therefore finer azimuth resolution. The process of forming the synthetic aperture to achieve the increased azimuth resolution is called azimuth compression.

During the time a target is in the beam, the range to the target is changing from pulse-to-pulse. After generating a SAR image we identify a target's location in the image by its azimuth and range position as shown in Figure 6.5. To select a unique range from the family of ranges that are changing from pulse-to-pulse during the synthetic aperture, the angle from the velocity vector to the target (or equivalently the Doppler frequency[2]) is specified for processing as shown in Figure 6.6.

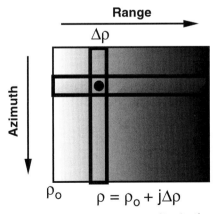

Figure 6.5 Shown above is a target imaged in the jth range bin.

---

[2] Doppler frequency is the shift in frequency that occurs when a transmitter and receiver are in relative motion. The Doppler frequency shift is a function of the angle between the relative velocity vector and line-of-sight between transmitter and receiver and the wavelength. SAR processors typically specify the Doppler frequency to coincide with where the antenna is pointing to get maximal signal strength.

The bold dashed line from pulse N-2 to the target indicates the desired Doppler (or equivalently angle) at which the target will be imaged. Observe that selection of the Doppler frequency not only affects the range at which a target is imaged but the corresponding position of the platform (and hence azimuth location) when the target is imaged.

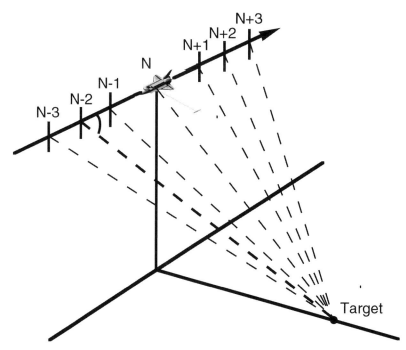

Figure 6.6 This figure shows the shuttle imaging a fixed point on the ground from a number of pulses in a synthetic aperture. The range at which a target appears in a synthetic aperture image depends on the processing parameters and algorithm used to generate the image. For standard range/Doppler processing the range is fixed by choosing the pulse which has a user defined fixed angle between the velocity vector and the line-of-sight vector to the target. This is equivalent to selecting the Doppler frequency.

It is useful for our subsequent discussion of IFSAR systems to distill the above information on SAR image coordinates to the simple geometry of the intersection of two surfaces. As discussed earlier, range information is obtained by measuring the time it takes a radar pulse to propagate from the antenna to a target and return. Azimuth location is determined from the Doppler frequency shift that is related to the angle from the velocity vector when a target is imaged. Viewing SAR target location geometrically, the range/azimuth location locus is the intersection of a sphere centered at the antenna with radius equal to the radar range and a cone with generating axis along the velocity vector with cone angle proportional to the Doppler frequency as shown in Figure 6.7. A target in the radar image could be located anywhere on the intersection locus which is a circle in the plane formed by the radar line of sight to the target and vector pointing from the aircraft to nadir. Since the intersection is a curve in three dimensional space, further information is required in order to locate a target uniquely.

Because the range direction is not parallel to ground coordinates as shown in Figure 6.8, SAR images are distorted relative to a planimetric view. In many applications this distortion can adversely affect data interpretation, particularly when one is not well acquainted with SAR imagery [Leberl, 1990]. IFSAR systems, being able to resolve the three dimensional coordinates of points in SAR imagery, can produce imagery having correct planimetric placement in regions where there are good interferometric phase measurements. These corrected images are often easier to interpret and

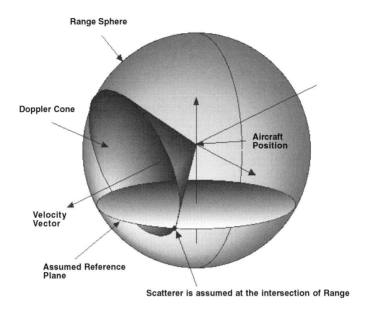

Figure 6.7 Figure showing the geometric view of target location in SAR imagery. Range information locates a target on a sphere centered about the SAR platform and the Doppler frequency locates a target on a cone centered about the velocity vector. The intersection locus of these two surfaces is a circle and thus the three dimensional location of a target cannot be uniquely determined from a single image.

are easier to register with other data layers required for analysis. Three common features observed in SAR imagery that bear particular mention are foreshortening, layover and shadow.

Foreshortening in radar imagery results from the fact that relief displacement is towards the direction of the radar. Because the range increases more slowly than ground coordinates on slopes facing toward the radar (higher elevations contend with increasing ground distance, slowing the range increase) they tend to appear bunched relative to a planimetric view. The opposite occurs on slopes facing away from the radar (lower elevations coupled with increasing ground distance speeds the range increase) where they tend to expand out when compared to a planimetric view. Both situations are illustrated in Figure 6.8. Note that foreshortening in radar images is opposite to that of optical imagery where relief displacement is away from the direction of the camera.

Layover is a limiting case of foreshortening where points arranged with increasing ground coordinates appear reversed in the radar imagery. Layover occurs because the range to objects with larger ground coordinates is less than the range to other objects with smaller ground coordinates. Geometrically this happens when the slope of the terrain is greater than the angle the incident radiation makes with respect to vertical. More importantly for our purposes is to note for interferometric radar systems layover causes a loss of useful signal and therefore precludes the determination of elevation in layover regions.

Shadow occurs when the radar beam cannot reach a portion of the terrain being imaged because it is occulted by other parts of the terrain or other objects in the scene. Where the terrain is shadowed the radar image will appear dark and the signal in these range cells is only due to thermal noise. As with layover regions, shadowed regions have no useful interferometric signal and consequently no elevation values can be determined.

Synthetic aperture radar systems are currently operating over a wide range of frequencies and resolutions depending on their intended applications. Operating frequencies vary from as low as

3 MHz to as high as 40 GHz. The choice of frequency is dictated by a number of factors including intended application, platform and power constraints, and availability of the desired frequency range. Table 6.2 shows the correspondence between frequency, wavelength and the band designation letter code (assigned in World War II for security reasons) that are often used to specify the operating frequency of the radar.

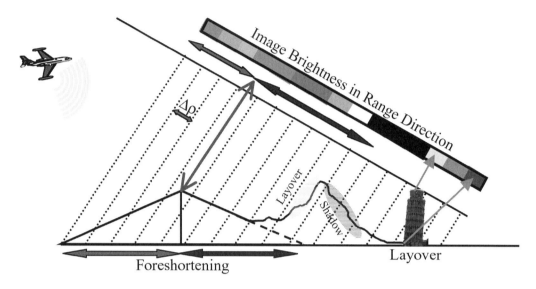

Figure 6.8 The three-dimensional world is collapsed to two dimensions in conventional SAR imaging. After image formation, the radar return is resolved into an image in range-azimuth coordinates. This figure shows a profile of the terrain at constant azimuth, with the radar flight track into the page. See color plate in Appendix C.

Table 6.2 Frequency and Wavelength Relationship Table.

Frequency Band (MHz)	Wavelength Range (cm)	Band Identification
26500-40000	1.13-.75	Ka
18000-26500	1.66-1.13	K
12500-18000	2.4-1.66	Ku
8000-12500	3.75-2.4	X
4000-8000	7.5-3.75	C
2000-4000	15-7.5	S
1000-2000	30-15	L
300-900	100-33	P or UHF
30-300	1000-100	VHF
3-30	10000-1000	HF

To appreciate why particular radar frequencies (wavelengths) are selected for a given application, it is necessary to have a cursory understanding of how radar signals interact with terrain [Elachi, 1988], [Raney, 1999]. Each pixel in a SAR image is a complex number having a magnitude and phase determined by the terrain surface properties and the image geometry. A radar signal impinging on a resolution element (area of the surface contained within a single range and azimuth bin) will in general scatter energy in all directions. The signal reflected back toward the radar is referred to as the backscatter. Backscatter strength is a function of the composition of the surface and its structure. Electrical composition of a surface is characterized by its dielectric constant. The dielectric constant of a material determines how much energy is absorbed or reflected from the surface and depends on the radar frequency. Surface structure is usually characterized by roughness, a measure of how much the surface varies in a resolution element. Roughness is measured in terms of the incident radiation's wavelength, so surfaces that are smooth at one wavelength may appear rough at another wavelength. As a general rule of thumb the rougher the surface the greater the backscatter. For example, a road that is relatively flat and free of potholes or other major imperfections may appear very smooth when imaged using a L-band (23 cm wavelength) radar because a typical road's micro-topography may be less than 5 mm. However, the same road imaged with a Ka-band (7.5 mm wavelength) radar may seem quite rough and appear bright in a radar image. Figure 6.9 illustrates in a qualitative sense how radar interacts with different types of ground cover, and Figure 6.10 shows the same area imaged at X and P-band with the GeoSAR radar.

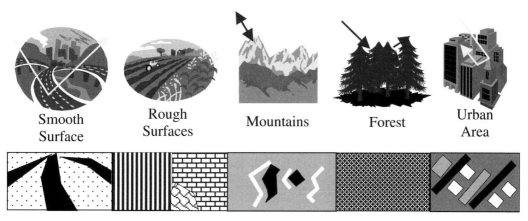

Smooth Surface Rough Surfaces Mountains Forest Urban Area

Figure 6.9 Above are five common ground cover types found in SAR imagery. Smooth surfaces such as roads or water tend to reflect energy away from the radar and appear dark in radar images. Rough surfaces, such as often found in fields and cropland, exhibit a type of checkerboard pattern of fields with the texture and brightness level varying with crop and field condition. Extremely bright lines running parallel to the look direction as a result of layover coupled with shadowed regions is typical of that found in mountainous regions. Forested areas generally appear relatively bright since the rough nature of the canopy at most wavelengths generates high levels of backscatter. Depending on the resolution of the SAR, urban areas can show individual buildings or groups of building and the associated roadways. See color plate in Appendix C.

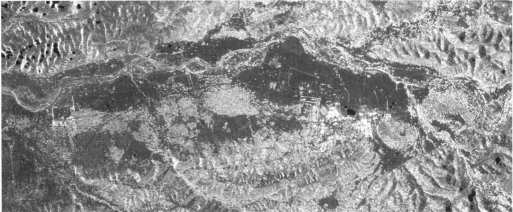

Figure 6.10 GeoSAR X-band (top) and P-band (bottom) orthorectified SAR images of Hunter Liggett. Notice how the vegetated areas in the center portion of the image have much greater contrast at P-band (85 cm wavelength) than X-band (3 cm wavelength). This contrast differential results from open areas appearing smoother at P-band than X-band whereas the vegetated areas appear rough at both wavelengths. In the hilly regions at the top-left and bottom-right portions of the image are some areas of shadow and layover.

Although the above discussion primarily concentrated on the observed magnitude in a SAR image, it is the phase that is needed for interferometry. The two primary components of the phase measurement consist of a systematic and a random part. The systematic part is the range to the resolution elemoment converted to phase modulo 2π. Even though there may be many millions of wavelengths (hence many multiples of 2π) from the antenna to a resolution element, only the principal value (a number between $-\pi$ and π) can be extracted from a complex-valued resolution element.

The random component is a result of a thermal noise contribution and the coherent sum of contributions from all the elemental scatterers in a resolution element. The elemental scatterers are points within a resolution element that dominate the signal value, and their contribution depends only on the viewing geometry and the composition of the scatterers. In general, because the distribution of elemental scatterers within a resolution element changes from element to element and the range converted to phase modulo 2π to a resolution element is randomly distributed, phase values in SAR images are randomly distributed. Because these effects cannot be separated, phase values from a single SAR image are generally ignored. It is important for the IFSAR discussion to follow to note that if the viewing geometry is nearly unchanged, and the elemental scatterers within a resolution cell are undisturbed, then this portion of the random phase remains the same. Thus the thermal noise is random in time and the scatterer noise is random in space.

Because radar primarily interacts with structures that have lengths comparable to the wavelength or larger, longer wavelength (lower frequency) radars tend to penetrate deeper into the vegetation canopy or ground surface. The amount of penetration in a vegetation canopy depends on the structure and density of the vegetation. Radar wavelengths less than roughly 10 cm mostly sense the upper portions of canopies while wavelengths longer than 20 cm sense deeper into a canopy. This differential penetration effect for lower frequency radars has led to the development of radar systems designed to exploit this phenomenon. Ground surface penetration depends on the type and composition of the ground layers, ground cover and soil moisture. Longer wavelength radars have been known to penetrate several meters or more in dry sandy soil and even deeper into certain types of ice.

IFSAR Overview

By augmenting a conventional SAR system with another spatially separated receiving antenna, as illustrated in Figure 6.11, it is possible to extract topographic information. More detail on IFSAR systems and processing can be found in [Rosen et al, 2000], [Madsen and Zebker, 1999], [Franceschetti, 1999] and [Bamler and Hartl, 1998]. While radar pulses are transmitted from the conventional SAR antenna, radar echoes are received by both the conventional and an additional SAR antenna. If the received signals from the two antennas are combined *coherently* for each imaged point to measure the phase difference, then the system forms an interferometric SAR. Here the interferometric phase difference is essentially related to the geometric path length difference to the image point, which depends on the topography. With knowledge of the interferometer geometry, the phase difference can be converted into an altitude for each image point. By having a third measurement, the interferometric phase, in addition to the standard along and cross track location of an image point obtained with conventional SARs, it is possible to determine the three-dimensional location of a point.

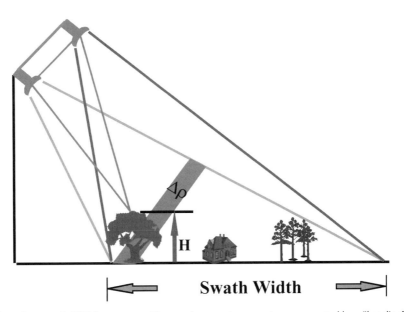

Figure 6.11 Interferometric SAR for topographic mapping uses two apertures separated by a "baseline" to image the surface. The phase difference between the apertures for each image point, along with the range and knowledge of the baseline, can be used to infer the precise shape of the imaging triangle (in red) to determine the topographic height of an object. See color plate in Appendix C.

Previously, it was shown that knowing the SAR coordinates of a target restricted its location to be on the intersection locus of a sphere and cone that from Figure 6.7 was seen to be a circle. Parameterizing the location on this circle by an angle, referred to as the elevation angle, θ, reduces the three dimensional target location problem to determining this angle. For this we need the interferometric measurement. Assume two identical antennas, A1 and A2, are receiving radar echo signals from a single source as shown in Figure 6.12.

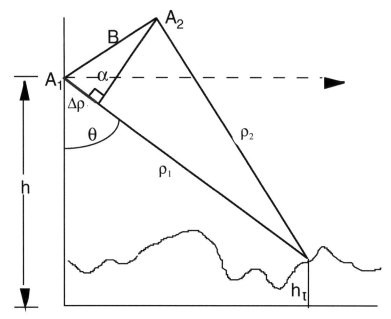

Figure 6.12 Simplified broadside looking (zero Doppler) radar interferometry geometry. The difference in range from the two observing antennas to the target is approximately equal to the projection of the baseline vector onto the line-of-sight vector shown in blue. This range difference can be related to a phase measurement using equation 6.1 and forms the primary interferometric observable. See color plate at Appendix C.

The path length difference, $\Delta\rho$, of the signals received by the two antennas is approximately given by

$$\Delta\rho = |\vec{\rho_1}| - |\vec{\rho_2}| \approx B\sin(\theta-\alpha) \qquad (6.4)$$

where $\vec{\rho_i}$ indicates the vector from antenna 1 to the target, B is the length of the baseline vector which is the vector pointing from antenna 1 to antenna 2, θ is the desired elevation (or look) angle and the baseline orientation angle, α, is the angle the baseline vector makes with respect to the horizontal. Observe that the range difference to a good approximation for most systems is simply the length of the projection of the baseline vector onto the line-of-sight. The range difference, $\Delta\rho$, may be obtained by measuring ϕ, the phase between the two interferometer signals, using the relation

$$\phi = -\frac{2\pi m\Delta\rho}{\lambda} \qquad m = 1,2 \qquad (6.5)$$

where λ is the radar wavelength and m equals 1 when the path length difference is associated with the one-way path difference, or 2 for the two-way path difference as is the case for Ping-Pong or repeat pass systems described below. Geometrically, the phase measurement provides a second cone with cone axis the interferometric baseline. Intersecting the phase cone with the range sphere and Doppler cone determines the elevation angle to the target and therefore the target's full three-dimensional location as shown in Figure 6.13.

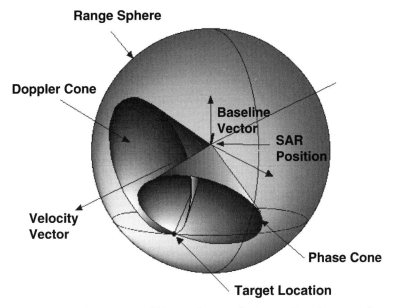

Figure 6.13 Target location in a SAR image could be anywhere on the intersection of a range sphere and Doppler cone thereby providing no information on the target's elevation. 3-D information is obtained by the intersection of the phase cone with range sphere and Doppler Cone.

Using the simplified geometry of Figure 6.10 the height of a target, ht, is given by

$$h_t = h - \rho\cos(\theta) \tag{6.6}$$

where h is the altitude of the radar antenna and ρ is the slant range from the antenna to the target. Since the signal phase is sensitive to displacements between images of a fraction of a wavelength, the interferometric technique provides a very accurate means of determining topographic heights. Using Equations 6.4 and 6.5 the elevation angle can be determined to be

$$\theta = \sin^{-1}\left(\frac{\lambda\phi}{2\pi mB}\right) + \alpha \tag{6.7}$$

It is immediate from Equations 6.6 and 6.7 that determining the height of a target requires knowledge of the platform position, the range, the interferometric baseline length, the baseline angle and the interferometric phase. Generation of accurate topographic maps using radar interferometry places stringent requirements on the knowledge of the platform and baseline vectors. Figure 6.14 shows interferometric phase measurements and amplitude images.

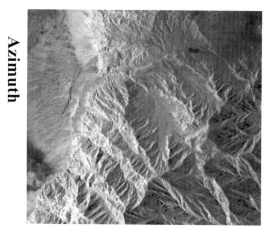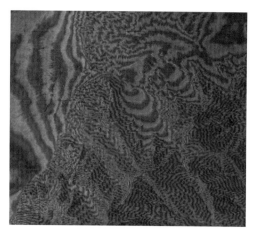

Azimuth

Range

Figure 6.14 Interferometric phase and associated amplitude image of the Mojave Desert, CA, generated from repeat pass observations using the SIR-C radar. See color plate in Appendix C.

Understanding conditions when interferometric phase measurements useful for topographic mapping are possible requires us to examine more closely what happens to radar signals within a resolution element. Consider a resolution cell with elemental scatterers arranged throughout as shown in Figure 6.15. Each elemental scatterer will contribute a portion of the backscatter that is added coherently with the other elemental scatterers to produce the return from the cell. Since the return from the elemental scatterers adds coherently, the relative phase or distance between the scatterers affects the magnitude and phase of the total signal. Conceptually, the phase can be decomposed into a systematic and random component by selecting the center of the cell as reference. The systematic component is the phase from the antenna to the center of the cell and is the portion of the signal needed for interferometry. The random component is the coherent sum of the signals from the randomly arranged elemental scatterers within the cell to the center of the cell. This component, although random from resolution element to resolution element, remains the same (or nearly the same) if the viewing geometry is nearly identical and if the relative position of the elemental scatterers within a cell remain the same (or nearly the same) as shown in Figure 6.15.

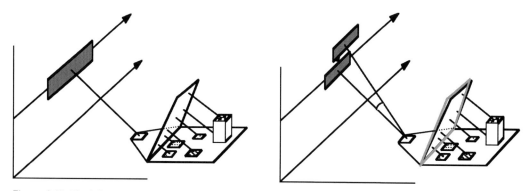

Figure 6.15 The left portion of the figure shows a notional arrangement of elemental scatterers within an imaging cell. Each elemental scatterer may have different surface roughness and dielectric properties as indicated by the different shading patterns. The right portion of the figure shows that if the imaging geometry is nearly the same the relative distance between scatterers is preserved and cancels out in the interferometric phase measurement.

For interferometric applications, where the viewing geometry of the interferometric pair is nearly the same, the random component arising from the elemental scatterer arrangement cancels and leaves only the difference between systematic components. This phase difference is the interferometric phase measurement and equals the phase in Equation 6.5 modulo 2π. Another random component, which does not cancel, is thermal noise. Thermal noise is different for each receiving antenna, and depending on its magnitude relative to the desired signal degrades interferometric phase measurement. The above discussion is summarized below.

$$\text{phase} = \underbrace{\begin{array}{c}\text{range from antenna} \\ \text{to center of cell}\end{array}}_{\substack{\text{Systematic component desired} \\ \text{by interferometric measurement}}} + \underbrace{\begin{array}{c}\text{Coherent sum of elemental} \\ \text{scatterers arranged randomly in cell}\end{array}}_{\substack{\text{Random component that if look direction is nearly the same} \\ \text{and scatterers within cell do not move relative to each other} \\ \text{this component cancels in the interferogram formation process.}}} + \underbrace{\begin{array}{c}\text{thermal noise}\end{array}}_{\substack{\text{Random component that does} \\ \text{not cancel and results in} \\ \text{interferometric phase noise}}}$$

It is important to appreciate the consequences of the fact the interferometric phase measurement is made modulo 2π. The total range difference between the two observations that the phase represents in general can be many multiples of the radar wavelength, or expressed in terms of phase, many multiples of 2π. It is this value that is required in order to make height measurements. The standard approach for determining the unique phase that is directly proportional to the range difference is to first determine the relative phase between pixels via the so-called "phase unwrapping" process. Unwrapping of IFSAR imagery is a non-trivial process for which a number of algorithms have been developed. Complications arise in avoiding unwrapping errors in regions of shadow, layover and low signal return. The connected phase field after unwrapping may still need to be adjusted by an overall constant of 2π. The step that determines the overall constant of 2π is referred to as absolute phase determination.

Interferometric correlation, a measure of the similarity of the signal received at the two antennas, can be estimated directly from the image data of the two interferometric channels [Zebker and Villasenor, 1992]. Correlation measurements have values between 0 and 1, with 1 designating perfect correlation between the channels. Sometimes it is more convenient to refer to the amount of interferometric decorrelation, which is defined as one minus the correlation. The amount of decorrelation due to the slightly different viewing geometry is called geometric decorrelation. Thermal noise induced signal decorrelation is called noise decorrelation. Shadowed regions suffer from noise decorrelation and areas on steep slopes exhibit geometric decorrelation that increases phase noise and can preclude useful phase measurements altogether. Another form of decorrelation occurs when there is a vertical distribution of scattering elements within a resolution element as shown in Figure 6.16. Not only is the signal decorrelated, the point within the resolution cell corresponding to the interferometric phase measurement depends on the wavelength and the scatterer distribution in the cell. This form of decorrelation is called volumetric decorrelation and can be used to infer information about the vertical structure of the volume. Recently, there has been a great deal of activity using volumetric correlation to estimate tree and canopy structure within the interferometric SAR community.

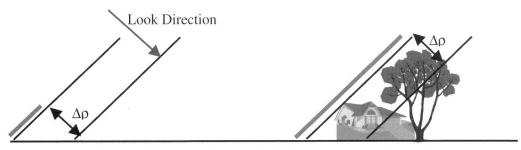

Figure 6.16 Vertical structure of scatterers within a resolution element due to vegetation or other structures present in the cell cause increased decorrelation. This form of decorrelation can be used to infer information about vertical structure within a resolution element. The increased decorrelation results from the increased size of the range cell projected back toward the direction of the radar (shown in magenta) when compared to a flat surface.

There is an upper value on the useful baseline length known as the critical baseline [Rosen et al, 2000]. The critical baseline is reached when the amount of phase change per resolution element exceeds 2π radians. This limitation is a result of the fact that the interferometric phase measurement is made only modulo 2π. As the baseline approaches the critical baseline, the phase values from the two antennas become completely decorrelated. However, as the baseline increases, the sensitivity of phase to height increases improving the accuracy of interferometric SAR systems. Practical mapping systems must select baselines with a balance between adequate phase to height sensitivity to meet mapping requirements and excessive decorrelation with corresponding processing difficulties.

Combining the SAR image formation process, interferometric phase measurement, unwrapping and height determination into an automated processing algorithm has a process flow that is shown in Figure 6.17 [Madsen et al, 1993]. An understanding of the steps involved is useful for understanding IFSAR calibration and for identifying potential error sources in IFSAR generated DEMs. Raw data are collected and stored onboard for batch processing. The first processing step is decoding the byte data, followed by range compression for each of the two interferometric channels. Using the platform motion information obtained from Inertial Navigation System (INS) and Global Positioning System (GPS) measurements, as well as any other baseline metrology devices, the data are compensated for perturbations in aircraft motion from a reference path[3] and then azimuth compressed. This generates two single-look complex images.

One image of the single-look complex image pair is resampled to overlay the other. This registration must be done to a small fraction of a pixel (typically less than .1 of a pixel) in order to avoid phase decorrelation. Multiplying the complex pixel value in one image by the complex conjugate of the corresponding pixel value in the second image forms an interferogram. The resulting interferogram is multi-looked, by spatially averaging the complex pixels in a box about a given pixel to reduce the amount of phase noise.

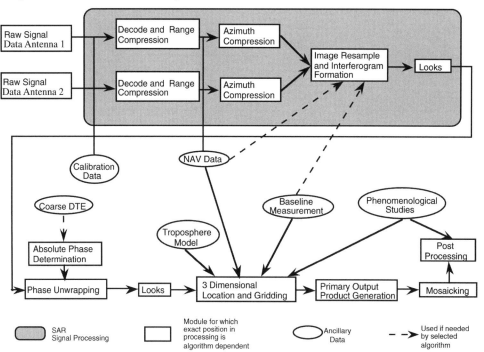

Figure 6.17 Interferometric processing block diagram.

---

[3] The process of correction for motion away from an ideal path is referred to as motion compensation. Motion compensation corrects for motion on the order of fractions of a wavelength in order to generate well focused SAR imagery. The requirements for motion compensation are even more demanding for IFSAR systems and place stringent requirements on the platform and baseline metrology systems.

After the multi-looked interferogram has been generated the phase for each complex sample is computed. To generate a continuous height map, the two-dimensional phase field must be unwrapped. After the unwrapping process an overall multiple of 2π is estimated and added to the unwrapped phase (the estimated value may be 0).

Subsequent to determining the absolute phase for each pixel in the interferogram and possibly taking additional looks, the 3-dimensional target position can be determined. Phase corrections are applied to the interferometric phase to account for tropospheric effects, and the range is corrected to account for the speed of light changes in the atmosphere. Using accurate baseline and platform position information, the phase and range information for the target position is computed. A relief map is generated by gridding the unevenly sampled 3-dimensional target locations in a natural coordinate system aligned with the flight path. The gridded products include the target heights, the SAR image which has been orthorectified, a correlation map, and a height error map described below. These four products will be referred to as primary mapping or strip map products. The resulting radar relief map may be measuring the heights above the ground, within the vegetation canopy or beneath the surface, in arid regions. To convert this map into a true ground surface DEM corrections based on phenomenological studies, e.g. using scattering or semi-empirical curves to correct elevation measurements based on the amount of decorrelation in the canopy, must be incorporated into either the 3-dimensional location algorithms or into a post-processing step.

One of the unique aspects of interferometric SAR systems is the ability to determine the statistical height error, that is the degree of height noise from pixel to pixel, estimated from knowledge of the correlation, γ [Hensley and Webb, 1994]. The amount of phase noise between the two channels is simply and directly related to the correlation and number of looks used to reduce phase noise[4]. The Cramer Rao bound relating the phase variance, σ_ϕ, to the correlation coefficient, γ, is given by

$$\sigma_\phi = \frac{1}{\sqrt{2N_L}} \frac{\sqrt{1-\gamma^2}}{\gamma} \tag{6.8}$$

where N_L is the number of looks. From Equations 6.6 and 6.7 the height error, σ_h, as a function of the phase noise is found to be

$$\sigma_h = \frac{\lambda \rho \sin(\theta)}{2\pi m B \cos(\theta - \alpha)} \sigma_\phi \tag{6.9}$$

Equations 6.8 and 6.9 allow the generation of an error map showing the local height accuracy for each post in an interferometrically derived DEM.

Typically, the post spacing of the IFSAR topographic data are comparable to the fine spatial resolution of SAR imagery while the altitude measurement accuracy generally exceeds stereo-scopic accuracy at comparable resolutions. The registration of the two SAR images for the interferometric measurement, the retrieval of the interferometric phase difference and subsequent conversion of the results into digital elevation models of the terrain can be highly automated, representing an intrinsic advantage of the IFSAR approach. The performance of IFSAR systems is largely understood both theoretically and experimentally enabling these system to be designed and built to meet specific mapping objectives. These developments have led to airborne and spaceborne IFSAR systems for routine topographic mapping.

---

[4] The Cramer Rao bound used to relate the phase noise to correlation and number of looks is only valid when the number of looks exceeds 4 or 5. The number of looks in most interferometric systems used to generate topographic maps usually is much larger than 4. A notable exception is the SRTM system (described later in the chapter) where the number of looks varied between 1 and 4.

For the remainder of this chapter IFSAR is defined as an airborne or spaceborne interferometric radar system, flown aboard rotary or fixed wing aircraft, or any space based platform, that is used to acquire 3-dimensional coordinates (these coordinates must be convertible to a specified geographic datum) of terrain and terrain features that are both manmade and naturally occurring. IFSAR systems consist of a platform, GPS and attendant GPS base station(s) if needed, INU and interferometric radar system including commanding and data acquisition systems. The system may also include other ancillary equipment such as baseline metrology systems as necessary for accurate map generation. These systems form synthetic aperture images of terrain surfaces from two spatially separated antennas over an imaged swath that may be located to the left, right or both sides of the imaging platform.

DEVELOPMENTAL HISTORY

Radar interferometry has a relatively short history, with the first instances occurring in the late 1960's for planetary radar observations. Rogers and Ingalls [Rogers and Ingalls, 1969] reported using interferometry to remove the "north-south" ambiguity in range/range rate maps of the planet Venus from Earth-based antennas. Later, Zisk [Zisk, 1972] applied a similar methodology to measure the topography of the Moon.

Radar interferometry for Earth based topography measurement had its genesis with an airborne SAR system by Graham in the early 1970's [Graham, 1974]. Graham modified the system with an additional physical antenna displaced in the cross-track plane from the original SAR antenna to form an imaging interferometer. By mixing the signals from the two antennas in hardware, the Graham interferometer recorded amplitude variations that represented the relative phase of the signals. As discussed above these relative phase changes are sensitive to the topography of the surface and thus the resulting fringe patterns tracked the topographic contours.

The rapid advance in digital processing techniques and hardware in the late 1970's and early 1980's enabled subsequent IFSAR systems to record and process the complex amplitude and phase information digitally for each antenna. This obviated the need for combining the signals in hardware as done in the Graham interferometer, thereby overcoming the difficulty of trying to invert the amplitude fringes for quantitative topography measurements. Demonstrations of the first airborne [Zebker and Goldstein, 1986] and spaceborne [Li and Goldstein ,1990] interferometric systems employing this technique were conducted by researchers at the Jet Propulsion Laboratory in the late 1980's.

Rigorous assessment of SAR interferometry for topography mapping was first done using the NASA/JPL TOPSAR interferometric radar system [Madsen et al, 1993]. TOPSAR, an extension of the multi-purpose JPL AIRSAR radar system that features fully polarimetric C-, L- and P-band frequency radars, originally consisted of a C-band (5.6 cm wavelength) interferometer [Zebker et al, 1992]. It was later augmented with an L-band (24 cm wavelength) interferometer. The TOPSAR system uses two C-band antennas that are flush mounted on the left side of the JPL/NASA DC-8 aircraft as shown in Figure 6.18. With an approximately 12 km swath and 2-3 m height accuracy at 5 m postings, TOPSAR proved (and continues to prove) a valuable testbed for understanding the capabilities and limitations of interferometric radar systems.

Although the first demonstrations of spaceborne interferometric SAR used the L-band SAR aboard the SEASAT satellite and the Magellan S-band SAR that mapped the surface of Venus, it was the launch of the European ERS-1 (1991) and ERS-2 (1995) satellites that spawned international interest in interferometric SAR research. ERS satellites collect interferometric data in the so-called repeat pass mode where data is collected on two nearly identical flight tracks separated in time. Repeat pass observations can be used to generate topographic maps and surface deformation maps [Zebker et al, 1994]. Topographic maps generated from repeat pass observations have two additional error sources resulting from changes between observation times. See below for a more detailed discussion of repeat pass interferometry. The first error source is due to changes in

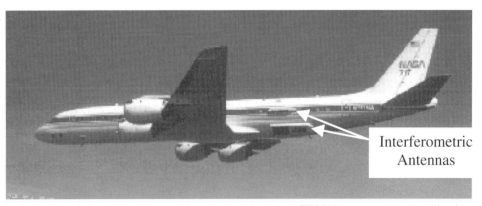

Figure 6.18 View of the NASA DC-8 in flight with the AIRSAR and TOPSAR antennas clearly visible where they are mounted on the fuselage. See color plate in Appendix C.

the surface (recall these only need to be on the order of a wavelength) that cause decorrelation and therefore increased height noise. The second source is due to changes in the atmosphere between observations that cause phase distortions. To demonstrate the capability of this approach on a global scale, the European Space Agency has operated the ERS-1 and ERS-2 satellites in a so-called "tandem mission" approach. The two spacecraft obtained SAR measurements for a significant fraction of the earth's surface with measurements from one spacecraft one day after those from the other, with the two spacecraft in nearly the same orbital configuration. The one day separation in the observations was chosen to minimize the changes in the surface and atmosphere mentioned above. Although a detailed quantitative report is not yet available, rather severe temporal decorrelation, even with a one day repeat observation interval, has been observed especially in heavily vegetated areas. When a detailed quantitative report from this large data set becomes available, it will be an important resource for DEM users and future IFSAR mission designers to assess the potential accuracy of such products.

In the early 1990's, based on the success of TOPSAR and other results, the Defense Advanced Research Projects Agency (DARPA) saw the potential for radar interferometric mapping systems to meet a variety of military and civilian needs. Under DARPA sponsorship the IFSARE radar system [Sos et al, 1994], designed and built by ERIM with system engineering support and an interferometric processor supplied by JPL, was the first system specifically engineered to meet a set of topographic mapping requirements. A key system requirement for IFSARE was to map absolute elevations, without the need for ground control, to meter level accuracy. Flown on a LearJet36 with operational altitudes up to 10,000 m, IFSARE uses a combination of differential GPS (DGPS) and a state of the art INU to obtain accurate position and attitude information. To insure baseline stability as a function of temperature, the interferometric antennas are mounted on an Invar frame attached to the bottom of the aircraft. A series of rigorous tests designed to evaluate system performance versus engineering predictions showed the system met or exceeded all mapping requirements. Subsequently, the IFSARE system, renamed to STAR-3i and operated by Intermap, became the first commercially operational interferometric mapping radar.

In 1994 NASA twice flew the third in a series of Space Imaging Radars (SIR-C) in partnership with the Italian and German Space agencies. SIR-C/X-SAR was fully polarimetric at C- and L-bands and operated in the vertically polarized state at X-band. For the last three days of the second mission, the shuttle position was controlled to have nearly exact repeat orbits separated by 1 day. Some of the data collections in the second mission were designed for repeat pass observations over sites collected during the first mission six months earlier. Interferometric studies from SIR-C/X-SAR contributed to a further understanding of the relative temporal decorrelation rates at X-, C-, and L-bands, increased the understanding of atmospheric propagation effects, and provided the first insights into how polarization affects interferometric phase.

The two very successful flights and the high quality interferometric products generated during the mission led to a dedicated interferometry space mission. This mission, the Shuttle Radar Topography Mission (SRTM) has finally achieved a 3 decades long elusive goal of obtaining a highly accurate globally consistent topographic map of the Earth's surface [Farr and Kobrick 2001].

The National Aeronautics and Space Administration (NASA) in conjunction with the National Imagery and Mapping Agency (NIMA) – now the National Geospatial-Intelligence Agency (NGA) of the US – developed SRTM to address some of the limitations of repeat pass interferometry discovered by ERS and SIR-C/X-SAR. The SIR-C/X-SAR radar was augmented with radar antennas mounted on a 60 m deployable boom. Radar interferometric data was collected at C- (5.6 cm wavelength) and X- (3 cm wavelength) bands. The SRTM C-band radar system collected data for 99.97% of the Earth's landmass between –57° and 60° latitude during an 11 day mission in February, 2000. By combining the data from both ascending and descending orbits a seamless mosaic of the Earth's topography was generated. The topography data have an absolute height measurement accuracy (90% confidence level) of about 9 meters with a post spacing of about 30 m. This is the first synoptic measurement of the Earth's topography processed in a globally consistent fashion. Data from SRTM at a 90 m posting is freely available for download for all areas mapped worldwide and at 30 m posting for the US and its territories. It has already had many scientific, civilian and military applications.

Continued proliferation of interferometric SAR systems for topography and other applications is a testament to the success of the technology. Today there are over a dozen airborne interferometers operated by governments, universities and commercial organizations. There have been a large number of spaceborne SAR instruments flown in recent decades: ERS-1 and ERS-2 satellites operated by the European Space Agency, JERS-1 operated by the National Space Development Agency of Japan, RadarSAT-1 operated by the Canadian Space Agency, and SIR-C/X-SAR operated by the United States, German, and Italian space agencies. Planned spaceborne SAR instruments such as ENVISAT by the European Space Agency, ALOS PALSAR by National Space Development Agency of Japan, and RadarSAT-2 by the Canadian Space Agency will continue to spawn new technology and applications.

TYPES OF SENSORS

Interferometric SAR systems come in a variety of configurations and operate over a diverse set of frequency, resolution and accuracy regimes. Here we outline elements common to all interferometric mapping systems and describe some of the tradeoffs between the various configurations. This treatment is geared for DEM users who need to understand how best to select a system that accommodates their mapping requirements.

Categorizing IFSAR systems by the platform type, airborne or spaceborne, and method of data collection, single-pass (SPI) or repeat-pass (RPI), yields four major implementations with various relative strengths and weaknesses. Regardless of implementation these systems have a number of elements in common. Constructing accurate height maps using radar interferometry requires precise knowledge of the platform position, attitude, and interferometric baseline as well as knowledge of the radar operating parameters. Phase stability and tracking of any phase changes not a result of topographic variations are also key considerations for IFSAR mapping systems.

Interferometric observations are made with both antennas on the same platform[5], referred to as single-pass interferometry (SPI), or from multiple observations separated in time, referred to as repeat-pass interferometry (RPI) as illustrated in Figure 6.19. Repeat pass observations may be separated by as little as a fraction of a second or may be many years apart. RPI is possible when

---

[5] In principal the antennas could be on separate platforms flying in formation. Several global IFSAR mapping missions have been proposed using formation flying satellites to achieve the required baseline lengths, however to date none has flown [Zebker et al, 1994].

the flight tracks are separated by less than the critical baseline length and when the surface has not changed enough to cause decorrelation. Atmospheric changes between observations, particularly those attributed to tropospheric water vapor, can dramatically alter interferometric phase measurements [Goldstein, 1995], [Zebker et al, 1997] and [Tarayre and Massonnet, 1996]. Spatial scales for atmospheric phase distortion effects are typically on the order of kilometers and scale indirect proportion to wavelength. The effect on interferometric height measurements can be a meter to hundreds of meters depending on the amount of distortion and the baseline length. Spaceborne SARs flying above the ionosphere (orbits above 300 km) also experience phase distortions due to changes in the ionosphere between repeat observations, however these changes typically have larger spatial scales of 10-100 kilometers and have a non-linear wavelength dependency. The non-linear wavelength dependence offers the possibility of removing iono-spheric distortion by flying a multi-frequency system, similar to the way GPS corrects for the ionosphere using two frequencies.

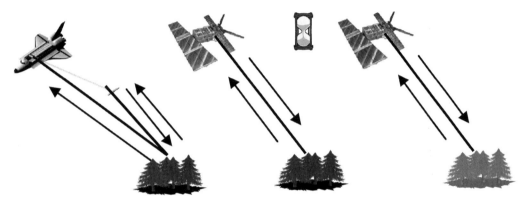

Figure 6.19 Interferometric radar topographic measurements are made with single pass and repeat pass systems. With single pass systems two spatially separated antennas (usually on the same platform) are arranged to collect echoes from the terrain simultaneously. The left side of the figure shows the SRTM mapping radar, which had two antennas separated by a 60 m retractable boom and made interferometric radar observations for much of the Earth's surface. With repeat pass systems the scene is imaged at least twice separated by an interval of time that may be seconds to years. The right side of the image shows the ERS radar satellite imaging the same area twice. The time interval for repeat pass ERS observations were as short as 1 day during the tandem phase of operation and have spanned many years.

Surface change between observations has two effects on the interferometric measurement. The first, discussed previously, is loss of correlation when change occurs within a resolution element. These changes need only be a fraction of a wavelength, such as vegetation blowing in the wind or snow falling, to cause decorrelation severe enough to make topographic mapping impossible. Secondly, the surface can deform in a systematic manner such that the elemental scatterers within a resolution element remain largely unaltered. Examples of this include inflation from volcanoes, earthquake displacement, subsidence due to water or oil pumping, and glacier motion. In contrast to topography where the amount of phase change depends on the length of the baseline, phase distortions due to surface motion are independent of baseline. The direct coupling of surface motion interferometric phase measurement to the range rather than the baseline results in a much greater sensitivity of the interferometric phase to surface motion than to topographic variability. Placing this in perspective, for a typical IFSAR configuration the sensitivity of phase to topography is roughly a change of 2π radians for a hundred meters of relief, whereas the phase changes by 2π radians from surface motion of centimeters[6]. For RPI

---

[6] More precisely, surface motion of half a wavelength results in a change of 2π in the interferometric phase.

topographic mapping applications, it is essential to avoid areas where there has been surface motion between observations as this results in major distortions to the topographic map. However, with proper processing techniques it is possible to exploit the sensitivity of IFSAR observations to surface motion to measure millimeter level surface deformation of very wide areas. These observations have become an essential part of the investigations of many solid earth scientists studying earthquakes, volcanoes, and glaciers. The possibility of using these observations for making topographic map corrections is discussed later in the chapter.

Position, Attitude and Baseline Metrology

Position measurement with the advent of GPS and DGPS systems and very good INSs enables very accurate motion measurement on a broad range of time scales. Kinematic GPS used with either airborne or spaceborne platforms achieves decimeter absolute position accuracy with a 2 Hz sampling rate. Although 2 Hz sampling of the motion works for satellites that have relatively smooth trajectories, faster sampling of 20 Hz or greater is required for airborne IFSAR applications. INU systems provide the faster motion and attitude update rates needed for motion compensation. Blending of kinematic DGPS and INU data is an increasingly common method of optimizing position and attitude data to have a high effective sampling rate and excellent absolute position accuracy necessary for airborne applications..

For interferometric applications it is knowledge of the antenna locations that is essential and required for baseline determination and motion compensation. Rarely are the motion metrology systems mounted to the center of the antenna, therefore platform attitude measurements coupled with measurements of the antenna location relative to the motion sensors is needed. Absolute angle determination with accuracy of approximately a few thousandths of a degree is off-the-shelf technology today with tightly coupled INS/GPS systems, significantly improving the critical determination of the baseline orientation angle. For spaceborne platforms, star trackers provide absolute attitude measurements with 1-10 arcsecond accuracy. If faster update rates are needed then star tracker measurements are coupled with IMU measurements.

It is not always possible to design IFSAR systems such that the antennas remain fixed relative to the motion measurement system. When this is the case additional metrology devices are required to track antenna motion with respect to the platform. Very few systems thus far have been fitted with active baseline metrology systems but those that have used a combination of optical ranging and target tracking devices. Update rates for these systems are matched to the expected motion of the antenna relative to the platform to insure proper baseline determination.

Spaceborne radars, until recently, have relied upon Doppler tracking for orbit determination. Doppler tracking can determine satellite positions with accuracy from 10 cm to 100 m depending on the orbit and the amount of tracking data available. The highest accuracy Doppler derived orbit position data may fall short of the accuracy requirements needed for RPI topographic mapping. Baselines that must be known to a centimeter or even sub-centimeter accuracy cannot be determined strictly using Doppler tracking data. Ground truth in the form of existing DEMs or radar identifiable ground control points are used to determine the baseline for RPI topographic applications when adequate metrology is not available.

Frequency Selection

Frequency selection is often a trade among scientific considerations, technology readiness, platform constraints, frequency availability and cost. Ideally, the choice of frequency would be tailored to electromagnetic properties of the surface of interest. However, the varied nature of the Earth's terrain precludes any single frequency from satisfying all possible application requirements. For example, higher frequency systems interact with the leafy crowns and smaller branches so the interferometric height more closely follows the top of the vegetation canopy. Lower frequencies penetrate deeper into the canopy and interact more with the larger branches and ground-trunk junctures so the measured height more closely follows the ground surface. One estimate or the other may be more desirable depending on the application. For RPI topographic systems, lower frequency systems are usually preferred since temporal decorrelation is less than for higher frequency systems, particularly in vegetated regions.

Practical considerations may also be important, especially when there are platform constraints on weight, power or volume. For a given baseline length the higher the frequency the greater the sensitivity to topographic variation. Therefore, for a platform where the baseline length is fixed, one way to increase the mapping accuracy is to increase the frequency. Antenna size is inversely proportional to the wavelength so lower frequency systems generally need larger antennas. Propagation differences for different frequencies can also affect selection. Spaceborne radars flying above the ionosphere experience greater phase propagation distortion as the frequency decreases. Both international and national organizations regulate frequency spectrum usage that further restricts selection. In particular, mapping systems that require a wide bandwidth for fine resolution mapping may have more difficulty in certain bands.

Airborne-Single Pass

Single pass aircraft systems are well suited for generating fine resolution regional scale DEMs. An example of regional mapping using TOPSAR, an airborne IFSAR system, is shown at Figure 6.20. Aircraft systems have a great deal of flexibility in scheduling data acquisitions, orientation of flight lines, and modes of operation. Single pass systems are best suited for generating high quality topographic maps to a specified absolute accuracy since they do not suffer from temporal decorrelation or from atmospheric phase distortion problems.

Figure 6.20 Radar DEM of the Napa Valley. This view of Napa Valley, California and the surrounding area was created with data from NASA's Airborne Synthetic Aperture Radar while it was being flown in its topographic (TOPSAR) mode on a NASA DC-8 aircraft. The colors in the image represent topography, with blue areas representing the lowest elevations and white areas, the highest. Total relief in the image is approximately 1400 meters. The height information has been superimposed on a radar image of the area, which was collected simultaneously. The image is 70 by 90 kilometers with the Napa Valley the broad flat long area (green–blue) in the center left of the image. Lake Berryessa is the dark area in the center right of the image. See color plate in Appendix C.

Two modes of aircraft interferometric data collection are common; single antenna transmit (SAT) mode where one antenna transmits and both receive and Ping-Pong mode where each antenna transmits and receives its own echoes as shown in Figure 6.21.

Single Antenna Transmit

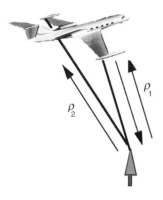

Transmission from one antenna
Reception through both antennas simultaneously

Ping-Pong

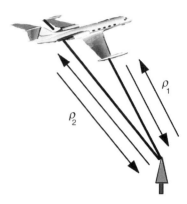

Alternately transmitting out of two antennas
Reception through the same antenna used for transmission only

Figure 6.21 Illustration showing the two means of data collection used on SPI IFSAR systems. In Single Antenna Transmit mode (SAT) a pulse is transmitted from one antenna and the echo recorded from two receiving antennas whereas for Ping-Pong systems each antenna separately transmits and receives.

In SAT mode, the total phase difference is

$$\delta\phi = \frac{2\pi}{\lambda}\{\rho_1 + \rho_1 - (\rho_1 + \rho_2)\} = \frac{2\pi}{\lambda}\{\rho_1 - \rho_2\} \tag{6.10}$$

where ρ_i is the range from antenna A_i to a point on the surface. In Ping-Pong mode, the interferometric phase is given by

$$\delta\phi = \frac{2\pi}{\lambda}\{\rho_1 + \rho_1 - (\rho_2 + \rho_2)\} = \frac{4\pi}{\lambda}\{\rho_1 - \rho_2\} \tag{6.11}$$

Equations 6.10 and 6.11 show that the interferometric phase in Ping-Pong mode is twice that of SAT mode, such that Ping-Pong operation effectively implements an interferometric baseline that is twice the physical baseline. The advantage of operating in Ping-Pong mode is the larger effective baseline increases the interferometric height acuity by a factor of two compared with SAT mode. However, the increased baseline length causes the phase to change faster and in steep terrain can lead to areas that cannot be unwrapped. For those systems that have a choice of operating in either mode, the selection depends on the amount of topographic relief.

Airborne-Repeat Pass

Airborne repeat pass IFSAR systems for topographic mapping enjoy the same operational flexibility as SPI IFSAR systems, namely, scheduling of data acquisitions, orientation of flight lines, and modes of operation [Gray and Farris-Manning, 1993]. In principle, repeat pass systems have increased baseline flexibility because repeat tracks could be flown having any desired baseline length and orientation. Intelligently matching the baseline length to the terrain, or by combining multiple data sets with varying baselines, opens the possibility of generating topographic products with increased accuracy. In practice, controlling the repeat flight pass geometry with precision is extremely difficult. Typically, useful baseline lengths are in the range of 10-100 meters and, to avoid variable quality problems, should remain parallel. Standard flight management systems do not support such accuracy. Several IFSAR mapping systems have been modified to support repeat pass interferometry, including the Danish EMISAR system [Madsen et al, 1996], which is operated on a Royal Danish Air Force Gulfstream G-3 and Aerosensing's Turbine Commander aircraft. The EMISAR system has demonstrated a track repeatability of 10 m which is sufficient for many applications but certainly falls short of being able to fly with any desired baseline.

Although repeat pass systems have increased baseline flexibility they suffer from several problems not present in SPI system. Temporal decorrelation in foliated areas and changes in the terrain even for very short time intervals can be severe. Figure 6.22 shows airborne repeat pass interferometric data at C-, L-, and P-bands acquired using the NASA/JPL AIRSAR system [Hensley et al, 1995]. Although the flight tracks were only separated by 20 minutes, the windy conditions caused decorrelation at all three frequencies. The amount of decorrelation increases as the wavelength decreases. Atmospheric changes between passes can cause phase distortions that lead to height errors that are difficult to detect and remove.

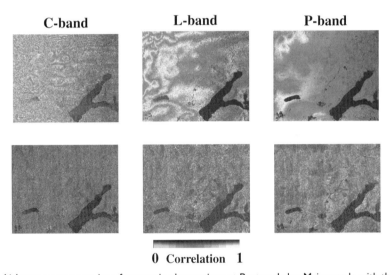

0 Correlation 1

Figure 6.22 Airborne repeat pass interferometric observations at Portage Lake, Maine made with the AIRSAR system. The top row shows the interferometric phases for C-, L- and P-bands. At bottom are the corresponding correlation maps. Conditions were windy when the data was collected and the branch movement resulted in greater decorrelation at shorter wavelengths. See color plate in Appendix C.

To generate accurate topographic maps using RPI IFSAR systems, the baseline must be accurately determined. Kinematic DGPS solutions for aircraft motion have an accuracy of 2-3 cm. Typical interferometric baseline accuracy requirements are at the millimeter level, an order of magnitude finer than the capability of current metrology. Determining the baseline at this level of accuracy must be done using the data and some form of ground control. Aircraft motion, unlike spacecraft motion, is not very smooth and solving for airborne RPI baselines is quite difficult. Because of this it has thus far proven very difficult to calibrate these systems for absolute accuracy.

Spaceborne-Single Pass

Spaceborne platforms have the advantage of global and rapid coverage and accessibility. Increased coverage for spaceborne systems comes about from the combination of the faster velocity by a factor of 30 and the larger swath widths ranging from 50-500 km. Spaceborne systems also avoid airspace restrictions that make aircraft operations difficult in certain parts of the world. Typical baselines for spaceborne IFSAR system making topography measurements range from 100-1000 meters. Baseline accuracy requirements are similar to airborne platforms, requiring millimeter length and arcsecond orientation angles knowledge. This poses a difficult metrology problem regardless of whether the antennas are connected to the same platform or are on separate platforms flying in formation. Tracking phase instability of the radar hardware and antennas, which may go through a hundred degrees Celsius or more of temperature change in an orbital period, requires special hardware. SRTM is the only spaceborne SPI IFSAR system to have flown thus far and will be described in greater detail later.

Recently approved is the Tandem-X mission whereby the German space agency, DLR, in partnership with EADS Astrium GmbH and InfoTerra GmbH, plans to fly two nearly identical X-band SAR systems with tightly controlled orbits with the goal of producing global DTED-3 (12 m posting with better than 2 m height accuracy) for the world. The system has numerous other modes and capabilities (e.g. ocean current and traffic velocity mapping) that will tested after is planned launch in 2009. Of particular interest to the topographic mapping community is that Tandem-X system is fully polarimetric offering the possibility to estimate the vegetation bias (at least for some vegetation types) using the recently developed techniques of polarimetric radar interferometry. Topographic data generated by Tandem-X will be available commercially through the industrial partners of DLR. Tandem-X is posed to be the successor to SRTM and provide the next generation higher resolution and accuracy global DEM of the Earth.

Spaceborne-Repeat Pass

Repeat pass interferometric observations have their greatest utility in measuring surface deformation over wide areas for geophysical applications such as earthquake monitoring, volcano inflation and deflation, and glacier motion. Nonetheless, RPI IFSAR has been used to make topographic maps in many parts of the world, often exceeding the accuracy of the best topographic maps currently available in those regions. Figure 6.23 shows a map of Ft. Irwin, CA made with repeat pass SIR-C. Comparison with a TOPSAR mosaic of the same area showed the height accuracy of $RMSE_z = 16$ m. The height difference map in Figure 6.23 shows tropospheric water vapor induced error that in this case was the dominant error source. If DEMs from multiple independent pairs of repeat pass observations are available, these can be averaged to reduce both atmospheric and random noise.

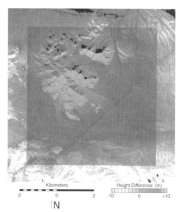

Figure 6.23 IFSAR DEM of Ft. Irwin, CA generated using SIR-C C-band one day repeat pass data collected during the October, 1994 flight of the instrument. The limiting source of error is most likely a result of changes in tropospheric water vapor between passes. See color plate in Appendix C.

Besides tropospheric or ionospheric propagation effects to the interferometric phase as seen in the last example, the other major limiting factor to RPI IFSAR topographic map generation is temporal decorrelation. Figure 6.24 shows decorrelation on the island of Hawaii, for one, two and three day repeat observations, using C-band and L-band data acquired during the second SIR-C mission. Similar to the aircraft RPI example shown earlier, the lower frequency L-band is better correlated than the C-band data for all repeat intervals. The unpredictability of the amount of decorrelation, (in this case the 3 day repeat interval had greater correlation than the two day repeat interval), complicates the process for obtaining suitable repeat pass pairs.

Table 6.3 summarizes the discussion of the various types of IFSAR systems.

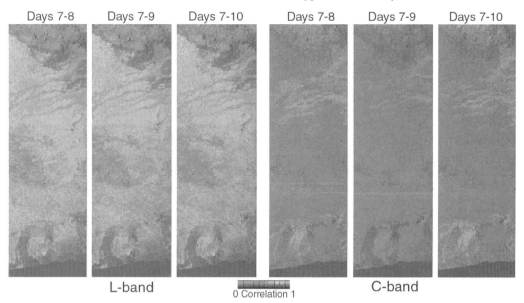

Figure 6.24 Correlation maps produced for one, two and three day repeat pass intervals at C-band and L-band obtained during the second SIR-C mission. See color plate in Appendix C.

Table 6.3 Summary of Types of IFSAR Systems.

	Single Pass	**Repeat Pass**
Airborne	Regional Coverage Affordable Fine Resolution Necessary Motion Compensation Benign Atmospheric Effects No Temporal Decorrelation No Ionospheric Effects Possible Need for Active Baseline Metrology	Regional Coverage Affordable Fine Resolution Necessary Motion Compensation Problematic Atmospheric Effects Temporal Decorrelation Effects No Ionospheric Effects Difficult Track Repeatability Difficult Baseline Estimation Change Detection Possible Increased Baseline Flexibility
Spaceborne	Global Coverage Costly Fine Resolution Benign Motion Compensation Benign Atmospheric Effects No Temporal DecorrelationProblematic Ionospheric Effects Baseline Metrology Required	Regional Coverage Costly Fine Resolution Benign Motion Compensation Problematic Atmospheric Effects Temporal Decorrelation Effects Problematic Ionospheric Effects Difficult Track Repeatability Benign Baseline Estimation Change Detection Possible

PRESENT OPERATING STATUS

With widespread availability of spaceborne radar data acquired in the 1980's by ERS and RadarSAT, many companies now offer RPI-based IFSAR DEMs and associated products. Several of these also sell software that allows users themselves to generate products from raw data. The quality of these products depends on the number of repeat pass pairs available over the region of interest, the amount of decorrelation and atmospheric distortion, and baseline length for the interferometric pairs. The principal companies marketing these technologies and products are Gamma, MDA, TerraSAR and Vexcel. However, the most accurate and reliable sources of IFSAR DEM data are generated using SPI systems. The remainder of this chapter, with one exception, is devoted to brief descriptions of currently commercially operational or soon to be commercially operational SPI IFSAR systems. These systems are airborne systems designed for commercial operational mapping and are operated by Intermap Technologies Inc. and EarthData International. SRTM is the exception since DEMs generated from this government mission are appearing in many commercial and civilian applications.

Intermap Technologies / STAR Systems[7]

Intermap Technologies Inc. currently operates three airborne IFSAR systems with two additional systems under development that will be in operation by late 2006. Intermap's first IFSAR system, STAR-3i®, has been operated by Intermap since 1996. It was initially developed by ERIM (Environmental Research Institute of Michigan) and referred to as IFSARE in the early literature. STAR-3i is an X-band, HH polarization IFSAR flown on a Learjet 36 [Tennant and Coyne, 1999]. In the last few years, Intermap has replaced all of the software and most of the hardware in order to improve product quality and efficiency of operation. In particular this has led to higher resolution images, and better vertical accuracy of the DEMs. Equally important, software automation has led to improvements in processing throughput. The net result of the modifications is higher quality data sets moving toward decreasing costs and wider availability.

Intermap's second system is named TopoSAR® (formerly called AeS-1). It is one of several systems developed by AeroSensing GmbH [Schwäbisch and Moreira, 1999], still operated by Intermap and is currently flown on an Aerocommander turbo-prop platform. In addition to X-Band, HH single-pass IFSAR, it supports repeat-pass, fully polarized P-Band IFSAR. Intermap modified this system in 2005 to allow simultaneous acquisition of the X-Band and P-Band channels. While the system design philosophy originally was quite different from that of the STAR-3i system, the processing stages and the specifications of the X-Band products are now identical. This commonality is achieved via the STAR-4 architecture, technology developed by Intermap in 2003 incorporating the best of the preceding architectures. The STAR-4 architecture was designed to provide the improved products and increased capacity needed to satisfy Intermap's NEXTMap nation wide acquisition programs. Intermap's third system is based completely on the new STAR-4 architecture and is flown in a King Air prop-jet. Two new systems based on the STAR-4 architecture are under construction in 2006 and will be flown in Lear Jet and KingAir platforms and will be named STAR-4 Lear2 and STAR-4 KA2. Current specifications of all five systems are summarized in Table 6.4. Plans are also in place to upgrade STAR-3i to the STAR-4 architecture.

To ensure the final product is precise, accurate and consistent, all Intermap systems utilize a stable fixed baseline on which the antennae and inertial measuring device are co-located. This fixed baseline is critical to accuracy as 1-mm of error in baseline length translates to several meters of elevation error. Co-location of the IMU improves accuracy as it allows accurate measurement of the baseline position and orientation; small errors in these parameters lead to large errors in the elevation solution. All Intermap systems use a single transmit/receive chain which provides double the effective baseline as the interferometer operates in ping/pong mode. A single chain also minimizes calibration errors as all signals travel the same system paths. The motion data and

---

[7] This section was provided by Intermap to describe the operating status of their IFSAR systems.

auxiliary radar data are stored on the control computer for subsequent processing. All sensor positioning is managed using post-processing DGPS/INS processing SW that was developed by Intermap. There is no radar processing on board; radar signal data are recorded directly to an onboard disc system capable of storing over 1 Terabyte which is sufficient to acquire 4 – 5 lines, 450km in length, in one flight. Data are transcribed to LTO-3 data tapes in the field and are transferred to the processing center for generation of the final products.

Table 6.4 System Parameters of Intermap IFSAR.

Parameter	STAR-3i	STAR-4 KA1	STAR-4 Lear2	STAR-4 KA2	TopoSAR X-Band	TopoSAR P-Band
Operational year (Initial)	2002 (1996)	2004	2006	2006	2005 (1996)	2005 (2000)
Platform	Lear 36	King Air 200T	Lear 36	King Air 200T	Aero Commander 685	Aero Commander 685
Wavelength	3 cm	3 cm	3 cm	3 cm	3 cm	74 cm
Peak Transmit Power	8 kW	8 kW	8 kW	8 kW	2.5 kW	1.1 kW
Center Frequency	9.605 GHz	9.605 / 9.675 GHz	9.605 / 9.675 GHz	9.605 / 9.675 GHz	9.605 GHz	375 MHz
Bandwidth	135 MHz	135 / 270 MHz	135 / 270 Mhz	135 / 270 MHz	135 MHz	67 MHz
Antenna Beam Width	1.45°	3.95°	1.45°	3.95°	8.1°	33°
Baseline Length	0.92 m	1.02 m	1.04 m	1.02 m	0.92 m	Typ 80 m
Polarization	HH	HH	HH	HH	HH	Quad-Pol
Baseline Tilt Angle	1.5°	1.3°	1.5°	1.3°	1.5°	---
Platform Altitude	6 – 12 km	4 – 8.5 km	6 – 12 km	4 – 8.5 km	4 – 8.5 km	4 – 8.5 km
Swath Width (km)	8 – 15 km	6 – 11 km	8 – 15 km	6 – 11 km	6 – 11 km	4 – 10 km

Figure 6.25 The three images show the STAR-3i, TopoSAR and STAR-4 platforms respectively. TopoSAR is the only system with antennas not enclosed within a radome. Figure courtesy of Intermap Technologies Inc. See color plate in Appendix C.

The process begins with data acquisition and ends with an independent review of data quality for the products created. Acquisition efforts start with the creation of a detailed flight plan using Intermap planning SW that accounts for terrain variation and accuracy requirements. From this acquisition, logistic plans are developed. Acquisition begins with site preparation; installation of GPS ground stations and, if the requirement is for Type I or II elevation accuracy, the installation of radar corner reflectors. Flight logistics and motion processing are managed via a central facility. Upon completion of data acquisition, centrally processed motion data and raw data tapes are sent to one of the two Intermap processing centers. These processing centers are semi-automated and have the same capacity as the aircraft. The processing center utilizes 64-bit blade computation servers that generate the intermediate strip map products which are mosaiced into image tiles. Upon completion of the mosaic, a bare earth model is created using proprietary software, and all data products are finalized for delivery to the Intermap store where they are made available for licensed purchase.

The core products include an Ortho-rectified Radar Image (ORI), a Digital Surface Model (DSM) and the bare earth Digital Terrain Model (DTM). X-band images are at 1.25-m resolution with similar horizontal accuracy. DSM and DTM are posted at 5m spacing. The elevation products are available in three standard accuracy specifications as illustrated in Table 6.5 below. It is worth noting that all four of the STAR family of sensors are able to achieve these product specifications despite the nuance of individual system design or platform specifics. Apart from these CORE specifications, other accuracies and image/DEM resolution can be supported to meet specific customer requests. Optical/radar merged products are now also becoming available. Figures 6.26 and 6.27 are visualizations of Type II products acquired during the NextMap Britain program.

Data Availability

Data can be obtained from Intermap by either of two methods: custom project or off-the -shelf. In order to make the latter approach feasible, Intermap has been developing country-wide mapping programs under the name NEXTMap. This approach is intended to address the market issues of currency, timeliness, cost and availability. To meet these market demands the approach is to provide licensed data to the users so that ultimately the acquisition/production cost is shared by multiple users.

Table 6.5 Intermap Elevation Accuracy Specifications.

Product	Measures of Vertical Accuracy			
	Specifications		Nominal	
	RMSE	95%	Mean	Standard Deviation
DSM Type I	0.5	1.0	0.3	0.3
DSM Type II	1.0	2.0	0.7	0.7
DSM Type III	3.0	6.0	2.0	2.0
DTM Type I	0.7	1.5	0.5	0.5
DTM Type II	1.0	2.0	0.7	0.7

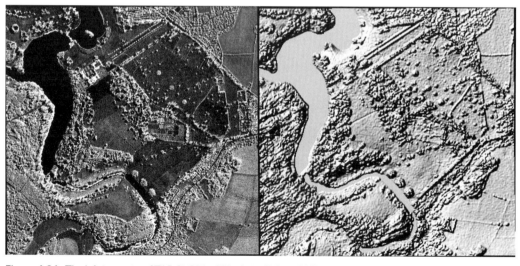

Figure 6.26 The left image is a STAR-3i ORI of Blenheim Palace, U.K. and the surrounding area while the right image is a shaded relief representation of the corresponding DSM. The images are about 2.3 km x 2.3 km. The palace is clearly defined in the upper left quadrant. Individual trees and shrubs are defined in both ORI and DSM. The texture in the open field DSM corresponds to the limiting STAR-3i elevation 'noise' - about 50 cm in this case. Figure courtesy of Intermap Technologies Inc.

Figure 6.27 The image is a three-dimensional visualization of an area in northern Wales U.K. A color air-photo has been merged with the STAR-3i DSM and presented as a perspective view or 'hill-shade'. The air-photo was supplied by GetMapping plc. Figure courtesy of Intermap Technologies Inc. See color plate in Appendix C.

TopoSAR P-band Capability

In addition to the standard X-band capabilities described above, the TopoSAR system can generate P-Band DTM products by synthesizing the interferometric baseline from two individual passes. To achieve the closer flight-line tolerance required for dual-pass interferometry, the flight management system consists of an on-line kinematic DGPS system coupled with a Honeywell LaserRef III inertial sensor. The DGPS corrections are obtained from the global OmniStar system and are downlinked to the aircraft allowing real-time 1m accuracy kinematic tracking of the flight path. This information is displayed along with the deviation relative to the desired flight track and enables the pilot to keep the position error between the actual and desired flight path to less than 10 m. The repeat-passes are usually separated in time by less than an hour, and typically at interferometric baselines of 50 to 80 meters. Tests have shown that an 80 meter baseline allows DTM extraction beneath forest canopies up to 40 meter height at the vertical accuracy level of 1.5 – 4 meter RMSE [Mercer, 2004] when working in quad-pol mode. An example of a P-Band derived DTM beneath heavy forest canopy is presented in Figure 6.28.

EarthData International/GeoSAR

GeoSAR was a program to develop a dual frequency airborne radar interferometric mapping instrument designed to meet the mapping needs of a variety of users in government and private industry. Program participants are the Jet Propulsion Laboratory (JPL), EarthData International (previously Calgis, Inc.), and the California Department of Conservation with funding provided initially by DARPA and subsequently by the National Geospatial-Intelligence Agency (NGA). Begun to address the critical mapping needs of the California Department of Conservation to map seismic and landslide hazards throughout the state, GeoSAR is currently undergoing tests of the X-band and P-band radars designed to measure the terrain elevation at the top and bottom of the

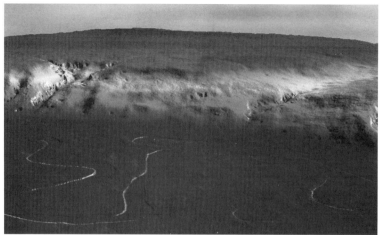

Figure 6.28 TopoSAR quad-pol P-Band DTM of test area within King County, WA, USA. The river valley was relatively bare while the steeply sloped terrain and plateau region included dense mixed forest of 10-35 meters height. Comparisons with control points and lidar 'truth' indicated RMSE differences of about 1.5-2.5m RMSE in the heavily forested plateau region but with differences growing with slope to several meters RMSE in the strongly sloped zone. Figure courtesy of Intermap Technologies Inc. See color plate in Appendix C.

vegetation canopy. Maps created with the GeoSAR data will be used to assess potential geologic/ seismic hazard (such as landslides), classify land cover, map farmlands and urbanization, and manage forest harvests. This system is expected has been fully operational in 2003.

The GeoSAR radar flies onboard a Gulfstream-II aircraft and is a dual-frequency (P- and X-band) interferometric Synthetic Aperture Radar (SAR), with HH and HV (or VV and VH) polarization at P-band and VV polarization at X-band [Hensley et al, 2001]. The radar hardware onboard the Gulfstream-II aircraft is supplemented with a Laser-Baseline Measurement System (LBMS) which provides real-time measurements of the antenna baselines in a platform based coordinate system that is tied to onboard Embedded GPS/INU (EGI) Units. GeoSAR maps a 20-km swath by collecting two 10-km swaths on the right and left sides of the plane as shown in Figure 6.29.

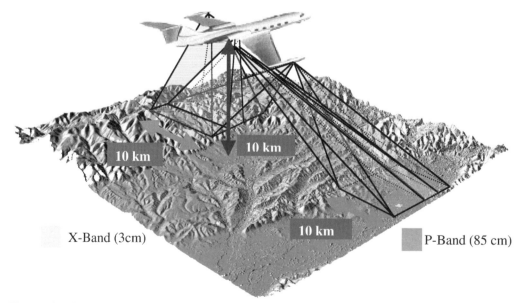

Figure 6.29 GeoSAR collects 10 km swaths simultaneously on both left and right sides of the aircraft at both X- and P-bands. See color plate in Appendix C.

The P-band antenna system is mounted in the port and starboard wingtip pods providing a long antenna-baseline of about 20 meters. X-band antennas are mounted in pairs under the wings with an antenna-baseline of 2.5 meters. Radar operations are controlled by a command disk generated preflight by the Mission Planning Software. Real-time data collection is controlled in-flight via an Automatic Radar Controller (ARC) that sets data collection windows, performs Built-In Test (BIT's) before and after each datatake, and automatically turns the radar on and off during a data acquisition. Raw radar data is recorded on high-density digital tape recorders for subsequent, post-flight processing. The onboard data collection via the Automatic Radar Controller also records navigation data from the aircraft's GPS/INU system, the laser-based antenna-baseline measurement system, and raw signal data from X- and P-band radars. Table 6.6 gives a summary of the main system parameters.

Table 6.6 GeoSAR System Parameters

Parameter	P-Band Value	X-Band Value
Peak Transmit Power	4 kW	8 kW
Bandwidth	80/160 MHz	80/160 MHz
Center Frequency	350 MHz	9.755 GHz
Baseline Length	20 m and 40 m	2.6 m or 5.2 m
Baseline Tilt Angle	0°	0°
Platform Altitude	5,000 m to 10,000 m	5,000 m to 10,000 m

Processing of the data is done on a cluster of Origin computer systems equipped with hundreds of processors and hundreds of Gbytes of RAM. The processor incorporates a number of new algorithms used to remove radio frequency interference (RFI) at P-band, focus the P-band data with its large synthetic aperture and for regridding and mosaicking the data. The expected map accuracy of the X-band system is sub-meter in bare surface regions and 1-4 m in vegetated areas through a combination of X-band and P-band data. Figure 6.30 shows height maps generated using the X-band and P-band radars over Monarch Grove, CA. The eucalyptus tree stand highlighted in the imagery shows up extremely well at X-band but is nearly undetectable in the P-band data because of the increased penetration into the canopy.

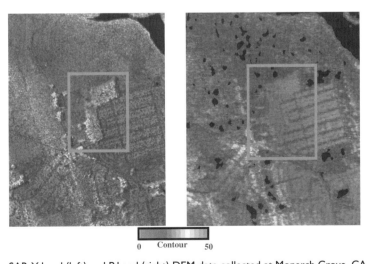

0   Contour   50

Figure 6.30 GeoSAR X-band (left) and P-band (right) DEM data collected at Monarch Grove, CA. Note the elevation contours of eucalyptus tree stand inside the orange box is clearly visible in the X-band data but barely detectable in the P-band data. The GeoSAR mapping system will use a combination of X-band and P-band data to generate bare surface elevation maps in vegetated regions. See color plate in Appendix C.

The system has undergone a number of upgrades since in began operational service. First the system incorporated a smaller and more accurate second generation LBMS to track the interferometric baselines greatly increasing the mapping swath at X-band and reducing multipath from the LBMS fairing leading to better calibrated products. Secondly, the system was augmented with a lidar mapping system that collects nadir pointing elevation data with 15-20 cm mapping accuracy. Lidar data are used to provide very accurate control for large area topographic mapping projects. Upgrades to the digital system replaced the high-speed tape based storage system with new disk based storage devices thereby increasing the amount of data that could be collected in a single flight line. The system is now capable of collecting data in continuous strips greater than 500 km in length. Also, upgraded at the same time were the analog-to-digital converters to provide higher fidelity radiometric and height mapping products.

NASA-NGA/SRTM

The Shuttle Radar Topography Mission system is the only spaceborne SPI IFSAR flown to date [Farr and Kobrick, 2000]. The mapping instrument consisted of modified versions of the SIR-C C-band and X-band radars that were flown on the shuttle in 1994. The most prominent modification was the 60 m retractable boom seen in Figure 6.31, with C-band and X-band receive-only antennas attached to its end. To meet the stringent mapping requirements, the SRTM mapping instrument was equipped with a specially designed motion metrology system. Absolute position information was determined from two GPS receivers located on the outboard antenna. Attitude information was derived from a combination of star tracker and IRU measurements. The interferometric baseline was measured using a combination of an optical target tracker, which measured the angles to several targets located on the outboard antenna structure, and an electronic ranging device used to measure the distance between inboard and outboard antennas. Key system and operating parameters are listed in Table 6.7.

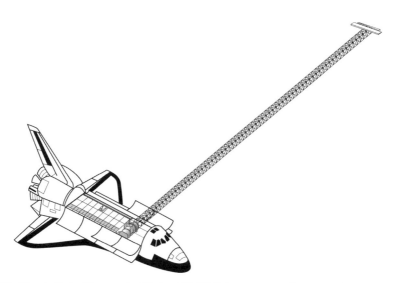

Figure 6.31 The Shuttle Radar Topography Mission (SRTM) flight system configuration. The SIR-C/X-SAR L-, C-, and X-band antennas were located in the shuttle's cargo bay. The C- and X-band radar systems were augmented by receive-only antennas deployed at the end of a 60 m long boom. Interferometric baseline length and attitude measurement devices were mounted on a plate attached to the main L-band antenna structure. During mapping operations, the shuttle was oriented so that the boom was 45 degrees from the horizontal.

Table 6.7 SRTM System Parameters

Parameter	Value
Baseline Length	62 m
Baseline Orientation Angle	45°
Wavelength	.0566 m
Burst Length	60 -100 pulses
Platform Altitude	240 km
Platform Velocity	7.5 km/s
Look Angle Range	30°-60°
Antenna Lengths	12 m/8 m
PRF Range	1330 - 1550 Hz

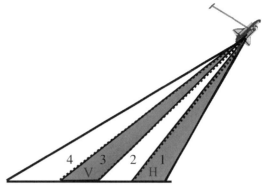

Figure 6.32 The SRTM C-band radar collected data in two subswaths simultaneously using horizontal (H) and vertical polarization (V). The four ScanSAR subswaths are numbered 1-4 starting from nadir as shown above.

To map the world in the 10 days allotted for the mission required the C-band radar to operate in ScanSAR mode. The C-band interferometry data was collected in swaths comprising four subswaths each as shown in Figure 6.32. ScanSAR mapping modes alternately switch between two (or more) beam positions in the cross track direction to increase the swath width at the expense of along track resolution. Exploiting the C-band polarization capability, the SRTM C-band radar operated in ScanSAR mode on vertical (V) and horizontal (H) polarizations to achieve an effective swath width of 225 km while maximizing the signal-to-noise over the swath.

Data collected onboard the shuttle was stored on approximately 300 high density tapes (approximately 6 TB of raw data). During data collection most of the mappable area was imaged two or more times from ascending and descending vantage points. Combination of these data will reduce the noise from each individual strip height map, and allow fill capability for those areas missed in a particular data acquisition (e.g. from shadow and layover). An SRTM datatake is defined as the four subswaths of ScanSAR data collected from radar collection initiation to radar collection termination. Datatake initiation usually commenced just prior to an ocean to land crossing or the start of an island group (or series of island groups) and terminated just after a crossing from land to ocean or the end of an island group (or series of island groups).

Briefly, the processing flow is as follows. Processing is done on a continent basis. All datatakes over a continent are processed from beginning to end. Each of the four subswaths of a datatake is processed independently using a specially designed ScanSAR interferometric processor. The processor generates geocoded strips of height, magnitude, correlation and height errors in coordinate system aligned with the shuttle flight direction for storage efficiency[8]. The strips then needed small adjustments to overcome small imperfections in the metrology or radar system. In conjunction with ground control points these estimates are used to adjust the data relative to the WGS-84 datum. Quality assurance measures are made after both strip map processing and mosaicking. In the event anomalies are detected, the data is queued for further analysis and potential reprocessing. Finally, the data are combined and formatted into 1° DTED 2 cells (1 arcsecond posting). Subsequent to strip map and mosaicking at the JPL the data was shipped to NGA who provided the data to two contractors who did the final data editing and brought the data set in the required DTED products specifications [Slater, et al 2006].

---

[8] Geocoding data in a sensor aligned coordinate system has other advantages. DEM errors are more easily identified and traced to their root cause when aligned with the collection geometry. Moreover, DEM mosaicking can be optimized to solve for the minimal correction parameters based on the geometry of the errors intrinsic to the sensor.

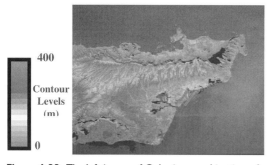

Figure 6.33 The left image of Oahu is a combination of radar backscatter with color contours overlain. Each color cycle, i.e. going from green to blue and back to green again represents 400 m of elevation change. Honolulu International Airport, Waikiki, and Diamond Head are clearly visible in the image. The right image is a perspective view using the SRTM generated topography with Landsat imagery overlaid. See color plate in Appendix C.

An example of SRTM topographic map data processed during the mission is of the island of Oahu in Hawaii. The Oahu data are from beam 2 and are posted at 30 m. These data can be combined with other sensor data shown in Figure 6.33.

An extensive validation of SRTM data has been conducted by JPL, NGA and a number of other investigators throughout the world, that showed that the SRTM data set exceeded all its accuracy specifications[9]. JPL's assessment of the SRTM data is summarized in [Rodriguez, et al, 2006] which is a condensed version of a more extensive report [Rodriguez, et al, 2005]. Analysis consisted of comparisons with continental scale kinematic GPS tracks distributed throughout the world, corner reflectors, a database of nearly 100,000 ground control points and DEM chips distributed globally. Comparison with these ground truth data sets indicated a global height accuracy of 8m (90 % confidence level) and a planimetric accuracy of better than 20m which exceeded the SRTM requirements by a factor of two. The spatial structure of the errors and the sources of these errors are described more fully in the references sited above,

All X-SAR data are the property of the German Aerospace Center DLR and the Italian Space Agency ASI. Therefore all X-SAR data except over Italy are processed, archived and distributed at full resolution by DLR. Apart from selected sensitive areas no restriction will apply. C-band raw data are owned by NGA. One arcsecond (30 m) data over the US will be publicly available, as will 3 arcsecond (90 m) data over the world. NGA will restrict access to 1 arcsecond data outside the US, however for NASA's principle scientific investigators special requests can be made to NGA via NASA. The time and method of distribution is still being decided at the time of this writing.

CALIBRATION PROCEDURES

As with any instrument designed to make quantitative measurements IFSAR systems must be properly calibrated in order to meet accuracy requirements and deliver consistent products to the user. Determining height from interferometric phase measurements requires knowledge of the platform position, range, baseline length and orientation, interferometric phase, wavelength, velocity and Doppler. Estimating systematic corrections to these parameters to obtain consistently accurate topographic maps is the essence of IFSAR calibration. First, an overview of how several key parameters effect topographic height measurement and where errors in these parameters arise is presented. This is followed by a description of the IFSAR calibration procedure.

---

[9] The March, 2006 issue of Photogrammetric Engineering and Remote sensing was devoted to papers assessing the accuracy and utility of SRTM data

Calibration Parameters

Platform Position

DGPS and INS measurement accuracy are generally the limiting factors effecting platform position errors. An error in platform position translates output position measurements in the direction of the position error. Platform position error is the only error source that is completely independent of target location. Figure 6.34 illustrates how an error in platform position translates into DEM errors.

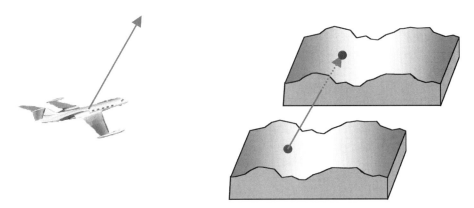

Figure 6.34 An error in platform position, indicated by the red vector in the figure, causes a translation error in the IFSAR DEM equal to the platform position error. See color plate in Appendix C.

Range

Radar range is measured by converting the time it takes for a signal to propagate from the radar antenna to the target and return to distance. Hardware timing offsets and unknown physical delays in the transmitter and receiver chains in the radar system are the major sources of range error. Range errors cause the target location to be translated along the line-of-sight vector as shown in Figure 6.35. The line-of-sight is varying across track, it moves progressively away from vertical as the cross track distance gets larger. Regardless of location within the mapping swath, horizontal and vertical distortions to the DEM are smaller in magnitude than the size of the range error.

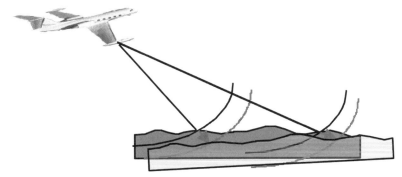

Figure 6.35 Range errors cause displacements along the line-of-sight. Points in the near range are displaced more vertically than horizontally whereas points in the far range are displaced more horizontally than vertically as illustrated above. See color plate in Appendix C.

Baseline Length and Orientation

As previously indicated, very accurate baseline knowledge is necessary to generate accurate topographic maps. Typically, the baseline length must be known to a fraction of a millimeter and baseline orientation angle to a thousandth of a degree. Surveying baselines to this level of accuracy after installation on the aircraft is often difficult or infeasible. The phase center of an antenna, which is usually not the geometric center of the antenna, is the point on the antenna needed for baseline measurements. Analytical methods for determining the phase center from the physical and electrical properties of an antenna are not sufficiently accurate for interferometric applications. Baseline errors generate target location errors on the perpendicular to the line-of-sight as shown in Figure 6.36. The magnitude of the error depends on target location.

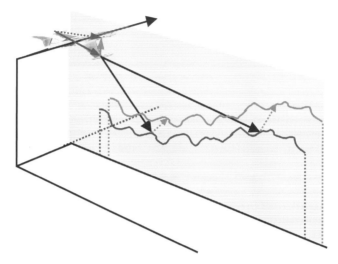

Figure 6.36 Baseline errors cause displacements perpendicular to the line-of-sight and the magnitude of the error is a function of cross track location. The correct baseline is the solid blue arrow on the aircraft, the red arrow is the baseline error (in this case mostly baseline orientation) and the dotted blue arrow is the incorrect baseline. The blue squiggly line represents topographic heights processed using the correct baseline and the red squiggly line the topographic heights with the incorrect baseline. The dotted red arrows point perpendicular to the line-of-sight from the correct to incorrect height. See color plate in Appendix C.

Phase

The differential phase between interferometric channels can have unknown phase delays due to variations in the phase center of the two antennas or from phase delays in the receiver chain. Temporal variation in either of these types of phase delay is tracked by introducing a signal of known relative phase into both channels and tracking the difference. The residual constant phase is then estimated as part of the calibration procedure. Phase errors translate into differential range errors that distort the observation triangle and lead to height errors in the topographic map as shown in Figure 6.37. The magnitude of the height error depends on range, and like baseline errors is perpendicular to the line-of-sight. A constant phase error causes a tilt and shift in the topographic map.

Another type of phase error occurs when reflected energy from the aircraft is received along with the desired signal from the surface as shown in Figure 6.38.

This type of phase distortion is referred to as multipath and introduces a range varying sinusoidal phase error. Roughly speaking, the amplitude of the error depends on the magnitude of the reflected signal compared to the direct signal from the surface, and the frequency of the sinusoid depends on the distance from the antenna. Figure 6.39 shows the effect of multipath on the TOPSAR system.

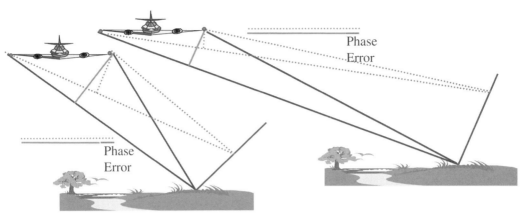

Figure 6.37 Phase errors viewed as differential range errors distort the interferometric observation triangle. The blue triangles represent the nominal interferometric observation triangles with the differential range indicated by the solid green lines. A phase error is introduced by changing the differential range by an amount equivalent to the length of the solid red line. The dotted red triangles show the resulting observation triangles. The position differences lie on a line perpendicular to the line-of-sight, the purple lines, and the amount of height error is range dependent as seen from the near range (left image) and far range (right image) examples. See color plate in Appendix C.

Figure 6.38 Signal reflected from the aircraft, blue line, that is received at the same time as the direct signal return from the surface, red line, introduce a range varying phase error. See color plate in Appendix C.

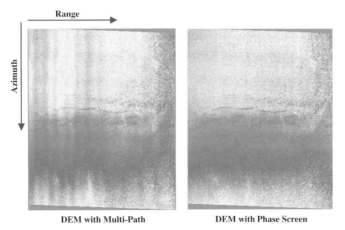

Figure 6.39 Topographic map of Mojave Desert, CA created with and without using a phase screen. Note the cross track ripples 1-10 m in amplitude in the map without the phase screen characteristic of multipath. See color plate in Appendix C.

Radiometric Calibration

Although there is no radiometric accuracy requirement imposed on the imagery for purely DEM applications of IFSAR data, most providers radiometrically correct imagery for antenna pattern and range effects. Prior to mosaicking strip imagery, additional radiometric balancing of the image data to reduce swath-to-swath brightness variations caused by drift in radar system parameters or radar system parameter changes may be necessary. Imagery may be used to aid in breakline determination, terrain use classification and identification of potential water constriction features.

Calibration Site and Procedure

Determining the calibration parameters requires a site with an arrangement of radar identifiable fiducial points (surveyed corner reflectors) over which repetitive overflights are made. In addition, a site with a high accuracy DEM covering an area larger than the cross track direction of the swath and of sufficient size in the along track direction is needed to determine an elevation angle dependent phase correction. Described below are the key calibration parameters, how they are determined, and their effect on DEM accuracy.

To separate the effect the various calibration parameters have on height error, the differing cross track dependencies of the error sources is exploited. A site, preferably with little or no vegetation, is prepared with radar identifiable fiducial points arranged in the cross track direction as shown in Figure 6.40.

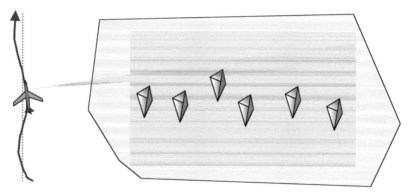

Figure 6.40 IFSAR calibration site is equipped with an array of corner reflectors deployed across the imaging swath of the radar (shown in green). A high accuracy DEM covering the range swath (shown in blue) may be co-located with the corner reflector array or at a different site. Multiple lines are flown at the corner reflector array, and the DEM location if different, in order to determine the calibration parameters. See color plate in Appendix C.

There are several ways of making radar identifiable fiducial points, however the most popular means are passive devices known as corner reflectors. Corner reflectors are metallic objects, shaped either as trihedrals or dihedrals (hence the name corner reflector), that show up as bright objects in radar images. Moreover, trihedral corner reflectors behave as point scatterers, that is the reflected energy acts as if it emanates from a single point (the apex), thereby providing a well defined point from which range measurements may be calibrated. Corner reflector locations are GPS surveyed (and often monumented) to centimeter accuracy. Examples of both types of corner reflectors are shown in Figure 6.41.

Calibration begins with repetitive overflights of the calibration site or sites exercising all the IFSAR mapping modes and configurations. Several flight altitudes may be flown for each mode or configuration to verify stability of the calibration parameters or to generate altitude dependent corrections. The data are first processed to form slant range images. Corner reflector locations, range and along track coordinates, in the slant plane imagery can be predicted from the surveyed locations of the corner reflectors and platform ephemeris data. The predicted range is compared with the measured range and the difference forms the common range delay correction. Range pixel location can be determined to better than a tenth of a pixel by oversampling the slant plane

Figure 6.41 The two types of corner reflectors normally deployed for SAR calibration are a trihedral shown in the left of the figure and a dihedral shown in the right of the figure. Physical size of a corner reflector used for calibration is a function of the wavelength, radar transmit power, antenna size and range. The trihedral is this figure is approximately 2.6 m measured along a diagonal edge and the dihedral is about 2 m high.

imagery. Because range measurements to the two interferometric channels may differ, a differential range correction is computed, by measuring range offsets between the two channels. Differential range measurements are accurate to better than a hundredth of a range pixel and insure proper range registration of the channels during interferogram formation.

After determining the common and differential range corrections, the data are reprocessed and strip map DEMs and orthorectified imagery are generated. Planimetric positions of the corner reflectors are measured using oversampled orthorectified imagery. The height of the corner reflectors is obtained by interpolating the interferometric DEM to get the height at the measured planimetric location of the corner reflector. By comparing the surveyed 3-D locations of the corner reflector array to the interferometrically observed positions, correction estimates for baseline length, baseline orientation angle, and phase are made via a least squares technique. Finally, the high accuracy DEM is used to generate a phase screen that provides elevation angle dependent phase corrections for effects such as multipath and switch leakage. Radiometric calibration of the imagery using corner reflector brightness can be done at this stage if desired or required for the system.

Checking Calibration

Calibration of the IFSAR system is usually done on a regular basis or if the system has undergone any significant change that may affect the calibration. The interval between calibrations depends on the system and its overall stability. Calibration may be linked to major system deployments or occur on a regularly scheduled basis. Periodic checks may be made by deploying a small number (3-4) of surveyed corner reflectors at a site and verifying planimetric and vertical accuracy or comparing height measurements with other data sources or equal or better quality. Kinematic GPS surveys, static GPS survey points, lidar or photogrammetric DEMs provide excellent sources to verify calibration.

PLANNING CONSIDERATIONS

Careful planning and execution of IFSAR data collections are needed to ensure that customer requirements are met and to avoid costly operational errors. Planning considerations can be divided into four phases: requirements definition, mission planning, site operations and data collection. The basic aspects for each planning phase of an airborne SPI data collection are described. Many of these same considerations equally apply to spaceborne and RPI data collections.

Requirements Definition

In the requirements definition phase, the customer and data provider agree upon the overall objectives for a project. First, the customer provides the data provider a description of the site to be mapped, planned use of the data, and their expectations for data quality. The data provider evaluates whether the customer's expectations and planned use of the data are realistic and provides recommendations to the customer as to whether to proceed or not. Customers that have not worked with IFSAR data may be shown sample products to aid their assessment of the applicability of IFSAR data to their project.

Next collection requirements for the region to be mapped are established. Boundaries of the site or sites to be mapped are identified geographically. The customer specifies the desired mapping accuracy. Accuracy requirements may vary spatially, for example flat areas may require one level of accuracy whereas mountainous or vegetated areas may have another. The customer specifies special operational logistics, for example required time of day or year, coordination with ground activity at the site, or coordination with other sensor collections. Mission timing can be critical to obtaining maximal information from IFSAR derived DEMs. Time of day or year may be specified to coincide with low tide in littoral regions or leaf-off conditions in deciduous areas. Mapping in agricultural areas might be linked to a specific time in the growing season or to the post harvest period to avoid mapping seasonal crops. Depending on the wavelength of the radar, it may be necessary to avoid collections during times when the ground is covered by snow levels the radar is unable to effectively penetrate. Coordination with ground activity may be needed if the customer has need for IFSAR data contemporaneous with other activity at the site, or they may wish to deploy their own ground control (e.g. corner reflectors) for the data collection. The amount of allowed voids and multiple passes should be specified. Again these requirements may vary spatially to coincide with areas of greater interest or greatest need. For example, urban areas may need to be mapped on two or more passes from different look direction to prevent holes from shadow and layover in the map products.

IFSAR systems generate a number of data layers in addition to DEMs such as orthorectified SAR imagery and height error maps. Desired output products from the collection must be specified. The customer specifies the datum, geoid and map projection. If the data provider does not support the desired datum, geoid or map projection then the customer may select alternates that can be converted to the desired data representation. With the proliferation of data formats and storage media, it is essential that the customer and data provider agree upon format and delivery media.

To aid in mission operation the customer and data provider should review existing data at the site. This may include DEMs, paper maps, or other relevant reports that provide insight on restrictions or problems affecting either ground or air operations. Finally, a careful review of the expected results between customer and data provider can help avoid mission replans that may increase cost or cause delay in schedule.

Mission Planning

The mission planning phase transforms the data collection requirements into a data collection plan that includes flight lines, instrument parameters, and required coordination activities. A review of overall mission logistics determines the tasks that must be accomplished and the items that must be scheduled, coordinated and tracked. Based on customer input and aircraft availability, the data flights are scheduled. Usually, flight operations are scheduled with contingency days which can be used to recover data lost due to equipment failure or other unforeseen events.

A suitable base of operations is needed for sites outside the data provider's home base operating sphere. Locating an airport within the aircraft's operating range to the site and with runway and hangar facilities equipped to support the data provider's aircraft is one of the first priorities. Additional facilities, possibly remote from the airport, include hotel and meeting areas near the site to support ground activities. A check is made for existing ground control available to support DGPS data collection, and if nothing suitable is located, provisions for establishing control are arranged. The amount of coordination required for spectrum use depends on the operating frequency of the data provider's IFSAR system and the country where the site is located.

Data providers have a great deal of flexibility in scheduling flight lines to generate a DEM having the required posting, accuracy, and data voids based upon their system's operating parameters. An analysis of the project area, project requirements, topography, proximity to restricted airspace, flight altitude, radar parameters and other factors will determine the flight path configuration. The spacing between flight lines will depend on the desired amount of swath overlap between adjacent mapping strips and the steepness of the terrain. Multiple incidence angles are often used in steep terrain in order to fill data gaps caused by radar shadow or layover. Missions consisting of multiple parallel flight tracks should include crossing tracks spaced roughly 10 swathwidths or less apart to help maintain control between flight lines as shown in Figure 6.42.

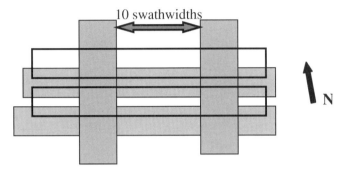

Figure 6.42 IFSAR providers need to plan sufficient overlap between adjacent swaths to avoid data gaps due to terrain effects and should allow for crossing swaths to help maintain control between parallel mapping swaths.

Planning to avoid significant shadow and layover dropouts in areas with significant relief is required. An image mask indicating the predicted image voids for each strip can be generated using existing DEMs such as those available from the USGS. Although the accuracy of the predictions will vary with the quality and post spacing of the planning DEM, this exercise helps verify radar command parameters are set properly. Data masks are generated for each flight line individually and mosaicked together to predict the amount and location of voids in the final product. Figure 6.43 shows a mosaic of the predicted data voids and overlap between flight lines for a TOPSAR data collection over Orange County, CA. Adjacent to the prediction mosaic is shown the mosaicked image and DEM for that collection. Tools such as the one illustrated help ensure both the customer and data provider that the planned data collection will meet coverage requirements. At this point the customer gives the final approval to proceed with mission.

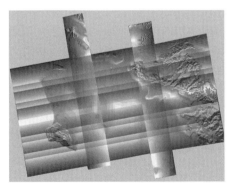 

Figure 6.43 The left figure is a mosaic of image masks from 8 flight lines used in planning an Orange County data collection. Visible is the planned overlap of a quarter of a swath (3 km) between the 6 adjacent east-west flight lines and the 2 orthogonal flight lines used to maintain control. The right figure is a mosaic of the processed TOPSAR data from the Orange County collection. Each color cycle used to depict elevation contours represents 100 m of elevation change. Brightness in the image mask mosaic is derived from a shaded relief of the USGS DEM used to make the mask whereas in the TOPSAR mosaic it is the radar backscatter. See color plates in Appendix C.

Site Operations

Site operations are the initial steps in executing the mission plan. A pre deployment visit to the airport, DGPS base station, base of operations and the site are made to confirm mission planning assumptions are valid. Major variances with the planning assumptions can lead to modifications to the mission plan. All necessary paperwork to conduct flight and ground operations such as visas, flight permits, data export licenses, landing authorizations and spectrum allocation are obtained and verified. A pre-deployment check of the aircraft, radar and ground support equipment is conducted to verify everything is working properly.

Equipment and personnel that must be on site prior to data collection are transported to the base station. Equipment may include flight spares, additional DGPS stations and corner reflectors. The status of activities that need to be completed or initiated prior to data collection such as corner reflector deployments or other ground truth activities are checked. At this point the aircraft and flight crew are deployed to the site and a final check of flight systems is conducted. Agencies such as Air Traffic Control (ATC) are contacted and permission for flight operations confirmed. Finally, the aircraft and ground crew review pre-mission contingencies and mission abort criteria.

Data Collection

If all mission operations could be executed exactly as planned, site operations would mark the end of planning considerations. However, events unforeseen during the mission planning phase can force alteration to the planned data collection strategy. Briefly, a data collection proceeds as follows. A pre-flight briefing between the aircrew, radar operator, and ground crew is conducted the day before or on the day of the data collection to make sure there have been no changes to plans and to coordinate with any other ground truth or sensor collections that may be taking place. The DGPS is deployed to the DGPS base station and data collection is begun approximately one hour prior to takeoff. The aircraft and radar systems go through a pre-flight checklist. Radars with Built-In-Test (BIT) equipment go through their pre-flight sequence. After takeoff and arriving at the site, collection of the planned datatakes commences. The radar operator monitors radar, INU and DGPS, and other metrology systems to check for any operating anomalies. After the mission a post flight briefing is conducted to note any anomalies with the air or ground operations. If warranted, alterations to the mission to facilitate operations or correct deficiencies are made. Data is periodically forwarded to the processing center for further checks of data integrity and system health. This continues until the mission is complete.

COMPARISON WITH OTHER TECHNOLOGIES

Photogrammetry and lidar systems are other remote sensing technologies designed to make topographic measurements (see Chapters 5 and 7 for a detailed discussion of these sensors). Each type of sensor is sensitive to different aspects of the surface under observation and therefore measures height differently depending on surface type and ground cover. All of the above sensors make height measurements that depart from an "idealized height sensor" that gives the height measurement at precisely one point. Only for simple surfaces or after appropriate post-processing of the data can the height measurements of the three types of sensor be directly compared with point measurements like those obtained by DGPS surveys.

The desired elevation measurement is application dependent. Floodplain applications require DEMs to have all vegetation and buildings removed, and water constriction features such as bridges, fences and power poles edited from the data. However, for flight obstruction or forest mapping it is desired to leave some or all of the elevations unaltered. Each of the different sensor technologies has strengths and weaknesses depending on the desired height measurement for a particular application. In fact, a synergistic combination of measurements from two or more of the above sensors can produce the best possible product.

As the variety of IFSAR, lidar and photogrammetric sensors is quite numerous, and performance parameters continuously improving for all three types of sensors, only very general comparisons of the sensor characteristics are presented[10]. The primary characteristics that distinguish the sensors and their height measurements are shown in Figure 6.44. Lidar[11] and IFSAR systems are active sensors supplying their own illumination source, IFSAR and photogrammetric systems are imaging sensors, and lidar and photogrammetric are optical sensors.

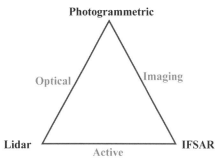

Figure 6.44 Figure showing the primary sensor characteristics shared by the three pairs of sensor combinations.

Photogrammetry

Photogrammetric sensors, like IFSAR systems, generate both imagery and height data and have been operated on both airborne and spaceborne platforms. Unlike aerial or spaceborne photogrammetry, IFSAR missions can be flown without regard to sun angle. Flights may take place at night or in conditions of inclement weather provided the conditions are such that the image formation process is not degraded. Airborne optical cameras continue to generate extremely fine resolution (often sub-meter) imagery without the troublesome layover and shadow problems of radar. However, radar interferometers are proving to be a cost-effective method for wide area, rapid mapping applications, and do not require extensive hand-editing and tiepointing. Additionally, because IFSAR systems often fly at greater altitudes, they can operate in congested air-traffic corridors that are often difficult to image photogrammetrically. Mapping in tropical regions that are often cloud-covered can be done more reliably with IFSAR systems that penetrate clouds. Urban mapping is a challenging venue for mapping by IFSAR systems due to the extremely complex scattering environment. Although some high resolution systems have shown promise for urban mapping, photogrammetry still has inherent advantages for this application.

Densely vegetated surfaces can be problematic for both sensors if bare surface elevations are desired. Photogrammetric true ground surface heights can only be obtained if sufficiently large gaps are present in the canopy. These points, usually determined manually, are then extrapolated to other portions of the canopied area to produce bare surface height maps. Heights measured by IFSAR systems are reflective surface heights and can lie anywhere within the canopy. Longer wavelength systems penetrate deeper into the canopy but the exact location within the canopy corresponding to the height measurement is not easily determined. IFSAR correlation has information about the vertical structure of the canopy and has the potential of providing corrections to measure bare surface elevations [Hagberg et al, 1995], [Rodriguez et al, 1999] and [Hokeman and Varekamp, 2001].

Unlike photogrammetric and lidar systems, IFSAR systems can generate height error maps on a pixel-by-pixel basis [Hensley and Webb, 1994]. These images provide an estimated relative statistical height error as described earlier. These products are extremely useful for ascertaining whether an IFSAR derived DEM is suitable for a particular mapping application and for locating problematic regions within the DEM. Figure 6.45 shows a height error map of Long Valley, CA made using the TOPSAR system and a comparison with measured statistical height errors from kinematic GPS measurements.

---

[10] Many detailed sensor comparisons between sensors have been made like the ones discussed in [Madsen, 1993], [Hensley and Webb, 1994] and [Mercer et al, 1999].

[11] Previously, operating commercial lidar systems did not record the reflected lidar signal level that could be used to form a lidar image. However, intensity images are now being offered by lidar vendors, as explained in Chapter 7.

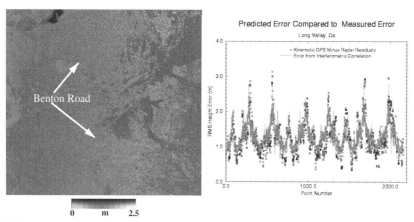

Figure 6.45 Local height errors computed from the interferometric correlation data were compared with kinematic GPS measurements by computing the "local" RMS height difference between the TOPSAR and GPS measured heights along Benton Road in LongValley, CA. See color plate in Appendix C.

Lidar

Lidar like IFSAR is an active sensor providing its own illumination and similarly records the time delay between transmit and receipt of reflected signals from the surface. Employing a very narrow beam so that the projected footprint on the ground is typically 10 meters or less from space (several feet from airborne sensors), lidar systems obtain one or more height measurements per pulse. The number of height measurements is dependent upon the vertical structure of objects within the beam and the type of lidar system as shown in Figure 6.46. Some lidar systems are equipped to only record a single time delay per pulse whereas other systems record time delays for multiple samples exceeding a signal level threshold. By scanning cross track to either side of the nadir point of the aircraft and rapidly pulsing the laser reasonable mapping swaths are obtained. Operating at optical instead of microwave frequencies, lidar systems do not penetrate clouds and other atmospheric obscurants.

Figure 6.46 Lidar systems like IFSAR systems are active sensors that measure range. Liears use narrow scanning beams to localize their targets spatially. Some lidar system measure the height of multiple returns (denoted by blue bars next to object in scene) exceeding a specified threshold (sample echo in blue with threshold in green next to plane) thereby providing additional information about the vertical structure of objects in the scene. See color plate in Appendix C.

Unlike IFSAR systems lidars are not imaging sensors. Applications where contextual information that is not easily derived from height data alone favor IFSAR and photogrammetric mapping sensors. Classification studies and resource inventory surveys are examples where imagery plays a vital role in separating and identifying vegetation and crop types, geologic structures, and various anthropogenic uses. Water body mapping and delineation is often possible with IFSAR systems depending on the frequency of operation and the roughness of the water body surface, whereas lidar systems do not obtain good height measurements over water.

Lidar systems have become the sensor of choice for mapping vegetated regions when elevation measurements beneath the canopy are needed. True ground surface elevation measurements are obtained after a post-processing step to insure the reflective surface does not arise from within the vegetation canopy. As previously noted, heights measured by IFSAR systems are reflective surface heights and can lie anywhere within the canopy, but with proper frequency selection and use of correlation data has the potential of providing corrections to measure bare surface elevations. Larger swaths possible with IFSAR mapping systems can substantially reduce the time to collect data over large areas.

POST-PROCESSING

Processing and post-processing of IFSAR data affect the accuracy and quality of final map products. The division between processing and post-processing is somewhat arbitrary, however for the purposes of this chapter post-processing will be defined to begin after the interferometric phase is transformed to a position and elevation measurement. Many aspects of IFSAR post-processing are nearly identical to standard photogrammetric or lidar post-processing. The type and amount of post-processing is application dependent and is tailored to meet specific user requirements. In this section some of the most common IFSAR post-processing steps are described.

Regridding

Critical to understanding the final DEM is the posting to smoothing window ratio. Smoothing of the interferometric phase measurements is done to reduce phase noise and aid in the unwrapping process. Typically this involves spatially averaging the phase over a window by an amount that is set by the processor operator. This window is often larger than the post size of the DEM. Thus the effective resolution of the DEM may be less than post size depending on the spatial frequency spectrum of the underlying topography.

Unwrapped phase measurements lie on a uniform grid in range and azimuth, however the position measurements determined from the phase measurements are distributed unevenly with respect to the processor ground projection. To obtain an elevation map on a uniform ground projection grid the data is interpolated or resampled to the desired posts in the regridding process. The regridding algorithm employed affects the resulting height accuracy and spatial resolution of the IFSAR map products. Regridding algorithms include the simple nearest neighbor algorithm where the point closest to the desired post within a specified radius is used to more sophisticated algorithms such as surface fitting or more general interpolation algorithms. Adaptive regridding algorithms adjust the smoothing spatially based on the amount of topographic relief with more smoothing done in flat areas to reduce the height noise and less smoothing done in areas with substantial relief to maintain spatial resolution.

Map Mosaics

Mosaicking is the process whereby multiple images and/or DEMs are merged into a single image and/or DEM with a common datum, map projection and data format. The mosaicking process may involve DEMs in multiple coordinate systems that can be derived from multiple sources (e.g. interferometric, USGS, DTED, photogrammetric or lidar), have different data types (e.g. floating point, integer) and have different units (e.g. m, ft). Mosaicking of elevation data is inherently a 3-dimensional process and uses algorithms capable of manipulating and combining 3-dimensional data sets in order to produce high quality seamless mosaics. The mosaicking process can be divided into four steps: determination of the data sets to be mosaicked, finding ground control and tie points, mathematical adjustment of the data sets based on the tie and ground control point data, and combining of the multiple observations into a seamless map product.

If geolocation of the individual map components is sufficiently accurate, mosaicking is done via dead reckoning, that is placement of pixels in the final mosaic is based on the *a priori* positioning data of the individual components. A combination of ground control and tie points can be used to improve absolute and relative geolocation accuracy. Ground control points are points in the component data sets that are identified with external data having known absolute positions. These data are used to remove both relative and absolute positioning errors depending on their distribution within the data sets. Typically, these points are generated from corner reflectors or from manually identified points. Tie points are points identified to be the same point in two or more of the component data sets. These data can be used to remove relative position errors between the data sets, but do not provide absolute position information. Tie points are generated using automated matching algorithms to match either the imagery or elevation data.

Before the data can be combined into a final mosaic, a mathematical framework that includes the required coordinate conversions and position corrections based on tie and ground control point data must be established. The model may be sensor based if only one type of data is to be combined (e.g. IFSAR or photogrammetric data) or based on a more generic error function such as affine transformations[12]. Regardless, care must be taken to avoid fitting for parameters in the model that are not well constrained by the distribution of tie and ground control points.

The final step in the mosaicking process interpolates the individual data sets into the map mosaic coordinate frame and combines what may be multiple observations into the final map product. Combining multiple data sets from the same sensor or from multiple sensor seamlessly uses a smooth blending from one data set or combination of data sets to another called feathering. Feathering adjusts the relative weighting of the different data sets over a specified distance to smoothly transition from one data set or combination of data sets to another. The feathering weights may be further adjusted to reflect the height accuracy of the individual points by incorporating the height covariance estimates determined from the correlation measurements. In this way posts in the final map mosaic favor the most accurate IFSAR mapping data.

Datum/Geoid and Map Projection

The user specifies the desired datum, geoid and map projection for the final DEM. During the mosaicking process the individual IFSAR mapping strips are projected into a common coordinate system that is normally the desired user map projection and datum thereby avoiding unnecessary data interpolations. Correcting the heights to the desired geoid can be part of the mosaicking process or done in a separate post-processing step.

Hole Fill

Data gaps from layover, shadow or low signal regions may be present after mosaicking is complete. Filling these data gaps may be required for some applications. There are three basic methods used to fill gaps in the final DEM. Data may be specially acquired over the gap regions, data from alternate sources may be used, or analytical methods for filling gaps may be employed. Specially acquired data to fill residual gaps is the most expensive means of filling gaps in the DEM and may require a delay in product delivery to allow for data collection and processing. This

---

[12] Affine transformations are linear transformations plus a translation. Affine transformations can be decomposed into rotational, scale, skew and translation components and for most sensors small errors are well modeled by these terms.

option has the benefit of maintaining uniform quality data throughout the DEM but is usually warranted when there are excessively large data voids in critical portions of the DEM. Data from previous data collections or other data sources (e.g. USGS DEMs) may also be used to fill in gaps in the data. These data in general may not meet the same accuracy or resolution requirements of the IFSAR data, however alternate source data often proves adequate for small gaps. By incorporating these alternate sources during the mosaicking process, a seamless final product is achieved, provided there has not been extensive change to the topography between the time of the IFSAR data collection and the time the alternate source data were acquired. A myriad of algorithms is used to analytically fill gaps in topographic data. Surface fitting, kriging methods, and polynomial interpolators are among the most commonly employed algorithms for hole filling. The choice of algorithm depends on the size of holes to be filled and the intended application for the DEM.

Data Editing

Data editing is used to correct errors in the DEM detected during the quality control process or to manipulate height values so that they conform to a user prescribed mapping standard. Unwrapping errors occur when an incorrect multiple of 2π is added to the interferometric phase measurement. This results in the IFSAR elevation measurements being too high or too low by a multiple of the ambiguity height, a quantity that is determined from the interferometric system parameters and mapping geometry. Unwrapping errors are detected and edited from the DEM by searching for height discontinuities that are multiples of the ambiguity height. Spikes and wells are isolated points in the DEM whose elevation differs from surrounding heights by an unphysical amount. These points are edited from the final DEM and marked as data voids or filled in using a combination of the surrounding elevation values. Some map products (e.g. DTED products) require that water bodies have single elevation value. IFSAR DEMs over water are usually noisy and have intrinsic height variation that depends on the amount of thermal noise. Water body editing consists of identification of the water body and setting the elevation to the desired value. Water body identification using IFSAR data is a difficult problem and is a significant portion of the editing process.

Vegetation Removal

Applications that require bare surface DEMs need to have IFSAR reflective surface elevation measurements corrected to bare surface elevations. Correction of reflective surface elevation measurements is called vegetation removal. Vegetation removal involves identifying vegetated regions and then correcting the elevation measurements to the bare surface. Identification of vegetated region uses combination of imagery, elevation measurements and correlation data. Correction to bare surface elevations may employ algorithms similar to lidar and photogrammetric sensors where elevation measurements that penetrate to the bare surface are used in combination with surface fitting algorithms to make elevation adjustments. More sophisticated algorithms that use the image brightness, correlation and elevation measurements along with a model of the vegetation are now being employed by some IFSAR sensors for vegetation removal.

Derived Products

In addition to the IFSAR image and DEM products, several derived products based on the IFSAR data may be generated during post-processing and provided to the customer. Classification maps that delineate water body boundaries, urban and vegetated areas, as well as other classes are possible using IFSAR data or IFSAR data in combination with other sources such as Landsat imagery. Slope and curvature maps necessary for hydrological and seismic hazard assessment and landslide potential studies can be derived from the height and height error maps. Semi-automated road identification based on a combination of IFSAR imagery and elevation measurements can provide an updated cartographic layer for map generation. Breakline identification and water body constriction removal are post-processing steps usually required in floodplain mapping applications.

QUALITY CONTROL

Quality control is a task or series of tasks that scrutinizes all, or a sample, of the IFSAR products issued during, or at the end of, the IFSAR map generation process in order to ensure that the final product meets or exceeds requirements [Ackerman, 1994], [Burrough, 1986] and [Positional Accuracy Handbook, 1999]. This scrutiny involves a combination of review, inspection and quantitative measurements, against well-defined criteria that are outlined in references. Additional quality controls determined by the data provider are used for other map products such as SAR imagery and other IFSAR specific derived products. Many data providers certify their QA/QC processes to the ISO-9002 standard. An overview of some of the standard qualitative and quantitative quality control procedures is presented in the following sections.

Visual Accuracy Checks

Visual quality control begins by looking for gross processing errors associated with incomplete phase unwrapping, large spikes and wells, large tilts on water bodies and features that seem out of place. The maximum and minimum elevations in the IFSAR DEM are compared to the maximum and minimum values represented by contours or spot elevations available on the most recent available map. A check for completeness in the project size and for continuity along mosaic seams and data gap boundaries is also made. Overlay the IFSAR map products on available map data to check if geo-referencing is correct. Spot check selected pixel values such as corner and center pixel values against heights on published maps. Use a DEM viewing workstation with the appropriate software tools to aid in the identifications of blunders such as spikes and holes. Blunders are generally identified through a combination of color banding of elevation contours, stereoscopic viewing using anaglyphic filters, shaded relief enhancements and use of histograms. Artifacts identified during the visual accuracy checks are documented and quantified noting the location and source, for example: terrain masking, radar shadow, DEM sub-patch boundary, land/water boundary, vegetated regions, wind motion, or other factors.

Ground Truth

Quantitative assessment using ground truth data is an important component of the quality control procedure. A selected set of ground control points, typically greater than 20 for any region or sub-region to be tested, is compared with the corresponding IFSAR generated height measurements. For a rectangular area that is believed to have uniform positional accuracy, check points may be distributed so that points are spread at intervals of at least 10% of the diagonal distance. At least 20% of the points are to be located in each quadrant. The independent source of higher accuracy shall be of the highest accuracy feasible and practical to evaluate the accuracy of the IFSAR data. To make a rigorous accuracy assessment usually requires truth data that is three times more accurate than the product tolerance. Each checkpoint must be well defined (NMAS, ASPRS and NSSDA mapping standards – see Chapter 3) in the context of the image resolution, resolution and features that are present. A well-defined point represents a feature for which the horizontal position is known to a high degree of accuracy and for which the absolute position with respect to the map product geodetic datum is known. Kinematic GPS measurements taken along major highways and trunk roads provide excellent data sets for quality control and accuracy assessments. Kinematic GPS transects should be collected away from urban areas where multipath in the radar and kinematic GPS data is often problematic.

Height accuracy is slope dependent for IFSAR mapping systems. Accuracy assessments grouped according to slope magnitude ease the comparison with the National mapping standards. The National Map Accuracy Standards (NMAS) and the ASPRS accuracy standards for large-scale maps states that for the purposes of checking elevations the map position of the ground point may be shifted in any direction by an amount equal to twice the limiting RMSE position accuracy. Implicitly this allows for spatially varying height accuracy that may be slope dependent. Evaluating the accuracy in different sub-regions grouped by slope and using the standard specified above gives a better overall assessment of map accuracy.

Height Error Map Accuracy Analysis

One of the valuable map products generated by IFSAR mapping systems is the local statistical height error map generated from the correlation measurements using Equations 6.8 and 6.9. The error map provides the user with a point by point assessment of the vertical accuracy of the DEM. Evaluation of the height error map accuracy is done using areas of bare surface. The height error map accuracy is assessed using the local relative height error at a point p, σ_{h_p}, which is defined as

$$\sigma_{h_p} = \sqrt{ \frac{1}{\#(B)} \sum_{q \in B} \left(h_{r_q} - h_{t_q} \right)^2 - \left[\frac{1}{\#(B)} \sum_{q \in B} \left(h_{r_q} - h_{t_q} \right) \right]^2 } \qquad (6.12)$$

where h_r is a radar height value, h_t is the corresponding ground truth height value, B is the set of points in a neighborhood of the point p (to be defined), and $\#(B)$ is the number of points in B. B should be a box centered at p with size equal to 5 pixels as shown in Figure 6.47. The estimate of σ_{h_p} should be considered valid if and only if $\#(B)$ is greater than or equal to 10.

Figure 6.47 This figure shows the neighborhood, B, about a point, p (yellow circle), where the local statistical height accuracy is being measured. A sufficient number of control points (shown in red) should be present in order to make a valid assessment. See color plate in Appendix C.

Control points are usually derived from either kinematic GPS measurements or a high accuracy photogrammetric or lidar DEM with relative height accuracy at least three times better than the expected IFSAR mapping accuracy. Height error estimates are assumed valid if 90% of the points have a local statistical height error that is within 20% of the IFSAR predicted statistical height error.

USER APPLICATIONS

Fine resolution topographic measurements have applications throughout the commercial, civilian, and military sectors. Applications include, for example, land slope stability and land-slide characterization, land-use classification and change monitoring for agricultural and military purposes, floodplain and hydrological modeling, littoral zone mapping, and archeological and geological applications. The accuracy and resolution depend on application, and a number of technologies are usually available that can meet any particular application requirements. The ability to generate accurate IFSAR DEMs at regional or global scales quickly and at a reasonable cost has seen the rapid infusion of this technology into a variety of applications.

Hydrology

The insurance industry as well as local and national governments have become increasingly concerned about proper risk assessment associated with flooding. Risk assessment is needed for flood warning, floodplain control and financial liability studies. Floodplain mapping and risk assessment uses a combination of topography and surface cover type along with propagation models to determine depth of flooding. Airborne derived IFSAR DEMs with the combination of accuracy and resolution and cost have proved ideal for regional flood risk assessment as has been shown in several studies both in the United Kingdom [Galy and Sanders, 2000] and in the United States.

---

[13] Mapping water body surfaces is usually only possible for higher frequency systems (C-band and above) and when there is sufficient wind or current to make the water appear rough at the imaging wavelength.

Littoral Zone Mapping

Littoral zone mapping is an area where IFSAR mapping is playing an increasingly important role because it maps from the near shore regions out onto the water surface[13]. Photogrammetric and lidar systems have greater difficulty mapping these regions because neither type of system makes height measurements over water bodies. By mapping at low tides IFSAR systems should provide some of the most complete and detailed maps of the littoral zone.

Seismic Hazards

Slope and along-slope and cross-slope curvature estimates are needed for slope hazard analysis. Special care must be taken in computing slope and surface curvature from interferometric DEMs because point-to-point height noise can be comparable to a significant fraction of the post spacing. Studies have shown that when this is taken into account, IFSAR derived DEMs improve classification of areas of landslide induced seismic risk [Real et al, 1997].

Urban Mapping

Urban mapping varies from the relatively low density and simple structures of a suburb to the extremely complex and high density environment of a modern major city. Multiple scattering, shadow and layover make urban mapping a challenging application environment for IFSAR systems. High resolution airborne IFSAR systems have shown some utility for this application particularly in medium to low density urban areas [Mercer and Gill, 1998]. System resolution and the degree of algorithm optimization for urban environments greatly affect the achievable mapping accuracy.

Archeology

Understanding where, how and when ancient civilizations modified and controlled their physical environment is an aspect of archeological research where SAR and IFSAR systems have made important contributions. Multiple frequency observations that penetrate into dense vegetation coupled with accurate topographic information is providing archeologists with unique regional scale observations of ancient sites such as Angkor Wat in Cambodia and the Great Wall in China. Because of the unique perspective SAR and IFSAR systems can provide, the use of these data in future investigations is expected to increase.

Vegetation Mapping and Land Use Classification Maps

The use of interferometry for land use classification and vegetation parameter determination is a rapidly expanding area of research. The use of multi-frequency IFSAR systems that exploit the relative penetration into the canopy, and the use of interferometric correlation which is sensitive to the vertical structure of the canopy, have shown great promise for extracting canopy parameter elevations [Hagberg et al, 1995], [Rodriguez, Martin and Michel, 1999], [Hokeman and Varekamp, 2001] and [Hensley et al, 2001]. Land use maps that have classification accuracy in the 90% level have been demonstrated using data from airborne IFSAR systems [Rodriguez, Martin and Michel, 1999] although significant ambiguities were observed under certain conditions. Specifically, problems arose due to the sensitivity to the absolute calibration of the radar backscatter and from changes in backscatter as a function of incidence for the same ground cover type. Using multi-frequency, multi-temporal or other optical data sources can significantly reduce classification error.

Geology

Topographic maps have traditionally played an important role in geological applications. IFSAR system height and image data can simultaneously provide topographic information at two scales. Using the topographic data directly, topography at the DEM posting provides information about geologic structures such as faults, volcanic structures, and alluvial fan size and extent. The associated SAR imagery, which is sensitive to the surface roughness on the scale of the radar wavelength, provides information about the micro-topography of the surface. The combination of the two scales can be used to infer information about the surface geology such as the relative age of lava flows.

DATA DELIVERABLES

Data deliverables can be divided into three categories, pre-project deliverables, post-project deliverables, and map products including DEMs, imagery and other derived products. Depending on whether data is specifically collected to support a project or purchased from archived sources, not every deliverable category is applicable. The main goal of this chapter is to provide the DEM user with a list of the type of deliverables that may be available throughout the course of a project. Selection of those deliverables most useful for a particular project will depend on the type of data needed and the application.

Pre-Project Deliverables

Pre-project deliverables are designed to insure that the desired data is collected and will meet project accuracy and coverage requirements. Project planning, as covered earlier, is integral to the success of any project. Clear communication by appropriate pre-project deliverables can help the data provider and data user effectively communicate cost (and cost versus data quality tradeoffs), data quality expectations, data collection constraints, and schedule.

- A map (typically, U.S. Geological Survey maps are desirable for the purpose) showing the study area boundaries, flight paths and mapping swaths at a medium scale (1:50,000) or small scale (1:100,000).
- A shaded relief map of each swath indicating the area lost to layover, shadow or where the phase is unwrappable.
- A shaded relief composite mosaic of all the mapping swaths showing those gaps that will be filled in during the mosaicking process.
- A table giving the estimated amount and type of data voids on each swath and in the data mosaic must be provided.
- Documentation specifying altitude, airspeed, heading, start and end location, flight time, radar pulse spacing, bandwidth, center frequency and polarization, interferometer configuration (ping-pong or single antenna transmit), pulse width, and other flight and equipment information deemed appropriate. Maximal tolerance on flight or radar parameters before a line must be aborted should also be included.
- A schedule indicating expected date and time of flights, processing and data delivery dates.

Post-Project Deliverables

Post-project deliverables provide the DEM user with information about how closely the planned data collection objectives were met. Ancillary data may also include additional information about weather, ground control, or other pertinent data to facilitate use of the data in its intended application.

- An IFSAR data system report includes discussions of: data processing methods used both for strip map production and DEM mosaicking, sensor configuration parameters for each datatake, accuracy and precision of IFSAR data collected, accuracy of the topographic surface products, and any other data deemed appropriate.
- A flight report documents the mission date(s), time, flight altitude, airspeed, heading, start and end points of the data take, look angles to the near and far edge of the swath, radar mode parameters and any other information deemed pertinent. The report usually includes information about the aircraft motion including GPS derived flight information, INS data including attitude angles and attitude angle rates. Comparisons between planned and actual flight paths and radar parameters should be given with any deviations exceeding the maximal specified tolerances explicitly noted.
- A ground control report includes all the pertinent base station information and mission notes, including information on GPS station monument names and stability.
- A data processing report summarizes the parameters for processing the data and identifies any anomalies encountered during the processing.

- A system calibration report indicates the time when and data used to calibrate the sensor for the project and an assessment of how accurately the sensor was calibrated.

Map Products

Map products are defined as any data deliverable that is derived from the IFSAR data. The range of products depends on the application and the amount of post-processing done to the data. Most providers will accommodate a range of map projections, geoid choice, data format and delivery media to satisfy customer needs and requirements.

COST CONSIDERATIONS

The cost of IFSAR products depends on many factors. Some of the factors are accuracy, project size, geographic location, ground post spacing, terrain type and density, and type of the vegetation cover. Current reported prices for IFSAR generated DEMs are grouped into two categories: (1) project specific, where data is collected by the data provider to meet a specific customer mapping requirements, and (2) archival data where data is purchased from previously collected (and possibly processed) IFSAR mission data [Global Terrain Prices, 2001].

Project Specific

For project specific IFSAR, DEM prices range from $30/km² to $100/km² depending upon the site location, terrain ruggedness, foliage density and extracted vector data.

Archival Data

Archival data prices are lower than project specific prices and depend on whether the data must be reprocessed or can be used as previously processed. Archival data purchases are possible when the data collector, usually in exchange for a reduced collection and processing price, has reserved the data rights for a data collection. In affect, the data collector licenses the data to his client for a narrow use and retains distribution rights for all other uses. Data archive prices range from $11/km² to $25/km² for DEMs and $7/km² for IFSAR images. Table 6.8 shows a summary of prices for different postings and geographic locations.

Table 6.8 IFSAR X-band Prices.

Commercial X-Band Data Warehouse Prices			
Post Spacing(m)	Vertical RMSE(m)	Price Range per km²	
		DEM	DEM and Image
5	1.0	$20-$100	$23-$110
10	1.5-2.0	$12-$55	$14-$60
10	2.0-3.0	$10-$45	$12-$50

TECHNOLOGICAL ADVANCEMENTS

A number of innovations in IFSAR technology and methodology are pressing toward finer resolutions and height accuracy, and improved characterization of the surface heights.

Airborne IFSAR systems continue to progress to finer resolutions and height acuity. At Ku band and other available bands, cm-scale resolutions are possible in the cross-track direction. In azimuth, spotlight mode processing can achieve sub-meter resolutions. Experimental systems by Sandia and ERIM have demonstrated this capability. With such fine resolution, it is straightforward to achieve relative accuracy that is sub-meter because of the large amount of averaging that is possible.

The challenge for future systems is unambiguously differentiating the heights of the various physical surfaces on the ground, from treetop to bare earth. Systems such as GeoSAR, with X- and P-band interferometry and dual-polarization, are the first attempt to address this issue [Hensley et al, 2001]. In the future, we expect to see fully polarimetric interferometers, possibly at multiple frequencies, as the next technological leap. Scattering from randomly oriented objects like leafy canopies tends to randomize the polarization of the electromagnetic signal, while scattering from tree-trunks and sloped surfaces has a more deterministic effect on the polarization. With the full polarization matrix available, scattering from treetops can be separated from surface interactions [Cloude and Papathanassiuo, 1997]. With interferometric polarimetry, it is then possible to assign a height to the treetops and to the surface independently. This is an active area of research, however no systems have been built as polarimetric interferometers at sufficient accuracy to quantify the performance of the concepts.

Numerous space mission concepts to produce global topography beyond the level attained by SRTM have been forwarded to NASA and the Department of Defense, but none have yet been funded by these agencies. Some of these proposed missions were to have two spacecraft orbiting in formation with precise inter-craft metrology systems and with the radar operating at L-band frequencies. Others proposed to configure a boom with dual apertures to form the interferometer, and with the radar operating at the higher frequencies. The proposed cost of these missions was high, and can only be justified in terms of global map production. While the need for targeted accurate topography worldwide is well-established, the need for global maps has been insufficient to justify the cost.

Several nations, however, following an innovative concept proposed by D. Massonnet of CNES, are considering a new SAR constellation known as an interferometric cartwheel [Massonnet, 2001]. In this concept, a standard orbiting SAR serves as a signal source for an interferometer. Several receive-only satellites orbit in phased, elliptical orbits such that, in the frame of the mean circular orbit, the satellites execute epi-cyclic motion around an ellipse once per orbit. These receive-only satellites act as the interferometer apertures, with baseline lengths highly variable in time. The baselines are typically several kilometers, so the height acuity is excellent. Though the antennas are very small compared to standard SAR antennas, to reduce cost, it can be shown that the usual performance degradation one would expect due to ambiguities are greatly reduced when the baseline is long. Planners expect to be able to generate global topography in about 1 year of mapping at 1 m accuracy at a resolution determined by the signal source, but enhanced by super-resolution techniques. The first demonstration experiments are expected in the next few years, when the details of baseline metrology and calibration will be examined. Operational systems may arise in about a decade.

Topography can change on very rapid time scales, so there is a continuing need to update topographic maps, particularly at the finest resolutions and accuracy. Future systems may map topographic change as it evolves from the vantage point of geosynchronous orbit. Topographic change mapping using IFSAR can be done when either the interferometric baseline is zero, or the base topography is known and can be removed from the interferometry data. Any change in the range from the radar to the surface can be mapped at the millimeter scale. From geosynchonous orbit, the baselines will be very small, and topographic change can be measured from hour to hour as the system continuously points at a site of interest.

AUTHOR BIOGRAPHIES

The principal author for this chapter is Scott Hensley, Radar Science and Engineering Section, Jet Propulsion Laboratory, 4800 Oak Grove Drive, Pasadena, California 91109. Contributing authors to this Chapter are Riadh Munjy from Earth Data International, Inc., and Paul Rosen from the Jet Propulsion Laboratory.

Scott Hensley received his BS degrees in Mathematics and Physics from the University of California at Irvine. He received a PhD in Mathematics from the State University of New York at

Stony Brook where he specialized in the study of differential geometry. Hensley is currently a Principal Engineer and GeoSAR Project Manager at the Jet Propulsion Laboratory. He has developed processors for both airborne and spaceborne interferometric applications and leads the processor development activity for the GeoSAR program. Current research includes studying the amount of penetration into the vegetation canopy using GeoSAR data as well as simultaneous L and C band TOPSAR measurements and repeat pass airborne interferometry data collected at lower frequencies. He was the technical lead of the SRTM Interferometric Processor Development Team.

Riadh Munjy is Professor of Geomatics Engineering at California State University, Fresno. He is also the chief scientist at Earth Data International, Inc. working on the development of the GeoSAR System. He has over 30 years of experience in mapping. Munjy obtained his BSc in Civil Engineering from the University of Baghdad, Iraq in 1976 and MS in applied mathematics, MSCE and PhD in Civil Engineering from the University of Washington , Seattle respectively in 1978, 1980 and 1982.

Paul Rosen is supervisor of the Interferometric Synthetic Aperture Radar Algorithms and System Analysis Group at the Jet Propulsion Laboratory, and visiting faculty member and lecturer at the California Institute of Technology. Rosen's assignments at JPL include independent scientific and engineering research in methods and applications of interferometric SAR. He has developed interferometric SAR processors for airborne topographic mapping systems such as the JPL TOPSAR and ARPA IFSARE, space-borne topographic and deformation processors for sensors such as ERS, JERS, RadarSAT, and the Shuttle Radar Topography Mission (SRTM). Rosen is the Project Element Manager for the development of topography generation algorithms for SRTM. He has also led several proposals for surface deformation satellite missions.

ACKNOWLEDGEMENTS

The authors would like to thank all those who supplied figures and the research and management staff at Jet Propulsion Laboratory who have helped directly or indirectly in making this work possible. Special thanks go to Elaine Chapin who supplied some of the figures and reviewed the manuscript and to Tom Farr, Dave Imel and Yunjin Kim for their insightful comments and suggestions. Although the authors have worked assiduously to maintain accuracy we apologize for any errors that have inadvertently gone undetected. This chapter was written at the Jet Propulsion Laboratory, California Institute of Technology, under contract with the National Aeronautics and Space Administration. The Intermap Technologies section of this chapter was provided by Bryan Mercer, Chief Scientist, assisted by Tim Coyne, Keith Tennant and Ian Isaacs.

REFERENCES

Ackermann, F., 1994. Digital elevation models - techniques and application, quality standards, development, *International Archives of Photogrammetry and Remote Sensing*, 30(4): 421-432.

Bamler, R., and P. Hartl, 1998. Synthetic aperture radar interferometry, *Inverse Problems*, 14, R1-54.

Burrough, P.A., 1986. *Principles of Geographical Information Systems for Land Resources Assessment*, Oxford University Press, Oxford.

Cloude, S.R., and K.P. Papathanassiou, 1997. Polarimetric optimization in radar interferometry, *Electronics Letters*, 33(13): 1176-1178.

Curlander, J.C., and R.N. McDonough, 1991. *Synthetic Aperture Radar Systems and Signal Processing*, Wiley-Interscience.

Elachi, C., 1998. *Spaceborne Radar Remote Sensing: Applications and Techniques*, IEEE Press, New York, NY.

Farr, T., and M. Kobrick, 2000. Shuttle radar topography mission produces a wealth of data, *EOS, Trans. of American Geophys. Union,* 81(48): 583-585.

Franceschetti, G., and R. Lanari, 1999. *Synthetic Aperture Radar*, CRC Press.

Galy, H.M., and R.A. Sanders, 2000. Using SAR imagery for flood modeling, *RGS-IBG Annual Conference Prec.*

Global Terrain Prices, 2001. URL: http://www.globalterrain.com.

Goldstein, R.M., 1995. Atmospheric limitations to repeat-track radar interferometry, *Geophys. Res. Lett.,* 22, 2517-2520.

Graham, L.C., 1974. Synthetic interferometric radar for topographic mapping," *Proc. IEEE,* 62(6): 763-768.

Gray, A.L., and P.J. Farris-Manning, 1993. Repeat-pass interferometry with an airborne synthetic aperture radar, *IEEE Trans. Geosci. Rem. Sens.,* 31(1): 180-191, 1993.

Hagberg, J.O., L.M.H. Ulander, and J. Askne, 1995. Repeat-pass SAR interferometry over forested terrain, *IEEE Trans. Geosci. Rem. Sens.,* 33(2): 331-340.

Hensley, S., and F.H. Webb, 1994. Comparison of Long Valley TOPSAR data with kinematic GPS measurements, *IGARSS Proceedings*, Pasadena, CA.

Hensley, S., J. Klein, P.A. Rosen, E. Chapin, S.N. Madsen, and F.H. Webb, 1995. Repeat pass aircraft interferometry results at Portage Lake, Maine, and Innisfail, Australia, *Proc. of the AIRSAR Sci. Workshop.*

Hensley, S., E. Chapin, A. Freedman, C. Le, S. Madsen, T. Michel, E. Rodriguez, P. Siqueira, and K. Wheeler, 2001. First P-band results using GeoSAR mapping system, *Proceedings of IGARSS 2001*, Sydney, Australia.

Hokeman, D., and C. Varekamp, 2001. Observation of tropical rain forest trees by airborne high-resolution interferometric radar, *IEEE Trans. Geo. Sci, Rem. Sen.,* 39(3).

Kovaly, J., 1976. *Synthetic Aperture Radar*, Artech House Inc., Boston, MA.

Leberl, F.W., 1990. *Radargrammetric Image Processing*, Artech House Inc., Boston, MA.

Lewis, A.J., and F.M. Henderson, 1999. Radar fundametals: The geoscience perspective, in *Manual of Remote Sensing*, Artech House Inc., Boston, MA, 3(3).

Li, F., and R.M. Goldstein, 1990. Studies of multibaseline spaceborne interferometric synthetic aperture radar, *IEEE Trans. Geosci. Remote Sensing*, 28: 88-97.

Madsen, S.N., H.A. Zebker, and J. Martin, 1993. Topographic mapping using radar interferometry: Processing techniques, *IEEE Trans. Geosci. and Rem. Sens.,* 31(1): 246-256.

Madsen, S.N., N. Skou, J. Granholm, K.W. Woelders, and E.L. Christensen, 1996. A system for airborne SAR interferometry, *Intl. J. Elect. Comm.,* 50(2): 106-111.

Madsen, S.N., and H.A. Zebker, 1999. Synthetic aperture radar interferometry: Principles and applications, in *Manual of Remote Sensing*, Artech House Inc., Boston, MA, 3(6).

Madsen, S.N., J.M. Martin, and H.A. Zebker, 1993. Analysis and evaluation of the NASA/JPL TOPSAR across-track interferometric SAR system, *IEEE Trans. Geosci. Rem. Sens.,* 33()2): 383-391.

Massonnet, D., 2001. Capabilities and limitations of the interferometric cartwheel, *IEEE Trans. Geo. Sci, Rem. Sen.,* 39(3).

Mercer, J.B., and M. Gill, 1998. Radar-derived DEMs for yrban areas, *Proceedings of the ISPRS Commission IV Symposium,* Stuttgart, Germany.

Mercer, J.B., J. Bryan, and S. Schnick, 1999. Comparison of DEM from Star3i and scanning laser, *ISPRS Commission III Workshop*, La Jolla, CA.

Positional Accuracy Handbook, October, 1999, Minnesota Planning Land Management Information Center, URL: http://www.fgdc.gov/standards/status/sub1_3.html.

Raney, K., 1999. Radar fundamentals: Technical perspective," in *Manual of Remote Sensing*, Artech House Inc., Boston, MA, 3(2).

Real, C., R.I. Wilson, and T.P. McCrink, 1997. Suitability of airborne-radar topographic data for evaluating earthquake-induced ground failure hazards, *12th Int. Conf. on Appl. Geol. Rem. Sens.,* Denver, CO.

Rodriguez, E., T. Michel, D. Harding, and J.M. Martin, 1999. Comparison of airborne InSAR-derived heights and laser altimetry, *Radio Science,* in press.

Rodriguez, E., J.M. Martin, and T. Michel, 1999. Classification studies using Interferometry, *Radio Science*, in press.

Rodriguez, E., C. Morris, E. Belz, 2006. A global assessment of the SRTM performance*, Photogrammetric Engineering and Remote Sensing*, 72(3): 249-260.

Rodriguez, E., C. Morris, E. Belz, E. Chapin, J. Martin, W. Daffer, and S. Hensley, 2005. An assessment of the SRTM topographic products, Technical Report JPL D-31639, Jet Propulsion Laboratory, Pasadena, CA.

Rogers, A.E.E., and R.P. Ingalls, 1969. Venus: Mapping the surface reflectivity by radar interferometry," *Science*, 165: 797-799

Rosen, P.A., S. Hensley, I.R. Joughin, F.K. Li, S. Madsen, E. Rodriguez, and R.M. Goldstein, 2000. Synthetic aperture radar interferometry, *IEEE Proc.*, 88(3).

Schwäbisch, M., and J. Moreira, 1999. The high resolution airborne interferometric SAR AeS-1, *Proceedings of the 4th International Airborne Remote Sensing Conference and Exhibition*, Ottawa, Canada.

Slater, J., G. Garvey, J. Haase, B. Heady, G. Kroenung, J. and Little, 2006. The SRTM data finishing process and products, Photogrammetric Engineering and Remote Sensing, 72(3): 237-247.

Sos, T.G., H.W. Kilmach, and G.F. Adams, 1994. High performance interferometric SAR description and capabilities, *Proceedings of Tenth Thematic Conference on Geologic Remote Sensing*, San Antonio, TX, 2.

Tarayre, H., and D. Massonnet, 1996. Atmospheric propagation heterogeneities revealed by ERS-1 interferometry, *Geophys. Res. Lett.*, 23(9): 989-992.

Tennant, J.K., and T. Coyne, 1999. STAR-3I Interferometric Synthetic Aperture Radar (INSAR): Some lessons learned on the road to commercialization, *Proc. of the Fourth Intl. Airborne Rem. Sens. Conference and Exhibition/ 21st Canadian Symposium on Remote Sensing*, Ottawa, Ontario, Canada.

Zebker, H.A., and R.M. Goldstein, 1986. Topographic mapping from interferometric SAR observations, *J. Geophys. Res.*, 91: 4993-4999.

Zebker, H.A., S.N. Madsen, J. Martin, K.B. Wheeler, T. Miller, Y. Lou, G. Alberti, S. Vetrella, and A. Cucci, , 1992. The TOPSAR interferometric radar topographic mapping instrument, *IEEE Trans. Geosci. Remote Sensing*, 30.

Zebker, H.A., and J. Villasenor, 1992. Decorrelation in interferometric radar echoes, *IEEE Trans. Geosci. Rem. Sens.*, 30: 950-959.

Zebker, H.A., T.G. Farr, R.P. Salazar, and T.H. Dixon, 1994. Mapping the world's topography using radar interferometry - the TOPSAT mission, *Proc. IEEE*, 82(12): 1774-1786.

Zebker, H.A., C.L. Werner, P.A. Rosen, and S. Hensley, 1994. Accuracy of topographic maps derived from ERS-1 interferometric radar, *IEEE Trans. Geosci. Rem. Sens.*, 32: 823-836.

Zebker, H.A., P.A. Rosen, and S. Hensley, 1997. Atmospheric effects in interferometric synthetic aperture radar surface deformation and topographic maps, *J. Geophys. Res.*, 102, 7547-7563.

Zisk, S.H., 1972. A new Earth-based radar technique for the measurement of lunar topography, *Moon*, 4: 296-300.

Chapter 7

Topographic and Terrestrial Lidar

Robert A. Fowler, Andre Samberg, Martin J. Flood, and Tom J. Greaves

INTRODUCTION

This chapter of the "DEM Users Manual" has been modified considerably from the first edition. For those who wish to know more about the physics which is used in laser and the types of lidar systems and their history, there is a much expanded introduction. There is also a section added on the use of lidargrammetry and specific information about ground based or terrestrial scanners.

The two types of lidar used for digital terrain model production are airborne and terrestrial, and many of the principles are common to both so there is much overlap. These general principles are dealt with first, followed by the specific issues relating to airborne systems and then ground based systems. The information regarding lidargrammetry has been included in the airborne section, but the software can also be effective for terrestrial lidar data.

A number of abbreviations have been used throughout the chapter, not because they are used in everyday conversation but simply to shorten the text by avoiding continually repeating the terminology in full.

Chapter 14 includes additional details regarding lidar data processing.

Lasers, Lidar and What Makes it Work

Lasers have been used in commercial measuring equipment for more than 30 years. Today, laser scanning is a mature technology. This technology is a complex integration of the fields of optics, opto-mechanics, and electronics. It is applied in many different fields, such as barcode scanning, as-built documentation, noncontact inspection, 3D modeling, rapid prototyping, civil engineering, oil exploration, architecture, topography, mining, health sciences, reverse engineering, archaeology, quality assessment, and mechanical dimensional inspection. The list of applications is vast, but this chapter will focus on the use of lidar for topographic mapping and field surveying.

Lidar (LIDAR or LiDAR) is an acronym for LIght Detection And Ranging, and like radar and sonar, lidar is now commonly written in lower case. It makes use of several of the laws of physics which will be reviewed briefly.

Gravity is a phenomenon with which we are all familiar, although scientists still struggle with the precise nature of this energy of attraction. There is still considerable conjecture in the scientific world whether there is such a thing as a "graviton," the theoretical element of gravitational energy. If it does exist, the force is so weak it is practically unmeasurable. Despite popular science fiction, it is thought there is no anti-graviton as gravity acts on the total energy or mass not on the charge states of a mass. Gravity is, of course, what keeps us on the ground, but it has the peculiar property of varying depending on where on the ground one happens to be. The density of the rocks you stand on can affect the "amount" of gravity you experience. While the human brain cannot discern small changes in gravity, scientifically it is measurable and it does make a difference to certain sensitive equipment. Because the density of the earth is not consistent, the center of gravity of the earth is different from the center of its shape.

Furthermore, while for years scientists have known the center of the earth is molten, until the advent of GPS satellites it was not definitively known that the earth's center of gravity is not in a constant location and that, indeed, it moves around. In fact, some claim it can move up to one meter per day because of the molten center of the earth, coupled with the distortion of the earth's surface from the pull of the moon. GPS has also allowed us to prove that not only are the oceans subjected to tidal effects but the earth's hard surfaces (ground) are also affected by diurnal tides. The land in Washington D.C., for example, rises and falls approximately 20-30 centimeters (8-12 inches) twice a day. Because everything on the earth in our immediate surroundings moves up and down by the same amount this is not at all obvious and really makes no difference to anything – unless one is conducting accurate measurements using satellite technology.

See Chapter 2 for further references on gravity and geoid modeling.

Time is another required element in the lidar package. However, time as an element is arbitrary. There is a lot of cosmology which posits that time and space are interwoven (Einstein) and may be manifestations of the same phenomena. This is not at all intuitive, and it is doubtful that many outside of professional cosmologists understand this! But for practical purposes here on earth, time is a construction based on the periodicity of the duration of the orbit of the earth around the sun, manifested and measured in base 6 mathematics, originating from the ancient Sumerian civilization. There is considerable argument that the base 6 math was derived from the approximate time it takes the earth to circumnavigate the sun (360 days), and also the Sumerians apparent dislike of fractions (360 is neatly divisible by 1,2,3,4,5,6,8,9,10, and multiples thereof). But while no one knows for sure why the Sumerians came up with a base 6 rather than base 5 or 8 or 10 math, their legacy is we have both time based on days broken into hours, minutes and seconds, and circles that have 360 degrees, 60 minutes in a degree, and 60 seconds in a minute, which works very handily in geometry.

Light is both a wave and a discrete particle of energy. The particle is known as a photon. Coherent light is the phenomenon generated by the laser part of the lidar package. Visible light is just a small portion of the electromagnetic spectrum which encompasses a wide range of what we often tend to consider different energies, from radio waves to gamma rays. However light is really no different from any of the other parts of the spectrum. Light is simply the portion of the electromagnetic spectrum which is visible to human eyes. It is a narrow part of the spectrum ranging in wavelength from 400 to700 nanometers (one nanometer is 10^{-9} meters or 0.000000001m). Our eyes have developed the ability to correlate this part of the spectrum and provide us with information about the physical world that enables us to function relatively efficiently.

Interestingly, the speed of light was first measured by a Scandinavian, Olaus Roemer, in 1676. He calculated it from observing aberrations in the predictions of the orbits of the moons of Jupiter. He was not very accurate – coming up with an answer of about 225,000 Km/second, but it was a remarkably innovative approach and result for that period of history. Yet, only 50 years later an Englishman, James Bradley, calculated the speed of light to be 301,000 Km/second – which is amazingly very close. In fact, the speed of light was fixed in international agreement only in 1983 at 299,792.458 Km/second, based on the time it takes light to travel 1 meter through a vacuum. (1/ 299792458 second). As a final historical note, it should be said that Roemer did not have an accurate measure of the diameter of the Earth for use in his computations, but if he had, his calculations would have yielded a figure very close to the correct value.

All of the electromagnetic spectrum travels at this speed, and it is the frequency or length of the waveforms in parts of a meter which vary and provide us with different properties (for example colors). In terms of energy, the shorter the wavelength, the larger the energy. At one end of the spectrum, radio waves are long and relatively weak forms of energy, and at the other end of the spectrum gamma rays are very short but disastrously (for life) very strong forms of energy.

Infrared waves are longer in wavelength than visible light and thus slightly outside the visible spectrum. Most airborne and terrestrial lidars operate on or close to 1.064 microns (1064 nanometers) in the infrared portion of the spectrum, but there are quite a number of systems using lasers in the green wavelength at 532 nanometers.

Since the mid-1990s, Airborne Laser Scanning (referred to henceforth as ALS) and Terrestrial Laser Scanning (TLS) have become fully accepted and proven technologies because of their abilities to supply the surveying and mapping communities with precise and directly georeferenced spatial information about the shape of the earth or objects. Using these laser-based remote sensing techniques, it is possible to conduct a 3D survey mission in a more cost-effective and speedier way, especially when data cannot be collected easily by any other means.

There are several features which make laser-based remote sensing techniques very attractive.

Firstly, these are active systems, generating their own energy to survey the target. This means a survey mission can be carried out any time of day and night and, subject to some general weather conditions, during any season.

Secondly, typically all ALS systems and some TLS systems are integrated with a positioning and orientation system, which can include an onboard GPS (Global Positioning System), and a type of Inertial Measurement Unit (IMU). Once a GPS receiver locks on to four or more GPS satellites, it can triangulate its location on the Earth from the known positions of the GPS satellites. The IMU, which also includes accelerometers, measures the exterior orientation of the sensor in its own coordinate system related to gravity, as well as velocity. By combining the results of calculations from the GPS receiver and the IMU, the X, Y, Z coordinates of the location of a footprint of a laser beam in 3D space can be determined with a very high accuracy. In the case of ALS, the accuracy is typically better than 15 cm (6 inches) vertically, and 30 cm to 5 meters (1 to 16.5 feet), depending on the system, horizontally. In the case of TLS, the distance measurement accuracy can be on the order of 20 mm under normal conditions, and the average angle accuracy is on the order of ±0.05°. See Chapter 10 for details on GPS and IMU technologies.

From the point of view of photogrammetry and mapping, the integration of GPS and IMU allows the calculation of X, Y, Z coordinates of the laser footprint on the target surface directly from distance measurements, thus speeding the production of orthoimages or contours.

Thirdly, these laser-based remote sensing techniques have provided mapping professionals with a powerful means for high-speed acquisition of data in forests, vegetated and rugged areas which were previously difficult or impossible to access. It is relatively easy to derive a bare earth DEM from a collection of laser points. Therefore, forest managers and hydrologists can obtain accurate and complete vegetation cover maps and surface models for further development and improvement of slope and hydrology models.

Since the first edition of the "DEM Users Manual," continuing advances have been made in the development of ever more sophisticated topographic laser-based remote sensing systems. Commercial ground based (terrestrial laser scanners) 3D laser scanning systems are available from several equipment manufacturers. This type of measuring equipment consists of a laser rangefinder on a tripod, which scans the scene in front of it. The TLS systems are applicable for producing 3D data with very high accuracy for various applications both indoor and outdoor (e.g., the survey of oil refinery pipelines, building facades, and bridge constructions).

As mentioned earlier, there are no principal differences between the optical and mechanical aspects of ALS and TLS systems. ALS basically performs measurements from an airborne platform. TLS collects the 3D data of the target in front of a TLS system mounted on the ground, moving vehicle or sometimes a boat. In general, the installation and calibration procedures of the ALS system are more complicated than the installation and calibration procedures of the TLS system.

Background

In 1917, Albert Einstein first proposed the process that makes lasers possible, called stimulated emission. In 1954, the first papers about the maser (or MASER) were published as a result of investigations carried out simultaneously and independently by Townes and his co-workers at Columbia University in New York and by Basov and Prokhorov at the Lebedev Institute in Moscow. MASER stands for Microwave Amplification by Stimulated Emission of Radiation. A laser is a maser that works with higher frequency photons in the ultraviolet (UV), visible light (VIS) or infrared (IR) spectrum. For this work they were awarded the 1964 Nobel Prize in Physics. The optical maser or the laser dates from 1958, when the possibilities of applying the maser principle in the optical region were analyzed by Schawlow and Townes as well as in the Lebedev Institute. Laser spectroscopy was developed by Schawlow and his associates at Stanford University. The first laser was operating in 1960. It was a ruby laser generating strong pulses of red light.

With respect to laser-based remote sensing, in 1964 NASA launched the Beacon B satellite followed by Lunar laser ranging with the tracking of a corner cube reflector on the moon. Since the 1960s, a global network of ground stations has been developed to measure ranges to satellite-borne reflectors, and satellite laser ranging is still an integral part of NASA's space geodesy program.

In 1975, a joint NASA, NAVOCEANO, and NOAA program sponsored the Airborne Oceano-graphic Lidar (AOL). This was conceived as an airborne test bed for new applications of laser remote sensing. The AOL was a laser fluorosensor that measured a variety of oceanographic properties such as chlorophyll and other biological and chemical substances in the world's oceans. The original design also provided some topographic information. In 1994, a separate airborne lidar system dedicated to topographic mapping was developed and called the Airborne Topographic Mapper (ATM). The AOL remained for collecting the laser-induced fluorescence (LIF) spectrum in a contiguous region covering the spectral band from 370 nm to 740 nm, for each laser pulse. In addition to the LIF, the AOL collects passive (solar-induced) ocean color radiance data and sea surface temperature (from an ancillary infrared radiometer).

Further investigations and development of laser-based remote sensing systems were carried out at the Laser Altimeter Processing Facility (LAPF) at NASA's Goddard Space Flight Center. As the results of those efforts, SLICER (Scanning Lidar Imager of Canopies by Echo Recovery), RASCAL (RAster SCanning Airborne Laser Altimeter), SLA-01 (Shuttle Laser Altimeter I), and SLA-02 (Shuttle Laser Altimeter II) appeared.

Traditionally, terrestrial field surveyors and engineers have used a group of instruments for measuring horizontal and slope distances, vertical distances, and horizontal and vertical angles. Angular measurements were produced using theodolites. These, used with separate microwave instruments (Tellurometers) in the 1940s for measuring distance, allowed horizontal distances to be calculated. Later in the 1970's, Electronic Distance Measuring Equipment (EDME) devices penetrated the market. EDMEs were originally often mounted on top of a theodolite. Their operating principle is the same as a rangefinder which transmits a narrow laser beam to a reflecting surface, and measures the time it takes to go and return. Eventually the total station was developed which combined the features of a theodolite and rangefinder in a single package.

TECHNOLOGY OVERVIEW

In theory, any light source can be used to create a lidar instrument, but in practice all modern lidar instruments use a definable laser as the source. In a nutshell, light detection and ranging is the science of using a laser to measure distances to specific points. Lasers can technically use any wavelength in what is considered the "light portion" of the electromagnetic spectrum.

A laser can be thought of as a tube with a mirror at each end. One of the mirrors has a small hole in its center. If the outer shell of the tube includes a light source which is flashed on and off, the photons from the light source are emitted in all directions. Inevitably a number of the photons will start to bounce back and forth between the two mirrors. If two photons collide, they also have the ability to split and create two more photons. Also, inevitably, some photons will escape through the hole in the mirror and they will create a virtually (but not completely) parallel light source at the specific frequency of the emitting light source. While this may sound as if the laser has managed to solve the impossible by creating more photons than were initially generated, in fact there is considerable atrophy and indeed lasers are notorious energy hogs. It is common for the emitted laser light to be between only 5-20% of the source power. It should be remembered, however, that all lasers are potentially damaging, even the laser pointers used by teachers and lecturers. Lidar manufacturers are very cognizant of these dangers and lidar units are manufactured to be used within certain parameters.

Laser scanning systems can be classified in different ways. They can be pulsed and continuous wavelength laser systems or noncontact optical profilometers depending on their transmitting and receiving components. Different beam steering devices can produce a scan of a laser beam across-track or scanning can be spot-wise vertical profiling. From the operational point of view, laser scanning systems can be installed on different carrying platforms. Depending on the chosen laser sources and the reflective measuring features of the objects, different laser-based remote sensing units operate at different wavelengths.

Laser-based remote sensing systems, which are used for topographic purposes, can be classified in the following ways, by:

- Operating principles
- Mounting
- Scanning techniques
- Operating wavelengths

Operating Principles

Figure 7.1 shows a classification path of different operating modes of the laser-based remote sensing systems from the point of view of operating/measuring principles.

The pulsed laser system works in the following way. It transmits laser pulses, then amplifies the light that is scattered back through an optical telescope receiver and photomultiplier tube. The distance to the object is determined by recording the time the transmitted pulse travels to the target and back by using the speed of light.

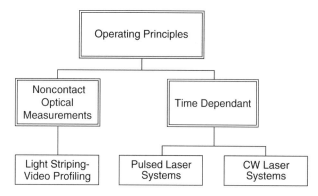

Figure 7.1 Operating principles of laser-based remote sensing.

The continuous wave (CW) laser system transmits a continuous signal, and ranging is carried out by modulating the light intensity of the laser light. Typically, it is a sinusoidal signal which is received with a time delay. The travel time is directly proportional to the phase difference between the received and transmitted signal.

There is also one type of laser measurement principle which is based on a combination of a laser light stripe generator and a video camera. It is a so-called noncontact optical measurement. In this case the laser source is separate from the video camera, which can be digital. The laser light is visible and follows along the target surface on a continuing basis. This line is considered as a surface profile. Then, during the movement of a carrying platform, the profile maps are registered to the same 3D coordinate system by an iterative surface matching algorithm. The laser light is transmitted through a cylindrical lens. This lens produces the laser beam which is very narrow in one direction and expanded in the other direction. Typically, this form of the laser beam is so-called a line. The laser light sheet is usually perpendicular to the illuminated surface. Thus, if an observer looks down on the flat surface, he/she will see a straight line. However, a (digital) video camera apart from the laser source registers a 3D surface profile. If the surface is flat, then the profile is a straight line. If the surface is rough, then the profile is a curve. The digital image processing is based on a projective transformation between the image plane of the camera and the plane of the laser sheet, and also the direction of scanning with respect to the plane of the laser sheet. The refinement is obtained through weighted least squares matching of multiple profile maps acquired from different points of view, and registered previously using an approximate calibration.

In current lidar systems, the pulsed laser systems are most frequently used because they can produce a high power output at a very high pulse repetition rate. Therefore, the operating distance can be more than 1 km (0.62 mi).

Mounting

The laser sensor is used for collecting a dataset about a remotely located object. All of these sensors are differentiated by how they are mounted as noted in Figure 7.2 and are basically classified as airborne or ground based.

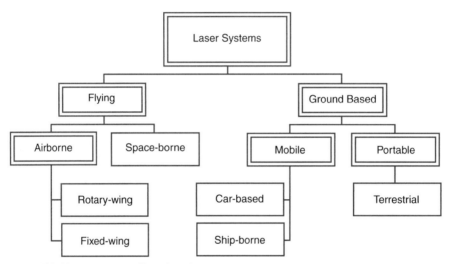

Figure 7.2 Mounting types of laser-based remote sensing systems.

The laser systems installed onboard airborne carrying platforms are typically known as airborne laser scanners. They can be mounted onboard a fixed-wing aircraft or a helicopter (rotary-wing). Usually, airborne laser scanners are across-track or push-broom scanners. An airborne laser profiling system, which is essentially a laser altimeter, has very limited use. This type of airborne laser profiling system can be still applied in remote sensing of forest and forestry-oriented applications, although these systems are no longer economically efficient.

Regarding airborne applications, there are those that work over water called bathymetric laser scanning systems, and those that work over land called airborne terrain mapping systems or topographic systems. The bathymetric ALS systems operate mainly in the blue/green portion of the spectrum. Infrared radiation is partially absorbed by water, and near infrared lasers do not reflect much of a return when used over water bodies. The blue-green lasers usually frequency-double the wavelength to create one pulse which is reflected off the water's surface, and one which penetrates to the sea floor. The differentiated distance is the bathymetric depth. Current systems provide a return for depths of up to three-four times what can be seen by the naked eye. So, simply stated, if you can see down through water to a depth of 10 feet, a laser will provide a return up to a depth of 30-40 feet (providing it hits a reflecting surface in that distance). See Chapter 8 for the technical review of Airborne Lidar Bathymetry. The wavelengths of both ALS and TSL systems are mostly near-infrared (NIR).

Spaceborne topographic laser systems are typically laser altimeters which are applied for surface profiling of the Earth. This remote sensing technique is widely used for the study of geosciences such as measuring of forested ecosystems, global monitoring of ice fields, mapping of polar sea-ice freeboard and thickness, high-resolution mapping of ocean eddies, glacier topography, and lake and river levels. For forest land-cover applications, estimating forest canopy heights and canopy closure is based on the analyses of the waveform of the returned laser signal. It should be noted that the footprint of space-borne lasers is usually large (in the tens of meters) and absolute accuracy is not appropriate for engineering.

Ground based laser systems can be divided into two groups: mobile and fixed portable. The mobile laser systems can be either vehicle-based or ship-borne. Fixed systems are usually set on a tripod on or at a specific location.

Ship-borne laser systems are mostly applied in environmental monitoring, pollution detection and bathymetry. Those laser systems, which are used for environmental monitoring and pollution detection, are basically based on LIF technology described above. Furthermore, more modern LIF-based laser remote sensing systems can also be installed on board a flying platform. Typically, they are profiling systems. Advanced airborne LIF-based laser remote sensing systems can be operated in two modes: across-track scanning or vertical profiling.

Laser Scanning Techniques

Laser beam steering is one of the key technologies implemented in the laser-based remote sensing systems used for topographic and terrestrial mapping purposes. This is a well established technology that is thoroughly described in numerous literature sources. Figure 7.3 shows how laser-based remote sensing units can be grouped from the point of view of scanning techniques.

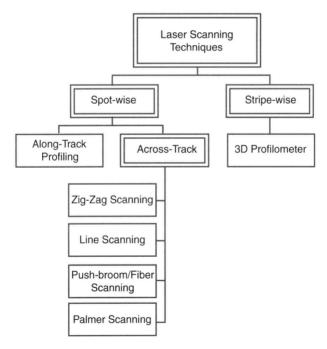

Figure 7.3 Laser Scanning Techniques.

In theory there are no special reasons why one scanning technique is preferable to another. Historically, spot-wise along-track profiling was the first laser use in remote sensing.

Continuous research and development in the opto-mechanics and electro-optical industries led to improvements in beam steering technologies. Subsequently, laser beam steering opto-mechanical devices became robust and very well controlled. The most common scanner is a polygonal scanner, which consists of a polygonal mirror, a drive system and a bearing system. Typically, because of the forward motion of the aircraft a polygonal scanner produces a zigzag pattern of scanning.

Oscillating Mirror (Zig-Zag Scanning)

In systems using an oscillating mirror, the mirror rotates back and forth between limited extents. Thus, a zigzag line is produced on the surface of the target area (Figure 7.4). The major advantage of this method is that the mirror is always pointing towards the ground so data collection can be continuous and theoretically all pulses of the laser are used. In most systems the user can generally control the mirror's field of view and scan rate (the angle through which the mirror swings and the number of times the mirror oscillates per second). Changing the field of view provides additional flexibility as it allows points to be collected over a shorter span (thus effectively closer together) or a wider span (further apart). But there are a number of disadvantages to the oscillating mirror principle. Some of these are due to the mirror having to start from one end of its travel, accelerate to full scan speed, and then stop at the other end of its travel. The changing velocity and acceleration of the mirror cause torsion between the mirror and the angular encoder. The changing velocity also means that the measured points are not equally spaced at the beginning and ends of travel. The point density increases at the edge of the scan field where the mirror slows down, and decreases at nadir. Manufacturers have solved these problems by essentially ignoring the last points on a scan and modelling the distortions caused by changing speed using a computer program.

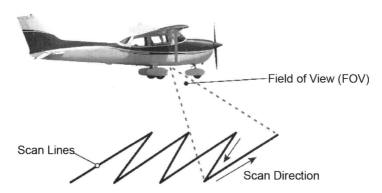

Figure 7.4 Zig-zag or Z-scan pattern (ALS, ALTM, TopEye). Courtesy of Dewberry.

Rotating Mirror (Line Scanning)

In this approach, the mirror is rotated continuously at a constant velocity in one direction by a motor. The measurements of the angles are carried out either directly from the motor rotation or from an angular encoder directly mounted to the mirror. The result is measured points are in parallel lines on the ground (Figure 7.5). The main advantage is that the constant velocity doesn't induce any acceleration type errors in the angle observation. However, there are also several disadvantages. The major disadvantage is that observations cannot be taken during a significant amount of time during each mirror rotation because the mirror is pointing away from the target. So while the laser may be firing at 100,000 times per second it could be that 70,000 of those pulses are not aimed at the target area. The other disadvantage is the field of view cannot be changed as the mirror must rotate 360 degrees.

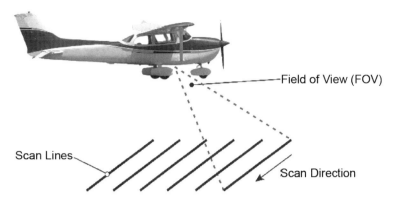

Figure 7.5 Line scan pattern. Courtesy of Dewberry.

Push Broom (Fiber Scanning)

Figures 7.6 and 7.7 show a push broom, fiber-optical or nutating scan pattern used by Toposys and Falcon. The 127 fibers are arranged at one end in a circle and at the other end in a fixed linear array. The laser pulsed energy is transmitted into one of the fibers arranged in a circle. There it is formed to a narrow laser beam and transmitted to the ground. The reflected light is focused to the corresponding fiber in a linear array at the receiving side. There it is guided to the circular array and coupled into the center fiber leading to the detector. The direction of a transmitted laser beam is defined by each individual fiber. It is stable. Any misalignment within this arrangement will lead to a loss of energy but not to a false direction. The fiber scanner guarantees a precise knowledge about the beam direction with respect to the fiber scanner itself. The fiber scanner and IMU are mounted close together. Thus the orientation between them becomes invariable against any mechanical forces induced by the aircraft or forced by thermal variations. The bore-sight alignment is established by at minimum one specific calibration flight. This can be a flight over a large building where the coordinates of the roof corners are well known or can be measured conventionally to centimeter accuracy. In order to reduce the influence of errors caused by the weather conditions to the positioning, such a calibration flight is done during the most favorable conditions.

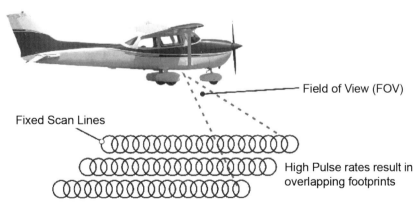

Figure 7.6 Push-broom, fiber-optical or nutating scan pattern (Toposys and Falcon). Courtesy of Dewberry.

Scan Pattern

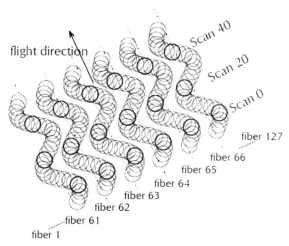

Figure 7.7 Toposys/Falcon fiber optical scan pattern. Courtesy Toposys.

The scan pattern of the Toposys/Falcon laser scanning system (Figure 7.7) looks like push-broom ranging from the right to the left side of a swath with a constant separation between adjacent fibers. Due to the high scan rate of 650 Hz and a slight swiveling with amplitude of about 1 mrad (0.06 deg), adjacent footprints are overlapped. The nominal scan lines are only about ½ foot apart. In a flat area, adjacent measurements can not largely differ. If there are single measurements deviating from their neighbours they can be considered as erroneous. Unlike widely separated spot-wise measurements this method provides a high reliability of the resulting DEM coming close to the reliability of EDME.

Palmer (Elliptical) Scanning

Figure 7.8 shows the Palmer scanning pattern, used by ScaLARS, which produces an elliptical pattern with redundant data that can be used for calibration.

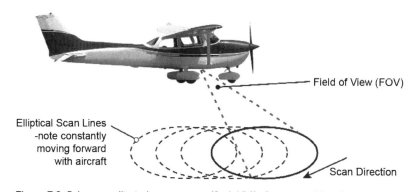

Figure 7.8 Palmer or elliptical scan pattern (ScaLARS). Courtesy of Dewberry.

Stripe-Wise Scanning

As shown in Figure 7.9, non-optical measurements are performed by means of a combination of a laser line generating unit and a video camera in a way similar to a structured light 3D scanning in close-range photogrammetry. The laser projector and the video camera are apart from each other. The video camera looks at the profile, the deformation of the pattern on the subject, and uses a technique similar to triangulation to calculate the distance of every point on the line. Due to the triangulation angle and the fixed optical image formation the X, Y coordinates of one profile of the object can be calculated. The system is moved in defined steps along the moving direction, i.e., the flight direction. Thus, the 3D shape of the object is scanned slice by slice. In general, the scanned pattern may be 1D or 2D. An example of a 1D pattern is a single line. The 2D pattern is formed when single profiles are collected in a grid manner. The deformation of the pattern is usually registered on the CCD sensor. Then, a fairly complex algorithm is used to calculate the distance at each point in the pattern. In the simplest case, one could analyze an image and assume that the left-to-right sequence of stripes reflects the sequence of the lasers in the array, so that the leftmost image stripe is the first laser, the next one is the second laser, and so on. In non-trivial targets having holes, occlusions, and rapid depth changes, however, this sequencing breaks down as stripes, are often hidden and may even appear to change order, resulting in laser stripe ambiguity. One of the big advantages of using such a 3D profilometer is speed. Stripe-wise scanning scans multiple points or the entire field of view at once. Therefore, the problem of distortion from motion can be significantly reduced or even eliminated. However, the commercial application of the 3D profilometer is limited because of the complex data processing and analyses regarding surface reconstruction.

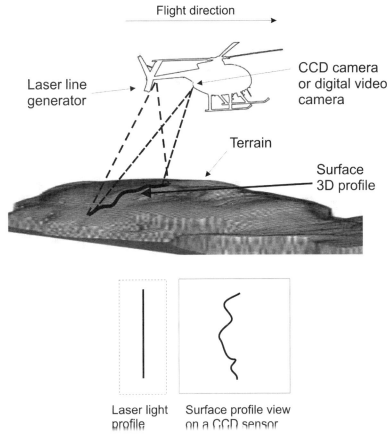

Figure 7.9 The principle of stripe-wise scanning (3D profilometer).

MAIN OPERATING PRINCIPLES

Laser rangefinder (LRF) technology is very suitable for applications where there is a demand for the speedy gathering of very accurate 3D information. The accuracy of distance measurement can be on the order of 20-30 mm accuracy for outdoor applications depending on the distance between the laser sensor and the study object. Having very high accuracy is possible because of low divergence of the laser light beam, which is typically on the order of 1-2 milliradians.

From the physical point of view, there are no major differences between the operating principles of commercial airborne and terrestrial systems. The main measuring principles are the same as in a LRF. They can be divided into two groups: pulsed wave LRF and continuous wave (CW) LRF. The pulsed wave LRF can measure the Time-Of-Flight (TOF) of the transmitted pulse or determine the distance between the transceiver and the object surface using a Frequency-to-Distance Conversion (FDC). Continuous wave LRF can be CW-AM (Amplitude Modulation) and CW-FM (Frequency Modulation). In reality, the operating principle of the typical commercial laser scanning systems, either airborne or terrestrial, is pulsed-wave based.

The typical pulsed terrestrial LRF consists of a laser transmitter, the transmitting and receiving optics, and a time-to-digital converter. The transmitter emits a short optical pulse (2 to 20 nanoseconds) to the surface of the target, and back at the speed of light. A quartz-stabilized clock is used to measure the time difference between the transmitted pulse and received echo. The range is calculated by halving the two-way travel time and multiplying by the speed of light. An image of the object is created point by point by sweeping the transceiver through the specified zenith and azimuth angles.

In the FDC LRF, a time period is proportional to the distance to the target. The measurement is usually accomplished either by comparing two very short pulses, or using a continuous amplitude or frequency modulated wave, and measuring the phase difference or beat frequency. Furthermore, in the measured signal the amplitude of the received waveform is proportional to the intensity of the received light. The phase difference between the waveform reflected from the surface of the target and the reference signal gives a direct measurement of the distance to the object point.

The use of a phase-sensitive detector can give a more accurate indication of TOF, and hence distance, than a simple pulsed system, in which a direct time measurement is made on an intermittent burst of laser energy. In this case, the accuracy can be on the order of 1 mm (close range measurements).

In CW-AM LRF, a sinusoidal signal modulates in amplitude the transmitted signal. The phase shift between the transmitted and received modulated signals is proportional to the distance to the target. The phase measurement is periodical in time. Thus, the measuring result is valid for range values which are less than one wavelength of the modulated signal determining a distance ambiguity interval. If there are no ambiguity resolving mechanisms (i.e., instructions from an operator, or from some heuristic rule), the depth of field is constrained to less than one wavelength. If higher modulating frequencies are used, better depth resolution is obtained. If lower modulating frequencies are used, a larger depth of field is obtained.

In CW-FM LRF, a transmitting signal is modulated by a linearly time-varying frequency. The returned signal is mixed with a reference signal producing a beat frequency which is proportional to the distance. The advantage of this method is that the absence of phase measurement in this method excludes the existence of an ambiguity interval.

All laser scanning devices operate by directing a laser light beam to the object to be measured, then detecting and measuring the signal from the light reflected by the object surface. Unlike conventional photography, which records images reflected from ambient light, laser scanning systems record the strength of the echoes (reflectance). The intensity value of the returned echo can be useful for processing purposes, but it should be remembered that laser light is monochromatic.

The operating distance of laser scanning systems depends on several factors such as the output energy of the laser source, the operating wavelength, and the eye safety limitations at a particular wavelength. Additionally, light mist, fog or clouds will cause a situation where the received signals are severely attenuated, as much as 100 db less than the transmitted signal. In heavy fog or clouds lidar systems are unusable. A rule of thumb is: if you cannot see the target because of haze or fog, then the laser will also not penetrate to the target.

Current advanced airborne systems can be operated above the ground surface, depending on the system, from 80 – 6,100 meters (260 - 20,000 feet). The flight altitude depends on the strength of the laser, weather conditions and, in terms of the final deliverables, the mission planning parameters. Terrestrial systems typically measure ranges from 3 – 1,000 meters (10 – 3,280 feet) with range uncertainties of the order of millimeters to centimeters. Ground based systems operate by measuring range distances sweeping through both azimuthal and zenith angles in small steps on the order of tens of microradians.

The main tradeoff between TOF scanners and phase-based scanners is between the speed of acquisition and dynamic range. TOF devices typically capture data at a rate between hundreds and thousands of points per second. By contrast, phase-based devices capture hundreds of thousands of points per second. Phase-based devices are faster, and in many applications this makes them the tool of choice. However, TOF devices have a much greater dynamic range of useful measurement than phase-based devices. At the time of writing this manual, the upper range limit of commercial phase-based devices is 80 m (262 feet).

The tradeoff of acquisition speed versus dynamic range stems not only from the measurement principles but from other operational considerations. The pulse repetition rate of a TOF laser system governs in part how the device is classified in terms of eye safety because the mean output power is proportional to the pulse rate. Eye safety is a substantial issue affecting acceptance of laser scanners in some industries. Of course, the speed of light provides a physical upper bound. Each laser pulse must have time to return to the detector before the next one is sent out. If the signal is making a 2-kilometer round trip, the speed of light would limit the signal rate to 150,000 pulses per second, even before allowing for latency in the detector.

Phase-based scanners are also restricted in their output power for eye-safety reasons. Increasing the measurement range of phase-based devices requires higher output power. Another limitation on the measurement range of phase-based scanners is that the modulation waveform increases with range. Accuracy suffers over longer ranges because of the resolution of the measurement of the phase angles.

Sensor Position and Orientation
While it is fairly simple to measure distances using a laser, the positioning of the footprint of the laser beam in 3D space creates additional problems if the laser source itself is moving. If the laser is mounted in an aircraft, ship or ground vehicle, then the relationship between the observer and the observed is not easy to solve. It would be even worse if the surveyor is on a moving vehicle and the object surface being surveyed is also moving. While the distance between the surveyor and object will indicate if it is getting closer or further away, there is no way of knowing whether the object is moving at the same speed or at an angle towards or away from the surveyor, or at a different speed, or possibly not moving at all.

The movement issue was long a problem with mounting a laser ranging system in an aircraft. The distance from the aircraft to a point on the ground could be accurately measured, but this distance was not relevant because there was no method of determining whether the laser was vertical or ranging off-vertical. In addition, the actual position and attitude of the aircraft in relation to a ground coordinate system was impossible to determine. The result was no one could say for certain exactly what spot on the ground was being measured.

Consequently, airborne laser technology requires two additional technologies to enable it to become a useful tool for terrain modeling and mapping. The first is inertial measurement technology and the second is global positioning systems. Both of these technologies are discussed in detail in Chapter 10, Enabling Technologies.

Inertial technology uses two fairly old and well-known laws of physics. The first is that an object spinning very rapidly tends to keep its relative orientation in space; and the second is that on earth, a rapidly spinning object typically aligns itself with gravity. This can be checked by making a toy top spin very fast on a board. The top will rotate around the true vertical, pulled by the force of gravity. If the board is tilted, the top will still stay upright. Modern, robust gyroscopes (the scientific spinning top) rotate a mass within a gimbal or cage. Recently, the mass in gyroscopes is kept in electromagnetic suspension to reduce the influence of friction. If the cage is attached and aligned to the laser head, then the angle of the laser, from vertical, can be measured. Typical inertial navigation systems (INS) also contain accelerometers to measure the velocity of a moving object. An accelerometer may be visualized as a weight suspended on a string from the top center of a cardboard box. If the box is given a shove, the box itself moves and the weight takes a fraction of a second to catch up with the movement. Incorporating a high precision clock and a method of measuring angles, an accelerometer can measure both the speed and direction of movement. However, no accelerometers can be relied upon to remain accurate for long periods of time. There are a number of reasons for this, some of which are mechanical, and some of which relate to external influences such as gravity and rotation of the earth. Consequently, even if the precise starting point is known, once it has been moving for a while, the accelerometer tends to lose its precise location. In order to solve this problem, GPS measurement of position is used together with INS orientation of the lidar sensor.

The GPS satellites orbit the center of gravity of the Earth and transmit radio signals that are received by the GPS receivers. Using a minimum of four satellites whose precise orbits are known, it is theoretically possible to compute the position of the receiver. However, in practice it has been determined that for the very precise locations required for accurate positioning, lock on at least six GPS satellites is desirable. There are a number of other considerations that have to be addressed with the GPS technology. The GPS is relatively simple in theory (basic 3D geometry), but it is complicated by irregularities in the earth's gravity, the shape of the earth, the map projection to be used, as well as inconsistencies in atmospheric conditions and other phenomena such as sun spots.

AIRBORNE LIDAR SYSTEMS

There are a variety of different systems in use around the world, some of which were developed for specific purposes and some developed for more generalized purposes. Earlier in the chapter it was mentioned that the commercial laser scanning systems utilize mostly pulsed wave lasers. Regardless of the manufacturer of laser scanning systems, all laser scanners are characterized by describing their features which are as follows: pulse energy measured in µJ, pulse duration measured in nanoseconds, pulse repetition rate (PRR) measured in kHz, field of view of scan measured in degrees, and scan rate measured in Hz. The Encyclopedia of Laser Physics and Technology defines those parameters as follows: Optical pulses are basically flashes of light, in most cases delivered in the form of laser beams. The pulse energy is simply the total energy content of a pulse. Pulse duration is most frequently defined as the Full Width at Half Maximum (FWHM) of the optical power versus time. The pulse repetition rate (or pulse repetition frequency) of a light source which periodically emits pulses is defined as the number of emitted pulses per second. For example, a 50 kHz system generates 50,000 pulses of laser energy in one second. The scan rate is the number of times per second a scanning device samples its field of view. Scan period is the period taken by a scanner to complete a scan pattern and return to its starting point. The field of view is the part of the observable world that can be sampled. Varying some of these parameters will change the effective results of the survey.

Some airborne systems have been developed specifically for very low level surveys (typically using helicopters) for corridor applications, and some are for more generalized mapping. NASA has continued development of its own space-borne systems: their SLICER (Scanning Lidar Imager of Canopies by Echo Recovery) and LVIS (Laser Vegetation Imaging Sensor) are both tools for measuring the detailed canopy structure of vegetation. These units have an unusually broad footprint of about 9 meters (30 feet) for data analysis of forest cover. Commercial off-the-shelf (COTS) units, such as those offered by most lidar manufacturers, provide a middle-of-the-road "general" unit for accurate mapping of topography.

Compared to the earlier versions of laser scanning systems, which were capable of recording only one pulse at low pulse repetition rates, today's lidar systems are much more advanced. Manufacturers have developed sensors which can record simultaneously multiple echoes (currently up to 5) for each transmitted laser pulse, and reflected intensity for each echo and recently full waveform digitization has been introduced.

A case of multiple returns from a single pulse can happen when a laser beam reaches the roof of a building. If the beam is broad enough, then it can partly hit the roof edge of a house and the rest of the laser beam travels to the ground. The return beam detector registers one reflection of the rooftop edge, and one reflection from the ground, subsequently providing two different elevations from the single pulse. The elevation computed for the rooftop is called the "first return," and the elevation computed for the ground is called the "last return." Thus, a digital surface model (DSM) and a digital terrain model (DTM) can be created. Figure 7.10 shows elevations from first-return lidar data of Baltimore, Maryland, with variable elevations color-coded from dark blue (lowest elevations) to dark red (highest elevations).

Figure 7.10 First return lidar data of Baltimore, MD. Note the ships at dock in the harbor at "3 o'clock." Courtesy of the Joint Precision Strike Demonstration Project Office (JPSD-PO), Rapid Terrain Visualization (RTV) Advanced Concept Technology Demonstration (ACTD), Fort Belvoir, Virginia. See color plate in Appendix C.

In a forest, the situation is more complicated. When the laser beam from a multi-return system hits a tree, then the first return is usually assumed to arrive from the top of the canopy. The last return, perhaps the fifth, is assumed to come from the ground. The intermediate returns, i.e., 2nd, 3rd and 4th, are expected to be caused by tree branches and understory vegetation between the top of the canopy and the ground. However, sometimes, the vegetation is so thick that the laser beam never penetrates through to the ground. Typically the rule of thumb is: if a person walking through a forest cannot see the sky above then the lidar system probably cannot "see" the ground beneath the canopy.

Full waveform digitization offers even more choices in that it allows for many multiple returns with short separation to be collected from a single laser shot. The down side is the more returns collected the more data there are in storage, and more complex data processing is required. In reality, at the present time, with the exception of vegetation studies, there are no significant beneficial advantages for more than first and last returns.

In addition, most laser scanning systems are capable of storing the information about the intensity of each detected echo. Intensity capture of the return pulse, either through waveform digitization or return pulse peak capture, is becoming an increasingly common practice. This information is valuable for classification purposes, and considerable research and study is taking place to make more use of these data (see also lidargrammetry later in this chapter). Regardless, by reviewing the intensity returns it is possible to distinguish between different objects and general vegetation cover. As a general rule, objects with high reflectivity of visual light, such as a metal roof, show a higher return energy than objects such as a newly paved, black-tarred roadway. Continued development and improvement of software are needed in order to transfer the knowledge about the intensity into more useful information about different types of surfaces. Also, this information can be valuable for automated feature extraction. Figures 7.11 and 7.12 provide two examples of lidar intensity return images. However, it should be remembered that as stated previously lidar systems are monochromatic – that is they record reflected energy from a single wavelength, compared to photography which collects reflective data from a wide variety of wavelengths.

Figure 7.11 Lidar intensity return image of Baltimore, Md. Compare with Figure 7.10. Note that stripes can be seen on the football field. Note also the speckled returns from water in Baltimore Harbor (3 o'clock). Courtesy of the Joint Precision Strike Demonstration Project Office (JPSD-PO), Rapid Terrain Visualization (RTV) Advanced Concept Technology Demonstration (ACTD), Fort Belvoir, Virginia.

For reference, the characteristics of typical commercial lidar instruments in operation today are included in Table 7.1. It should be noted that the new capabilities and functionality are being introduced on a regular basis so "typical" characteristics are changing over time. Also individual lidar systems may be developed for specific purposes, so not all lidar units have the range of characteristics noted.

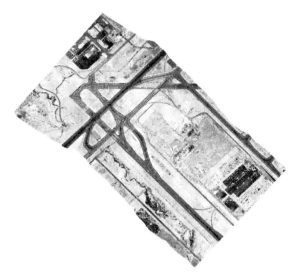

Figure 7.12 An example of intensity data over Toronto's Pearson Airport. Courtesy of Optech, Inc.

Table 7.1 Characteristics of Typical Commercial Lidar Systems.

Specification	Typical Value
Wavelength [a]	1.064 m
Pulse Repetition Rate	10-150 kHz (150 kHz max)
Pulse Energy	100s μJ
Pulse Width	10 ns
Beam Divergence	0.25 – 2 milliradian
Scan Angle (full angle)	40° (75° max)
Scan Rate	25 – 90 Hz
Scan Pattern	Zig-zag, parallel, elliptical, sinusoidal
GPS Frequency	1 – 2 times per second
INS Frequency	50 - 200 times per second max
Operating Altitude	80– 3,000 m (6,000 m max)
Footprint	0.25 – 2 m (from 1,000 m)
Multiple Elevation Capture	1 – 5
Grid Spacing	0.3 – 2 m
Vertical RMSEz	10+ cm
Horizontal RMSEr	15-100 cm
Post-Processing Software [b]	Proprietary
Price (standard)	$850,000 - $1,500,000 US$
Price (custom)	$1,000,000 - $2,000,000 US$
Delivery (standard)	20 – 26 weeks

[a] generally diode-pumped Nd:YAG, Nd:YLF and Nd:YVO$_4$ although there are some systems operating at 1.5 m

[b] refers to geo-referencing of laser slant ranges to an established reference frame, normally WGS84

State-of-the-Art

The earliest versions of laser remote sensing systems were more scientific and prototype than commercial instruments useful for topographic purposes, but in the 1980s early commercial endeavors involved the use of laser profilers to generate a single line profile of the ground beneath an aircraft. However, it wasn't until the 1990s that the development of the enabling technologies reached a degree of sophistication for accurate airborne use. The 1990s also saw the development of laser scanners (as opposed to profilers) and the development of the current lidar instruments.

Two predominant companies were involved in the initial development of commercial systems: Azimuth Corporation of Westford, Massachusetts (now owned by Leica Geosystems), and Optech, Incorporated of Toronto, Canada. Today, in the number of current operating units, the market is dominated by Optech and Leica.

Azimuth Corporation developed laser rangefinders as subsystems for profilers and military target tracking starting in the late-1970s and through the 1980s. Azimuth supplied rangefinder subsystems to several early entrants into the laser mapping field including EagleScan and Southern Applied Technology (now Aerotech). They subsequently delivered a complete Aeroscan system in 1998, a 15 kHz system capable of flying up to 6,000 meters above ground. Leica has subsequently delivered progressively more advanced systems of increasing pulse rates. As of 2006, Leica's state-of-the-art lidar system is the ALS50, shown at Figure 7.13, with pulse repetition rate of 133,000 pulses per second.

Figure 7.13 Leica ALS50 Lidar Sensor, 133 KHz.

In the early 1980s, Optech, Inc. developed airborne profilometers based on a series of compact, rugged laser rangefinders for industrial applications. Optech, Inc. was also involved in the development of several airborne laser bathymeters: the LARSEN 500 in 1984 with Terra Surveys Ltd. (now Terra Remote Sensing Inc.) and the Canadian Hydrographic Service, FLASH in 1988, and ALARMS in 1988. They next built the prototype ALTM (Airborne Laser Terrain Mapper) in 1993, which was a 2 kHz instrument, and delivered the system to TopoScan GmbH in Germany. A re-packaged commercial design was offered for sale in 1995 as the 1020 model. Optech, Inc. delivered an enhanced model 1020 (5 kHz) in 1996 and upgraded the earlier 2 kHz models. A custom 1025 (25 kHz) system was delivered in Japan in 1997. Optech subsequently produced an ALTM 1210 system (10 kHz) system for commercial sales in 1998 and a new 1225 enhanced model (25 kHz) in 1999. In 2000, they delivered a 33 kHz lidar system followed by a 50 kHz system and most recently a 100 kHz system (see Figure 7.14). They are also the only commercial source of continued development of bathymetric lidar systems (see Chapter 8).

Figure 7.14 Optech 3100 Lidar Sensor, 100 KHz.

SAAB Survey Systems AB in Jönköping (Sweden) delivered a commercial version of the TopEye system in 1996. This system was a result of a joint development of a hydrographic airborne laser scanning system, the hardware of which was originally designed by Saab Dynamics (Sweden) and Optech, Inc. Later, TopEye AB was spun off from Saab. It continues to mostly offer a helicopter-based system, although a fixed-wing version of TopEye is also available and the company is now part of the Blom group.

About the same period of time, TopoSys GmbH (Germany) introduced the TopoSys-1 airborne laser scanning system. This type of ALS system is different from traditional ALS systems because it is based on a glass fiber technology. Today, it has been replaced by the latest development called the Falcon-III. The TopoSys system has also a polygon scanner, which employs the wide angle full wave form digitization of a laser scanner from Riegl GmbH.

Since the beginning of the 21st century, GeoLas Consulting (Germany) together with IGI GmbH (Germany) has been providing its own commercial airborne laser scanning system called LiteMapper.

Riegl Laser Measurement Systems GmbH (Austria) has been in the field of the development of laser radar systems for more than two decades. Currently, the company supplies hardware for both airborne and terrestrial laser scanners.

There are a number of other companies and organizations which have developed and built customized laser scanning systems for supporting specific applications. One of the earliest was FliMap developed by John Chance Land Surveys, Inc. (USA). FliMap is a rotary-wing laser scanning system used for the corridor mapping purposes where a very high point density on the ground and a very high precision of a terrain model is required. Terrapoint, Terra Remote Sensing, Aeroscan and a number of others have all developed in-house systems. Another example is ScaLARS, which has been developed in the Institute for Navigation, University of Stuttgart (Germany). ScaLARS uses the Palmer scanning pattern (see Figure 7.8).

The advantage of in-house lidar development (compared to commercial off-the-shelf, manufactured systems) is a group can decide on its research program or market niche and develop a system that will meet that specifically by combining the type and quality of laser, inertial system and GPS to meet its specific needs. The disadvantage is a high degree of knowledge in optical,

optical mechanical, and electrical systems is required to engineer the disparate parts into a working whole, and then develop software to ensure all of the systems are working as a unit, and able to process the data efficiently and accurately. While considerable monetary savings can be achieved by buying all of the hardware (compared to a manufactured unit), development costs of making everything work together can be extremely high.

While specific objectives are usually the reason for in-house development of airborne lidar systems, the major manufacturers are constantly expanding the capabilities of their systems and in reality almost all airborne lidar systems are, in effect, custom built.

There are also existing 3D flash laser imaging systems which are capable of producing 3D imagery of the scene. However, this type of laser system is not discussed further because it is mostly applied for a close-range image acquisition in non-commercial applications. The principle of operation is based on laser radar using a flash-lamp-pumped laser light source.

Calibration

The most frequently asked questions many lay people ask lidar operators are: How do you know the system is working properly, and how do we know the elevations you give us will be of the ground (or various objects)? These are two very simple questions with quite complex answers.

Lidar systems collect a lot of data. (See lidar "hit" pattern in Figures 1.21 and 1.24, Appendix C). Even the lower kHz instruments (the 5,000-25,000 kHz machines by today's standards) collect an incredible amount of data. Obtaining a data point 5,000 times per second provides a dense picture of whatever the laser pulses are hitting, as can be seen in the point cloud illustrations in this chapter (e.g., Figure 7.15). (*Point cloud* is a term used by many lidar system operators to describe all of the returns received by the instrument, and is best imagined as a collection of dots of light hanging in space indicating the spot where each reflection originated.) Depending on the width of the beam when it hits something, the laser will record a variety of phenomena. Obviously, if the beam hits a flat roofed building in a shopping center or a paved parking lot, there is a clear and unambiguous return reflection.

However, if the beam hits a tree, a number of things can happen. The beam could exactly hit the center of a large trunk or stem and bounce back. However, there is more likelihood that, on the pulse's downward path, it will hit some leaves and then some branches. If the tree is sparsely branched and there is enough laser energy, some may eventually hit the ground and be reflected back. Depending on the system, it may be set up to record the first return, the last return or multiple returns. Regardless, whichever the case, a minimum of one position and elevation will be recorded for every pulse, unless the laser energy is absorbed (by water, for example).

Under most circumstances, by comparing the relative 3D positions (and intensity, if the system has this feature), software or an interpreter can usually identify man-made features such as road surfaces, buildings, parking lots, and often fences and overhead wires. On the other hand, wherever there appears to be random 3D spacing of points, this is a good indication of returns reflected from vegetation.

The interpreter can use one of several software packages to view point cloud data vertically or horizontally as shown in Figure 7.15. It is generally obvious there is a layer, which appears to be (and most likely is) the ground. This is represented by a mass of points appearing to be lowest in the data set. Above this "ground layer" are other mass points that appear to be understory while other points are suspended higher in the air. These are the points that were bounced back from various intermediate reflectors and are usually "weeded out" by software. However, when there are a number of points floating apparently uniformly above ground and indicating a specific surface, there is a strong indication that the system is recording a man-made structure or perhaps a dense agricultural field such as wheat, corn or sugar cane.

Depending on the client and the intended use for the data, the intensity returns may be sufficient for interpretation. However, many lidar systems are operated along with some sort of tracking device, such as a video or frame camera, which is time-tagged by the GPS. This imagery

First Return
Second Return
Third Return
Fourth Return

Figure 7.15 When viewed horizontally, we can see lidar "point clouds" in trees. Note that many of the first returns (yellow) reach the ground, whereas some of the 3rd returns (red) are still in the trees. Many pulses do not even receive 3rd and 4th returns, so their last returns may still be in the trees. From Stoker, et al. 2006. See color plate in Appendix C.

allows the interpreter to check and verify processed data. Further, with the development of more and more sophisticated frame cameras with larger array chips, digital imagery captured at the same time as the lidar is often used in conjunction with the lidar data to provide ortho-rectified imagery with pixels equivalent to 15 cm (6 inches) or even smaller. At current writing, there are still some limitations with frame cameras because array sizes still do not approach the larger format digital mapping cameras (which tend to work as line scanners rather than frame capture) and because download times of images to hard drives, and refreshing the CCD array for speedy acquisition, is still a concern.

The ultimate question often asked, however, is: How do you know that what appears to be ground at any one location really is the ground and not a tuft of grass or a piece of garbage someone threw there? Generally, the lidar operator cannot be 100 percent sure that ground points can be correctly defined all of the time, unless the technician can see the feature clearly on the video or frame camera record. However, the dynamics of the technology are such that there are so much data being recorded that any aberrations are few overall, and in most cases the final product will be more accurate than other surface modeling methodologies.

Addressing the other question on the proper operation of the equipment is more complex. Depending on the system, it can be difficult to know that everything is functioning perfectly during the flight and data acquisition. One of the reasons, as previously mentioned, is that a lidar system is three separate components that are basically operating independently. Consequently, the lidar operator has to validate that the laser, GPS, and inertial systems are all functioning and logging correctly. Luckily, the operator of the lidar system has some empirical indications when the data are being recorded in the aircraft. If the laser is not getting sufficient returns, it means one of two things: the aircraft is flying over something that is not reflecting the signals (a lake, for instance – water absorbs infrared energy), or the laser is experiencing some mechanical or electronic problem. The actual light source is straightforward to verify and can be thought of in terms of a light bulb, i.e., while all laser diodes tend to deteriorate and lose some power over time, they generally either work or don't, and when they burn out, it becomes fairly obvious.

In real time, watching the data being recorded from the IMU should indicate a general progression as the aircraft takes off and gathers momentum and elevation, the same as with the GPS unit. If either of these subsystems shows erratic or inconsistent data, there is obviously something wrong.

Monitoring the data during collection is only part of the process to assure proper operation of the equipment and ultimately, data quality. The independence of the GPS, inertial and laser data sets can also be used to give a first pass assessment of the data quality and relative accuracy of the data after processing. While the individual data sets are logged independently, they are precisely time tagged and used together to calculate the X,Y,Z offsets from the local survey ground control to the individual 3D coordinates of each collected point. If the entire system is not working properly, it is often readily apparent in the data. By examining the geometric relationships between groups of points that define features such as overhead wires, roads or buildings, an operator can recognize specific problems. For example, if any of the subsystems is not working correctly or is misaligned, then regular features will appear as irregular and random.

However, all subsystems may be indicating correct operating parameters (precision), but that doesn't mean that together they are providing accurate answers. The only way to validate the collection process is to run some calibration tests, much the same as would be done with any other instrumentation. These procedures allow the operator to know if the subsystems have been set up properly and if there are any inherent biases in the instrumentation.

As with any scientific testing, a series of conditions are required, measured by an independent technology of higher accuracy. Most lidar operators test their equipment over a calibration site for which they have a large amount of data, acquired by using another survey technology. There are guidelines for calibration and system operation from both the American Society for Photogrammetry and Remote Sensing (ASPRS) and the U.S. Federal Emergency Management Agency (FEMA). For complete calibration the lidar operator selects an area and proceeds to complete a ground survey of it. Typically, the area is not completely flat, and contains a variety of different 3D features. For example, a suitable site could contain a large commercial building with a flat roof, a large flat parking area, a ravine, a small wooded area, some roadways and some other buildings. The survey is often done on the ground using kinematic GPS or on rooftops and surrounding terrain using static GPS surveys. What are needed are positions and elevations for a large number of features, surveyed with procedures that are more readily verifiable than the lidar system being calibrated. (See Figure 7.16).

When the lidar is flown over this test area in two opposing directions and normally with additional cross-flights at 90 degrees to the former, the airborne results in each direction are then compared not only with the "ground truth" results but also with results of the other flight directions. Calibrations are normally performed on a regular basis, since factors that cause lidar systems to lose their calibration result covertly from routine usage rather than from known incidents. As major calibrations are time consuming, a limited calibration is usually flown on every flight mission. A limited calibration could be as simple as flying in both directions over the airport runway before starting a survey mission.

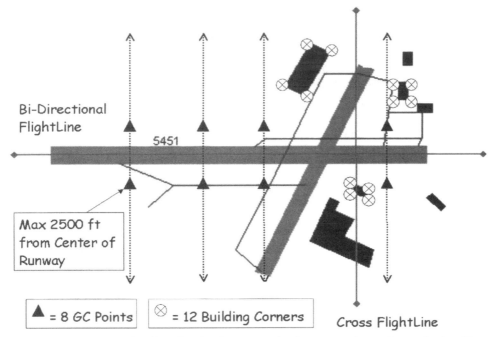

Figure 7.16 Lidar Calibration Test Site. Sample of a test area showing measured ground control points. Courtesy EarthData International.

The analysis of the airborne results has to take into account the relationship of the subsystems to each other as well as the relationship of the subsystems to the ground. This is quite complicated. For example, the GPS antenna on the aircraft is generally placed outside the top of the fuselage, but as near as possible to the laser head unit and usually directly above it. The relationship between the antenna and laser head must be surveyed precisely as any offsets will affect the absolute accuracy of the final results. If the lidar is moved to a different aircraft, obviously a new calibration survey must be done each time a new installation is carried out. Periodically a check survey should be completed to ensure calibration integrity.

Similarly, having the IMU bolted onto the laser scanner is not just a matter of measuring the offset between the laser head and the center of the IMU, as this does not necessarily mean they are perfectly aligned with each other. Minute differences of a thousandth of an inch in vertical alignment on the test bench are magnified tremendously when the beam is extended from three thousand feet in the air. However, calibration flights allow systematic errors to be calculated and then corrected using software.

This empirical methodology is quite typical of scientific testing. When the aircraft is flown in one direction over the test site, then turns 180 degrees and flies back in the opposite direction over the site, any misalignments should appear as offsets of features: i.e., on the second flight, roads or buildings will not appear to be in the same place as they were on the first. In this way, any systematic rotations in roll and pitch of the system as mounted in the aircraft can be determined and then modeled.

Depending on the laser operations, there are other tests that have to be performed. Most airborne laser scanners scan from side to side accomplished with a swinging mirror galvanometer that goes back and forth, reflecting the laser beam down to the ground. There are both electrical and mechanical aspects to this. First, there is what is called latency - the lag in time from the encoder on the scanning mirror. Typically, this is very small, in the range of 3 microseconds, but the greater the number of pulses sent out by the laser the more significant this becomes. Secondly, the bigger problem is what is generally called "windup." As the mirror starts its travel from left to right it commences from stop to full speed to stop at the end of its travel, then it reverses for the trip back. The acceleration from dead stop to full speed (torque) can cause a flat surface on the ground to appear "convex/concave looking" if the unit is not modeled or calibrated correctly.

As mentioned earlier, there are some lasers that scan using a rotating prism. This method would initially seem to solve the swinging mirror problem, as the prisms can rotate at a constant speed. There is, however, a more difficult timing problem in calculating angle changes with a system that doesn't have a complete stop at any point. So, the rotating prism system solves one problem at the expense of another. Further, because all of the data are collected only in one direction, it is somewhat more difficult to ascertain any biases or, worse, accumulating biases. Conventional wisdom currently seems to favor the bi-directional mirror technology.

The careful lidar operator is aware of these technical problems and watches for any indications of trouble in the data. If the calibration flights do not result in the required tolerances for the system, then bench testing or further investigation is required.

DATA PROCESSING

Because a lidar system's hardware is complicated, the data processing is also complicated. The data collected by the hardware components of lidar systems are called the raw data and these are in a unique format because each lidar system (or series of systems) has its own combination of hardware and internal operating software. Following the processing of the raw data which is often called pre-processing, additional processing is used to develop the final product. The additional processing is called post-processing. Much of the data processing has become more automated over the last few years and there is every reason to believe this trend will continue as better and more effective algorithms are developed. The following schematic shows a traditional processing chain.

As shown in Figure 7.17, the laser data processing procedure starts with three different raw data sets, namely: positioning, orientation, and laser point ranges. In almost all cases it is necessary for these raw data to be processed by the company or agency which collects the data because the initial processing software has been developed specifically for that lidar system or model series.

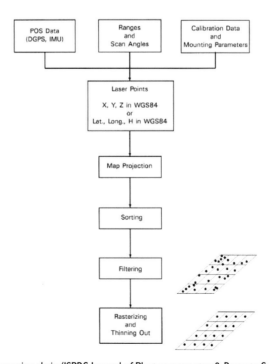

Figure 7.17 Typical data processing chain (ISPRS Journal of Photogrammetry & Remote Sensing 54 (1999), pp. 68–82).

While there are two existing positioning systems (GPS and GLONASS) and a third (Gallileo) in development, at the present time all airborne lidar systems use the GPS. All GPS based systems use the satellite reference system called the World Geodetic System (WGS). There are well developed and solid transformation programs to transform WGS coordinates and elevations into every major map projection used throughout the world.

In most lidar systems the GPS data are correlated with the IMU data to provide a more solid positional reference, while the inertial data are used concurrently to provide the orientation of the system. Inertial systems are typically subject to wild fluctuations not only for the shifting attitude of the aircraft but also for a number of electro-mechanical reasons, miniaturization, as well as others due to gravity, speed of rotation of the earth (which varies according to latitude – being approximately 1600 Km/hour at the equator and virtually zero at the poles) and various other physical effects. Therefore a set of software filters are used to average the IMU output to make it usable.

The laser system and its photo sensor receiver outputs ranges, or distances, and these are then combined with the other data to produce positions and elevations in relation to the World Geodetic System. Additional software models any system calibration effects and applies these to the final output.

As a brief digression it should be noted that the WGS is an average system developed for use around the world. It is not particularly suited, therefore, for any particular region or country. As a result almost all users require final data in a map projection which is more suited to where they are located. All map projections, including the WGS, are essentially based on a regular (globe shape) figure of the earth based on a circumference calculated at sea level. Because the earth is not regular, the geoid, the real shape of the earth, usually only fits any map projection in spots. For the rest of the map projection, the geoid can be above or below the surface represented by the map projection. This peculiar situation is not at all intuitive, as it means that you can have real elevations of zero mean sea level which could be above the "map projection zero sea level" in some areas and below the "map projection zero sea level" in others. This becomes important as it means the elevations which are computed in the WGS projection can be wildly different to local sea level datum in the area of the survey. It is further confused by the fact, as mentioned earlier, that the center of gravity of the earth moves on a continuing basis and all of the earth is subject to tidal influences. From this is it obvious that some reference is needed to place the WGS coordinates recorded on the aircraft back into the real world coordinates being used on the ground.

The easiest way to do this is to do what is done in any precision kinematic GPS survey: that is to have a GPS base station operating on a known coordinated survey point on the ground within a reasonable distance of the kinematic survey unit. When this is done the GPS base station will collect the same satellite data as the kinematic GPS unit in the aircraft and this eliminates virtually all of the same effects of atmospheric, tidal and other physical phenomena errors which can affect GPS data, and being tied to a survey monument with a specific coordinate in the user's map projection allows transformations of all of the aircraft data to that same projection, coordinate system and elevation datum.

While technically the WGS output could be sent to the user to complete the processing, in almost all cases the operator of the lidar system will effect the transformations and also do some quality checks by comparing lidar output data to field survey elevations on the ground. However, at this stage the laser data set is still unsorted and unclassified. It is a cloud of randomly distributed laser points in elevation and position.

As a lidar system is an undiscriminating sensor, it collects data for every point from which it receives a return echo. The result is a tremendous number of data points from objects that may have no value for a specific project. A user who wants only the bare earth ground data is not interested in returns from towers, rooftops, branches or leaves, or other objects that are above the ground. The lidar data, therefore, need all of these irrelevant returns removed. This data processing is accomplished by utilizing software delivered with the lidar system, proprietary software developed by the consultant, or with a commercially available package, all of which involve a wealth of sophisticated algorithms and expertise to review data to its nearest neighbors and weight them accordingly before removing what are considered either buildings, vegetation or other outliers.

There are several conditions which can cause erroneous outlier laser points. There might be reflections from objects in the background, reflections from objects between a laser scanner and an object (birds, moving persons or traffic, atmospheric effects such as dust or moisture etc.), partial reflection only of the laser spot at edges, multiple reflections of the laser beam, range differences originating from systematic range errors caused by different reflectivity of the surface elements and erroneous points caused by very bright objects. Therefore, this step in post-processing is the classification of laser points as ground or non-ground. This procedure is also sometimes called *sorting*. In this phase the points, which do not represent the surface of the target, are removed. Bare earth ground points are essentially a DTM.

Additional filter techniques can be applied for further classification of the remaining laser data with respect to vegetation and man-made objects like buildings, bridges or power lines. Different vendors have implemented various filtering methods in their software packages. Those methods can be morphological, autoregressive process, techniques based on least squares interpolation, or using geometrical values like distances and angles as filter criteria.

Each laser point is originally randomly located. In many cases, not all points may be required in order to define the terrain surface or objects on it. A technique called thinning is often used in order to remove those points which are not of interest. The most common way of thinning is using nearest neighbor algorithms to compare adjacent points and remove any that do not add to the definition of the required object. Thinning the amount of the laser points also helps post-processing to be completed much more speedily.

Depending on the final use of a data set, another task often conducted during lidar data processing is surface generation or reconstruction. Because the original laser points are irregularly spaced, and many users prefer a regular, gridded surface, gridding is also often completed before the data set is delivered. This process can also be used to reduce the size of the data set if the end-user is using subsequent software which does not handle large file sizes or the user wants to review large areas of data at a time. Gridding is a standard processing task and there are many software packages available. Often it is done on a one, two, three or five meter grid. Studies have shown that a raster cell of 1m × 1m gives a very good and detailed representation of the earth.

There are conditions which affect the return signals that can have an effect on the data processing. The strength of the signal returned to the laser scanner detector, which limits the signal to noise ratio, is influenced by multiple factors including a function of the measured range, angle of incidence of the transmitted signal, atmospheric conditions, albedo (reflectivity) of the measured surface, and the wavelength of the transmitted signal.

Laser spot size, which increases at ranges beyond the focal length of the instrument, necessarily results in mixed pixel effects when measuring edges. In such cases when the beam strikes a surface edge, part is returned by the object and part is returned by whatever is behind or adjacent to an edge. This results in unavoidable range ambiguity or noise. Signal returns from oblique angles of incidence are typically weaker than from surfaces more perpendicular to the transmitted beam and consequently are noisier.

Figure 7.18 shows color-coded last-return lidar elevations prior to post-processing (left image) and data voids (right image) where no lidar returns were received. Figure 7.19 shows the same color-coded last-return lidar elevations after completion of post-processing; these represent the bare-earth elevations required for a normal DEM. Note that the right image in Figure 7.19 shows all the additional data voids caused by automated and manual post-processing to reclassify lidar returns on features elevated above the ground, to include bridges (removed and placed in a separate file) as part of the hydro-enforcement process discussed in Chapter 1.

 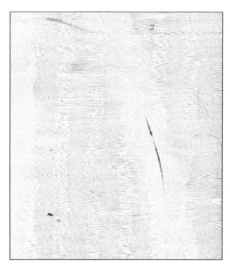

Figure 7.18 Last return lidar data of Lakewood, CA prior to post-processing. The image to the right shows pixels (in black) where there were no lidar returns, presumably absorbed or not reflected by water in the ditches or ponds. Images courtesy of the U.S. Army Engineer Research and Development Center (ERDC), Topographic Engineering Center (TEC). See color plate in Appendix C.

Figure 7.19 Last return lidar data of Lakewood, CA after post-processing. The left image now represents the bare-earth. The right image shows pixels where elevation points were moved due to reclassification of points on rooftops and dense vegetation. Images courtesy of U.S. Army Engineer Research and Development Center (ERDC), Topographic Engineering Center (TEC). See color plate in Appendix C.

Manual Post-Processing

Whereas automatic post-processing algorithms typically reclassify approximately 90-95 percent of elevation points that do not represent the bare earth terrain, the remaining 5-10 percent can be very labor intensive to determine. Indeed, to "clean" the remaining ten percent may consume 90 percent of the post-processing budget. Thus, determining just how "clean" a bare-earth dataset needs to be may be the principal cost-driver for some lidar projects. On the other hand, the proliferation of both COTS and individual company processing software has resulted in processing costs being reduced dramatically. Whereas five or six years ago manual processing might have represented 60 percent of a project budget, in many cases that has declined to 20 percent of the budget.

Still, while the automated post-processing software is quite sophisticated, it requires some operator intervention at times to ensure that the algorithm isn't making blunders. For example, in a flood area lidar surveyed and processed south of Winnipeg, Canada the software removed the berms around farmhouses, assuming they were hedges. The use of the data was flood protection and remediation, so the berms were necessary in the final deliverable and had to be re-inserted in the delivered files. Occasionally, some apparent data anomalies appear in the file which require identification to see what they are, and the lidar analyst may review aerial photography, digital imagery or a videotape to identify features.

Manual post-processing can also include the generation of 3D breaklines along approximate stream centerlines and/or shorelines, in order to generate hydrologically-enforced DEMs, TINS, and contours to highlight "islands" of higher terrain along stream channels (see Figure 1.5b in Chapter 1).

Full Waveform Digitizing

One of the latest developments in laser scanning technology is so-called full waveform digitizing (FWD). FWD provides a more detailed description of the structure of objects, more accurate range measurements, and extraction of additional and more detailed information from the data using an off-line processing step. Using FWD it is, in principle, possible to access almost unlimited number of returns per laser pulse, high multiple-target resolution, estimates of surface roughness and slope, and estimates of a target's laser cross section. The foreseen areas of applications are: details about canopy, sub-canopy structures, ground vegetation, improved detection of discontinuities and breaklines, transparent accuracy analysis from user-definable parameters, and target detection and range calculation in post-processing. For example, low vegetation may be separated from the ground, and canopy height measurements may be improved. At the time of writing this chapter, however, this development is rather experimental. There is more than one lidar system which offers this data collection mode but at present there are no commercial software packages which can use this type of data in a commercial setting.

Artifacts

Figure 7.20 shows artifacts that remained after automated post-processing was performed on this dataset. The entire corn field to the top-left of this image is an artifact that does not represent the bare-earth terrain and needs to be removed manually for DTM generation. However, the noisy surface on the right side of this image is a forest floor that actually undulates as shown. Noisy surfaces are not artifacts although often erroneously considered as such. Chapters 12 and 13 both address the smoothing and potential over-smoothing of noisy data.

As mentioned, the cost of manual post-processing may represent 90 percent of the total cost for post-processing. Lidar project costs can be reduced significantly if some artifacts are allowed to remain un-cleaned. Similarly, noisy data typically identifies subtle terrain features and are often within the desired accuracy of the project.

Edge Matching

Post-processing includes edge matching along adjacent lines and the removal of surplus data at the edges. Cross check lines are imported and again reviewed against the main survey lines for consistency and integrity. Any places where data do not match are investigated for possible cause. If there is no reasonable explanation, then the data may need to be re-acquired.

Tiling

The final aspect of the post-processing is to cut the data into the tiles or file sizes the client requires and is able to import and manipulate in the software format of choice (see Chapter 13).

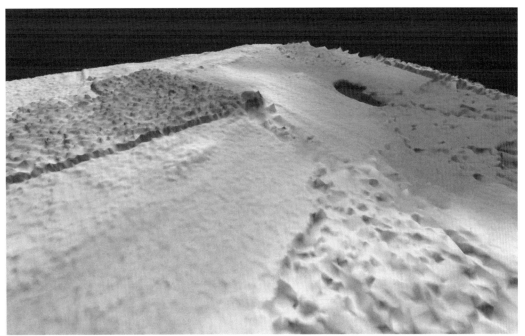

Figure 7.20 Artifacts may be small or large, as per the entire corn field shown here (top left) that should have been removed from the bare-earth DTM. The noisy area to the right, however, does not depict artifacts but true undulations in a forest floor after removal of trees.

LIDARGRAMMETRY[1]

Words ending in "grammetry" generally define noncontact measurements of objects from some form of imagery. Various measuring techniques refer to "-grammetry," for example: photogrammetry, videogrammetry, radiogrammetry, radargrammetry, and lidargrammetry. In this case, lidargrammetry is the direct exploitation of stereo imagery generated from lidar data.

With the increasing availability of lidar as a tool for generating high-resolution, high accuracy 3D terrain models of the earth, techniques are being developed to extract greater information from the basic lidar data sets now available from commercial vendors. These are somewhat similar in conception to earlier developments in "radargrammetry" which was developed by Intermap Technologies and essentially employs similar software to produce a 3D image by creating overlapping stereo pairs from a single radar "intensity" image and the 3D information from the direct elevation and position measurements. The basic software to accomplish this is found in most softcopy photogrammetric software.

In simple terms, a photogrammetric software package utilizes the reconstructed rays from standard film based aerial photography to produce a 3D image which can be measured at the intersection of the light rays forming that image. (Digital images may be constructed from frame cameras or push broom technologies - the latter of which require different software.) The photogrammetrist can see the images in 3D and thus the changes in elevation. In radargrammetry and lidargrammetry, theoretically the same algorithms are used in reverse. The input now, though, is one image of the ground from the amplitude of the radar or lidar return signal plus the elevation data. Therefore two pseudo images called a pseudo stereo pair (PSP) can be constructed which will then allow a photogrammetric system operator to "see" in 3D and use this facility to better determine the location of ground features.

---

[1] Some of the techniques discussed here are based on algorithms developed by GeoCue Corporation and implemented in their GeoCue software suite. GeoCue Corporation has patents pending on certain aspects of its point cloud processing techniques, including specific aspects of its implementation of point cloud processing, rendering and "synthetic stereo."

Early commercial lidar sensors provided only spatial information, the X,Y,Z locations of the returns from the target surface. The ability to capture the amplitude of the return signal, usually referred to as the intensity, was introduced by sensor manufacturers and rapidly adopted by commercial providers starting circa 2000. Intensity data has not, in general, been used to generate additional mapping products directly from the lidar data. Rather it has predominantly been used to create ancillary data, such as pseudo black and white images of the project site, as secondary data to improve automated classification of the point data, or as a tool to improve sensor calibration routines. With the recent deployment of lidar sensors with repetition rates of 100 kHz or more, it has become attractive to look at other techniques for exploiting the intensity-capture capabilities of the sensors by generating traditional mapping products directly from the intensity images. One such approach is to use the intensity information as the source data for generating stereo models of the project area directly from the lidar data itself rather than from ancillary imagery.

By creating appropriate PSPs from the lidar intensity images, it is possible to generate stereo models that can be directly exploited using existing photogrammetric workstations and the traditional photogrammetric workflow in areas such as feature extraction or breakline compilation. Using the lidar intensity data to generate stereo models allows data providers to improve the overall efficiency of their lidar data processing while also allowing established mapping firms to continue to exploit their existing infrastructure when working with lidar data sets. Data providers can directly integrate proven photogrammetric workflow with the accurate elevation information available from the lidar sensor, rather than having to rely on less well-established and usually less well-understood point cloud manipulation techniques. By leveraging established workflows, "lidargrammetry" enables the deployment of lidar technology while still exploiting an organization's existing environment (infrastructure), current skill sets (people), and preserving client satisfaction with proven and accepted processes (reputation).

A primary driver of the recent interest in lidargrammetry has been to create improvements to overall production efficiencies when working with lidar point data. Even with the increasing sophistication of automated classification algorithms for point data, lidar data can still require significant manual editing to finish the map product. A technique such as lidargrammetry, which reduces the manual editing time required, has an obvious impact on overall production efficiency and improved product quality. The technique is also useful in determining if an end-to-end 'lidar-only' workflow is practical for a particular project. Finally, capturing the cost reductions lidargrammetry can create is of obvious benefit to both data producers and end users.

There are established techniques for rendering an orthorectified image into stereo using an ancillary elevation model. The *stereo mate* technique works by creating two images from an orthorectified source image and a corresponding elevation model. However, with lidar point data, no true image exists. Rather, the source data consists of actual 3D "object space" points and their intensity value. In normal stereo vision systems a pair of 2D images, each taken from a slightly different perspective, is used to derive 3D object space points by performing triangulation. Technically, lidargrammetry works by reversing this process, taking 3D object space points and rendering a PSP of 2D images. The images are generated as if captured at positions determined via an inferred *base-height* parameter and related parameters of the data set. As a result, the algorithms required for lidargrammetry are somewhat different from the stereo mate process, although stereo mate techniques have been used to generate models from original 3D data. The process involves introducing parallax (displacement of the image pixels in the X direction) and generating the pseudo images. The parallax introduced is proportional to the difference of the actual elevation value for a pixel from a fixed elevation value (average) across the image. The object information being used to generate the image, usually the intensity, determines the brightness value of the pixel.

Once generated from the 3D object space points using appropriate algorithms, the PSP can be used directly in the traditional photogrammetric workflow. When applied to lidar data, the readily available 3D elevation values and additional co-registered object information, such as intensity, make the lidargrammetry concept relatively easy to implement. Practically, PSP generation can be applied to any set of 3D point data, ideally with associated object information suitable for generating the image. The source data are input into a software tool capable of generating the pseudo images and implementing them with the appropriate math model for the particular stereo viewing software to be used in downstream production. The resulting lidar stereo model is accurate to the same level of accuracy as the lidar data itself; in other words, the lidar stereo rendering supports the planimetric and vertical accuracy of the source lidar data.

To achieve the best results for these PSP techniques with lidar data, a dense data set is required for accurate image creation, hence the need for higher pulse repetition rate lidar sensors to efficiently exploit the technique. It should also be noted that setting proper sensor parameters during the field data collection work is critical to intensity image quality and the resulting quality of the stereo image. As could be expected for any stereo image process, areas with low vegetation or obscured ground surfaces can cause some problems with the resulting stereo models, but these are usually far less severe than the corresponding issues with models generated from traditional imagery. While the lidargrammetry technique is in this instance applied primarily to airborne lidar data sets used for the generation of map products, it is generally applicable to any 3D point cloud data set and can, for example, be used to generate a pseudo stereo model of a building façade captured using a terrestrial (ground-based) laser scanner.

As mentioned, once generated, the images can be viewed as a stereo model in standard photogrammetric software. Because the resulting images are orthographically correct, production technicians can use established viewing, measurement, and compilation techniques to extract breaklines and features from the image, exactly as if working with a standard stereo model created from traditional imagery. The extracted features are 3-dimensionally correct at time of collection. This creates several significant advantages when using the technique with lidar point data. It allows for a shorter turnaround time from sensor to exploiter. In fact, when properly set-up and with the appropriate integrated software tools, stereo imagery can often be available ahead of the completion of automated and manual editing of the lidar point data itself. Given the large amount of point data usually collected by lidar sensors and the fact even the most sophisticated auto-mated classification routines don't provide 100 percent accurate feature extraction, manual editing is required to finish map products generated from lidar data. The manual editing of the point data, even if just for final clean-up and QA/QC, can be extensive enough that the time required actually exceeds the time required to extract the same features directly from lidar stereo imagery using traditional photogrammetric methods.

The lidargrammetry technique also allows pseudo stereo models to be created independent of lighting conditions, including generating images from data acquired at night and/or under clouds. Obviously, the fact that the production operator can exploit the images with existing stereo display hardware and software is a significant benefit to organizations with established infrastructure. Because a standard stereo model is created, *automated* 3D feature extraction techniques can be more easily implemented than in the point domain alone. Features in the lidar point cloud can be readily screened and identified using attributes such as morphology, color, and elevation in the stereo model and the information extracted or fed back into the point cloud processing environment.

It is also important to note that the collection area, the area coverage per PSP, can be much larger than for traditional imagery, so fewer set-ups may be needed per project. Lidar stereo models can be generated from point clouds of 200+ million points (equivalent to a $15,000 \times 15,000$ pixel image). Thus, a lidar stereo model can be used to visualize huge amounts of point data in a single stereo viewing session. As an example, a pilot lidar project of 600 square miles with 1 billion lidar points was covered by only six stereo models. Thus, it becomes very efficient to inspect very large data sets using existing digital photogrammetric workstations. Because the pseudo stereo images are directly generated from the point data itself, there is no need to use hybrid techniques to import the raw lidar points into the stereo environment, for example, to find anomalies in the point classification routines. Qualitative assessments from early pilot projects with PSP images generated from lidar point data also indicate that shorelines are not as easily obscured by vegetation, so actual horizontal positioning of a water body is more accurate than when compiled from corresponding imagery. Experience also indicates that the production operator can measure more accurate water levels and hydro breakline locations, and flow direction is very easy to determine.

An added advantage when using software for PSP generation that is tightly integrated with the stereo viewing/editing software is that production operators can use iterative refinement schemes for selective improvement of specific areas of interest in the image. Because the stereo models are generated synthetically from single pass data (no *stereo overlap* is required), one can set any desired base-to-height ratio. Regeneration of problem areas, or areas of interest with greater stereo exaggeration, is easily accomplished. For example, a production operator can very quickly regenerate a stereo model over a particular portion of a project area and increase the base-to-height ratio to increase the stereo exaggeration. This can allow the operator to easily detect and follow even small relief changes in that area of the image, such as shallow ditches in relatively flat areas.

The lidargrammetry technique also provides for enhanced interpretability of lidar point cloud features by a production operator. Feature extraction from stereo images has been demonstrated to provide a much faster manual editing environment for a trained production operator versus working with traditional lidar point displays. While still a relatively new technique on the production floor to date, lidargrammetry has been applied to lidar data in actual production to allow rapid breakline delineation for terrain modeling (improved contours), planimetric feature capture and for final QA/QC of results from automated point classification routines (bare earth extraction). While there are few, if any, independent quantitative results published, qualitative evidence from early adopters of lidargrammetry indicates breaklines collected from stereo images generated from 2 meter posting lidar data is equivalent to 1"=200' scale imagery (horizontally).

Applying lidargrammetry to lidar point data is a relatively new technique for lidar and photogrammetric professionals, so much work is being done to validate the technique and look at areas for further improvement. These include working with increased resolution lidar imagery, examining *class-based* stereo images (point data classification translated directly into color-coding in the stereo image) and using color images created by modulating elevation values with intensity data or classification values with intensity data. Because the technique is independent of the object information used to create the *image*, the generation of pseudo stereo models from lidar imagery fused with other data, for example hyperspectral data, is also of significant interest. In mainstream production, lidargrammetry offers obvious advantages as a supplemental technique to automated feature extraction, whether the automation is done in the point domain or the image domain. Since the technique can be applied retroactively, work with legacy/historical lidar data sets to add additional value or improve previous results is also possible.

Perhaps the most exciting area under investigation is the use of lidargrammetry to enable direct manual re-classification of point data at the stereo workstation. Techniques are already being implemented that allow a production operator to create and manipulate points in the 3D environment with a direct connection back to point classification software tools. For example, a production operator at a stereo workstation working in Intergraph's SSK can view PSP lidar images generated in GeoCue (from GeoCue Corporation) software, review the results of automated point classification routines, directly tag misclassified areas and either manually reassign the points or assign and run a classification macro from a tool such as TerraScan (by Terrasolid Ltd.) software. With these techniques rapidly developing, and given the relatively onerous and less intuitive manual editing environments that exist in the point domain, lidargrammetry techniques offer a way for mapping firms to eliminate the difference between 'lidar editors' and 'stereo compilers' and deploy lidar technology with far less disruption to their established workflow.

QUALITY CONTROL OF AIRBORNE LIDAR DATA

Quality control of airborne lidar DTM data is a continuing procedure throughout the cycle of any project. The subsystems of the lidar unit are checked before flight and monitored during flight. The operator should ensure there is no loss of lock on the GPS satellites during the turns, and that the roll of the aircraft is always less than 20 percent.

On completion of the flight, a review of the data logs should be conducted to ensure nothing was missed during the flights. Because lidar data are geo-referenced directly at the time of collection, decimated data sets (for example, every 10th point) may be reviewed in GIS software in-situ following the flight.

The GPS processing can be completed both forward and backward if there is evidence of cycle slips. The inertial data must also be reviewed for consistency.

The lidar operator ensures that data are checked thoroughly at each stage of the operation primarily because it is expensive to mobilize and re-acquire data if a problem occurs.

During the post-processing, quality control is also performed using the ground control survey data for verification/validation, adherence to final product requirements, and completion of the metadata report. Many quality control steps involve manual review of the 3D surfaces.

See Chapter 12 for details of QC of lidar and other digital elevation datasets.

CAPABILITIES AND LIMITATIONS

Airborne lidar is capable of collecting large data sets that can provide exceptional ground surface detail. The advantage of high volume data collection includes the fact that lidar data may be collected in circumstances when other sensors may not be suitable. Lidar systems can be flown in overcast, cloudy conditions (as long as the clouds are above the aircraft operating height) or even at night when visible spectrum sensors cannot be used. The data can be collected in any season, although results may be hampered by leaves on trees. However, except in the thickest of canopy cover, lidar can usually penetrate between vegetation sufficiently to provide a terrain model that may not be obtainable by any other methodology during leaf-on seasons. Lidar needs only a single near-vertical laser pulse to penetrate between the trees (or through the trees) to measure the ground elevation, whereas photogrammetry requires two different lines-of-sight to see the same points on the ground from two different perspectives. This is the reason why photogramme-trists often identify "obscured terrain" and map the topography with dashed contour lines to estimate elevations on the ground that could not be seen on stereo photography. Thus, lidar will have far fewer areas where the terrain is obscured by trees that block the lines-of-sight. Incidentally, lidar energy is reflected extremely well from snow covered ground; however, it should be noted that this might be valuable only if there is minimum snow cover although lidar surveys have been used to assess snow accumulation. Lidar energy is reflected from the top of the snow; it cannot penetrate through the snow.

Lidar data cannot be collected in rain, mist, fog, smoke, or during snowstorms or high winds. Unusually turbulent conditions (high winds and turbulence) tend to introduce unacceptable variables within the inertial system. As a final limitation, because of the operational costs (mobilization, calibration, validation surveys, etc.) involved in this technology, it is not generally a suitable approach for very small project areas.

Lidar has several disadvantages when compared with photogrammetric terrain mapping:
- Lidar returns on water are unreliable. It can be difficult to determine the edge of lakes and rivers from lidar data alone unless lidargrammetry is used. Normally, digital orthophotos are used to determine the limits of water boundaries (2D breaklines), and lidar returns within those water boundaries are discarded. However, limited lidar returns from lakes and reservoirs may be used to establish the surface elevations of such level waterbodies.
- Lidar data are ill suited for determination of breaklines. If lidar pulses have a nominal point spacing of 5 meters, for example, it is hard to determine the location of breaklines

at the tops and bottoms of stream banks that fall somewhere between the elevation points 5 meters apart, especially when data in the stream itself are also unreliable. Thus, 2D breaklines estimated from digital orthophotos or photogrammetrically compiled 3D breaklines are often used to augment the lidar data as needed for hydraulic modeling.

- Lidar is a relatively new technology, and standard procedures have not yet been developed to yield data with predictable accuracy comparable to that from photogrammetry where flying height, focal length, and established photogrammetric procedures consistently yield predictable results.

- Whereas contour lines produced manually by photogrammetric compilation are normally smooth, and "cartographic license" is used to generate contours that cross streams, roads and ditches in a manner that appears logical to human map interpreters, contour lines generated automatically from any source (including lidar) are more jagged and commonly show high and low "islands" in the vicinity of streams and elsewhere. Imagine, for example, that there is a large boulder in the middle of a creek. Lidar would measure this high point and generate contours as though there was a dam across the creek. In reality, water flows around the boulder and moves down stream. Human cartographers routinely discard such high (or low) points, whereas contours generated automatically from lidar data would not recognize this aberration unless detected during manual post-processing.

- "Hydrologic enforcement," explained in Chapter 1, is routinely performed by photogrammetrists, but special manual procedures are required to hydro-enforce a lidar dataset for either contours, TINs or DEMs.

On the other hand, several companies are now working on software which will incorporate either intensity data or digital imagery acquired at the same time as the lidar data to provide answers to some of these problems.

COMMERCIALIZATION

Adoption Curve

While research and scientific laser altimetry systems have been deployed for many years by government and academic institutions, only during the past decade has there been a large growth in the number of commercial organizations operating airborne lidar systems on a "for profit" basis. As a relatively new technology, the adoption curve is an indicator of the rate at which airborne laser altimetry is being deployed and accepted as a standard operational tool in the commercial sector. It provides insight into trends in the implied demand for services based on the technology and can be used as the basis for estimating the projected instrument base and the resulting competitive environment for survey companies using airborne laser altimetry.

A review of the commercial sector from 1995 through 2000 then through 2005 shows the number of installed instruments increased rapidly during the first five year period then almost doubling during the next. A breakdown of the annual rate at which commercial firms took delivery of instruments, either COTS or proprietary designs, is presented in Table 7.2. The number of new sensors deployed each year is listed. The numbers clearly demonstrate significant year-over-year growth in the installed instrument base. Each of these systems represents an investment of approximately $1 million or more.

Of these systems in use in 2000, approximately one-third were proprietary systems produced by research groups or commercial entities primarily for their own market niche – some operating at up to 50 kHz pulse repetition frequency (PRF). The proprietary instruments include a number of legacy instruments that were already built or in development prior to the widespread availability of COTS systems. Because of the large developmental costs, it is not clear if the organizations operating these proprietary sensors will replace their systems with COTS instruments or continue their own proprietary development if they need to expand their instrument base. At the present time there appears to be some will to continue individual system development, possibly because so much time and effort has been expended in the initial development that the lesser cost of upgrades is more easily justified, although this may now be changing.

Table 7.2 Airborne Laser Scanners by Year 1995 – 2005.

Year	New Instruments	Total Instruments
1995	3	3
1996	6	9
1997	2	11
1998	9	20
1999	18	38
2000	20	58
2001	13	71
2002	7	78
2003	17	95
2004	32	127
2005	20	147

Regardless of any future price changes, custom-built systems will remain attractive for those organizations that can leverage existing laser/lidar expertise during their design process or for those organizations that require advanced functionality not yet offered by COTS systems. There are, of course, advantages to proprietary systems, including application-specific design that COTS systems cannot attain with their wider market entry requirements, although lately COTS manufacturers have significantly engineered more flexibility into their products. It remains to be seen if the peak number of systems coming on line in 2004 is a real peak or whether the reduced number in 2005 is an aberration. However, it should be noted that these figures were compiled from known custom built units and a survey of all existing manufacturers units "sold" per year. Systems sold in a year may not have been delivered in that year.

Present Operating Status

As noted earlier, an estimated 58 airborne systems (See Table 7.2) were in operation around the world at the start of the year 2001. Some were operated by governments or research institutes, but the vast majority of them were commercially operated, with the largest number of systems concentrated in North America. Today (in 2006) it is difficult to know exactly how many systems are currently being used. Manufacturers report total yearly sales but there is no real way of determining how many units stay in operation. Likewise, companies that have developed their own systems also tend to count every system produced. The reality is many early systems that may still be technically operational are no longer used because they lack the efficiency or accuracy demanded by today's market conditions. Companies that may report owning four units may only actually use two of them. At an estimated total, the actual number of systems currently in use is probably around 110, assuming that most systems older than about five or six years are probably no longer competitive in the commercial market.

PLANNING CONSIDERATIONS

Planning for a lidar project, as with any project, must consider the required final results and use of the data. This can be summed up with the following questions:

- What is the intended use for these data?
- How accurate do they need to be in relative terms and absolute terms?
- How far apart are data points required?
- How large is the area?
- Is accessibility and terrain slope an issue?
- Is lidar technology applicable, and does the cost/benefit ratio make it attractive?

The use of the data will depend on each client's special requirements. Whether or not lidar is suitable essentially depends upon accuracy, cost and other factors described in detail in Chapter 13 that includes a "User Requirements Menu" of choices.

Lidar decisions are often driven by economies of scale. For very small projects of a few acres, there is little doubt that unless there is some very compelling reason a ground survey using traditional or GPS methodology is most appropriate. (A compelling reason for using remote sensing may be the growing challenge of special environmental concerns, or simply being unable to access the site.)

From the experience of most operators today, projects smaller than 5-6 square kilometers (approximately two square miles) or a corridor shorter than 16 kilometers (10 miles) are probably best done using alternative technologies.

Accuracy is usually a driving consideration. As mentioned, the laser itself is remarkably accurate over a wide range of distances, usually within one inch (2-3 centimeters) in normal aircraft operating elevations 300 to 6,000 feet (100-2,000 meters) above ground. The IMU accuracy will vary somewhat according to flying height above ground. While the accuracy of the IMU's measured angles does not change, the higher the aircraft is above ground the greater the horizontal circle of error becomes (thus the use of helicopters by firms requiring high accuracy in specific applications). Finally, there is the accuracy of the GPS to consider. A properly set up GPS with adequate ground stations and multiple satellite linkages will provide an airborne GPS accuracy of ± 2–3 inches (5-7 cm). Adding all of these error combinations together results in a typical 15 cm (6-inch) error budget in elevations and positions. In summary, while the errors in the subsystems can (and often may) cancel each other out, the best vertical accuracy that can be guaranteed from current technology is 15 cm ($RMSE_z$), slightly better than the 18.5-cm $RMSE_z$ required for 2-foot contours. On some lidar systems, particularly low level flying configurations, this error may be reduced somewhat, but even then the $RMSE_z$ will not be better than 9.25 cm (required for 1-foot contours). As explained in Chapter 13 (Table 13.2), lidar DTMs equivalent to 1-foot contours have a vertical RMSE ($RMSE_z$) of 9.25 cm (0.30 ft) which equates to absolute vertical accuracy of 0.50-ft at the 90% confidence level (per the National Map Accuracy Standard) and absolute vertical accuracy of 0.60-ft at the 95% confidence level (per the National Standard for Spatial Data Accuracy).

Lidar operators are dealing with real, quantifiable results that are consistent, even though the final products are a result of cumulative error budgets for combinations of technologies. Even so, accuracy statements are only valid when the lidar system being used is properly calibrated and operated. In support of this, a "report of survey" usually accompanies the data collection describing the system calibration, the GPS log, any ground survey point referenced, the design accuracy, the validation process, and a statistical summary of the results.

Lidar accuracy continues to be a point of discussion because there are many other aspects that apply to overall accuracy of final products. One typical aspect is the spacing of lidar data points. It is, for example, somewhat pointless (unless there is a uniform slope) having survey data accurate to half an inch if each point in the data set is one hundred yards apart. In this instance, a lidar survey with a ground data point every three feet to $\pm$ six inches, on average, is likely to be a more accurate representation of the ground than the former, although the precision of any single point is not as good. Consequently, the accuracy of a specific data set involves more than simply the accuracy of the point at a single location.

The mass of data points is actually one of the big advantages of lidar. Lidar, depending on the type of system and how fast it is being flown, will provide multiple data points both along and across the track. For example, a 15 kHz system being flown at 120 miles per hour at 5,000 feet above ground with a 20° field of view will collect a data point a maximum of every 6 to 7 feet (2 meters) cross track (along the left to right to left swing of the mirror). These points will be spaced the same maximum distance apart along the line of flight, although, the distances of points apart along the flight track will vary because the back and forth swing of the mirror results in points along the track of the mirror forming an elongated "v" shape. Points on one arm of the "v" are closer to points on the next arm of the "v" when they are close to the vertices, even though they may be 6 feet apart along the scan. If the project requires different point spacing, a faster air speed or wider scan angle may be considered. If positional accuracy may be relaxed, a higher flying altitude may be suitable, with swaths being correspondingly greater. Conversely, if positional accuracy is critical or a client requires a more detailed survey, a slower and lower flying helicopter platform with high-density laser hits per square meter might be more suitable. (Figure 1.21 in Appendix C shows the high density of lidar pulses from the cross track (east-west) swing of the mirror for the line of flight which is nearly north-south.)

From a lidar operator's point of view, planning any project involves a number of considerations. All of the operator's decisions, however, will be based on the client's required accuracy and the desired designed spacing of data points.

Bearing these factors in mind, the pulse rate of the specific laser system will greatly influence the aircraft flying speed and altitude, the swath width and the number of flight lines required. On some systems the footprint size can be controlled and may also enter into the equation. On many systems the width of swath can also be changed, with data points collected closer together in a narrower swath or further apart in a broader swath.

If the project area is a block, the operator must decide the optimum distance between flight lines. A minimum 30 percent side lap between adjacent lines usually guarantees gapless coverage, although the type of terrain and features also affect the design of sidelap. If the area is a city with a high density of tall buildings, or a forest of tall trees, or the terrain is steep and rugged, lidar flight lines are typically flown closer together (with a larger overlap), so that the beam will not miss an *urban canyon* or lack an overlap on steep-sided hills. If the project is a corridor, the flight planning will likely include two parallel lines, preferably flown in opposite directions, if not on each segment at least on a representative fraction thereof. This procedure is a quality control requirement to ensure there are no data collection biases. The data from adjacent lines in overlap areas should be within the tolerance for the system and the project specifications. In a larger block (more than a couple of lines), a couple of cross flight lines will add a measure of confidence and validation in the system and the data.

Finally during planning, the operator needs to determine where the ground GPS base stations should be established (for the translocation computation requirements) as well as suitable locations for the quality control ground checkpoint data. Ground GPS base stations for positional control of the lidar aircraft should normally be within 12 miles (20 km) of the operations area in order to limit airborne GPS errors to 5 to 7 cm. The flight timing should ensure an adequate number of the same satellites (a minimum of 5) are visible, both on the ground as well as in the air for the GPS with a Positional Dilution of Precision (PDOP) of <3.

User Applications

Lidar data can be put to use in any of the myriad ways for any digital terrain data. These are limited to the needs, imagination (and available software) of the users. In this respect, lidar terrain data are no different from surface model data from any other source. Lidar data are advantageous for the client because they can be collected more quickly, accurately, often less expensively, and under conditions that are challenging or impossible with other technologies.

Depending on the survey application, lidar or laser altimetry can be viewed as another complementary technology for the development of surface model generation. For many survey applications, airborne laser altimetry is currently deployed in conjunction with other more traditional sensors including standard aerial film cameras, digital cameras, multispectral-hyperspectral scanners, or hybrid imagery. In such cases, lidar is used to provide the base DTM upon which additional value-added products are created. In general, laser altimetry is evaluated as an addition to the remote sensing toolbox that can add significant value to the data products produced by providing high-resolution DEMs used as an independent product or in conjunction with other sensor systems. Deploying airborne lidar within a field survey can provide additional value depending on project specific goals and deliverables. Since each individual client has particular needs and specifications, laser altimetry may or may not meet these expectations without support from traditional survey methods. In certain applications, such as forestry or coastal engineering, lidar offers unique capabilities not achievable with any other technology. A brief review of several primary applications of commercial activity follows.

Forestry

The use of airborne lidar in the forestry industry was one of the first commercial areas investigated. Accurate information on the terrain and topography beneath the tree canopy is extremely important to both the forestry industry and natural resource managers. Accurate information on tree heights and densities is also critical information that is difficult to obtain using conventional techniques. Airborne lidar technology, unlike radar or satellite imaging, can simultaneously map the ground beneath the tree canopy as well as relative tree heights. Post-processing of the data allows the individual laser returns to be analyzed and classified as vegetation or ground returns allowing DTMs of the bare ground to be generated and representative tree heights to be calculated from DSMs. Emerging techniques from the research sector using regression statistics and/or full waveform analysis of the return laser pulse to investigate details of canopy structure are also receiving greater attention as the technology gains acceptance in the commercial sector. Consequently, airborne lidar mapping is an extremely effective technique for obtaining both DTMs and DSMs in forested areas when compared to photogrammetry or extensive ground surveys.

Coastal Engineering

Beach and sand dune mapping of coastal regions are excellent examples of airborne lidar technology, offering state-of-the-art type performance with significant advantages over existing survey techniques. Because traditional photogrammetry is difficult to employ in areas of limited contrast and width, such as beaches and coastal zones, an active sensing technique such as laser altimetry offers the ability to complete surveys that would be cost prohibitive using other methods. In addition, highly dynamic environments, such as coastal zones, often require constant updating of baseline survey data.

Airborne lidar mapping offers an effective method to perform this type of mapping on a routine basis. Lidar is also used for mapping and monitoring of shore belts, dunes, dikes and coastal forests. In combination with airborne lidar bathymetry, it is a very powerful, integrated coastal analysis tool.

Corridor or Right-of-Way Mapping

Airborne lidar mapping allows rapid, cost-effective, accurate mapping of linear corridors such as power utility rights-of-way, gas pipelines, railroads, highways and telecommunications corridors. A major commercial market is mapping power line corridors to allow for the modeling of conductor catenary curves, sag, ground clearance, encroachment and accurate determination of tower and attachment locations. For example, the use of data acquired through airborne laser surveys can be combined with simultaneous measurements of air and conductor temperature and load currents to establish admissible increases in load-carrying capacity of power lines.

Lidar used on corridor mapping projects for power lines, pipeline or other right of way surveys provides significant advantages. Often these types of surveys cover terrain with few roads or access points. An airborne lidar survey can be completed in hours that would take months to survey by ground methods.

Floodplain Mapping

Accurate and updated modeling of floodplains is critical both for disaster planning and flood insurance purposes. Airborne lidar offers a cost-effective method of acquiring the topographic data required as input for various floodplain modeling programs; numerous projects have been completed for this discipline.

As part of its Map Modernization Program, the Federal Emergency Management Agency (FEMA) in the U.S. is currently using lidar data for Flood Insurance Studies and Digital Flood Insurance Rate Maps and related products of the National Flood Insurance Program (NFIP). FEMA has guidelines which state specifications that are to be used for the application of laser altimetry systems for gathering the data necessary to create bare-earth DTMs and other NFIP products.

Urban Modeling

As shown at Figure 7.21, accurate DSMs of urban environments are required for a variety of applications including telecommunications, microclimate modeling, wireless communications, law enforcement and disaster planning. (See also the virtual city fly-through demonstration on the attached DVD, as explained in Chapter 15. That virtual city results from the merger of a lidar DSM and oblique imagery from Pictometry.) In addition, lidar terrain models are ideal for storm water management in flood prone areas. An active remote sensing system such as lidar offers the ability to accurately map urban environments without some of the disadvantages of other technologies.

Figure 7.21 Example of digital elevation data used for urban modeling of San Francisco. Courtesy of Optech. See color plate in Appendix C.

Disaster Response and Damage Assessment

Major natural disasters such as hurricanes or earthquakes stress an emergency response organization's abilities to plan and respond. Airborne lidar mapping allows for timely, accurate survey data to be rapidly incorporated directly into on-going disaster management efforts and allows rapid post-disaster damage assessments. Lidar is particularly useful in areas prone to major topographic changes during natural disasters — areas such as beaches, river estuaries or flood plains.

Wetlands and Other Restricted Access Areas

Many environmentally sensitive areas such as wetlands offer limited ground access due to vegetation cover and soil characteristics, and are difficult to map with traditional photogrammetry. Airborne laser altimetry offers the capability to survey these areas and can also be deployed to survey toxic waste sites or industrial waste dumps.

Other

In addition to the commercial applications discussed above, various efforts are under way to investigate other application areas where airborne lidar may offer significant advantages. Due to this tool's versatility and ease of deployment, unique applications are being explored including the use of lidar in large area models for special effects in major motion pictures, golf course and ski resort modeling, for state-of-the-art video games, extremely high-resolution terrain modeling for locating archeological features of interest, sub-canopy vegetation mapping for wildfire fuel characterization, slope-stability assessments for landslide hazard analysis and erosion, avalanche prediction using snow depth and slope parameters, and urban modeling for realistic flight simulators, such as the virtual city fly-through demonstration included on the attached DVD.

Data Deliverables

Data deliverables of lidar digital terrain data (or ground-based lidar) are no different than digital data from other sources. Essentially the data at the completion of post-processing are delivered as a point data ASCII file composed of easting, northing and elevation. As such, they are directly importable into practically any GIS or CAD software. It is relatively safe to state that all lidar terrain data producers can deliver data in any specific format. (See a menu of choices at Chapter 13.

Cost Considerations

Costs, as in any business, are usually broken into two types. There is the base capital cost of the equipment which, depending on the manufacturer and the unit purchased, is currently between $800,000 and $2,000,000 (USD) for an airborne system. It is reasonable to assume that the capital investment for such high-tech equipment should be amortized over no more than five years, even though units may continue to operate longer. An average system worth $1,300,000 amortized over five years is a monthly expense of slightly in excess of $21,700. However, there are continuing maintenance costs, which could add another $10,000 per month, and the costs related to financing if the system is not purchased with available cash.

The costs associated with a COTS system are actually not dissimilar to those experienced by groups that have developed their own proprietary systems. While the component parts of a lidar system are less expensive to purchase individually, there is a correspondingly greater cost in time and labor for system development, integration, and the difficult task of developing proprietary software, testing, and validation.

Regardless, service providers must amortize the capital investment costs of their sensors, whether it is around $1,500,000 for a COTS system, or offsetting the costs of funding their own research, development and lidar system support infrastructure for those operating custom-built sensors. In addition, many providers who have developed their own systems have to support in-house software efforts to address proprietary software development, whereas those who buy COTS have these costs buried in COTS system acquisition and maintenance prices.

The operational costs begin with a minimum of two trained technicians to maintain and operate the lidar system as often as possible. When the amortization costs are between $20,000-$30,000 per month or close to $1,000 per day whether used or not, there is a high motivation to use it as much as possible.

The amount of data the system will collect will require a number of robust computers, and highly trained technicians and analysts to operate them. While some potential purchasers of lidar systems might be initially under the illusion that the system magically does it all, almost everyone who has operated lidar for a period of time knows there are numerous other costs related to recovering the investment whether it is developing specific software – or purchasing COTS software, training staff, marketing and so on.

These base costs are all monthly expenses that are paid regardless of whether the system works, needs servicing, or sits idle.

Following the capital investment costs, there are the project specific costs. The cost of mobilization from the home base to the project site is a factor, as is the number of lines and length of the lines. For example, if the lines are many and short, an operator may be taking more time to turn the aircraft on the shallow turns (to avoid loss of lock on satellites) at the end of lines than actually flying the on-line data acquisition. When a block area is being flown, the accuracy, type of terrain, type of features, flying height, line spacing, and desired overlap between lines all influence the costs. Then there are other local conditions which may also be a factor; for example, a major airport near the project area may mean flights have to be scheduled for specific times, or the aircraft has to go into holding patterns between lines to avoid incoming and outgoing aircraft. There may be weather constraints or GPS satellite availability issues that may be expected to cause delays.

Remarkably, if a lidar system can be kept reasonably busy during the year, the lidar cost factors indicate the technology can be very competitive with other geospatial technologies. There are times it will be far less expensive than standard photogrammetry, but there will be conditions where it is not. Typically, the larger the project, the more efficient it is to collect terrain data with lidar.

Pricing

Detailed pricing for lidar DEMs is difficult to generalize due to the variety of data products that can be produced, the lack of a defined and accepted benchmark products for comparative pricing, the many input and delivery variables unique to a given project, and the various applications that can be addressed. In addition, pricing strategies in the past have varied considerably among providers.

Most lidar operators now quote on a margin basis, calculating their costs to complete the project and then adding their profit margins. However, there are some who price strategically, determining price based on business drivers such as minimizing idle capacity, maximizing regional coverage, capturing market share, excluding competitors, servicing favored clients, pricing to approved contracting agency budgets, or leveraging out revenues and cash flow. This type of pricing eventually has its drawbacks for the company unless it has extensive financial resources.

In the past, providers may have used different pricing strategies to satisfy their business model or sometimes a combined approach, with the resulting bids appearing to a contracting organization to be fictitious rather than a rational, predictable pricing scheme.

However, with the gradual maturity of the provider base, along with increased automation and experience with the technology, the prices are expected to stabilize.

As mentioned earlier, the primary cost drivers for a given level of lidar-derived DEM point density and accuracy are:
1. project scope,
2. mobilization and demobilization costs,
3. project boundary shape, and
4. project deliverables.

Secondary factors include terrain relief, vegetation, culture, features, access and extent of available ground control sites and data, and sometimes the season of the year.

However, these costs alone do not determine the pricing that an end user can expect to see at this writing. During 2001, lidar DEM pricing in the domestic U.S. market, for a data product capable of supporting 2-foot contour-interval mapping, could be found ranging from less than $1.00 per acre to well in excess of $250 per acre. Companies focusing on linear corridors do not quote prices per acre, but generally per linear mile or kilometer, based on the swath coverage required. These, again, can vary from averages between $150 and $1,250 per kilometer depending on the type of survey, its location and the deliverables.

There are several published benchmark lidar contracts in the public domain for large rectangular areas (see for example the Puget Sound Lidar Consortium; Kitsap County Survey, and the North Carolina - Floodplain Mapping Program which can act as pricing guidelines for large area lidar surveys). In 2000, the general range for these large area projects was running between $0.50 and $1.00 per acre for the basic lidar DEM product, largely depending on the amount of manual post-processing to be performed. By 2005, however, costs for some major projects had dropped considerably with some operators working for as little as 0.25 cents per acre for data acquisition. However, because it is difficult to know what exactly was included in the contract price, such published information should be viewed with the proverbial grain of salt.

It is important to remember, however, that a prospective client should not count on rates at 25 or 50 cents an acre for lidar DEMs, as these are based on very large area surveys with basic deliverables and the system operator is likely gambling on the very large volumes to make a profit. As in any industry, the pricing structures used by various companies may take into account approaches such as gaining access to a market, maintaining work flow, dealing with immediate cash requirements, and attempting to maintain a specific market or niche, but it has to be remembered that bids based on the presumption that "everything will go right, the weather will cooperate" and so on are gambles that can result in surprises. Few companies survive for long if they operate with negative cash flow. All this is to say that the client who is seeking a lidar survey for 50 square kilometers must be prepared for reasonable and competitive pricing compared with rates with other technologies. While a few clients want a bare minimum effort, there are many who want data that is quality controlled and processed to the point where it is ready to be loaded into whatever software they are using at a design stage.

In many cases for end users, the lidar pricing is often buried in a larger per acre cost that includes additional value-added components such as imagery, planimetrics, or contouring, making isolated lidar costing difficult to determine if not specifically requested. However, as mentioned above, most clients require more than the raw data files which, depending on the lidar system, may not be useful to the client anyway as proprietary software and expertise is required to generate useful products.

Published pricing on smaller projects, ranging down to several hundred acres, is much more difficult to obtain.

As examples of the general domestic U.S. pricing levels in 2006, a 2,000 square mile (1,280,000 acres) effort near a lidar provider's base, rectangular in shape, with minimal terrain relief and features and vegetation, along with plenty of suitable control and access, flown in summer or fall might find pricing as low as the $350 per square mile ($0.55 per acre) range. Projects priced at lower costs per square mile are typically completed with minimal if any manual processing, or with manual processing performed off-shore with low-cost labor.

At the other extreme, a 1 square mile (640 acres) project more distant from a base, with inefficient limits such as a winding stream or transportation corridor, in rugged terrain with heavy vegetation and no access or available control would yield a price of at $25,000 per square mile ($39.00 per acre), and perhaps as much as $40,000 ($62.50 per acre) in the midst of the busy flying season. In the latter case, the daily cost to mobilize the lidar system combined with factored lost opportunity costs by the lidar provider pushes the per unit cost to these higher levels. Again, providers focusing on linear corridors price their outputs in a distinctly different fashion, typically on a line kilometer or line mile basis, depending on the complexity of deliverables.

For even smaller projects, on the order of tens of acres, the per-acre cost becomes significantly higher due to the fixed costs of mobilizing the lidar sensor. For many standard mapping applications this increase pushes the price point well beyond the level that can be justified by the end user, leaving lidar beyond the reach of most of these smaller mapping projects. Therefore, while lidar projects enjoy significant cost advantages on larger projects (compared with photogrammetric methods), the unit cost of smaller projects can be significantly higher. For this reason, the minimum break-even point for employing lidar ranges upwards from a minimum of 2,000 acres, depending upon the location of the project and the service provider chosen. In short, the present market pricing from leading service providers offers lidar DEM data at a 20-50% discount off photogrammetrically derived DEMs, once that breakeven point is surpassed.

While these price levels are current for the published date of this book, changes in operational costs (aircraft fuel, general inflation, etc.) and technical advances will have an impact in either direction.

COMPARISON WITH OTHER TECHNOLOGIES

Airborne lidar compares favorably with several competing/complementary technologies primarily because of its accuracy, active sensor capability and ability to penetrate between foliage.

The "look angle" of lidar, for example, is generally from vertical to typically 20 degrees either side of vertical. This means that if there are any holes in a forest canopy, the lidar beam will "see" to the ground. The same applies for the deep "canyons" between high rise buildings which occur in large city centers. While some systems have a wider field of view angle than 20 degrees, if the look angle is stretched too far from vertical then the beam starts to hit building sides, tree trunks and so on rather than the ground, resulting in erroneous or ambiguous returns.

The ability of lidar to obtain a direct distance (and angle) from the sensor to the ground in forested areas is far superior to photogrammetry in these conditions because, while an aerial camera may see to the ground in one aerial photo, the succeeding aerial photo will not see through the same opening. The photogrammetrist will, therefore, only see in stereo at the top of the canopy and will not be able to map an elevation on the ground.

The speed and nature of lidar data acquisition are also an advantage for many clients. The data are directly in digital format and are essentially deliverable after post-processing of the GPS translocation information. However, most often, a client requires a specific data set, such as the bare earth DTM. Additional post-processing, therefore, removes all of the extraneous data and can take a period of one to several weeks to complete, depending on the size of the project. Nevertheless, this is normally three to five times faster than a similar area completed using photogrammetry or ground methods. It should be noted, though, that the speed of acquiring lidar surveys has to be regarded with some measure of reality. It is unlikely the lidar operator is sitting on the ground just waiting for a client to call about a survey to be done tomorrow, especially during the traditional busy seasons of spring and fall. Other work in progress is normally a factor in all delivery schedules and costs. Many service providers try to be fair to their clients by completing work more or less in the order in which it is booked. Client flexibility on delivery dates often leads to lower costs, whereas insistence on an expedited schedule may dictate a requirement for overtime (and higher labor costs) to complete the delivery on time.

Finally, the opportunity to use lidar during all seasons (except when there is heavy snowfall) means clients used to photogrammetric data acquisition do not have to wait until there are no leaves on the trees. As mentioned earlier, heavy tree canopy can decrease the number of points providing bare earth lidar data, but the technology is still the best available for providing DEM data for projects that are urgent or cannot be delayed until a leaf free period.

By comparison, elevation and position data from radar technology are based on side looking acquisition of the DSM or DTM data. That is, the radar beam used by most commercial producers of radar terrain models is transmitted at a considerable angle off-vertical to one side of the aircraft. Some erroneous data is bounced back from the sides of trees and buildings. The nature of the side looking system also leaves radar "shadows" sometimes called "data voids" in the area behind the building, vegetation, and sometimes hills where there are no radar data because of the shadow effect of the feature in front of it.

While considerable advances have been made in the processing of data, and newer hardware advances have improved the accuracy of radar data, radar data do not yet approach the consistency and accuracy of data surveyed using lidar. Radar (IFSAR) data typically also suffers from "smoothing techniques" in the processing. Lidar, by comparison, tends to show sharper edges to features and more realistic building shapes. However, IFSAR terrain models have significant advantages for broad area based terrain mapping and modeling and usage in areas that suffer from persistent low-level cloud cover. Radar systems are also typically flown at higher altitudes which allow for a measure of safety in very rugged, mountainous terrain.

Typically lidar DTMs compare favorably with the cost of producing the same data using photogrammetry, and are less expensive than IFSAR DTMs except for very large area coverages where IFSAR has the cost advantage. Obtaining field measured DTM data using total stations, kinematic GPS or other ground based techniques may be more accurate, but are also far more costly if the area is more than a few acres in size.

Figure 7.22 compares IFSAR data with last-return lidar data, both before and after post-processing. Note that IFSAR collected more tree canopy data than did the last-return lidar data, and IFSAR is excellent for this purpose. Lidar is better for penetrating the vegetation to collect more elevations of the ground beneath the tree canopy. The left-most image at Figure 7.22 shows the bare-earth terrain upon completion of post-processing.

Bare earth LIDAR   **Last return LIDAR**   **IFSAR**

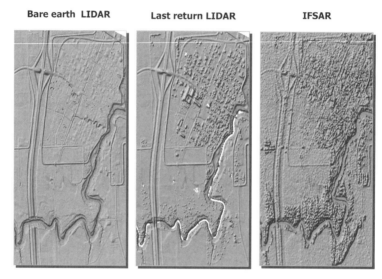

Figure 7.22 The left image shows the last-return lidar data after completion of post-processing. The center image shows the last-return lidar data prior to post-processing. The right image shows IFSAR data that includes the tree canopy. Lidar data and IFSAR datasets often complement each other. Figures courtesy of the U.S. Army Corps of Engineers. See color plate in Appendix C.

TECHNOLOGICAL ADVANCEMENTS

Predicting the future in any technology is difficult, particularly when the technology is evolving rapidly. It is quite possible that by the time this book is printed that some remarkable new aspect to lidar surveying could be announced. Most developers of systems maintain confidentiality regarding new developments for fear of losing market advantage. Conservatively, the future of lidar will undoubtedly result in "higher, faster, and maybe slightly less expensive" systems, with more built-in safety features; though past history indicates that any reductions in the pricing of component parts has been offset by the introduction of increased features and flexibility. It is also worth noting that airborne lidar systems tend to be manufactured as ordered and being a limited specialty market are not mass produced. (A review of the figures in the adoption Table 7.2 shows that currently five manufacturers are selling an average of less than 20 units a year.) So the economies of a production line do not apply as they do for mass market consumer products.

The current pulse repetition rate for lidar data capture, at least theoretically, is reckoned to be about 160 kHz. The reason for this is the time it takes for a pulse of laser data to be sent and received. If a second pulse is sent before the first pulse is received back there will be occasions where deciphering one pulse from another may be impossible, thus creating ambiguities and errors. It should also be stated that the theoretical limit of lidar pulse rates per second may not be the same as the practical rate of lidar pulses per second. This is not to say that someone will not come along and develop a new way of "tagging" lidar pulses, which is theoretically possible, but currently this is very difficult if not impossible to do within the cost constraints of the market.

The effective computation of waveform digitization data may well be the next major advance for most systems in order to capture multi-levels of information (especially through vegetation). There may also be a degree of more specialization of systems and, conversely, the development of COTS systems that can be adapted for many different types of surveys without the hassles of reconfiguring hardware.

The use of intensity data will become more meaningful, based on the fact that software and applications are already developed to take advantage of this feature.

Most lidar operators will testify that processing software continues to need improvement. On the other hand, remarkable progress has already been made especially over the last few years, and software is continually under development by a number of large and small organizations that will make the processing of these huge data files both faster and easier.

Like many areas of remote sensing, lidar operators are continuing to look for the "holy grail" of automated feature recognition, and large strides have been made in this direction. With the use of intensity data and alternate imagery sources such as aerial photo and multiband sensors, this is now not so far in the future. Indeed, in simple cases this has already been achieved. The main difficulty lies in areas where there are multiple layers of information: such as where trees partially cover building roof lines, where buildings have multiple complex roof lines, and where constructions lie vertically on top of one another, such as complex road interchanges where there may be three or more levels of roadway at the same horizontal coordinates.

Regardless, while developments will undoubtedly continue, lidar is now a mature technology that has unique advantages over many other DEM development technologies, and should be considered for accurate detailed mapping projects.

GROUND BASED (TERRESTRIAL) LIDAR SYSTEMS

Technology Overview

Terrestrial laser scanners come in two main types: time-of-flight (TOF) devices and phase-based devices. A third type of scanner, with a slow data collection rate, uses optical triangulation to yield very high accuracies over short ranges – usually less than one meter, though one commercial device has specified range up to 25 meters; triangulation is the technology least often used for terrestrial applications and will not be discussed further here.

All laser scanning devices operate by directing structured light to the object to be measured, then detecting and measuring the signal from light reflected by the object surface. In this sense, ground laser scanning is analogous to flash photography, one pixel at a time. Unlike conventional photography which records images reflected from ambient light, laser scanning and flash photography come with their own light sources. The orientation of the laser beam is determined by its zenith and azimuth angles which are recorded as part of the measurement.

Scanning devices operate by sweeping a beam through both azimuth and zenith angles in small steps of the order of tens of micro-radians. The orientation of the laser beam, in combination with the range to the reflected surface characterizes the components of the recorded measurement. The beam orientation is determined by recording the zenith and azimuth angles of the instrument; the range distance is determined by timing the round trip of the transmitted beam and reflection of that beam.

The measured surfaces are typically rough, at least at length scales comparable to the wavelength of the laser light used in these devices, meaning there is nearly always some component of the surface that is normal to the light source. Laser wavelengths vary by terrestrial instrument manufacturers and are typically in the green or infrared part of the spectrum. The received signals are severely attenuated – as much as 100 db less than the transmitted signal – which requires sensitive detectors tuned to the frequency of the transmitted laser beam and sophisticated signal processing electronics. Terrestrial laser scanning typically involves measuring ranges from 1m to up to 1000m with range uncertainties of order of millimeters to centimeters.

Adoption of Ground Based Lidar

The technologies underpinning today's terrestrial laser scanning hardware can be traced to instruments developed for robotic machine vision, airborne lidar systems and total station survey instruments. Articles about the use of reflected range data for scene analysis date back to the mid-1970s. In the 1980s and the first half of the 1990s, development advanced in research laboratories; the first commercial instruments began to appear in the second half of the 1990s. Commercial acceptance did not take off until 2000. At the end of 2005 the worldwide market for laser scanning hardware, software and services was approximately $200 million and enjoying robust growth.

The number of ground based lidar systems has increased dramatically since they were introduced in the late 1990s and now, world wide, number close to 2000.

The adoption curve for terrestrial scanners came along much later than the start of airborne units, as shown in Figure 7.23.

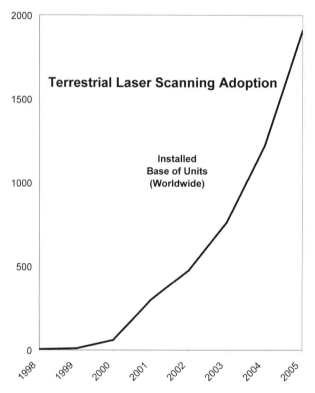

Figure 7.23 Adoption curve for terrestrial laser scanners.
Courtesy of Spar Point Research LLC.

Calibration

Instrument calibration for ground based scanners is typically performed at the factory. However, in most cases it is not necessary to return instruments to the factory to verify calibrations.

Today no test facility exists to provide controlled and independent verification of instrument accuracy. Some university research facilities around the world have conducted investigations into scanner accuracy; however, the results are far from complete. Rapid developments in hardware make it a formidable task to keep this information current. The National Institute of Standards and

Technology, Gaithersburg, Maryland, is developing a suite of protocols for this purpose, and a preliminary report on this was expected in late 2006.

Planning

For ground based lidar scanners, the planning is similar to traditional ground survey planning. Consideration must be given to the type of project, where set-up stations are to be located, and where suitable ground control can be utilized for the work involved. This may mean selecting a ground station location that is coordinated along with some targets surveyed within the scanned scene. Depending on the use of the data and the accuracy of location, these considerations may warrant a separate survey or include standard field survey equipment along with the laser scanner.

Limitations of Terrestrial Laser Scanning

The strength of the signal returned to the laser scanner detector, which limits the signal to noise ratio, is influenced by multiple factors including the measured range, angle of incidence of the transmitted signal, atmospheric conditions, albedo (reflectivity) of the measured surface, and the wavelength of the transmitted signal.

Laser spot size, which increases at ranges beyond the focal length of the instrument, necessarily results in mixed pixel effects when measuring edges. In such cases when the beam strikes a surface edge, part is returned by the object and part is returned by whatever is behind the edge. This results in unavoidable range ambiguity or noise. Signal returns from oblique angles of incidence are typically weaker than from surfaces normal to the transmitted beam and consequently are noisier.

Atmospheric conditions such as dust, steam or rain can introduce spurious range measurements. Most instruments are rated to operate between 0 °C (32 °F) and 40 °C (104 °F) which restricts their utility for outdoor work in either hot or cold climates. Absent compensation mechanisms, temperature variations can also result in drift in measurement electronics.

Laser scanning systems are limited in their capabilities to measure very reflective surfaces such as polished stainless steel. Surfaces that absorb nearly all incident light such as coke coated surfaces in refineries are also notoriously difficult to image. In these cases, range accuracy can be degraded significantly. Practitioners will sometimes coat a very reflective surface with a fine powder to obtain better results but this is not always practical.

Laser wavelengths are determined by the semiconductor material used to fabricate the laser and are selected by the manufacturer for eye safety concerns and noise rejection properties. Lasers that operate in the visible part of the spectrum are more influenced by ambient light. Measuring green objects with a red laser is to be avoided for example.

Ground Lidar Data Post-Processing

Following data collection, the first step in post-processing is to align multiple scans to a common coordinate system, a process known as scan registration. Typically raw scan data are captured without knowing the precise location of the scanner. A scan is registered to another scan by translating and rotating the data so that both sets are in a common coordinate system. There are two main methods to register point clouds, cloud-to-cloud registration and global or target-based registration.

Cloud-to-cloud registration is achieved by matching distinct features that can be seen in both scans. With this method, it is not necessary to reference any external data and no independent survey is used to align the coordinates of the scans. A rule-of-thumb is to ensure at least 20% overlap of data between scans to ensure reasonable registration. Obviously the technique is more effective when there are distinct and recognizable features that are visible in each scan.

Global or target-based scan registration involves locating and surveying targets in the scan scenes prior to scanning operations. A minimum of three overlapping targets between scan scenes is required for subsequent registration; often four or five targets are overlapped between scenes to provide redundancy. Targets are usually spheres of known and stable dimensions which can be fixed with magnetic or threaded attachments, or paper targets that can be taped to surfaces that will be measured or reflector targets commonly used by surveyors for conventional total station work. Usually targets are surveyed with total stations and either referenced to existing benchmarks and/or monuments or located with GPS or other instruments. Most laser scanning software has the capability of automatically recognizing and locating scene targets. For example, spheres can be fitted with high accuracy even if part of the sphere surface is occluded. (Spheres are useful in that the center is fixed for all viewing angles. Paper targets have patterns which are well defined for recognition purposes. Location of control targets is part of the art of successful laser scanning practice. Targets must be well distributed in a scene to allow scan registration. Too few targets cause scan registration to be difficult or impossible. Too many targets consume precious schedules needlessly.

Survey control problems can arise from errors in the initial survey. Benchmarks and monuments may be located incorrectly from previous work. Techniques that work for land survey, i.e. closing a loop and subsequent bundle adjustment, may be inadequate or impossible for industrial plant or shipbuilding projects. The measurement uncertainty of laser scanners approaches that of total stations in many instances; when discrepancies are observed it is not always clear which instrument is at fault.

Registering scan data and survey data to CAD geometry introduces another level of complexity. Many CAD systems assume – even insist on – orthogonality of elements such as structural steel. As-built geometry typically is different from as-designed geometry; steel columns may be aligned on a 2D drawing but may not have been installed correctly, for instance. Such differences are called "clashes."

Deliverables

Client deliverables vary significantly depending on the application. In some cases a spreadsheet table of measurements, for example minimum bridge height clearances, may be all that is required. In other cases a watertight 3D solid model based on the scan data may be required. Automobile manufacturers invest as much as 50 hours of post-processing effort for every hour of scanning in order to create 3D models of complex production equipment assemblies; these models are in turn used to feed sophisticated kinematic simulations.

The ability to extract point-to-point measurements often provides high value for clients. Low cost point cloud visualization tools that allow simple measurements can be used for design review or construction monitoring purposes. Some of today's visualization tools enable users to extract piping centerlines by selecting just a patch on a section of scanned piping and similarly create geometry primitives.

Beyond visualization, point cloud data can be displayed in some native CAD or design review applications to allow clash detection and reporting between existing conditions data, i.e. the scan data and design geometry generated from the CAD application. Clash detection and reporting has yielded significant construction rework reductions on industrial plant modification projects. Equipment demolition and installation sequencing simulations, e.g., crane movement simulation in a nuclear reactor, typically require some sophisticated modeling but become reliable construction management and training tools when based on accurate scan data. Some users have developed computational fluid dynamics (CFD) models based on scan data; because the simulations are based on as-built data, they are considered to be superior to those developed from idealized design data.

For transportation and civil infrastructure projects often the client needs 2D deliverables, i.e. line work or TIN meshes for road work. Dense point cloud data can be sectioned and traced to yield line work; TIN meshes can be generated semi-automatically.

Some users of point cloud data object to the large file sizes created by most scanning systems. Some work processes have been developed to thin or decimate the data by as much as

90% in order to make the files manageable. Fractious debates at industry meetings about the efficacy of this approach suggest that its benefits and drawbacks are far from settled.

Post-Processing Software

When commercial scanning systems first became available, point cloud databases with one million points were considered large. Processing points as individual CAD objects burdens most CAD systems to unmanageable levels at 100,000 points. Today in some applications it is routine to register hundreds of millions of points together to create databases with billions of points. The ability to manipulate these very large databases with modest computing hardware advances is expected to continue to advance. In the not-too-distant future it will not be exceptional to manipulate tens of billions of points.

Demand is robust for solutions that allow point cloud data to be manipulated inside native CAD environments without decimation or vectorization. Such solutions allow 3D visualization of existing geometry together with new design geometry. Beyond visualization comes clash or interference detection and reporting between existing conditions data and design geometry. Users can expect significant improvement in this kind of capability in the near term. The ability to annotate and tag point cloud data with non-geometric attributes promises to deliver asset management value to scan data. This capability will increase in functionality in the near term also.

Solutions that allow seamless navigation of hybrid databases based on scan data, airborne scan data, digital photography, CAD geometry, GIS data, and other sensor data remain as unfinished work with attractive economic incentives for completion. Google Earth, Microsoft Virtual Earth and other recent software development point the way to simple user interfaces for interacting with complex data from multiple sources.

Applications of 3D Terrestrial Laser Scanning

Terrestrial laser scanners are used in a wide variety of applications. Using scanners to create as-built documentation for revamping process plants and modifying and upgrading power generation facilities has yielded significant reductions in project costs and schedules because of the high accuracy and detail of the data. The technology is beginning to be used for monitoring construction of greenfield projects as well as for sequencing demolition, fabrication and installation of equipment in these facilities. Harnessing the technology for asset management purposes by annotating the point cloud databases produced by scanners is underway as pilot projects at some firms. Architects use scans of building facades for potential future reconstruction of new and old buildings to original as-built conditions; this is especially important for historical buildings.

Terrestrial laser scanners are also used for the design, construction and operation of transportation and civil infrastructure projects as well as buildings. For transportation infrastructure projects often the key benefit is safety – because laser scanning allows remote data capture, surveyors need not be exposed to high speed traffic and lane closures can be reduced. Combining data from airborne sensors and ground-based instruments for planning and engineering of transportation infrastructure projects is also getting wider acceptance. Creating 3D tunnel profiles to monitor deformation and to design remediation is finding wider acceptance for rail organizations.

Other applications for terrestrial laser scanning include crime and accident scene mapping for forensic purposes. Innovative uses of the technology for forensic purposes include measuring vehicle crush which can in turn be correlated with accident vehicle speeds, measuring blood spatter geometry to determine bullet trajectories, and measuring crime scene backgrounds to extract perpetrator geometry from surveillance images.

Scanning is used by geotechnical specialists for creating digital outcrop models, monitoring cliff erosion, measuring landslide and earthquake damage, quarry mapping, landfill surveying, measuring and monitoring mining volumes, and monitoring dam deformation.

Discrete manufacturing industries also are beginning to use terrestrial laser scanning not only for capturing the geometry of production facilities for revamp purposes but also for capturing the geometry of production line equipment. Automobile manufacturers, who are among the world's most sophisticated users of 3D modeling for product design, often find that information about their production assets is limited to out-of-date 2D drawings if they exist at all. Scanning provides a significant improvement over manual methods of data capture to produce as-built, as-maintained equipment geometry which in turn can provide advanced production simulation models. Other discrete manufacturing industries ranging from shipbuilding to aerospace also are beginning to deploy scanners for modeling production facilities and tooling.

The entertainment industry uses laser scanning to capture accurate as-filmed set geometry. Post-processing, to incorporate special effects, requires precise information about lighting and camera position and trajectories. Post production rendering processes are streamlined with high quality geometry obtained from scanning.

Figures 7.24 and 7.25 are images of phase-based terrestrial lidar. These images look like black and white photos. Figure 7.24 is a scan of the gun deck of the USS *Constitution*. Figure 7.25 is a high-resolution scan at a refinery. What is truly astonishing about all these images is that each pixel has xyz coordinates. In other words, they're not just pretty pictures. They contain valuable engineering grade information, the reason why this technology is expanding so rapidly. They clearly have a different look and feel than the airborne lidar intensity images shown at Figures 7.11 and 7.12 above.

Cost Considerations

List prices for phase-based scanners range from $65,000 to $165,000, while time-of-flight devices list for $31,500 to $150,000; prices for most time-of-flight devices are in the upper two-thirds of this range. As-sold prices vary according to hardware configuration and software and maintenance options. Annual hardware maintenance is approximately 20% of the list price of the hardware.

Point cloud processing software prices range from free (included with the purchase of laser scanning services) to approximately $25,000 for a high function, stand-alone perpetual license.

Fees for scanning services vary considerably. Capturing as-built data on an oil platform off the coast of Nigeria will be in the range of $5,000 to $10,000 per day for a two-person crew plus instrument, net of travel and lodging expenses. In North America conventional bridge, road and tunnel survey work is often less than $2,000 per day for a crew and instrument. Back-office post-processing of the data is typical billed by the hour at CAD operator hourly rates that range from $40 to $80.

Competing and Complementary Technologies of Terrestrial Lidar

Terrestrial laser scanning competes with manual measurement using spirit levels, plumb bobs and measuring tapes, electronic measurements based on total station or hand held disto instruments as well as traditional photogrammetry. Manual measurement is still superior to laser scanning in cost and speed when the geometry is uncomplicated and readily accessible and only a small number of measurements need to be collected.

Total station technology is widely adopted by the surveying community. Surveys for building construction and civil and transportation infrastructure projects are often conducted with total station instruments. Scanning has some distinct advantages over total station measurements in that the data sets are typically more complete – millions, even billions of points collected rather than hundreds or thousands. Nearly every project manager has occasion to rue missing measure-ments; it is often difficult, impossible or simply uneconomic to return to the job site to capture a missing measurement. For example the opportunity to capture measurements in a nuclear power plant dry well is limited even during planned outages. Sending a survey crew 200 kilometers offshore in a helicopter to get a missing measurement on an offshore oil platform is expensive.

In most instances total station technology complements the use of terrestrial laser scanning for establishing survey control. One method of registering multiple scans involves accurately surveying targets in the scan volume which in turn are detected by the scanner. A minimum of

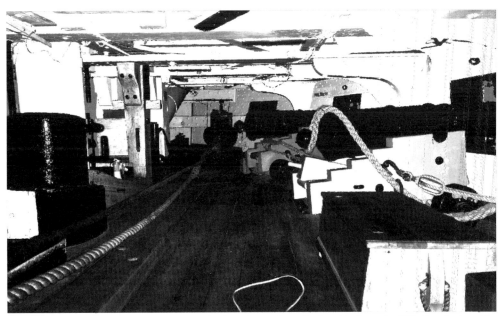

Figure 7.24 Image from a high resolution scan looking forward on the Gun Deck on the USS *Constitution*. The 360 scan is one of 20 shots taken with a phase-based scanner to profile the as-is conditions for upcoming historical preservation and restoration work. Each pixel represents a 3D xyz spatial coordinate. Image courtesy Meridian Associates, Inc.

Figure 7.25 High-resolution laser image of a fluid catalytic cracker (FCC) in a refinery captured with a phased-based scanner. Each pixel represents a 3D xyz spatial coordinate. Image courtesy of Quantapoint, Inc.

three matching targets are used to align the scan to survey control or another scan pair. The scans' origin is rotated and translated to the common coordinate system, which in turn is geo-referenced to survey located benchmarks.

Close range photogrammetry has some advantages over laser scanning in environments where it is difficult or impossible to capture the data from a stable platform. Most of today's scanners require stability for the duration of each scan. For example, capturing the geometry for an offshore production platform from a boat is usually better suited to photogrammetric techniques. Photogrammetry has significlant limitations – no position information is available along homogenous surfaces. Matching images is sometimes difficult, and unreliable results are obtained by practitioners without a high level of expertise and experience. The limitations are particularly pronounced when there are significant depth variations in the images.

Many of today's scanner systems allow capture of both digital photographs and scan data from the same setup, allowing a combination of photogrammetry and terrestrial scanning post-processing. The high semantic content of digital photographs, particularly with color images, can accelerate post-processing modeling of point cloud data. For example, it can be easier to distinguish curb breaklines from leaves or other road debris with RGB data registered to scan data than with monochrome scan data alone.

AUTHOR BIOGRAPHIES

Robert Fowler was the primary author of this chapter. Andre Samberg contributed much additional information, especially in the lidar and scanning explanations and expanded history of airborne lidar. Martin Flood completed a first edit and added text to the original chapter in the first edition, and he wrote most of the section on lidargrammetry added in this second edition. Tom Greaves supplied the detailed information, text and photos about ground based lidars.

Robert Fowler was an Ontario Land Surveyor and worked in the survey and mapping industry after joining the Ordnance Survey of the U.K. in 1960. He moved to Canada in 1964 and worked for four different mapping companies as a field surveyor and photogrammetrist. He wrote for numerous technical journals in the survey, remote sensing and mapping fields and was editor of *Northpoint* magazine for ten years. Most rectently, Fowler was Vice President Sales and Marketing for a lidar service provider, Lasermap Image Plus/GPR, working from their Bristol, Québec, Canada office. Shortly after completion of this chapter, he passed away.

Andre Samberg has been in the field of remote sensing since 1989. His primary research interest was and still is laser remote sensing, in particular, imaging laser scanners. He is the CEO of AVAPROedu/Training and Consulting based in Finland. He currently serves as Chair of the ASPRS Lidar Committee, Co-chair of SPIE/Technical Group of Robotics and Machine Perception, and an expert to ISO (International Organization for Standardization).

Martin Flood is currently employed by GeoCue Corporation (formerly NIIRS10), a workflow software provider specializing in geospatial data production management tools. Martin provides technical consulting services to GeoCue clients and manages GeoCue's operations in Canada. He also serves as the company's domain expert in lidar technology and sensor systems. Prior to joining GeoCue, Martin worked for several mapping firms specializing in providing lidar data and related products and worked at Optech Inc. during the development of the ALTM family of instruments. He holds BS and MS degrees in Physics and served as Chair of the ASPRS Lidar Committee from 2001-2005.

Tom Greaves is a co-founder and managing partner of Spar Point Research LLC in Danvers, Massachusetts. Previously he served as an analyst and marketing executive at Daratech, Inc., Cambridge, Massachusetts; product manager at Wexxar Packaging, Vancouver, Canada; and wireline engineer for Schlumberger Overseas S.A., Abu Dhabi, Kuwait, and Oman. He holds a BSc in physics from Queen's University at Kingston, an MSc in physics from the University of British Columbia, and a master's from the Sloan School of Management at the Massachusetts Institute of Technology.

ACKNOWLEDGEMENTS

Significant contributions are gratefully acknowledged for other personnel. Bob Kletzli, previously with Spectrum Mapping, allowed many of his technical materials to be plagiarized from his May 2000 ASPRS conference workshop: "Problems and Pitfalls in LIDAR." Mike Renslow, technical editor of *Photogrammetric Engineering & Remote Sensing* (*PE&RS*) performed pre-editing and provided suggestions. David Maune, senior project manager at Dewberry and senior editor of this manual, provided many of the images and performed additional editing of this chapter. The staff at Lasermap provided many of the technical suggestions and lessons learned materials for this chapter.

The authors also acknowledge their receipt of a large number of illustrations from various companies and regret that not all could be used. Fowler and Maune made the final decisions on materials included and excluded.

READINGS

A large number of papers have been written about applications of both airborne and terrestrial lidar over the last ten years, and may be found in PE&RS, and many trade publications. Many can be searched on-line. A number of web sites offer additional information on lasers, the electromagnetic spectrum and the enabling technologies. Optech's web site, www.optech.on.ca is a good source for general information on lidar (and of course Optech Instruments). Topeye, previously Saab, which manufactures helicopter mounted lidar systems has a web site at www.topeye.com and Dornier GmbH the aircraft manufacturer spun off their Toposys Division in 1995. Toposys' web site can be found at www.toposys.com. The Leica-Geosystems website at www.leica-geosystems.com covers a wide range of scientific instrumentation including both their airborne and terrestrial lidar systems. Several university sites such as The University of Florida and University of Western Ontario, as well as a number of research institutes and NASA, have sections of their web sites devoted to lidar. Most lidar service providers also have information on their web sites. A number of terrestrial lidar manufacturers also have information on their web sites including as mentioned previously Leica, Optech, and Reigl. While for the most part the authors have tried to avoid a lot of commercial brand "naming," in some cases it was necessary or integral to the history to mention specific company names. These names however, are not all inclusive and it is up to individuals who are considering purchasing equipment to investigate the market themselves. With today's search engines on the internet that is not an onerous task.

REFERENCES

AOL History - WFF AOL (http://aol.wff.nasa.gov/index.php?module=pagemaster&PAGE_user_op =view_page&PAGE_id=3&MMN_position=3:3).

Bachman, C. G., 1979. *Laser radar systems and technologies*, Artech House, Inc.

Beiser, L., 1992. *Laser Scanning Notebook*. SPIE.

Boehler, W. et al., 2002. 3D scanning software: An introduction, Close-Range Imaging, Long-Range Vision, ISPRS Commission V, Symposium 2002, September, 2002, Corfu, Greece (http:// www.i3mainz.fh-mainz.de/publicat/korfu/p11_Boehler.pdf).

Buckner, R. B., 1991. Surveying measurements and their analysis, Landmark Enterprises, 3rd edition,

Encyclopedia of Laser Physics and Technology. (http://www.rp-photonics.com/ encyclopedia.html).

Farrell, J. A. and Barth, M., 1999. *The Global Positioning System and Inertial Navigation*. McGraw-Hill.

Jelalian, A. V., 1992. *Laser Radar Systems*, Artech House.

Jenkins, T. E., 1987. *Optical Sensing Techniques and Signal Processing*, Prentice Hall International.

Karim, A., 1990. *Electro-optical Devices and Systems*, PWS-KENT Publishing Company.

Katzenbeisser, Rolf, 2003. About the calibration of lidar sensors, ISPRS Workshop, 3D Reconstruction form Airborne Laser-Scanner and InSAR Data, 8-10 October 2003, Dresden.

Katzenbeisser, Rolf, 2004. Calibration and data validation of a lidar fiber scanner, ASPRS Annual Conference, 24-27 May 2004, Denver, CO.

Laser Challenge, (http://nobelprize.org/physics/educational/laser/facts/history.html).

Löffler, G., Aspects of Raster DEM Data Delivered From Laser Measurements, (http://www.natscan.uni-freiburg.de/suite/pdf/040108_1534_1.pdf).

Marshall, G. F., 1985. *Laser Beam Scanning* (G.F. Marshall, editor), Marcel Dekker, Inc.

Measures, R. M., 1984. *Laser Remote Sensing*, Krieger Publishing Company.

Merhav, S., 1996. *Aerospace Sensor Systems and Applications,* Springer-Verlag.

Morin, Kristian. *Calibration of Airborne Laser Scanners*, master's thesis, UCGE reports No 20179, Department of Geomatics Engineering, University of Calgary, Canada (http://www.geomatics.ucalgary.ca/Papers/Thesis/NES/02.20179.KrisMorin.pdf).

Persson, Å., et al., 2005. Visualization and analysis of full-waveform airborne laser scanner data, *Proceedings of ISPRS WG III/3, III/4, V/3 Workshop, Laser scanning 2005*, September 12-14, 2005, Enschede, the Netherlands.

Pfeifer, N. and Rottensteiner, G., 2001. The Riegl laser scanner for the survey of the interiors of Schönbrunn Palace, *Proceedings of 5th Conference on Optical 3D Measurement Techniques*, Vienna, Austria, http://www.uibk.ac.at/geographie/personal/pfeifer/publication/vienna_terrestrialls_pfeifer.pdf)

Renslow, M.S., Development of a bare ground DEM and canopy layer in NW forestlands using high performance lidar, (http://gis.esri.com/library/userconf/proc00/professional/papers/PAP808/p808.htm).

Samberg, A., 1997. The design of an airborne laser 3D imaging instrument, ACSM/ASPRS Annual Convention & Exposition, Seattle, 7-10 , April 1997, Bethesda ,MD, ASPRS, American Congress on Surveying and Mapping, Resource Technology Institute, pp. 359-363.

Samberg, A., 2004. Introduction to eye-grammetry, Internal report of AVAPROedu.

Sequeira, Vitor, 3D image acquisition using laser range finders, (http://sir.jrc.it/3d/3DReconstruction/3DSensors/3DSensors.htm).

Sithole, G. and Vosselman, G., 2003. Comparison of filtering algorithms, *Proceedings of the ISPRS working group III/3 workshop, 3D reconstruction from airborne laserscanner and InSAR data*, 8-10 October 2003, Dresden, Germany.

Stoker, Jason M. et al., 2006. CLICK: The new USGS Center for Lidar Information Coordination and Knowledge, *Photogrammetric Engineering and Remote Sensing*, 72(6): 613-616.

Wehr, Aloysius and Lohr, Uwe, 1999. Airborne laser scanning—an introduction and overview, *ISPRS Journal of Photogrammetry & Remote Sensing*, 54, pp. 68–82.

Chapter 8

Airborne Lidar Bathymetry

Gary C. Guenther

INTRODUCTION

Airborne laser (or lidar) bathymetry (ALB) is a technique for measuring the depths of moderately clear, near-shore coastal waters and lakes from a low-altitude aircraft using a scanning, pulsed laser beam (Hickman and Hogg, 1969; Guenther and Goodman, 1979; Penny and Phillips, 1981; Guenther, 1985; Muirhead and Cracknell, 1986; Guenther, 1989; Estep, 1993). It is also known as airborne lidar hydrography (ALH) when used primarily for nautical charting. The more generic term, ALB, will be used predominantly throughout this chapter. The term "lidar" is an acronym which stands for LIght Detection And Ranging, but, as with "sonar" and "radar", it is in such common usage that it has become a word in its own right and is no longer capitalized.

Why is this technology important? It is well known that the hydrographic charts for many of the world's coastal areas are either out of date or nonexistent (Nordstrom, 2000). Almost 50% of the maritime states have no national hydrographic capability; developing coastal nations often lack adequate data and charts. The overall status of hydrographic surveying and nautical charting world wide is rated in the range from "poor" to "fair" (UN, 1989). Conversely, the use of coastal areas by commercial and recreational concerns is growing at a rapid pace. There is reason to believe that hydrography, in the U.S. and around the world, is in a state of crisis regarding the ability of professional hydrographic organizations to provide the needed and desired products within their budgets and in a timely manner (Featherstone, 2001). Additionally, coastal zone engineers and managers need coastal bathymetric data for a wide variety of environmental applications. A technology that can deliver faster and cheaper shallow-water surveying for both hydrographic and bathymetric purposes is critically needed. ALH/ALB is that technology.

Based on many years of operations, ALB has proven to be an accurate, cost-effective, rapid, safe, and flexible method for surveying in shallow water and on coastlines where sonar systems are less efficient and can even be dangerous to operate (LaRocque and West, 1999; Wellington, 2001a; Skogvik and Axelson, 2001). In addition to traditional nautical charting, applications for bathymetric data, such as monitoring engineering structures and the movement of sand, environmental protection, and resource management and exploitation, are expanding rapidly (Wozencraft and Millar, 2005). The growth in the recognition, utilization, and demand for ALH and ALB surveys has become explosive around the world and is beginning to outstrip availability.

The costs of operations for all current ALB systems are reported most often as 15-30% of the standard survey cost, depending on location, depth, and survey density. Soundings are densely spaced, typically on a 2-5 meter grid, within a wide swath under the aircraft, whose width is typically greater than half of the aircraft altitude. Gross coverage rates as high as 77 km^2/hour (23 nmi^2/hour) are reported (Wozencraft and Lillycrop, 2003). The major limitation is water clarity. For areas with very clear water, the advantage of surveying a wide swath at aircraft speeds can be obtained for depths as great as 50 meters or more. Only in this way can the enormous survey backlogs of many countries (UN, 1989) be significantly reduced in a timely manner. The fact that airborne lidar can also measure land topography and survey simultaneously on both sides of the land/water boundary (Guenther et al., 1998; Irish et al., 2000; Wozencraft and Lillycrop, 2003) is highly beneficial and attractive to coastal engineers. Figure 8.1 presents a graphic comparison of lidar and sonar operations in shallow water.

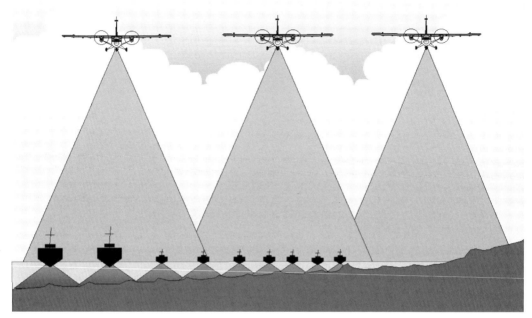

Figure 8.1 Depiction of lidar and multi-beam sonar operation in shallow water to emphasize lidar capabilities and efficiency. See color plate in Appendix C.

The essential qualities required for a successful ALB system are accuracy, capability, and cost effectiveness. Over the past twenty-five years, developments in lasers, optics, electronics, and computers have made it somewhat easier to construct viable airborne lidar systems with varying purposes, and an increasing number are being constructed (mostly for topographic use). Fewer than ten airborne lidar bathymeters exist in the world today, however, because of the complexity, the large initial monetary investment which must be amortized, relatively limited (but rapidly growing) demand, and because it remains a challenge to meet vertical accuracy standards. It is relatively easy today to build a lidar system that can detect the sea bottom, and it is not hard to get approximate depths from a system. It takes a great deal of understanding and effort, however, as with shallow-water multibeam sonar, to obtain depths (and elevations) that will meet international vertical accuracy standards and the operational requirements of the typical customer (Guenther et al., 2000). A great deal of care, time, and money has been put into the design, construction, testing, calibration, and operation of the present ALB systems to ensure that they meet the accuracy standards of the International Hydrographic Organization.

Two basic system strategies are in current use. Several bigger ALB systems are permanently installed in larger aircraft with the capability to execute lengthy survey sorties or transit long distances to remote survey sites. Other more compact systems have been designed for efficient mobilization and demobilization in somewhat smaller and less expensive "aircraft of opportunity". Both types can be deployed world wide and can exhibit similar performance specifications. The trend is toward smaller, lighter, cheaper, more flexible systems which can be flown in smaller aircraft and fielded in larger numbers, as survey tools, with no loss of performance (Lillycrop et al., 2001). Newer systems are often paired with complementary airborne sensors and more powerful lidar processing algorithms that characterize more aspects of the marine environment than just depths or elevations (Tuell and Park, 2004; Tuell et al., 2005a).

This chapter presents the numerous applications for which the technology is used. How it works, in terms of requirements, theory, hardware design strategies, performance, and limitations, is described. The features and capabilities of systems currently in use are examined. Factors affecting costs are analyzed, and comprehensive comparisons with overlapping systems and technologies are discussed for bathymetry and coastal zone mapping. Detailed information is provided on operational procedures, including calibration, tides, horizontal positioning, mission planning, data processing, and products, that have been developed to provide the basis for systems which will meet required accuracy standards while maintaining efficiency and cost-effectiveness. The chapter ends with a thorough examination of where this inviting new approach to shallow-water surveying is headed.

Quality control is integrated throughout the hardware, software, procedures, and production aspects of ALB systems and will hence be integrated throughout the corresponding sections of this chapter rather than being presented as a separate topic. A major emphasis of this chapter is how recognized error sources are managed and how accuracy is obtained and maintained from sensor to chart. The primary considerations in the design, construction, and operation of an airborne bathymeter must be data quality, depth measurement accuracy, and automation. Both the physical environment and system hardware components contribute error sources that must be overcome. This requires thoughtful hardware and software system design and construction (Guenther et al., 2000), as well as the prediction, modeling, and application of appropriate correctors (Guenther, 1985). Operational procedures for quality control, calibration, and maintenance must be established and followed. Although data processing must be largely automated, as dictated by data collection rates as high as 10.8 million soundings per hour, limited manual interaction during data processing continues to be a critical step.

The quantum leap from sound to light has been made. The first steps have been taken with excellent and exciting results. As of spring 2006, eight systems are presently engaged in ALB operations. Several of the current-generation bathymetric systems have been operating successfully for over twelve years for diverse applications. The accuracy, capabilities, and cost-effectiveness of these novel bathymeters are now being widely recognized and respected by the user community, and demand for contract surveys and new systems is increasing rapidly. Several new systems are on the drawing board, and prospects for expanded services and new products are very positive.

USER APPLICATIONS

Airborne lidar bathymetry is an accurate, capable, and highly cost-effective alternative to traditional, waterborne sonar in areas with appropriate depth and water clarity. With the production of high-density, three-dimensional digital bathymetric data, it offers a number of important products, services, and applications in coastal waters. Under appropriate circumstances, finished survey products may be delivered within 24 hours (Sinclair, 1999b; Lillycrop et al., 2000). ALB is often optimal in relatively shallow areas where sonar is less efficient. It can also survey safely in areas where sonar cannot, including, for some systems, above-water structures and dry land. ALB is, however, not a substitute for sonar because ALB surveys are limited by water clarity and depth. Furthermore, it cannot be expected to detect one-hundred percent of bottom hazards with size on the order of a one-meter cube unless an expensive, unusually high-density survey is conducted. Regions where ALB and sonar capabilities overlap are thought of as areas of cooperation rather than of competition.

Operational ALB systems have been and can be deployed to locations around the globe. Applications for ALB (Cunningham et al., 1998; Sinclair, 1999b; Irish et al., 2000; Wellington, 2001a) include bathymetric surveys of large offshore coastal areas, islands, coral reefs, navigation channels, lakes, ports and harbors, shore protection projects such as jetties and breakwaters, beaches, shorelines, mud banks, and dredge disposal sites. Surveys have been completed economically and safely in disparate areas. These include everything from large, relatively shallow, mostly flat areas with sink holes and patterns of sand waves, as in the Bahamas (LaRocque and West, 1999), to complex areas composed of myriad small islands, channels, and shallow banks, as in Norway (Sinclair, 1999a) and Sweden (Skogvik and Axelsson, 2001), to deeper, rocky areas rife with pinnacles which pose a serious danger to surface vessels, as in New Zealand (Graham et al., 1999; Sinclair, 1999b). Large, stable regions, such as coral reefs, can be surveyed one time only, while rapidly changing areas like the sandy coast of Florida, 40% of which is suffering serious erosion, may be surveyed every year or two to monitor change (West and Wiggins, 2000b).

Each existing ALB system has begun with a specific concept of operations, but, through use and experience, new applications have evolved or been identified as well suited for airborne lidar. Today's primary missions are nautical charting, port and harbor surveys, coastal zone mapping, and military applications.

Large-scale nautical charting has been the chief survey requirement for most of the airborne lidar survey systems. This is due to the enormous backlog in the production of modern charts needed for safe navigation world wide (Setter and Willis, 1994; Nordstrom, 2000; Featherstone, 2001). A large percent of the backlog areas is in relatively clear, shallow waters (less than 50 m) which are well suited for ALB. This mission requirement is not likely to diminish over the next 20 years because even though tens of thousands of square nautical miles have been surveyed with LARSEN, LADS, Hawk Eye, SHOALS, LADS Mk II, SHOALS-1000, CHARTS, EAARL, and Hawk Eye II, many more times this area is in critical need of surveying. These systems will be discussed in later sections. ALB is particularly important for use in complex coastal areas because of its cost, speed, and safety. Nordstrom (2000) said it succinctly for the Swedish Maritime Administration: "the use of a helicopter-borne laser-beam system (in Sweden) is essential, especially in shallow and narrow waters in the archipelagos."

Port and harbor surveying is a similar requirement (Irish et al., 1995), but one whose goals are to define navigation channel conditions for safe navigation and to determine and quantify potential dredging requirements. These surveys are typically concerned with harbor approaches and the condition of the navigation channel in terms of sediment shoaling. The most successful surveys are in harbors that have good flushing and mixing with clearer ocean waters. This mission requirement is not expected to diminish over the next 20 years as the need for deeper navigation channels, prone to shoaling, is expected to grow.

Perhaps one of the more rapidly growing survey requirements is for large regional surveys to map, monitor, and manage coastal shorelines (Watters and Wiggins, 1999; Wozencraft and Irish, 2000; Strock, 2006). This is particularly true along sandy shorelines that are subjected to severe storms, but also along more stable, even rocky shorelines where the effects of storm waves and flooding are of concern. Natural boundaries are eroding, and entire land masses disappear as new ones grow. Over the past few years, requirements for this application emerged in diverse locations such as Canada, Italy, the Marianas Islands, the Middle East, Spain, Portugal, the United Kingdom, Puerto Rico, and many of the coastal states in the United States, to name only a few examples. At the federal level in the United States, the Army Corps of Engineers has established a national coastal mapping program designed to map the entire coast on a cyclical basis. ALB flown with complementary sensors is the main source of data for this program (Wozencraft and Lillycrop, 2006). This survey requirement is expected to increase over the next 20 years, driven by growing potential for property damage associated with increased population along the coasts of the world and fueled by the need for responsible shoreline growth and management.

The development of airborne lidar systems originated with military requirements for submarine hunting (Sorenson et al., 1966). Although the ability to measure bottom depths was originally somewhat serendipitous, it was not long before the military applications of ALB were recognized. One such current application is "rapid environmental assessment" which includes sending military assets to collect data to characterize potential amphibious landing sites where data may be dated or non-existent. Sites may be denied areas and may range in size from a few kilometers to hundreds of kilometers. The support of rapid regional reconnaissance and surveying is an emerging requirement for which airborne lidar has great potential.

It is instructive to look at a more detailed enumeration of the diverse uses to which this technology has already been applied:

- Large-area charting for navigational purposes (Pope et al., 1997; Sinclair, 1999b),
- Monitoring of shoaling in navigation channels (Irish et al., 1997a),
- Support of oil and gas exploration and production (Sinclair, 1999b),
- Coastal engineering studies of sediment transport (Irish and Lillycrop, 1997; Irish et al., 1997b; Wozencraft et al., 2001),
- Baseline turning point and Exclusive Economic Zone (EEZ) delimitation (Sinclair, 1999b),
- Design and evaluation of coastal engineering structures for shoreline stabilization (Mohr et al., 1999; Irish and White, 1998),
- Monitoring seasonal change (McClung, 1998),
- Marine resource and coral reef management,
- Fisheries management,
- Water level management on controlled lakes (Wozencraft et al., 2002),
- Rapid-response storm damage assessment after hurricanes such as Opal (Morang et al., 1996),
- Establishment of sediment budgets and monitoring sand as a local resource (West and Wiggins, 2000b),
- Storm surge modeling (West and Wiggins, 2000a),
- Resolution of historic bathy/topo shoreline inconsistencies (Parker et al., 2001),
- Submarine pipeline planning and construction,
- Low impact surveys in ecologically sensitive areas (West et al., 2001a),
- Rapid shoreline assessment for tactical military operations (Lillycrop et al., 2000), and
- Strategic defense applications.

As a bonus, several of these requirements can sometimes be satisfied simultaneously (Ebrite et al., 2001).

The primary advantages of this technology are that it provides:

- the ability to perform surveys accurately and quickly, in both large and small project areas, in a more cost-effective manner (Enabnit et al., 1978; Sinclair and Spurling, 1997; LaRocque and West, 1999);
- the capability to survey where it would be difficult, dangerous, or impossible to use water-borne techniques (Graham et al., 1999);
- the facility to simultaneously survey the sea bottom, the adjacent beach, and coastal engineering structures (both above and below the waterline) (Guenther et al., 1998; Mohr et al., 1999);
- the mobility to perform yearly monitoring of dynamic areas and rapid assessments of seasonal change (McClung and Douglass, 1999) and storm damage (Irish et al., 1996; Irish and Truitt, 1995); and
- the capacity to quickly complete surveys during favorable environmental windows in areas which are unavailable to traditional techniques for long periods due to conditions such as ice cover (Vosburgh and Banic, 1987) or high river flow (Millar et al., 2005).

ALB is rapidly achieving acceptance in the diverse user community as these capabilities become more widely recognized and exploited. New capabilities continue to be attained, exciting new applications are being found, and new products will be developed. ALB provides unique survey opportunities, capabilities, and products, in shallow water and across the land/water boundary, which would be worth having even if they cost much more.

DEVELOPMENTAL HISTORY

The concept of ALB grew out of efforts in the mid 1960's to use the newly invented laser to find submarines (Ott, 1965, Sorenson et al., 1966) and as an "airborne laser fathometer" (Sorenson, 1966). The seminal paper confirming the ability to perform near-shore bathymetry was written by Hickman and Hogg (1969) based on work done at the Syracuse University Research Center.

In the early 1970's a number of first-generation airborne lidar systems were successfully tested by the U.S. Navy (Ott et al., 1971; Cunningham, 1972; Rankin, 1975; Witt et al., 1976), by the National Aeronautics and Space Administration (NASA) (Kim et al., 1975), in Canada (Bristow, 1975; O'Neil et al., 1978), and in Australia (Abbot and Penny, 1975). Much of the early work in the Soviet Union (Ivanov, 1972), Sweden, and Canada (Carswell and Sizgoric, 1974) was ship-borne. A system sponsored by the U.S. Air Force was successfully tested from a tower over the Gulf of Mexico (Levis et al., 1973). Several symposia, co-sponsored by the National Oceanic and Atmospheric Administration (NOAA) and NASA, were convened to establish user requirements and design goals for the use of the second-generation NASA Airborne Oceanographic Lidar (AOL) for hydrography (Goodman, 1975; Goodman, 1976). Successful bathymetric field testing of the AOL was conducted in 1977 (Guenther and Goodman, 1978; Guenther et al., 1979; Hoge et al., 1980). As a result, the existence of environmentally-induced biases in both surface and bottom returns were discovered (Guenther, 1981). Other second-generation systems were built and tested in Canada (O'Neil, 1981), in Australia (Penny, 1981; Abbot, 1981), and in the Soviet Union (Balandin and Volodarskiy, 1979). The Canadian system, augmented with a scanner, was also tested in Sweden (Steinvall et al., 1981). The attractiveness of this technology is that it promises faster and cheaper accurate shallow-water surveys (Enabnit, 1981).

The 1980's began with the 4th Laser Hydrography Symposium in Australia; a great many breakthroughs were reported (Penny and Phillips, 1981). Thereafter, the LARSEN (Anderson et al., 1983; Banic et al., 1986) was developed in Canada by Optech Incorporated for the Canadian Hydrographic Service and the Canada Centre for Remote Sensing to support nautical-charting missions in the Arctic during the few weeks a year the region is ice free. Based on surveys performed in the Canadian Northwest Territories, it became the world's first operational ALH system (Casey, 1984; Casey et al., 1985; Casey and Vosburgh, 1986; Conrad, 1986; Vosburgh and Banic, 1987). Additional surveys were conducted in the Great Lakes, the St. Lawrence River, and off the East and West coasts of Canada. Testing of the Australian WRELADS II was successfully completed (Penny et al., 1986; Billard and Wilsen, 1986; Billard, 1986a); design and construction was begun at BHP/Vision Systems on the operational version called LADS (Compton and Hudson, 1988; Penny et al., 1989) for the Royal Australian Navy. Design and testing of a number of systems such as the U.S. Navy HALS (Harris et al., 1986; Curran et al., 1988) and the Swedish FLASH (Alexsson et al., 1990; Steinvall et al., 1992) continued. Three multi-purpose research systems (GOI, Chaika, and Makrel-II) were actively tested in the Soviet Union (Bunkin et al., 1984; Abroskin et al., 1986; Abramochkin et al., 1988; Tsvetkov, 1991; Feigels and Kopilevich, 1993a), and work was also conducted in China on their BLOL (Liu, 1990). In 1988, the U.S. Army Corps of Engineers began the SHOALS program with Optech (Pope and Lillycrop, 1988; Banic et al., 1990). The promise is beginning to be realized.

In the 1990's, LADS became operational in Australia (Setter and Willis, 1994; Nairn, 1994), SHOALS became operational in the United States (Lillycrop et al., 1993; Lillycrop et al., 1994; Lillycrop et al., 1996; Lillycrop et al., 1997), and Hawk Eye became operational in Sweden (Steinvall et al., 1994; Koppari et al., 1994; Steinvall et al., 1997). LADS is flown in a dedicated Fokker F-27 fixed-wing aircraft. SHOALS originally operated from either of a pair of NOAA Bell 212 helicopters, while two Hawk Eye systems were borne in Bell 212 and Boeing Vertol helicopters. The LARSEN system continued to perform in a variety of fixed-wing aircraft (Hare, 1994). Late in the decade, SHOALS added the capability of using kinematic GPS (KGPS) as an optional vertical reference (Guenther et al., 1998); this permits topographic mapping over land to be conducted in conjunction with bathymetric missions and also permits operation without concurrent tides data. The pulse-repetition rate of SHOALS was doubled (Irish and Lillycrop, 1999), and the system was transitioned from the helicopters to a deHavilland Twin Otter (Dash 6) fixed-wing aircraft (LaRocque and West, 1999). The LADS Mk II system, with many added capabilities such as a much higher pulse-repetition rate and improved computer and navigation functions, was built by Tenix LADS Corp. to perform contract surveys world wide and became operational in a faster deHavilland Dash 8 200-series aircraft (Spurling and Perry, 1997; Sinclair, 1998). The promise has come to fruition. ALB surveys have proven to be accurate, rapid, flexible, and significantly less expensive than waterborne surveys in appropriate locations.

ALH surveys were conducted by the government hydrographic agencies of Australia and Sweden with their dedicated LADS and Hawk Eye systems, respectively, and contract surveys with LARSEN, SHOALS, and LADS Mk II were widespread for a variety of applications. The governments of Canada, Australia, Mexico, New Zealand, Norway, Indonesia, Barbados, Puerto Rico, the United Arab Emirates, and Finland, and also NATO, contracted surveys with the above systems, as did commercial organizations such as gas and oil and ocean engineering companies. Contracts were also let by various U.S. federal and state government agencies such as the Army Corps of Engineers, the Navy, the Geological Survey, NOAA's National Ocean Service, the Federal Emergency Management Agency, and the Florida Department of Environmental Protection.

The first decade of the 2000's has been a time of busy surveying (Wozencraft and Lillycrop, 2006), of the development of new systems, of a breakthrough into the commercial arena, and of thoughtful planning for a bright future. The pace-setting LARSEN, the world's first operational ALB, active for an impressive 16 years, was retired in 2001 (R. Quinn, personal communication, 2006). Wellington (2001b) reported the addition of topographic ability for LADS Mk II. The SHOALS system was upgraded to 1000 pulses per second (pps) (LaRocque et al., 2004; Wozencraft, 2002) and 3000 pps. A SHOALS-1000 system was purchased by the Japan Coast Guard (Iwamoto et al., 2004). USACE obtained a SHOALS-3000TH system called "CHARTS" with new, high-rate topographic and hyperspectral capabilities (Wozencraft and Millar, 2005; Tuell et al., 2005a). Optech built an additional SHOALS-1000T "demo" system which can be made available for use by interested parties. Most notably, Fugro Pelagos became the first commercial surveyor to purchase an ALB system when they received a SHOALS-1000T (Lockhart et al., 2005). The NASA Experimental Advanced Airborne Research Lidar (EAARL) of unique design (Feygels et al., 2003) was fielded in 2001 (Wright and Brock, 2002) to provide topographic and limited bathymetric surveys combined with imagery from a down-looking RGB digital camera and a high-resolution multi-spectral color infrared (CIR) camera, often in support of U.S. Geological Survey projects. Recently, a new consortium called Admiralty Coastal Surveys AB was formed in Europe to develop and provide surveys with the Hawk Eye II system built by Airborne Hydrography AB in Sweden.

As this is updated in 2006, eight systems are engaged in operational hydrography. Looking ahead, plans are underway for a new system for the Royal Australian Navy to replace their workhorse LADS, and design has begun for a next-generation system for USACE, to be built by Optech International (Kiln, MS) in conjunction with the University of Southern Mississippi, called the Coastal Zone Mapping and Imaging Lidar (CZMIL), which may include some exciting new technologies.

CONCEPT

The Challenge

The accuracy standards generally accepted for hydrography are established by the International Hydrographic Organization (IHO) in Monaco and disseminated in Special Publication 44. The current version is the 4th Edition (April 1998); this is also excerpted in Federal Geographic Data Committee (FGDC) Geospatial Positioning Accuracy Standards, Part 5: Standards for Nautical Charting Hydrographic Surveys (see Chapter 3 of this book). Many hydrographic surveys are conducted to "Order-1" specifications, with some at "Special Order" for shallow shipping channels, and some, typically in waters deeper than 30 meters, at the less demanding "Order-2" (Engstrom and Axelsson, 2001). In its simplest form, the Order-1 vertical-accuracy requirement for shallow water hydrography can be paraphrased as a total of ±0.50 m (95%) from all sources, including tides.

The operational production of reliable ALB depths accurate to these IHO standards involves detailed understanding of the characteristics of the laser and optics, of the data collection electronics, and of a number of physical interactions between the laser beam and the environment. Each of these factors contributes important error sources that must be ameliorated (Guenther, 1985). The development of a system must begin with proper hardware and software design in which all major error sources are recognized and minimized so that flight data have desirable characteristics and all necessary system outputs are available (Guenther et al., 1996; Guenther et al., 2000). The detection requirements for small objects on the sea bottom, also covered in S-44, are a further difficulty which will be discussed separately. The corresponding Order-1 horizontal requirement of 5 m (95%) is not as hard to meet using modern Global Positioning System (GPS) techniques.

There is a danger to believe that, if a generic water-lidar system can detect returns from the sea bottom, it can be used as a hydrographic system. That is not necessarily the case, because one of the biggest problems that must be solved in the design of a bathymetric lidar involves the accurate and reliable determination of the location of the air/water interface, for each laser pulse, for a wide variety of environmental circumstances (Guenther et al., 1994). For reasons that will be detailed, the use of green "surface" returns alone has not been considered to be an acceptable solution. It is necessary to have a surface detection channel at a wavelength such as infrared (IR) which has no significant penetration into the water (Tyler and Preisendorfer, 1962). In order to maintain the highest accuracy for every laser pulse, to not restrict the operational envelope, and to cover full ranges of water depths and environmental constraints, it is beneficial to have a second surface channel at the Raman-shifted green wavelength in the red. In the future, the development of sophisticated software routines may enable the use of green surface returns for the accurate determination of the air/water interface location.

A second generic problem that must be solved is the handling of the more than six orders of magnitude of amplitude dynamic range between strong water interface returns and weak bottom returns. That difference, which occurs in only a matter of tens or hundreds of nanoseconds, must be handled by the detector without anomalous effects and must be compressed into the useful input range of the digitizer, which is typically only two or three orders of magnitude. The choice of the scan pattern and beam nadir angle(s) has a major impact on this aspect of system design.

The laser transmitter is one of the most critical system components. The requirements for an ALB laser in terms of pulse energy, pulse-repetition rate, pulse width, beam quality, lifetime, and reliability in the field under flight conditions seem to be only a little easier to achieve with today's technology than they were 25 years ago. Appropriate lasers have continued to be custom units not generally available off the shelf, and their performance cannot be taken for granted.

These challenges have been successfully met by several manufacturers, and operational ALB systems are providing highly productive, low-cost surveys at many locations around the world.

Theory

The general technique of ALB (Guenther, 1985; Guenther and Goodman, 1978; Hoge et al., 1980; Guenther and Thomas, 1983) involves the use of a pulsed laser transmitter with both green and IR output beams. [A continuous-wave (CW) heterodyne approach was studied (Mullen et al., 1996) but was not fielded.] Green is selected for sea bottom detection because that is the wavelength which penetrates typical coastal waters with the least attenuation (Jerlov, 1976). This very penetration causes it to be a less than satisfactory sea surface detector under some circumstances. Infrared light penetrates very little and can be used for unambiguous detection of the sea surface location for most wind conditions. Depending on system design, the IR beam may be nearly collimated and scanned collinearly with the green beam, or it may be broader and constrained at nadir. Red energy generated in the water from green-excited Raman backscatter (Walrafen, 1967) immediately beneath the air/water interface (and from incidental laser-induced fluorescence) may also be used as a surface return by correcting its arrival time to the interface (Guenther et al., 1994). The problem of accurate and reliable surface detection across the entire operational envelope is more complex than can be dealt with here. The reader is directed to the "Water surface detection strategy" section of Guenther et al. (2000) for more details.

A conceptual green lidar return waveform (amplitude vs. time), as seen in an airborne receiver, is shown in Figure 8.2 with the three principal components — surface return, volume backscatter return, and bottom return — identified. Volume backscatter denotes the signature of pulse energy reflected from particulate materials in the water column. The amplitudes of the green interface returns vary statistically with wind/wave conditions over many orders of magnitude because they depend on surface wave-slope statistics. The amplitudes of the near-surface, green volume-backscatter peaks are generally relatively constant because they depend on water clarity. Although the interface return component is illustrated in Figure 8.2 as being roughly equal in magnitude with the volume return to which it is added, this is not generally true. The interface component can be significantly stronger or weaker on a pulse-to-pulse basis (Guenther and Mesick, 1988b). If the green interface return is significantly weaker than the volume-backscatter return, the latter may be incorrectly detected as the surface. The resulting surface time bias (and hence depth bias) is unacceptably large (Guenther, 1986). For this reason, the use of generic green surface returns is problematic, and a system using only green pulses is generally unsuitable (Guenther et al., 1994; Guenther et al., 2000) except for unique technical approaches involving extremely short laser pulse widths and tiny receiver field of view and/or the application of an innovative software solution. The logarithmic slope of the volume backscatter can be used as a measure of water clarity.

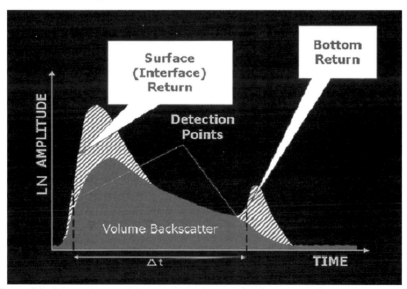

Figure 8.2 Schematic green lidar waveform showing the three principal signal components.

In turbid waters, the volume backscatter can be a limiting noise source for the bottom return.

The transmitted green laser pulses are partially reflected from the water surface and from the sea bottom back to the airborne receiver. The arrival time differences between the surface and bottom returns, representing the round-trip times through the water column, are typically on the order of tens or hundreds of nanoseconds. With knowledge of the speed of light in air and water and the beam nadir angle in water, distances to the local sea surface and bottom could be calculated by measuring the times of flight of the pulses to those locations. These measured surface and bottom distances at each pulse location could be differenced to provide local water-column depths, but this is not the desired result.

The required product may be the mean water depth at each pulse location with respect to a tidal datum such as "mean lower low water" (MLLW) or "lowest astronomical tide" (LAT), or it may be the bottom elevation with respect to a given ellipsoidal datum. In the former case, the mean water level, and wave heights about it for each pulse, are first estimated by modeling a large number of surface return distances in a so-called wave-correction algorithm. These models may use Kalman filters (Billard, 1986a) or other sophisticated techniques (Thomas and Guenther, 1990) involving the use of vertical acceleration data (Krabill and Swift, 1981b). The mean water depths at each pulse location at that time are then determined by differencing the bottom return times from the mean water level times, converting to distance with the speed of light in water, correcting for the effect of the measured wave height, and using the water nadir angle to convert from slant distance to vertical depth. Unlike the situation with sonar where the speed of sound is a sometimes elusive quantity and can lead to large depth errors, the speed of light in water is only a very weak function of salinity and temperature and can be easily handled, for example, with three crudely differentiated values representing "fresh", "brackish", and "salty".

For charting purposes, these mean-water-level depths are reduced to the desired geodetic (tidal) datum with the application of the simultaneously measured tidal time series. Alternately, with the use of kinematic GPS with on-the-fly ambiguity resolution (KGPS/OTF), also known as post-processed kinematic (PPK), to establish the vertical datum, instead of using the mean water level, bottom elevations may be determined directly with respect to the WGS-84 ellipsoid (Krabill and Martin, 1987), or to any datum known with respect to the ellipsoid, across the project area (Guenther et al., 1998). In this case, mission concurrent water-level measurements are not needed, and unlimited topographic surveys may be conducted over land. This greatly improves the efficiency of surveying both sides of the land/water boundary in areas of irregular coastline geometry.

In practice, the green and IR beams are purposely expanded to a diameter of at least several meters at the water surface in order to achieve eye-safe operation with sufficient pulse energy to provide reasonable signal-to-noise ratios. (This is not necessary with EAARL and its low pulse energies.) More spreading of the green beam in the water is caused by the optical effects of waves on refraction angles at the water surface. The resulting redirection of the beam also contributes to small random depth errors (Guenther, 1985). In all but very shallow water, however, most of the beam spreading, for typical operating conditions, is caused by scattering from particulate materials in the water column.

Although laser beams are commonly envisioned as being highly collimated with a small cross section (as they are in space or over short distances in air), this is not the case in water. Here, as seen in Figure 8.3, scattering causes even the narrowest beam to expand into a cone whose interior angle and cross section increase significantly with depth. [It should be noted that Figure 8.3 is a cartoon, and the beam spreading depicted has been exaggerated for clarity.] For most operating conditions, the 3-db (half-energy) beam diameter at the sea bottom will range between ten and thirty percent of the depth; for extreme conditions near extinction, it could be as great as half the depth. Related propagation-induced depth measurement biases must be corrected (Guenther and Thomas, 1984a). The resulting net expansion in irradiated bottom area is beneficial to the detection probability for significant bottom features (Guenther et al., 1996) but, as with broad sonar beams, can be detrimental to depth accuracy when very high-relief features are present.

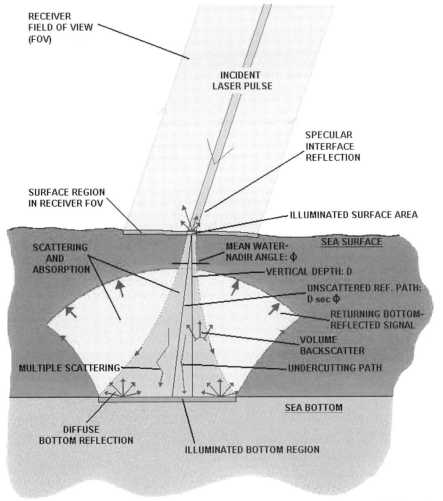

Figure 8.3 Schematic diagram of the effects of scattering on the green lidar beam (not to scale). See color plate in Appendix C.

Approach

Airborne laser bathymetry is a comparatively young and growing discipline which depends on state-of-the-art engineering in areas of lasers, optics, electro-optics, and electronics. Although detailed specifications and implementations vary somewhat from system to system, there is a fair amount of generic commonality because the designs are driven by the same physical principles and available engineering, and by similar user requirements. Data collection and processing are all digital. This enables flexibility in product generation to meet varied user requirements and facilitates fusion with data from other sources. Two competing design philosophies are extant for full-capability systems, one supplied in North America by Optech Incorporated (Toronto, Ontario), and in Sweden by Airborne Hydrography AB, and the other supplied in Australia by Vision Systems Ltd. (now part of Tenix Defence Systems Pty Ltd.). They differ in their scan patterns, surface detection strategies, and means of handling the signal-amplitude dynamic range. Both approaches have been extensively demonstrated to provide excellent performance. NASA's EAARL offers a different, unique technique based on a combination of very short, low-energy laser pulses and a very small receiver field of view to achieve good resolution and accuracy in an all-green system. This provides a system with excellent topo/bathy capability at the shoreline, but also leads to a limited depth capability (Feygels et al., 2003).

Systems are mounted in both helicopters and fixed-wing aircraft, depending on requirements. For the former, the transceiver is typically carried in an externally mounted pod, while for the latter, it is generally mounted internally. Typical aircraft altitudes are in the 200-500 meter range. An optical scanner provides coverage of a broad swath under the aircraft track. Scan patterns vary from system to system; with semi-circular, rectangular, and elliptical scans in use. The scan patterns must be automatically compensated in real time for variations in aircraft roll and pitch in order to yield swaths with straight edges and even spot spacing. This can be accomplished with a mirror servoed in two axes under computer control with compensation for attitude measurements or with a scanner mounted on a gyroscopically stabilized platform.

The maximum scanner nadir angles in use are 15-22 degrees; this leads to surveyed swaths with widths from fifty to eighty percent of the aircraft altitude. Larger angles would cause unacceptably large pulse timing errors in both surface and bottom returns due to the more extreme geometry. Coverage is dense; surveys are performed with soundings spaced in a regular pattern. The densities vary from system to system. Nominal spacings for current-generation systems range from two to ten meters. These densities are achieved with laser pulse-repetition rates from 168 to 5000 pulses per second or more. Higher sounding densities from the same pulse rates may be utilized for special purposes with a corresponding decrease in swath width and increase in survey cost. All current systems have the capability to vary sounding density within certain limits. An example of SHOALS data collection with a constant nadir angle and 4-m spacing is seen in Figure 8.4.

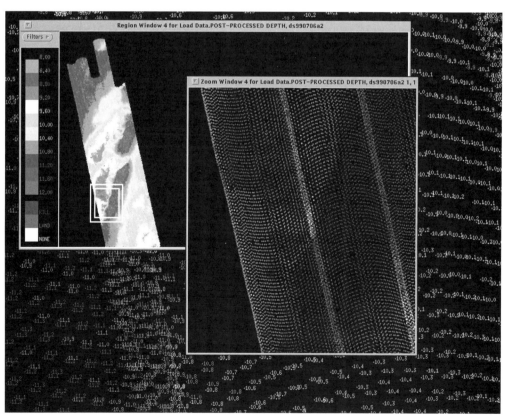

Figure 8.4 Example of region and zoom displays of overlapping swaths flown in opposite directions with semi-circular scan and nearly constant nadir angle. See color plate in Appendix C.

The laser currently used universally is a solid-state Nd:YAG source which produces radiation at an IR wavelength of 1064 nanometers (nm). That wavelength is appropriate and used for one type of surface detection. The bonus is that a fraction of the IR laser output can be diverted and frequency doubled, in a crystal with nonlinear optical properties, to produce a simultaneous output at 532 nm, which is the green light needed for penetration of the water column. Recent laser systems are diode pumped, rather than flashlamp pumped, to provide smaller size, much better electrical efficiency, and longer lifetimes. All systems are carefully designed to be eye-safe at operational altitudes; typical green pulse energies are on the order of 5 millijoules, except for EAARL. Accurate depth measurement requires reasonably-narrow temporal pulse widths; customary values are under 7 ns, the smaller the better. For a given spatial sounding density requirement, the area that can be covered per unit time depends on the laser pulse-repetition rate. Higher rates permit faster aircraft speeds, higher altitudes, and lower survey costs, or higher survey densities important for small-object detection. This combination of pulse energy and width is not an easy set of requirements for laser manufacturers to meet at the higher pulse rates noted above.

The laser pulses reflected at two or three different wavelengths from the water surface, near surface, and sea bottom are detected in the airborne receiver. A typical lidar receiver consists of a telescope, various optical filters and field-of-view controls, light detectors, amplifiers, analog surface-detection logic for real-time system control, a digitizer, and a magnetic storage device or removable hard drive. Both the transmitter and receiver are operated under detailed computer control. Light at different wavelengths is split into separate channels for independent detection and timing. Two types of light detectors, photomultiplier tubes (PMT's) and avalanche photodiodes (APD's), are in common use, and a typical receiver may contain both. Details of receiver design vary widely between systems because various approaches are taken in solving the problems associated with handling the extremely large amplitude dynamic range between strong surface reflections and weak bottom returns. Some systems utilize multiple channels and, possibly, logarithmic amplifiers for this purpose, while others use gain-controlled PMT's. The returning pulse waveforms are digitized in one or two-nanosecond increments and stored on magnetic media, along with a great deal of supporting data, for processing after acquisition, typically on the ground.

Because of the complexity of the environment and of the interactions of the lidar beam with the environment (such as returns from fish and underwater scattering layers), it has not been possible to calculate all depths with highest accuracy and reliability in the air in real time. Approximate depths are calculated in real time for feedback to the system operators for quality-control purposes, but precise depths, involving more-detailed calculations and a limited amount of manual intervention for difficult cases, are determined on the ground via post-flight processing of digitized and stored waveforms. In some systems, a down-looking video or digital camera is used to provide a permanent record of the survey area to assist hydrographers in the identification of shoreline phenomena, engineering structures, navigation aids, and the origin of anomalous data.

For the interested reader, a complete technology overview is included in Guenther (2000). This includes more detailed information on the selection and effects of the beam nadir angle, handling the amplitude dynamic range, parameter measurement accuracy requirements, waveform recording, the scanner, vertical references, the use of a vertical accelerometer, and other optics and electronics considerations.

Performance

Coverage Rate

The single most obvious benefit of ALB is coverage rate. Gross coverage rates, in units such as km²/hour, are easily calculated as the flight speed times the swath width. The less obvious but controlling factors are the required survey density and the available laser pulse-repetition rate. These two quantities determine the speeds and swath widths that can be used. Two bounding examples will be given. On the low end, one can consider a system with a 100-kt speed and a 110-m swath width that yields a gross survey rate of 5670 m²/sec which is equivalent to 20.4 km²/hour. This is easily ten times the rate that could be achieved with a multibeam sonar system. On the high side, a 175-kt speed with a 240-m swath gives nearly 78 km²/hour, an additional factor of 3.8. The value of this technology is very apparent.

At the present time, the performance of the systems in the field falls within these bounds. Net coverage rates depend on many factors such as swath overlap, flight-line length and time spent in turns, airspace restrictions, and percentage of reflies needed. For a typical day's work of one 6-hour mission or two 3-hour missions with a 20% overlap and a conservative 65% on-line fraction, between 64 km² and 243 km² can be surveyed per day. Longer flightlines with more time on target will increase these to even larger values. If the detection of small objects on the bottom is required, surveys may have to be flown much slower with a special scanner pattern, or multiple coverage may be required, to achieve higher sounding densities. For cases such as these, the productivity of shallow-water multibeam sonar surveys is greatly reduced, as well (Skogvik and Axelsson, 2001).

Vertical Accuracy

The results from lidar surveys have been compared with sonar surveys many times, by many different organizations, with excellent results. Results for LADS systems, for example, have been described on a number of occasions (Setter and Willis, 1994; Nairn, 1994; Sinclair and Spurling, 1997; Sinclair, 1999a). Perry (1999) reports 95% of soundings within 0.24 meters for a LADS Mk II benchmark of 84,500 points for depths ranging from 6-30 meters. This significantly exceeds IHO Order-1 vertical accuracy requirements of 0.50 m.

First field trials of the SHOALS system (Lillycrop et al., 1994; Lillycrop and Estep, 1995) revealed very accurate performance, and only a few small adjustments were required. Subsequently, SHOALS results were compared with an operational NOAA, National Ocean Service sonar survey (Riley, 1995) in Tampa Bay (Florida) to 20-m depths. The accuracy of SHOALS for that test was determined to be 0.28 meters at the 95% confidence level. This also greatly exceeds IHO Order-1 requirements. In a shallow-water comparison with data from the U.S. Army Corps of Engineers (USACE) "coastal research amphibious buggy" (CRAB) mobile reference platform at Duck, NC, the SHOALS results were even better (Lillycrop et al., 1997). SHOALS topographic accuracy was confirmed over an optical test facility at the Stennis Space Center (Mississippi). The accuracy of Hawk Eye for a variety of trials over natural sea bottoms and large man-made targets, as described by Steinvall and Koppari (1996), like that for SHOALS, was reported to be 0.28 meters at the 95% confidence level, well within IHO requirements. Field trials for the U.S. Naval Oceanographic Office Compact Hydrographic Airborne Rapid Total Survey (CHARTS) system included accuracy assessments for the SHOALS-1000 and SHOALS-3000 (Wozencraft and Lillycrop, 2006). Accuracy of both systems over a depth range from 7 to 50 meters is 0.30 meters at the 95 % confidence level. Topographic accuracy of both systems is better than 0.15 meters for both the infrared and green lasers. Tests of the Japan Coast Guard SHOALS-1000 in Japan demonstrated horizontal and vertical accuracy results well within IHO requirements for bathymetry and topography (Iwamoto et al., 2004). Independent accuracy tests of the SHOALS-1000T carried out by Fugro Pelagos (Lockhart et al., 2005) indicate lidar depths matching the multibeam control results to within IHO accuracy requirements at the 98% level for normal bottoms and 93-94% with wrecks included. In general, accuracy in ALB systems is maintained operationally by various combinations of daily benchmark comparisons or comparisons of depths in swath overlaps and crosslines, automated software quality-assessment routines, and regular checks of absolute system timing and angle calibrations.

It should be noted that, in general, the accuracy of any ALB system degrades somewhat from the above values for cases of weak signals near the penetration limit, for situations with extremely dirty water, and for depths associated with steeply sloping bottoms and small targets. The environmental problems are avoided by appropriate survey management.

Steep bottom slopes represent a geometry problem and a vertical and horizontal measurement problem for lidar as they do for sonar. Because of the finite beam width, the tendency is to bias the depth toward the shoalest point in the beam, while horizontally the slope moves slightly away from its true location. Results will also vary somewhat depending on the direction of flight with respect to the slope because of the off-nadir beam angle (Steinvall and Koppari, 1996). Extremely sophisticated algorithms would be needed to improve performance for this case. Perhaps a better way of looking at the situation is to consider that, for the most part, the error is not really a vertical error, but just a slight horizontal displacement of an otherwise accurate vertical measurement. The horizontal accuracy requirements are generally forgiving enough to accept this shift without a problem. This can, however, cause a problem with volume measurements in channels with steep sides and with the apparent size and location of engineering structures. These errors can be compensated for with appropriate software.

Small objects pose a particularly difficult situation. The maximum detection depth of small objects on the bottom is less than the detection depth of the underlying bottom. This fact must be taken into careful consideration by the survey manager. The depth-measurement accuracy of the objects is somewhat less than for that of the underlying bottom because of geometric effects involving the finite beam size and the uncertain (random) location of the object within the beam spot.

The hydrographers of Australia, Sweden, Canada, Mexico, New Zealand, Indonesia, Norway, Japan, and the U.S., to name just a few, have demonstrated by their actions that they are convinced that the accuracy of a well-designed and properly-operated ALH system can meet required accuracy standards.

Horizontal Accuracy

The location of the sounding is based on three components: the location of the aircraft, the location of the lidar surface spot with respect to the aircraft, and the location of the bottom sounding with respect to the surface spot location. The location of the aircraft is determined by whatever variant of GPS is required to meet survey needs. Practical details are discussed later under "Operational Considerations". The location of the surface spot with respect to the aircraft location is known with very high accuracy by default because it depends on the nadir angle of the lidar beam and the aircraft altitude above the water surface. Both of these quantities are known to high accuracy because they are crucial to the vertical measurement accuracy of the system, which is far more stringent than the horizontal accuracy requirement. One would not expect this component to exceed ± 0.20 m RMS in a well-designed system.

The effective location of the sounding on the sea bottom relative to the surface spot location is a far more complex situation because it is subject to uncertainties related to surface waves, the effect of water clarity on beam propagation through the water column, and bottom topography. Wave slope effects and water column scattering can increase horizontal error. The existence of bottom features with high relief can also contribute unique horizontal biases for individual soundings.

Surface waves affect the direction of beam entry through the water surface on a pulse-to-pulse basis. The mean direction is the same as for a flat surface, and the RMS variation is a function of the beam nadir angle arriving at the surface and RMS wave slopes which vary with wind speed and fetch. There are also factors related to the relative size of the laser spot diameter at the surface, compared to the wavelengths of the water waves, which make it difficult to achieve a precise error estimate. Based on airborne measurements of RMS gravity-wave slopes by Cox and Munk (1954), a reasonable horizontal error estimate for a 20-degree nadir angle and 10-knot winds is ± 0.36 m RMS per ten meters of depth. These are random errors from pulse to pulse.

The effects of scattering in the water column have been described above and pictured in Fig. 8.3. Because the photon paths in the region undercutting the unscattered ray from the surface to the bottom are shorter, they encounter less total path attenuation. This causes the spatial energy peak, and hence the effective sounding location, to be located in the undercutting region. The magnitude of the shift of the effective sounding location from the unscattered ray for a flat surface depends on various water clarity parameters (such as the scattering phase function and the single-scattering albedo) and depth. Because these water clarity parameters cannot be known from the air, the exact sounding location is a bit uncertain. For constant or slowly-varying water clarity conditions, this horizontal error will be a bias. The magnitude of this shift has been predicted by Monte Carlo simulation for various water clarity conditions. The value of the predicted mean shift, averaged over bounding water clarity conditions, can be applied as a horizontal bias corrector leaving the variation about the mean as a residual bipolar uncertainty of reduced magnitude. Depending on circumstances, recommended mean shift magnitudes are on the order of 10%-30% of the distance from the unscattered ray to the nadir point. Residual horizontal errors after the bias correction, which increase linearly with depth, are estimated at ±0.32 m RMS per ten meters of depth. These are bias errors that are constant from pulse to pulse and vary only with water clarity properties. The quoted variation relates to the statistical uncertainty of the water clarity.

The net result of the above effects, on a windy day at a 30-m depth, for example, with software that applies an appropriate predicted horizontal bias corrector for scattering, is an expected bias error on the order of ±1 m RMS and an expected random error of 1 m RMS. For most applications, these errors are well within the overall horizontal error budget.

For low-density surveys, the apparent location of a small object on the bottom detected only in the off-axis part of a single laser footprint could be shifted by several meters from its true position. For survey density appropriate to the accuracy and scale of the survey, that same object will be irradiated on-axis by a neighboring pulse and properly located to within the above tolerances. The net effect will be to slightly magnify the horizontal extent of the object.

Limitations

The limitations, as seen below, have proven to be operationally acceptable and, for the most part, pose no more than logistical problems that are dealt with by appropriate planning and survey management.

Water Clarity

The most significant limitation for ALB systems is water clarity, which limits the maximum surveyable depths (Guenther and Goodman, 1978). The maximum surveyable depth is the greatest depth, at a given time and location, for which depth measurements can be obtained whose accuracy meets obligatory standards. This requires that the bottom-return signals be reasonably strong and free from excessive noise so that their arrival times can be accurately estimated. This depth will be somewhat less than the greatest depth from which weak, noisy lumps of bottom-return energy are barely detectable in the signal waveforms. The maximum surveyable depth depends on a number of system hardware, software, and logistical parameters in addition to environmental conditions. The former include such items as green laser-pulse energy and width, receiver optical bandwidth, aperture, and field of view, optical system efficiency, electronic noise figures, and flight altitude. The latter are primarily water clarity, bottom reflectivity, and solar background. Of the environmental factors, water clarity is by far the more important because it enters as a negative exponential factor, while bottom reflectivity is a linear factor.

For a typical, eye-safe system, maximum surveyable depths range from greater than 50 meters in very clean offshore waters to less than 10 meters in murky near-shore waters. For extremely turbid conditions, surveying may not be possible. It is not uncommon, in a given area, to be able to survey in deeper water and not in the shallowest water because the water is typically much clearer farther from shore. As a rule of thumb, for a full-capability system, one can expect successful operations to depths between 2 and 3 times the Secchi depth. [The Secchi depth is an old and intuitive water clarity measure which is the depth at which a standard white (or black and white) disc, deployed over the side of a boat, is no longer visible to the human eye (Tyler, 1968).] The Secchi depth is not a particularly good predictor of performance, however, because its relationship to the proper optical parameter, the diffuse attenuation coefficient, varies with the scattering-to-absorption ratio of the water (Gordon and Wouters, 1978). The factor of two applies where the water has a significant amount of absorption (which reduces energy), while the factor of three is appropriate for waters dominated by scattering (which redistributes energy). The ratio of scattering to absorption in sea water depends on the quantities and types of suspended organic and inorganic particulates and on the amount of dissolved organic material in the water. This varies strongly with location, season, tidal cycle phase, and weather.

In the more specific terms of ocean optics, the water property which most nearly dictates the received bottom-return pulse energy in a well-designed, full-capability ALB system is the "diffuse attenuation coefficient", "K", at the green laser wavelength. The concepts surrounding various definitions and measures of K are far too complex to describe here (Gordon et al., 1975; Gordon, 1989), but in simple terms, K is the exponential factor by which the downwelling vector irradiance of the incident light field, at a given wavelength, decreases with increasing depth. The bottom-return peak power, typically used in ALB pulse detections, decreases slightly more rapidly than pulse energy with increasing depth due to pulse stretching caused by scattering (Guenther, 1985). The value of K is very different from the so-called "beam attenuation coefficient", c, which is the sum of the scattering and absorption coefficients. For a full-capability system, c is not a good measure of the maximum surveyable depth. [The ratio K/c, is always less than unity and for green light typically ranges between one-sixth and one-half for coastal waters. It depends strongly on the scattering-to-absorption ratio of the water column (Timofeyeva and Gorobets, 1967), often expressed in terms of the so-called "single-scattering albedo", and also, to a lesser extent, on the scattering "phase function" (Guenther, 1985).]

If the receiver field of view (FOV) is sufficient, at the given altitude and depth, to integrate a major fraction of the returning bottom-reflected energy, the system attenuation coefficient for pulse energy, "k", will approach K (Krumboltz, 1979; Steinvall et al., 1992). If the FOV is insuffi-cient, k tends in the direction of the larger value of c (Gordon, 1982), and a potentially severe depth penalty will result. The EAARL system was purposely designed in this small-FOV regime for certain practical reasons (Feygels et al., 2003), and it is for this specific reason that EAARL is not a "full-capability" system in terms of maximum penetration depths.

The maximum surveyable depth for a given water clarity can be expressed roughly as n/K, where "n" is a constant. For typical, eye-safe ALB systems, under customary operational circum-stances, the value of n will be around 3 to 4 for daytime operation and perhaps 5 at night (Guenther, 1985) but with smaller values for the detection of small objects on the bottom (Engstrom and Axelsson, 2001). In other words, if, for example, the water clarity can be expressed in terms of a value of $K=0.1$ m^{-1}, then one would expect to be able to survey to a depth of 30-40 meters during the daytime. The daytime value of n depends on the extent of solar background and sun glint present during operations and on the optical filter bandwidth of the system. Nighttime operation is preferred from a performance standpoint, because there is no sun glint to avoid, and the shot noise associated with the ambient, reflected solar background in the optical filter bandwidth is absent. Flying at night for extended periods, at low altitude over water, however, may be taxing on pilots, and can be more dangerous, particularly near land. For safety and practicality, most operations are consequently conducted during the daytime, with concomitant reduction in performance.

In many areas, if the water is too dirty for a survey to be successfully performed on a given day, it may only be necessary to return to that site at a different tidal phase, or several days later when the weather has changed, to find acceptably clear water. This is one of the logistics factors that must be managed in survey planning for ALB systems. Given that many government agencies involved in bathymetric surveying have a large hydrographic backlog in areas with moderately clear waters, as well as the need for periodic monitoring in sites with dynamic bottoms, there is more than enough work within these water clarity limits for a number of ALB systems (Lillycrop et al., 1995).

Small-Object Detection

The use for which current ALB systems are not appropriate is in proving, beyond any doubt, that a navigation channel is free of small objects on the bottom with a size on the order of a 1-meter cube or slightly larger. ALB is not a substitute for side scan sonar. Its spatial resolution is not as good as for modern high-frequency sonars, and some small targets may not be detected, even if illuminated (Guenther et al, 1996). The problem is that it is either difficult or impossible, depending on which part of the laser beam hits the target, to resolve the small target return in the presence of the much stronger and immediately following bottom return. To be confidently detected, the small target must be in the part of the illuminated bottom area closest to the aircraft where the light path-lengths are shorter than those for the remainder of the bottom return energy. Such objects may not be detected at all for the case of near-nadir beam angles as used by the LADS systems.

The standard, and most-effective, approach for increasing the detection probability for small objects is to significantly increase the survey density. This technique is expensive and does not guarantee 100% detection unless the density becomes extremely high. In general, objects with a combination of larger surface areas and smaller heights (than a one-meter cube) are well detected, as are objects with reasonably small areas and larger heights (Guenther et al., 1996). This is true because the target returns for such cases are better separated from the sea bottom returns. Small-object detection probabilities become smaller with increasing depth more rapidly than the bottom-return probabilities, even if water clarity is sufficient, because the ratio of object size to bottom illuminated area decreases as the laser pulse expands geometrically. The maximum depth to which a small object can be reliably detected is not nearly as great as the depth to which a relatively flat bottom can be detected. Survey plans and parameters must be adjusted according to object-detection requirements (Engstrom and Axelsson, 2001). For example, this problem can be mildly ameliorated by using a small receiver field of view (Steinvall and Koppari, 1996), but that is an expensive solution because it increases the spot density requirement and reduces the maximum penetration depth for flat bottoms.

The reliable detection of small objects on the sea bottom depends on a properly designed lidar transceiver, sophisticated automated pulse-processing software, a well-designed survey strategy, knowledge of system hardware and software capabilities, well-trained and experienced human data processors, and a knowledgeable and attentive survey manager. A failure in even one of these areas could result in a large object being missed. Such an oversight would not be a failure of ALB, but, rather, a failure of implementation.

It should be noted that multibeam sonars, by themselves, have the same problem in that it is also difficult for them to detect one-meter cubes on the bottom (Hughes Clark et al., 1999) for similar reasons. Modern channel-clearance surveys, such as done by the U.S. National Ocean Service, for example, require waterborne sonar using a combination of multibeam and redundant side scan techniques.

Logistics

Environmental factors, other than water clarity, which can cause problems with ALB surveys include rain, fog, low clouds, high winds, high waves, surf zone, sun glint, very steep slopes, and kelp beds (Steinvall et al., 1994; Guenther, 1985; Nairn, 1994). Surveys are not generally conducted in the rain because the laser beam is severely backscattered to the receiver by the raindrops. The ALB technique does not operate through fog or clouds. A notable exception, however, is the typical wisps of morning mist ("sea smoke") which can form at a few meters' height over calm water. Systems using only IR or green surface returns will not perform well here because these signals are backscattered by the mist, and this can result in false surface heights. A system such as SHOALS with a red channel to receive water Raman backscatter and laser-induced fluores-cence can effectively see through light mists without degradation in performance because the concentration of water molecules in the mist is much lower than in the underlying liquid water. Heavy sea smoke would degrade performance by reducing green signal strengths. Tropical clouds can often be defeated by lowering the flight altitude below 500 meters.

High winds are bad for several reasons. First, they can pose a danger to the aircraft, particularly when flying near coastal mountain cliffs. High tail winds can also pose a problem if the aircraft is attempting to survey at a ground speed near its stall speed. Second, they cause whitecaps and large waves that can cause false land detections and degrade system penetration and accuracy. Third, they create a spray of water drops above the surface that, like mist, can cause false surface returns at IR and green wavelengths. This is not a problem for a red channel for water Raman backscatter because, again, the water molecule concentration is too low to create a false detection. Fourth, strong headwinds and tailwinds can cause changes in survey density if the pilots fly by airspeed instead of ground speed.

Low winds can also be a problem because capillary waves are needed to reflect the off-nadir laser energy from the water surface back to the airborne receiver. Without sufficient wind, the capillary wave slopes are insufficient for this need, and as the interface becomes glassy, the IR and green interface returns will become unusably weak at larger nadir angles. Again, this is not a problem for a system like SHOALS with a red surface channel, because the water Raman returns are received regardless of wind or wave structure (Guenther et al., 1994). Conversely, with the glassy case, near-nadir green and IR interface returns can be virtually mirror-like and so excessively strong (Petri, 1977) that they can saturate the receiver and possibly cause anomalous pulses in the green PMT. This is not generally a problem for systems that utilize larger, nearly constant nadir angles.

Large wave heights and wave lengths pose problems, both directly and indirectly, for several reasons. As wave heights grow, the accuracy of the measurements of the mean water level and the local wave heights degrade, regardless of the surface detection technique. This reduces the accuracy of the resulting depth or elevation measurements. Larger wave slopes also affect the direction of the beam as it passes through the interface and add an additional small random depth error. Perhaps the biggest problem with large waves is that they tend to stir up loose bottom sediments and cause a significant decrease in water clarity which may prevent sufficient penetration or which can add a scattering layer above the bottom which can be falsely detected as the bottom. Interestingly, SHOALS was able to operate successfully in Portugal when the winds and waves were so great that they forced the survey boats to remain in port (Lillycrop et al., 2000).

Very long wavelengths (swell), can cause a problem with the determination of the mean water level because of the difficulty of sufficient sampling. This is more of a problem for a system like LADS which determines the mean water level by averaging across the swath (Penny, 1992) than for SHOALS which uses a vertical accelerometer and averages a longer and adjustable distance along the swath (Guenther et al., 2000). Swell is not a problem if KGPS/OTF is used as the vertical reference instead of the mean water level. The surf zone is a particularly difficult area in which to work because of the large quantities of foam which can give false land indications, the resuspended bottom material which can make the water virtually opaque, and the fact that the correct mean water level is difficult to discern.

Sun glint is a noise source that, if sufficiently strong, can effectively blind the airborne receiver. For this reason, operations are sometimes scheduled to avoid flight times around local noon. LADS, for example, flies its missions in the late afternoon and early evening (Sinclair and Spurling, 1997). A properly designed receiver, however, can work successfully in moderate glint if the bottom return signal strength is sufficient.

Underwater masses of kelp growing from the bottom toward the surface provide strong false returns throughout the water column and, when dense, are nearly impossible to penetrate to the bottom. Sonar has a similar problem, plus the danger of vessel entanglement. It is possible at least to delineate the boundaries of the kelp beds. Less obtrusive but nevertheless dense bottom vegetation may be detected and may cause a slight shoal bias depending on height, density, and reflectivity.

CURRENT OPERATING STATUS

Background

As of Spring 2006, eight systems (LADS, LADS Mk II, EAARL, three SHOALS-1000s, CHARTS, and Hawk Eye II) are in active use around the world. These systems, based on three differing technical design philosophies, have all proven to be highly effective, and they demonstrate excellent accuracy. By adding succeeding generations, the venerable LADS and SHOALS systems have been providing operational hydrographic and bathymetric surveys virtually full-time for 13 and 12 years, respectively. EAARL has been in operation for the past 5 years, collecting shallow-water bathymetry and topography for projects like coral reef and post-hurricane mapping. The new Hawk Eye II has recently joined the ranks of available systems.

On the other hand, it is important to note that ALB remains a youthful technique that utilizes state-of-the-art technology and requires knowledgeable implementation. It is far from mature, and a new generation of systems and techniques is now being initiated which will improve performance and availability even more.

The growing list of sites successfully surveyed to date, using the operational systems described below, includes the Northwest Territories of Canada, many of the coastal areas of Australia including the Coral Sea, the Timor Sea, the Gulf of Carpentaria, and the Great Southern Ocean, the East and West coasts of Canada, the East, West, and Gulf coasts of the United States, the Great Lakes, the St. Lawrence River, Sweden, New Zealand, Indonesia, Mexico, Barbados, Alaska, Norway, six of the Hawaiian Islands, the Bahamas, Puerto Rico, the United Arab Emirates, Portugal, the Madeira Islands, Lake Tahoe, Finland, Guam, American Samoa, Wake Island, the Republic of Marshall Islands, the Commonwealth of Northern Mariana Islands, the Federated Sates of Micronesia, the Republic of Palau, the Australian Antarctic Territory, the United Kingdom, Honduras, Okinawa, Kenya, Philippines, Israel, Japan, and Montserrat. Since 1993, LADS has been used to survey over 100,000 km^2 in Australia alone; this is at least 50% of the total area surveyed by the Royal Australian Navy Hydrographic Service in Australian waters each year (Sinclair, 1999c). It is fair to say that coverage is world wide, extensive, and expanding.

LADS (Laser Airborne Depth Sounder)

In 1971, only about 15% of the Australian continental shelf, the critical area for safe navigation, was charted to modern standards (Setter and Willis, 1994). The estimated backlog was 50 survey years using conventional ship-based acoustic equipment. Half of this area has depths less than 50 meters, and one quarter is less than 30 meters. In 1972, CAPT J.H.S. Osborn, the far-sighted Hydrographer of the Royal Australian Navy (RAN), asked the Department of Defence's Weapons Research Establishment (later the Electronics Research Laboratory of the Defence Science and Technology Organisation) in Salisbury, South Australia to evaluate whether an airborne lidar system could be used for accurate, high-speed surveying in shallow water. Two successful prototypes, WRELADS I (Abbot and Penny, 1975) and WRELADS II (Penny et al., 1986), were subsequently developed in Salisbury under the direction of Mike Penny.

In 1989, a contract was awarded to BHP Engineering Pty. Ltd. and to Vision Systems Ltd. of Australia to develop a turn-key, operational system from the WRELADS II design. In January 1993, LADS entered service in the RAN, internally mounted in a dedicated Fokker F-27 500-series aircraft (Nairn, 1994). LADS is operated by the RAN LADS Flight with logistics support from the system manufacturer, Tenix LADS Corporation Ltd. (formerly BHP/Visions Systems), a wholly owned subsidiary of Tenix Defence Systems Pty. Ltd. LADS operations are conducted solely by and for the RAN which uses LADS data in the production of Australia's IHO-compliant chart series. The use of LADS, in conjunction with the RAN surface fleet, will reduce the survey backlog to an estimated 15 years (Sinclair, 1999a). LADS surveys at 20 times the rate of conventional surface vessels. While surveying half of the total area surveyed by the RAN, it was found to be four times more cost effective than the surface fleet on an absolute basis, not taking into consideration the added difficulty of the shallower survey areas.

LADS uses a 168-pps laser to provide a sounding spacing of 10 meters in a 240-m swath width from a 500-m altitude. At a speed of 75 m/s, this yields a gross area coverage of 50 km^2 per hour. The scanner was augmented to permit 3-m and 5-m spacing across the scan, at reduced swath widths, for more detailed investigation of least depths on critical shoals (Sinclair and Spurling, 1997). The system has green and IR channels, and the design involves the use of a scanning green beam and a vertically-fixed IR beam, both transmitted from a gyroscopically-stabilized platform (Penny et al., 1989). The scan pattern is rectangular with a widely-varying nadir angle whose maximum value is 15 degrees. The IR beam is used for surface detection, while the green beam is used for bottom detection and to augment surface detection. The digitizer has 2-ns time bins with 6 bits of amplitude resolution. Positioning is by P-code GPS.

On one of its first RAN shakedown test flights in Spencer Gulf, LADS discovered a dangerous and previously uncharted granite pinnacle rising to an 11.9-m depth from an otherwise flat, 20-m bottom. The feature was first designated "Laser Shoal" and then, more aptly, renamed Penny Shoal. This sophisticated and reliable system has surveyed an estimated 10,000 km^2 per year in Australia. Much of this area is strewn with dangerous reefs that would have been difficult to survey in any other way.

LADS Mark II

A significantly upgraded version of LADS, named the LADS Mk II, was developed as a commercial system to meet government and industry needs. Built by Vision System's LADS Corporation, now owned by Tenix Defence Systems, it provides fixed-price contract surveys. It has been operational since 1998 in a relatively-large, fast deHavilland Dash 8-202 aircraft that has the capacity to deploy world-wide and execute long survey sorties or transit long distances to remote survey sites (Spurling and Perry, 1997; Sinclair, 1997). The aircraft flies at a transit speed of 250 knots at altitudes up to 25,000 feet, with an endurance of up to eight hours, and a transit range of 2000 nautical miles. Survey operations are conducted from altitudes between 400 m and 700 m at ground speeds between 140 and 210 knots.

The basic design configuration is the same as LADS, with a vertical IR beam and a rectangularly-scanned green beam. As with all current ALB systems, LADS Mk II consists of airborne data collection and ground-based data-processing subsystems. The design has been augmented with a great deal of newer technology and has benefited from many lessons learned by operating the RAN LADS. It has an improved laser, computer, and navigation technology enabling the collection of higher-density data at deeper depths and at higher productivity, and the depth accuracy has been improved to meet IHO Order-1 standards for depth, position, and target detection (Sinclair et al., 1999). Maximum depths of roughly 70 meters can be measured in extraordinarily clear water. KGPS capability (Sinclair et al., 1999) and topographic ability (Wellington, 2001b) have been added.

The survey planning and data processing requirements for LADS Mk II surveys have evolved as a result of the huge RAN LADS output and the differing requirements and survey standards of the contract survey customers. These challenges have required continued improvements in survey planning, data collection, data processing, data validation procedures, quality control, data output formats, and data visualization. The data processing to data collection ratio is better than 1:1.

The wide range of hydrographic applications of ALB systems can be demonstrated by reviewing LADS Mk II survey operations during the first six months of 2002. It conducted surveys for users engaged in oil and gas development, coastal zone management, and nautical charting. Survey operations were conducted in both the northern and southern hemispheres, including the North West Shelf of Western Australia, the Norwegian Sea, Qatar in the Middle East, and the Irish Sea (Sinclair, 2002). Environmental conditions ranged from -10° C overnight in Stavanger, Norway to 50° C on the tarmac in Doha, Qatar. The system recorded depths to 50 meters in the cold Norwegian Sea and 35 meters in the hot waters of the Arabian Gulf. Over the years, surveys have also been conducted in a wide range of conditions and other locations such as the other coasts of Australia (Wellington, 2001a), New Zealand, the Australian Antarctic Territory, Finland, Alaska (Sinclair, 2004), Connecticut (Sinclair, 2005), the Canary Islands, Florida, Scotland, Italy, Dubai, and Bermuda.

A Nd:YAG laser, riding on a stabilized platform, operates at a 900-pps rate and is set to provide 5 x 5 meter laser spot spacing in the main line sounding mode of operation across a swath width of 240 meters. For a typical 88-m/s aircraft speed, this yields a survey rate of 64 km²/hour. The electro-mechanical scanner can also provide higher-density modes of operation with laser spot spacings of 4 x 4, 3 x 3 and 2 x 2 meters, according to survey requirements, at reduced swath widths, as well as a 6 x 6 meter reconnaissance mode. Returning green laser energy from the sea surface and the sea floor is captured by the green receiver and digitized and logged onto digital linear tape. The broad infrared laser return determines the height of the aircraft, supplemented by an AHRS inertial height reference and KGPS height. The LADS Mk II system can operate by day and night; operations at night are enhanced by the removal of the day-filter from the receiving optics to improve the optical efficiency. Real-time positioning is provided by WADGPS, and raw GPS (since "selective availability" was turned off on 1 May 2000). Off-line GPS signal logging for use in determining post-processed DGPS and KGPS positions is also included (Sinclair, 2005). The ground-based data processing subsystem consists of a portable Compaq Alpha Server ES40 that can be transported in the aircraft to the deployment site.

SHOALS (Scanning Hydrographic Operational Airborne Lidar Survey)-1000

The USACE operates and maintains thousands of miles of navigation channels throughout the U.S. In the late 1980's, it initiated a development program to produce the SHOALS system (Lillycrop, et al. 1996; Guenther, et al., 1996; Lillycrop et al., 1997). SHOALS systems are built and maintained by Optech Incorporated, Toronto, Ontario, Canada. The SHOALS-200 began survey operations in 1994, and it was upgraded to the SHOALS-400, with a doubled pulse rate and new capabilities such as KGPS, in 1998. Many hundreds of projects were surveyed world wide for a variety of customers and applications from the Great Lakes (Mohr et al., 1999) to New Zealand (Graham et al., 1999), from the Bahamas (West and Lillycrop, 1999) to Hawaii (West, 2001), from Lake Tahoe (West et al, 2001a) to Portugal (Lillycrop et al., 2000), and from Mexico (Pope et al., 1997) and Puerto Rico (West et al., 2001a) to a long list of Pacific Islands. SHOALS-1000 is a further generational advancement of the original SHOALS technology, based on nine years of operations (Wozencraft and Lillycrop, 2003).

Design of the SHOALS-1000 focused on creating a more compact, lightweight, and portable system whose size and power requirements are conducive to operations on photogrammetric aircraft of opportunity, and to integration with other sensors. Digital, geo-referenced, RGB imagery captured at one frame per second replaces SHOALS analog down-look video. New flight planning and survey tracking software support operations. Redesigned data processing software requires less manual intervention from the survey engineers and maintains collection-to-processing ratios for the faster bathymetric laser and optional integrated topographic laser. New 3D data-editing tools improve visualization and speed during manual data cleaning.

SHOALS-1000 comprises a 1000-pps bathymetric laser and a DuncanTech (DT)-4000 digital camera (LaRocque et al., 2004). A 9000-pps topographic laser, technology similar to that discussed in Chapter 7 of this book, is available as an option. The topographic laser is integrated into the same hardware box as the bathymetric laser system and digital camera. The lasers share an optical path of scanners, mirrors, telescopes, and receivers, but do not operate at the same time. Typical operational altitudes have ranged between 300 and 400 meters, and the swath width is roughly three-fourths of the altitude. Standard survey densities are 2 to 5 meters according to customer needs. All survey scan patterns are of the form of a section of a circular arc, and the beam is maintained very nearly at a constant 20-degree nadir angle. The lidar and RGB imagery are located using an integrated Applanix Pos AV. Positioning may be accomplished using either pseudorange or carrier-phase based GPS techniques. At survey speeds from 125-180 knots, coverage rates range from 14 to 77 km²/hour depending on survey density.

The collinear laser design puts both green and IR beams at the same location on the surface. SHOALS has the unique capability of measuring Raman backscattering from the water, in conjunction with the infrared air/water interface reflection, to provide the most sophisticated and accurate water surface detection strategy of any ALB system (Guenther et al., 1994). Green surface returns are never used for depth calculation due to the inherent ambiguity of their origin. The receiver has four independent channels in which to measure surface and bottom returns: two green, one IR, and one red. The overlap areas provide an excellent ability to monitor system calibration. A special software algorithm permits acquisition of depths from the problematic region of less than one meter of water (Brooks et al., 1998; Millar et al., 2005). This permits seamless operation across the land/water boundary. The green channels are radiometrically calibrated to enable extraction of bottom reflectance from the lidar waveforms (Tuell et al., 2005b). The computer data-processing to data-acquisition ratio is better than 1:1.

Three SHOALS-1000 systems are currently operating: Fugro Pelagos makes SHOALS-1000 surveys available commercially; the Japan Coast Guard uses its SHOALS-1000 to support its charting mission; and one system is available for lease from the manufacturer. The SHOALS-1000 systems are operated to meet both USACE "Class 1" and IHO "Order 1" hydrographic accuracy standards for most applications.

CHARTS (Compact Hydrographic Airborne Rapid Total Survey)

CHARTS is the U.S. Naval Oceanographic Office program name for its airborne coastal mapping and charting sensor suite (West et al., 2001b; Heslin et al., 2003). CHARTS is technically a SHOALS-3000TH instrument that comprises an Optech SHOALS-3000T lidar and an ITRES Research Ltd. CASI-1500 hyperspectral imager. The SHOALS-3000T is itself an integrated instrument containing a 3000-pps bathymetric laser, a 20,000-pps topographic laser, and a DT-4000 RGB digital camera. The SHOALS-3000 is the same technology as the SHOALS-1000 described in the previous section, but the lasers and scanner operate at higher rates. The CASI-1500 is a visible/near-IR pushbroom hyperspectral instrument whose design was specified for integration with the CHARTS system. The SHOALS-3000 and CASI-1500 occupy a single rigid platform and view window in the aircraft, and the hyperspectral imagery is geo-referenced using the position/orientation data stream from the Pos AV in the SHOALS-3000. The SHOALS-3000 and CASI-1500 require separate operator consoles.

CHARTS is managed and operated by the Joint Airborne Lidar Bathymetry Technical Center of eXpertise (JALBTCX) in Kiln, MS. Surveys are conducted world wide. CHARTS collects lidar bathymetric soundings spaced from 2-5 meters and topographic lidar postings spaced from 1-2 meters. The DT-4000 captures one image every second with a ground resolution near 20 cm per pixel. Typical aircraft altitude (400 m) and flight speed (150 knots) result in more than 50% overlap between the images in the flight direction. The CASI-1500 features high spatial and spectral resolution from 0.25 m to 1.50 m and 288 bands, respectively. It is tuned to the marine environment, operating over 675 nm that is programmable between 375-1050 nm. The depth, water column attenuation, and bottom reflectance derived from the lidar data pulses are used to constrain the inversion of a radiative transfer model, resulting in bottom reflectance data of all bands of the hyperspectral imagery (Tuell and Park, 2004; Tuell et al., 2005c; Kopilevich et al., 2005).

EAARL (Experimental Advanced Airborne Research Lidar)

The NASA Experimental Advanced Airborne Research Lidar (EAARL) is a pulsed, blue-green airborne laser altimeter with capabilities for high-resolution surveys of emergent and submerged, shallow aquatic topography. It was developed by C. Wayne Wright at the NASA Wallops Flight Facility, Wallops Island, Virginia to map sandy beach topography, three-dimensional coastal vegetation structure, shallow bathymetry, coral communities, and near-shore benthic habitats simultaneously (Wright and Brock, 2002; Brock et al., 2004; Nayegandhi et al., 2005). Changes in these features can be detected by returning to sites on multiple occasions. [Much of the information in this section was obtained from a number of small articles at http://coastal.er.usgs.gov, the site of the USGS Center for Coastal & Watershed Studies.]

EAARL has been operational since the summer of 2001, when it surveyed the coral reef tract in the northern Florida Keys. Subsequently, surveys have been carried out in a variety of coastal communities around the Gulf of Mexico and in the Caribbean. EAARL data have been used extensively by the USGS and USACE for hurricane storm damage evaluation and response, respectively. In the 2004 and 2005 hurricane seasons, EAARL collected topographic data immediately before and after major storms.

EAARL represents a unique design philosophy for ALB. There are two main features that separate the EAARL from traditional airborne bathymetric lidars. It uses very-short, low-energy green laser pulses with a radically-narrowed receiver field of view (FOV) and produces 20-cm laser footprints at a nominal 2-m spacing at 300-m altitude and 97-knot flight speed. It operates at a single green wavelength (532 nm) with little of the traditional ambiguity in surface location detection because of the combination of 1.2-ns laser pulses and a 1.5 - 2-mr receiver field of view. The shorter pulse increases depth-measurement accuracy and enhances the pulse resolution, while the narrower receiver FOV aids in improving the spatial resolution of the bathymetric system while minimizing geometrically-induced temporal return pulse broadening. Moreover, the small FOV aids in rejecting ambient sunlight and also rejects laser light which has been widely scattered in the water column. The smaller FOV results in much less temporal broadening of the surface and bottom return pulses and therefore provides more precise determination of both surface and bottom temporal position within each laser return waveform, consequently improving the measurement accuracy.

On the other hand, the narrower receiver FOV inevitably causes a more rapid decay of the bottom-return signal amplitude with increasing depth and therefore a decrease in operational depth of the lidar (Feygels et al., 2003). Unfortunately, the small FOV and low pulse energy limit depth penetration for EAARL to roughly 1.5 Secchi-disc depths. Based on proof-of-concept tests performed over Carysfort Reef off the upper Florida Keys, the maximum EAARL survey depth should be on the order of 25 m under ideal, extremely-clear water conditions. The system can make a topographic range measurement with accuracy on the order of 2 - 5 cm, depending on variations in the target reflectivity from pulse to pulse. The lidar system was determined to be capable of separately ranging signal returns down to a minimum separation of about 0.5 m.

The EAARL sensor suite includes a water-penetrating, adaptive lidar transceiver, a down-looking RGB digital camera with 80-cm resolution operating at one picture per second, a 3-band multispectral, color/infrared camera with 20-cm resolution operating at one picture per second synchronized to the GPS, two precision dual-frequency, kinematic carrier-phase GPS receivers, and an integrated miniature digital inertial measurement unit that provide sub-meter geo-referencing of each laser sample. The nominal EAARL platform is a twin-engine Cessna-310 aircraft, but the instrument may be deployed on a range of light aircraft. A single pilot, a lidar operator, and a data analyst constitute the crew for most survey operations. Aircraft costs are reduced due to the compact design, low power requirement, and the substitution of an array of GPS antennas in the place of an Inertia Navigation System. All of these innovations minimize the airborne payload and enable the use of light aircraft that are commonly available at low cost.

EAARL's lidar is a raster-scanning, waveform-resolving system with the capability to detect, capture, and automatically adapt to each laser backscatter return in real time. Although the laser can operate up to 5000 pps, its pulse-repetition frequency is computer controlled and varied to produce nearly equal cross-track sample spacing, thus equalizing the sample density within the swath. The laser also concurrently generates a 3-ns, 1064-nm (IR) pulse that can be used to double the sample density for non-submerged topographic targets. The receiver system uses a "digitizer only" design which eliminates all hardware-based, high-speed, front-end electronics, start/stop detectors, time-interval units, and range gates, typically found in lidar systems. It can accommodate a large signal dynamic range through the use of multiple channels with high-speed waveform digitizers. It has the capability to sense the vertical complexity of the surface target "on the fly" during a given survey. This enables automatic, adaptive acquisition of dramatically different surface types, thereby reducing data volume over bare terrain while simultaneously enabling the capture of detailed reflected pulse waveforms over forests and shallow water. This makes it well suited for mapping emergent coastal vegetation, submerged coral reefs, and bright sandy beaches in a single flight.

Hawk Eye II

In the middle 1980's, the Swedish Defense Research Establishment (FOA) worked with Optech Incorporated to develop the FLASH airborne lidar system to evaluate object detection and the performance of emerging ALB technology (Steinvall et al., 1994). The success of this program led to development of two identical Hawk Eye systems, largely derived from the SHOALS design, in the early 1990's by Saab Instruments AB (later Saab Dynamics AB) and Optech Incorporated. The two pod-mounted systems were purchased by the Swedish Defence Material Administration (FMV) — one for the Royal Swedish Navy and one for the Swedish Maritime Administration. They were designed for helicopter operation in a Boeing Vertol and a Bell 212, and were deployed in 1994 and 1995 for the dual purposes of hydrography and submarine detection (Steinvall et al., 1997; Skogvik and Axelsson, 2001). These systems are no longer active.

Airborne Hydrography AB (AHAB) was formed as an employee buyout of the lidar work at Saab Dynamics AB to supply state-of-the-art laser bathymetry and terrestrial systems and hydrographic laser survey services. In 2004, AHAB and TopEye AB of Sweden and Admiralty Holdings Limited in the United Kingdom formed a unique collaboration, Admiralty Coastal Surveys AB (ACSAB), to create and produce an ALB and topography service based around their new Hawk Eye II lidar system. Admiralty Holdings Limited is a wholly government-owned subsidiary of the United Kingdom Hydrographic Office (UKHO) created to provide a route through which partnerships can be formed with industry. Blom ASA of Norway became a partner in ASCAB when it purchased TopEye in 2005.

Hawk Eye II Laser Bathymetry and Topography System was tested in 2005 and delivered to ASCAB in early 2006. Surveys have been performed in France, Germany, Denmark, Estonia, Norway, UK, and Sweden. The Hawk Eye II system is a considerable improvement on its forerunners. It simultaneously collects 4000-pps bathymetric soundings, 64,000-pps topographic soundings, and geo-referenced, high-resolution digital color images. The hydrographic and topographic lasers use the same 2-axis, servo-controlled scanner mirror. This large (25-cm diameter) mirror and sensitive receivers assure a great depth range. The mirror is geo-stabilized and compensates for flight deviations in roll, yaw, pitch, altitude, speed, and side position, to distribute the scan pattern optimally. This reduces the needed overlap between flight lines and minimizes the errors between the hydrographic and the topographic survey data. Operational altitudes for Hawk Eye II are between 200 and 450 meters, with a typical swath with of one-half of the altitude; the aircraft speed range is from zero to 250 knots. The bathymetric sounding density is programmable between 0.5 m and 3 m, depending on customer needs.

With a total system weight of less than 180 kg and electrical power consumption of less than 1.4 kW, Hawk Eye II is designed for easy installation in most small-to-medium, fixed-wing or rotary-wing aircraft. The system can be installed within one hour and is operated by one operator and one spotter. Hawk Eye II is delivered with the operator's console used for survey planning and airborne operation, and an extensive coastal-survey software package that includes advanced post-flight processing and data analysis and the costal survey viewer (a tool for the end customer). Specific software algorithms have been developed for detection of very shallow depths (less than 0.3 meters), which permits seamless presentation of the boundary between the topographic and bathymetric data.

Hawk Eye II enables ACSAB to provide fast and accurate surveys, with full coverage of shallow waters, land, coastlines, shores, and islands, crossing from one to the other in a single mission. Survey results fulfill IHO S44 Order-1 accuracy requirements.

Summary

In the first decade of the new millennium, the vintage LARSEN, augmented with the VideoMap digital camera system by Terra Remote Sensing Inc., succumbed to Moore's Law and flew its last mission. LADS, fully and heavily utilized by the Royal Australian Navy in reducing the survey backlog on the Great Barrier Reef, is in need of replacement. SHOALS-1000, CHARTS, LADS Mk II, and Hawk Eye II, representing the current generation of full-capability lidar bathymeters, are fully involved around the world providing hydrography and a wide variety of related bathymetric services and products, as noted in the User Applications section, for a variety of customers. EAARL is used to support the coastal change and coastal mapping initiatives of the US Geological Survey.

Because the uses of these systems are so varied, it is difficult to select an example of a typical product. As one sample, Figure 8.5 provides a small-scale presentation of a survey product from the SHOALS system. It illustrates the navigation channel between jetties, and the ebb tidal shoal at Fort Pierce, Florida (Irish et al., 1995). The depths are color coded; land is represented as brown. If desired, the land topography can also be color coded.

The successes of all these systems are responsible for rapidly growing interest in this technology in many countries. Two new systems, now in the design stage for the Royal Australian Navy and the U.S. Army Corps of Engineers, promise evolutionary improvements in performance, utility, and survey cost. Exciting opportunities lie ahead.

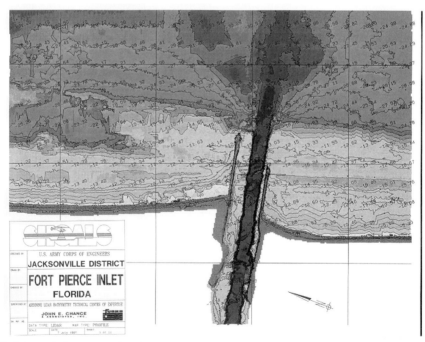

Figure 8.5 Color-coded contours of the Jetties and navigation channel at Fort Pierce, Florida. See color plate in Appendix C.

COST CONSIDERATIONS

Background

Costs for hydrographic surveying are highly variable and depend on environmental and logistical circumstances. They change with time and technology relative to the costs of other services, and they have historically been hard to assess because they were most often conducted by government agencies who may or may not have always considered all of the overhead costs involved. In the last century, surveying techniques and costs underwent a succession of great changes as a result of improving measurement technology. We now take sonar and lasers and GPS for granted, but it was not that many years ago that surveyors were throwing graduated, lead-weighted lines overboard and positioning with sextants. Techniques and relative costs will continue to change. One of the primary reasons for the development of ALB systems is their significant cost advantage in shallow water.

In the past, there may have been only one way to conduct a survey. Today, a hydrographer has choices. There may be more than one method possible for solving a given survey problem, and, after accuracy, cost must be one of the most important considerations. More attention is being paid to the detailed calculation of costs now due to tight budgets and the advent of a transition in many countries to some fraction of contract surveying. Although the costs may be better known, they are now often considered a somewhat confidential matter due to commercial competition, and they may not be readily obtainable. Without a comprehensive cost analysis using carefully controlled and well-defined evaluation criteria for a given survey scenario, there is always the risk of drawing false conclusions. Even the results of such studies depend on many assumptions and can vary. Published values must be understood in context, their sources recognized, and their validity carefully considered.

The true costs associated with surveying in general are highly dependent on location and geography. Flat, smooth, nearby coastlines like the Gulf Coast of the U.S. are cheaper to survey than the remote, rocky coastlines of Alaska by a factor of two or three. According to a recently published report (Featherstone, 2001), the cost of waterborne sonar hydrography, averaged over a number of different areas, some easy and some hard, varies between $4400/km^2 for NOAA surveys and $13,300/km^2 for contract surveys. Indications are that the latter number may be a little on the high side. This report is undoubtedly controversial, and more may yet be heard in this arena.

Modern hydrographic surveying is clearly a very expensive and labor intensive task. This is one of the reasons for the large hydrographic backlogs being experienced by many countries (UN, 1989). NOAA now has only four hydrographic vessels in the field (RAINIER, FAIRWEATHER, THOMAS JEFFERSON, and RUDE), down from eleven in the 1970's, due to budget and pressure from the private sector to use contract surveys. Most of the world's coastal charts are outdated, both because the coastal environment is a region of significant change and because earlier measurement techniques were not as accurate as presently (Featherstone, 2001). The cost of surveying is a significant contributing factor in the lack of resolution of this problem in most countries.

In the U.S., only the 40 highest priority sites, which primarily involve river entrances and harbors heavily used for commercial shipping, are being addressed by NOAA's Office of Coast Survey. A great deal of time and attention must be paid to these areas because of the continuing reductions in under-keel clearance being utilized by very large ships to gain economic advantage. Even for this limited goal, the backlog is reported to be 25 years due to limited ship time and budgets. This says nothing, however, of the needs of coastal resource managers and recreational boaters. The above critical areas represent only 1.3% of the total coastal responsibility. There is clearly a need for a faster and cheaper approach to provide coverage in the 98.7% of less critical areas where small-object detection is not as important a requirement.

For many applications in waters less than 50-m deep, where the guaranteed detection of 1-m cubes is not required, that approach can and should be ALB. Although it offers many adjunct products which are utilized and appreciated by a variety of customers, the primary reasons for the use of ALB are its ability to perform hydrographic surveys much more rapidly and at a much lower cost per unit area.

Qualitative Factors

Costs are important at two times: when a job is being planned and bid, and when the job is done. A cost estimate prior to a lidar survey is based on two generic factors — logistics and risk. Once a price bid or cost forecast is accepted, the ultimate survey cost depends on planning, logistics, survey management, and luck. Contract surveys are typically bid at fixed prices; the price must also include factors for profit and recovery of initial investment. Contract surveys with higher environmental risks must be bid at higher rates with the understanding that actual profit margins will vary from mission to mission according to uncontrollable circumstances.

Risks which must be considered in survey planning and bids involve the statistical consideration of the uncontrollable factors such as the expected effects of water clarity, wave heights, local and regional weather, refly probability, and time on site. Water clarity varies with location, season, tidal phase, and weather. Water clarity problems can be managed by choosing the optimum month for a given location and, once on site, by selecting the best time of day and by having alternate targets in neighboring areas with different characteristics — such as two sides of an island, or protected bay areas compared to exposed offshore areas. Weather varies on both daily and seasonal time scales and, as with water clarity, can be managed by selecting optimum seasons and times of day, and having alternate targets. Some days will be lost to weather. This is true of sonar as well as lidar. Those days are rarely wasted because they are generally well spent in performing needed system maintenance, planning future surveys, and catching up on data processing. For hydrographic surveys, areas known to have coral heads and fish schools or high winds will require a higher percentage of reflies to resolve anomalies and holidays. Time on target may be affected by winds. Flightlines may have to be flown in only one direction, for example. In some congested airspace near urban areas, time can also be lost to the aircraft "loitering" while awaiting clearance from the air traffic controller to access the survey area. In some cases, daytime flights may be proscribed altogether, requiring a shift to nights where, in some cases, increased dangers near land could reduce production rates.

Lidar survey operation and maintenance (O&M) costs depend strongly on project characteristics. Survey scenarios and costs can vary widely. The characteristics with the largest effects on costs are project location, size, horizontal density requirements, survey accuracy "order", the possible requirement to resolve all questionable points by reflying, the physical shape of survey area and if it includes surf zone or high cliffs, the positioning method employed, and extant environmental conditions on site. Many of these same factors apply to sonar costs.

Two aspects of project location are important: the distance of the airfield to be used from the preceding mission site and the distance of the project area from the airfield being used. Transit (mobilization) costs can be a significant fraction of the total. Greater costs are obviously incurred by flying halfway around the world than by flying to the next county or state. For this reason, it is important to be able to plan ahead as far as possible and plot a "grand tour" route in which surveys fall in logical geographical and environmental progression. On a single continent, survey crews can drive to their next location, but for travel over water, regardless of the size of the survey aircraft, many of the survey crew fly to their destinations by commercial air carriers. A great deal of computer and positioning hardware, spares, and other equipment must also be transported. This greatly increases the costs for distant locations. The size of the survey must be large enough to amortize these costs. Simply put, large areas are cheaper to survey per unit area than small areas. Interestingly, however, increased costs at remote areas are sometimes nevertheless a cost advantage, because some sites may be so remote or dangerous that they cannot practically be accessed other than from the air. In such a case, greater costs may be justified.

Once on site, the project location with respect to the aircraft's base of operations has a large influence upon the survey cost. Each aircraft type has specific flight endurance, and the time spent in transit to reach and return from the survey area reduces the time available for data collection. Aircraft time in the air is money, whether it is in transit to the project location, to the survey site, or in actual surveying.

For a given system, the spatial data density required is another strong contributor to the project cost. This is true for both lidar and sonar. Most current lidar systems offer a means of decreasing or increasing "spot" density from their standard value, in order to deal with special circumstances. Spot spacing is typically controlled by varying the coverage swath width of the aircraft flight line and the ground speed of the aircraft while collecting data. There is a direct correspondence between required survey density and the required aircraft time and cost to complete a survey. Economics dictate that surveys should be performed at the lowest density acceptable to achieve the desired products. If surveys are required to prove or disprove the existence of small objects with high probability, the data processing time and refly percentage will also increase. In other words, hydrographic surveys are more expensive than bathymetric surveys.

The physical shape of the project is also a large factor in cost determinations. Generally speaking, large, rectangular shaped, open-water areas are the most efficient for ALB surveys, and irregular shorelines tend to be least efficient. Data collection plans over a specific survey area can be broken into two parts: collection lines and line changes (time in turns). The most efficient survey areas incorporate the longest possible collection lines, within reason, and the least number of lines. The efficiency of the survey is best indicated by the ratio of time "on-line" to time "off-line"; the higher this number the more efficient the survey. Another consideration for near-shore areas is whether the flightlines are flown parallel with the shore or perpendicular. Various logistical concerns may dictate one or the other. Flights perpendicular to the shore are less efficient because they spend more time over land. This may not necessarily be true, however, if topographic heights over land are part of the product. Areas with large surf zones are less efficient because the large areas of white foam can require reflies. High cliffs adjacent to the shore can disrupt desired flight patterns for shoreline surveys, and the winds associated with them can be dangerous to the safe operation of the aircraft. It is noteworthy that a factor that is not very important to ALB cost considerations is depth, because the lidar swath is constant. This is very different from the situation with multibeam sonar for which the swath decreases as the depth decreases, and the shallow-water sonar costs soar.

Additional items affecting costs are the positioning system used and the environmental conditions. The use of wide-area differential GPS (WADGPS), if available, is less expensive than placing and manning differential stations on the ground. The use of kinematic GPS, if needed, requires more equipment, more work on the ground, and more data processing. Although this increases the cost over DGPS, it is somewhat ameliorated by the lack of need to record, collect, and incorporate concurrent water levels. Finally, as noted above under risk management, it is well known that a certain number of days are going to be lost to rain, dirty water, high waves, and high winds. The associated costs are included as part of risk assessment. Savvy survey management and the availability of alternate survey areas can reduce the associated losses.

Quantitative Aspects

Costs can be broken down into four main categories: initial system costs, upgrade costs, operations, and maintenance. It is not hard to deal with the first two by establishing a simple model. If one assumes, for the sake of argument, an ALB system cost of, say, $5,000,000, a system lifetime of 10 years, and a yearly survey total of 10,000 km² (the rather extraordinary yearly survey rate of the RAN LADS for the last seven years), then the sunk cost works out to $50/km² over the lifetime of the system. If an average system may only survey 5,000 km² in a year and incurs an additional cost of, say, $1,000,000 for technology and software upgrades, and needs to return 6% on the initial investment if the system is commercially backed, this value is still only on the order of $150/km². The cost of future systems is expected to be significantly lower when they are produced in greater numbers. Similarly, the design of future systems is based on a greater base of experience than in the past, and the probability of a need to upgrade is reduced. Nevertheless, these figures are virtually in the noise compared to the O&M costs reported above for sonar, and further discussions will center on the O&M costs for ALB. There are much more-complicated ways of making this estimate, but this simple approach provides a reasonable estimate and can be scaled for different assumptions.

There are two ways to relate the O&M costs of ALB: as hard numbers for given circumstances, or as an estimated fraction of what the corresponding waterborne sonar survey cost would be. As noted above, even the latter are either not well known or vary over a great range. Different user and provider groups have different ideas, needs, philosophies, and experiences. Because ALB costs depend strongly on the above factors and may be closely held because of increasing commercial competition, only broad ranges and averages can be discussed. To put this important subject into full perspective, the topic will be approached, therefore, first by reprising two historic predictions, second by examining a common-sense, semi-quantitative model result, third by referencing the relative costs experienced by the Royal Australian Navy, fourth by repeating the predictions of a model published by an equipment manufacturer, and finally by quoting unofficial but often heard estimates.

NOAA became interested in ALB in the mid-1970's. Because one of the primary benefits proposed for the new technology was cost savings, a cost-effectiveness study was immediately commissioned. The results (Enabnit et al., 1978), calculated over a variety of survey scenarios, indicated a predicted cost of $123/km^2 for ALB and $772/km^2 for launch sonar. Note that the ratio was a 6:1 advantage for ALB and that these were 1976 dollars. Assuming an average 4.75% inflation rate over the last 25 years, these costs inflate by a factor of 3.2 to a prediction for 2001 of $394/km^2 for ALB and $2470/km^2 for sonar. This sonar value was low by a factor of two for NOAA surveys, according to Featherstone (2001), and the ALB figure is consistent with the low end of concurrent predicted and quoted values seen below.

Cost figures in a 1990 study (Golaszewski et al., 1990) for a government-owned, contractor-operated ALB system predicted a cost benefit for ALB over sonar of 2.7 with ALB costs (converted to 2001 dollars) of $4980/km^2 and sonar costs of $13,460/km^2. Interestingly, the latter figure is consistent with the sonar contractor values reported by Featherstone (2001) but overestimate actual NOAA vessel survey costs by a factor of three and typically mentioned ALB costs by a factor of between four and ten.

A simple model involving benchmark cost and coverage rates can be enlightening for determining the ballpark cost-benefit ratio of ALB. For coverage, the assumptions will be a lidar swath width equal to three times the sonar swath width (appropriate at a 20-m depth for a 200-m ALB swath width or a 10-m depth for a 100-m swath width) and a 20x aircraft speed advantage (say, 150 knots compared to 7.5). For actual operations, the swath-width ratio would be a very strong function of depth because the sonar swath width is a linear function of depth. For costs, the daily expense of operating an aircraft will be assumed to be about half again as much as for a vessel, and, furthermore, it will be considered that the vessel will collect data 2.5 times longer each day (say, 15 hours compared to 6 hours). A factor of two in extra cost for ALB over sonar will be included based on the hypothesis that the data processing and the maintenance of the more complex hardware might each be about 40% higher. With these numbers, the coverage ratio favors ALB by 60x, and the cost ratio favors sonar by 7.5x. The net ALB cost benefit per unit area becomes a factor of 8:1. This crude estimate is only slightly more favorable than the original, much more carefully calculated 1978 NOAA prediction, and corresponds very well with Australian field experience, as noted directly below. This ratio will decrease as the depth increases and multibeam sonar becomes increasingly efficient. All of these factors obviously vary from system to system and from project to project, but the proposed values indicate very simply the primary factors involved, their rough magnitudes, and the basic reason for the ALB advantage.

Sinclair (1999c) reports that as a result of using LADS in combination with its survey vessels, the RAN has experienced long term cost reductions to 20-30% of traditional total survey costs. Sinclair (1999a) emphasizes further that this global average factor of four benefit is not a one-to-one comparison because it does not take into consideration that the ships are being used where they are more cost effective and LADS is being used where the vessels would be less cost effective. If the ships were used in the same locations where LADS is being used, the direct cost comparison factor would be much larger. Considering that LADS surveys roughly the same total area as the RAN vessels each year, if one hypothesizes that LADS is surveying in waters which are, on average, at least two times shallower than the ships, the fact that the swath width and cost effectiveness of the vessels would be reduced by that same factor in those areas, indicates that the true cost benefit of LADS is at least a factor of 8. This is the same figure estimated by the rough model above. This high ratio is possible with LADS' relatively low laser pulse rate because the survey density is correspondingly low. The ratio for LADS Mk II may be a bit higher because of slightly increased aircraft speed, but much of the increased laser pulse rate goes instead into increased sounding density, and LADS Mk II also has a relatively high initial system and aircraft cost to be amortized.

A detailed cost model for a large, complex survey area has been published by Axelsson and Alfredsson (1999) of Saab Dynamics AB with input from the Swedish Hydrographic Department. The survey logistics are broken down by depth range and associated accuracy requirements and discussed in terms of the selection of the proper mix of airborne and water-borne resources. Table 8.1 contains a sampling of the predicted costs per square kilometer presented therein for 100% use of each sensor technology in given regimes. The ALB values are for a proposed "Hawk Eye" 1000-pps system mounted in a helicopter. Information on the cost categories involved and on the origin of their estimates is not reported. It is surmised that these values are for "local" surveying and do not include transit or mobilization costs from a distant location.

Table 8.1 Estimated O&M costs per unit area (Dollars/km^2) from Axelsson and Alfredsson (1999).

Depth (m)	4	8	8	8	16	16	32
S44 Order	1	Special	1	2	1	2	2
Hawk Eye	$378	$2413	$378	$249	$336	$221	$210
Boat	$16434	$12791	$8217	$3819	$2407	$1119	$497
Ratio	43.5 : 1	5.3 : 1	21.7 : 1	15.3 : 1	7.2 : 1	5.1 : 1	2.4 : 1

Although these results are quite interesting from a relative perspective and emphasize the great variability with depth and accuracy requirements, it should be noted that the predicted vessel costs for the depths in which the vessels normally operate are significantly lower than the values quoted by Featherstone (2001) for NOAA and NOAA contractors, and the predicted lidar cost numbers also appear to be lower by a factor of from two to four than practical experience would dictate.

As implied by the variety of cost figures in Table 8.1, actual costs will vary over a considerable range depending on the many factors discussed above. Based on unofficial comments, it appears that O&M costs for typical airborne hydrographic charting surveys of reasonably sized areas, not involving excessive transit distances or other complications, will range between $400/km^2 and $1500/km^2 depending primarily on location, size, and survey density. Less stringent bathymetric surveys will tend to the low side, while difficult shoreline areas could be somewhat more. Prices charged will also vary according to risk, rate of recovery of initial investment, and profit margin.

In summary, the O&M area cost ratio between ALB and multibeam sonar depends very strongly on the survey depth, the lidar survey density, the pulse-repetition rate of the airborne system, and the location of the survey. For most practical cases, it appears that a realistic factor is probably between 3 and 10 in favor of ALB for depths under 50 meters. Regardless of the exact numbers, it is quite clear that ALB offers a significant cost advantage in addition to its other advantages of coverage rate, rapid-response capability, safety, and overall flexibility.

COMPARISON WITH OVERLAPPING TECHNOLOGIES

Bathymetry

Background

The most compelling attributes of airborne lidar bathymetry are its proven accuracy, its numerous, varied, and unique capabilities, and its advantages in terms of high coverage rates, flexibility, mobility, efficiency, safety, and low cost per unit area. Although airborne lidar bathymetry is most frequently used alone, to good advantage, it is generally complementary with traditional survey technologies (Calder and Penny, 1980), including both sonar and land-based topographic elevation data-collection methodologies. This is due, in no small way, to the fact that ALB technology and techniques were conceived for this purpose. Both sonar and ALB have strengths and weaknesses. The most obvious difference is that sonar is optimal in deeper waters while lidar is more efficient and safer in depths less than about 50 meters as long as the water is reasonably clear. The overlapping boundaries of optimal performance provide the opportunity for cooperation, rather than competition, to maximize overall survey efficiency and safety. Lidar and sonar, and their products, have been used together with excellent success (Graham et al., 1999).

A good example of the complementarity of lidar and sonar working together is Lake Tahoe on the California - Nevada border. This is one of the world's deepest and clearest lakes. Unfortunately, visitors and neighboring development are negatively impacting the finely balanced environment, and water clarity is suffering. The U.S. Geological Survey mapped the lake in 1998 with multibeam sonar for depths greater than 10 meters, but 72 miles of shoreline remained unsurveyed because of the shallow water limitations of the sonar. The near-shore area, however, is a critical focus for studies of shoreline erosion and runoff that encourages the growth of algae. Because of this, SHOALS was called in to complete the mapping of the lake's near-shore depths. Together, the SHOALS and multibeam data present a complete picture and their complementary nature permits the production of a survey invaluable to understanding and predicting natural and manmade lakeshore processes (West et al., 2001a).

Survey planners are increasingly challenged to identify the types and locations of surveys needed and to assign the appropriate mix of data collection sensors in order to maximize survey efficiency and minimize cost. Conceptually, this has always been the aim, but it has only been in recent years that emerging technologies such as ALB have broadened the array of sensors available and made this a real possibility. Perhaps the most prominent manifestation of this has been the supersedence of the traditional, scale-driven approach to surveying by one that is usage driven and allows broader interpretation of survey data density and resolution. This approach is still suffering growing-pains and currently offers pitfalls along with the opportunities, since many survey planners are still not fully educated to the relative merits of these emerging technologies, especially ALB. The synergy between ALB and sonar can provide great benefits (Skogvik and Axelsson, 2001). Careful consideration must be given to understanding or properly defining true user requirements, to understanding the effects of geography on user requirements, to recognizing the proper mix of technologies, to meeting but not exceeding user requirements, and to managing the relationships among techniques and costs relative to those requirements (Axelsson and Alfredsson, 1999). The system and flight parameters of future ALB systems will be able to be adapted according to the S-44 survey Order required (Engstrom and Axelsson, 2001).

One trend that is lending impetus to this evolution in survey philosophy is the growing worldwide move to having some fraction of surveys provided to government agencies by private contractors (DeBow et al., 2000) who can provide access to a mixture of new and varied technologies. Land Information New Zealand (LINZ) is New Zealand's national topographic and hydrographic mapping authority. They have been at the forefront of the movement to providing contractors with greater autonomy and flexibility in instrument selection and in July of 1998 introduced full contestability for most of its mapping and charting requirements. A primary factor behind this move was the aim to identify better and less expensive ways to undertake inshore surveys, while also ensuring the safety of conventional hydrographic survey craft in uncharted areas. One of the first contracts to be tendered was for a survey of the two Sub-Antarctic Island groups, Snares and Solander, which lie 60 miles SW and 120 miles S of the New Zealand mainland, respectively. This presented an enormous challenge to mobilize, during an extremely short weather window, a total survey effort that could work in a complex seabed environment that ranged from water several hundred meters deep to exposed rocky coasts. ALB was the enabling component with its ability to meet all the inshore requirements while also defining the areas in which conventional acoustic platforms could safely work. The winning consortium stated that they would have considered declining the contract if the use of ALB had not been acceptable to LINZ (Graham et al., 1999).

Ships or launches surveying near-shore waters at slow speed in potentially hazardous conditions are exposed to precisely the same dangers that they are tasked with delineating. For this reason ALB is attractive as a means of both defining safe operating areas prior to deployment of surface platforms and as a method of surveying areas which are declared to be too hazardous for such vessels to operate in. In Australia this concept has revived the 'No Bottom At' (NBA) classification which was historically used to indicate depths apparently deeper than the maximum length of a lead line. NBA is now used to describe areas that LADS and LADS Mk II has 'cleared' of hazards to the assumed lidar extinction depth (Nairn, 1994; Perry, 1999). These areas may be surveyed later by sonar without fear of danger to the vessel. Although this approach entails a certain inherent risk regarding water clarity estimation, the term is officially endorsed for LADS surveys by the Australian Hydrographic Office of the Royal Australian Navy. A prudent mariner will apply the same degree of caution to such an annotation on the chart whether it comes from lead line or laser.

The ability of ALB to bridge the topographic and marine survey worlds is one of its most useful features. The disparate topographic and hydrographic communities have recently been brought together to resolve a historic land/water juncture problem (of inconsistency between respective shoreline locations) which has significant social, economic, legal, and safety implications (O'Reilly, 2000). The National Oceanic and Atmospheric Administration (NOAA) National Ocean Service (NOS) and the U.S. Geological Survey (USGS) conducted a "bathy/topo" demonstration project to resolve their procedural differences in terms of methodologies, datums, and standards with the goal of producing a single digital elevation model (DEM) initially referenced to the ellipsoid (Parker et al., 2001). Data sets from various airborne and satellite remote sensing instruments were used to create a high-resolution "shoreline elevation zone" in the DEM, which will, for the first time ever, be used to produce a number of internally consistent "shorelines" by moving the water level in the DEM to the desired tidal datum heights (Parker, 2002; Parker et al., 2003). The United States has over 95,000 miles of shoreline to map and third-party data will be used wherever possible. ALB data can be very useful in supporting this effort.

Nowhere are the relative merits of ALB versus traditional surface-based technologies more clearly emphasized than in the dilemma of how to map environmentally sensitive or dangerous coastal areas without the need to put potentially damaging or vulnerable assets on the surface. Such areas can pose difficult surveying problems because they may be difficult to access from the shore due to logistical or legal restrictions or because they may pose a threat to the surveyor. Examples range from the areas offshore from the rain forests of Puerto Rico to sensitive sand-grass dunes to the rocky coasts of Hawaii or New Zealand. Survey boats are often required to operate in very shallow water; this is not only time-consuming but also presents the possibility of damaging either the boat or the environment. In extremely shallow waters, as in Florida Bay, depths less than a meter may even be acquired by the manual use of a calibrated staff from small boats or hovercraft — a very tedious and expensive approach. The lidar survey aircraft are relatively quiet and complete their missions with a minimal impact on fauna and flora. ALB provides the capability to undertake such tasks rapidly, safely, efficiently, and with minimum disruption of the environment (Guenther et al, 1994). In several cases such as New Zealand's remote, uninhabited, rocky islands of Solander and Snares (which are important marine sanctuaries), Puerto Rico's Vieques conservation zones, and Hawaii's Molokai coral reefs, SHOALS survey projects have been completed that would have been all very slow, difficult, dangerous, and expensive for conventional systems (West et al., 2001a). LADS Mk II also surveyed under similar circumstances in New Zealand (Sinclair, 1999b).

Acoustic Technology

The development of ALB from the 1970's parallels the commercial development of multibeam echosounders. Early systems were rather slow and ponderous, but advances in underlying technologies have made both ALB and multibeam much more effective today. A number of very capable multibeam echo sounders have been developed for use in increasingly shallow water depths. Although these acoustic swath, shallow-water multibeam (SWMB) systems represent a significant improvement in performance versus the single-beam echosounder, they maintain one feature in common with the single-beam systems: they are waterborne and thus seriously limited in the speeds at which they can safely survey, particularly in shallow waters.

Although ALB was developed specifically to cover the shallow-water areas that are inefficiently surveyed with sonar technology, it is important to remember the limitations of ALB. As has been noted, lidar works only in relatively optically clear waters and only out to limited depths. In deeper or dirtier waters, sonar is, and will remain, the tool of choice. It is relatively straightforward for an appropriately trained hydrographer to recognize how a survey area will naturally break down into overlapping areas alternatively best served by ALB and by acoustic approaches based on considerations involving depth, bottom character, water clarity, safety, and weather limitations (Graham, et al., 1999; Axelsson and Alfredsson, 1999). Configurations using combinations of ALB for depths under 50 m and SWMB for greater depths have much lower annual costs. In short, ALB is not, and was not intended to be, a general replacement for sonar. It is, rather, a new tool that can be utilized, with great cost, speed, and coverage benefit under the proper circumstances, as an adjunct to sonar.

Vertical-Beam Echosounder (VBES)

A VBES (also known as a "single-beam echosounder") is only able to provide data along the profile delineated by the vessel's track. Surveys using VBES require large amounts of ship time to provide dense enough data to characterize an area, and they nevertheless include areas devoid of data between profiles. Shoal features between lines are typically detected with the use of concurrent side scan sonar and developed by increasing the profile density of the area with the VBES, or, in exceedingly rough bathymetry, through planned profiles at high density without the use of side scan sonar. For this reason, VBES is rapidly being demoted to a subordinate, near-shore role in large marine surveys to provide preliminary data before sending in expensive SWMB systems. Despite this, relatively inexpensive initial capital equipment costs mean that its use is still widespread among lower-end users who predominantly have limited or small survey requirements. ALB could be economical for such users if a group of nearby projects can be combined.

In the past, sediment management has been a significant use for VBES. Traditionally, coastal monitoring conducted by agencies such as the Florida Department of Environmental Protection has been based on a combination of cross sections surveyed using VBES and land-leveling at 1000-foot intervals. These cross sections extend from an established baseline, marked by survey monuments, to either the 30-foot contour line, or 2,400 feet from the shoreline, whichever is closer. Time and cost, including the maintenance of dense control points, limit the scope of such an exercise, and it is for these reasons that ALB now provides a cost-effective alternative, while also providing a greatly enhanced data density (West and Wiggins, 2000b). Single-beam echosounders are currently the focus of a new sediment characterization mission, in which the returning backscatter is analyzed and categorized relative to known sediment types.

Shallow-Water Multibeam Echosounder (SWMB)

If resolution were the only consideration for a shallow-water bathymetry survey, ALB might be judged as inferior to the SWMB. This is because a modern SWMB typically employs beams that are formed tighter than 2 degrees in both the fore/aft direction and the across-track direction. Some of the most modern SWMB systems use beams as narrow as 0.5 degree. Waterborne survey and data processing costs are relatively high, however, and users' requirements often do not need such a high level of resolution. SWMB systems are least efficient in very shallow waters because their cross-track angular coverage provides a swath width that decreases proportionally with decreasing depth. This degradation in efficient performance in very shallow waters is further accentuated by the need to compensate for smaller footprints (resulting from the narrow beam angle) by slowing the speed of advance to ensure overlap of footprints along track. In shallow waters, the time and cost of a SWMB survey increases rapidly with decreasing depth. In contrast, ALB systems, with high speeds and wide swath widths nearly independent of depth, are very efficient in relatively shallow waters. For ALB, the along-track speed is linked to density requirements and laser repetition rate, because object detection often remains a primary purpose for the hydrographic mission.

As noted earlier, theory and practical experience have shown that although ALB is able to reliably detect only a fraction of isolated bottom features the size of a one-meter cube, a modern SWMB is also unable to resolve such objects except in the near-nadir situation when the vessel passes almost directly over them (Brissette and Hughes Clarke, 1999; Hughes Clarke et al. 1999). For this reason, SWMB, like VBES, is typically operated in conjunction with side scan sonar when small-object detection is important. IHO "Special Order" (more accurate than Order 1) survey specifications require full bottom search for all objects of 1-meter cube size, and only side scan sonar, properly acquired and processed, can currently meet that specification. NOAA Office of Coast Survey Hydrographic Survey Specifications and Deliverables (http://chartmaker.ncd.noaa. gov/hsd/specs/specs.htm) do not require IHO Special Order, but instead require side scan sonar usage when small-object detection is needed.

ALB using a constant 20-degree nadir angle and three or four meter sounding spacing is expected to resolve a very high percentage of 2-meter cube objects (to limiting depths) (Guenther et al., 1996), while such objects were noted to be resolved only over the inner 45 degrees of swath for a particular SWMB system (Hughes Clarke et al., 1999). It should be noted that each SWMB product has special characteristics to ensure that it can be differentiated from its competitors, and that some may perform a mission better than others. Some newer, specialized multi-beam systems combine angle-independent imagery, similar to side scan sonar; this permits better small-object detection at large nadir angles. Other systems are optimized for normalized backscatter by beam to enable accurate segmentation of bottom characteristics. Still others are optimized for little user interaction, which makes them good only as "beginners" bathymetric systems. In terms of target resolution, it appears that for most systems, SWMB used by itself offers little advantage over ALB.

One important, but often underestimated, aspect of SWMB is the quantity of the data and the resultant amount of time necessary to create a product. The data acquisition speed of SWMB is very high, even higher than ALB, in terms of bytes per knot over ground. The special characteristics of the near-shore environment make the resultant data highly dependent on boundary conditions, and environmental effects on the acoustics can make SWMB systems quite inefficient. The data management of SWMB is a very large factor which must be considered in the deployment of the system, because processing rates of from 3:1 to 6:1 (one hour acquisition requires up to six hours manual processing for high-confidence hydrography) must be factored in (G. Noll, personal communication, 2001). Repeating coverage in shallow areas which were not accurately sounded on first attempts costs many hours of lost production. Planned double coverage with ALB, at relatively lower cost, has been used in some missions by the U.S. Navy to ensure that the final hydrographic accuracy goals and object detection criteria were reached.

Side Scan Sonar

Conventional side scan sonar provides no bathymetric depth measurement capability. It is typically used in conjunction with VBES and SWMB surveys because it is an invaluable tool for feature reconnaissance in coastal waters. Although a side scan only measures seabed backscatter, defined in time (commonly correlated to slant range) and azimuth, it provides a superior method to all other sensors for detecting small (< 2-m cube), off-nadir targets with a high level of confidence. This is because it is conventionally deployed in a submerged tow-body 10-15 meters above the seabed, which results in a geometry with low grazing angles such that targets protruding above the general seabed surface will cast telltale shadows. As a consequence, however, double coverage of the bottom is required in order that the detection gap at nadir is covered by the active area of the adjacent swath. Although side scan sonar yields good target detection capability, it typically suffers from poor positioning, which can be of the order of tens of meters, due to uncertainty in tow-body location — except in cases where a short baseline acoustic transponder is used (Hughes Clarke et al., 1999). There is also the possibility of damaging the sensor on an unexpected hazard. The best results are now being obtained from systems with an angle-independent imagery option.

In shallow water, the height of the tow body above the bottom may need to be decreased. This decreases the effective swath width and increases the danger of grounding. Beams are quite narrow in the along-track direction, and, in shallow water, either speed over the bottom has to be reduced in order to avoid excessive spatial gaps or the listening time of the sonar must be decreased, which further reduces the true swath width. Surface noise and motion effects become more pronounced in shallow water. Unless sea conditions are extremely calm, it is difficult to operate a towed side scan in waters less than roughly 15-m deep without a significant degradation in performance. Tow speed in waters less than 10-m deep is often 4 knots or less, which results in extremely slow coverage rates. An alternative for waters less than, say, 20 m deep is to use a method pioneered by NOAA (Huff, 1993) in which the side scan transducers or towfish are fixed directly to the vessel hull, and speeds may be increased to between 6 and 8 knots. Still, the coxswain and equipment owner both need nerves of steel for such survey tasking. This presents a striking contrast to an ALB system operating safely overhead at a speed in excess of 100 knots and with a swath width of 100-200 meters. The survey customer needs to be very sure of his target detection requirements to justify the costs associated with waterborne techniques versus use of an ALB system.

Satellite Bathymetry

Depths may be estimated from passive, multispectral satellite data for clean waters (Lyzenga, 1978; Philpot, 1989). This method does not meet IHO hydrographic accuracy standards, but it can provide a meaningful bathymetric model if lesser accuracy can be tolerated. The results depend very strongly on the algorithms used to process the measured irradiances, and the atmospheric correction is crucial. Many models have been used over the years for data from a variety of systems. A standard algorithm for determining depth in clear water from passive sensors exists, but it requires tuning of five parameters and does not retrieve depths where the bottom has an extremely low albedo. As one example of a new approach, Stumpf et al. (2003) report that to address these issues, they developed an empirical solution using a ratio of reflectances that has only two tunable parameters and can be applied to low-albedo features. The standard linear transform and the new ratio transform were compared through analysis of IKONOS satellite imagery against lidar bathymetry. Both algorithms compensate for variable bottom type and albedo (sand, pavement, algae, coral) and retrieve bathymetry in water depths of less than 10-15 m, the latter being the practical limit for the linear transform. The coefficients for the ratio algorithm were tuned manually to a few depths from a nautical chart, yet performed as well as the linear algorithm tuned using multiple linear regression against the lidar. The ratio approach is more robust and can sometimes work in deeper depths, water clarity permitting; but it tends to have less resolution and to be noisier in that regime.

Shoreline Mapping

Shoreline mapping can be described simply as the delineation of the location of the land/water boundary. This is, however, a gross oversimplification because of legal and environmental considerations. The shoreline is typically defined in terms of the water level at the time of a particular tidal datum. For charting purposes, the mean high water line is typically used. For legal purposes, various nations and, indeed, various states in the U.S. use many different definitions in relationship to rights of ownership, rights to use resources, etc. For some legal purposes, the shoreline may be defined by the mean high water; for others, it may be the mean lower low water or something else. The beauty of a complete digital elevation model of a coastal area is that different shorelines may be determined, as desired, simply by selecting the appropriate water level on the computer. The problem lies in the frequent lack of consistent historical elevation data and the great expense of collecting, to modern accuracy standards, what is needed for contemporary purposes. NOAA has developed a national vertical datum transformation tool called "VDatum" that allows the transformation of elevation data between any two vertical datums, among a choice of 28, which can be categorized as three general types: tidal, orthometric, and 3D ellipsoidal datums (Parker et al., 2003). NOAA is presently engaged in creating the VDatum database that must be populated for all geographic locales by making the necessary measurements. Some areas currently covered include Tampa Bay, a section of the Louisiana coast, New Jersey, Delaware Bay, Chesapeake Bay, North Carolina, and Puget Sound (Myers, 2005).

The selection of a remote sensing tool for shoreline mapping should be based on criteria such as cost, speed, products, and data quality. A brief description of some typical sensors follows.

Aerial Photogrammetry

Aerial photographs have been acquired for many decades to support shoreline-related applications. Almost all high-water shoreline on hydrographic charts comes from photogrammetry (O'Reilly, 2000). The mapping of shoreline using photogrammetry is simpler than the construction of a full DEM and more pragmatic. High-resolution, stereoscopic, geo-referenced black-and-white infrared aerial photography can be acquired at flight times carefully coordinated with the desired water levels. The water comes out dark, and the land comes out light. Clouds are a problem. The further use of color photography permits the construction of stereo models from which land elevations above (and perhaps slightly below) the water can be determined. From such photos, often also taken to identify and locate land features, it may be possible to determine a high water datum from berms or debris fields. Photographs may cover widths as great as 9200 meters for a 1:40,000-scale survey. Even though a metric camera can be flown in a small aircraft, aerial data collection and processing are, nevertheless, expensive and must be limited to high-priority targets. More information may be found in Chapter 5 of this book.

Satellite Imagery

High-resolution black-and-white satellite imagery is, perhaps, the most promising approach to large-scale shoreline definition and precision mapping projects, but a number of hurdles remain. Coverage is global, but, as with aerial photography, it must be tide coordinated and cloud free. Spatial resolution varies considerably from satellite to satellite. Geo-referencing is difficult due to off-nadir angles and atmospheric distortions, and high resolution and accuracy are expensive to obtain. Products of varying resolutions are available and priced accordingly. The accuracy of most typical current products is borderline for some applications. Satellite images are now being assessed by NOAA's National Geodetic Survey as a reconnaissance tool to define areas of rapid change that may need more-frequent aerial investigation and to evaluate the current validity of previously compiled shoreline data. More satellites and data suppliers are needed to create a competitive atmosphere that will promote improved accuracy at reduced prices for all users.

Airborne IFSAR

Airborne interferometric synthetic aperture radar (IFSAR) is another very promising technology for shoreline mapping. There is no water penetration, and, as for the techniques above, data collection must be tide coordinated. A major benefit of this approach is that it works through even heavy clouds. This ability is needed for areas that are frequently cloud covered such as Alaska and areas in the tropics. The spatial resolution is good with 2.5-m pixels. DEMs can be generated above the extant water line. Missions are typically flown from relatively high altitudes, on the order of 6000 meters, with swath widths of several thousand meters. The resulting high coverage rate is a cost advantage. NOAA's National Geodetic Survey has sponsored several successful commercial IFSAR shoreline surveys in Alaska. More information on IFSAR may be found in Chapter 6 of this book.

Airborne Lidar Topography

Over the past three decades, airborne lidar terrain mapping (ALTM) systems have been developed into extremely capable and popular land surveying tools with many applications. They have also been used for water surface applications (Jelalian, 1968; McClain et al., 1982). Although the land/water boundary is qualitatively evident in the results of many ALTM systems (Gutierrez et al., 1998), formally defined, quantitative shoreline has not been a common product. The feasibility and cost effectiveness of this promising approach are being assessed for the production of new and enhanced charting products (O'Reilly, 2000). For shoreline applications, ALTM results must be tide coordinated and will provide a three-dimensional digital data set from which DEMs can be generated for elevations above the extant water line. Shorelines defined at higher hypothetical water levels can be derived from the DEM. System specifications vary by manufacturer, of which there is a large and growing number, but areal coverage is generally very dense, effective pixel size is small, and vertical accuracy is excellent. Typical operating altitudes are in the 1000-2000 meter range, and swath widths are generally about seven-tenths the altitude, or about 1000 meters on average. Infrared wavelengths are used, and, as with all approaches except for IFSAR, it cannot work through clouds.

The ability to resolve land from water is sometimes a problem, particularly if surf is present. Most ALTM systems do not have software optimized for distinguishing between land and water for each laser pulse. Water is qualitatively evident as a result of reduced signal strengths. Signal dropouts often occur, particularly at larger nadir angles, but the combination of variable nadir angles and wind speeds leads to a very wide and confusing range of signal amplitudes from water. The location of water areas is often inferred manually in a geographic context. The shoreline accuracy required for some applications may not be easily achieved without additional software development. Some excellent qualitative results have been reported in complex estuarine environments (O'Reilly, 2000). Chapter 7 of this book contains detailed information on ALTM systems.

Airborne Lidar Bathymetry

Early examples of surveying across the land/water boundary were conducted with the NASA Airborne Oceanographic Lidar (Krabill and Swift, 1981a). The performance of ALB systems at the land/water interface varies with design. LADS is used primarily over water. Most now have augmented capabilities to provide services in this critical regime. SHOALS was the first to perform bathymetry and topography simultaneously with an optional KGPS vertical datum and special software algorithms which give it the capability to operate seamlessly at the shoreline if environmental conditions permit (Guenther et al., 1998; Brooks et al., 1998). The major advantage is that there is no need for tide coordination. The elevation data are collected both above and below the water surface for the development of a DEM on which any desired water level may be added on the computer to determine the related shoreline. LADS Mk II also supports KGPS and added a topographic capability (Wellington, 2001b). Woolard et al. (2003) report encouraging results in a NOAA study using LADS Mk II data from a test area at Shilshole, Washington. EAARL and Hawk Eye II are also designed to work at the shoreline.

One possible drawback of using an ALB system for shoreline definition is that the presently available survey density (typically 4 m at full swath width) may not be as great as desired for some applications, although it should be sufficient for many uses. Additionally, as noted previously, system performance degrades in a heavy surf zone due both to large areas of white foam and to the water being opaque with re-suspended bottom material. Both of these conditions can cause a false land indication. This is not an ideal area for shoreline operations because the land detection algorithms are not foolproof, particularly in such difficult circumstances. Because the methods used to distinguish water from land typically involve relative factors such as pulse return amplitudes and shapes (Swift et al., 1981), performance will vary from system to system.

If a bathymetric or bathy/topo survey is already being conducted at the shoreline, the "shoreline" product can have excellent quality and be a nearly cost-free result — except possibly for additional data processing and reporting. On the other hand, if shoreline mapping is the only product desired, airborne lidar may not necessarily be a good competitor with aerial photogrammetry, satellite imagery, or IFSAR, in terms of coverage rate and cost, particularly for complex coastline geometries, because bathymetric lidar typically flies at relatively low altitudes with associated narrower swaths (less than 300 meters). If a full DEM is desired, however, and coordination with tides is onerous, then airborne topo/bathy may provide the best approach. Now, innovative approaches for shoreline topo/bathy include multiple lidars working together on one platform and lidar married with hyperspectral techniques, but coverage rate and cost will probably remain a comparative problem if there is no complementary reason for the system to be there.

OPERATIONAL CONSIDERATIONS

Calibration Procedures

As noted in an earlier section, low-order IHO accuracy requirements are quite rigorous, and the ability to achieve and maintain them cannot be taken for granted. ALB, like other systems, has a number of inherent and potential error sources that must be carefully managed and monitored. These are exacerbated by the aircraft altitude and the need to pass through the air/water interface. Proper system design is of primary importance. The hardware and software designs must be predicated on producing the best possible precision and accuracy of recorded and processed data by minimizing sensitivity to uncontrollable environmental effects while not introducing any uncorrectable errors (Guenther et al., 2000). Recognized biases must be removed in software. Because field operations take place in harsh environments, the precision, repeatability, and absolute accuracy of the system must be checked on a regular basis by performing occasional intercomparisons against independent standards, both on the ground and in the air, and through constant monitoring of survey overlap areas between swaths and flying periodic cross lines.

A great deal of attention, during both design and operation, must be paid to the precise and accurate measurement of times and angles. Optical and electronic time delays through the system, both fixed and variable, must be carefully determined, and errors must be either eliminated or calibrated and corrected in software. Typical examples are signal transit time variations in a photomultiplier tube (PMT) as a function of high voltage and in a logarithmic amplifier as a function of signal amplitude. Inputs related to aircraft attitude and location are typically recorded at a rate slower than the laser pulse rate. Such measurements must be temporally deskewed and appropriately interpolated on a pulse-to-pulse basis. Computer latencies must be well understood and carefully handled. The stability of laser pulse characteristics such as pulse risetime, width, and energy is very important and must be monitored. It is important to design the system such that any correctors are small so that errors in the correctors do not have a substantial impact on overall system performance. Timing calibration must be measured and corrected to sub-nanosecond accuracy, and it should demonstrate good stability. This calibration for each receiver channel should be checked occasionally by firing the system in calibrated target ranges on the ground, and it must be repeated when new components which can affect the timing are added or when problems are suspected. Constants thus derived are used in the software. Systems such as SHOALS that have multiple receiver channels have the added benefit of continuous, full-time timing intercomparisons as a consistency check.

System installation angles, aircraft orientation angles, and the resulting beam nadir angle in the world frame must be known to high accuracy for every pulse because their effect on distance measurements is magnified by the aircraft altitude. For example, at a 400-m altitude and with a nominal 20-degree nadir angle, a system angle error of 0.05 degrees (<1 mradian), which equates to a nadir angle error of 0.10 degrees after reflection off a misaligned mirror, would yield a 25-cm error in the estimated vertical height of the aircraft. This would be unacceptably large for many applications. It is desirable to limit system error components to about 5 cm and thus system angle errors to about 0.01 degrees. The measurement of system alignment angles in the aircraft to such a tolerance would be very difficult. This calibration can be accomplished with the needed accuracy by applying an inverse algorithm to slant ranges to the water surface from flight data collected occasionally for the specific purpose of angle calibration. Calibration passes should be made whenever the optical system is disturbed, as when laser heads are switched.

The green light beam in the water spreads out because of the effects of surface waves and of scattering from entrained organic and inorganic particulate materials. Scattering is generally the dominant effect. The complex phenomena involved were diagrammed in Figure 8.3. The beam spreading is both spatial and temporal and affects both the effective location of the sounding and the arrival time of the bottom return at the receiver. The basis for timing measurements for the slant path to the bottom is the so-called "unscattered ray". Scattering causes simultaneous "long" biases due to increased photon path lengths and "short" biases due to the fact that a significant amount of energy is scattered into the "undercutting" region in the direction closer to the aircraft than the unscattered ray. The results of Monte Carlo simulation studies of underwater light propagation (Guenther and Thomas, 1984b; Guenther, 1985) indicate that net propagation-induced depth measurement biases vary with nadir angle, depth, and water clarity parameters and exhibit larger magnitudes, and larger variations versus water clarity parameters, near nadir. The resulting net depth-measurement biases must be predicted by such modeling. These predicted biases, after their accuracy has been confirmed by field intercomparisons, are then applied in software as correctors to the raw measured depths.

For each aircraft installation, the precise location of the GPS antenna must be determined relative to the location of the timing datum in the transceiver. This can be accomplished to within a few centimeters either by using a total station or by geodetic GPS observations from an arbitrary baseline. For systems that utilize measured vertical accelerations, the location of the inertial reference unit is also calibrated with respect to the center of rotation of the aircraft.

The philosophy regarding the need to confirm vertical and horizontal accuracy in field intercomparisons, or "whole system checks", varies from system to system. The frequency of benchmark survey intercomparisons depends on system design, the recommendations of the system manufacturer, and the propensity of the user. The LADS systems employ a strategy of benchmark surveys on every flight (Setter and Willis, 1994; Sinclair, 1999b), while other systems do not embrace the need for such a procedure on a regular basis because long-term calibration stability has been well established. Both approaches appear to be quite satisfactory. LADS vertical accuracy is assessed against acoustic benchmarks, wherever possible, on each operational sortie using an automated comparison routine in post-flight processing (Perry, 1999). Other systems, such as SHOALS, rely on occasional benchmarks, rigorous periodic timing and angle calibrations, proven calibration stability (Guenther et al., 2000), and monitoring survey data quality with continuous checks of internal system consistency in overlaps between adjacent swaths and in cross-lines. The latter checks, performed either manually or in software, are potentially the most reliable method for identifying system errors. For systems with topographic capability, topographic benchmark surveys are also required.

When making these intercomparisons, it must be taken into consideration that both lidar and sonar systems are designed to meet the same accuracy standards and that the accuracy of a properly designed lidar system is as good as that for sonar (Setter and Willis, 1994). There is a danger in the popular conception that, when lidar results are compared with those from older techniques, the latter are correct. This is not necessarily the case. Indeed, laser surveys have "brought to light" errors in associated sonar surveys.

Although surveys using KGPS to provide the aircraft height, and resulting measured elevations, with respect to the WGS-84 ellipsoid are nominally very precise and accurate, practical experience has shown that some form of gross vertical accuracy checking is required when performing KGPS surveys because they are highly susceptible to errors in datum information and data quality, the latter particularly at times of active sunspots. Project datums are most often related to tides. New control surveys are sometimes needed because the height difference between the project datum and the WGS-84 ellipsoid can change throughout the project area (Guenther et al., 1998).

Satisfactory horizontal accuracy for nearly all applications can be obtained from appropriate implementations of GPS. Differential GPS (DGPS) is most commonly used. Gross horizontal-error checks can be made by confirming the location of identifiable features in down-look video imagery, but these depend on the alignment of the camera and the reference grid utilized. More accurate results can be obtained by parking the aircraft over control points on the runway and by comparing the measured and known locations of objects detected in the lidar pulses themselves (Graham et al., 1999).

Positioning the Aircraft

All existing ALB systems use some form of GPS for horizontal positioning of the aircraft. Developments in GPS positioning capabilities over the past decade to provide the ability to accurately position aircraft "over the horizon" have had a major impact on the efficiency of ALB operations. Earlier positioning systems such as microwave ranging were less accurate, and their use was unwieldy. The accuracy of stand-alone GPS is marginal, at best, for most modern surveying purposes even with selective availability (SA) switched off.

Two methods of overcoming large portions of the propagation and SA errors associated with stand-alone GPS are Precise (P) Code and differential (DGPS). Although P-code (originally available only to military organizations) is less accurate than DGPS, it continues to be useful for the RAN LADS (Sinclair and Spurling, 1997). DGPS achieves substantial improvement in accuracy by using one or more GPS "base stations" at known locations for measuring local errors in the GPS pseudo-ranges (ranges to the satellites derived by an iterative process) and generating corrections. Range errors are transmitted, by one of several methods, to users and applied as correctors to the observed user pseudo-ranges to the same satellites. DGPS positioning, typically accurate to better than 3 meters, is used by most or all systems.

Finally, sub-decimeter accuracy, both horizontal and vertical, can be obtained through the use of carrier-phase measurements in so-called kinematic GPS (KGPS) which became practical with the implementation of a technique variously called "on-the-fly (OTF) ambiguity resolution" (Remondi, 1991) or "integer ambiguity resolution". This combination is alternately known as KGPS/OTF or DGPS with KAR (kinematic ambiguity resolution) or post-processed kinematic (PPK). Its primary use for ALB is to provide an alternative vertical reference, the WGS-84 ellipsoid, independent of the water surface. Because of the previously mentioned uncertainties in the bottom-sounding horizontal location relative to the surface location, caused by beam spreading, its additional use as the horizontal reference would probably be of little practical benefit.

In the early days, differential corrections were applied during post-flight processing of recorded user data, but now DGPS systems not only generate the corrections but also utilize some type of wireless transmission system for getting the correctors to users in near real time. This communication may be VHF systems for short ranges (FM broadcast), low-frequency transmitters for medium ranges (beacons), and geostationary satellites (L-Band) for coverage of entire continents. All of these methods have been employed for ALB. Prior to the demise of SA, the correction update rate and transmission bandwidth required consideration, but this concern is now significantly reduced.

Over short ranges (less than roughly 50 km), VHF transmission presents several advantages. Once the user has purchased the portable differential base station, it is under his full control. It can be established over any selected known point, and there are no further costs. A second advantage lies in the high update rate that allows accuracy to be easily maintained. Major drawbacks, however, are associated with the limited range, the associated potential need for a large number of base stations, and the multiple sources of interference in that part of the electromagnetic spectrum. Although the use of VHF was common in the earlier days of ALB, it is now seldom used both for the reasons outlined above and because of the availability of other independently maintained systems.

Medium or low frequency beacons operated almost continuously, independent of the user, by organizations such as the U.S. Coast Guard, offer much enhanced ranges over VHF (up to about 200 km). Despite the fact that use of such beacons is essentially free to the user (except the cost of purchasing a DGPS-compatible receiver), they suffer from several problems that can, in some circumstances, compromise their usefulness for ALB purposes. These include both slower update rates and occasional atmospheric interference effects. Notwithstanding this, ALB systems have successfully used such beacons for a number of years.

By far the most flexible solution is provided by Wide Area DGPS (WADGPS) in which corrections are provided via satellite broadcast. This enables both high update rates and reliable communications over continent-size footprints. The broadcast has ample power within the footprint that a small omnidirectional antenna may be used for receiving, and the frequency used is sufficiently close to that of GPS that, in most instances, a common, single antenna may be used. This particular feature is highly attractive to ALB because it reduces the need for modifications to the external fuselage of the aircraft that may have certification implications. A further key feature of WADGPS is "Virtual Base Station Solution" (VBS), which uses a weighted solution from multiple base stations to provide every user with corrections optimized for their specific location. This is an attractive feature to ALB since the aircraft is provided with a solution that is consistently accurate regardless of proximity to any particular base station. A number of providers have established WADGPS subscription services; OmniSTAR, Starfix, Skyfix supplied by Fugro, and CNAV supplied by C&C Technologies are probably the best known. Incorporating up to 80 permanent reference stations and two or three regional network control centers, these services are designed to provide uninterrupted and accurate positioning via L-Band geostationary communications satellites to up to 95% of the globe. This versatility and robustness is offered at reasonable subscription rates. WADGPS is currently in wide use for ALB operations (Lillycrop and Brooks, 1996; Sinclair, 1998).

KGPS/OTF provides a methodology for sub-meter positioning of the aircraft in all three dimensions. Although this accuracy may not be needed for horizontal positioning, it has been noted that the optional use of this technique for the defining the vertical aircraft reference provides the benefits of unlimited operation over land for beach profiling and topographic mapping, as well as operation over water without the need for concurrent water-level measurements. These advantages, however, are not without costs. The biggest drawback to the use of KGPS for ALB is the burdensome logistics requirements, which are a function of the number of base stations required. To ensure the highest possible reliability and accuracy, a procedure that utilizes multiple baselines to detect and prevent erroneous initializations should be used (Lapucha and Barker, 1996). This requires the placement, monitoring, and maintenance of multiple base stations at sites locked to an extremely accurate vertical control network.

Estimates of the maximum distance from the base station at which KGPS can be operated vary from 10-30 km, but this figure is dependent on a number of factors. First among these is the extent of the unobstructed horizon at both the base station and the aircraft. While the possibility that high buildings and/or trees may obstruct the clear horizon at the base station is easily appreciated, care also has to be taken that line of sight to satellites is not obstructed on the aircraft either by poor antenna location or through aggressive maneuvering of the aircraft. In optimum conditions, maximum range from base station to mobile can be achieved if both have in view a common set of satellites, even when some of these may be at relatively low elevations. Conversely in less ideal conditions, obstructions can limit base and mobile to the use of only high-elevation satellites, resulting in the need to establish a tighter network of base stations. This problem is further compounded when it is considered that the main benefactor of KGPS technology is coastal resource management projects that are characterized by long stretches of coastlines which consequently require an extended linear network of base stations. Consequently, while logistics costs discourage its general use, KGPS offers a viable solution to areas with specific problems such as complex tides or the need to survey both topography and bathymetry simultaneously.

Although some applications benefit from performing calculations in near-real-time using a technique known as "real time kinematic" (RTK), there is little or no currently perceived benefit for its application to ALB, and the carrier-phase data is recorded in both the aircraft and base stations receivers for subsequent post-flight processing and quality control. During flight, positional control is typically maintained using a DGPS solution.

Water Level ("Tidal") Measurement

The water level at a given time and location on a body of water is a function of an astronomical component (the tide) which can be predicted and a meteorological component which cannot. Depending on the location, the tidal variation may range from a few decimeters to over ten meters. Florida's Atlantic coast, for example, has tidal ranges that vary from a maximum of 2.01-m in the North to 0.56-m in the South. ALB surveys break down into two categories: those using the extant mean water level at the time and location of the survey as the vertical measurement reference and those using KGPS/OTF. For the former, traditional approach, water level measurements at the survey site, concurrent with the survey, are required. For the latter method, they are not. This is one of the major advantages of the KGPS/OTF approach.

For a traditional survey, depths measured with respect to the local mean water level will be reduced to the tidal datum of choice by applying either predicted tides or measured tides. A low order (high accuracy) survey requires the latter because predicted tides do not include the effects of meteorology and are often inaccurate. The collection and application of a water-level time series for the survey time and location must be carefully planned and executed. The accuracy of this measurement is a critical component of the depth error budget. Data from existing water-level gages, such as those maintained by the National Ocean Service, is used wherever possible. It takes at least a month to establish datums at a new gage (traditional spelling). For the large areas covered rapidly by airborne surveys, a single water-level gage is often insufficient. A further complicating factor occurs in areas of restriction, such as an inlet. Because of access issues and the need to protect gages from storm action, tide stations are often located inside inlets where incoming and outgoing tides create a build up of water during high flow and can cause tidal reductions to be erroneous for areas outside the inlet. In these situations, a water-level gage network may be needed, and the further procedure of tide zoning between gages will be needed to avoid steps in the modeled surface. In complex geographic situations, integration of modeled tides and *in situ* gages may be required to maintain desired accuracies.

For KGPS/OTF surveys, the surface and sea bottom elevations measured with respect to the WGS-84 ellipsoid are often reduced to a local tidal datum for charting or mapping purposes. This does not require a survey-concurrent, water-level time series, but, as noted above under "Calibration", it does demand accurate knowledge of the ellipsoidal heights of the vertical control monuments to which the local tidal datums are referenced. This may necessitate a vertical and horizontal control survey of the existing monuments or the creation of new reference stations that can be tied into the monument network. This type of survey tends to be more expensive, due to the added logistics, and is therefore only conducted when needed. The accuracy may be degraded somewhat during times of high solar activity. In order to permit assessment of the accuracy of baseline closure at the time of the survey, the control survey should be conducted prior to the hydrographic survey. It should be noted that knowledge of the ellipsoidal elevations of the control monuments alone is not necessarily sufficient to correct a KGPS survey to the tidal datum. An accurate zoning model of the datum separation (geoid to ellipsoid) over the entire survey area is needed, and these are not always available. Unmodeled variations in the separation will result in errors in reported depth, with respect to a true geoidal datum at that location, much as errors in tidal zoning result in depth errors for the traditional method.

Survey Planning and Management

Mission planning can be thought of in terms of three epochs: the basic survey plan, detailed scheduling and logistics, and on-site survey management. Given a potential mission requirement, the first agenda involves the development of a plan consisting of a feasibility study, the estimation of logistical considerations, the determination of data requirements, and a cost assessment. The success or failure of a survey can depend on how well it is planned, how those plans are executed, and the ability to deal with unforeseen circumstances.

The feasibility study involves both theoretical and practical aspects. The first determination that has to be made is expectation of success based on depth requirements and expectations of water clarity. For many areas, the water clarity and meteorological factors may vary seasonally and dictate the month(s) appropriate for the survey. The next matter is ascertaining the availability of the system at that time and location. Availability conflicts may need to be resolved. Planning a geographical "Grand Tour" can be very important in reducing costs. Customer priorities and requirements must be taken into consideration. If the survey is judged feasible, the next considerations are logistical. The distance from the expected system location to the new survey is determined. The size of the survey area is considered with respect to projected travel costs. The nearest appropriate airport to the survey site is located and contacted. The availability of suitable facilities and equipment for aircraft and personnel are evaluated. Special features such as mountains and potential air space restrictions or conflicts will be factored in.

Discussions with the potential sponsor about data requirements will have indicated whether the survey is to be a bathymetric survey or a hydrographic survey and defined the associated data density, vertical and horizontal accuracy, and small target requirements. The need for surf-zone, shoreline, or topographic products will have been identified. Known features of particular emphasis will have been denoted. It will first be decided whether the survey will be traditional or use KGPS/OTF as the vertical reference. For a traditional survey, the availability of suitable water-level gages and their condition must be ascertained. In extreme cases, an *ad hoc* gage may need to be installed. The method to be used for horizontal control is selected. For a DGPS survey, the source of differential correctors (wide area or local) must be determined. If local, consideration must be given to the coverage area, range limits over land and water, the number of stations needed, and practical sites along coast. For a kinematic survey, the number of base stations needed is determined, availability of control monuments and locations for base stations is identified, and the possible need for a control survey must be considered. Experience has proven that things are not always where they were thought to be. Finally, a cost assessment is made based on the logistical considerations, data requirements, and perceived risks.

If it is to be a contract survey, this is where the technical and cost proposals would be made, assuming the survey is deemed appropriate for the technology. With a determination to proceed, the second step is to supplement the basic plan with a schedule and detailed logistics for items such as aircraft and equipment needs, environmental considerations, transportation requirements, personnel assignments, office space, and housing arrangements.

The third and final process can best be categorized as survey management. This involves the implementation of the plan, mobilization of equipment and personnel, establishment and manning of control and water level stations, conducting needed system calibrations, day-to-day selection and planning of specific survey areas and laying out flightlines consistent with data requirements, monitoring weather and water clarity, management of flight times to avoid sun glint and meet the needs of the air crews, coordination with tidal cycles if desirable, reacting to winds, weather, and wave conditions, selection of alternate sites, planning reflies, modification of plans as necessary, selection of data processing protocols, evaluation of data quality, production of the required output products, maintenance of the equipment, conducting necessary remedial actions to ensure the successful completion of the survey, and demobilization. This is a complex and demanding task that requires a great deal of both expertise and experience.

Post-flight Data Processing

Software design features and algorithms are equally important with hardware for performance and accuracy. A detailed description of post-flight data processing software and procedures is beyond the scope of this document, but a brief summary is presented here to emphasize important features and typical characteristics. The major generic software components are the Automated element, the Manual element, Visualization and Editing, and Production. Data processing techniques vary considerably from system to system, but they have a number of aspects in common. Early work was reported by Billard and Wilsen (1986) and Guenther and Mesick (1988a). More recent details have been provided for LADS by Perry (1999) and for SHOALS by Guenther et al. (1996; 2000). Depth-measurement accuracy is the primary goal. Post-flight data processing software seeks to maximize sea-bottom detection probability while minimizing false alarms. As a major part of this effort, it is absolutely critical that small objects (such as rocks, coral heads, and man-made debris) be properly identified. The processing corrects several unavoidable but predictable biases from the environment as well as removing effects inherent to the hardware configuration. Its automated component provides efficiency, while the manual components provide flexible operator interaction to handle differing survey requirements and special environmental circumstances. Visualization tools were originally used to assist with a final sanity check, but these powerful programs are now being customized for specific systems and taking over more of the manual processing functions. The production element provides the required survey output products for the customer.

A practical measure of data processing can be expressed in terms of the effective laser pulse-repetition rate that can be handled by a single work station and operator while maintaining the needed data throughput. In order to minimize personnel and computer requirements in the field, systems with higher pulse rates will have to compensate with faster computers, more efficient processing, and less need for manual interaction.

Automated Algorithms

The following list highlights some of the major functions performed by the post-flight waveform processor and depth determination algorithms. Flexible operator interaction is provided to handle special cases through the use of a set of software control parameters. Timing latencies in measured scanner angles, attitude, and altitude data are deskewed. Low-rate sensor data are interpolated for each pulse. A tracking algorithm may be applied to surface times. Surface and bottom returns are discriminated using signal-to-noise ratio and possibly near-neighbor confidence as criteria. Algorithms containing heuristic rules (Guenther and Mesick, 1988a) are helpful in rejecting noise, system artifacts, and false targets in the environment such as fish and scattering layers. The algorithms must handle complex waveforms associated with a variety of circumstances from extremely strong shallow returns to extremely weak deep returns as well as difficult returns in turbid waters (Perry, 1999). It is vitally important to have a reliable capability to identify small objects on the sea bottom. Recorded waveforms, which have been nonlinearly processed in hardware, are linearized, and precise pulse arrival times are estimated. Studies have shown that the most accurate and precise pulse-location algorithm is a half-peak-height amplitude threshold applied to the linear waveform (Guenther and Thomas, 1981). Timing calibration correctors are applied for hardware and environmental time delays. This should include delay versus amplitude tables because transit times through nonlinear components tend to acquire a certain amount of amplitude dependence. Predicted biases associated with the measured sub-surface water Raman-scattered surface times (Guenther, 1986) are added in the case of SHOALS.

Several types of automated channel priority logic may be available for selection of the optimal surface return for each pulse. The local mean water level is calculated. This acts as the primary depth reference and permits the removal of wave heights from the measured water-column depths (Billard, 1986a; Thomas and Guenther, 1990). The depths are determined in a manner consistent with the quality of available surface data and the goals of the survey. Two possible bottom returns per waveform are saved in order to permit valid depths to be calculated in the presence of fish and other biota in the water column. This is also a critical for small-object detection. Depths from both detections, if available, can be presented for possible manual inspection. Automated depth selections may be manually swapped to an alternative if desired. When KGPS/OTF is used as the primary vertical reference, bottom elevations are calculated with respect to the ellipsoid (Guenther et al., 1998). A predicted corrector for propagation-induced bias is applied as a function of depth and nadir angle (Guenther, 1985). The positions of the soundings are calculated taking into consideration parameters such as aircraft position, altitude, attitude, scanner angles, and depth.

A number of internal consistency checks are conducted during processing, and various confidence and accuracy statistics are gathered. For each pulse, an overall level of "confidence" in the result is provided as a key parameter. For a traditional survey, predicted tides or measured water levels are applied. For LADS systems, benchmark depth comparisons are flown and automatically processed for every flight. Prerecorded data is generally available for defined, small areas that have been surveyed using high-accuracy acoustic techniques. The comparison cross-line and benchmark statistics are calculated and recorded for subsequent viewing (Perry, 1999). In SHOALS, quality control of surface data is augmented by calculating difference statistics for independent but redundant times in the two surface channels. In addition to bathymetry, topo-graphic heights may be calculated for pulses on land. The horizontal position of each laser shot on the bottom is determined. At this point, for LADS systems, a subset of soundings is produced by a selection process aimed at producing a decimated data set suitable for conventional fairsheet presentation at the scale of the survey. SHOALS defers decimation until the production step.

Manual Processing

Interactive data displays and automatically calculated statistics are available to facilitate quality control and validation of results. Calculated depths are typically color-coded and may be presented in a variety of display formats. The user may "zoom" in to view selected geographic regions of interest. Pulses not returning depths may need to be examined. Areas of indicated land might need to be verified, particularly in surf zones. The time-stamped down-looking video record or digital images may be consulted for ancillary geographic information. Difficult or questionable data segments can be reprocessed, within limited geographic boundaries, with parameters optimized for the situation. Multiple or false depths due to environmental effects such as schools of fish or turbidity layers can be investigated by the operator to ensure the use of the underlying true bottom depths. The automated decision may be reversed if necessary. Problem soundings or areas are marked for further investigation or reflies.

Most importantly, recorded raw waveforms, along with important parameters, can be accessed for selected soundings and displayed for careful evaluation by the operator (Brooks et al., 1998; Sinclair et al., 1999). According to the laws of statistics, assuming a normal distribution, one pulse in every hundred is beyond the three-sigma level. If a relatively short 13-km flight line contains, say, 100,000 or more pulses, then that flight line will contain at least 1000 pulses whose depths are outside the three-sigma bound. A few of such statistically inevitable errors may leak through automated quality tests and need to be studied, and possibly removed, manually. Waveforms with multiple bottom returns may need to be examined, particularly for the presence of small objects when invoking hazard-detection procedures.

Especially rigorous hazard detection techniques and quality control procedures are used for nautical charting data (Brooks et al., 1998; Perry, 1999). The waveforms of questionable soundings are examined and compared to those from neighboring points to assist interpretation. The distinction between fish and coral heads or a wreck is not always clear. For nautical charting work, if no conclusive evidence exists to discredit an apparent anomaly, additional flight data are collected to confirm or disprove its existence. Some surveys are flown with 200% original coverage to improve the detection probability of small objects. In this case, the data are examined to determine if the anomalies exist in both flightlines. A software or operator failure at this point will lead to very dangerous, or, at best, embarrassing circumstances. The job of data processing is not any easy one. The survey manager must be aware of problematic data and maintain control over these procedures. For less-stringent general bathymetry not for navigation purposes, such as reconnaissance or "condition" surveys or modeling work, similar examinations of the anomalies and neighboring soundings are made, but additional data are not normally collected; the decision to keep or discard is made based on the existing data.

For LADS systems, the possibility of assigning "No Bottom At" depths is assessed. For SHOALS, depths in the problematic 0-1 meter depth range can be examined for validity and selected by the operators if desired (Brooks et al., 1998). Additionally, SHOALS provides access to internal and value-added parameters for calibration, analysis, correlation, and plotting through the use of optional relational database and spreadsheet programs. Utility programs for tasks such as angle calibration may be executed. The various systems employ numerous other analytical features that are beyond the scope of this article.

All flight lines are planned to overlap adjacent lines. Areas of missing coverage ("holidays") caused by missing or unresolvable data, data edits, or incorrectly positioned flightlines are identified for further investigation or reflying. The consistency of overlap results, throughout the survey area, is monitored for quality control. Periodic cross-lines are flown and analyzed for the same purpose. Quality control is also augmented by monitoring redundant surface time statistics. For LADS systems, previously calculated cross-line and benchmark statistics are reviewed and evaluated.

Powerful visualization software tools have become commercially available. Manufacturers are willing to customize these tools to meet the unique needs of specific users. This permits the migration of much of the editing previously done in *ad hoc* two-dimensional manual processing schemes to be accomplished more efficiently in a pseudo-three-dimensional visualization environment.

Visualization and Spatial Editing

Three-dimensional visualization programs may be used as a check for holidays and wild depths in geographic context and for spatial data editing. These permit color-coded data to be viewed interactively from various perspectives and typically include a variety of features such as rotations, contouring, shadow rendering, and profile views. Excellent commercial programs are available, and these are often customized to provide *ad hoc* features such as efficient access to the raw waveforms. LADS and SHOALS, for example, use the Fledermaus Professional Edition from IVS 3D to great effect (Francis et al., 2003). In general, such software must be able to provide simple and rapid rotations of very large data sets. Shadowing has proven to be a quite useful feature. Profiles, in addition to being a quality control feature, may be an output product in some cases. Data sets acquired at different times or with different sensors may be combined and tested for agreement. An effective visualization program will provide the ability to find suspicious step offsets which could indicate problems such as errors in positioning, water-level correctors, or angle calibration. Pseudo three-dimensional views are valuable for discovering any remaining random outliers that have avoided two-dimensional manual quality checks. All data sets for a project area are cleaned and saved.

Deliverables

Products, procedures, and deliverables vary far too much from system to system, customer to customer, and over time, to be described in any but the most general terms. Deliverables may be paper or digital; most often, both are required. Typical digital products from a survey, provided to the customer in agreed-upon formats, would be the cleaned and verified full xyz survey data set, a decimated xyz data set, TINs, Computer-Aided Design (CAD) and Geographic Information System (GIS) files, plot files, and a metadata file compliant to FGDC standards. Paper products may include two-dimensional forms such as charts, maps, smooth sheets, contour plots, or profiles and pseudo three-dimensional, color-coded, shaded displays. Some customers may desire higher-order products, based on further analysis of the data, such as bathymetric differences from previous years or dredge volumes.

All raw data and processed results should be permanently recorded for possible later review during chart verification and production, as well as for archiving. If decimation has not already been done, it would be done at this point to the cleaned xyz files. The raw survey density is far too great for presentation to many customers, and a large percentage of "unimportant" soundings may need to be removed in the generation of final products. The decimation process retains the critical soundings, particularly the shoals, according to the scale of the survey. Overlapping soundings and unneeded data on uniformly sloping areas are removed according to specified horizontal and vertical tolerances. Commercial or custom software programs may be used. The result is saved in an appropriate digital format for distribution and may be used to generate paper products. In the near future, the digital data may be used for the creation of Electronic Nautical Chart (ENC) files.

When paper products are required, the cleaned or decimated data are typically passed into commercial chart or map production software. The scale is determined by customer needs and the size of the project. The complete data set would generally only be used to create very large-scale charts (1:1200 or larger) for small projects, because the large file size is not justified by the minimal increase in information in the final product. The basic element of the mapping process is the triangulated irregular network (TIN) that represents the depths or elevations. Each individual sounding is a mass point in the TIN. TINs are used as intermediate products in the generation of a variety of deliverables such as color-coded elevation grids, contours, and profiles. Hard breaklines are rarely needed or used when dealing with high-density bathymetric data. Along the shoreline or on land, however, breaklines may be used along road centerlines, toes and crowns of dikes, levies, jetties, and walls, and anywhere they are needed to prevent the software from connecting data points that fall on opposite sides of a physical discontinuity.

Individual CAD and/or GIS files may contain single data representations such as color-coded elevations, contours, profiles, geo-referenced photographs, and sounding elevation text (individual soundings shown on the final chart) which can be overlaid in various combinations. Contours are usually generated on intervals ranging from 0.5 m to 5.0 m depending on the chart scale and intended use of the data. The elevation text is produced by a method that reads the complete or decimated data file. The overlaid data files must be on, or converted to, the same datum and the same projection but need not all cover identical geographic areas. Composite products can be generated by retrieving all data within a selected overlay frame and writing it into a "sheet" file. The sheet file will also contain items such as the title block, legends, notes, index maps, scale bars, and borders. Plot files can be created from these sheet files. Charts and maps may be printed on site in the field, but, more often, cleaned complete and decimated files will be sent to a centralized production and distribution facility for final validation and printing. The customer may perform additional data verification measures according to their standard procedures.

Digital GIS products can provide access to the valuable information contained within the bathymetric lidar and accompanying datasets, especially in cases where customers do not have the knowledge or hardware required to deal with large datasets. These products include raster images, or grids, built from TINs of the combined topographic and bathymetric elevation data. From these grids, a shoreline or other contour of interest is extracted and stored as a shapefile. For topographic data, images of first and last returns are analyzed to extract building footprints and bare earth models. Topographic lidar intensity and bathymetric seafloor reflectance data are used to discriminate between discrete land use areas and bottom types, respectively. These classifications are improved by combining lidar elevation and intensity/reflectance with RGB or hyperspectral image data in complex data fusion algorithms (Tuell et al., 2005c).

FUTURE ADVANCEMENTS

Background

The ALB systems operating in the world today are largely derived from Canadian, Australian, United States, and Swedish government programs, and these governments were primarily responsible for defining the user requirements. Airborne lidar-bathymetry systems of the current generation have matured, and the services of several are now available from industry. With up to twelve years of successful operations, including thousands of hours of experience in logistics, data collection, data processing, and product generation, representatives from the latter three national governments re-evaluated their needs and formulated more ambitious ALB requirements that go well beyond the current capabilities. Serious consideration was being given to defining where the technology and systems must be in five to ten years to meet anticipated needs in areas such as nautical charting, port and harbor mapping, coastal zone management, and military rapid environmental assessment for site characterization. Each early system was developed based on different survey requirements and program goals, each program has traveled a different path, and each has experienced different successes and failures, but the representatives discovered that they all shared the same vision for the future (Lillycrop et al., 2001). Industry will continue to be quite challenged to meet these new requirements for enhanced data collection capabilities, lower unit cost, size constraints, and the ability to integrate with complementary sensors.

The missions described in detail in the User Applications section are expected to continue to be the primary applications over the next five years or more. At the present time, there are two general philosophies of system configuration in terms of aircraft size and utilization. One approach is to use a large, high-performance lidar system in a dedicated, long-range aircraft. In this way, the system can be flown directly to any location in the world within a few days. Long sorties may consist of lengthy surveys if flown at a location near the airport or shorter surveys performed at a great distance from the airport. The latter capability is an important asset for reaching remote locations, and it is expected that there will be continued demand for contract services from such a system. Few such systems, however, will be needed. The second approach is the proliferation of smaller, portable, shorter-range systems that can be installed in local "aircraft-of-opportunity". These have the advantage of lower cost, the ability to fly from smaller and less developed airfields, and the potential for greater acceptance as a general survey tool by both service providers and clients.

The consensus opinion of government and industry representatives was that the emphasis in the future will be on smaller size and lower cost for the lidar sensor and associated electronics, potential for use in smaller aircraft, greater flexibility in the use of aircraft-of-opportunity, more sophisticated automated data processing with integrated survey planning, and utilization of more off-the-shelf equipment for easier maintenance. These characteristics will reduce the survey cost per unit area by reducing the initial investment, flight costs, field crew size and training, and manual data processing complexity.

More information about the environment should be extracted from the raw lidar return signals to better quantify the physical characteristics of the survey area and add value to the already existing bathymetric products. Once the cost has been expended to operate the aircraft for lidar depths and elevations, valuable additional environmental characterization can be obtained at a very low cost if appropriate software algorithms are available. The ability to use multiple lidars, and lidar in conjunction with complementary sensors such as multispectral and hyperspectral imagers, to produce a broader range of information and products, will lead to new applications and missions. There are undoubtedly other sensors that lidar could complement to improve the ability to rapidly and accurately characterize and quantify the coastal zone. The potential applications are broad, but require ALB systems that are small, flexible, relatively inexpensive to purchase and operate, and easy to operate and integrate with a variety of other techniques.

Driving Factors

There are two types of ALB customers — system customers who wish to own and operate their own systems and survey customers who wish to contract for surveys. The first category includes both government agencies and private companies. The latter ranges from national governments with huge survey backlogs and multi-million dollar budgets to local governments or private entities with a small budget and a little project. While there are already a sufficient number of the former, there could be a very large number of the latter if costs are attractive and knowledge and availability of the technology become widespread. With few exceptions, the needs of this diverse customer base are very similar.

The vision for future ALB systems is driven by the following factors.

- All customers desire more affordable ALB systems and surveys.
- Most survey customers do not have large enough requirements or budgets to justify the purchase cost of a system.
- Most system customers wish to operate systems in smaller aircraft to reduce overall operating costs, because aircraft costs are the dominant cost in ALB operation.
- Systems of the future must be extremely flexible to meet the varied and changing requirements of the survey community.
- Lessons learned from existing systems and programs must be incorporated, and preferably automated, into the new ALB systems.
- Compact airborne laser terrain mapping (ALTM) systems, adapted for operation on small photogrammetric aircraft-of-opportunity and providing accurate, high-density terrain elevation data, are enjoying world-wide success. This implies the existence of a large potential user base and act as a role model for more complex ALB systems.
- Expectations of the international hydrographic community are shifting towards higher standards for hydrographic mapping, including nearly 100% bottom coverage and the ability to detect small features on the bottom.
- Many survey customers would be able to make use of value-added products related to environmental characterization.
- Military organizations desire to put even smaller systems (generation-after-next) into unmanned airborne vehicles for covert operations.

It is envisioned that in the future, as with ALTM systems now, the majority of ALB systems will be procured by aerial survey companies which will then provide survey services to clients as required. A minority of systems will be purchased by government agencies who will want to own and operate their own equipment. Many government agencies will make use of contract surveys.

Performance Characteristics

New advancements in ALB technology and software algorithms will be able to provide the user with a combination of increased capability, improved performance, new products, and lower operating costs in a smaller package than has been available with earlier-generation ALB systems. As performance improves, the locations and types of applications will increase. It is crucial to remember, however, that the penetration and accuracy of existing systems has been hard won and must not be compromised in new systems for the sake of cost and size reductions. An ineffective or marginalized system is not a bargain and is not acceptable. Standards must be maintained, and lessons learned must not be forgotten.

To support the applications described above, the ALB systems of today must evolve. This section lists some of the desired performance characteristics and identifies key focal points for research and development to provide the changes needed to enhance today's sensors and systems. Until these characteristics are adopted by industry, government programs will be the only method of evolving airborne lidar hydrography. If these criteria are met, the entire survey community, both industry and governments, will add ALB to their capabilities. Only then will systems mature and evolve based on the needs of the many.

Platform and Logistics

Size and power requirements of existing ALB systems make them somewhat platform-specific. For systems not intended to be operated from a dedicated aircraft, achieving an airborne sensor design that is fully platform-independent will allow the use of aircraft-of-opportunity. To increase operational flexibility with respect to mission type, sensor fusion, and survey cost, most systems of the future will be small, portable, and modular in design. Regardless of application, these three criteria will ensure that future systems can utilize standard photogrammetric aircraft of opportunity (including utility helicopters), be easily shipped worldwide to utilize these aircraft, and be capable of operating integrated with other sensors. A smaller sensor may be operated from a smaller aircraft, thus reducing the cost of hourly survey flight operations. Reduced costs for sensor mobilization and demobilization will also be realized. The size must also be reduced so that lidar can become a viable sensor for unmanned aerial vehicles (UAV). This is important to the military of the future, one that must project itself in a moment's notice around a region or around the world.

Existing systems require several specially-trained personnel to mobilize them into the aircraft. Once installed, they require complex procedures to calibrate. Future systems, as a goal, should require fewer and less-specially-trained personnel to mobilize equipment and initiate survey missions. Targets for size and training requirements should be similar to those for acoustic multibeam survey systems. System maintenance should be modular and self-diagnosing to reduce the amount of training required of the field survey crew. Finally, the level of automation versus operator control must advance such that the system itself is capable of monitoring the progress of the mission and assessing the quality of the data to reduce the needed expertise level and workload of the operator, or in the case of a UAV application, to operate autonomously.

Lasers

Since airborne lidar bathymetry began, a primary performance metric has been laser pulse-repetition rate. Faster lasers are very desirable. Higher sounding rates will allow even greater area coverage rates, with associated reduction in survey cost, and/or denser coverage. Higher area density, particularly to achieve 100% overlap at the surface, would improve the detection probability for small objects on the bottom. Along with high repetition rates, the pulses must have sufficient energy and narrow width. Narrow pulse widths provide higher peak power, and hence higher signal-to-noise ratio, for a given pulse energy. They also help improve performance in turbid waters and, additionally, can improve the technical aspects of depth measurement accuracy. Diode-pumped solid-state laser technology has advanced to the point where compact systems in the field today have pulse-repetition rates of 5000 pulses per second or more, with appropriate characteristics. In the future, there is expectation of even higher repetition rates and narrower pulse widths. The limitations then will shift to digitizers, associated electronics, and computers that can keep up. As such performance improves, however, it will still be desired to maintain system compatibility with smaller aircraft of opportunity. As pulse rates increase, in conjunction with the need for the same pulse energy, average power requirements would naturally increase. It will be important to find compensating efficiencies to prevent this. For the far future, tunable lasers (wavelength and energy) capable of adjusting to maximize performance under given environmental conditions could improve maximum depth performance and possibly extend the locations and missions where ALB systems are capable of operating.

Technology

In current systems, many components were custom built or in limited availability. This can lead to maintenance and support problems as the system ages. In future systems, maximum use should be made of commercial off the shelf components. For platform-dedicated systems, which can be larger in size and more expensive, the ultimate performance envelope can be extended with the use of cutting-edge, highly sophisticated components regardless of size. Portable systems of limited cost and size will be built to meet but not exceed ad hoc operational requirements. The sophistication in this case will be in miniaturization.

In order to achieve the above goals, recent and upcoming advancements in several key areas of ALB technology will be utilized. In addition to the lasers already discussed, these include the following:

- Lightweight and compact optical scanning systems are now becoming available that can provide the high scanning rates required by future ALB systems. The scanner must be flexible, programmable, and capable of operating in a variety of configurations to match the survey requirements. This might involve altering sounding density in the range between 1 m and 10 m. This and other mission survey parameters must be able to change for each survey line. A new generation of scanners may be necessary to keep up with increasingly high laser repetition rates.

- New waveform digitizers are now commercially available that are much more compact and provide 1-ns digitization on one board, without the need for interleaving separate digitizer boards. For systems with extremely narrow laser pulses, sub-nanosecond digitizers are needed, once again pushing the envelope of the possible.

- Significant advances have been made in the development of compact inertial measurement systems, such as the POS AV, that are now integrated with GPS. Future systems will continue to use a wide range of different positioning systems such as GPS, DGPS, and KGPS.

- High-pulse-rate ALTM systems are now providing ALB systems with enhanced capabilities for terrain mapping and allowing mapping of coastal areas on both sides of the land-water interface at appropriate densities. The trend is toward even more capable and flexible combinations.

- Computer technology has taken enormous strides with the development of new functional boards and faster processors, which will provide tremendous increases in data acquisition and data processing speeds. Fewer computer boards will be required for airborne data acquisition and control. This computing power will also be harnessed by incorporating sophisticated software and algorithms to provide increased automation in both airborne operations as well as post-flight data processing.

- Lightweight, flat-panel displays have replaced large, heavy computer monitors used for operator displays in earlier-generation systems.

- Geo-referenced high-rate digital photography is a highly desirable feature that is being incorporated into current systems. More sophisticated products will be produced from these systems.

- Developments in compact narrow-band optical filters will be closely monitored because these can improve the signal-to-noise ratio, and hence the maximum depth penetration capability, for daytime operations.

The above technological advancements, when simultaneously incorporated into future-generation ALB systems, will yield a powerful combination of superior performance in a miniaturized package.

Ground-Based Processing

Survey operations, including survey planning, data acquisition, and data processing, will become faster and more automated, thereby providing the user with a quicker turnaround and reducing the number of personnel required to support system operations. Software and algorithm development to provide more automated data processing with less manual interaction is essential in making ALB a mainstream hydrographic tool. Minimizing hydrographer interaction through streamlining and optimizing ALB data processing will increase data throughput and provide greater uniformity in final products. This is particularly important in light of ever-increasing laser pulse-repetition rates. Improved algorithms are needed for the complex surf zone and land/water interface where large areas of white foam and suspended solids complicate depth measurement and shoreline differentiation. Delineating where the land ends and the water begins, whether for coastal zone management or military rapid environmental assessment, can be very difficult and time consuming. An accurate, repeatable, automated methodology is required and should be achievable with more aggressive use of existing raw data. In addition, a variety of new, sophisticated data processing options could be used to meet application and mission-specific goals.

Some existing ALB systems appeared before conventional shallow-water acoustic multi-beam survey systems became wide spread, but this acoustic technology has already significantly helped ALB. Shallow-water multibeam echosounders can produce as much data as ALB systems, and this has caused a boom in tools to manage, edit, and visualize large spatial data sets. These tools, and their successors, can be integrated into future ALB systems in order to improve depth extraction and processing efficiency. Today, many weeks of special training in lidar technology is required to process data accurately. Only through an integrated approach that automatically processes ALB data by considering raw lidar signals, nearest neighbors, and statistical variations simultaneously with survey mission parameters and historic survey data, can the amount of additional training be reduced and a typical hydrographer conduct ALB processing. To maximize the incorporation of ALB into commercial visualization and editing packages, an open architecture must be adopted by the lidar manufacturers so that existing software manufacturers and universities can evolve this capability.

Future Capabilities

A comprehensive ALB system of the future could include a variety of potential capabilities. Added features could include bottom and water-column characteristics, hydrodynamic characteristics, and feature imaging. Airborne technologies and data processing algorithms have demonstrated the potential to measure such parameters as bottom reflectivity and type, water wave properties, and surface currents. More detailed interrogation of raw ALB waveforms to extract value-added information may provide an independent means for quantifying certain environmental parameters. The integration of ALB with existing operational sensors such as geo-referenced digital photography, topographic lidar, and multispectral scanners is beginning to meet additional data requirements. Multi-sensor data fusion with ALB is beginning to provide a most efficient and reliable means for mapping additional environmental parameters.

Added ALB-only Products

Bottom Reflectivity

With a radiometrically calibrated system, bottom return amplitudes can be converted into estimates of bottom reflectivity. This can be a very valuable value-added product of bathymetric surveys. It is equivalent to the "intensity" product offered by a number of lidar altimeter systems. This parameter is now being estimated from SHOALS and CHARTS data (Tuell et al., 2005b). It is also an important input into the processing of multispectral data (Tuell and Park, 2004).

Water Clarity

There is much more information contained in the digitized and recorded raw green lidar return waveforms than only water depth. The development of algorithms to extract value-added information from on-wavelength returns is possible for applications such as the quantification and three-dimensional mapping of various water clarity parameters and associated environmental factors. This has been a popular topic since the availability of practical lasers in the late 1960's, particularly due to military applications. The literature abounds with hundreds of highly technical and increasingly sophisticated references dedicated to theoretical studies and field measurements, from surface vessels and aircraft, of the propagation and scattering of light in hydrosols (see, for example, numerous volumes from the biennial Ocean Optics conferences published by SPIE). A great deal of work is also reported in the Soviet literature (Bunkin et al., 1984; Vlasov, 1985). Of greatest interest for this application is solving the so-called "inverse" problem, i.e., estimating the parameters from the measured light field, rather than predicting the effects of the parameters on the light field. It should be noted, however, that from a practical point of view, much more effort and funding is put into off-wavelength (fluorescence) and passive multispectral techniques because of the benefits these offer, particularly for living resources. The chief advantage of a lidar system over passive techniques is related to its ability to penetrate much deeper and to estimate the parameter depth profiles.

From depth-resolved green pulse returns, the optical diffuse attenuation coefficient can certainly be estimated (Gordon, 1982; Billard, et al., 1986; Steinvall et al., 1992; Feygels, et al., 2003), and water clarity parameters, such as some form of scattering coefficient, may be possible (Reuter, 1982; Phillips et al., 1984; Billard, 1986b). For some users, mapping the three-dimensional distribution of a parameter may be of more value than its precise value. Such applications have been discussed, for example, by Hoge et al. (1988), Feigels and Kopilevich (1993), and Feigels and Kopilevich (1994). The spatial concentration of suspended materials could be used, for example, to evaluate dredging operations or measure the impact of effluents on a region. Systems have also been designed for the detection of fish schools (Murphree et al., 1974; Kronman, 1992; Churnside et al., 1997), but that type of operation would require dedicated missions and probably not be conducive to simultaneous operation with a bathymeter.

Wave Spectra
In order to calculate most accurate depths, the wave heights about the mean water level at each pulse location must be measured. These estimated wave heights are presently not being used as value-added products by the operational bathymeters. This should change. The size and direction of waves is important for many coastal engineering applications such as measuring sediment transport rates and in military operations such as determining limiting conditions for safe ingress and egress routes. Early one-dimensional experiments with airborne profiling lasers were carried out by Ross et al. (1970), Schule et al. (1971), Liu and Ross (1980), and McClain et al. (1982). Spatial and statistical wave height characteristics including the two-dimensional vector wave-number spectra can be obtained from a scanning system. These dynamics can be obtained with airborne topographic lidar systems (Hwang et al., 1998), and the results could also easily be reported for ALB missions.

One difficulty which requires careful attention to detail is the fact that the waves and the aircraft are both moving and at very different rates and directions. The sampled wave heights are thus neither synoptic nor stationary, and special algorithms are required to provide a useful product (Walsh et al., 1985). One possible drawback with the present scenario is the spatial data density. The 4-m spacing typically used by today's bathymeters may not provide sufficient sampling density for many wave applications. If future systems have higher sounding densities, the wave-height products would be of greater value. It should be noted that wave heights over the entire swath under all environmental conditions can only be reliably measured by systems with collinear green and infrared beams.

Multi-Sensor Fusion
More information than is currently collected is needed to better quantify the environment. Lidar sensors are now being combined with other airborne sensors on a single airborne platform because of the resulting economy and utility in simultaneously collecting information from many sensors with the same reference data. More importantly, the synergy between synoptic products can provide environmental information that neither sensor alone could produce. As noted above, lidar and geo-referenced digital photography were pioneered in LARSEN. Most ALB systems now have digital cameras, and geo-referencing is being done at various accuracy levels depending upon needs.

The use of lidar provides the unique ability to survey ground elevations at the same time as depth soundings, thus integrating land and water measurements in the same data set. Land elevations are being collected on a regular basis by some existing ALB systems, but the pulse-repetition rate of current bathymeters is not as great as desired for land operations, and they consequently lack the horizontal resolution necessary to fully define topographical features such as small structures, dune lines, seawall break points, and other fine detail. High-resolution renderings of these shoreline structures and coastal features provided by existing ALTM systems are capable of being merged with ALB underwater data, thus producing a seamless product. The solution has two approaches depending on where you start: add topographic capability to a bathymeter or bathymetric capability to a topographic system.

The merging of a combined terrain and bathymetric lidar system with a digital camera creates an excellent data collection tool with numerous applications. Further addition of hyperspectral capability completes the picture and will provide capabilities not yet contemplated. The ALB systems of the future will be capable of sharing a single airborne platform with a variety of complementary sensors. Early proof of concept studies and tests successfully brought together ALB with topographic lidar and ALB with hyperspectral imaging (Borstad and Vosburgh, 1993). All these sensors now form the standard suite for CHARTS missions (Tuell et al., 2005a; Tuell et al., 2005c). Other possibilities include ALB with airborne electromagnetic sensors or with IFSAR.

Multiple Lidars

Combinations of independent bathymetric and topographic lidars on one platform provide great flexibility in the coastal zone. The CHARTS and Hawk Eye II systems now include independent high-rate topographic lidar capability to sample land elevations at a higher rate than the water depths. The two sensors do not operate simultaneously, but data collection is interchangeable from flightline to flightline. EAARL provides high-rate topographic coverage and bathymetry with a single lidar, but at the cost of some bathymetric performance.

Bathymetric Lidar with Digital Imagery

Digital, geo-referenced imagery has been used traditionally as a base photograph on elevation and depth contour plots. With the use of Geographical Information System (GIS) software, elevations and imagery can be integrated, possibly with other data, to yield more interesting displays, and more sophisticated and valuable products. Existing lidar data have been used with separately collected aerial photographs or even satellite imagery, but precise geo-rectification of the individual products can be a serious problem. When imaging ability is deployed on the lidar aircraft to collect simultaneous data, this synoptic information can be more accurate, more meaningful, and less expensive. LARSEN, for example, made extensive use of this feature to provide products such as mapping of shorelines, coral reefs, and fish habitats. Flying with Terra Remote Sensing's proprietary VideoMap imaging system, the LARSEN bathymeter provided the Coastal Zone Management Unit of the Barbados Government with lidar, geo-referenced video, and ortho-rectified still images, all of which were combined with sonar data, to provide a complete solution for shipping and navigation, shoreline erosion, and coastal features (Quinn, 2000). Most current ALB systems have been designed or upgraded to include high-rate digital imagery which can be geo-rectified to the extent desired. Uses include both quality control of the lidar data and the production of new, value-added products.

Bathymetric Lidar with Multispectral or Hyperspectral Scanner

Multispectral and, more recently, hyperspectral imagers are perhaps the most valuable of all remote sensing tools for both land and water. World-wide attention was drawn to them with the satellite launches of Landsat in 1972 and the Coastal Zone Color Scanner in 1978 (Austin, 1979). These increasingly capable tools are being used from satellites and aircraft to discern a myriad of environmental parameters. Extremely sophisticated algorithms have been developed and proofed to estimate everything from crop health and the location of minerals on land to many physical, optical, and biological parameters from the sea. There is no room here to delve much deeper, but innumerable books, journal articles, and conferences have been dedicated to this very broad subject (see, for example, Volume II of ERIM, 1998).

Several facts are worth mentioning. The radiances measured at various wavelengths from shallow water by imagers can be used to estimate approximate depths (to a maximum depth of somewhat less than one Secchi depth) (Lyzenga, 1978), but even with sophisticated algorithms these depths are not reliable and do not meet IHO requirements (Fay and Miller, 1990; Morel and

Lindell, 1998). These same high-density depths from the imager, however, can be accurately calibrated with the simultaneous use of a low-density lidar bathymeter in a so-called "active-passive" mode (Cooper, 1981). This capability was further demonstrated in a test in which the Compact Airborne Spectrographic Imager (CASI) was successfully flown simultaneously with LARSEN (Borstad and Vosburgh, 1993).

The multispectral radiances measured by the scanners, if processed with appropriate algorithms, can provide the ability to map a wide variety of aquatic features such as oil slicks, near-surface fish schools, bottom types, sea grass, coral and other benthic plants, phytoplankton in the water column, and suspended sediment plumes, to name only a few (Quinn, 1992). As with estimated depths, however, when radiances are used to estimate many environmental characteristics, assumptions must be made, and an uncertainty or ambiguity exists in the results if the bottom depth is unknown. Again, the active-passive combination of a bathymetric lidar with the imager provides a major synergy that permits significant improvements in the accuracy of the products, both quantitative and qualitative, that can be derived from the imager. For example, lidar depths were used to calibrate multispectral imagery in the Environmental Research Institute of Michigan (ERIM) M8 scanner (Lyzenga, 1985). Two additional examples are provided by Hoge et al. (1986). In a later experiment, SHOALS depths were used to calibrate CASI multi-spectral imagery collected on a separate flight (Lillycrop and Estep, 1995). It was determined that it is possible to classify and map bottom types in gross terms (i.e., sand, sea grass, mud, etc.), but more research and experimentation are needed.

There is a great deal of interest in the mapping, monitoring, health, and conservation of coral reefs (McManus and Noordeloos, 1998; CRTF, 1998). It is expected that an active-passive approach could provide accurate, high-resolution information on characteristics such as coral reef location, health, and speciation which neither sensor alone could produce.

There is much important and interesting work to be done in environmental characterization and mapping. The first integration a hyperspectral scanner with an operational bathymetric lidar has now been accomplished in CHARTS, and an entire new field of study has begun. Algorithms developed at Optech International constrain the inversion of the hyperspectral radiative transfer model using parameters extracted from the lidar waveform (Tuell et al., 2005a; Tuell et al., 2005b; Tuell et al., 2005c; Tuell and Park, 2004; Kopilevich et al., 2005). Active-passive sensing will be a dynamic area of research in the future as more compact, relatively inexpensive, portable ALB systems become available. Both sensors involve very complex technology and algorithms, and numerous technical, scientific, and financial challenges will have to be met.

AUTHOR BIOGRAPHY

Gary C. Guenther is retired from government service after 35 years with the National Security Agency and NOAA's National Ocean Service, Coast Survey Development Laboratory. He has participated in airborne laser bathymetry projects sponsored by NOAA, NASA, U.S. Navy, and U.S. Army Corps of Engineers for over 25 years. Contributions have been made in areas of modeling, simulation, performance prediction, error analysis, system design, data-processing algorithm development, test design, and data analysis. Gary received the Department of the Army Commander's Award for Public Service, the Department of Commerce Silver and Bronze Medals, and the Optical Society of America Engineering Excellence Award. He earned BS and MS degrees in engineering and physics from Northwestern University. He is currently working part time as an advisor for Optech International in support of SHOALS and following systems.

ACKNOWLEDGEMENTS

The author is indebted to Jennifer Wozencraft of the Joint Airborne Lidar Bathymetry Technical Center of Expertise for providing substantial assistance with updates for this Second Edition.

The author would like to sincerely thank Jeff Lillycrop and Geraint West at the U.S. Army Corps of Engineers Joint Airborne Lidar Bathymetry Technical Center of Expertise in Mobile, Alabama for generously supplying significant written material for several of the above sections. Many other people graciously provided their time, thoughts, written material, positive criticism, and support in this endeavor. The author would like to extend appreciation to John Banic, Sebastian Sizgoric, Paul LaRocque, Rick Quinn, Carl Kuhnke, Eddie Wiggins, Jen Irish, Mark Sinclair, Mike Aslaksen, Bruce Parker, Jerry Mills, Guy Noll, Don Carswell, and Russ Ives.

The author wishes to recognize the teams of dedicated professionals on three continents who have worked for decades to bring this important airborne lidar bathymetry technology to fruition and promote its use. The pioneering efforts of Dan Hickman, Mike Penny, Allan Carswell, Sebastian Sizgoric, Capt. Mike Calder (RAN), Mike Casey, Bob O'Neil, Jim Vosburgh, Ralph Abbot, Dave Phillips, Ken Petri, Mike Contarino, Mike Rankin, Ove Steinvall, Mike Cooper, Hongsuk Kim, Frank Hoge, Bob Swift, Lowell Goodman, Bob Thomas, Dave Enabnit, Max Houck, and Merlin Miller, to name only a few of the many, must be remembered.

It is also very important to acknowledge the invaluable contributions of the field teams and flight crews who are responsible for daily operations of these systems around the world. Special thanks must go to all these people, who labor long days far from home, for their hard work and dedication.

REFERENCES

Abbot, R.H., 1981. WRELADS II trials, *Proc. 4th Laser Hydrography Symposium, ERL-0193-SD*, Defence Research Centre Salisbury, Sept. 30 - Oct. 3, 1980, Salisbury, South Australia, 188-215.

Abbot R.H.and M.F. Penny, 1975. Air trials of an experimental laser bathymeter, *Tech. Note WRE-TN-1509*, Weapons Research Establishment, Dept. of Defence (Australia), Salisbury, South Australia, 39 pp.

Abramochkin, A.I., V.V. Zanin, I.E. Penner, A.A. Tikhomirov, and V.S. Shamanaev, 1988. Airborne polarization lidars for atmospheric and hydrospheric studies, *Optika atmosfery*, 1(2): 92-96, (in Russian).

Abroskin, A.G., A.F. Bunkin, D.V. Vlasov, A.L. Gorbunov, and D.M. Mirkamilov, 1986. Full-scale experiments with laser aerial sounding at the Chayka facility, *Works of the General Physics Institute: Remote sensing of the ocean* (Trudy IOFAN: Distantsionnoye zondirovaniye okeana), Vol. 1, Moscow: Nauka, 29-47.

Anderson, N., P. Bellemare, M. Casey, K. Malone, R. MacDougall, D. Monahan, R. O'Neil, and S. Till, 1983. Beginning the second hundred years — the laser sounder, *Proc. Centennial Canadian Hydro. Conf., Spec. Pub 67*, Fisheries and Aquatic Services, Ottawa, Ont.

Austin, R.W., 1979. Coastal zone color scanner radiometry, *Proc. SPIE Ocean Optics VI*, Vol. 208, 170-177.

Axelsson, R. and M. Alfredsson, 1999. Capacity and capability for hydrographic missions, *Proc. U.S. Hydrographic Conference*, April 26-29, Mobile, AL, (paper 9-4 on CD), 9 pp.

Axelsson, R., O. Steinvall, and P. Sundberg, 1990. Programmable scanner for laser bathymetry, *Int'l. Hydro. Rev.*, 67(1): 161-170.

Balandin, V.N. and R.D. Volodarskiy, 1979. Laser instruments for measuring the depth of shallow water, *Geodeziya i kartografiya*, 2, 58-61.

Banic, J., S. Sizgoric, and W.J. Lillycrop, 1990. Second-generation airborne lidar system for hydrographic applications, *Proc. Oceanology Int'l.*, March 1990, Brighton, England.

Banic, J., S. Sizgoric and R. O'Neil, 1986. Scanning lidar bathymeter for water depth measurement, *Proc. SPIE Laser Radar Tech. and Appl.*, Vol. 663, Quebec City, Quebec, 187-195.

Billard, B., 1986a. Estimation of a mean sea surface reference in the WRE-LADS airborne depth sounder, *Appl. Opt.*, 25(13): 2067-2073.

Billard, B., 1986b. Remote sensing of scattering coefficient for airborne laser hydrography, *Appl. Opt.*, 25(13): 2099-2108.

Billard, B., R. Abbot, and M. Penny, 1986. Airborne estimation of sea turbidity parameters from the WRELADS Laser Airborne Depth Sounder, *Appl. Opt.*, 25(13): 2080-2088.

Billard B. and P.J. Wilsen 1986. Sea surface and depth detection in the WRELADS airborne depth sounder, *Appl. Opt.*, 25(13): 2059-2066.

Borstad, G.A. and J. Vosburgh, 1993. Combined active and passive optical bathymetric mapping: using the LARSEN lidar and the CASI imaging spectrometer, *Proc. 16th Canadian Symposium on Remote Sensing*, June 7-10, Sherbrooke, Quebec, 153-157.

Brissette, M.B. and J.E. Hughes Clarke 1999. Side-scan versus multibeam echosounder object detection: a comparative analysis, *Proc. U.S. Hydrographic Conference*, April 26-29, Mobile, AL, (paper 6-1 on CD), 11 pp.

Bristow, M., 1975. CCRS program, *Laser hydrography user requirements workshop minutes*, L.R. Goodman (ed.), National Aeronautics and Space Administration, Wallops Island, VA, January 22-23, 1975, Rockville, MD, 25-34.

Brock, J.C., C.W. Wright, T.D. Clayton, and A. Nayegandhi, 2004. Optical rugosity of coral reefs in Biscayne National Park, Florida, *Coral Reefs*, 23, 48-59.

Brooks, M.W., E. Culpepper, G.C. Guenther, and P.E. LaRocque, 1998. Advancements and applications of the SHOALS laser bathymetry system, *Proc. ION GPS 98*, Institute of Navigation, Sept. 15-18, Nashville, TN, 8 pp.

Bunkin, A.F., D.V. Vlasov, A.S. Galumyan, D.V. Mal'tsev, D.M. Mirkamilov, V.P. and Slobodyanin, 1984. Versatile airborne laser system for remote probing of ocean, atmosphere, and farmland, *Sov. Phys. — Tech. Phys.*, 29(11): 1284-1287.

Bunkin, A.F., D.V. Vlasov, D.M. Mirkamilov, and V.P. Slobodyanin, 1984. Airborne laser probing of turbidity profiles and mapping of phytoplankton distribution, *Sov. Phys.-Dokl.*, 29(11): 932-934.

Calder, M. and M.F. Penny, 1980. Australian overview, *Proc. 4th Laser Hydrography Symposium, ERL-0193-SD*, Defence Research Centre Salisbury, Sept. 30 - Oct. 3, 1980, Salisbury, South Australia, 1-21.

Carswell, A.I. and S. Sizgoric, 1974. Underwater probing with laser radar, *Proc. The Uses of Lasers for Hydrographic Studies, Report No. SP-375*, National Aeronautics and Space Administration, Wallops Island, VA, Sept. 12, 1973, Wallops Station, 89-103.

Casey, M.J., 1984. Deploying the lidar on hydrographic surveys, *Proc. 9th Canadian Symp. on Rem. Sens.*, St. Johns, Newfoundland, 165-175.

Casey, M.J., R.A. O'Neil, and P. Conrad, 1985. The advent of LARSEN, *Proc. Canadian Hydro. Conf.*, Halifax, N.S., 7-12.

Casey, M.J. and J. Vosburgh, 1986. Chartmaking with LARSEN, *Canadian Surveyor*, 40(3).

Churnside, J.H., J.J. Wilson, and V.V. Tatarskii, 1997. Lidar profiles of fish schools, *Appl. Opt. LP*, 36(24): 6011-6020.

Compton, J.S. and M.A. Hudson, 1988. New charting technology in Australia: the Laser Airborne Depth Sounder, *Int'l. Hydro. Rev. LXV*(2), Monaco, 145-157.

Conrad, P., 1986. Reaping the harvest — the processing of LARSEN data, Internal report, Canadian Hydrographic Service, Sidney, B.C., 25 pp.

Cooper, M.T., 1981. An active/passive multispectral scanner for airborne hydrography, *Proc. 4th Laser Hydrography Symposium, ERL-0193-SD*, Defence Research Centre Salisbury, Sept. 30 - Oct. 3, 1980, Salisbury, South Australia, 305-335.

Cox, G. and W. Munk, 1954. Measurement of the roughness of the sea surface from photographs of the sun's glitter, *JOSA*, 44(11): 838-850.

CRTF, 1998. National action plan, The U.S. Coral Reef Task Force (CRTF), *Executive Order #13089 on Coral Reef Protection*, President W.J. Clinton.

Cunningham, L.L., 1972. Test report on Pulsed Light Airborne Depth Sounder (PLADS), *Naval Oceanographic Office Tech. Note 6620-102-72*, U.S. Navy, 53 pp.

Cunningham, A.G., W.J. Lillycrop, G.C. Guenther, and M.W. Brooks, 1998. Shallow water laser bathymetry: accomplishments and applications, *Proc. Oceanology International: The Global Ocean*, March 10-13, Brighton, England, Vol. 3, 277-288.

Curran, T., T. Keck, V.M. Contarino, M.M. Harris, S.P. and Haimbach, 1988. Digital ABS Laser Sounder bathymetry, *Proc. SPIE Ocean Optics IX*, Vol. 925, 242-249.

DeBow, S.P., C.B. Greenawalt,and J. Ferguson, 2000. NOAA contractor partnership: How NOAA uses private industry to support nautical charting, *Int'l. Hydro. Rev.*, 1, 1 (June), 7pp.

Ebrite, S., R.W. Pope, and W.J. Lillycrop, 2001. A multi-agency solution for coastal surveys – SHOALS in the Pacific, *Proc. Oceans 2001*, MTS/IEEE, Nov. 5-8, Honolulu, Hawaii.

Enabnit, D.B., 1981. An evaluation of airborne laser hydrography, *Proc. 4th Laser Hydrography Symposium, ERL-0193-SD*, Defence Research Centre Salisbury, Sept. 30 - Oct. 3, 1980, Salisbury, South Australia, 85-95.

Enabnit, D.B., L.R. Goodman, G.K.Young, and W.J. Shaughnessy, 1978. The cost effectiveness of airborne laser hydrography, *NOAA Technical Memorandum NOS 26*, National Oceanic and Atmospheric Administration, Rockville, MD, 56 pp.

Engstrom, R. and R. Axelsson, 2001. Laser bathymetry and its compliance with IHO S44, *Proc. Hydro 2001*, The Hydrographic Society, Special Pub. 42, March 27-29, Norwich, England, Paper 18, 10 pp.

ERIM, 1998. *Proc. 5th Int'l. Conf. on Remote Sensing for Marine and Coastal Environments*, ERIM International, October 5-7, San Diego, CA.

Estep, L., 1993. A review of airborne lidar hydrographic (ALH) systems, *The Hydrographic Journal*, 67(1): 25-42.

Fay, T.H., and H.V. Miller, 1990. Bathymetric analysis of "in-water" upwelling radiance data, *Proc. SPIE Ocean Optics X*, Vol. 1302, 641-654.

Featherstone, S., 2001. NOAA is sinking, *Boating*, 74(2): 150-155.

Feigels, V.J.and Y.I. Kopilevich, 1993a. Russian airborne lidar for oceanography, *Proc. Symp. on Russian Airborne Geophysics & Remote Sensing*, SPIE, Vol. 2111, Sept. 13-17, 1992, Golden, CO, 127-141.

Feigels, V.I. and Y.I. Kopilevich, 1993b. Remote sensing of subsurface layers of turbid sea water with the help of optical lidar system, *Proc. Underwater Measurements, SPIE*, Vol. 2048, Tromso, Norway, 34-42.

Feigels, V.I. and Y.I. Kopilevich, 1994. Applicability of lidar remote sensing methods for vertical structure investigation of ocean optical properties distribution, *Proc. SPIE Ocean Optics XII*, Vol. 2258, 449-457.

Feygels, V.I., C.W. Wright, Y.I. Kopilevich, and A.I. Surkov, 2003. Narrow-field-of-view bathymetrical lidar: theory and field test, *Proc. Ocean Remote Sensing and Imaging II*; SPIE, Vol. 5155, 1-11.

Feygels, V.I., Y.I. Kopilevich, A.I. Surkov, J.K. Yungel, and M.J. Behrenfeld, 2003. Airborne lidar system with variable field-of-view receiver for water optical properties measurement, *Proc. Ocean Remote Sensing and Imaging II*; SPIE, Vol. 5155, 12-21.

Francis, K., P. LaRocque, L. Gee, M. and Paton, 2003. Hydrographic lidar processing moves into the next dimension, *Proc. U.S. Hydro 2003*, The Hydrographic Society of America, March 24-27, Biloxi, MS, paper 5.3, 18 pp.

Golaszewski, R., D. Barol, J. Phillips, W. Zyskowski, and E. Maillett, 1990. Economic evaluation of proposed helicopter lidar bathymeter system, *Contract Report CERC-90-1*, Gellman Research Associates Inc., Jenkintown, PA, 304 pp.

Goodman, L.R. (ed.), 1975. *Laser hydrography user requirements workshop minutes,* National Aeronautics and Space Administration, Wallops Island, VA, January 22-23, 1975, Rockville, MD, 143 pp.

Goodman, L.R. (ed.), 1976. *Laser hydrography technical review workshop minutes,* National Oceanic and Atmospheric Administration, Rockville, MD, August 25-26, 1976, Rockville, MD, 127 pp.

Gordon, H.R., 1982. Interpretation of airborne oceanic lidar: effects of multiple scattering, *Appl. Opt.,* 21(16): 2996-3001.

Gordon, H.R., 1989. Can the Lambert-Beer law be applied to the diffuse attenuation coefficient of ocean water?, *Limnol. Oceanogr.,* 34(8): 1389-1409.

Gordon, H.R., O.B. Brown, and M.M. Jacobs, 1975. Computed relationships between the inherent and apparent optical properties of a flat homogeneous ocean, *Appl. Opt.,* 14(2): 417-427.

Gordon, H.R. and A.W. Wouters, 1978. Some relationships between Secchi depth and inherent optical properties of natural waters, *Appl. Opt.,* 17(21): 3341-3343.

Graham, T., K. Smith, J. Spittal, and G.R. West, 1999. Improving the efficiency, safety and economy of the New Zealand national nautical charting program through the integrated use of the SHOALS system in a multi-sensor survey, *Proc. U.S. Hydrographic Conference*, April 26-29, Mobile, AL, (paper 9-5 on CD), 11 pp.

Guenther, G.C., 1981. Accuracy and penetration measurements from hydrographic trials of the AOL system, *Proc. 4th Laser Hydrography Symposium, ERL-0193-SD*, Defence Research Centre Salisbury, Sept. 30 - Oct. 3, 1980, Salisbury, South Australia, 108-150.

Guenther, G.C., 1985. Airborne laser hydrography: System design and performance factors, *NOAA Professional Paper Series*, National Ocean Service 1, National Oceanic and Atmospheric Administration, Rockville, MD, 385 pp.

Guenther, G.C., 1986. Wind and nadir angle effects on airborne lidar water surface returns, *Proc. SPIE Ocean Optics VIII*, Vol. 637, 277-286.

Guenther, G.C., 1989. Airborne laser hydrography to chart shallow coastal waters, *Sea Technology*, 30(3): 55-59.

Guenther, G.C., M.W. Brooks, and P.E. LaRocque, 1998. New capabilities of the SHOALS airborne lidar bathymeter, *Proc. 5th Int'l. Conf. on Remote Sensing for Marine and Coastal Environments*, ERIM International, October 5-7, San Diego, CA, Vol. I, 47-55. [reprinted in 2000, *Remote Sens. Environ.*, 73, 247-255.]

Guenther G.C., A.G. Cunningham, P.E. LaRocque, and D.J. Reid, 2000. Meeting the accuracy challenge in airborne lidar bathymetry, *Proc. 20th EARSeL Symposium: Workshop on Lidar Remote Sensing of Land and Sea*, European Association of Remote Sensing Laboratories, June 16-17, Dresden, Germany, (paper #1 on CD), 28 pp.

Guenther, G.C., T.J. Eisler, J.L. Riley, and S.W. Perez, 1996. Obstruction detection and data decimation for airborne laser hydrography, *Proc. 1996 Canadian Hydro. Conf.*, June 3-5, Halifax, NS, Tues., 51-63.

Guenther, G.C. and L.R. Goodman, 1978. Laser applications for near-shore nautical charting, *Proc. SPIE Ocean Optics V*, Vol. 160, 174-183.

Guenther, G.C. and L.R. Goodman (editors), 1979. *Proc. Airborne Laser Hydrography Symp. III*, National Oceanic and Atmospheric Administration, Rockville, MD, October 5-6, 1977, Rockville, MD, 103 pp.

Guenther, G.C., L.R. Goodman, F. Hoge, R.N. Swift, R.W.L. Thomas, and D. Bright, 1979. AOL project: results to date, *Proc. Airborne Laser Hydrography Symp. III*, National Oceanic and Atmospheric Administration, Rockville, MD, October 5-6, 1977, Rockville, MD, 62-103.

Guenther, G.C., P.E. LaRocque, and W.J. Lillycrop, 1994. Multiple surface channels in SHOALS airborne lidar, *Proc. SPIE Ocean Optics XII*, Vol. 2258, 422-430.

Guenther G.C. and H.C. Mesick, 1988a. Automated lidar waveform processing, *Proc. U.S. Hydro. Conf. '88*, Spec. Pub. 21, April 12-15, Baltimore, MD, 52-59.

Guenther G.C. and H.C. Mesick, 1988b. Analysis of airborne laser hydrography waveforms, *Proc. SPIE Ocean Optics IX*, Vol. 925, 232-241.

Guenther G.C. and R.W.L. Thomas, 1981. Error analysis of pulse location estimates for simulated bathymetric lidar returns, *NOAA Tech. Rpt. OTES 01*, National Oceanic and Atmospheric Administration, Washington, D.C., 51 pp.

Guenther, G.C. and R.W.L. Thomas, 1983. System design and performance factors for airborne laser hydrography, *Proc. Oceans '83*, IEEE/MTS, Aug. 29 -Sept. 1, San Francisco, CA, 425-430.

Guenther G.C. and R.W.L. Thomas, 1984a. Effects of Propagation-induced Pulse Stretching in Airborne Laser Hydrography, *Proc. SPIE Ocean Optics VII*, Vol. 489, 287-296.

Guenther, G.C., and R.W.L. Thomas, 1984b. Prediction and correction of propagation-induced depth measurement biases plus signal attenuation and beam spreading for airborne laser hydrography, *NOAA Tech. Report NOS 106 CGS 2*, National Oceanic and Atmospheric Administration, Rockville, Md., 121 pp.

Guenther, G.C., R.W.L. Thomas, and P.E. LaRocque, 1996. Design considerations for achieving high accuracy with the SHOALS bathymetric lidar system, *Laser remote sensing of natural waters: From theory to practice*, V.I. Feigels, Y.I. Kopilevich, SPIE, Vol. 2964, 54-71.

Gutierrez, R., J.C. Gibeaut, M.M. Crawford, M.P. Mahoney, S. Smith, W. Gutelius, D. Carswell, and E. MacPherson, 1998. Airborne laser swath mapping of Galveston Island and Bolivar Peninsula, Texas, *Proc. 5th Int'l. Conf. on Remote Sensing for Marine and Coastal Environments*, ERIM International, October 5-7, San Diego, CA, Vol. I, 236-243.

Hare, R., 1994. Calibrating LARSEN-500 lidar bathymetry in Dolphin and Union Strait using dense acoustic ground truth, *Int'l. Hydro. Rev.*, Monaco, LXXI(1), 91-108.

Harris, M.M., G.D. Hickman, and R. Booker, 1986. Development of the Airborne Bathymetric Survey system, *Proc. Hydro USA '86*, National Oceanic and Atmospheric Administration, Rockville, MD, March 25-27, 1986, Norfolk, VA, 50-55.

Heslin, J.B., W.J. Lillycrop, and R.W. Pope, 2003. CHARTS: An evolution in airborne lidar hydrography, *Proc. U.S. Hydro 2003*, The Hydrographic Society of America, March 24-27, Biloxi, MS, paper 5.2, 4 pp.

Hickman, G.D. and J.E. Hogg, 1969. Application of an airborne pulsed laser for near-shore bathymetric measurements, *Remote Sens. of Env.*, 1, 47-58.

Hoge, F.E., R.N. Swift, and E.B. Frederick, 1980. Water depth measurement using an airborne pulsed neon laser system, *Appl. Opt.*, 19(6): 871-883.

Hoge, F.E., R.N. Swift, and J.K. Jungel, 1986. Active-passive ocean color measurement: two applications, *Appl. Opt.*, 25, 48.

Hoge, F.E., C.W. Wright, W.B. Krabill, R.R. Buntzen, G.D. Gilbert, R.N. Swift, J.K. Yungel, and R.E. Berry, 1988. Airborne lidar detection of subsurface oceanic scattering layers, *Appl. Opt.*, 27(19): 3969-3977.

Huff, L.C., 1993. High-resolution multibeam focussed side-scan sonar, *Proc. Institute of Acoustics*, Vol. 15, (2) 389-405.

Hughes Clarke, J.E., L. Mayer, J. Shaw, R. Parrott, M. Lamplugh, J. and Bradford, 1999. Data handling methods and target detection results for multibeam and side-scan data collected as part of the search for Swiss Air Flight 111, *Proc. Shallow Survey-99*, Australian Defence Science and Technology Organization, Oct 18-20, Sydney, Australia, Paper 6-2, 11 pp.

Hwang, P.A., W.B. Krabill, W. Wright, E.J. Walsh, and R.N. Swift, 1998. Airborne lidar remote sensing of coastal waves and breaking distribution, *Proc. 5th Int'l. Conf. on Remote Sensing for Marine and Coastal Environments*, ERIM International, October 5-7, San Diego, CA, Vol. II, 1-8.

International Hydrographic Organisation, 1998. IHO Standards for Hydrographic Surveys, *Special Publication No 44*, 4th Edition. http://www.iho.shom.fr/publicat/free/files/S-44-eng.pdf.

Irish, J.L. and W.J. Lillycrop, 1997. Monitoring New Pass, Florida with high density lidar bathymetry, *J. Coastal Research*, 13(4): 1130-1140.

Irish, J.L. and W.J. Lillycrop, 1999. Scanning laser mapping of the coastal zone: The SHOALS system, *ISPRS Journal of Photogrammetry & Remote Sensing*, 54(2-3): 123-129.

Irish, J.L., W.J. Lillycrop, and L.E. Parson, 1997a. Accuracy of Sand Volumes as a Function of Survey Density, *Proc. 25th International Conference on Coastal Engineering*, American Society of Civil Engineers, September 2-6, Orlando, FL, Vol. 3, 3736-3749.

Irish, J.L., J.K. McClung, , and W.J. Lillycrop, 2000. Airborne lidar bathymetry: the SHOALS system, *The International Navigation Association, PIANC Bulletin*, No. 103, 43-53.

Irish, J.L., L.E. Parson, and W.J. Lillycrop, 1995. Detailed bathymetry of four Florida inlets, *Proc. 1995 National Conference on Beach Preservation Technology*, Florida Shore and Beach Preservation Association, January 25-27, St. Petersburg, FL, 243-258.

Irish, J.L., J.E. Thomas, L.E. Parson, and W.J. Lillycrop, 1996. Monitoring storm response with high density lidar bathymetry: The effects of Hurricane Opal on Florida's Panhandle, *Proc. 2nd Int. Airborne Remote Sensing Conf.*, June 24-27, San Francisco, CA., Vol. III, 723-732.

Irish, J.L. and C.L. Truitt, 1995. Beach Fill Storm Response at Longboat Key, Florida, *Proc. 1995 National Conference on Beach Preservation Technology*, Florida Shore and Beach Preservation Association, January 25-27, St. Petersburg, FL, 103-117.

Irish, J.L., C.L. Truitt, and W.J. Lillycrop, 1997b. Using High-resolution Bathymetry to Determine Sediment Budgets: New Pass, Florida, *Proc. 1997 National Conference on Beach Preservation Technology*, Florida Shore and Beach Preservation Association, 183-198.

Irish, J.L. and T.E. White, 1998. Coastal engineering applications of high-resolution lidar bathymetry, *Coastal Engineering*, 35(1-2): 47-71.

Ivanov, A.P., A.L. Skrelin, and I.D. Sherbaf, 1972. Study of optical characteristics of water media using pulsed sounding, *ZhPS*, 17(2): 232-240.

Iwamoto, H., T. Ono, H. Shirana, H. Yajima, and G. Cunningham, 2004. Field testing results for the Japan Coast Guard SHOALS-1000 system, *Proc. 5th Annual Coastal Mapping and Charting Workshop*, Joint Airborne Lidar Bathymetry Technical Center of Expertise, June 9-10, St. Petersburg, FL, CD "Cunningham."

Jelalian, A.V., 1968. Sea echo at laser wavelengths, *Proc. IEEE*, 56(5): 828-835.

Jerlov, N.G., 1976. *Marine Optics*, Elsevier Scientific Pub. Co., Amsterdam, 231 pp.

Kim, H.H., P. Cervenka, and C. Lankford, 1975. Development of an airborne laser bathymeter, *NASA Tech. Note TND-8079*, National Aeronautics and Space Administration, Washington, D.C., 39 pp.

Kopilevich, Y., V. Feygels, G. Tuell, and A. Surkov, 2005. Measurement of ocean water optical properties and seafloor reflectance with Scanning Hydrogrpahic Operational Airborne Lidar Survey (SHOALS): I. Theoretical background, *Proc. Remote Sensing of the Coastal Oceanic Environment*, SPIE, Vol. 5885, 106-114.

Koppari, K., U. Karlsson, and O. Steinvall, 1994. Airborne laser depth sounding in Sweden, *Int'l. Hydro.*, Rev. LXXI(2), Monaco, 69-90.

Krabill, W.B., and C.F. Martin, 1987. Aircraft positioning using global positioning system carrier phase data, navigation, *J. Inst. of Navigation*, 34(Spring): 1-21.

Krabill, W.B. and R.N. Swift, 1981a. Preliminary results of shoreline mapping investigations conducted at Wrightsville Beach, NC, *Proc. Army Corps of Engineers Remote Sensing Symposium*, December, Nashville, TN, 20 pp.

Krabill, W.B. and R.N. Swift, 1981b. Removal of aircraft vertical motion from airborne laser data, *Proc. 4th Laser Hydrography Symposium, ERL-0193-SD*, Defence Research Centre Salisbury, Sept. 30 - Oct. 3, 1980, Salisbury, South Australia, 490-491.

Kronman, M., 1992. Lidar: laser technology could revolutionize aerial fish finding, *National Fisherman*, April, 40-42.

Krumboltz, H., 1979. Experimental investigation of system attenuation coefficient for HALS, *Report No. NADC 80035-30*, Naval Air Development Center, Warminster, PA, 103 pp.

Lapucha, D., and R.A. Barker, 1996. Dual Baseline Real-time OTF Kinematic GPS, *Proc. ION-GPS '96*, Sept. 17-20, Kansas City, MO, 883-888.

LaRocque P.E., J.R. Banic, and A.G. Cunningham, 2004. Design description and field testing of the SHOALS-1000T airborne bathymeter, *Proc. Laser Radar Technology and Applications IX; SPIE,* Vol. 5412, 162-184.

LaRocque P.E. and G.R. West, 1999. Airborne laser hydrography: an introduction, *Proc. ROPME/ PERSGA/IHB Workshop on Hydrographic Activities in the ROPME Sea area and Red Sea,* October 24-27, Kuwait, 16 pp.

Levis, C.A., W.G. Swarner, C. Prettyman, and G.W. Reinhardt, 1973. An optical radar for airborne use over natural waters, *Proc. Oceans '73,* 76-83.

Lillycrop, W.J. and M.W. Brooks, 1996. Two years of operating the SHOALS airborne hydrographic survey system, *Proc. Hydro 96,* 10th biennial symposium of the Hydrographic Society, Sept 24-26, Rotterdam, Netherlands, paper #14, 8pp.

Lillycrop, W.J. and L.L. Estep, 1995. Generational advancements in coastal surveying and mapping, *Sea Technology,* 36(6): 10-16.

Lillycrop, W.J., L.L. Estep, J.L. Irish, and L.E. Parson, 1995. Determination of areas in coastal United States waters that are appropriate for airborne lidar hydrographic surveying, *Miscellaneous Paper CERC-94,* U.S. Army Corps of Engineers Waterways Experiment Station, Vicksburg, MS, 171 pp.

Lillycrop, W.J., J.L. Irish, and L.E. Parson, 1997. SHOALS system: Three years of operation with airborne lidar bathymetry - Experiences, capability and technology advancements, *Sea Technology,* 38(6): 17-25.

Lillycrop, W.J., J.L. Irish, R.W. Pope, and G.R. West, 2000. GPS sends in the marines: rapid environmental assessment with lidar, *GPS World,* 11(11): 18-28.

Lillycrop, W.J., P. Johnson, U. Lejdebrink, and R.W. Pope, 2001. Airborne lidar hydrography: requirements for tomorrow, *Proc. Oceanology International,* April 3-5, Miami, FL, paper 5-7, 9 pp.

Lillycrop, W.J., L.E. Parson, L.L. Estep, P.E. LaRocque, G.C. Guenther, M.D. Reed, and C.L. Truitt, 1994. Field testing of the U.S. Army Corps of Engineers airborne lidar hydrographic survey system, *Proc. U.S. Hydro. Conf. '94,* The Hydrographic Society, April 18-23, Norfolk, VA, Special Pub. No. 32, 144-151.

Lillycrop, W.J., L.E. Parson, and G.C. Guenther, 1993. Processing lidar returns to extract water depth, *Proc. Int'l. Symp. Spectral Sens. Res.,* Nov. 1992, Maui, Hawaii.

Lillycrop, W.J., L.E. Parson, and J.L. Irish, 1996. Development and Operation of the SHOALS airborne lidar hydrographic survey system, *Laser Remote Sensing of Natural Waters: From Theory to Practice,* V. I. Feigels, Y. I. Kopilevich, SPIE, Vol. 2964, 26-37.

Liu, Z.S., 1990. Estimate of maximum penetration depth of lidar in coastal water of the China sea, *Proc. SPIE Ocean Optics X,* Vol. 1302, 655-661.

Liu, P.C. and D.B. Ross, 1980. Airborne measurements of wave growth for stable and unstable atmospheres in Lake Michigan, *J. Physical Oceanography,* 10(11): 1842-1853.

Lockhart, C., D. Arumugam, and D. Millar, 2005. Meeting hydrographic charting specifications with the SHOALS-1000T airborne lidar bathymeter, *Proc. U.S. Hydro 2005,* The Hydrographic Society of America, March 29-31, San Diego, CA, paper 7-3, 8 pp.

Lyzenga, D.R., 1978. Passive remote sensing techniques for mapping water depth and bottom features, *Appl. Opt.,* 17(3): 379-383.

Lyzenga, D.R., 1985. Shallow-water bathymetry using combined lidar and passive multispectral scanner data, *Int. J. Remote Sensing,* 6, 115.

McClain, C.R., N.E. Huang, and P.E. LaViolette, 1982. Measurements of sea-state variations across oceanic fronts using laser profilometry, *J. Physical Oceanography,* 12(11): 1228-1244.

McClung J.K., 1998. High density lidar data: A monitoring tool for East Pass Florida, *Proc. 5th Int'l Conf. on Remote Sensing for Marine and Coastal Environments,* ERIM International, October 5-7, San Diego, CA, Vol. I, 75-82.

McClung, J.K. and S.L. Douglass, 1999. Observing changes in an ebb-tidal shoal, *Proc. 4th International Symposium on Coastal Engineering and Science of Coastal Sediment Processes*, American Society of Civil Engineers, June 21-23, Long Island, NY, Vol. 1, 734-749.

McManus, J. and M. Noordeloos, 1998. Toward a global inventory of coral reefs (GICOR): remote sensing, international cooperation, and reefbase, *Proc. 5th Int'l. Conf. on Remote Sensing for Marine and Coastal Environments*, ERIM International, October 5-7, San Diego, CA, Vol. I, 83-89.

Millar, D., J. Gerhard, and R. Hildale, 2005. Using airborne lidar bathymetry to map shallow river environments, *Proc. Coastal Zone 2005 Conference*, July 17-21, New Orleans, Louisiana.

Mohr, M.C., J. Pope, and J.K. McClung, 1999. Coastal response to a detached breakwater system; Presque Isle, Pennsylvania, USA, *Proc. 4th International Symposium on Coastal Engineering and Science of Coastal Sediment Processes*, American Society of Civil Engineers, June 21-23, Long Island, NY, Vol. 3, 2010-2025.

Morang, A., J.L. Irish, and J. Pope, 1996. Hurricane Opal morphodynamic impacts on East Pass, Florida: Preliminary findings, *Proc. 1996 National Conference on Beach Preservation Technology*, Florida Shore and Beach Preservation Association, January, St. Petersburg, FL, 17 pp.

Morel, Y.G. and L.T. Lindell, 1998. Passive multispectral bathymetry mapping of Negril Shores, Jamaica, *Proc. 5th Int'l. Conf. on Remote Sensing for Marine and Coastal Environments*, ERIM International, October 5-7, San Diego, CA, Vol. I, 315-324.

Muirhead, K. and A.P. Cracknell, 1986. Airborne lidar bathymetry, *Int. J. Remote Sensing*, 7(5): 597-614.

Mullen, L.J., P.R. Herczfeld, and V.M. Contarino, 1996. Hybrid lidar-radar ocean experiment, *IEEE Trans. Microwave Theory and Techniques*, 44, 2703-2710.

Murphree, D.L., C.D. Taylor, and R.W. McClendon, 1974. Mathematical modeling for the detection of fish by an airborne laser, *AIAA Journal*, 12(12): 1686-1692.

Myers, E., A. Wong, K. Hess, S. White, E. Spargo, J. Feyen, Z. Yang, P. Richardson, C. Auer, J. Sellars, J. Woolard, D. Roman, S. Gill, C. Zervas, and K. Tronvig, 2005. Development of a national VDatum, and its application to sea level rise in North Carolina, *Proc. U.S. Hydro 2005*, The Hydrographic Society of America, March 29-31, San Diego, CA, paper 9-3, 25 pp.

Nairn, R., 1994. Royal Australian Navy laser airborne depth sounder, The first year of operations, *Int'l. Hydro. Rev.*, Monaco, LXXI(1), 109-119.

Nayegandhi, A., J.C. Brock, and C.W. Wright, 2005. Classifying vegetation using NASA's Experimental Advanced Airborne Research Lidar (EAARL) at Assateague Island National Seashore, *Proc. ASPRS Annual Conference*, March 7-11, Baltimore, MD, 15 pp. [CD-ROM].

Nordstrom, G., 2000. The Swedish Hydrographic Service on the eve of a new millennium, *Integrated coastal zone management*, Spring Edition, 37-40.

O'Neil, R.A., 1981. Field trials of a lidar bathymeter in the Magdalen Islands, *Proc. 4th Laser Hydrography Symposium*, ERL-0193-SD, Defence Research Centre Salisbury, Sept. 30 - Oct. 3, 1980, Salisbury, South Australia, 56-84.

O'Neil, R.A., V. Thomson, J.N. de Villiers, and J.R. Gibson, 1978. The aerial hydrography program at CCRS, *Proc. Coastal Mapping Symp.*, Aug. 14-16, 1978, Rockville, MD, 125-132.

O'Reilly, C., 2000. Defining the coastal zone from a hydrographic perspective, *Backscatter*, (Alliance for Marine Remote Sensing Association), 11(2): 20-24.

Ott, L.M., 1965. Underwater ranging measurements using blue-green laser, *NAVAIRDEVCEN Report No. NADC-AE-6519*, Naval Air Development Center, Warminster, PA (CONFIDENTIAL).

Ott, L.M., H. Krumboltz, and A.K. Witt, 1971. Detection of submerged submarine by an optical ranging and detection system and detection of pulses by a submarine, *Proc. 8th U.S. Navy Symp. of Military Oceanography (Vol. II)*, May 18-20, 1971, Naval Postgraduate School, Monterey, CA (CONFIDENTIAL).

Parker, B., 2002. The integration of bathymetry, topography and shoreline, and the vertical datum transformations behind it, *Int'l. Hydro. Rev.*, 3(3): 35-47.

Parker, B., D. Milbert, R. Wilson, K. Hess, J. Bailey, C. Fowler, D. Gesch, and R. Berry, 2001. A Tampa Bay bathymetric/topographic digital elevation model with internally consistent shorelines for various datums, *Proc. Hydro 2001*, The Hydrographic Society, Special Pub. 42, March 27-29, Norwich, England, Paper 11, 11 pp.

Parker, B., K. Hess, D. Milbert, and S. Gill, 2003. A national vertical datum transformation tool, *Sea Technology*, 44(9): 10-15.

Penny, M.F., 1981. Laser hydrography in Australia, *Proc. Int'l. Conf. on Lasers '81*, Dec. 14-18, 1029-1042.

Penny, M.F., 1992. LADS, the Australian laser airborne depth sounder, part 1, *Proc. Int'l Hydro. Symp.*, Monaco, II-5, 9 pp.

Penny, M.F., R.H. Abbot, D.M. Phillips, B. Billard, D. Rees, D.W. Faulkner, D.G. Cartwright, B. Woodcock, G.J. Perry, P.J. Wilsen, T.R. Adams, and J. Richards, 1986. Airborne laser hydrography in Australia, *Appl. Opt.*, 25(13): 2046-2058.

Penny, M.F., B. Billard, and R.H. Abbot, 1989. LADS — the Australian Laser Airborne Depth Sounder, *Int'l. J. Rem. Sens.*, 10(9): 1463-1479.

Penny, M.F. and D.M. Phillips, (editors), 1981. *Proc. 4th Laser Hydrography Symposium, ERL-0193-SD*, Defence Research Centre Salisbury, Sept. 30 - Oct. 3, 1980, Salisbury, South Australia, 554 pp.

Perry, G.J., 1999. Post-processing in laser airborne bathymetry systems, *Proc. ROPME/PERSGA/ IHB Workshop on Hydrographic Activities in the ROPME Sea Area and Red Sea*, October 24-27, Kuwait, 13 pp.

Petri, K.J., 1977. Laser radar reflectance of Chesapeake Bay waters as a function of wind speed, *IEEE Trans. Geoscience Electronics*, GE-15(2): 87-96.

Phillips, D.M., R.H. Abbot, and M.F. Penny, 1984. Remote sensing of sea water turbidity with an airborne laser system, *J. Phys. D: Appl. Phys.*, 17, 1749.

Philpot, W. D., 1989. Bathymetric mapping with passive multispectral imagery, *Appl. Opt.*, 28(8): 1569-1578.

Pope, J. and W.J. Lillycrop, 1988. Development of a helicopter lidar bathymeter system, *Proc. U.S. Army Corps of Engineers Surveying Conf.*, Fort Belvoir, VA, 213-216.

Pope, R.W., B.A. Reed, G.R. West, , and W.J. Lillycrop, 1997. Use of an airborne laser depth sounding system in a complex shallow-water environment, *Proc. XVth Int'l Hydro Conference*, April 21-22, Monaco, 10 pp.

Quinn, R., 1992. Coastal base mapping with the LARSEN scanning lidar system and other sensors, *Fifth Biennial International Hydrographic Conference*, National Ocean Service, Feb 25-28, Baltimore, MD, 219-221.

Quinn, R., 2000. Bathymetry with airborne lidar & videography, *Backscatter*, (Alliance for Marine Remote Sensing Association), 11(2): 8-17.

Rankin, M., 1975. Naval Air Development Center program, *Laser hydrography user requirements workshop minutes*, L.R. Goodman, (ed.), National Aeronautics and Space Administration, January 22-23, 1975, Rockville, MD, Wallops Island, VA, 49-74.

Remondi, B.W., 1991. Kinematic GPS results without static initialization, *NOAA Technical Memorandum, NOS NGS-55*, National Geodetic Information Center, Rockville, MD.

Reuter, R., 1982. Lidar investigations of hydrosols: notes on the determination of scattering matrix elements, *Appl. Opt.*, 21, 3762.

Riley, J.L., 1995. Evaluating SHOALS bathymetry using NOAA hydrographic survey data, *Proc. 24th Joint Meeting of UJNR Sea-Bottom Surveys Panel*, November 13-17, Tokyo, Japan.

Ross, D.B., V.J. Cardone, and J.W. Conaway, 1970. Laser and microwave observations of sea-surface conditions for fetch-limited 17 to 25-m/s winds, *IEEE Trans. Geoscience Electronics*, GE-8(4): 326-336.

Schule, J.J., L.S.Simpson, and P.S. DeLeonibus, 1971. A study of fetch-limited wave spectra with an airborne laser, *J. Geophysical Research*, 76(18): 4160-4171.

Setter, C. and R.J. Willis, 1994. LADS — From development to hydrographic operations, *Proc. U.S. Hydro. Conf. 1994*, The Hydrographic Society, Special Pub. No. 32, April 18-23, Norfolk, VA, 134-139.

Sinclair, M., 1997. LADS Mk II Aircraft Launched, *Hydro International*, 11, December, 29-31.

Sinclair, M., 1998. Australians get on board with new laser airborne depth sounder, *Sea Technology*, June, 19-25.

Sinclair, M., 1999a. Airborne laser bathymetry in 1998/1999, *EEZ Technology*, 4(2): 69-72.

Sinclair, M., 1999b. Application of laser airborne depth sounder for EEZ delimitation and management, *EEZ Technology*, 5(2): 95-99.

Sinclair, M., 1999c. Laser hydrography — commercial survey operations, *Proc. U.S. Hydrographic Conference*, April 26-29, Mobile, AL, (paper 9-2 on CD), 10 pp.

Sinclair, M., 2002. Airborne laser surveys for resources development, *Sea Technology*, 43(9): 4pp.

Sinclair, M., 2004. Hydrographic lidar operations in Alaska, *Sea Technology*, 45, 10.

Sinclair, M., 2005. Hydrographic lidar survey – Experiences from Long Island Sound, *Proc. U.S. Hydro 2005*, The Hydrographic Society of America, March 29-31, San Diego, CA, paper 7-4, 27 pp.

Sinclair, M.J. and T. Spurling, 1997. Operational laser bathymetry in Australia, *XVth International Hydrographic Conference*, International Hydrographic Organization, April 21-22, Monaco, Session IV, 4.1-4.17.

Sinclair, M., D. Stephenson, and T. Spurling, 1999. High resolution surveys in shallow water — LADS, *Proc. Shallow Survey-99*, Australian Defence Science and Technology Organization, Oct 18-20, Sydney, Australia, Paper 3-2, 9 pp.

Skogvik, J. and R. Axelsson, 2001. Experience and results from Swedish laser surveys and post-processing of laser bathymetry data, *Proc. Hydro 2001*, The Hydrographic Society, Special Pub. 42, March 27-29, Norwich, England, Paper 20, 13 pp.

Sorenson, G.P., 1966. Proposed airborne fathometer system for high-speed offshore beach mapping, *Technical Note,* Stanford Research Institute.

Sorenson, G.P., R.C. Honey, and J.R. Payne, 1966. Analysis of the use of airborne laser radar for submarine detection and ranging, *SRI Report No. 5583*, Stanford Research Institute.

Spurling, T. and G. Perry , 1997. A new generation laser airborne depth sounder, *XVth International Hydrographic Conference*, International Hydrographic Organization, April 21-22, Monaco, Session IV, 1.1-1.16.

Steinvall, O., H. Klevebrant, J. Lexander, and A. Widen, 1981. Laser depth sounding in the Baltic Sea, *Appl. Opt.*, 20(19): 3284-3286.

Steinvall, O and K. Koppari, 1996. Depth sounding lidar — an overview of Swedish activities and future prospects, *Laser Remote Sensing of Natural Waters: From Theory to Practice*, V. I. Feigels, Y. I. Kopilevich, Editors, SPIE, Vol. 2964, 2-25.

Steinvall, O., K. Koppari, and U. Karlsson, 1992. Experimental evaluation of an airborne depth sounding lidar, *Proc. SPIE Lidar for Remote Sensing*, Vol. 1714, 108-126.

Steinvall, O., K. Koppari, and U. Karlsson, 1994. Airborne laser depth sounding: system aspects and performance, *Proc. SPIE Ocean Optics XII*, Vol. 2258, 392-412.

Steinvall, O., K. Koppari, U. Lejdebrink, J. Winell, M. Nilsson, R. Ellsen, and E. Gjellan, 1997. Theories and experience of the Swedish airborne laser system, *Proc. XVth International Hydrographic Conference*, International Hydrographic Organization, April 21-22, Monaco, Session IV, 3.1-3.23.

Strock, C.A., 2006. Regional sediment management, *Sea Technology*, 47(1): 11-12.

Stumpf, R.P., K. Holderied, and M. Sinclair, 2003. Determination of water depth with high-resolution satellite imagery over variable bottom types, *Limnol. Oceanogr.*, 48(1, part 2), 547–556.

Swift, R.N., W.B. Krabill, and F.E. Hoge, 1981. Applications of the Airborne Oceanographic Lidar to shoreline mapping, *Proc. 4th Laser Hydrography Symposium*, ERL-0193-SD, Defence Research Centre Salisbury, Sept. 30 - Oct. 3, 1980, Salisbury, South Australia, 151-187.

Thomas, R.W.L, and G.C. Guenther, 1990. Water surface detection strategy for an airborne laser bathymeter, *Proc. SPIE Ocean Optics X*, Vol. 1302, 597-611.

Timofeyeva, V.A. and F.I. Gorobets, 1967. On the relationship between the attenuation coefficients of collimated and diffuse light fluxes, *Isv. Atmospheric and Oceanic Physics* (Acad. of Science USSR) 3, 291-296 (166-169 in translation).

Tuell, G., and J.Y. Park, 2004. Use of SHOALS bottom reflectance images to constrain the inversion of a hyperspectral radiative transfer model, *Proc. Laser Radar and Technology Applications IX*, SPIE Vol. 5412, 185-193.

Tuell, G., J.Y. Park, J. Aitken, V. Ramnath, and V. Feygels, 2005a. Adding hyperspectral to CHARTS: early results, *Proc. U.S. Hydro 2005*, The Hydrographic Society of America, March 29-31, San Diego, CA, paper 7-1, 10 pp.

Tuell, G.H., V. Feygels, Y. Kopilevich, A.D. Weidemann, A.G. Cunningham, R. Mani, V. Podoba, V. Ramnath, J.Y. Park, and J. Aitken, 2005b. Measurement of ocean water optical properties and seafloor reflectance with Scanning Hydrographic Operational Airborne Lidar Survey (SHOALS): II. Practical results and comparison with independent data, *Proc. Remote Sensing of the Coastal Oceanic Environment*, SPIE Vol. 5885, 115-127.

Tuell, G., J.Y. Park, J. Aitken, V. Ramnath, V. Feygels, G. Guenther, and Y. Kopilevich, 2005c. SHOALS-enabled 3-d benthic mapping, *Proc. SPIE Vol. 5806, Algorithms and Technologies for Multispectral, Hyperspectral, and Ultraspectral Imagery XI*, S. Chen and P. Lewis eds., 816-826.

Tsvetkov, E.A., 1991. Lidar related shipboard and aircraft measurements, *Technical Seminar on Issues in Lidar and Ocean.*, Oct. 1-2, Naval Ocean Systems Center, San Diego, CA.

Tyler, J.E., 1968. The Secchi disc, *Limnol. Oceanogr.*, 13, 1-6.

Tyler J.E. and R.W. Preisendorfer, 1962. *The Sea* (M.N. Hill, editor), Wiley-Interscience (New York).

UN, 1989. Status of hydrographic surveying and nautical charting world-wide, *4th United Nations Regional Cartographic Conference for the Americas*, January 23-27, 81/INF/9.

Vlasov, D.V., 1985. Aerial laser sounding on the upper layer of the ocean, *Bull. Acad. Sci. USSR: Phys. Ser.*, 49(3): 433-442.

Vosburgh, J. and J. Banic, 1987. Airborne laser surveys of the Northwest Passage, *Proc. XIIIth Int'l. Hydro. Conf.*, Monaco.

Walrafen, G.E., 1967. Raman spectral studies of the effects of temperature on water structure, *J. Chem. Phys.*, 47(1): 114-126.

Walsh, E.J., D.W. Hancock, D.E. Hines, R.N. Swift, and J.F. Scott, 1985. Directional wave spectra measured with the surface contour radar, *J. Phys. Oceanogr.*, 15, 566-592.

Watters, T. and C.E. Wiggins, 1999. Utilization of remote sensing methods for management of Florida's coastal zone, *Proc. U.S. Hydrographic Conference*, April 26-29, Mobile, AL, (paper 93 on CD), 7 pp.

Wellington, M., 2001a. The Laser Airborne Depth Sounder (LADS) — a broad range of applications, *Proc. Hydro 2001*, The Hydrographic Society, Special Pub. 42, March 27-29, Norwich, England, Paper 19, 11 pp.

Wellington, M., 2001b. The Laser Airborne Depth Sounder (LADS) - a broad range of applications, environmental conditions, and commercial models, *Hydro International*, 5, 3 (April), 6-9.

West, G.R., 2001. In deeper waters, *POB (Point of Beginning)*, 26(7): 22-26.

West, G.R. and W.J. Lillycrop, 1999. Feature detection and classification with airborne lidar — practical experience, *Proc. Shallow Survey-99*, Australian Defence Science and Technology Organization, Oct 18-20, Sydney, Australia, Paper 3-4, 8 pp.

West, G.R., W.J. Lillycrop, and R.W. Pope, 2001a. Keeping a low profile — using airborne laser bathymetry in sensitive hydrographic scenarios, *Hydro International*, 5, 4 (May/June), 28-31.

West, G.R., W.J. Lillycrop, and R.W. Pope, 2001b. Utilizing airborne lidar bathymetry technology for rapid environmental assessment, *Sea Technology*, 42(6): 10-15.

West, G.R. and C.E. Wiggins, 2000a. Airborne mapping sheds light on Hawaiian coasts and harbors, *EOM*, 9(4): 25-27.

West, G.R. and C.E. Wiggins, 2000b. Airborne lidar bathymetry in the management of Florida's coastal zone, *ICZM*, 2(2): 69-73.

Westwood, J., 1999. EEZ surveys — costs and benefits, *EEZ Technology*, 4(2): 61-67.

Witt, A.K., J.G. Shannon, M.B. Rankin, and L.A. Fuchs, 1976. Air/underwater laser radar test results, analysis, and performance predictions, *Report No. NADC-76005-20*, Naval Air Development Center, Warminster, PA, 293 pp. (CONFIDENTIAL).

Woolard, J., M. Aslaksen, J. Longenecker, and A. Ryerson, 2003. Shoreline mapping from airborne lidar in Shilshole Bay, Washington, *Proc. U.S. Hydro 2003*, The Hydrographic Society of America, March 24-27, Biloxi, MS, paper 5.1, 11 pp.

Wozencraft, J. M. and J.L. Irish, 2000. Airborne lidar surveys and regional sediment management, *Proc. 20th EARSeL Symposium: Workshop on Lidar Remote Sensing of Land and Sea*, European Association of Remote Sensing Laboratories, June 16-17, Dresden, Germany, (paper #2 on CD), 11 pp.

Wozencraft, J.M. and W.J. Lillycrop, 2003. Airborne coastal mapping, past, present, and future, *J. Coastal Research*, Special Issue, 38, 207-215.

Wozencraft, J.M. and W.J. Lillycrop, 2006. JALBTCX Coastal Mapping for the USACE, *Int'l. Hydro. Rev.*, (in press).

Wozencraft, J.M. and D. Millar, 2005. Airborne lidar and integrated technologies for coastal mapping and charting, *Marine Technology Society Journal*, 39(3): 27-35.

Wozencraft, J.M., K. Francis, and J. Pope, 2002. SHOALS airborne laser hydrography to support Lake Ontario-St. Lawrence River water level study, *Proc. Canadian Hydrographic Conference 2002*, Toronto, Ontario, Canada.

Wozencraft, J.M., J.L. Irish, and W.J. Lillycrop, 2001. Sand volumes and transport pathways for Gulf of Mexico Regional Sediment Management, *Proc. Coastal Dynamics '01*, June 11-15, Lund, Sweden.

Wright, C.W. and J.C. Brock, 2002. EAARL: A lidar for mapping shallow coral reefs and other coastal environments, *Proc. Seventh International Conf. on Remote Sensing for Marine and Coastal Environments*, May 20-22, Miami, Florida.

Chapter 9

Sonar

Lloyd C. Huff and Guy T. Noll

TECHNOLOGY OVERVIEW

SONAR is an acronym for (So)und (Na)vigation and (R)anging. Sound and acoustic are terms that can be used interchangeably, although the latter is a broader term. The former is most often used to describe acoustic frequencies within the range of human hearing, which leads to terms like ultrasonic and sub-sonic for acoustic frequencies that are respectively, above and below the range of human hearing.

Sound waves have a physical character that differs from that of other types of propagating waves, i.e. light and radio waves. Acoustic waves are based on vibrations of the actual material of the medium and are manifested as periodic variations of pressure in the medium. As a result of this physical nature of acoustic waves, the exact composition of the material through which an acoustic wave travels will impact the energy that is necessarily lost as the wave propagates through the material. When a propagating acoustic wave encounters a sudden change in the properties (sound speed and/or density, but specifically the product of sound speed and density) of the actual material of the medium, a portion of the acoustic wave will change its propagation direction. That portion of the acoustic wave that reverses its propagation direction is the echo which echo sounders are designed to exploit for distance measurements. Figure 9.1 shows the basic principle of an acoustic wave reflecting from the ocean floor and the simple formula for reducing the time of flight to a depth value.

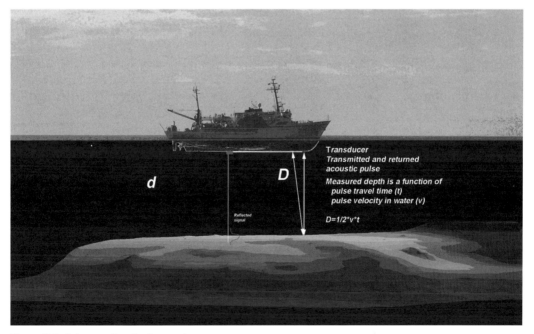

Transducer
Transmitted and returned acoustic pulse

Measured depth is a function of pulse travel time (t) pulse velocity in water (v)

$D = 1/2 * v * t$

Reflected signal

d

D

Figure 9.1 Echosounding fundamentals.

If the transmission and reception of acoustic energy can be confined to a singular narrow angular sector, the detection of an echo at some time after a pulse is transmitted provides both the range and bearing to the point in space where the echo was generated. Measuring the local configuration of the seabed with acoustics is that basic: transmit acoustic energy toward the bottom and precisely detect the arrival times and directions of the acoustic energy that returns from the bottom. The measured ranges and 3-dimensional directions to points where the echoes were generated can be converted into 3-dimensional locations, relative to the transducer. Finally it is necessary to transfer the echo generation locations from the transducer frame of reference into the ship's frame of reference and finally into the appropriate reference frame for presenting the survey results.

The accuracy standards for hydrographic surveys are set forth in Special Publication 44 (SP 44). SP 44 is issued by the International Hydrographic Organization (IHO) in Monaco and updated from time to time with the fourth version of SP 44 published in April 1998. Chapter 3 of this DEM Users Manual discusses the various Orders of IHO vertical and horizontal charting specifications along with issues concerning detection of features on the bottom. While reading this chapter on sonar, it is sufficient to keep in mind that shallow water hydrographic surveys, which are typically conducted to "Order-1" specifications, must meet the requirement that depths, corrected relative to chart datum, are within 50 cm of the true depth, with 95% confidence. Thus, much of the final accuracy is dependent upon the precision and accuracy of the corrections applied through a robust process.

DEVELOPMENTAL HISTORY

The earliest methods for sounding water depths were simple and direct, and a natural extension of the forms of propulsion in use, such as poles and oars. A weight attached to a rope served the needs of early man to measure depths that were too deep to measure with a pole. In approximately 450 BC, Herodotus, a Greek chronicler, reported a water depth of 11 fathoms at a distance of one day's sailing distance off the Egyptian coast (Harre, 1992). In the early part of the nineteenth century when the advent of oceanic submarine cables accelerated the need for soundings in deep water, the measurement tool was naturally a technology similar to a weight attached to a rope. It was a lead weight attached to a wire line. Note: The action of measuring depth is known as taking a sounding, based on the old French verb *sonder*, meaning to probe the unknown, and was not derived from the English "sound". The use of sound to take a sounding was an invention made in the early part of the twentieth century. Nevertheless, in the twenty-first century, a graduated wire line with an attached lead weight remains an accepted means to confirm the correct operation of modern echo sounders.

In 1490, Leonardo da Vinci wrote, "If you cause your ship to stop and place the head of a long tube into the water and place the other extremity to your ear, you will hear ships at a great distance from you." This is generally accepted as the earliest documented reference to acoustics in the sea (Bell, 1962). In 1827, documented investigations into the propagation of sound in water (Lake Geneva) were conducted. In 1877, Lord Rayleigh described the basic mathematics of acoustic waves in "The Theory of Sound." In 1912, one month after the RMS Titanic collided with an iceberg, a patent application was filed with the British Patent Office for echo ranging with underwater sound. That device was intended to detect submerged objects, like for example, the underside of an iceberg. In 1914, the outbreak of World War I provided the impetus for developing the capability to detect submerged objects, such as an enemy submarine.

Echo sounders were commercially available for use in deep water by 1925 (Klein, 1968). Depths were determined by measuring the time interval required for a short sequence of sound waves (acoustic pulse) to travel from the ship to the ocean bottom (where the sound waves are reflected, producing an echo) plus the time for the subsequent echo to return to the ship. One-half of that time interval multiplied by the speed of sound gives the depth. These early echo sounding designs were limited by the technology for making precise measurements of short time intervals. Consequently, the measurement of acoustic time-of-flight was unsuitable for application to measuring shallow depths until a decade later. It is interesting to note, that in this same era, acoustic travel times were also employed in the determination of horizontal positions (Hawley 1931). In 1935, the U.S. Coast and Geodetic Survey began employing shallow water echo sounders for hydrographic surveys. Note that these improvements in technology and techniques precede and are paralleled by the recent evolution of lidar.

The development of acoustic echo sounders advanced considerably as a result of acoustics research in World War II that was directed toward the detection of submarines and radar research for the development of electronic wave forming. That research resulted in improved electronic circuitry, and in improved materials for use in constructing acoustic transducers, which are necessary to convert between electrical energy and mechanical (acoustical) energy, and vice versa (Tucker, 1966). Those improvements led to scientific investigations to better understand the transmission of sound in the oceans (Horton, 1957) and the physical mechanisms involved in generating echoes through the interactions of sound with the seabed (Urick, 1956). These investigations demonstrated that the interactions at the seabed depended on the acoustic frequency, the angle of incidence, and physical properties of the seabed, like roughness, porosity and grain size. (Owaki, 1963) (Hamilton, 1971). In 1958, acoustic waves were first used to purpose-fully map geologic surface features of the seabed utilizing acoustic backscatter (Chesterman, Clynick, and Stride, 1958).

BASIC PRINCIPLES OF SONAR SYSTEMS

All sonars must have the capability to generate electrical signals that are converted to acoustic energy via a transmit transducer, thereby emitting into the water column a short burst or pulse of acoustic energy at a particular frequency. All sonars must also have the capability, via a receive transducer, to convert the acoustic energy of the returning echoes into electrical energy and separate those echoes from the background sound. Additionally, all sonars require the ability to accurately associate time, particularly time relative to the time of transmission, with the returning echoes. The details of the transmit transducer, receive transducer, echo processing, and the interpretation of the echo returns are what distinguishes a particular sonar product as vertical beam, multibeam, or side scan, etc.

Acoustic Sources

If a short pressure fluctuation were to be inserted at a point in the water column that is a large distance from either the surface or bottom of the sea, that pressure fluctuation would spread equally in all directions as a spherical wave. This is termed omni-directional, because the pressure fluctuations are the same in all directions projected from the source. As the radius of the spherical wave increases, the cross-sectional area over which the pressure fluctuation is spread increases according to the squared distance from the point of origin. This is the basis for the well-known "inverse-square law" which describes the decrease in the pressure fluctuation of an acoustic wave as it moves through the water. Assuming that the seabed below the point of the initial pressure insertion is horizontal, the intersection of the expanding spherical shell of the pressure fluctuation starts as a point, which expands to a circle of radius "R" and then transforms into an expanding annulus of width "R." Echoes can only be generated where the spherical shell is intersecting with the bottom. The vertical angles between the intersection points and the initial insertion point are continually increasing from an initial value of zero. Echoes resulting from the interaction between the pressure fluctuation and the seabed will propagate back toward the insertion point of the initial pressure fluctuation and over time will arrive from a continually changing vertical direction.

All of the echoes from any given annulus will arrive at the insertion point at the same time. In order to identify which specific section of the seabed generated a particular echo, it is necessary to estimate the vertical and azimuthal angle of arrival of any particular echo. Those angular estimates are not possible to make if the echoes are received using an omni-directional receiver. In order to estimate the vertical and azimuthal arrival angle of an echo, it is necessary to use receive transducers that are directional and it is also preferable to use a directional transmit transducer.

In the case of a sonar system, directionality of the transmit and receive transducers and the techniques of achieving that directionality is one of the major factors that distinguish one sonar type from another.

Directional Transmit/Receive Transducers

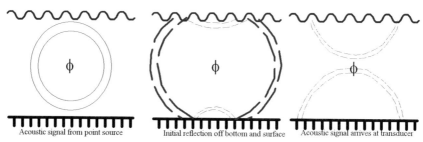

Figure 9.2 Signal reflection off surface and bottom from point source.

It has already been stated that acoustic energy will spherically radiate from a point source. Let us consider what would happen if two point sources, in close proximity to each other, were activated at a particular frequency (local pressure caused to alternate periodically between being above and below the local ambient pressure) using the same driver. There would be a set of spherical waves expanding around each of the point sources, as seen in Figure 9.2. Because the sources are driven periodically, the spherical waves might be visualized as a set of expanding concentric spherical shells where adjacent spheres alternate between being an increase in pressure and a decrease in pressure. Since there is a set of expanding spheres centered on each of the point sources, the shells must intersect at a number of places. If at the intersection between two shells, each shell is an increased pressure shell, the pressure at that point in space will be doubly increased relative to the ambient pressure. Likewise, if at the intersection between two shells, each shell is a decreased pressure shell, the pressure at that point in space will be doubly decreased relative to the ambient pressure. The third possible combination of two intersecting shells is the combination where one is an increased pressure shell and the other is a decreased pressure shell, resulting in the pressure at that intersection point being the ambient pressure. Once that mental picture has been formed, imagine that the two sources were activated by two different drivers operating at the same frequency such that the pressure at one point source is being increased relative to ambient pressure while the other point sources is decreased relative to ambient pressure. The radiating concentric shells will be essentially as before, but with one important difference. At the shell intersections where both shells were previously either increased or decreased pressure relative to ambient pressure, the resultant pressure will now be ambient rather than a pressure that is doubly increased or decreased relative to ambient pressure.

Figure 9.3 illustrates this point in two, rather than three, dimensions. In the right half of the figure, the phase of one of the point sources has been shifted by one-half a cycle relative to the cyclic pressure of the other point source. The darker areas represent increased pressure and the white areas represent decreased pressures, relative to ambient pressure. The figure demonstrates how the simple act of changing the relative phase angle between the two point source drivers has

Figure 9.3 Interference pattern from two wave sources.

completely changed the two-dimensional spatial pattern of pressure fluctuations relative to ambient. If this two point source example were expanded to a series of point sources regularly spaced in a straight line, there would still be concentric shells of pressure increases and decreases around each point source. There also would be a complicated set of points in space where all of the shells would intersect with different combinations of pressure increases and decreases relative to ambient. As in the two point source example, the relative phases with which the individual point sources are driven can dramatically alter the three-dimensional spatial pattern of pressure fluctuations relative to ambient. Selecting the proper combination of relative phases can cause the pressure to be zero or near zero everywhere in space except along a particular direction from the long axis of a line drawn through each of the point sources. In this manner a transmit transducer can be caused to direct a spherically spreading acoustic pulse into a particular direction, rather than into all directions as was the case with the omni-directional point source. Since echoes can only be generated from sections of the seabed where the spherically spreading pressure fluctuations from the transmitter have intersected with the seabed, it is possible to reduce the uncertainty in which specific section of the seabed generated a particular echo.

The main lobe of a transmit/receive transducer is defined as having a beam width equal to the angular sector between the half-power points of the transducer response. The characteristics of the main lobe and associated side lobes of a transmit/receive transducer depend on the actual frequency and physical size of the transducer. For example, the width of a transducer's main lobe in a given plane will be reduced as the dimension (measured in acoustic wavelengths) of the transducer in the perpendicular plane increases. When discussing the physical dimension of a transducer like its length, width or diameter, it is common practice to express the dimension in multiples of the acoustic wavelength (Urick, 1967, 1975, 1983). In the case of a horizontal- looking, rectangular shaped transducer, the vertical beamwidth is controlled by the vertical height of the transducer, whereas the horizontal beamwidth is controlled by the (horizontal) length of the transducer. The angular width of a line shaped transducer's main lobe in a particular direction is roughly 50 degrees divided by the extent of the transducer in that direction, expressed in number of wavelengths. In the case of a circular transducer, the beamwidth in the direction perpendicular to the transducer face is controlled by the diameter of the transducer. The angular width of a circular transducer's main lobe is roughly 60 degrees divided by the diameter of the transducer, expressed in number of wavelengths.

A receive transducer, like the transmit transducer described above, can be caused to respond only to acoustic energy that arrives at the receive transducer from a particular direction relative to the long axis of a line drawn through each of the linearly arranged point receivers. To accomplish this feat, it is necessary that the electrical signals from each of the point receivers be phase shifted (aka time-shifted) relative to each of the other point receivers and then summed to provide one composite electrical signal. If a directional transmitter and a directional receiver are mounted such that their main lobes are co-aligned, then it is possible to determine with considerable assurance which specific section of the seabed generated a particular echo.

Acoustic survey systems are generally constructed such that the transmit/receive transducers have negligible response in one hemisphere and finite response in the other hemisphere. They are mounted in such a manner that the responsive hemisphere is aimed in the direction where echoes of interest might be generated, like the seabed. The basic physical shapes of the transducers used in acoustic survey systems are circular arcs and linear lines. The lengths of the line transducers are usually ten to twenty times their width.

The transducer design and its associated beam characteristics fundamentally enable or restrict the ability of a particular type of sonar to associate a specific and unique direction, relative to both nadir and the heading of the vessel, with each echo that the system receives. An acoustic survey system can only respond to echoes that are generated in the region on the seabed where the projection of the main lobe of the transmit beam onto the seabed and the projection of the main lobe of a receive beam onto the seabed coincide. Object detection is also directly linked to the extent of differentiation of bottom return to the other sources of sound in the water column. An object must typically comprise at least one-half the "volumetric" measurement of the sonar ping, measured by duration of intersection of the first and last part of the ping with the bottom and object, to be recognized by the sonar processor as distinct from the bottom alone. However, this is also significantly affected by the bottom type, the amount of signal returned, and the frequency of the sonar used. Higher frequency sonars with shorter ping periods and smaller beams typically have higher resolution.

TYPES OF SONARS

Four types of sonar survey systems are discussed. Vertical beam sonar, multibeam sonar, interferometric sonar, and side scan sonar broadly represent the types of sonars that are used to obtain information about the configuration and condition of the seabed. There are important differences and obvious similarities in the functional designs of these four types of sonar.

Vertical Beam Sonar

Vertical beam sonars are primarily designed to produce quantitative information about water depths. Vertical beam sonars have one, and sometimes two, transducer(s) that are each used for both transmitting and receiving acoustic energy at a given frequency. The vertical orientation of the beam(s) means the transmitted acoustic waves will most likely interact with the bottom at near vertical incidence, which will maximize the energy in the echo returns. The received echoes are processed to determine the onset time of the first echo's arrival defined by the "leading edge" of the echo envelope waveform. The time measured by a vertical beam echo sounder is associated with the shortest distance from the ship to a point on the seabed. Depending on characteristics of the transducer and the configuration of the local seabed, that distance may not be the depth directly beneath the survey vessel, also referred to as nadir. However, it is generally assumed to be nadir because in shallow depths the error in position is likely not great, and in deeper depths the footprint is so large as to include the nadir at nearly all realistic vessel attitudes.

In detecting the vertical beam sonar echo return, one is looking for a significant rise in voltage level above the mean level of the noise fluctuations that are also present in the output of the receiving transducer. The ability to distinguish one arrival time from another is limited by the bandwidth of the receiver. Wider bandwidths are associated with greater ability to precisely measure the arrival time of an echo. The amount of noise present in the output of the receive transducer depends on both the amount of acoustic noise in the water and the bandwidth of the receiver. The engineering aspects of designing and building a vertical beam sonar deal with the tradeoff between time resolution and rejection of noise which allows weaker echoes to be reliably detected. Other factors that the sonar engineer may change to improve the vertical beam sonar performance for a particular application, like measuring into the seabed (sub-bottom profiling), are acoustic frequency, transmit power, transducer beam width, and the signal processing technique (Urick, 1967, 1975, 1983) (Chramiec and Morton, 1970) (Mayer and LeBlanc, 1983).

Vertical beam echo sounders point in the direction of their main lobe, which is directed vertically toward the seabed except when the vessel is experiencing high values of roll and/or pitch. Vertical beam echo sounders generally have main lobe angular widths between five and twenty-five degrees. Since vertical beam sonars are characterized as looking in only one direction, it is therefore evident that for each transmitted pulse, there is only one area on the seabed where transmit and receive beams coincide. This provides a high degree of confidence, but not an absolute guarantee, that the echoes measured in a vertical beam echo sounder originate from a point that was located in the direction that the main lobe of the transmit/receive transducer was pointing. If a narrow main lobe is not orientated vertically, there will be a horizontal displacement on the seabed between where the leading edge of the echo is generated and where the leading edge of the echo would have been generated if the beam were orientated vertically. The result is that the measured depth is vertically offset from true depth. The vertical offset associated with a non-vertical beam will always make the measured depth appear to be deeper than it is and the offset will scale with true depth. Figure 9.4 illustrates an example where a depth offset is produced as the result of a horizontal displacement caused by vessel roll. This case is more often observed in areas of extremely steep bottom relief, such as channel boundaries or fjords, in which small changes in pointing angle have a high impact on the measured acoustic travel time.

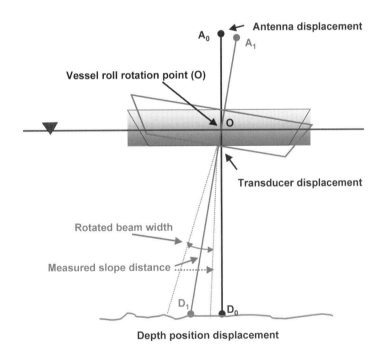

Figure 9.4 Horizontal displacement and depth offset caused by roll rotation of vertical beam.

Because the reduction to half-power in the transducer's angular response occurs on both transmit and receive, the half-power point specified for the transducer is actually the quarter-power point for the system throughput. As a word of caution, relentless pursuit of narrower and narrower beamwidths comes at the cost of greatly increasing the size of the transducer or greatly reducing the operating range of the sonar by greatly increasing the frequency to the point where the acoustic energy suffers increased attenuation by absorption. Furthermore, if a very narrow beam width is achieved, then even small values of vessel roll and pitch can negate the basic assumptions of vertical beam echo sounders, which are that the received echoes were generated directly beneath the vessel and consequently that the time after transmit of the leading edge of the echo relates to the depth directly beneath the vessel (MacPhee, 1979).

To achieve additional confidence in the accurate delineation of the sea bottom with vertical beam echo sounders, a narrow beam transmitting/receiving at one frequency may be operated in conjunction with a broad beam transmitting/receiving at another frequency. There are numerous echo sounders on the market that incorporate two simultaneous vertical beam depth measurements at different frequencies (for example 50 and 200 kHz). Figure 9.5 presents an Odom Hydrographic Systems ECHOTAC MKIII dual channel vertical beam echo sounder. The computer screen has been configured (left-right) to present acoustic returns from the higher and lower frequency channels, respectively.

Figure 9.5 Dual Channel Vertical Beam Echo Sounder.

In dual-frequency vertical beam echo sounders, the beamwidths may be the same, but that is the exception rather than the rule. Usually the lower of the two frequencies has a broader beamwidth. These systems can increase the robustness of the solution, both as a "check" and by bringing additional information to the measurement, such as density differences in the sediment or excluding vegetation returns from the primary bathymetry.

The received echoes in a vertical beam depth sounder may be subjected to various signal processing schemes, which provide information that allows the user to infer variations in the interaction of the transmitted acoustic pulse and the seabed that might, in turn, imply spatial variations in the composition of the seabed.

A notable variation of the vertical beam echo sounder is the multiple vertical beam echo sounder, or sweep sonar. The bottom coverage is a function of transducer spacing, beam width, and water depth. However, the dependence of its bottom coverage on water depth is much less than that of multibeam sonar. That fact makes a sweep sonar attractive for surveys in very shallow water. Sweep sonar is simply a series of standard single beam transducers vertically mounted on a boat, barge, or other stable platform. Sweep systems may use any number of transducers. Two or more transducers may be mounted permanently in the vessel hull. Additional transducers may be mounted on "over-the-side" outriggers or, more commonly, from hinged, retractable booms deployed to port and starboard. In 1985, the Detroit District of the U. S. Army Corps of Engineers was the first in the U.S. to install a 32-channel, vertical-looking multi-channel echo sounder (Rougeau, et.al. 1992). The more common systems deploy between 3 and 12 transducers on combinations of hull and retractable boom mounts. Figure 9.6 illustrates a sweep sonar with two hull mounted transducers and 12 transducers mounted on booms.

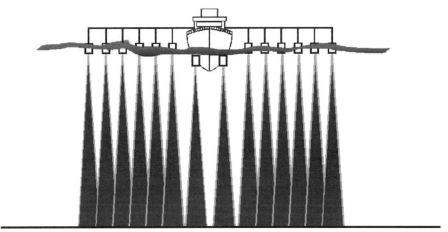

Figure 9.6 Sweep Sonar.

Sweep systems are normally used on shallow surveys where sea state conditions are typically calm. Thus, full X-Y-Z inertial motion sensors, as discussed in Chapter 10 of this book, are rarely added to a sweep system unless sea states cause excessive errors. Roll correction may be required to correct for vertical motion at the outer transducers, or a mechanical dampening system may be used to reduce the effects of roll on the booms. Regardless of roll, to maintain the full positional accuracy of the navigation system for each of the multiple soundings, it is essential that corrections be made for eccentricities due to yaw (heading).

Multibeam Sonar

Multibeam sonars are primarily designed to produce quantitative information about the water depths. Multibeam sonars are first characterized as having significant system response and the ability to measure depths at angles that are non-vertical to the seabed, as well as, at nadir, earlier defined as the term used to describe "perpendicular to the seabed", or simply "vertical." Secondly, multibeam sonar is typically characterized as having separate transducers for transmit and receive. All multibeam sonars measure travel times between the echo sounder transducer and the seabed using a transmitted acoustic pulse. One of the major differences between multibeam and the other types of sonars is the manner in which the sonar processes/ interprets the echo waveforms that are received subsequent to the pulse transmission (Heald and Pace, 1996). Conventional multibeam sonars measure the acoustic time-of-flight to the seabed as a function of angle from nadir. Through the use of trigonometric functions, the travel times are converted to a set of points, each with a vertical and horizontal coordinate, relative to the multibeam transducer (depth and position). Seemingly minor errors in the beam angle relative to nadir can result in unacceptably large depth errors. Because of the non-vertical measurement geometry, it is absolutely essential that full X-Y-Z inertial motion sensors, as discussed in Chapter 10 of this book, be installed and operated on the survey platform along with the multibeam sonar, with precisely measured accurate time linkage between the system components.

The first multibeam sonars were designed in the mid-1960's and deployed for military applications, they were known as SASS, for Sonar Array Sounding System (Glen, 1970) (Satriano, 1991).

In 1977, the first non-military multibeam bathymetric sonar was placed into service (Farr, 1980) (Renard and Allenou, 1979). Being deep water systems, the frequencies of SASS and other early multibeam sonars were necessarily low, and the transducers were correspondingly large and expensive. The operating frequencies of subsequent shallow water sonars were considerably higher than the frequencies of the early deep-water sonars. By 1990, there were multibeam sonars operating at frequencies as low as 12 kHz and as high as 455 kHz (Harre, 1992) (Steenstrup, 1992).

A conventional multibeam sonar has a single linear transmit transducer oriented along track. Its width and length are such that the entire width of the depth measurement swath is insonified by the same acoustic transmit pulse. The main lobe of the transmit transducer is narrow in the along track direction (horizontal plane) and broad in the cross track direction (vertical plane). The receive transducer, which may be either a linear line or a circular arc, is orientated cross track and has multiple beams, each with its own main lobe that is relatively broad in the along track direction (horizontal plane) and narrow in the cross track direction (vertical plane). It is important to note that in the instance of a sonar with a linear line receiving transducer, the sound speed must be measured at the transducer as that sonar requires knowledge of sound speed at the receive transducer in order for the sonar to operate at the full potential of its measurement capabilities. Due to differences between beamforming for a circular arc and linear line receiving transducer, the sound speed at a circular arc receiving transducer is not an essential parameter.

Figure 9.7 presents the Reson Model 8101 multibeam sonar which utilizes a circular arc receiving transducer. The linear line transmit transducer is to the lower left edge of the unit and pointing into the picture. In an installation the unit would be oriented such that the transmit transducer was on the bottom and pointing aft.

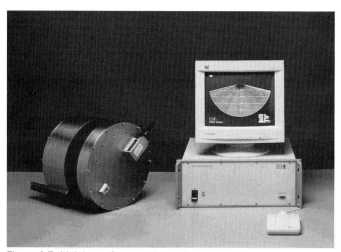

Figure 9.7 Multibeam Sonar with circular arc receiving transducer.

Figure 9.8 presents the Reson Model 8125 multibeam sonar which utilizes a linear line receiving transducer. The linear line transmit transducer is pointing straight up in this picture. In an installation, the unit would be orientated with the linear line receiving transducer extending in the atwartship direction. The linear line transmit transducer would be pointing aft.

For each pulse transmitted by a multibeam sonar, there are a large number of locations on the seabed where the projected main lobe of the transmit beam and the projected main lobe of a receive beam coincide. Collectively the multiple locations comprise the entire measurement swath, as shown in Figure 9.9.

Figure 9.8 Multibeam Sonar with linear line receiving transducer.

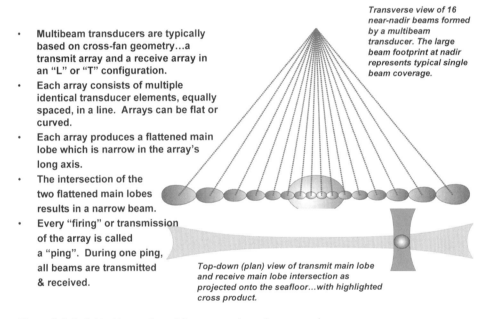

- Multibeam transducers are typically based on cross-fan geometry…a transmit array and a receive array in an "L" or "T" configuration.
- Each array consists of multiple identical transducer elements, equally spaced, in a line. Arrays can be flat or curved.
- Each array produces a flattened main lobe which is narrow in the array's long axis.
- The intersection of the two flattened main lobes results in a narrow beam.
- Every "firing" or transmission of the array is called a "ping". During one ping, all beams are transmitted & received.

Transverse view of 16 near-nadir beams formed by a multibeam transducer. The large beam footprint at nadir represents typical single beam coverage.

Top-down (plan) view of transmit main lobe and receive main lobe intersection as projected onto the seafloor…with highlighted cross product.

Figure 9.9 Individual beams in multibeam transducer form a swath.

The technique used in multibeam sonar to measure the acoustic time of flight may employ the amplitude of the echoes received in a given beam or the relative phases between the echoes received on adjacent beams. The amplitudes of the echoes received in each of the several beams are also measured and associated with horizontal coordinates relative to the transducer (Talukdar and Tyce, 1991). With suitable processing, the along track and cross track variations in the amplitudes of the received echoes provide qualitative information that may allow the user to infer spatial variations in the composition of the seabed. The variations in echo amplitudes may be presented in a planar view or presented as an overlay on the apparent surface of the seabed established by the multibeam sonar depths. Fundamentally, most sonar processing solutions use the area and shape of the amplitude-time series curve to determine seabed characteristics.

Interferometric Sonar

Interferometric sonar is another type of sonar that is primarily designed to produce qualitative information about depths and exhibits significant system response and the ability to measure depths at angles that are non-vertical to the seabed, as well as at nadir. Consequently, it sometimes is grouped under the general term of multibeam sonar. The measurement geometry of interferometric sonar is similar to that of side scan sonar. Consequently, it is sometimes called interferometric side scan sonar and grouped under the general term of side scan sonar. Interferometric sonar differs from multibeam sonar in that not only is the travel time of the echo measured but the vertical angle of arrival for each time sample of the echo must also be measured (Cloet and Edwards, 1986) (Denbigh, 1989). Interferometric sonar differs from side scan sonar in that not only is the amplitude of an echo measured for each time sample of the echo, but the vertical angle of arrival for each time sample of the echo is also measured.

Interferometric sonars have a single transmit transducer whereby the entire width of the depth measurement swath is insonified by the same acoustic transmit pulse. Interferometric sonars have multiple receive transducers, each with a relatively narrow main lobe response in the along track (horizontal) direction and a broad main lobe response in the cross track (vertical) direction. There is a small vertical separation between the several receive transducers which provides the physical geometry required to determine the vertical angles of arrival from the time samples of the received echoes. Because the geometry associated with echoes from near nadir is unfavorable for the accurate resolution of vertical angle of arrival, many interferometric sonars incorporate a vertical beam echo sounder to measure the depths directly below the vessel. As with multibeam sonar, it is absolutely essential that full X-Y-Z inertial motion sensors, as discussed in Chapter 10 of this book, be installed and operated on the survey platform along with the interferometric sonar.

Figure 9.10 presents the interferometric transducer of a GeoAcoustics GeoSwath wide swath bathymetry system. One of the system's transducers is facing out while the other facing into the picture is obscured. There is an attitude sensor mounted inside the Vee formed by the port and starboard transducers. Since this receiving transducer is in the general form of a linear line transducer, sound speed at the transducer is an important input parameter. In this picture a sound speed sensor clearly appears on the top edge of the transducer.

Figure 9.10 Interferometric transducer on pole for over-the-side deployment.

Interferometric signal processing techniques include determination of the amplitudes of the backscatter from the seabed, as well as determination of depths based on vertical angle of arrival. Those processing techniques provide a three-dimensional surface on which to view the along track and cross track variations in the amplitudes of the received echoes. Those spatial variations in echo amplitudes provide qualitative information that may allow the user to infer spatial variations in the composition of the seabed (Green, Hewitt, and Adams, 1993).

Due to the simplified design of the transducers and electronics, interferometric sonars are less costly than conventional multibeam sonars. The typically small transducer size means that they are quite portable and can be rapidly mounted onto small survey platforms, and also be configured for towing. However, if the transducer is towed, the roll/pitch and azimuth angles of the tow body must also be measured, as well as the depth of the tow body.

Manufacturers of interferometric sonars state that their systems can typically measure depths over a swath that is up to ten times the depth, or more particularly, the height of the transducer above the bottom. The data density in a beam-formed swath system (multibeam), and thus cross track resolution will halve if depth is doubled. The data density of a phase measurement swath system (interferometric) is far higher, typically hundreds of times higher, and stays roughly constant with depth. Therefore, the interferometric sonar can afford to average or statistically filter through many real data points and still provide soundings in a high spatial resolution grid. However, they also tend to provide depth measurements that are less accurate and precise than depths measured with beam-formed multibeam sonar. Factors contributing to the uncertainties in depths from shallow water interferometric sonar include: unraveling the true phase differences in light of the ambiguities in differential phases, interference from multipath arrivals, and interference due to simultaneous arrival of echoes with different vertical angles of arrival (such as echoes from both the sea surface and seabed). All of these factors are exacerbated in nearshore areas, but these are also the areas of greatest interest for interferometry due to the higher potential efficiency as compared to coverage that could be obtained with directional multibeam technology.

Side Scan Sonar

Side scan sonar is a widely-used tool for qualitative observations and supplements other quantitative measurement tools. The objective of side scan sonar is to provide a detailed presentation of the seabed features and manmade objects that may lie on the surface of the seabed, in the form of a planimetric image. The first side scan sonar was developed in 1960 at the Institute of Oceanographic Sciences (IOS) in England (Tucker and Stubbs, 1961). The first side scan sonar was a shallow water system, and most current versions of this technology are still used in estuaries, lakes, and bays. In 1969, ISO developed the Geological Long Range Inclined Asdic (GLORIA) side looking sonar for surveying in the deep ocean (Laughton, 1981). The fundamental physics remain the same as with other sonars, therefore higher resolution requires higher frequency and thus decreased range, consequently even in deep water, a towed side scan sonar must remain relatively close to the bottom to be effective.

As in multibeam sonar and interferometric sonar, a side scan sonar ensonifies the entire measurement swath with the same acoustic transmit pulse. Actually there are two pulses, one transmitted from a continuous line array transducer looking to port and one from a continuous line array transducer looking to starboard. The main lobe of the (port and starboard) transmit transducer is narrow in the along track direction (horizontal plane) and broad in the cross track direction (vertical plane), again due to the physics of the array size. Like vertical beam echo sounders, conventional side scan sonars use the same transducer for receive and for transmit. This provides a high degree of confidence, but not an absolute guarantee, that the echoes received by the side scan sonar originated from points that are located in the direction that the transducer is pointing. One of the greatest challenges facing the side scan sonar processor is removing multipath acoustic returns from the primary return. These can be reflections from the underside of the surface-air interface, objects in the vicinity, or even other vessels and their wakes.

The spatial resolution capabilities of side scan sonars are different in the cross and along track directions. Furthermore, the cross and along track resolutions each vary with the cross track distance from nadir and the character of those variations differs between the two directions. The along track resolution is determined by the horizontal beamwidth of the transmit/receive transducer and changes linearly with slant range. The cross track resolution is determined by the sonar's basic range resolution, largely dependent upon the duration period of the acoustic transmit pulse, and by geometric effects that vary nonlinearly with slant range, based on the height of the tow fish above the bottom and the cross track distance from nadir. The cross track resolution may be 50 to 100 times worse directly under the tow fish (zero cross track distance) as it is at the maximum cross track range. Thus, although the measured returns may be uniformly gridded, the returning acoustic signal varies considerably across the track, complicating the processing.

The basic range resolution of a side scan sonar, as well as a vertical beam echo sounder and a multibeam sonar, is determined by the bandwidth of the transmit pulse. In most systems the bandwidth of the transmit pulse is determined by the time duration of a short transmitted tone burst of a given frequency. However, in some designs the bandwidth is defined by the bandwidth of a long frequency-modulated transmit pulse. These systems are commonly referred to as "chirp" side scan sonars. The basic range resolution in meters is one-half the speed of sound divided by the bandwidth.

In the design of a side scan sonar a high premium is placed on achieving transmit/receive beams that are narrow in the along track direction to maximize resolution of features. Side scan sonars tend to use high frequencies in order to achieve narrow beamwidths with transducers of moderate length. Due to the high frequencies of side scan sonar, the useful operating range of a side scan sonar is typically less than 200 meters to either side of the tow fish. A notable exception is GLORIA II, which operates at a frequency of 6.5 kHz and has a maximum imaging range of 60 km (Figure 9.11, Mitchell, 1991).

 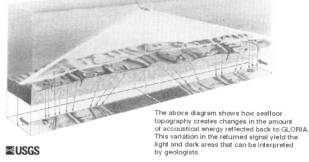

The above diagram shows how seafloor topography creates changes in the amount of accoustical energy reflected back to GLORIA. This variation in the returned signal yield the light and dark areas that can be interpreted by geologists.

USGS

Figure 9.11 Gloria II side scan sonar.

If the objective of a particular side scan sonar survey is to detect small objects, then the operating range may be limited by the spatial divergence of the beam in the horizontal plane as the acoustic pulse travels farther from the tow fish. For maximum ability to detect specific small targets at any given range, the along track width of the transmit/receive beam, at that range, should be less than the least cross section of that specific target, and the range resolution should be much less than the largest cross section of that specific target. Delineation of small details on large complex targets requires both narrow beamwidths and wide bandwidths.

The planimetric image of the seabed obtained via side scan sonar will almost always contain spatial variations in the intensity of the received backscatter signals. There are several possible effects that explain the majority of the spatial variations observed in the intensity of the received signals. The first possible cause of the spatial variation is an actual spatial change in the various materials that comprise the seabed. The relative backscatter characteristics differ for different materials. For example, rock and gravel will backscatter more of the incident acoustic signal than sand will backscatter. Sand will backscatter more of the incident acoustic signal than silt will backscatter, and silt will create stronger returns than decomposed organic matter. A second possible cause of the spatial variation is a change in the angle between the propagation direction of the outgoing (transmitted) acoustic pulse and the seabed, which is designated the incidence angle. The incidence angle varies systematically from ninety degrees directly below the tow fish to approximately five degrees at the maximum slant range expressed in the side scan imagery. Portions of the seabed with slopes that face toward the transducer on the tow fish (incidence angle is closer to ninety degrees) will backscatter more of the incident acoustic signal than surfaces with slopes that face away from the transducer (incidence angle is closer to zero degrees) will backscatter.

If the seabed is level and flat, the vertical beam pattern of the transmit/receive transducer approaches omni-directional, and the seabed is continually comprised of the same material over the entire cross track extent of the side scan imagery; then any variations in the intensity of the side scan sonar received signals that are observed along the survey track line can readily be attributed to variation in the material composition of the bottom. However, in general, most of those conditional statements are not simultaneously true, and the side scan imagery contains spatial variations that are due to local changes in both the incidence angle and the composition of the seabed. Consequently, manual interpretation of side scan sonar imagery requires considerable experience and first hand knowledge about the particular backscatter characteristics of various rock types, gravels, sands, and characteristic bed forms associated with them such as bedding, jointing, ripple marks, sand waves, etc. (Flemming, 1976) (Fish and Carr, 1990). Automated processing that includes interpretation is even more difficult to achieve, though software is continuously being improved with the intent of increasing the robustness of the classification achieved.

A side scan sonar is typically towed close to the seabed to control the geometry of the interactions between the acoustic transmit pulse and the seabed. When a tow fish is close to the bottom, the incident angle will change quickly from ninety degrees into a range of incident angles where the variation in backscatter is less sensitive to small changes in incident angle. The higher the tow fish is above the bottom the longer the incident angle is in the range where the variation in backscatter is more sensitive to small changes in incident angle. The geometry associated with towing the side scan sonar close to the bottom also enhances the generation of "shadows" behind areas of the seabed that distinctly rise above the surrounding area and consequently may represent a feature that warrants further investigation. Side scan sonar information is missing from these shadows, however, so full coverage is only achieved by combining two or more tracks. This allows the operator to also recover the nadir region under the tracks with improved incident angular coverage.

PRESENT OPERATING STATUS – PLATFORMS AND INSTALLATION

The obvious concerns in planning a sonar installation for a particular survey begin with the type of information that is required, along with any accuracy and precision requirements placed on that information. This gives the first indication as to what type of sonar(s) may be applicable, as well as the acoustic frequencies and consequently the transducer sizes that are required. Next, one must reconcile the primary engineering considerations of weight, size, volume, and power required by the sonar with the capabilities of a particular deployment platform. The next level of concern might be the definition of ancillary requirements, such as additional sensors beyond the sonar which are necessary components of a survey system, to include attitude sensors, heading device, sound speed profiler, navigational control, and whether to use a proprietary or open data acquisition format. Data processing, quality control and data visualization and presentation must be considered, particularly the extent to which those functions must be performed in near real time in the field for immediate delivery, or later in a shore facility.

Sonars of the types discussed above are deployable on a surface ship, a submarine, a small surface craft, a tow body, and sub–sea vehicles including remote-operated or autonomous vehicles (ROV and UUV/AUV). Virtually all combinations of sonars with all types of platforms are possible. Interferometric sonar may either be mounted to the hull of a vessel or incorporated into a tow fish (Tyce, 1986). Side scan sonars are generally incorporated into a tow body, or in one of the types of sub-sea vehicles. However, when mounted to the hull of a small surface craft, side scan sonars are also capable of providing quite satisfactory imagery in water depths less than 20 meters, (Huff, 1996). Figure 9.12 shows a Klein System 5000 side scan sonar mounted to the hull of a small surface craft. The bow of the craft and nose of the towfish are toward the left side of the picture. In this mode, the towing depressor and the tail fin surfaces are removed from the towfish and the position and attitude sensors on the small craft are used in developing a planimetric mosaic comprised of multiple survey lines throughout an area of interest. This arrangement improves the ability to accurately georeference the side scan imagery, which is important when an imagery mosaic is to be draped onto a DEM of the seabed.

Figure 9.12 Hull mounted side scan sonar.

Compact sized multibeam sonars are commonly mounted on small craft and used in shallow water to provide high spatial resolution while maintaining accurate positioning. Compact sized multibeam sonars are also sometimes operated on a sub-sea vehicle, as a means of achieving high spatial resolutions of small areas of the seabed (Steenstrup and Luyneburg, 1992). The transducers for multi-beam sonar that is applicable to deep ocean surveys are necessarily larger than those for application to shallow water surveys. The operating frequencies for deep water are necessarily lower than frequencies that are useable in shallow water. It is basically the difference in frequency that dictates the difference in transducer size.

CALIBRATION PROCEDURES

In a sonar there are only a few things to calibrate, namely the operating frequency, the pulse length, the transmit power, the main lobe amplitude of the transmit pulses, the main lobe sensitivity of the receive transducer, beam patterns of the transmit/receive transducer(s), and the accuracy of the time base. A user typically does not have the resources to calibrate many of these factors, and therefore relies on the manufacturer for the information. Even there, the normal practice is for manufacturers to provide typical or nominal response data, as opposed to the response function of a particular set of transducers and electronics.

Sound speed within the water column between the transducer and the seabed is an important parameter that affects the accuracy of sonars. It could be viewed as an extension of the accuracy of the sonar's time base. In a vertical beam echo sounder, the measured distance (depth) is the product of the total travel time, which transpires between the transmit pulse and reception/ detection of an echo, and the average sound speed along the travel path from the transducer to the seabed and back to the transducer. In multibeam and interferometric sonars, the distance measurement is further complicated by gradients in sound speed, which will cause the acoustic energy to travel along paths that are curved lines rather than straight lines. Errors due to sound speed are typically addressed by regularly measuring vertical profiles of sound speed at intervals in space and time throughout a survey.

Calibration becomes an issue when a particular sonar is incorporated into a survey system. In the instance of multibeam sonar and interferometric sonar, or fixed-mount side scan sonar, that means interfacing with additional equipment such as an attitude reference unit, heading device, navigational unit, and a data acquisition computer. The parameters that need to be calibrated are the locations, relative to the roll/pitch center of rotation of the platform, of the sonar transducer (acoustic center), the navigational (GPS antenna phase center) system, and the attitude reference unit (rotational center of heave/roll/pitch sensor), as seen in Figure 9.13.

Inaccuracies in these parameters impact the accuracy with which the measured acoustic travel

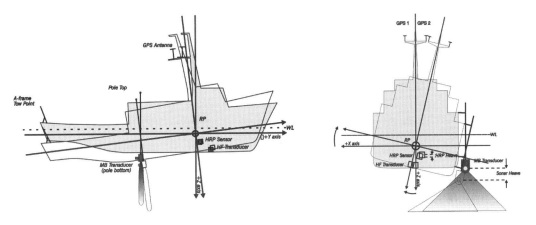

Figure 9.13 Pitch and roll effects on offsets of sensors.

times are converted to vertical and horizontal positions. There are also three angles that must be determined when the sonar and associated instrumentation are installed on the survey platform; the reduction of the data to compute these angles is more complex if the transducer is not installed squarely in the vessel frame of reference.

First, there is a calibration procedure, called a patch test (see Figure 9.14), which is used to calibrate the offset angles and timing. The exact offset angle between the azimuthal mounting of the transducer and the heading unit must be known in order to accurately convert acoustic travel times into horizontal positions relative to the transducer. The exact offset angle between the vertical angles (roll and pitch) of the transducer and the reference plane of the vertical reference unit must be known to accurately convert the acoustic travel times into vertical and horizontal positions relative to the transducer. Seemingly minor errors in the beam angle relative to nadir can result in unacceptably large depth errors. The patch test includes provisions for determining the offset angle between the vertical angles (roll and pitch) of the transducer and the reference plane of the vertical reference unit (Wheaton, 1988) (Godin and Ramalho-Marreiros, 1998).

The final calibration parameter (also determined during the patch test) is the time latency, which is the difference between the actual times when a measured parameter is reported from the

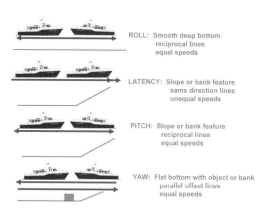

ROLL: Smooth deep bottom
reciprocal lines
equal speeds

LATENCY: Slope or bank feature
same direction lines
unequal speeds

PITCH: Slope or bank feature
reciprocal lines
equal speeds

YAW: Flat bottom with object or bank
parallel offset lines
equal speeds

Figure 9.14 Patch test lines for roll, timing, pitch.

depth sensor (sonar), the navigational unit (GPS), and heading unit is true, and the times which the data acquisition computer associates with those reports. For example if the survey vessel is running 5 meters per second and there was a one second time lag between when a GPS measured position is true and the computer time that is assigned to the GPS measurement, then the horizontal positions that are assigned to any particular sounding will be in error. The assigned positions will be displaced from the true positions by 5 meters in the direction the ship was traveling. In many gyroscopes, flux gate compasses and GPS heading devices, the output of the sensor is smoothed with a low pass filter to reduce unrealistic short-term fluctuations. The low pass filtering causes the output heading values to be presented at times after they were the true values for vessel heading. Timing latency in heading values will impact the horizontal positions assigned to any soundings that are taken while the vessel heading is changing.

A patch test calibration should be done each time the installation of the survey system is modified. For example if the vertical reference unit were to be replaced, that would be cause to perform a patch test to determine the roll/pitch offset angles between the transducer and the vertical reference unit. Effects on timing of data through changes to software and firmware should also be tested to ensure offsets are consistent after new software has been installed.

As shown in Figure 9.15, when a vessel's speed increases, it generally settles and squats (changes pitch trim), causing errors in depth measurement that must be corrected. In multibeam sonar the former is corrected by using settlement correctors and the latter is corrected by using the attitude (roll/pitch) sensor. In a vertical beam echo sounder, the effects of both settlement and squat are corrected by using a set of correctors. A settlement/squat test should be performed at least annually to determine the relation between boat speed and transducer height above or below the static sounding reference plane. It is important that the positions of the GPS antenna and the sonar transducer relative to the pitch center of the vessel be known accurately. Otherwise the effects of settlement and squat may cause depths to be reported that differ significantly from their actual values. Kinematic (dual frequency) GPS solutions that provide direct (absolute) antenna-transducer elevation eliminate the need for the settlement corrections, as the antenna height will record the settlement in real-time. However, if the Kinematic GPS system is set up to provide only the antenna height and is not configured to resolve the transducer elevation, then the squat correction must still be applied. Also, the final result must still be corrected for water level (tidal) changes.

Often it is desirable to establish a performance measure for each beam in a multibeam sonar. That performance measure can readily be accomplished by surveying a flat section of seabed in two perpendicular directions followed by comparing the data for internal consistency. First the area is surveyed using closely spaced survey lines like Swath B on Figure 9.16. Those swaths are processed into a gridded surface using primarily the central beam depths from the several swaths. Such a surface is designated as Reference Surface "B." The same area of seabed is also surveyed using track lines like Swath A, which are perpendicular to the survey lines used to develop the Reference Surface B. In this configuration the depths measured with each beam in Swath A can be compared to the spatially corresponding depths of the Reference Surface B. The differences between the Reference Surface B and depths measured in a particular beam of Swath A are expressed as the root mean square (RMS) of the differences. The Swath B and Swath A data sets should be acquired in a span of time that is too short for there to be changes in the water level and/or sound speed profile. With environmental factors constant, the depth differences are attributable to the slant range measurements of the bathymetric sonar, which are processed to depths using the vertical reference data. Low RMS values are desirable and necessary to satisfy the IHO depth measurement requirements.

If the RMS differences in any particular beam(s) are not less than seventy percent of the required specification, then it is doubtful that a hydrographic survey containing depths measured

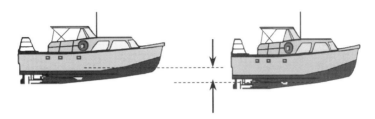

Settlement - At low speeds the effect of moving the hull through the water causes a local depression in the water surface around the hull. The effect of increasing speed on vessels with planing hulls is to cause them to lift out of the water.

Squat - Changes in vessel trim as it moves through the water. Little appreciable affect on transducer depth if transducer is located near amidships.

Figure 9.15 Effects of speed through water on sensor attitude and height.

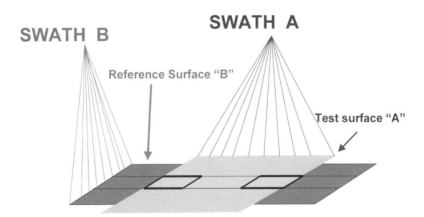

Comparison between two data set models:
• Center beam portion of "B" assumed fixed Reference Surface
• Outer beam array portion of surface "A" tested

Figure 9.16 System test using comparisons between surfaces. See color plate in Appendix C.

in those particular beams will meet the required survey accuracy. The seventy percent rule of thumb is based on the mathematical rule for propagation of uncertainties and on equally dividing the total allowable uncertainty between the measurement of depth and the knowledge of water level that is necessary to translate the measured depths, acquired relative to the actual water level, into depths relative to the MLLW chart datum.

During actual survey operations, the essence of this specific test can be accomplished through the use of cross line checks during the survey. However, in an actual survey the constraint for the same water level and the same sound speed profile are rarely met. Consequently, cross line checks exhibit elevated values of RMS depth differences, compared to those observed in a specific test between comparison surfaces. This shows that there is no substitute for understanding how the real-world constraints of operational sonar usage are deduced from the test measurements used in preparation for surveying after the equipment is installed.

Even when all of the factors which impact on the accuracy of a sonar's distance measurements are known, the measured depths reported by the sounder will undoubtedly be biased, relative to the actual depth reduced to charting datum. That is because the measured depths are relative to the sea surface at the times when each of the measurements were made and the depths for charting must be relative to the chart datum. In the U.S., the chart datum is mean lower low water (MLLW), whereas internationally it might be MLLW or lowest astronomical tide (LAT). The water level at a given time and location of a depth measurement is a function of a predictable astronomical (tidal) component and a meteorological component, which is much less predictable. Understanding how these components relate to the sonar measurements made throughout the survey area is critical to the task of creating a bathymetric grid of acceptable accuracy.

Depths measured with respect to the local mean water level must be reduced to the chart datum by applying either predicted tides or measured tides across zones of equal time (phase) and height relative to controlling gages of the world water level network. In the USA, this network is called National Water Level Observation Network (NWLON). Alternately, kinematic GPS with rapid ambiguity resolution (RTK-GPS) may be used to determine the depth with respect to the WGS-84 ellipsoid (Krabill and Martin, 1987), and later after applying the ellipsoidal height of MLLW using a tool like VDATUM (http://nauticalcharts.noaa.gov/csdl/vdatum.htm), determine the depth relative to chart datum.

PLANNING CONSIDERATIONS

Good survey products begin with proper planning of the data acquisition. Planning begins with understanding the survey requirements and the characteristics of the area to be surveyed. Planning culminates in the determination of the procedures, equipment, and software, which are linked and should always be considered carefully, so as to optimize the survey efficiency and effectiveness.

Surveyors have significant capital equipment costs, so they are often constrained to conduct a particular survey with the equipment on hand, rather than rent or purchase new equipment that might be particularly suited to a given survey. In such cases, consideration must be given to the capabilities and limitations of a given system and how to design the survey to maximize the quality of the results. The design of the survey will require a choice of line orientation, line spacing, vessel speed, and sonar ping duration and rates. Those will in turn depend on the distribution and configuration of depths in the survey area, expected types of objects or relief to be found, and the characteristics of the particular system that will be used to conduct the survey. Line orientation and line spacing may also depend or the relative importance of imagery and bathymetry in meeting the objectives of the survey. These factors are obviously regressive, so that there are many different "right" solutions to the problem of conducting an accurate survey; the main differences in modern surveys often will be in the efficiency with which the survey is completed to meet the desired data goals.

Any particular hydrographic sonar survey might be for one and often more than one of the following reasons: nautical charting, regional bathymetric mapping, engineering applications, geologic studies, military applications, habitat mapping, etc. The type of equipment used will often be driven by the primary objective, and influenced by the customer's interest in other data types that may potentially be collected.

Surveys for nautical charting are conducted for the purpose of safety of navigation and require very accurate bathymetry. However, the detection of all hazards to surface navigation such as wrecks and other obstructions is critical. This type of surveying is most often conducted with multibeam sonar and/or a sweep sonar, which might be augmented with towed side scan sonar to ensure full coverage of the seabed. If towing a side scan is not possible, many multibeam systems now collect reasonable side scan sonar backscatter data. However, such data have not been as reliable as towed systems for object detection in the past, so areas "swept" by multibeam are not necessarily free of isolated hazards (Wetzler, et. al., 2001).

Regional bathymetric surveys are conducted to determine the location and orientation of depth contours in water depths and areas where safety of surface navigation is not a major concern. This type of surveying might be accomplished with lidar systems, interferometric sonar, vertical beam echo sounder, or multibeam sonar. Because this type of survey is most often for coastal areas and possibly at considerable distance from a port, a sweep sonar is generally inappropriate, and imagery is acquired only if that parameter is an output of the specific survey system. These surveys are commonly used in support of water level modeling applications such as tsunami run-up models, storm surges from hurricanes, and flooding studies.

Surveys conducted for engineering applications include: pipe line and cable routing, dredging, and site selection for offshore platforms. This type of surveying must acquire information about bathymetry, sediment type, and the presence of abrupt features like rock outcrops. Systems most likely to be employed are multibeam sonar, vertical beam echo sounders (for sediment analysis), and side scan sonar with or without interferometry.

Geologic studies, both for mineral exploration and research, require bathymetry as well as identification of characteristics of the seabed that can potentially convey information about the geological processes that may have occurred in the past as well as geological processes that might be currently active. This type of survey might be accomplished with towed interferometric sonar or multibeam sonar, either of which will provide a level of detailed imagery to supplement the bathymetry. The limiting factor in these studies is often the *in situ* observations, so supplemental ground truth data acquired with remote vehicles is often necessary. Autonomous vehicles are becoming more prevalent in this market, such as the diamond mining off South Africa using the Maridan AUV (2001).

Mine countermeasures, also euphemistically referred to as "environmental assessment" is one military application that requires survey data. In surveys of this type, the ability to identify different sediment regimes and to detect targets of appropriate sizes and shapes throughout the water column are paramount in determining the selection of a sonar system. Side scan sonar, because of its superior ability to provide detailed imagery of the seabed and objects on the seabed, is a prevalent sensor for this type of survey.

Habitat mapping is a rapidly emerging application for sonar survey systems. This interest is based on requirements for fisheries management that relate geographic knowledge to fish population data acquired over huge areas, and these are still being defined. However, it is clear at present that habitat mapping requires information about sediment types, the prevalence and extent of plant cover on the seabed such as eelgrass and kelp, as well as bathymetry, both general trends and local rugosity, or surface roughness. These types of surveys might employ the entire suite of sonar systems discussed above. Vertical beam echo sounders and side scan sonars are widely employed in habitat mapping based on their ability for the identification/characterization of sediments by analysis of the individual echo waveforms or statistical analysis of "spatial patterns" in the backscatter imagery.

CAPABILITIES AND LIMITATIONS

Acoustic techniques for bathymetry are fundamentally limited by the ability of the sonar instrumentation to determine angle of return and time-of-flight. Multipath, the return of multiple echoes to the acoustic receiver, creates noise in the digital or analog recording. The uncertainty of the speed of sound in the water column, and the actual source of the returning echo from the sediment-water interface, also lead to uncertainty in the result. These problems can, to some extent, be eliminated through increasing the density of the acoustic measurements and doing inter-comparisons among neighboring echoes. Note that performing a trending analysis without independent check measurements can cause undue confidence in one's results. Therefore, using another source of data, if only for occasional comparison with the normal survey techniques, can prevent blunders in equipment or procedures from invalidating the survey product. In general, weather is responsible for the most variability in the operating conditions that limit effective work being performed. Weather, unfortunately, cannot be controlled. The continual requirement for the correct sound speed profile can also restrict the amount of acceptable data that can be acquired during a given period. This is particularly true if there are several different water masses in the survey area and the survey vessel must stop often to update the sound speed profile information because it is not possible to reorient survey lines to increase the survey time in a water mass. Using towed undulating sound speed instruments is becoming an increasingly common method to mitigate this problem and increase efficiency of the survey.

COMPARISONS WITH COMPETING/COMPLEMENTARY TECHNOLOGIES

As indicated above, many survey tasks require specific approaches and equipment. Complete, high-resolution bathymetric models have for decades been developed using vertical beam echo sounder techniques. However, a modern multibeam echo sounder does make quicker work of the job in water depths deeper than about twenty meters (60 feet). In calm waters shallower than ten meters, the use of a sweep sonar is very effective. Interferometric sonar sensors are quite effective at measuring bathymetry between 30 cm and 17 m (one and 50 feet) deep. As object size decreases, side scan sonar should become a more prominent method of the survey, and should be used whenever object detection is the primary reason for surveying. There is competition between the different sonar types with regard to which is best to use for a particular survey requirement, but they still represent the same basic acoustic technology.

Airborne lidar bathymetry technology is a survey technology which is distinctly different from sonar technology. Airborne lidar bathymetry is often thought to be a competing technology to that of sonar. However, the fact is that airborne lidar bathymetric systems were initially designed with the intent of complementing sonar survey systems. Chapter 8 of this publication discusses airborne lidar bathymetry in detail. It is important to point out that when airborne lidar bathymetric systems were initially designed, vertical beam echo sounders and side scan sonars were the primary survey tools for use in shallow water. It was initially envisioned that airborne lidar bathymetry would provide greater spatial density of soundings and be more efficient than sonar in water depths less than approximately 12 meters (36 feet). That vision was based on the standard vertical beam sonar procedure, which was to survey perpendicular to the depth curves, at a nominal spacing of 50 meter (150 feet) between lines. This vertical beam echo sounder procedure required a large amount of ship time to survey the areas between the 12-meter depth curve and the beach.

The technologies of multibeam sonar and airborne lidar bathymetry were developed at about the same time. With the change from vertical beam to multibeam sonar, there was a change in the sonar survey procedure, which switched from surveying perpendicular to the depth curves to surveying parallel to the depth curves. That switch was made because the cross-track angular coverage of multibeam sonar provides swath widths that vary proportionally with depth, narrower swaths are therefore associated with shallower depths. Another change in sonar survey procedure that accompanied the change from vertical beam to multibeam sonar was to adjust the survey speed to ensure along track overlap of footprints on successive pings. In shallow water this is an important factor because as the depths become shallower, the footprints become smaller and smaller, necessitating further reductions in survey speed to ensure the required overlap. Airborne lidar bathymetry is not subject to speed limitations in shallow water, though care must be taken to avoid loss of object detection using lidar.

Airborne lidar bathymetry has satisfied its design intent of complementing sonar survey systems by virtue of being an accurate, cost-effective, rapid, safe, and flexible method for surveying in shallow water and on coastlines where sonar systems are less efficient in obtaining data for bathymetric modeling.

POST-PROCESSING

Processing hydrographic survey sounding data is highly tailored to the goal of the survey. The marine bathymetric modeler may desire a smooth gridded surface, the nautical charting authority needs the more conservative shoal-biased binned data, and the dredge operator may want only high-density cross-sections. These and other different survey products that can be produced by a variety of software packages form a basis for differentiation of processing software. Each of several software vendors has optimized the features that the vendor's customers deem to be the most useful. There is industry-wide pressure to increase the speed and usability of the software that, in turn, provides further differentiation between the various vendors as they attempt proprietary data storage and automated processing techniques. The basic task of any processing software remains the same; take the acquired data, from one or more types of sonar acquisition packages, convert it to a common processed data format, remove incorrect bottom detection points, and output the cleaned data for visualization. Another important step is the re-application of corrector data based on updated knowledge of the vessel, sensors, or water column parameters, though this is not always performed.

Data density within a hydrographic survey has increased by orders of magnitude each decade in concert with improvements in computer technology. Similar strides have not been made in the human interface to the computer. The application of manual methods to cleaning high-density multibeam data is time-consuming and inefficient when faced with the volumes of data acquired in modern multibeam surveys. Fortunately, robust algorithms are being developed (Hou, et. Al., 2001) (Calder and Mayer, 2001) that promise significant improvement. Until these are implemented, the surveyor must educate the client with respect to the true cost of accurate high-density sounding data, and make particular note of the cost of processing the data, especially coastal data. As acoustic sensors improve and data become more spatially dense, it is likely that manual methods will succumb to mostly automated ones because operators will no longer be able to review the full data density at common screen resolutions, let alone edit it. However, there will always be a need for review of odd acoustic returns that the algorithms will flag as aberrant. These realities are reflected in on-going efforts by academia (Mayer, Calder 2002) to create standard metadata for bathymetric grids that will tie final products to the underlying measurements. The choice of processing software should reflect the surveyor's goals, including the type of product required, the degree of automation with which the client is comfortable, and the desired overall confidence in the survey.

QUALITY CONTROL

The higher the confidence with which the hydrographer can state the survey results, the more likely that the survey has been performed correctly. A quality control plan, or a control process, ensures that the final data will meet the desired specification when designed, implemented, and followed. No specification will magically create good data; the old maxim of "Garbage In-Garbage

Out" will apply to hydrographic survey data collected with the intent of good quality if the plan does not provide for the necessary controls.

One vital factor, which has considerable influence on the quality of the sonar data, is the sonar operator. The operation of the echo-sounder is carried out by hydrographers, who in the course of a hydrographic survey must review the incoming sonar data and set echo sounder system parameters like range scales, pulse lengths, transmitted power levels, and receiver gains in order to maximize the quality of the survey data that are acquired. Since hydrographers are expected to make the correct decisions regarding the operation of the echo sounder, they must be given specific training. It is not sufficient that the hydrographers simply understand the instrumentation. If the hydrographers are to collect meaningful data, then they must know which data are meaningful. Their training must provide some background in underwater acoustics, marine geomorphology and perhaps even a bit of marine biology, as well as extensive training in the operation of the sounding system and the on-line data quality control tools.

The quality control of hydrographic survey data requires an understanding of basic seabed conditions in the survey area and whether or not to expect the existence of man-made objects. The more complete that understanding, the higher the resultant confidence will be that features with a certain size and shape, will be mapped correctly. Thus, a hydrographer should reasonably expect that sand waves are found off a rocky sandstone headland, and that man-made objects generally are not found in a recently glaciated region. Extending this analysis, the hydrographer can estimate the likelihood of a given type and/or size of feature being detected, given the survey procedures and survey equipment that were employed. When absolute knowledge of the presence or absence of hydrographically significant objects is needed, then the hydrographer can focus resources on those areas which reflect the largest concern, and apply the appropriate procedures to locate the objects.

In addition to the extra attention that is necessary for potential problem areas in a survey, it is important to maintain the practice of acquiring data on survey lines that cross the main scheme of the survey (cross line checks) and comparing the resulting depths with those acquired on the main scheme survey lines. A patch test calibration, as discussed above, should be done when the character of the depths on either the main scheme survey lines or cross lines indicate that there might be something unnatural about the results. For example if the survey data always indicate that depths systematically decrease from port to starboard, regardless of heading of the survey line, that would be unnatural and indicate a problem with the roll sensor or the relative angle between the transducer and the vertical reference unit. Another example might be when the position of a particular localized feature, like a rock on the seabed that is measured on one survey line, does not agree with the position of the same localized feature that is determined on another survey line. This and the occurrence of a disjoint mismatch in a large-scale bottom feature, when viewed on different survey lines, may indicate one of several parameters about the installation of the sonar and its associated equipment have changed. Conducting a patch test calibration is just about the only way to resolve the root cause of such changes in performance of the survey system.

An important component of controlling the quality of survey data is for the sonar operator to assure that sound speed profiles in the survey area are adequately sampled in space and time. As part of this practice, it is necessary to maintain operator review of the swath data to quickly detect evidence that the sound speed profile being used to acquire/process the swath data differs from the actual sound speed conditions. In general, it is a fairly safe assumption that the seabed is comprised of large flat facets that may be tilted in one direction or another. Therefore, when the seabed seems to curve upwards or downwards to both port and starboard of the survey track, the sound speed profile of the water column is definitely not the same as the sound speed profile that is being used in the conversion of travel times at particular angles (beams) to vertical and horizontal positions. This situation should be remedied as soon as possible by measuring the local sound speed profile and using the new profile for converting acoustic travel times into depths and positions.

With many of the current acquisition systems, it is difficult, if not impossible, to efficiently re-process the measured acoustic information into new bathymetric solutions because of the manner in which the data are recorded. Thus, primacy of quality control during acquisition must be maintained. Normally, the use of equipment and software operating manuals, augmented by hydrographer's notes from past experience with the equipment, form the basis for this control. There are increasingly stringent requirements to maintain quality control at the operator's console and minimize the first-time usage of new technology on riskier projects. Training, improved software, mentored data acquisition operation, and management-by-results will provide users with the requisite tools and incentives to ensure adequacy of nearly all data, and all of these measures prove their worth over time.

Once collected, data may be analyzed in several ways. Traditionally, the manual methods discussed in the post-processing section above have been built around a dual-operator approach similar to the land surveying method of observing-recording. One person performs the tasks, one person checks the values acquired, and the initial operator double-checks the final results. Denser data sets now provide more measurements of the seabed, enabling the automation of the data inter-comparison and trending of statistical results, or stochastic analysis. These methods, still under development, will greatly simplify and generalize the quality control process in hydrography.

DATA DELIVERABLES

The traditional view of a complete survey — a drawing representing the area at a specific scale — is still produced for nearly all hydrographic projects today. However, provision of a digital data set that represents the survey area, with at least as much resolution as the plotted sheet, is becoming a best practice. The usefulness of this digital data, when combined with other Geographic Information System (GIS) data, is reliant upon its accuracy, so it must be scrupulously compared with interim products, including plotted sheets, to ensure the signed survey and the digital data are equivalent at the required scale. An example of a high-resolution DEM georeferenced to a nautical chart, a typical "blended product" now possible with a number of geographic information systems, is shown in Figure 9.17. A gridded product must similarly have requisite metadata that links back to the original source with relevant quality information. A new concept, called Bathymetric Attributed Grids (BAGs), should allow for broad agreement in metadata development to meet Federal and International standards for geographic data, and help the industry evolve away from scale-based products. Modern positioning and sonar methods have made the use of survey scale somewhat quaint, since accuracies are now more closely linked to the depth of the survey than the scale of the survey. A typical allowable error for a modern shallow water survey, at the 95% confidence level, would be expressed mathematically as:

$$\pm\sqrt{[a^2 + (b*d)^2]}$$

Where "a" is equal to 0.5 meters and represents the sum of all constant errors, (b * d) represents the sum of all depth dependent errors, "b" is equal to 0.013 and is the factor for depth dependent error, and "d" is depth in meters (NOAA, 2000).

COST CONSIDERATIONS

The costs for most hydrographic projects are driven primarily by the availability of personnel and platforms. When there are large numbers of petroleum and other high-cost deep-ocean projects in progress, qualified hydrographic personnel become scarce and expensive. Vessel time is similarly tied to the ocean industry, where daily vessel lease costs are several hundred to several thousand dollars per day, dependent on vessel size and equipment. Another major factor is the working area; remote regions require higher mobilization costs and strict adherence to vessel availability

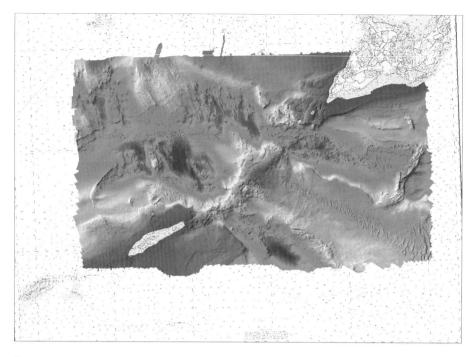

Figure 9.17 Digital Terrain Model on chart of Eastern Long Island Sound in 2003 by NOAA Ship Thomas Jefferson. See color plate in Appendix C.

schedules, whereas surveys of harbors near major metropolitan areas are easier to both equip and staff. Finally, the type of survey, as indicated above, has a very large effect on the potential costs of the work. Higher accuracy and confidences require more people with more knowledge to be involved in the work, thus increasing the project cost, and the length of the project affects the ratio of mobilization costs to overall survey production costs. The equation is not simple, and there are other factors that could affect final survey costs in measurable ways, but not in all situations. Surveying is a high-risk industry because it is closely linked to capital expenses, weather, and schedules mandated by these availability restrictions.

Costs for a hydrographic survey can easily range from $1,000 to over $100,000 per square nautical mile, a substantial range to be interpreted by an inexperienced surveyor bidding on contract work or a potential customer interested in procuring services. Proposing an expensive, technically challenging solution to the survey task is not always required. Often the smaller one- or two-person survey firms, with only a vertical beam echo sounder and analog side scan sonar, can do a job well and efficiently. Matching experience to the task at hand, these smaller firms can focus on one aspect of the hydrographic survey industry. They optimize their processes to the fullest extent, maintain their equipment through complete amortization, and thus maximize their profits while providing their customers with good survey products. Larger firms with higher values of investments in personnel and equipment can perform more remote and extended survey tasks.

TECHNOLOGICAL ADVANCEMENTS

The next major technology advancement in sonar systems, both bathymetric and imaging, will be in the manner in which beams are electronically formed. The present techniques will be modified to include the principle of focusing. Through the use of focusing, it is possible to achieve angular resolutions at ranges very close to the transducer that are as spatially acute as the resolutions that current technology achieves at ranges that are very far from the transducer. One benefit of focusing is readily apparent in a side scan sonar design that can simultaneously form several focused beams which lie parallel to each other in the along track direction. In such an instance, focusing provides the ability to considerably increase the speed at which side scan imagery can be obtained without having gaps in the along track coverage. That translates into a considerable reduction in ship time for a particular side scan survey, thus increasing survey efficiency. Another benefit of focusing is evident in a multibeam bathymetric system which forms focused beams. In such an instance, focusing can provide exceptional definition of bottom features and man-made objects on the seabed that have a vertical expression which is significant compared to the horizontal expression, for example a thin pile rising proudly from the bottom of a lake. This also translates into better definition of small details on large complex targets, which in turn provides improvement in the quality of range (depth) measurements that may translate into a cost benefit on many surveys. See examples of unfocused and focused images at Figure 9.18.

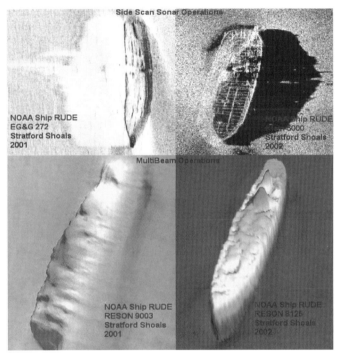

Figure 9.18 Examples of unfocused and focused images. See color plate in Appendix C.

Processing of side scan sonar data to account for the incident angle of the echo on the underlying bathymetry in near real time is a promising area of development. Using this and other techniques to improve the inter-comparison of data from different sensors should lead to faster surveys and increased confidence in the survey results, especially for object detection. Further research into the oceanographic properties of the littoral ocean, specifically the local variability of sound propagation, will also lead to operational efficiencies due to increased allowable swath widths in multibeam echo sounding. Automation of the processing algorithms used to clean multibeam echo sounding depths in near-real time, such as the Combined Uncertainty Bathymetric Estimation (CUBE) algorithm (Calder, CCOM/UNH, 2002) will lead to rapid acquire-review-submit cycles, and improve overall throughput from the surveyor. All of these advancements will enable hydrographic survey data to be an increasingly important facet of the GIS databases used for habitat preservation, municipal planning, and ecosystem development in the future.

AUTHOR BIOGRAPHIES

Lloyd Huff has more than 40 years experience in designing and using acoustic instrumentation for marine surveys of various parameters, including: tides, currents, surface waves, sediment transport, and depths. From 1985 to 1999, he was Chief of the National Ocean Service Hydrographic Technology Programs. Starting in 2000, he became a senior hydrographic researcher at the Center for Coastal Ocean Mapping/Joint Hydrographic Center, University of New Hampshire, Durham, New Hampshire. Huff has a BS in Physics from Southwestern University, a MS in Electrical Engineering from the University of Rhode Island, and a PhD in Ocean Engineering from the University of Rhode Island.

Commander Guy T. Noll, NOAA Corps, is currently the Commanding Officer, NOAA Ship RAINIER, a nautical charting-tasked hydrographic ship in the National Oceanic & Atmospheric Administration Office of Marine and Aviation Operations. He was formerly the Chief of the Hydrographic Systems and Technology Programs and Deputy Chief of the Hydrographic Surveys Division for the NOAA Office of Coast Survey in Silver Spring, Maryland. He has been with NOAA, both surveying operationally and in system development, for nineteen years. He was the lead systems integrator for the five multibeam echo sounder hydrographic systems installed aboard the NOAA Ship RAINIER from 1998 through 2000. CDR Noll has a BS in Civil Engineering from Columbia University and a BA in Physics/Mathematics from Whitman College.

ACKNOWLEDGEMENTS

The authors express gratitude to Al Rougeau of Odom Hydrographic Systems, Inc., who provided considerable background material for this chapter. They also acknowledge extended use of the US Army Corps of Engineers Publication EM 1110-2-1003, Hydrographic Surveying, and the NOAA Hydrographic Survey Specifications and Deliverables without specific citation.

REFERENCES

Bell, T.A., 1962. Sonar and Submarine Detection, U.S. Underwater Sound Lab Report 545.

Calder, B.R., and L.A. Mayer, 2001. Robust automatic multi-beam bathymetric processing, US Hydrographic Conference, May 21-24, 2001, Norfolk, VA.

Chesterman, W.D., P.R. Clynick, and A.H. Stride, 1958. An acoustic aid to seabed survey, *Acustia*, 8, pp. 285-290.

Chramiec, M.A., and R.W. Morton, 1970. High resolution near sub-bottom profiling, *Proceedings of Second Annual Offshore Technology Conference*.

Cloet, R.L. and C.R. Edwards, 1986. The bathymetric swathe sounding system, *The Hydrogr. Journal*, 40, 9-17.

Denbigh, P.N., 1989. Swath bathymetry: Principles of operation and analysis of errors, *IEEE J. Oceanic Engineering*, 14(4): 289-298.

Farr, H.K., 1980. Multibeam bathymetric sonar: Sea beam and hydrochart, *Mar. Geodesy*, 4, 77-93.

Fish, J.P., and H.A. Carr, 1990. *Sound Underwater Images: a Guide to the Generation and Interpretation of Side Scan Sonar Data*, EG&G, Lower Cape Pub., Orleans MA.

Flemming, B.W., 1976. Side-scan sonar: A practical guide, *Int. Hydr. Rev.* LIII (1), pp. 65-92.

Glenn, M.F., 1970. Introducing an operational multi-beam array sonar, *Int. Hydr. Rev.*, XLIII, pp. 35-39.

Geen, M.F., P.D. Hewitt, and A.R. Adams, 1993. The ISIS Interferometric Seabed Inspection Sonar, *Proceedings of the Institute of Acoustics, Acoustic Classification and Mapping of the Seabed, Vol 15 Pt 2*, University of Bath, England.

Godin, A., and J.P. Ramalho-Marreiros, 1998. Attitude and squat assessment for hydrographic launches using GPS positioning, *Proceedings 1998 Canadian Hydrographic Conference*, March 10-12, Victoria, BC, pp. 291-308.

Hamilton, E.L., 1971. Elastic properties of marine sediments, *Journal of Geophysical Research*, 76(2).

Harre, I., 1992. Multi-beam echosounders for inshore to rough-seas applications and the related data processing — An equipment survey, *Proceedings of The Eighth Biennial International Symposium of the Hydrographic Society, HYDRO '92*, IHO Special Publication No 29.

Hawley, J.H., 1931. *Hydrographic Manual, Special Publication No. 143*, Coast and Geodetic Survey, U S Department of Commerce, United States Government Printing Office, Washington.

Heald, G.J., and N.G. Pace, 1996. Implications of a bi-static treatment for the second echo from a normal incidence sonar, *Proceedings of 3rd European Conference on Underwater Acoustics*, pp. 649-554.

Horton, J.W., 1957. *Fundamentals of Sonar*, United States Naval Institute, Annapolis, MD.

Hou, T., L.C. Huff, and L. Mayer, 2001. Automatic detection of outliers in multibeam echo sounding data, *US Hydrographic Conference*, May 21-24, Norfolk, VA.

Huff, L.C., 1993. High-resolution multi-beam focussed side scan sonar, *Proceedings of the Institute of Acoustics, Acoustic Classification and Mapping of the Seabed, Vol. 15, Pt. 2*, University of Bath, England.

Hughes Clarke, J.E., et al., 1999. Data handling methods and target detection results for multibeam and side scan data collected as part of the search for Swiss Air flight 111, *Proc. Shallow Survey-99*, Australian Defense Science and Technology Organization, Oct 18-20, Sydney, Australia, Paper 6-2, 11 pp.

Klein, E., 1968. Underwater sound and naval acoustical research before 1939, *J. Acoust. Soc. Am,* 43:931.

Krabill, W.B., and Martin, C.F., 1987. Aircraft positioning using global positioning system carrier phase data, navigation, *J. Inst. of Navigation*, 34, Spring: 1-21.

Laughton, A.S., 1981. The first decade of GLORIA, *J. Geophys. Res.*, 86: 11511-11534.

MacPhee, S.B., 1979. Underwater acoustics and sonar and echo sounding Instrumentation, Canadian Hydrographic Service Technical Report.

Mayer, L.A., and L.R. LeBlanc, 1983. The CHIRP sonar: A new quantitative high-resolution profiling system, *Acoustics and the Sea-Bed* (N.G. Pace, ed.), Bath University Press, England.

Miller, J.E., J.E. Hughes Clarke, and J. Paterson, 1997. How effectively have you covered your bottom?, *The Hydrogr. Journal*, 83: 3-10.

Mitchell, N.C., 1991. Improving GLORIA images using sea beam data, *J. Geophys. Res*, 96: 337-351.

NOAA, 2000. NOS hydrographic surveys specifications and deliverables, p. 43, URL: http://ncd.chartmaker.noaa.gov.

Owaki, N., 1963. A note on depth when the bottom is soft mud, *Int. Hydr. Rev.*, XL, 2: 41-43.

Renard, V., and J-P Allenou, 1979. Sea beam, multi-beam echo-sounding in "Jean Charcot" description, evaluation, and first results, *International Hydrographic Review*, LVI (1).

Rougeau, A., L. Rosenbalm, and C. Sonnier, 1992. Integrated acoustic technologies form new shallow water survey system, *Mar. Geodesy*, 15: 187-198.

Satriano, J.H., 1991. Wide swath bathymetry for multi-beam sonar systems, *Proceedings of OCEANS '91, Ocean Technologies and Opportunities in the Pacific for the 90's*, Honolulu, HI, Vol 2, pp. 733-736.

Steenstrup, J.R., and R.W.E. Luynenburg, 1992. Multi-beam echo-sounder—On an ROV, *Sea Technology*, 33 (6): 17-21.

Steenstrup, P.R., 1992. New cost effective multi-beam echo sounder sytems for shallow water: 0 to 50 metres, *Proceedings of The Eighth Biennial International Symposium of the Hydrographic Society, HYDRO '92*, IHO Special Publication No 29.

Talukdar, K.K., and R.C. Tyce, 1991. Digital processing of sidescan images from bottom backscatter data collected by sea beam, *Mar. Geodesy*, 14: 81-100.

Tyce, R.C., 1986. Deep seafloor mapping systems—A review, *Mar. Tech. Soc. Journal*, 20: 4-16.

Tucker, D.G., 1966. *Underwater Observations Using Sonar*, Fishing News Books Ltd., London.

Tucker, M.J., and A.R. Stubbs, 1961. A narrow beam echo-ranger for fisheries and geological investigations, *British Journal of Applied Physics*, 12: 103-110.

Urick, R.J., 1956. Processes of sound scattering at the ocean surface and bottom, *J. Mar. Res* 15:134.

Urick, R.J., 1983, 1975, 1967. *Principles of Underwater Sound, 1st, 2nd. and 3rd editions*, McGraw-Hill, Inc.

Wetzler, N., and A. Van Den, 2001. Shallow water multi-beam system testing for object detection over a defined reference surface, US Hydrographic Conference, Norfolk, VA.

Wheaton, G.E., 1988. Patch Test, A system check for multi-beam survey systems, *Proceedings of the U.S. Hydrographic Conference '88*, Baltimore, MD, pp. 85-90.

Chapter 10

Enabling Technologies

Bruno M. Scherzinger, Joseph J. Hutton, and Mohamed M.R. Mostafa

This chapter describes the following recent technologies that have enhanced or in some cases enabled the major remote sensing systems for DEM data acquisition:
- Precise GPS positioning
- GPS-aided inertial navigation system
- Direct georeferencing system for airborne remote sensing
- Motion sensing system for multibeam sonar bathymetry.

PRECISE GPS POSITIONING

Technology Overview

The Global Positioning System or GPS has been extensively documented (see for example Parkinson and Spilker, 1996 or Hoffmann-Wellendorf *et al*, 2001). This overview describes its basic characteristics as introduction. More importantly, this overview describes how GPS is used to compute a position fix with decimeter accuracy.

GPS comprises three major segments. The space segment includes a minimum of 24 satellites that orbit the earth 20,200 km above the earth in 6 orbital planes with a 12-hour orbital period. The orbital planes are inclined 55 degrees with respect to the equatorial plane. The design of the space segment puts a minimum of 4 satellites in view at any time anywhere on the earth. Typical visibility in most parts of the world ranges from 5 to 10 satellites. Satellites transmit spread-spectrum modulated signals centered at 1575.42 MHz, known as the L1 signal, and 1227.6 MHz, known as the L2 signal. The spread-spectrum modulation comprises one or two pseudorandom codes. The Clear Access (also called Coarse Acquisition) or CA code has a repetition period of one millisecond and a bit or chip length of approximately 1 microsecond. Each satellite broadcasts a unique CA code on the L1 signal. The Precise or P code has a repetition period of 267 days and a chip length of approximately 100 nanoseconds. It is encrypted to form a Y code, the purpose of which is to deny unauthorized access to precise positioning and to prevent spoofing of the P-code by an adversary.

The control segment comprises the master control station (MCS), located in the Consolidated Space Operations Center (CSOC) at Schriever Air Force Base in Golden, Colorado, plus five tracking stations. One is located at the MCS, and the other four are located at Hawaii, Ascension Island, Diego Garcia in the Indian Ocean, and Kwajalein Island in the West Pacific. The control segment has the task of controlling the operation of the satellites and calibrating their orbits. The control station periodically uploads navigation and satellite clock correction parameters that the satellites then broadcast in their navigation messages.

The user segment comprises all user equipment, more commonly called GPS receivers, which perform positioning or time transfer using the GPS signals. A GPS receiver performs two fundamental functions: observables tracking and navigation solution computation. The GPS receiver contains a radio frequency (RF) section that interfaces with the antenna, plus 5 to 24 generic channels, each of which can track a combination of the GPS observables coming from a satellite. The observables comprise the CA or P pseudoranges, the L1 or L2 carrier phase and the Doppler frequency shift in the carrier phase. The receiver assigns one such channel to each L1 and possibly L2 signal from each satellite that it tracks. A single frequency receiver tracks only the CA pseudoranges and carrier phases on the L1 carrier from each satellite. A commercial dual frequency receiver tracks the L1 CA pseudoranges and carrier phase, and computes a derived L2 pseudoranges and carrier phase using the known cross correlation between the L1 and L2 code modulations. The receiver's computed pseudorange to each satellite is its estimate of the time of signal propagation from the satellite to the GPS antenna multiplied by the speed of light. The receiver maintains GPS time as measured by a crystal clock in order to determine the time of propagation. The computed pseudoranges comprise the true ranges between the satellites and the GPS antenna plus several pseudorange errors, the most dominant being the receiver clock error. The clock error is common in all pseudoranges, and contributes 30 centimeters pseudorange error per nanosecond. The clock error can be as large as one millisecond, which is an equivalent range error of 300,000 meters. Other errors include ionospheric delay, tropospheric delay, orbital error, multipath error and receiver noise. These are typically less than 10 meters, and hence negligibly small compared with the receiver clock error.

Figure 10.1 shows the vector position relationship between a GPS satellite and a receiver on the earth. If the receiver has access to the satellite position and the relative satellite to receiver position, then it can compute its position. In reality, the receiver measures the pseudoranges to the satellites and computes the satellite positions from the navigation data messages that the satellite includes in its transmitted signal. From these the receiver computes a navigation solution using trilateration of the pseudoranges. Figure 10.2 shows the basic geometry between a GPS antenna and four satellites. The lines between the satellites and the antenna indicate the line-of-sight ranges. The receiver requires a minimum of four pseudoranges to solve for four unknowns: three components of position on the earth and the receiver clock error. The geometry of the satellites impacts the position and time solution error. A position and time solution will have good accuracy in all dimensions if the satellites used in the solution are uniformly distributed across the visible sky. It will have poor accuracy in some dimensions if the satellites are located in one sector of the sky. This is captured in a figure of merit called the Geometric Dilution of Position (GDOP). In simplest terms, the position and time solution error standard deviation is given by the pseudorange error standard deviation multiplied by GDOP. GDOP can be decomposed into the Position Dilution of Position (PDOP) and the Time Dilution of Position (TDOP). PDOP is typically used as a figure of merit for coverage of a position on the earth by the GPS satellites. A position solution obtained from CA pseudoranges exhibits an error of 8 to 20 meters, depending on the satellite geometry.

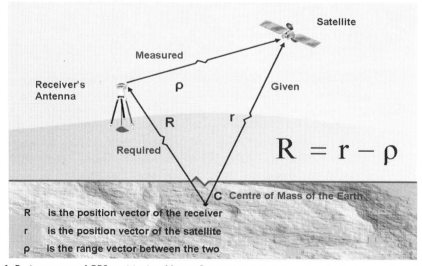

Figure 10.1 Basic concept of GPS positioning. Vector R + vector ρ = vector r in spherical geometry which accounts for the length and direction of each vector in 3-D space.

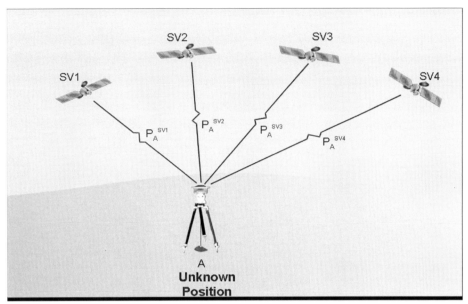

Figure 10.2 GPS positioning by trilateration.

Differential GPS

The key technology advancement that moved GPS into the commercial market was differential GPS. A DGPS system comprises one or more base receivers (also called reference receivers) at known positions and any number of roving receivers that move within an area covered by the base receivers. Figure 10.3 shows the geometry between two GPS antennas and four satellites. The lines between the satellites and each of the two antennas indicate the ranges. The baseline vector between the antennas is the DGPS solution. If the position of one antenna is known, then the position of the other antenna can be computed from the baseline vector. The base receivers both individually or collectively provide observations of the errors in the observables and broadcast navigation data. If the separation between a roving receiver and a reference receiver is within 100-200 km, then these errors are sufficiently correlated between the rover and reference receivers to allow their attenuation by the roving receiver using the data from the reference receiver. The attenuation increases as the baseline separation decreases. In a real-time DGPS system, the base receiver station broadcasts the corrections to the roving receiver over a data channel so that the roving receiver can correct its observables and achieve positioning accuracies on the order of one meter. DGPS corrections services that provide these corrections typically have continental coverage. In North America the DGPS services include OmniSTAR and the U.S. and Canadian Coast Guard differential beacon networks. OmniSTAR uses a continental array of base receivers to measure the atmospheric signal delays and broadcast orbital errors, and then transmit the differential corrections via satellite links. The U.S. and Canadian Coast Guard networks modulate the differential corrections on existing 500 kHz marine direction-finding beacons along coastal regions and inland waterways. Other parts of the world have their own services. The accuracy of a DGPS position solution obtained with broadcast correction is on the order of 1-3 meters.

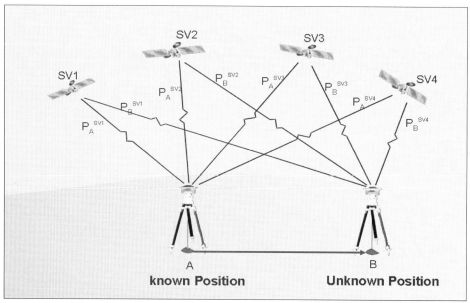

Figure 10.3 Differential positioning.

Precise Phase Interferometry Positioning

A more recent advancement in precise GPS positioning is integer ambiguity resolution. This technique uses the fact that a GPS receiver can track the L1 and L2 carrier phases modulo one wavelength coherently across the receiver channels with high accuracy. The receiver typically contributes L1 phase noise on the order of a few millimeters. Each reported L1 and L2 carrier phase contains among other errors an unknown integer number of wavelengths. A DGPS system with integer ambiguity resolution combines the phase data from two receivers so as to eliminate all significant errors other than the integer ambiguities. An integer ambiguity resolution algorithm is a statistical search for the set of unknown integer ambiguities among all feasible combinations of integers. Figure 10.4 shows the concept in a 2D plane. In this simple example, the intersecting carrier phases from two satellites define a grid of feasible positions in a search space. Each feasible point corresponds to one candidate set of two integer ambiguities. The carrier phase from a third satellite allows one of the feasible positions to be selected. Redundant L1 and L2 phase observations from two or more receivers each tracking five or more satellites provide the information for rapid unambiguous resolution. This method of signal processing can be thought of as coherent phase interferometry between two GPS receivers. Successful ambiguity resolution for baseline lengths between roving and base receivers of 10 kilometers or less typically requires 30 to 120 seconds of signal processing. Newer algorithms are providing single epoch or instantaneous ambiguity resolution under conditions of good satellite geometry (de Jonge, Bock and Bevis, 2000). Once the ambiguities are resolved, the corrected phases for each observed satellite become precise ranges that allow the computation of the baseline vector between the receivers with a typical accuracy of 2-10 centimeters.

Integer ambiguity resolution was first used to compute baseline vectors between stationary receivers as an alternative to conventional theodolite or total station survey methods. The receivers recorded the phase data, and the surveyor computed the baseline vectors in post-processing. Each receiver was required to occupy a station for 10-30 minutes so that phase errors could be averaged. The achievable baseline accuracy is less than one centimeter, which is within the requirements for network surveys. A more recent advancement in this methodology is kinematic ambiguity resolution (KAR) while one or both receivers are moving. This allows the relative positioning of one receiver with respect to the other with accuracies on the order of a few centimeters. If a fixed base receiver broadcasts the data requirement for KAR, then a roving receiver can compute its position in real time with decimeter accuracy. This is called real-time kinematic (RTK) positioning. It has become a preferred method of positioning for applications where up to 10 centimeters position error is tolerable. These include seismic surveying and construction site surveying.

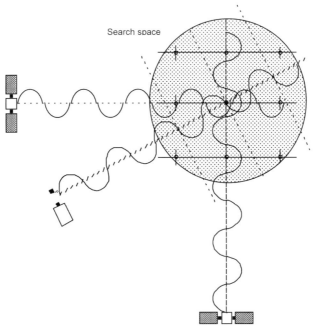

Search space

Figure 10.4 Example of integer ambiguity resolution in a 2D

Another application of RTK is attitude determination. The relative position vector between two antennas rigidly mounted with respect to each other in a horizontal plane is given in North, East and Down components. The heading of the baseline vector can then be computed as the arctangent of the ratio of East and North components. This concept can be extended to an array of three or four antennas to compute a complete roll, pitch and heading solution of the array. A GPS attitude measurement system thus becomes a possibly cost-effective alternative to an inertial system. The accuracy of the attitude array is dependent on the separation between antennas in the array. The attitude error can be computed as the RTK position error between antennas divided by the baseline length. Thus a one-centimeter position error divided by a one-meter baseline length yields a 10-milliradian or 0.5 degree attitude error. GPS attitude arrays by themselves are typically not suitable for continuous and accurate attitude measurement. However they can be used to shorten the alignment time and enhance the performance of a GPS aided inertial navigation system.

Network Differential GPS

Differential GPS in its simplest form relies on a strong correlation of atmospheric and satellite orbital and clock errors between the roving receiver and a single reference receiver at a known position. This allows the cancellation of these common-mode errors at various levels of accuracy, the most accurate being the phase interferometry methods described previously. Almost exact cancellation of common mode errors can be had on baseline lengths of 10 kilometers or less. Such short baselines may however be inconvenient or impossible to implement, for example in survey applications that cover larger distances. Examples are any type of airborne survey, large area road mapping and marine hydrography. An alternative approach to single baseline DGPS is network

DGPS. It uses multiple reference receivers to calibrate spatial models of the atmospheric signal delay errors that are applicable over large areas. As a simple example to illustrate the method, assume two reference receivers separated by 100 kilometers form a simple network. They respectively experience pseudorange delay errors of 3 and 5 meters due to the ionosphere. A simple model for the ionospheric delay along a line between the reference receivers is a linear function of distance from the first reference receiver with slope 0.02 meters per kilometer of distance. A network DGPS system will estimate a pseudorange delay of 4 meters for a roving receiver located between the reference receivers at 50 kilometers from the first reference receiver.

Actual network DGPS systems for precise positioning typically use 4 or more reference receivers separated by up to 50 kilometers to provide accurate spatial error models capable of calibrating atmospheric delay errors in the GPS observables to the decimeter-level accuracy needed for integer ambiguity resolution. An example of a network DGPS product is the Trimble Virtual Reference Station (VRS). It comprises a dedicated set of 4 or more reference receivers and a server that computes and transmits differential correction information to a roving receiver via a radio modem. It allows the roving receiver to implement RTK positioning accuracy over a 50x50 km^2 operational area instrumented by the VRS reference receivers as if a single reference receiver were always close by (hence the word *virtual* in VRS).

Satellite Based Augmentation Systems

A satellite based augmentation system (SBAS) is a network DGPS system with continental or global coverage, and uses satellites to relay the differential correction data to the roving receivers. The SBAS uses a network of reference receivers across the area of coverage to compute large scale spatial error models for atmospheric signal delay errors. It then relays the correction parameters to roving receivers operating in its area of coverage via L-band channels on geostationary communication satellites. OmniSTAR, a division of the Fugro Group, provides subscription DGPS services to users with two levels of accuracy. The OmniSTAR VBS service provides global meter-level positioning accuracy using standard global network DGPS techniques. The OmniSTAR HP service provides global decimeter-level positioning accuracy using a methodology called precise point positioning described later in this chapter. The wide area augmentation system (WAAS) was implemented and is maintained by the U.S. Federal Aviation Administration and the Department of Transportation for the purpose of en route and terminal guidance navigation for commercial aviation. It provides differential corrections with 1-3 meter positioning accuracy to users on an L-band channel that is compatible with the GPS signal structure so that a GPS receiver can receive and decode the signal without requiring a separate antenna and RF section. It uses 25 reference receivers located across the United States and two master stations that collect reference receiver data and compute the corrections. Europe has an equivalent SBAS called the European Geostationary Navigation Overlay System (EGNOS).

Development History

GPS first started development in 1973 with the formation of the U.S. Department of Defense NAVSTAR Joint Program Office (JPO) under the direction of Dr. (Col.) Brad Parkinson. An experimental constellation of 11 Block I navigation development satellites was used to test the concept and explore operational issues. The first Block I was launched in February 1978, the last on September 9, 1985. Thereafter, 24 Block IIA operational satellites were launched between 1989 and 1994 to replace the Block I satellites and achieve a fully operational constellation of a minimum of 24 satellites. In 1996, the first of 21 Block IIR satellites was launched to replace the aging Block IIA satellites as part of a GPS constellation replenishment program. The GPS modernization program was started informally with the May 2000 Presidential Decision Directive ordering the shutdown of selective availability (SA). This was part of an ongoing campaign to make GPS more accessible to commercial users and to respond to the emerging competitive challenge raised by the nascent European Galileo program. The GPS modernization program also includes an L2

Civilian (L2C) signal to allow commercial users access to dual frequency pseudoranges, and an L5 signal that provides commercial users with three carrier frequencies. The first Block IIR satellite broadcasting the L2C signal was launched in January 2006.

Commercial GPS activity began in 1984 when Trimble Navigation released its first GPS product. Since then Trimble and other companies have delivered GPS receivers and GPS-based products into the marketplace for a variety of applications. These include precision surveying, aircraft and ship navigation, commercial positioning for hiking and fishing and time transfer. In fact, most commercial transactions over electronic media such as wire transfers or the Internet are tied to GPS time.

Councilman first developed precise GPS positioning using carrier phase processing in 1980 (Councilman and Gourevitch, 1981). Hatch (Hatch, 1981) and Remondi (Remondi, 1985) conducted further developments in ambiguity resolution and decimeter level positioning. Their positioning methods required a static initialization of the roving receiver to identify the phase ambiguities. The first on-the-fly (OTF) ambiguity resolution was demonstrated in 1990. The first RTK receivers from Trimble, Leica and Novatel emerged during the early 1990's. Since then RTK GPS positioning has found extensive use in precision positioning applications such as land survey, structure and crustal motion monitoring, and control of construction and paving machines.

Figure 10.5 Example of a dual frequency OEM.

Types of Sensors

GPS receivers can be categorized as low cost and moderate performance for mass-market applications, and high performance for precision positioning applications that include surveying. The low-end receivers are single frequency (L1) receivers configured as original equipment manufacturer (OEM) components or chip sets for use in applications such as cell phones, car navigation systems and hand-held personal navigators. They are designed to deliver a position and time solution at minimum cost.

High performance receivers are dual (L1 and L2) frequency GPS receivers configured either as OEM boards for integration into high-end positioning and navigation systems (see Figure 10.5) or as self-contained instruments for a particular application (see Figure 10.7). Each of these requires a survey-grade antenna such as shown in Figure 10.6 that provides a stable phase center and a reception pattern that rejects ground-reflected signals. The first such application-specific receivers and antennas were designed for static survey applications. These receivers were designed for static occupation of survey points, and included a keypad and LCD screen for control and display,

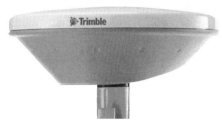

Figure 10.6 Example of a survey quality GPS antenna (courtesy Trimble Navigation).

and an internal data logging capability. The network adjustment was performed post-mission using companion post-processing software from the data recorded by the receivers. More recent receivers are designed to interface with a separate control, display and data-logging unit or to a laptop PC. They offer RTK functionality as an option, thereby allowing point-to-point surveys to be conducted in real time with occupation time per point on the order of seconds. This capability

Figure 10.7 Trimble R8 GNSS survey instrument (courtesy Trimble Navigation Inc.).

meets the requirements of applications such as seismic, construction and pipeline surveying. An example of a state-of-the-art RTK survey instrument is the Trimble R8 GNSS Surveyor shown in Figure 10.7. It combines a precision GPS receiver, dual frequency antenna, radio modem, data recorder and wireless interface to a handheld controller in a single "smart-antenna" enclosure.

Post-Processing

An alternative to real-time processing is to post-process the GPS observables and satellite ephemeredes recorded by GPS receivers during a mission. Several GPS manufacturers and third-party software developers offer GPS post-processing software. A GPS post-processing program takes advantage of the non-causal post-processing environment to compute a more accurate and more consistent ambiguity resolution solution than is possible in real-time. The simplest such technique is to compute position time histories forward and backwards in time and then combine them in some fashion to ensure maximum position accuracy at each time point. A simple data quality assurance method compares the separation between the forward and backward position time histories and thereby identifies ambiguity resolution failures or wrong fixes in either solution when the difference exceeds a few centimeters.

Precise point positioning (PPP) refers to the post-mission computation of a position using the observables from a single receiver using precise satellite orbit and atmospheric calibration parameters. The precise parameters can be downloaded over the Internet from several sources such as the International GNSS Service (IGS) typically several days after the mission. The IGS is a service established by the International Association of Geodesy (IAG) which officially started its activities on January 1, 1994 after a successful pilot phase of more than a year. It collects, archives, and distributes GPS observation data sets for a wide range of applications mainly via the Internet. For details on the IGS, see the JPL website: www.igscb.jpl.nasa.gov/components/prods.html.

Among a number of GPS and geodetic products, the IGS produces high accuracy GPS satellite ephemeris, satellite clock corrections, and ionospheric and tropospheric information. These products can be used in airborne surveys to refine the GPS data. GPS data refinement can be done on different levels. Firstly, if airborne GPS is operated in DGPS mode while the base station is more than 100 km away from the mapping area, using the IGS data minimizes orbital and atmospheric errors and, therefore, improves the positioning accuracy. Secondly, airborne GPS can be operated in single point positioning mode (no base station). In this case, using the IGS data improves the positioning accuracy down to a decimeter level and makes it possible to use GPS without a base station in some mapping applications.

The IGS accomplishes its mission through continuous GPS tracking stations, data centers, and analysis centers. The network of GPS tracking stations currently comprises some 250 globally distributed stations that continuously collect GPS data using quality dual-frequency receivers. Data centers are responsible for collecting data from tracking stations, reformatting and archiving data, and submission of data to analysis centers. Analysis centers are responsible for data processing and analysis. The products are then delivered to the Global Data Centers using designated standards on a regular basis. The IGS products are available after different periods of time and with different accuracy. Table 10.1 shows the IGS products, their accuracy and their timelines.

The Jet Propulsion Laboratory (JPL) offers a comparable precise orbit and clock data service on a commercial basis. It is the preferred choice for precise positioning services such as Fugro OmniSTAR and Navcom Starfire that require commercial-grade quality and reliability of data.

Table 10.1 IGS combined product accuracy and timelines (courtesy of IGS).

Product	Availability	Accuracy
Precise Ephemeris		
Ultra Rapid (Predicted half)	Real Time	0.10 meters
Ultra Rapid (Observed half)	3 hours	0.05 meters
Rapid	17 hours	< 0.05 meters
Final	13 days	< 0.05 meters
Satellite Clock Corrections		
Ultra Rapid (Predicted half)	Real Time	5 nanoseconds
Ultra Rapid (Observed half)	3 hours	0.2 nanoseconds
Rapid	17 hours	0.1 nanoseconds
Final	13 days	< 0.1 nanoseconds
Atmospheric Parameters		
Ultra Rapid Tropospheric Zenith Path Delay	2-3 hours	6 mm
Final Tropospheric Zenith Path Delay	4 Weeks	4 mm
Rapid Ionospheric TEC Grid	< 24 hours	2-9 TECU
Final Ionospheric TEC Grid	11 days	2-8 TECU

Capabilities and Limitations

GPS has become a significant utility to surveyors and navigators. It is capable of providing baseline position accuracies comparable with traditional survey methods, and requires significantly less expertise and training to operate. It is however sensitive to its environment, and can without proper planning and quality control give poor or misleading data. The two key limitations that a user of precise GPS positioning must plan for are *signal shading and multipath reflection* and *residual GPS errors*. These are described briefly below. For further details on the subject, see Parkinson and Spilker, 1996 or Hoffmann-Wellendorf *et al.*, 2001.

Signal Shading and Multipath Reflections

The 1.5 GHz GPS signal propagates along the line-of-sight from a satellite to a GPS antenna, and thus is prone to shading by obstacles. Also, the signal can be reflected off of fixed surfaces or refracted by foliage, both causing signals with multiple path lengths to impinge on the antenna. This is called multipath error. Multipath signals are always delayed compared to line-of-sight signals because of the longer travel paths caused by reflection. Code phase multipath can be as large as several meters if the antenna is stationary or slowly moving. For kinematic applications, the GPS antenna motion with respect to the signal reflectors tends to randomize the multipath error and thereby diminish its impact on positioning accuracy. Typical phase multipath does not exceed 0.05 centimeters. Consequently a GPS receiver must be operated with a clear view of the sky and away from reflecting surfaces. This is the key limitation to performance that operators of GPS equipment must be aware of when installing a GPS receiver or planning a survey mission.

Residual GPS Errors

GPS errors can be classified into three major groups as shown in Figure 10.8. DGPS processing can either eliminate or attenuate these errors provided that a GPS mission has been planned to account for these error sources. Such planning requires the separation between the base and roving receivers to be less than a maximum distance over which the residual common errors are small.

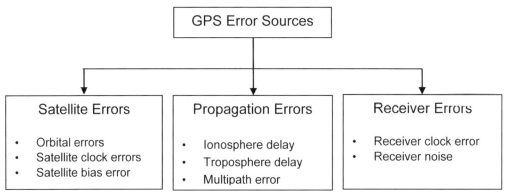

Figure 10.8 GPS errors.

Satellite Orbital Errors

A number of gravitational and non-gravitational forces affect each satellite in its orbit. The actual satellite orbit therefore deviates from its predicted elliptical form. The navigation message received by a GPS receiver includes the predicted (broadcast) ephemeris, which is a number of parameters from which the satellite trajectory is computed with respect to an Earth-Fixed Earth-Centered (ECEF) frame such as the World Geodetic System 1984 (WGS84). Satellite trajectory is required to be able to compute the position of the GPS receiver's antenna. Currently, the broadcast ephemeredes allow for satellite position computation with 2-10 m accuracy.

Satellite Clock Errors

Although GPS satellite clocks are very precise, small biases or drifts result in large GPS positioning errors (0.3 meters per nanosecond). Therefore, each satellite-transmitted navigation message carries three coefficients that a GPS receiver or GPS processing software uses to compensate for satellite clock errors. In post-mission, DGPS processing removes the satellite clock error. When using single point positioning (without a base station) in either static or kinematic positioning modes, the broadcast clock correction parameters are used with a residual error of 10 nanoseconds or 3 meters. Using single point GPS positioning together with the IGS-derived satellite clock corrections (accurate to 0.3 –0.5 nanoseconds) improves the satellite-to-receiver remaining range error to about 10 to 15 cm.

Selective Availability (SA)

Selective Availability is an intentional error imposed by the U.S. Department of Defense to limit the highest achievable autonomous (i.e. non-differential) GPS positioning accuracy to authorized military users. This is done by intentionally degrading the quality of the broadcast transmitted parameters in the CA signal that are required to compute each satellite position and clock corrections. SA limited the achievable autonomous positioning accuracy to 100 meters horizontal and 150 meters vertical. SA was turned off on May 2, 2000, and as a result the autonomous positioning accuracy improved to 8 meters horizontal and 15 meters vertical.

Propagation Media Errors

Another limitation that must be considered in planning GPS operations is the effect of the atmosphere. The ionosphere and troposphere introduce errors in the observables, which can contribute several meters of position error. GPS satellites transmit spread spectrum signals that propagate through about 20,000-26,000 km of media to be received by a GPS receiver. Signal transmission–to-reception time is about 0.07 seconds, during which the satellite signals pass through different layers of the Earth's atmosphere. Two major atmospheric layers affect the propagation of GPS satellite signals, namely the ionosphere and the troposphere.

Ionospheric Errors

The ionosphere has lower and upper limits of approximately 50 and 2000 km, within which ions and electrons are available in quantities sufficient to affect the propagation of GPS signals. The ionospheric distortion is due to the total electron count (TEC) along the signal path between a satellite and the receiver. It is affected by the daily radiation of the sun and by the 11-year solar cycle. The ionosphere is particularly active at equatorial and northern latitudes. The year 2000 was the most recent "solar max" at which the sun's electromagnetic radiation reached a peak and thereby caused a corresponding peak in ionospheric activity. The ionosphere's effect on the GPS signal, among other things, is a bending of the signal path, time delay of arriving code signals, time advance of arriving carrier phase signals, and scintillation. In some extreme cases of high solar activity, ionospheric scintillation causes rapid fluctuation of the GPS signal strength, which may prevent a GPS receiver from computing a position fix. Ionospheric errors can be dealt with using different approaches. Using DGPS significantly reduces the effect of the ionospheric error, especially when using dual-frequency receivers. In single point GPS positioning, the IGS-derived ionospheric grid helps reduce the ionospheric errors. In real time applications, either modeling or compensating for the errors using a differential GPS service is necessary.

Tropospheric Errors

The troposphere is the non-ionized portion of the atmosphere, and extends from the Earth's surface to about 50 km. It introduces a non-dispersive (i.e. frequency-independent) propagation delay of the GPS signals. The total effect can be divided into two main effects, the effect of the dry and the wet components. The dry component contributes about 90% of the total error and can be modeled to about 2% accuracy using meteorological surface measurements. The wet component is more difficult to deal with because of the variations of the water vapor content that cannot be correlated over time and space and, thus, can only be modeled to about 10-20% accuracy. Tropospheric errors can be reduced using DGPS. Modeling tropospheric errors is also used in either real time or post-mission.

Receiver Noise

GPS receiver noise comprises the CA code noise and the carrier phase noise. CA code noise is currently at the level of 0.1 to 0.5 meters. Carrier phase noise is usually at the level of one centimeter or less. The extremely low carrier phase noise is a key reason for the high accuracy of a kinematic ambiguity resolution position solution. DGPS processing combines the observables from two receivers, and typically increases the single receiver noise variance by a factor of 2.

DGPS Residual Errors

Generally, DGPS reduces atmospheric (ionospheric and tropospheric) and orbital errors, eliminates satellite and receiver clock errors, and increases the single receiver noise. Atmospheric and orbital errors are correlated with distance; the shorter the separation baseline between receivers, the greater the correlation between these errors at each receiver. These errors are almost the same at two receivers separated by short baselines (1 to 30 km), so that differential processing of the receiver data will effect the almost complete cancellation of the errors. Since these errors also distort phase data used in kinematic ambiguity resolution, the reliability of ambiguity resolution on short baselines is better than on longer baselines. For an overview on the subject, see Parkinson and Spilker, 1996. For details on the ionospheric errors, see Tiberius, 1998; on the tropospheric errors, see Collins and Langley, 1997. Table 10.2 briefly describes the DGPS remaining errors while Table 10.3 shows a summary for typical errors for GPS airborne differential positioning by carrier phase signal (c.f., Tiberius, 1998; Shi and Cannon, 1994).

Table 10.2 DGPS residual errors.

Error	Error Characteristics
Orbital	• Correlated between satellites • Significantly reduced by between-satellite differencing (DGPS) • Using precise orbits and satellite clock corrections improves positioning accuracy for long baselines
Ionospheric	• Frequency-dependent, thus, dual frequency data eliminates the error for long baselines. • Broadcast model reduces the error by 50% • In double difference airborne kinematic case error is typically 1-2 PPM for mid-latitudes between sunspot highs
Tropospheric	• Frequency-independent, thus, cannot be removed by dual-frequency data • Dry component can be modeled and removed • Wet component needs meteorological data and more difficult to model because of variable nature of water vapor • Over long baselines the wet component effect on positioning can be estimated for airborne applications
Multipath	• Site-dependent and, thus, cannot be removed using differential GPS • In kinematic applications, the multipath signature has a strong correlation with vehicle speed. Therefore, multipath gets random (and less) for higher speed

Table 10.3 Typical DGPS airborne relative positioning errors.

GPS Error Source	Typical Relative Positioning Error (PPM)	Relative Positioning Error For a 50 km baseline (m)
Orbital (SA is on)	1	0.05
Ionospheric	1-10	0.05 to 0.50
Tropospheric	2	0.10
Signal Multipath	0.01	0.05
Receiver Noise	0.001	< 0.025
Total Error	2.5 – 10.25	0.1 - 0.5

Planning Considerations and Quality Control

Use of GPS for precision positioning requires mission planning to avoid or diminish its limitations, discussed previously, and thereby ensure the quality of the data. The following aspects of a mission must be planned:

- the time of day of the mission,
- the expected mission trajectory,
- the baseline length(s) between receivers.

The ever-changing GPS satellite constellation provides different levels of coverage through-out a 12-hour period, ranging from 5 to 12 satellites. The time of day of the mission must be planned so that good satellite coverage is available throughout the mission with allowances for overrun of the expected mission duration. Mission planning software or services over the Internet (for example Trimble Navigation's web site) from some GPS manufacturers can be used to predict satellite coverage at a specified project area during a specified mission time. Figure 10.9 shows the Kalman filter Measurement residuals for a well-planned aerial survey (low PDOP). Note that Kalman filter residuals can always be used as a Q/C tool to capture some errors in the GPS/inertial integration process. Figure 10.10 and Figure 10.11 show the PDOP plot for a poor satellite sky distribution window, and the resulting Kalman filter measurement residuals, respectively. Note that the residuals in Figure 10.11 are much poorer than those displayed in Figure 10.9 due to the poor PDOP. In cases like these where the PDOP is rather poor during only a small period of time during the flight while the sun angle (for photography) is most suitable, the pilot could be instructed not to allow imaging data capture during that period of time, or to avoid flying over the mapping area during that period of time, if the flight control permits.

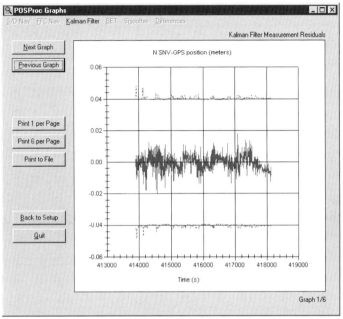

Figure 10.9 Kalman filter measurement residual for a well-planned flight mission (low PDOP).

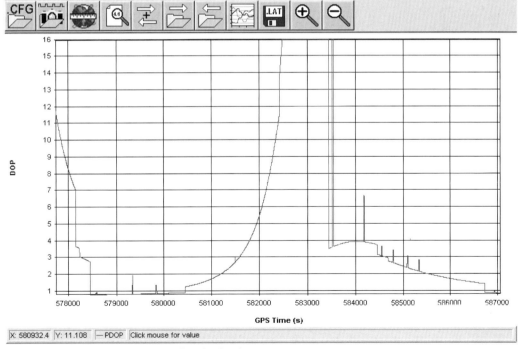

Figure 10.10 PDOP plot at poor satellite sky distribution.

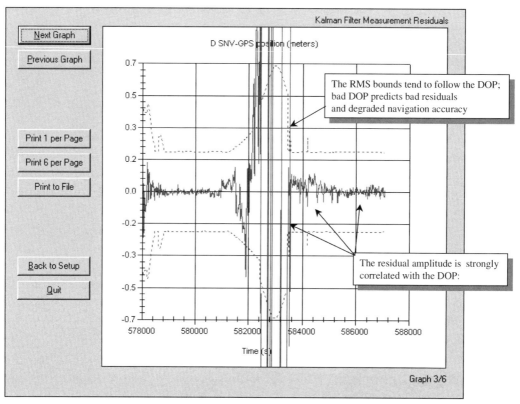

Figure 10.11 Kalman filter measurement residual in POSPac due to the poor PDOP shown in Figure 10.10.

Ionospheric activity during years of high solar activity can also compromise the quality of GPS data if not planned for. Where feasible, a mission-planning option is to conduct a survey at night when the ionosphere is quieter.

The mission trajectory should be assessed for sources of signal shading and multipath reflections. The 1.5 GHz GPS signal travels along its line of sight, and is easily shaded by structures and vegetation. Buildings and trees also can reflect the signal so as to generate multipath reflections to the antenna. Multipath error is the hardest error to control because it is local to one of the two antennas and therefore cannot be attenuated in a differential GPS solution. The best method to date of attenuating multipath is with an antenna ground plane or choke ring.

In order to achieve a KAR solution with 5-10 centimeters accuracy with low risk, the baseline length between two receivers used to generate the KAR solution should be limited to a maximum of 10 kilometers during high solar activity and 50 kilometers during low solar activity. It has therefore been considered a rule of thumb that the base station to rover separation is acceptable if it is within 25-30 kilometers. This ensures that common mode errors in the observables from the two receivers, most notably ionospheric and tropospheric delays, cancel almost exactly in the differential solution. If a longer baseline is contemplated, then two or more base receivers should be installed so that the roving receiver is within the maximum radial distance of any one receiver.

Comparison with Competing Technologies

Competing satellite navigation systems include GLONASS and Galileo. Competing methods of positioning in marine applications include microwave ranging systems (MRS) and Loran C. Among different past and present extraterrestrial positioning and navigation systems, three currently operated systems are briefly described below.

Competing GNSS

GPS has become the dominant method of positioning in remote sensing applications. It has significantly reduced the requirement for ground control points in airborne imaging such as photogrammetry. To date the Russian GLONASS is the only other global navigation satellite system (GNSS); however it has suffered from chronic underfunding and is not by itself a reliable method of positioning. It can however be used to supplement GPS. Some receiver manufacturers offer combined GPS/GLONASS receivers to provide enhanced satellite coverage for improved positioning reliability and faster ambiguity resolution. Recently the Russian government has embarked on a GLONASS modernization program with the intention of achieving full operational capability comparable to GPS in the next 5 years. The European Union (EU) and European Economic Community (EEC) have embarked on the development of their own GNSS called Galileo. The first Galileo satellite for in-orbit validation was launched in December 2005. Full operational capability is planned for 2008.

Microwave Ranging System

An MRS requires the installation of dedicated microwave transponders at surveyed positions along a shoreline near a project area. A vessel determines its horizontal position by trilateration from the measured ranges from the vessel to the transponders. It is sometimes used as an alternative positioning system to GPS in areas of high ionospheric activity.

Loran C

Loran C has been the traditional method of radio navigation before GPS appeared as an alternative. See Kayton and Fried, 1997 for a description of its method of operating and current status as a navigation system. Its limitation is its limited position accuracy, typically 100 meters, which is inadequate for survey applications.

Very Long Base Line Interferometry (VLBI)

VLBI is the most accurate yet least mobile among all extraterrestrial systems. VLBI signals use two bands in the microwave portion of the electromagnetic spectrum, namely the S band and the X band; the two bands are used so as to correct for ionospheric errors. As shown in Figure 10.12, the antennas of two or more radio telescopes receive signals from distant radio sources such as quasars or other extragalactic objects. After a well-defined data processing chain, the baseline between pairs of radio telescopes is computed based on the time delay of signal reception at different telescopes with mm accuracy. Using VLBI, the lengths of very long baselines (thousands of kilometres) are computed with the highest precision currently available. VLBI is mostly operated by government agencies, where networks of points are established continent-wide with high precision, which are then densified using GPS.

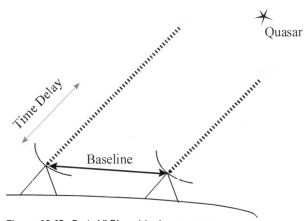

Figure 10.12 Basic VLBI positioning concept.

Satellite Laser Ranging

As shown in Figure 10.13, SLR positioning uses an intense laser pulse directed from a ground telescope to a satellite equipped with a reflector, which directs the laser pulse back to the ground SLR system. Measuring the elapsed time between transmission (T_1) and reception (T_2), one can determine the range to the satellite using the speed of light (c).

LLR is similar to SLR except that it uses the moon to carry reflectors, which were deployed on the lunar surface by the crews of Apollo 11, 14, and 15 (Wells *et al*, 1987).

Technological Advances

GPS was originally designed as a military global navigation system, but has become a core capability in many commercial products and services. Positioning accuracy using

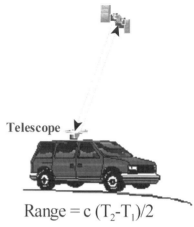

$$\text{Range} = c\ (T_2\text{-}T_1)/2$$

Figure 10.13 Basic concept of SLR.

DGPS and phase interferometry techniques have made GPS into a powerful survey tool. In order to extract this accuracy, the commercial GPS industry has designed around the intended and unintended limitations that the original GPS configuration had. The simplest circumvention of the original Selective Availability (SA) degradation of the CA signal was the basic DGPS configuration. Commercial receiver manufacturers developed codeless L2 phase tracking techniques to get around the L2 signal access limitation and extract dual frequency phases needed for reliable RTK positioning.

The U.S. government has recognized the importance of GPS as an important source of commercial economic activity. To improve GPS's accuracy and reliability in the commercial sector, the GPS JPO has launched a GPS modernization program. It will implement two new signals, L2C and L5, in the next generation of GPS satellites. L2C is a commercially accessible code modulated onto the L2 frequency. This will allow a commercial precision receiver to generate L2 pseudoranges so that the user can calibrate and remove the effects of the ionosphere in a position solution. It will also allow the receiver to track the L2 phase with lower noise than current semi-codeless phase tracking algorithms are capable of.

L5 is a new signal modulated onto 1176.45 MHz and transmitted with approximately 3 db more power than the L1 signal. It was designed primarily for civil aviation. The L5 carrier falls into the Aeronautical Radionavigation Services band, which allows the aviation community to manage interference in this band more effectively than is possible in the L1 and L2 bands. The implication to survey applications is a third frequency for constructing combinations with longer wavelengths than the currently used L1-L2 wide lane phase. A longer wavelength allows faster and more reliable phase interferometry with ambiguity resolution to be performed.

GPS-AIDED INERTIAL NAVIGATION SYSTEM

Technology Overview

"Direct georeferencing" (DG) is the direct measurement of the position and orientation parameters of a remote sensor. It is an enabling technology for quantitative data acquisition and mapping applications where precise orientation of the sensor in addition to its position is required. Such mapping applications include aerial photogrammetry, airborne multi-spectral scanners, airborne lidars and multibeam sonar bathymetry. In all of these applications, the sensors have a wide field of view of the terrain being mapped. A direct georeferencing system provides the position and orientation of the sensor that is required to stabilize and register the acquired data in geographic coordinates.

The state-of-the-art technology in DG systems is the GPS-aided inertial navigation system. The following discussion first describes the inertial navigation system, and then the concept of

GPS-aiding. More detailed descriptions of INS concepts and technology can be obtained in Britting, 1971; Kayton and Fried, 1997; and Siouris, 1993. See Parkinson and Spilker, 1996 (Volume 2) for an overview of GPS-aided INS. See Siouris, 1993 for a more detailed description.

Inertial Navigation System

An inertial navigation system (INS) has two main components. The first is the inertial measurement unit (IMU), which comprises three accelerometers, three gyros and the electronics to provide digitally encoded samples of the accelerometer and gyro data on a serial interface. The accelerometers are arranged into an orthogonal triad that measures the specific force vector experienced by the IMU. The specific force vector is the vector sum of the local gravity vector and the acceleration vector experienced by the IMU. The gyros are likewise arranged into an orthogonal triad that measures the angular rate vector experienced by the IMU. The angular rate vector comprises the sum of the earth rotation vector plus the angular rate vector experienced by the IMU with respect to the earth. A typical IMU outputs digitized samples at a 50-1000 Hz sampling rate of the total specific force and angular rate of the IMU with respect to a hypothetical stationary inertial reference system. High data rates are typically required to adequately sample short-term vibration dynamics as well as long-term vehicle dynamics.

The second component is the navigation processor. It solves Newton's equations of motion of the IMU on the rotating earth based on the measured accelerations and angular rates. In order to do so, the navigation processor must establish the local North, East and Down directions of a navigation coordinate frame using a procedure called alignment. Determining the Down direction is called leveling, and is based on the assumption that the local gravity vector is the vertical reference. Once leveling is completed, the horizontal axes of the navigation frame define a plane that is tangent to the local geoidal surface, and hence said to be locally level. Aligning a locally level navigation frame to the true North direction is called heading alignment. A mechanism called gyrocompassing uses the horizontal component of the earth angular rate vector as the heading reference. A stationary or otherwise non-accelerating INS uses the earth rate vector measured by the gyros to gyrocompass its navigation frame to true North. A typical aircraft INS must undergo a stationary alignment lasting 10 to 30 minutes to accurately align its navigation frame. Thereafter it navigates free-inertially, which implies that it computes its navigation solution using only the acceleration and angular rate data from the IMU without any subsequent corrections to its alignment or position solution.

The INS technology from the early 1950's to the late 1970's comprised the gimbaled platform. In a gimbaled platform INS, the accelerometer and gyro triads were located on a mechanical 4-axis gimbaled platform. The alignment process rotated the platform into alignment with the North, East and Down directions. Thereafter during navigation, the gyros measured the platform angular rate and provided the feedback signal to the gimbal axis motors to null the platform rotation with respect to the earth surface, thereby maintaining the platform locally level and aligned to true North in spite of the vehicle's angular rate. The accelerometers thus reported North, East and Down accelerations at all times, which the navigation processor integrated to compute North, East and Down velocity and from this updated latitude, longitude and altitude. The gyro technology used in these mechanical INS's was the floated spinning mass gyro. The platform gimbal axes were instrumented with synchro resolvers that measured the gimbal shaft angles. The mechanical design of the gimbaled platform caused the shaft angles to be the vehicle roll, pitch and heading, which formed a complete orientation solution for the vehicle. The INS thus computed a complete navigation solution for the vehicle comprising geographic position, North-East-Down velocity and orientation with respect to the North-East-Down directions.

The strapdown INS is the current state-of-the-art in inertial navigation. It emerged as the dominant INS technology during the late 1970's with the development of the ring laser gyro (RLG) and a class of avionics computers that could perform the numerically intensive strapdown navigation computations. It is so named because the accelerometers and gyros are hard-mounted, or "strapped down", to the INS case, and hence rotate with the vehicle. The accelerometers and gyros thus report the acceleration and angular rate of the INS resolved in the INS body frame. Using the angular rate data from the gyros, the navigation processor updates the direction cosine matrix (DCM) that describes the orientation of the INS body frame with respect to a mathematical navigation frame that is locally level and aligned to true North. The alignment process in the strapdown INS initializes this DCM and thereby establishes the alignment of the mathematical navigation frame. The body-to-navigation DCM is thus the mathematical equivalent of the mechanical gimbals in the platform INS. The strapdown INS then transforms the measured acceleration vector to the navigation frame and thereafter computes velocity and position in the same way as does the platform INS. The vehicle orientation parameters are derived from the components of the body-to-navigation DCM.

An INS is thus a sophisticated dead reckoning navigation system that navigates from an initial known position to its current position using only the measured accelerations and angular rates as measured by the inertial sensors. As with any dead reckoning method, it is prone to position drift, in this case caused by errors in the measured inertial data. A free-inertial navigator exhibits a position drift that on average grows linearly with time. An INS is typically classified in terms of the number of nautical miles that it drifts in one hour following a full ground alignment. A so-called medium accuracy INS that is used for aircraft navigation uses RLG's and typically exhibits an approximate one nautical mile per hour drift. Superimposed on this average position drift is the Schuler oscillation. This is a sinusoidal position error with an approximate period of 84 minutes, and is a consequence of the INS being constrained to navigate on the earth surface. It was first documented by Schuler, 1923. Higher accuracy INS's such as are used on ships and submarines are capable of better long-term position accuracies.

The dominant errors in an INS that cause a position drift are the alignment errors and the inertial sensor errors. The alignment errors are the deviation of the navigation frame alignment from locally level and North azimuth. A navigation frame tilt error from locally level causes the gravity vector to be projected into the horizontal components of the acceleration vector transformed into the navigation frame. The inertial navigation algorithm integrates these projected specific forces assuming they are real accelerations, and outputs an erroneous time-linear velocity and a position that grows as time squared. The dominant inertial sensor errors are the accelerometer and gyro biases. These are the non-zero outputs of the accelerometers and gyros when the INS is in fact inertially stationary (for example floating in deep space with no specific forces acting on it). The other major inertial errors are the accelerometer and gyro random noises. These are uncorrelated noises caused by a variety of mechanisms that includes analog amplifier noise, digital quantization error, and in the case of RLG's lock-in error. The inertial navigator algorithm continuously integrates these inertial sensor errors into INS velocity and position errors. In particular, the horizontal gyro biases translate to constant latitude and longitude error rates, which are the major components of the INS's position error rate. Smaller inertial sensor errors include scale factor error, input axis non-orthogonality and vibration rectification.

The inertial sensor errors are in fact the residual errors following a factory calibration of the IMU. An uncalibrated IMU will exhibit large biases, scale factor errors and input axis non-orthogonalities that vary with the internal temperatures of the inertial sensors. The calibration firmware in an IMU implements temperature-dependent models of these errors. A typical model is a 3rd to 6th order polynomial interpolation of an error as a function of temperature. An IMU calibration procedure estimates the model parameters at different test temperatures across the specified operational temperature range. Ideally, an IMU calibration will model the mean inertial sensor errors at any temperature, so that the residual errors are random from one IMU power-up to the next. A typical IMU performance specification thus quotes the standard deviations of these inertial sensor errors about their calibrated mean values.

GPS-Aided Inertial Navigation System

An aided INS (AINS) combines the components of an INS with navigation aiding sensors for the purpose of regulating the INS errors to those of the aiding sensors during vehicle navigation. Figure 10.14 shows a typical AINS architecture. The typical AINS uses a Kalman filter to estimate the errors in the inertial navigation solution and the inertial sensor errors. The Kalman filter uses measurements of the current inertial navigation solution differenced with aiding sensor navigation data to observe and estimate the INS errors. This is possible when the aiding sensor error characteristics are different from the INS errors. A GPS position solution contains errors that can be characterized as noisy and statistically bounded within an error ellipse of fixed volume. By contrast, the INS position errors are characterized as smooth but unbounded. These error characteristics are said to be complementary, and hence amenable to Kalman filter error estimation. The Kalman filter processes measurements that are the differences of the inertial navigator and GPS positions, and thus comprises the noisy but bounded GPS position errors plus the growing INS position error. The Kalman filter contains a model for these errors, and thereby is able to suppress the GPS short-term errors and estimate the INS errors. The accuracy of the INS error estimates depends on the magnitude of the GPS position error. It will obtain a better error estimate when the GPS solution is a kinematic ambiguity resolution solution with decimeter accuracy than when the GPS solution is an uncorrected CA solution.

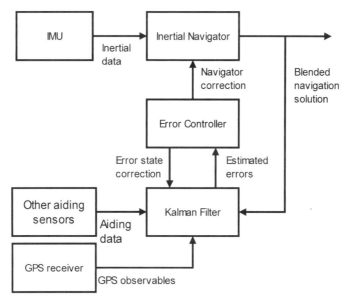

Figure 10.14 GPS-aided INS architecture.

The AINS uses the Kalman filter's estimated inertial navigation errors to correct the position, velocity and attitude computations in the inertial navigation algorithm. This error correction closes the loop around the INS and thereby regulates the INS errors to be consistent with the aiding sensor errors. In a GPS-AINS, it regulates the INS position and velocity errors to be consistent with the smoothed GPS position and velocity errors. It furthermore regulates the INS attitude errors and thereby continuously improves the INS alignment. Thus a GPS-AINS is able to align from a cold initialization while the vehicle is moving. This is called a mobile alignment, or in the case of an airborne AINS an "air-start."

A key capability of the GPS-AINS is an attitude solution whose accuracy is better than a free-inertial attitude solution. This admits the use of lower quality inertial sensors in an AINS than would be required in a free-inertial INS to achieve the same attitude accuracy. The AINS achieves this because its Kalman filter continuously calibrates the inertial sensor errors as part of its overall error estimation function. For example, the INS will integrate a constant accelerometer bias to a time-linear INS velocity error. A gyro bias will rotate the navigation frame out of locally level at a constant angular rate. The gravity vector will project increasingly into the horizontal accelerometer input axes, and the INS will integrate the resulting time-linear acceleration error to a time-quadratic velocity error. The AINS Kalman filter recognizes these INS velocity errors when it compares the INS and GPS velocities. The Kalman filter has a mathematical model that describes the velocity error as a function of the various sources of acceleration error, including the accelerometer and gyro biases. Using this error model, the Kalman filter is able to estimate these biases from the observed velocity error. The Kalman filter maintains the inertial sensor error estimates even as they undergo thermal drift. This ongoing calibration of the IMU provides for roll, pitch and heading accuracies that are significantly better than the INS could achieve without aiding. A GPS-AINS that uses a relatively inexpensive IMU can achieve roll and pitch accuracies on the order of a few arc-minutes and a heading accuracy on the order of 0.1 degrees or better.

Components of a GPS-AINS for Direct Georeferencing

A GPS-AINS system for survey and remote sensing applications typically comprises the following major components:

- IMU
- Roving GPS receiver
- Navigation computer system (NCS)

The following are optional components for obtaining differential GPS (DGPS) or real-time kinematic (RTK) position accuracies:

- Differential corrections receiver that receives corrections from a wide area differential corrections service
- Dedicated RTK subsystem: base receiver, radio modem transmitter and receiver

Those applications requiring the best achievable accuracy in post-processing will also include the following components:

- Mobile data acquisition system (DAS)
- Reference (base) receivers with self-contained data logging
- Data retrieval and post-processing computer

The IMU containing the accelerometers and gyros is ideally compact and unobtrusive so that it can be located at or close to the desired instrumentation point, for example an aerial camera perspective center. At the same time, its inertial sensors must be sufficiently accurate so that the overall system delivers the required orientation accuracy. These requirements typically conflict; high quality inertial systems are large, whereas tactical grade IMU's having the desired small size are not sufficiently accurate. A best compromise is achieved by using a small IMU with low noise inertial sensors in a GPS-AINS.

The NCS runs a software mechanization of the GPS-AINS algorithm described previously and computes a position and orientation solution in real-time. For some applications such as sonar bathymetry, the real-time solution is the primary data product of interest. For others requiring a post-processed solution, a real-time solution that meets its accuracy requirements provides quality assurance of the recorded data. A properly designed system will initialize and align while the vehicle is moving. The alignment and transition to full navigation performance is automatic and hence transparent to the operator after he has pushed the power switch.

The roving GPS receiver is typically embedded in the NCS. It must be capable of outputting L1 and L2 observables of sufficient accuracy and quality for computing a KAR position solution. The antenna must also be dual frequency capable and of sufficient quality to reject most multipath interference.

Without any source of differential corrections, the computed position accuracy is expected to be on the order of 10-15 meters, circular error probable (CEP). The optional RTCM differential corrections receiver provides GPS differential corrections in RTCM SC-104 format (Radio Technical Commission for Maritime (RTCM) Services, 1998) from a differential corrections broadcast service such as OmniSTAR, Navcom (shown in Figure 10.15), or the U.S. Coast Guard differential beacon network. With these corrections, the NCS computes position with a typical DGPS accuracy of 1-5 meters (CEP). The RTK subsystem comprises a base receiver that outputs RTK data and a radio modem transmitter and receiver that relay the data to the roving receiver. With the RTK data, the NCS computes position with an accuracy of 0.02-0.1 meters (CEP).

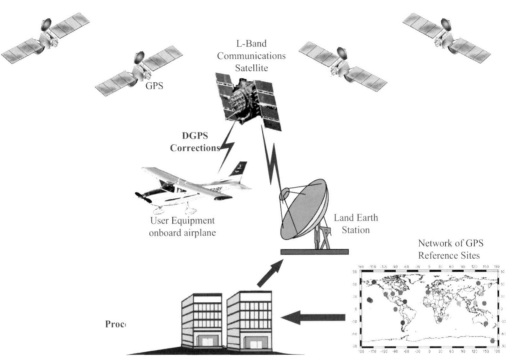

Figure 10.15 An example of real-time correction service via satellites (courtesy of NavCom).

The data acquisition system (DAS) is also typically embedded in the NCS. It records time stamped IMU and GPS data to a non-volatile storage media such as a hard disk or tape. The IMU time stamp accuracy must be 50 microseconds or better to ensure that the position and orientation solution is accurate at the sensor sampling time on a possibly fast moving platform such as an airplane. It is also required to ensure a good inertial-GPS integration in the GPS-AINS. A few hundred microseconds of time misalignment between the IMU and GPS data can cause the GPS-AINS to estimate incorrect accelerometer biases and hence compute inaccurate orientation data.

The base receivers with data logging are required to compute a precise position solution in post-processing. These are also dual frequency receivers, and they are located around or within a project area so that the distance from any one base receiver to the roving receiver is within 10-50 kilometers. This tolerable distance depends on the ionospheric activity in the project area at the time of the survey. Ionospheric interference with the GPS signals causes signal delay and scintillation. The data logging capability is either built into the receiver or is provided by a personal computer connected to the receiver.

The data retrieval and post-processing computer is used to retrieve and process the recorded data. The end product of post-processing is either the desired position and orientation solution formatted to the particular application, or parameters derived from the solution. For example, the end product for aerial photogrammetry is the set of exterior orientation parameters for each photo. These are essentially the position and orientation solution at the time of exposure in a particular industry standard format.

Development History

The aided INS concept emerged shortly after the development of the Kalman filter, a core component of the AINS. This technology was first developed for and deployed in military aircraft, beginning in 1968. More recently, the U.S. Air Force Embedded GPS-Inertial (EGI) program has spawned a standard GPS-AINS configuration.

The direct georeferencing concept for remote sensing has been postulated in technical research publications for several years (for example Schwarz et al, 1993). It has been put into practice in several experimental systems such as airborne multi-spectral scanners and laser altimeters. The orientation sensor typically was an aircraft INS that navigated free-inertially during the data acquisition. These systems demonstrated the DG concept, but were impractical because of the large size and high cost of the INS. An example is the early work performed by the Canada Centre for Remote Sensing (CCRS) which led to the development of the Multi-spectral Electro-optic Imaging Sensor (MEIS).

A practical DG system became feasible with the advent of GPS as a commercially available precise positioning system and the arrival of strapdown IMU's for tactical and motion sensing applications in military weapons systems. A "tactical" IMU is designed for short-term missile guidance. It is required to be small and light in order to fit into an air-to-air missile case, and relatively inexpensive in order to be affordable in an expendable weapon. It uses low cost inertial sensors such as fiber-optic gyros (FOG) to meet a 1-10 degree/hour performance requirement. Such an IMU is impractical in a free-inertial navigation application. Its gyro errors would drive the position error drift to upwards of 100 nautical miles per hour. It is however suitable in a GPS-AINS, which calibrates the inertial sensor errors on an ongoing basis. A "motion sensing" IMU is designed to measure the short-term motion of a platform such as a radar antenna for the purpose of signal error compensation. A typical application is a synthetic aperture radar (SAR) motion compensation system, which is required to measure the radar phase center displacement along the line of sight with an accuracy standard deviation of less than one centimeter over a 10-30 second integration time. Its inertial sensors exhibit stable and low noise errors that can be accurately calibrated on-line. These same characteristics become important for high accuracy orientation measurement such as required in the aerial photogrammetry application.

Applanix was the first organization to offer for sale a GPS-AINS specifically for commercial surveying applications. The Position and Orientation System for Land Vehicles (POS/LV) first appeared in 1993. The POS MV for multibeam sonar bathymetric survey was made available in 1994 (Scherzinger, Woolven and Field, 1997). Shortly thereafter, the POS AV for airborne remote sensing and POS/TG for railroad track geometry measurement were released (Hutton, Savina, and Lithopoulos, 1997).

DIRECT GEOREFERENCING SYSTEMS FOR AIRBORNE DIGITAL ELEVATION MODEL GENERATION

Types of Airborne DG Systems

There are currently three types of Direct Georeferencing Systems used in the commercial airborne market:

- Custom adaptations of military or commercial INS systems
- IGI AEROcontrol 3
- Applanix POS AV

In the first case, a ring-laser gyro based INS such as from aerospace manufacturers Honeywell or Litton is used to provide orientation measurements, while a traditional survey grade GPS receiver is used stand-alone to provide the position measurements. Neither the INS nor the GPS receiver provides data fusion capability, hence the aerial surveyor must incur engineering expense to develop a custom integration at some level for his particular installation. The INS is also usually too large to be used directly with an aerial camera.

Figure 10.16 Applanix POS AV (courtesy Applanix Corporation).

In contrast both the IGI and Applanix systems are designed specifically for commercial airborne mapping applications. The IMU used in the IGI system contains fiber optic gyros (FOG). The Applanix POS AV systems (see Figure 10.16) incorporate a number of different IMU's that use either FOG's or dry tuned rotor gyros (DTG), depending upon the accuracy requirements. The GPS receiver used in the DG systems are high quality, low-noise 12 channel L1/L2 survey grade receivers exemplified by the Trimble BD750, Ashtech Z12, and Novatel Millennium receivers.

Development History

Direct georeferencing has been the subject of fundamental research for many years. The first use of Inertial/GPS systems in airborne mapping was proposed by Schwarz et al (1984). Experimental systems that explored the feasibility of the technology have been developed by several university and government agencies (c.f., Schwarz, et al, 1993; Toth and Grejner-Brzezinska, 1998) Early DG systems used in the airborne survey market were adaptations of INS products. For an overview, see Schwarz et al, 1993 and Grejner-Brezezinska, 2001.

Applanix Corporation developed the first practical DG system for aerial photogrammetry in 1996 that was usable on existing cameras such as the Leica RC30 or Zeiss LMK (Hutton, Savina and Lithopoulos, 1997). The methodology proposed by Applanix to aerial photogrammetry companies was to aid or replace aerial triangulation (AT) with direct measurement of the camera exterior orientation (EO) parameters and thereby realize significant cost savings per project. Early adopters of this methodology pioneered its successful field usage and demonstrated its practicality to the industry during 1996-99 (c.f., Abdullah, 1997.) Since then, direct georeferencing has become an accepted alternative to the traditional AT methodology, to either totally replace or augment AT, based on the application.

Present Operating Status

Direct georeferencing systems are now an integral component of airborne lidar, Interferometric Synthetic Aperture Radar (IFSAR), and Digital Line Scanner systems such as the LH Systems ADS40. Direct georeferencing is in fact an enabling technology for these systems in precision airborne survey applications. DG systems are also being used with increased frequency with traditional aerial camera and multi-spectral scanner systems. For frame imagers, although not an enabling technology, direct georeferencing provides significant cost savings through the reduction or elimination of aerotriangulation in the photogrammetry process, as well as the manual ground work for ground control survey. It also enables corridor mapping, comprising single lines of photographs, for which aerotriangulation is not workable.

Technology Overview

The following discusses how the Direct Georeferencing (DG) systems are used in each of the previously mentioned applications.

Lidar

In an airborne lidar installation, a GPS-AINS DG system is used to measure the position of the laser reference point and the orientation of the laser range at the exact time of measurement. In a scanning lidar system, the laser reference point is the mirror; in a fiber optic system it is the fiber optic bundle. The orientation is given in Euler angles with respect to the North, East and Down directions. The DG INS or IMU is rigidly mounted to the lidar housing so that it is rigid with respect to the laser reference point. During a mission, the DG system records the IMU and GPS data and the time of each laser scan, all in a common time base such as GPS time. The DG post-processing software computes the time tagged position and orientation of the laser reference point at a high data rate, typically 200 Hz. The lidar post-processing software then interpolates the DG position and orientation data to the exact time of scan. With this data and the range measured by the laser, it computes the 3-dimensional ground spot coordinates of each laser range. Typically the software first computes the earth-centered-earth-fixed (ECEF, also called Cartesian) coordinates and then converts these to the desired mapping frame. The resulting three-dimensional elevation map contains the data required for a DEM.

IFSAR

In an Interferometric Synthetic Aperture Radar (IFSAR) system, the DG System is used to compute the relative displacement of the phase center of one SAR antenna with respect to another. The relative displacements are then used to correct the radar phase. This is the equivalent of stabilizing the IFSAR platform against aircraft motion due to maneuvers and air turbulence.

Digital Line Scanners and Aerial Cameras

In the case of a Digital Line Scanner or Aerial Camera (digital or film), the IMU is mounted as close to the camera perspective center as possible. The new digital line scanners and cameras from Leica Geosystems, Intergraph Z/I , Vexcel (now Microsoft), and Applanix have been designed to mount the IMU directly to the lens housing. See Figures 10.17 and 10.18 as examples. Retrofits of film cameras however usually require a special mount to be constructed to either place the IMU inside the lens cone or rigidly attach the IMU to the lens cone, as shown in Figure 10.19.

Figure 10.17 Large format digital imaging systems (from left to right: Leica ADS40, Intergraph DMC, and Microsoft Vexcel UltraCam).

During a photo-mission, the DG system records the IMU and GPS data, and the time of scan or mid-exposure pulse all in a common time base such as GPS time. The DG post-processing software then computes the perspective center positions and camera orientations at the scan or mid-exposure times. From these, it computes the exterior orientation parameters of each image or picture in a format suitable for entry into a stereo plotter. The DEM is then extracted from the stereo images generated by the stereo plotter. Figure 10.20 gives a visual example of how direct

Figure 10.18 The DSS: an example of a medium format digital imaging system.

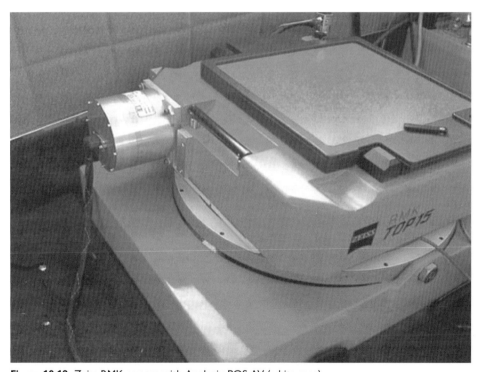

Figure 10.19 Zeiss RMK camera with Applanix POS AV (white case).

Figure 10.20 Georeferenced and mosaicked line scanner imagery.

georeferencing can be used to adjust airborne imagery. Shown on the left are two raw images from a line scanner, containing artifacts due to the roll and pitch motion of the aircraft. The image on the right comprises a mosaic of the raw images with the aircraft motion artifacts removed, using the position and orientation data from the DG post-processed position and orientation data.

Boresight Calibration Requirements

The IMU or INS usually does not provide an orientation reference for its inertial sensor input axes to the accuracy required by DG applications, hence the offset angles between the IMU and image sensor reference frame axes must be calibrated. This procedure is commonly called boresighting of the IMU. The methods will depend on the particular sensor.

Lidar

The mounting misalignment or boresight angles between the IMU and lidar reference frame are usually computed though a combination of laboratory and airborne calibration, or sometimes solely through an airborne calibration.

The laboratory calibration typically involves collimating the laser beam to achieve a perfect vertical reference, against which the roll and pitch output of the DG system are compared to determine the roll and pitch misalignment angles. Such a calibration requires a true horizontal reflecting surface. The laser beam is directed towards the horizontal reflecting surface and its scan angle is set to nadir. The complete lidar instrument is then rotated in roll and pitch until the incident and reflected beams are coincident and hence perpendicular to the horizontal reflecting surface. The roll and pitch angles reported by the DG system are then the roll and pitch misalignment angles of the DG IMU with respect to the laser beam. This procedure is repeated a number of times to average down the errors in the DG orientation.

The airborne calibration is usually done using a reference surface test. Here a series of opposing flight lines with 100% overlap are flown over a flat bare surface (usually a runway or parking lot). Cross sectional heights of opposing flight lines are then compared with each other. A roll misalignment angle will cause the cross sections to look like an "X" when they are overlaid, and hence can be estimated directly from the height differences. The pitch misalignment can similarly be determined by flying opposing flight lines over a bare sloped surface (i.e., a treeless hill). Along track sections are then compared to determine the pitch misalignment angle, which has the effect of offsetting the slope horizontally. Finally the heading misalignment is determined by flying opposing flight lines with 100% overlap over the corner of a building. The flight lines are then overlaid, and any heading misalignment will have the effect of the corner of the building to be translated horizontally between the opposing lines.

A variation of the reference surface test is to fly a block of opposing flight lines with 50% overlap and several cross strips. Then the overlapping surfaces can be adjusted in a least squares fashion to solve for the borcsight angles that minimize the height separation of the surfaces.

Some lidars also have the ability to provide intensity for each return. This allows specific points to be identified in a lidar "image", for which the ground coordinates can be surveyed, thus allowing traditional photogrammetric techniques to be used to determine the boresight angles.

No matter which method is used, the boresight flight must be designed such that the number of flight lines, flying height and overall geometry of the setup are enough to compute the misalignment angles to an accuracy level significantly better than the specified accuracy of the overall system. This can often be challenging, especially for the high-altitude systems that require better than 0.005 degrees of roll and pitch accuracy,

IFSAR

For an IFSAR system, the mechanical structure of the SAR antenna is usually machined to such a high level of accuracy that the INS or IMU can be mechanically aligned to the antenna in the laboratory to a sufficient accuracy. Then an airborne test using corner reflectors is conducted as a final check.

Digital Line Scanners and Aerial Cameras

Two approaches are followed to calibrate the boresight angles between the IMU and camera image plane (see Figure 10.21). The traditional absolute approach is to use aerial triangulation by flying over a test field having many ground control points. The boresight angles are computed by constructing the mean differences of the orientation angles from the bundle adjustment with the angles from the DG system. The other approach (the relative approach) is to directly and relatively solve for the boresight angles in the least squares filter without ground control. The relative approach is more or less the typical approach nowadays implemented in commercial boresighting softwares such as CalQC™ by Applanix. The relative approach allows for computing the boresight angles as a quality check using a small image block from any flight mission data and does not necessarily require flying over a test field unlike the case of the absolute approach, where ground control was always needed. For details, see Mostafa and Schwarz (2001)

It is recommended to fly two or more opposing strips with 60 percent along track overlap and 20 percent side overlap between the strips. For film cameras, for example, photo scale is typically between 1:5000 and 1:8000, and an even number of strips is used. Each strip has at least 5 to 8 photographs. Only one or two ground control points are needed for datum calibration only if the relative boresighting approach is used. However, signalized and well distributed ground control is needed if the absolute approach is used (Mostafa, 2002). One of the advantages of the relative approach is that the boresighting could be done anytime using a part of the flight mission data, as depicted in Figure 10.22, where only a small block of images is chosen at either the centre or the corner of the mapping area and run through CalQC™ to calibrate the boresight, camera, and datum as a quality check.

If the imaging sensor is a film camera, then one of the necessary steps is to automatically compute the interior orientation (see Figure 10.23). However for digital sensors such as the DSS, the UltraCam, or the DMC, this step is not necessary, and hence the boresighting operation is simplified by going straight to the automatic tie point generation mode, to collect some image tie points to be used in the boresight calibration engine. Figure 10.24 shows an example of tie point measurement operation (in CalQC™) using some of the DSS image data acquired during the mapping mission.

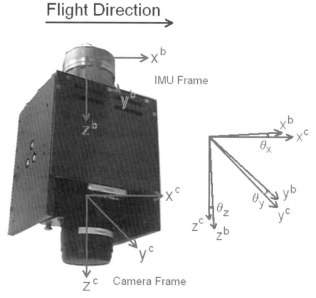

Figure 10.21 Boresight between camera and IMU frame of references. See color plate in Appendix C.

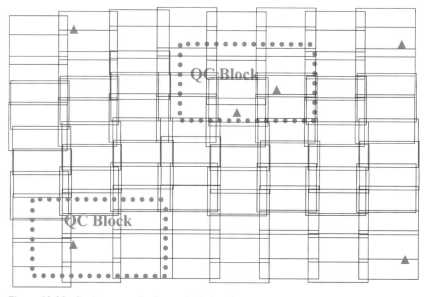

Figure 10.22 Quality control using real mission data.

Lever Arm Calibration Requirement

A lever arm is a relative position vector of one sensor with respect to another. It is usually convenient to define a sensor coordinate frame in which lever arms are cast, whose origin is the sensor reference point and the origin for all lever arm measurements. In a film camera installation, the sensor reference point is the camera perspective center. In a DG system installation, there are two lever arms that must be measured. The IMU lever arm is the relative position of the inertial center of the IMU with respect to the sensor reference point. The GPS lever arm is the relative

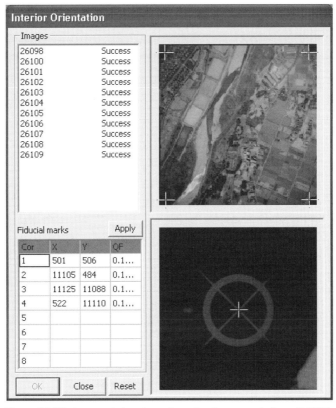

Figure 10.23 Automatic interior orientation (an example from CalQC). See color plate in Appendix C.

position vector of the phase center of the GPS antenna with respect to the sensor reference point. These two lever arm vectors characterize the installation of the DG system with respect to the sensor, and by vector subtraction provide the relative position of the GPS antenna with respect to the IMU required by the inertial-GPS integration software. As with the boresight angles, these lever arms must be measured to a better accuracy than the DG positioning accuracy in order for it not to contribute to the overall positioning error budget.

Post-processing

The final product of an airborne sensor such as a lidar or camera is generated by post-processing software. This implies that the airborne sensor essentially stores its raw data in some form during a mission. Likewise, a DG system for airborne applications logs its raw IMU and GPS data during a mission, and the position and orientation solution is computed post-mission with specialized GPS-AINS processing software. The software first implements a Kalman filter based GPS-AINS algorithm (see Figure 10.14) that generates the position and orientation time history. It then performs a smoothing operation backward in time on the data to generate a time history with improved accuracy. This method of post-mission processing generates the best achievable accuracy that can be had from the recorded inertial and GPS data. It is an important component of a high accuracy DG system capable of 20 arc-seconds orientation accuracy for aerial photogrammetry. Figure 10.25 depicts the "Reference" portion of the ADS40 process flow using Leica Geosystems GPro software which embeds Applanix POSPac software for the georeferencing processing of each scan line. This implies that the GPS/INS post-processing software is nowadays considered a part of the typical process flow of imaging data process flow.

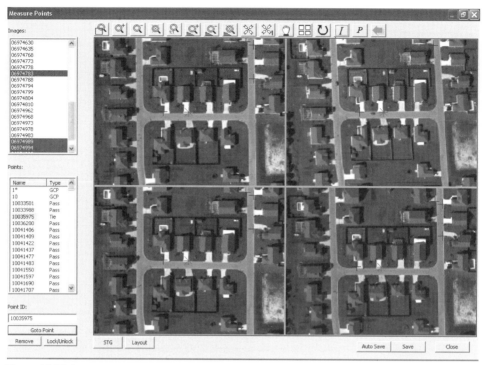

Figure 10.24 Image tie point measurement (an example from CalQC using the DSS images). See color plate in Appendix C.

Planning Considerations

The absolute accuracy of the blended position of a GPS-AINS DG system is limited to the absolute positional accuracy of the GPS. Hence it is important that proper mission planning be conducted to ensure that the best possible GPS accuracy is achieved. To this end, the generic GPS mission-planning considerations described previously apply here.

The best GPS positioning accuracy (2 to 15 cm) is achieved using carrier phase DGPS techniques described at the beginning of this chapter. To obtain this accuracy, a mission must be planned to provide conditions for reliable ambiguity resolution throughout the mission. Error sources that can prevent maintenance or re-fixing of integer ambiguities include ionospheric delays, multipath, and poor satellite geometry. Even if the correct ambiguities are found and maintained for the entire mission, these error sources can, if not properly managed, still degrade the accuracy of the solution. Airborne mission planning should therefore include the following components.

Static Data Collection

A mission should begin and end with a static data acquisition each lasting a minimum of 5 minutes. The static data allows the GPS post-processing software user the constant position information to obtain the correct initial and final ambiguities with high probability of success.

Minimizing Multipath

Multipath reflections can be a major source of position error and cause for integer ambiguity resolution failures. All base receivers should use antenna choke rings or ground planes to attenuate low elevation signals, and should be mounted at least 100 m away or above all reflecting surfaces.

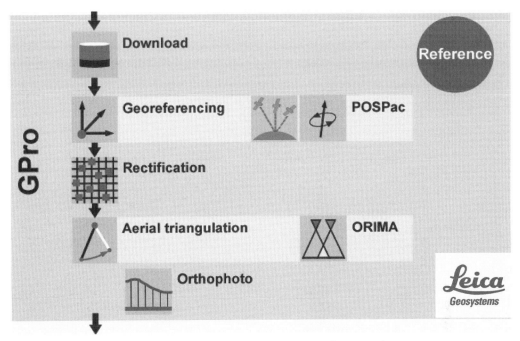

Figure 10.25 Process flow of the ADS40 using GPro (courtesy of Leica Geosystems).

Limiting Baseline Separation

If the mission requires the 2-10 centimeter position accuracy that a kinematic ambiguity resolution solution can provide, then the maximum baseline separation must be limited to 20 to 50 km depending on the diurnal and seasonal solar activity. This allows the GPS processing software to recover fixed integer ambiguities following cycle slips or loss of phase lock at any time during the mission. For missions with flight lines greater than 100 kilometers, multiple base receivers must be used to ensure the maximum separation between the aircraft and any base receiver is less than 50 kilometers. Current GPS processing software packages are able to combine data from the multiple base receivers to produce the optimal solution with the least amount of error. Continuously Operating Reference Stations (CORS) are becoming common nowadays such as the U.S. CORS (shown in Figure 10.26) or the Japanese GEONET. Both of these exemplify national efforts in different countries to establish a permanent tracking GPS networks for different applications. Both networks have more than 1000 permanent tracking GPS receivers from which data is accessible for free via the internet. Earlier analysis showed that, by using multiple base receivers, users achieve significant improvement in positioning accuracy, especially if baseline separation is greater than 5 Km (c.f., Bruton, et al, 2001).

Planning for PDOP

Theoretically, the flight mission should be planned during times of good satellite coverage and distribution (see Figure 10.27) so that PDOP is 3 or less throughout the mission. In aerial photography, the sun angle and air space are the other conflicting factors that have to be taken into account as well. Therefore, it's normally an optimization problem that the mission planner will work on for every flight mission, to achieve best sun angle for photography, best PDOP for highest precision GPS, and most suitable flight plan to account for air space regulations. At the time of writing, the GPS constellation comprises 29 satellites, which provides for a poor PDOP relatively infrequently. A simple satellite prediction software tool such as available from Trimble Navigation via their web site provides the information needed to plan for best PDOP.

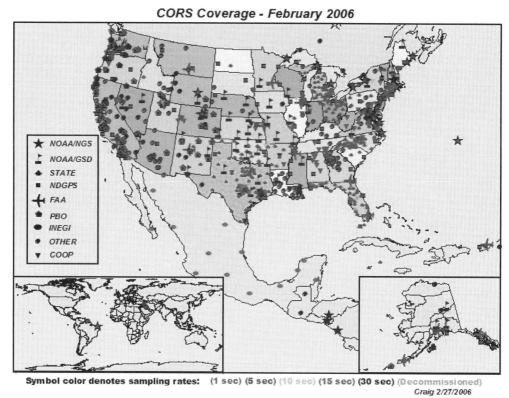

Figure 10.26 The U.S. CORS (courtesy of NOAA-NGS). See color plate in Appendix C.

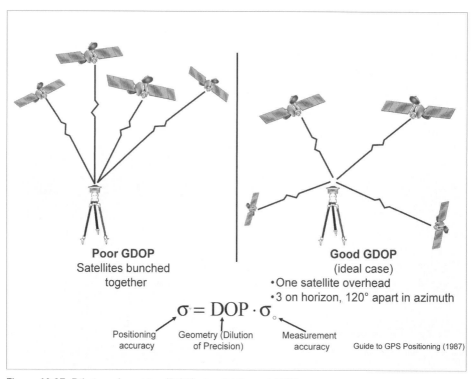

Figure 10.27 Dilution of precision (DOP) after Wells et al, 1987.

Inertial Navigator Alignment

If a stand-alone INS is used as part of a DG system, then the INS must undergo a stationary ground alignment prior to free-inertial navigation. The ground alignment lasts between 5 and 30 minutes, depending on the latitude. If the aircraft is buffeted by wind or by persons moving about its interior during this phase, constant tilt and heading errors outside of the specification for the INS can result. If a power interruption occurs in the air, the INS will lose its alignment and the mission must be aborted.

In contrast, a GPS-AINS can align itself while stationary or in motion. In fact, the in-air alignment is accelerated and the quality of the alignment improved if the aircraft performs an accelerating maneuver such as take-off or a turn. An in-air alignment requires about 3 minutes of nominally straight and level flight to allow the GPS-AINS to compute an initial roll and pitch, followed by a series of turns to align the heading. Thereafter the GPS-AINS improves its alignment with every maneuver. A typical zigzag survey pattern provides the maneuvers required by the GPS-AINS to maintain a high quality alignment.

Quality Control

The quality of the data generated by a DG system does not become directly apparent until it is combined with the imaging system data. Consequently quality control for a DG system becomes a process of managing each step in the data acquisition and post-mission processing phases to achieve a consistent and reliable quality assessment.

Proper mission planning as described in the previous section goes a long way towards obtaining repeatable results. Once the mission begins, the DG system must be monitored frequently for GPS dropouts or other data acquisition failures. A severe failure such as loss of GPS data for an extended time period may be grounds for aborting the mission. Once the aircraft has landed, the recorded data should be checked at the hanger for outages and other immediate indications of bad or missing data. This allows the mission to be re-flown possibly the same day.

If the recorded data are deemed to be acceptable, then the data are handed over to post-mission processing. The DG post-processing software typically has several quality assessment indicators. The most basic of these are the inertial-GPS residuals. These are the corrected differences between the inertial and GPS position solutions at each GPS epoch, and indicate the consistency between the solutions. The residuals will appear to be random in a successful inertial-GPS integration, indicating that the integration process has removed all sources of bias errors in the data. The processing software will typically perform a statistical analysis on the residuals and report a simple quality indicator to the user.

Once all the data have been processed and the georeferenced data assembled, the final quality indicator is given by the separation between computed and true positions of ground control points in the georeferenced data. This is the first direct measurement of quality, and comes at the end of the mapping process. If the previous steps have been managed properly, then the final quality measurement will be consistent, reliable and reproducible.

MOTION SENSING SYSTEM FOR MULTIBEAM SONAR BATHYMETRY

Overview

A multibeam sonar generates a fan of listening beams that spans $\pm$70-90 degrees. The bottom swath covered by the sonar fan has a width in excess of 7 times water depth. The multibeam sonar provides raw ranges from return echoes along each listening beam, which an on-line processing computer translates into georeferenced depth images. Figure 10.28 shows an example of a sea bottom DEM generated with a multibeam sonar. This process requires accurate measurement of the position and orientation of the sonar head at high data rates so that the sonar system can interpolate the sonar position and orientation to the time of echo reception. The International Hydrographic Organization (Special Publication No. 44, 1987) specifies an accuracy requirement of 1 percent of water depth greater than 30 meters and 0.1 meters for shallower depths. The depth error (as a ratio of water depth incurred in the outer beam of a multibeam sonar with fan angle) is:

$$\gamma = \delta\theta \tan(\theta)$$

where $\delta\theta$ is the error in the measurement of roll. Figure 10.29 shows the multibeam geometry. In order to achieve full utilization of a multibeam sonar, i.e. $\gamma = 0.01$ or 1 percent in the outer beam of a ±75 degree fan, the error standard deviation of the measured orientation must be better than 0.05 degrees. Heading error impacts the position error of each pixel in the bathymetry data. In order to obtain a 0.5 meter pixel position error in the outer beam of a ±75 degree fan at a depth of 100 meters, the heading error must be better than 0.05 degrees. Consequently the requirement for a high accuracy multibeam bathymetry system is 0.5 meters horizontal position error and 0.05 degrees orientation error in all three axes.

In addition, the heave of the vessel must also be measured to an accuracy of better than 0.1 meters to be consistent with the IHO standard. Absolute measurement of height with this accuracy is currently not feasible in a typical marine survey scenario that is far from the nearest shoreline where a GPS reference receiver or other form of positioning reference can be installed. Furthermore the datum for mean sea level does not necessarily correspond to a GPS zero altitude measurement. GPS uses the WGS-84 ellipsoid as the reference for positioning and an undulation model to compute height with respect to an approximate mean-sea level reference called the geoid. Consequently vessel heave for marine survey is specified as a relative displacement with respect to an assumed vessel waterline in calm water. Any offset between the assumed heave datum and true mean sea level is removed during the final map generation. A heave sensor is thus required to measure the non-constant or high frequency vertical displacement of the vessel, which is an approximately sinusoidal displacement with frequency given by the wave encounter frequency of the vessel. A simple heave sensor comprises a vertical accelerometer and a heave filter that performs a combined double integration and a high-pass filtering action on the measured vertical acceleration. The high-pass filter blocks the nearly constant accelerometer bias from reaching the double integrator, which in turn computes the vertical displacement of the vessel in the filter pass band. The heave filter must be tuned so that it provides the required accuracy in a pass band that includes the lowest expected wave encounter frequency when the vessel is moving downwind.

A roll-pitch-heave (RPH) sensor provides basic measurements of vessel roll, pitch and heave. It is typically a single unit that contains triads of accelerometers and gyros and a processor that implements a vertical gyro (VG) algorithm and the previously described heave filter. The VG algorithm computes roll and pitch with respect to an apparent vertical reference assumed to be the gravity vector. If the vessel does not accelerate, then the accelerometers will measure only the gravity vector that defines the true vertical. The VG algorithm computes the short-term roll and pitch motion with respect to the apparent vertical using the gyro data. It uses a complementary filter to block high frequency accelerations due to wave motion in the apparent vertical estimation and block low frequency gyro biases in the roll and pitch propagation. If the vessel experiences a sustained horizontal acceleration during a turn, then the apparent vertical will shift away from the true vertical and the computed roll and pitch will contain offsets. Once the sustained acceleration ends, the VG algorithm will exhibit a transient that decays within the complementary filter's settling time. A vessel that uses a RPH sensor must therefore allow a settling time (typically less than 5 minutes) at the beginning of a survey line following a turn before using the RPH data.

The state-of-the-art in high accuracy marine motion sensors is a GPS-aided INS. This technology provides all of the required motion data at the required accuracy to provide full utilization of a wide-swath multibeam sonar. The GPS-aiding provides for initialization, alignment and full accuracy motion sensing independent of vessel motion, as well as continuous refinement of the alignment and calibration of the inertial sensors. The GPS-AINS delivers full accuracy in any vessel dynamics, including sharp turns and severe accelerations and decelerations. It has no requirement to maintain a straight trajectory or to allow for a settling time after a turn, as does a VG-based RPH sensor. The IMU provides the vertical acceleration measurement for the heave filter. The heading accuracy is achieved with a dual-antenna azimuth aiding system. The Applanix POS MV exemplifies the state-of-the art in high accuracy marine motion sensing.

Figure 10.28 Greater Los Angeles continental shelf DEM generated with a multibeam sonar (courtesy U.S. Geological Survey). See color plate in Appendix C.

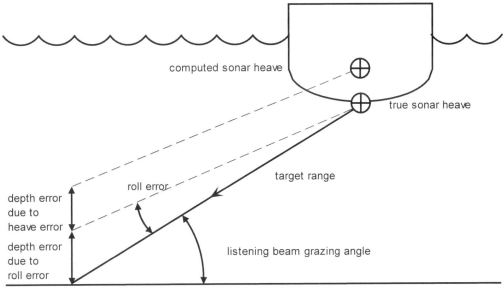

Figure 10.29 Bathymetric depth error in a multibeam sonar.

Development History

The Canadian Hydrographic Service (CHS) first recognized the possibility of marrying the multibeam sonar with a sufficiently accurate motion measurement system for quantitative bathymetry in 1992. Until then, the multibeam sonar, at that time a relatively new device, was used by oceanographers for seafloor imaging. The advantage of vastly improved production and data density over the traditional single-beam sonar became immediately apparent, and assured the eventual dominance of multibeam sonars for bathymetric survey. Applanix worked in partnership with the CHS to demonstrate the concept, and then developed the Position and Orientation System for Marine Vessels (POS MV) for this new application (Woolven, and Scherzinger, 1996). Since then the POS MV has become the dominant choice for high accuracy multibeam applications.

Types of Sensors

Motion sensors available for bathymetry range from simple roll-pitch-heave (RPH) sensors such as the TSS DMS or Kronsberg Seatex MRU series to a full GPS-AINS such as the Applanix POS MV (see Figure 10.30). The RPH sensors must be supplemented with a positioning system such as a GPS receiver and a heading sensor such as a gyrocompass. A GPS-AINS provides a complete position, orientation and heave solution in a single system and therefore requires no supplementary data.

Figure 10.30 Applanix POS MV (courtesy Applanix Corporation).

AUTHOR BIOGRAPHIES

The following authors wrote this chapter.

Bruno Scherzinger is the Chief Technology Officer at Applanix Corporation in Toronto Canada, where he is responsible for advanced navigation technology development and the core navigation technology in the Applanix product line. He has over 20 years of experience in GPS-INS integrated navigation, and is a member of the Institute of Navigation (ION) and the IEEE. Scherzinger obtained the BEng from McGill University in 1977 and the MSc and PhD in System Control Engineering from the University of Toronto respectively in 1979 and 1983.

Joe Hutton received his MSc in Aerospace Controls from the University of Toronto Institute for Aerospace Studies in 1991. He has been with Applanix Corporation since its inception and has over 15 years experience in Integrated GPS/Inertial technology as applied to airborne mapping. He is currently the Airborne Products Business Director, and is responsible for the management of the airborne product line.

Mohamed MR Mostafa is the Chief Technical Authority in Airborne Systems at Applanix Corporation and the chair of the Direct Georeferencing Committee of the ASPRS. He obtained a BSc and MSc from Alexandria University, Egypt in 1991 and 1994, respectively and a PhD from the University of Calgary in 1999. His research interests include mapping using multi-sensor systems.

REFERENCES

GPS

Ackermann, F., and H. Schade, 1993. Application of GPS for aerial triangulation, *Photogrammetric Engineering & Remote* Sensing, 59(11): 1625-1632.

Bruton, A.M., Mostafa, M.M.R., and Scherzinger, B.M., 2001. Airborne DGPS without dedicated base stations for mapping applications. *Proceedings of ION-GPS 2001*, Salt Lake City, Utah, USA, pp. 11-14.

Collins, J.P., and R.B. Langley, 1997. Estimating the residual tropospheric delay for airborne differential GPS positioning (a summary), *Proceedings of the 1997 Scientific Assembly of the International Association of Geodesy*, Rio de Janeiro, Brazil, 3-9 September, IAG Symposia, Vol. 118, Ed. F.K. Brunner, Springer-Verlag, 331-336.

Councilman, C.C., and S.A. Gourevitch, 1981. Miniature interferometer terminals for Earth surveying: Ambiguity and multipath for the global positioning system, *IEEE Transactions on Geoscience and Remote Sensing*, GE-19(4): 244-252.

de Jonge, P.J., Y. Bock, and M. Bevis, 2000. Epoch-by-epoch TM positioning and navigation, *Proceedings of ION-GPS-2000*, Salt Lake City, pp. 21-25.

Hatch, R., 1981. The synergism of GPS code and carrier measurements, *Proceedings of the 3rd International Geodetic Symposium on Satellite Doppler Positioning*, Las Cruces, New Mexico.

Hoffmann-Wellendorf, B., H. Lichtenegger, and J. Collins, 2001. *Global Positioning System Theory and Practice*, Springer-Verlag, New York, 5th edition.

IGS website, 2006. URL: http://igscb.jpl.nasa.gov/components/prods.html, (last date accessed: 16 March 2006).

Parkinson, B.W., and J.J. Spilker, 1996. Global positioning system theory and applications, Volume I, *Progress in Astronautics and Aeronautics Volume 163*, American Institute of Aeronautics and Astronautics.

Parkinson, B.W., and J.J. Spilker, 1996. Global positioning system theory and applications, Volume II, *Progress in Astronautics and Aeronautics Volume 163*, American Institute of Aeronautics and Astronautics.

Radio Technical Commission for Maritime (RTCM) Services, 1998. *RTCM Recommended Standards for Differential Global Navigation Satellite Systems Service*, Version 3.0, RTCM Special Committee, No. 104, January 15, 1998.

Remondi, B.W., 1985. Performing centimeter-level sSurveys in seconds with GPS carrier phase: Initial results, *Journal of the Institute of Navigation*, 32(4): 1985-86.

Tiberius, C.C.J.M., 1998. *Recursive Data Processing for Kinematic GPS Surveying*, NCG-Nederlandse Commissie voor Geodesie, Delft, Netherlands.

Wells, D., Beck, N., Delikaraorlou, D., Kleusberg, A., Krakiwsky, E.J.,Lachapelle, G., Langley, R.B., Nakiboglu, M., Schwarz, K.P., Tranquilla, J.M, and Vanícek, P., 1987. *Guide To GPS Positioning*, Canadian GPS Associates.

Inertial Navigation System

Britting, K.R., 1971. *Inertial Navigation System Analysis*, Wiley-Interscience, New York.

Chatfield, A.B., 1997. Fundamentals of high accuracy inertial navigation, *Progress in Astronautics and Aeronautics Volume 174*, American Institute of Astronautics and Aeronautics.

Proceedings of the IEEE, 1983. Special issue on global navigation systems, October 1983.

Schuler, M., 1923. The disturbance of pendulum and gyroscopic apparatus by the acceleration of the vertical, *Physikalische Zeitschrifte*, 24(7): 334-350.

GPS-Aided INS

Brown, R.G., and Hwang, P.Y.C., 1992. *Introduction to Random Signals and Applied Kalman Filtering*, 2nd edition, Wiley, New York.

Farrell, J.A., and M. Barth, 1999. *The Global Positioning System and Inertial Navigation*, McGraw-Hill, New York.

Gelb, A. (editor), 1984. *Applied Optimal Estimation*, MIT Press, Cambridge, MA.

Kayton, M., and W.R. Fried, 1997. *Avionics Navigation Systems, Second Edition*, Wiley and Sons, New York.

Rogers, R.M., 2000. *Applied Mathematics in Integrated Navigation Systems*, AIAA Education Series, 2000.

Siouris, G.M., 1993. *Aerospace Avionics Systems, A Modern Synthesis*, Academic Press, San Diego, CA.

Airborne Georeferencing

Abdullah, Q., 1997. Evaluation of GPS-inertial navigation system for airborne photogrammetry, *Proceedings, ASPRS/MAPPS Softcopy Conference*, July 27-30, Arlington, VA, pp. 237.

Grejner-Brezezinska, D.A., 2001. Direct sensor orientation in airborne and land-based mapping application, Report No. 461, Geodetic GeoInformation Science, Department of Civil and Environmental Engineering and Geodetic Science, The Ohio State University, Ohio, United States.

Heipke, C., Jacobsen, K., and Wegmann, H., 2001. Analysis of the results of the OEEPE test "Integrated Sensor Orientation". OEEPE Workshop, Integrated Sensor Orientation, Hannover, Germany, Sept. 17-18.

Hutton, J., Savina, T., and Lithopoulos, L., 1997. Photogrammetric applications of Applanix's Position and Orientation System (POS). ASPRS/MAPPS Softcopy Conference, July 27-30, Arlington, Virginia.

Ip, A.W.L., El-Sheimy, N., Hutton, J., 2004. Performance analysis of integrated sensor orientation. *International Archives of Photogrammetry and Remote Sensing*, ISPRS Comm. V, 35(B5), 797-802, Istanbul, Turkey.

Jacobsen K., and Wegmann, H., 2001. Dependencies and problems of direct sensor orientation. OEEPE Workshop, Integrated Sensor Orientation, Sept. 17-18, Hannover, Germany.

Madani, M., and M.M.R. Mostafa, 2004. Georeferencing the DMC images - Data flow and performance analysis. *Proceedings of the ASPRS Annual Conference*, May 22-28, Denver, CO., unpaginated CD-ROM.

Moffit, F., and E.M. Mikhail, 1980. *Photogrammetry,* Harper and Row, Inc., New York.

Mostafa, M.M.R., and J. Hutton, 2004. A fully integrated solution for aerial surveys: Design, development, and performance analysis, *PE&RS*, 71(4): 391-399.

Mostafa, M.M.R., 2002. Camera/IMU boresight calibration: New advances and performance analysis, *Proceedings of the ASPRS Annual Meeting*, April 21-26, Washington, DC.

Mostafa, M.M.R., J. Hutton, and E. Lithopoulos, 2001. Direct georeferencing of frame imagery - An error budget. *Proceedings of The Third International Mobile Mapping Symposium*, January 3-5, Cairo, Egypt.

Mostafa, M.M.R., and K.P. Schwarz, 2001. Digital image georeferencing from a multiple camera system by GPS/INS, *ISPRS Journal of Photogrammetry & Remote Sensing*, 56(2001): 1-12.

Mostafa, M.M.R., and K.P. Schwarz, 2000. A multi-sensor system for airborne image capture and georeferencing, *PE&RS*, 66 (12): 1417-1424.

Reid, D.B., E. Lithopoulos, and J. Hutton, 1998. Position and orientation system for direct georeferencing (POS/DG), *Proceedings of Institute of Navigation 54th Annual Meeting*, June 1-3, Denver, CO, USA, pp. 445-449.

Scherzinger, B., 1997. A position and orientation post-processing software package for inertial/GPS integration (POSProc). *Proceedings of the International Symposium on Kinematic Systems in Geodesy, Geomatics and Navigation (KISS 97)*, June 1997, Banff, Canada, pp. 197-204.

Schwarz, K.P., M.A. Chapman, M.E. Cannon, and P. Gong, 1993. An integrated INS/GPS approach to the georeferencing of remotely sensed data, *PE& RS*, 59(11): 1167-1674.

Schwarz, K.P., C.S., Fraser, and P.C., Gustafon, 1984. Aerotriangulation Without Ground Control, *International Archives of Photogrammetry and Remote Sensing*, 25 (Part A1), Rio de Janeiro, Brazil.

Shi, J and E.M. Cannon, 1994. Precise airborne DGPS positioning with a multi-receiver configuration: Data processing and accuracy evaluation, *Proceedings of the International Symposium on Kinematic Systems in Geodesy, Geomatics and Navigation*, Banff, Canada, pp. 393-402.

Škaloud, J., 1999. Problems in direct-georeferencing by INS/DGPS in the airborne environment, ISPRS Comm. III, WG III/1 Barcelona, Spain, Nov. 25-26.

Toth, C., and D.A., Grejner-Brzezinska, 1998. Performance analysis of the Airborne Integrated Mapping System (AIMS™), *International Archives of Photogrammetry and Remote Sensing*, 32 (2): 320-326.

Marine Georeferencing

International Hydrographic Organization (IHO), 1987. Special Publication No. 44, *IHO Standards for Hydrographic Surveys*, 3rd Edition.

Loncarevic, B.D., and B.M. Scherzinger, 1994. Compensation of ship attitude for multi-beam sonar surveys, *Sea Technology*, June, 1994.

Scherzinger, B.M., S. Woolven, and M. Field, 1997. Seafloor mapping solution, *Sea Technology*, March, 1997.

Woolven, S., and B.M. Scherzinger, 1996. An integrated position, attitude and heading solution for seafloor mapping with multi-beam sonars, *Proceedings of the IEEE Oceans 1996 Conference*, September, 1996, Fort Lauderdale.

Chapter 11

DEM User Applications

David F. Maune

DEM USES

This chapter summarizes major innovative DEM uses, but it is certain that many other uses are just waiting to be documented. When defining a DEM generically as "digital topographic and/or bathymetric data, in all its various forms," then DEM user applications are virtually unlimited. The following are the eight major DEM user application categories documented in this chapter:

- General Mapping Applications
- Coastal Mapping Applications
- Transportation Applications
- Underwater Applications
- Other Technical Applications
- Military Applications
- Commercial Applications
- Individual Applications

GENERAL MAPPING APPLICATIONS

The front cover of the May/June 2001 issue of *Imaging Notes* (Figure 11.1) was included in the original edition of this manual, and it is repeated in this 2nd edition because it foretold our emerging use of virtual city technology. The DVD enclosed with this manual includes a virtual city fly-through of Detroit, Michigan, explained in Chapter 15. Virtual cities and virtual landscapes summarize, in many ways, what this section is all about. How can modern maps keep pace with change? How can modern maps and Geographic Information Systems (GIS) address the ever-changing requirements for 3D spatial information that is accurate and up-to-date? How can users visualize cities and landscapes in 3D and efficiently analyze geospatial features?

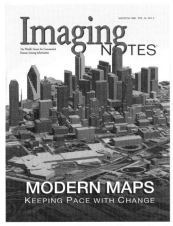

Figure 11.1 3D terrain and building model courtesy of Vexcel Corp., Boulder, Colorado. Copyright © 2001 Imaging NOTES Magazine.

Maps and GISs are widely used at all levels of government, academia and private industry. Although the uses are extremely diverse, they typically rely upon basic GIS foundation "layers" that include (1) digital orthophoto images, (2) digital elevation data, and (3) point/vector/polygon data base layers to include hydrography, transportation, structures and other planimetric features that can be photogrammetrically mapped from stereo aerial photography, as well as administrative boundaries and names that are not visible on aerial photos. On top of these basic GIS foundation layers, additional special purpose layers are georegistered so that they fit the basic foundation data.

Without elevation data, features photographed on individual aerial or satellite photos have *relief displacement* where features elevated above an established base elevation (e.g., the vertical datum) are displaced outward from the center of a vertical aerial photograph. This means that digital orthophotos, topographic maps, and planimetric maps that show no contour lines or elevation data, are not horizontally accurate unless elevations are accounted for in the mapping process.

Planimetric Maps

A planimetric map shows the horizontal location of features, but without contour lines or other means for displaying the 3D topography. The popular AAA road maps are a good example. Most planimetric maps are produced from aerial photography and stereo photogrammetry. Outside the mapping profession, it is not widely understood that digital elevation data are critical in the production of planimetric maps. The reason for this is *relief displacement*, mentioned above.

A single aerial photograph is a perspective view of the terrain as viewed from above. If the photograph is exactly *vertical*, i.e., photographed with the camera pointed straight down, elevated features on the photo will have a different scale than features closer to mean sea level. The magnitude of the relief displacement for a feature photographed with aerial photography is a function of the camera's focal length, the elevation of the feature mapped, and the feature's distance from the center of the photo. Relief displacement is corrected by stereo photogrammetric procedures that account for these variables. Furthermore, if the aerial photographs are not exactly vertical (they rarely are vertical because of aircraft dynamics), they also have *tilt displacement* caused by the roll and pitch of the aircraft at the instant a photograph is taken. Stereo photogrammetry corrects for *tilt displacement* in addition to *relief displacement*.

As stated above, planimetric maps are not normally horizontally accurate unless the elevations of mapped features are incorporated into the mapping process. Exceptions to this statement are parcel maps, administrative boundaries, and other features that are not mapped from aerial photographs and stereo photogrammetry, but from ground surveys of horizontal distances and angles. Since parcel and administrative boundaries are not visible on aerial photographs, land survey procedures are used.

The planimetric mapping requirement is normally satisfied by one of the stereo photogrammetric mapping procedures described in Chapter 5, perhaps in combination with additional land surveys of boundaries and other features not visible on the photos.

Topographic Maps

Topographic maps normally include planimetric features as well as topographic contours and spot heights. It goes without saying that topographic maps must include digital elevation data of some sort (to include DEMs or TINs converted into contours) in order to produce the critical elevation component of the topographic maps.

The topographic mapping requirement can be satisfied by stereo photogrammetry (see Chapter 5) or in combination with digital elevation data produced by IFSAR (see Chapter 6) or topographic lidar (see Chapter 7). Bathymetric contours are produced from airborne lidar bathymetry (see Chapter 8) or sonar (see Chapter 9).

Digital Orthophotos

Digital orthophotos include no elevation data per se, but they cannot be produced cost-effectively without DEMs. As described above under Planimetric Maps, aerial photographs are perspective views of the terrain. When these photographs are digitized, they still include *relief displacement* and *tilt displacement*. Aerotriangulation yields the six exterior orientation parameters for each photograph, as explained in Chapter 5, and computers can compensate for tilt displacement; but relief displacement is still present in the images. By projecting this image over a DEM, the "draped" image compensates for most of the relief displacement and provides an approximate orthographic projection, as though theoretically looking straight down from space. But this is true only for features at the ground elevation of the DEM used. Elevated features, such as buildings, towers and trees are still displaced outward, and the sides of buildings are shown, both as a function of their elevation and as a function of their distance from the center of the photograph "draped" over the DEM.

Because the sides of buildings are shown, most digital orthophotos in use today are not "true digital orthophotos." A true digital orthophoto would show the roof of a skyscraper directly over its foundation, and there would be no pixels showing the sides of a skyscraper, for example. However, the sides of skyscrapers are recorded on the perspective aerial photographs, and there are no simple solutions for deleting image pixels that have no place to go. Although there are several software programs designed to produce "true digital orthophotos," the process is still complex and expensive. For now, most digital orthophotos are not the perfect "straight down" views of the earth from infinity that we wish we had in a perfect GIS. For the foreseeable future, we will continue to rely upon DEMs to produce the forms of digital orthophotos in common use today.

Flood Insurance Rate Maps

Flood Insurance Rate Maps (FIRMs), produced by the Federal Emergency Management Agency (FEMA), are combinations of the above. The older FIRMs are essentially planimetric base maps overprinted with Base Flood Elevations (BFEs) and Special Flood Hazard Area (SFHA) boundaries (computed from hydrologic modeling of elevation data for entire watersheds, and hydraulic modeling of elevation data in floodplains), but they don't include actual contours.

If contour lines were printed on FIRMs, users would see that SFHA boundaries cross contour lines as the flood waters slope downstream in accordance with computer models for standard flood events (10%, 2%, 1% or 0.2% annual chance floods commonly referred to as 10-, 50-, 100-, or 500-year floods). A river doesn't simply flood to a specified elevation, but to variable elevations along different reaches of a river. In fact, FIRMs regularly show BFEs that are relatively close to other BFEs (upstream or downstream) that are, respectively, at least one foot higher or lower. Sometimes, a BFE immediately upstream of a bridge or culvert is several feet higher than a BFE immediately downstream of that bridge or culvert. This does not result from abrupt changes in surface topography, but from the bridge or culvert being undersized to carry the flow expected to result from a 1% annual chance flood (100-year flood), causing that bridge/culvert to act as a dam that increases the flood risk to buildings upstream.

FEMA's digital FIRMs (DFIRMs) often use digital orthophotos as the base map for overlay of georeferenced digital flood data. Figure 11.2 shows the concept behind the DFIRMs. It shows that the DFIRM results from the merger of (1) a digital orthophoto base map; (2) digital elevation data used to perform hydrologic and hydraulic (H&H) modeling and analyses; and (3) the digital flood data (BFEs and SFHAs) that result from such H&H modeling. The resulting DFIRM is the map designed to predict locations that have a 1% or greater chance of flooding during any given year.

FIRMs and DFIRMs are often obsolete because the risk of flooding is ever increasing, even for the same predicted amounts of rainfall, because land development activities (cutting down trees, and covering the land with concrete and asphalt) causes less water to be absorbed into the ground and more water to run off into the stream with each passing year, increasing the flood risk. Thus, although the shape of the topography may not change that much, the changing land cover on that topography continuously worsens the flood risks.

DFIRM Components

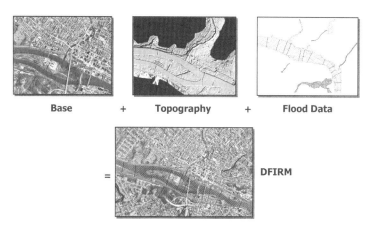

Base   +   Topography   +   Flood Data

=   DFIRM

Figure 11.2 Components of a Digital Flood Insurance Rate Map (DFIRM). Images courtesy of FEMA. See color plate in Appendix C.

A second problem is that hydraulic modeling performed on topographic data equivalent to 5' contours, for example, will be less accurate than hydraulic modeling performed on topographic data equivalent to 2' contours, but the higher accuracy topographic data are considerably more expensive.

Hydrologic modeling is performed on less-accurate DEMs available from virtually any source described in this manual, including Level 1 and Level 2 DEMs already available from USGS (see Chapter 4). The slope of the terrain (derived from DEMs) is one of the factors in determining the volume and speed of surface water run-off.

Hydraulic modeling is performed on more-accurate TINs, including various breaklines that define channel cross-section geometry and ditches, for example. The demanding requirement for hydraulic modeling requires TINs that are provided either by conventional stereo photogrammetric procedures described in Chapter 5, or topographic lidar described in Chapter 7. However, breakline generation is best performed by stereo photogrammetric compilation procedures, so lidar and photogrammetry may combine to deliver the optimal solution for hydraulic modeling necessary for FIRM production. As explained in Chapter 7, lidargrammetry is gaining acceptance for such breakline generation.

Wetland Maps

Photogrammetry, especially when using color infrared photography, is better able to delineate the boundaries between land and water; however, photogrammetry is not ideal for determining the elevations of the land in marshy areas because of difficulties in performing stereo correlation on ground features that are not distinctive and/or because of difficulties in penetrating through vegetation from two different angles, as required by stereo photogrammetry.

In 1999, USGS acquired topographic lidar data and produced accurate elevations of portions of the Florida Everglades, following wildfires that burned off the sawgrass and other vegetation, leaving the bare-earth relatively free of dense vegetation. However, without vegetation burn-off, a similar topographic lidar project of Pinellas County, Florida failed to penetrate the dense sawgrass and mangrove and tended to map the top surfaces of those features, even though last-return lidar returns were used. Although lidar is better than any other technology for mapping through dense vegetation, no technology yet known can map through features that it can't see through.

Researchers from the University of Connecticut and the University of New Haven worked with NOAA's Coastal Services Center to use lidar data for mapping estuarine wetland plant species in the Ragged Rock tidal marsh near Old Saybrook, Connecticut. Target classes included *Spartina patens* dominated pans, *Typha angustifolia*, and *Phragmites australis* which is a highly invasive wetland species that out-competes many native species. Spectral information from high resolution digital aerial imagery and vegetation height information from lidar data were used in a supervised classification of the tidal marsh. Two classification techniques were employed (feature analysis and image object segmentation) and different data inputs were tested (raw data and several derivatives). Quantitative accuracy assessments were generated for each permutation and the results indicated that the inclusion of lidar data improved the overall classification accuracy from 80% to 85%, and improved the user's accuracy of the *Phragmites* class by an additional 5%. Moreover, the results also indicated that classification techniques for using only the lidar derived information (for this particular application) yielded the same overall accuracy as that obtained using only the spectral information. This is but one of numerous applications that demonstrate that the merger of spectral imagery and lidar data has significant benefits.

Forestry Maps

As indicated in Chapter 7, accurate information on the terrain and topography beneath the tree canopy is important to the forestry industry and natural resource managers. Accurate information on tree heights and densities is also critical information that is difficult to obtain using conventional techniques. Airborne topographic lidar, unlike radar or satellite imaging, can simultaneously map the ground beneath the tree canopy as well as the tree heights, as shown in Figure 11.3.

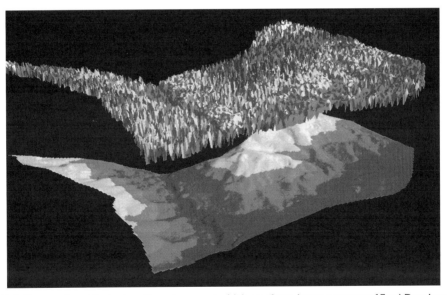

Figure 11.3 Bare-earth and first return (forest canopy top) lidar surfaces. Image courtesy of EarthData International. See color plate in Appendix C.

If Digital Surface Models (DSMs) are required of the tree canopy, then photogrammetric automated image correlation (see Chapter 5) or IFSAR (see Chapter 6) are optimum, and they produce DSMs of very large areas at lower costs than lidar.

Corridor or Right-of-Way Maps

As indicated in Chapter 7, airborne lidar mapping allows rapid, cost-effective, accurate mapping of linear corridors such as power utility right-of-ways, gas pipelines, or highways. Aerial access with highly detailed information has proven to be a major advantage that lidar offers over traditional methods to clients interested in engineering projects along these corridors.

In the case of powerline surveys, many of these projects cover terrain with few roads and require the definition of conductor catenaries, crossing catenaries, accurate attachment point elevations, DTM, encroachment and structure locations.

In the past, engineers would have to budget months for survey and mapping for critical projects. Topographic lidar significantly reduces the time and costs necessary to satisfy such engineering requirements along narrow and meandering corridors.

The National Map

In 2001, USGS released its plan for the "National Map," a seamless, continually maintained, nationally consistent set of basic spatial data to include digital orthorectified imagery; land characterization data; digital elevation data; vector layers to include transportation, hydrography, structures, and boundaries; and geographic names, similar to the prototype at Figure 11.4. Each of these framework datasets will have variable resolution and completeness. Each dataset will initially build upon the best available data, and improve throughout the decade with

Figure 11.4 The National Map prototype. Image courtesy of USGS. See color plate in Appendix C.

updates from various federal, state and local governments, private industry, and others. The National Map is to have around-the-clock Internet access, with user-specified combinations of data and geographic areas.

For topographic data, USGS will be the guarantor of national data completeness; the owner and organizer responsible for awareness, availability, and utility; the catalyst and collaborator for creating and stimulating data partnerships; the integrator of data from other participants; and the data producer when no other source exists.

The role of federal, state and regional government agencies is to identify needs, to coordinate consortia, identify changes and provide updates, and to collaborate on data.

The role of private industry is to provide tools, open standards, and data. The role of academia is to conduct research on producing and using the data.

The National Elevation Dataset (NED), explained in Chapter 4, is consistent with this vision of the National Map

Virtually all technologies addressed in this DEM Users Manual will contribute to this National Map. USGS is expected to be the repository for topographic data, while NOAA is expected to be the repository for bathymetric data; however, details remain to be worked out by the various agencies that comprise the National Digital Elevation Program (NDEP).

COASTAL MAPPING APPLICATIONS

Shoreline Delineation

NOAA has the responsibility to conduct surveys of coastal regions of the United States and its possessions for demarcating the nation's legal coastline. The national shoreline provides the critical baseline data for demarcating America's marine territorial limits, including its Exclusive Economic Zone, and for the geographic reference needed to manage coastal resources as well as many other uses. The National Shoreline is fundamental to the growth of the Nation's shipping, manufacturing, export, coastal development, and insurance industries. Therefore, accurate, consistent, up-to-date national shorelines are needed for incorporation onto NOAA nautical charts to facilitate safe marine transportation and navigation. The shoreline represented on NOAA nautical charts is based on a Mean High Water (MHW) tidal datum. This MHW tidal datum is defined as the average of all the high water heights observed over the National Tidal Datum Epoch (explained in Chapter 2). The utilization of remote sensing sensors that allow for derivation of high resolution DEMs allow the possibility for extraction of datum based shorelines (see Figure 11.5).

Figure 11.5 Extraction of a Mean High Water (MHW) tidal datum from a lidar derived DEM on Mullet Key, Florida. Image courtesy of NOAA. See color plate in Appendix C.

Research projects are currently being performed in conjunction with a vertical datum transformation tool to allow for consistent, non-interpreted tidally based coastal lines to be extracted from elevation data. NOAA is currently developing a software tool, VDatum that allows for transformation of elevation data expressed between any two differing vertical datums. VDatum currently supports 29 vertical datums that can be placed into three categories: 3-dimensional (realized through space-borne systems), orthometric (defined relative to a form of mean sea level), and tidal (based on a tidally derived surface). VDatum employs geoids, fields that represent departures of NAVD88 from mean sea level, and hydrodynamic models that depict variations in tidal ranges along the coastal environment. Extracting shorelines utilizing VDatum along with elevation datasets such as highly accurate lidar data has several advantages over traditional methods.

- Shorelines derived from highly accurate DEMs are accurately referenced to a tidal datum, which provides a routine that maximizes consistency with minimal interpretation.
- High resolution elevation data allows for deriving consistent tidal datum based demarcation lines across varying coastal environments, when compared to others such as the high water line, vegetative lines, and berms.
- The possibility of extracting multiple shorelines may be achieved from a single elevation data set, providing that data acquisition is properly coordinated with a specified tidal stage.

Sea Level Rise

Sea level rise is a significant issue that threatens coastal environments and communities. According to a report of the Environmental Protection Agency (EPA, 1997), this rise could be as high as one meter during the next century. When the White House asked the EPA for statistics on the number of buildings to be impacted by the predicted sea level rise, EPA attempted to use DEMs from the USGS, but found them to be unacceptable. The EPA lacked the DEMs accurate enough to perform this modeling effort. Without the appropriate elevation data, it is difficult to gather a good understanding of sea level rise impacts. This leads to problems for coastal zone managers and engineers needing to formulate strategies to mitigate the effects of a rise in sea level. The availability of accurate elevation data can help in understanding the possible effects of sea level rise on coastal morphology (erosion and deposition) and ecosystem habitats that have limited vertical and horizontal positions in the coastal environment, as shown at Figure 11.6.

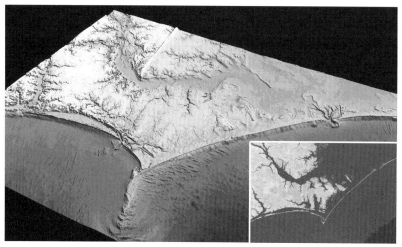

Figure 11.6 A seamless topographic/bathymetric elevation model utilized to simulate sea level rise scenarios. The inset illustrates an approximate one meter sea level rise based on the topo/bathy DEM. Image courtesy of NOAA.

Researchers at NOAA are trying to understand the effects of sea level rise in coastal states, such as North Carolina. One of the first steps to understanding this process is to construct an accurate DEM. In the case of North Carolina, a seamless topo/bathy DEM was constructed utilizing the most accurate elevation data available. The DEM utilized FEMA lidar data for topographic information and NOAA hydrographic soundings for bathymetric information to produce a continuous bathy/topo DEM relative to NAVD 88. Since this DEM was constructed from varying elevation data sets, these various data sets needed to be referenced to a common vertical datum. VDatum was used to transform the data to create a seamless topo/bathy DEM.

To assess the impacts of sea level rise, simulations can be developed by combining a finite element hydrodynamic model with the consistent, continuous elevation dataset. The scenarios can simulate tidal response, synoptic wind events, and hurricane storm surge propagation in combination with sea level rise. Accurate prediction of inundation patterns can be accomplished by merging the high resolution, continuous bathy/topo data with an accurate wetting/drying algorithm. Shoreline migration can then be dynamically computed from the algorithm's output as a function of sea level rise, and coupled to characterize the effects of sea level rise on coastal ecosystems. The availability of both high resolution bathymetric and topographic datasets holds an enormous possibility for helping understand the impact of sea level rise to the coastal environment.

Coastal Management

Coastal management organizations are regularly relying on lidar remote sensing data to provide high accuracy elevation models and contours for various scientific and regulatory applications. The Maine Geological Survey (MGS) uses lidar topographic data to help determine whether or not coastal development projects are located within Erosion Hazard Areas (EHAs), as defined by the state's revised Coastal Sand Dune Rules (http://mainegov-images.informe.org/dep/blwq/topic/dunes/355provisional.pdf). In Maine, an EHA is an area that may become a coastal wetland in the next 100-years through the combined effects of historic shoreline change, short-term erosion resulting from a 100-year storm, and flooding in a 100-year storm after 2-ft of sea level rise is taken into account, or any area mapped as an AO-zone by the effective FIRM. (An AO zone is a Special Flood Hazard Area with sheet flow, ponding, or shallow flooding.) To examine this, MGS uses the position of the frontal-and-back dune boundaries (D1 and D2), historic shoreline change data, short-term erosion data, FEMA FIRM data, highest annual tide levels, and lidar topographic data. This data is compiled within a GIS and overlain onto orthorectified aerial photographs. The topographic lidar data set is then color-gridded and draped over the orthophotographs (Figure 11.7). The ArcGIS lidar Data Handler, available from NOAA CSC, is then used to examine topographic transects along a project site in reference to published 100-year FEMA base flood elevations, in addition to projected future shoreline, washover, and highest annual tide (after 2-ft of sea level rise) positions and elevations (Figure 11.8). MGS uses EHA determinations to recommend whether or not a proposed structure should be placed on posts, acceptable flow-through foundation, or may use a full foundation.

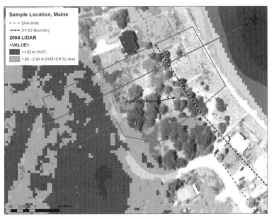

Figure 11.7 NOAA 2004 lidar draped over an aerial orthophoto showing the regulatory D1-D2 boundary, existing highest annual tide position (which defines the limits of a coastal wetland), and projected highest annual tide position after 2-ft of sea level rise. The transect A-A' shows topography across the site in Figure 11.8. See color plate in Appendix C. Image courtesy of Maine Geological Survey.

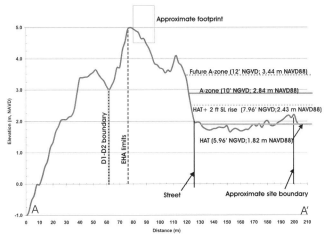

Figure 11.8 Topography along the transect A-A' shown in Figure 11.7 in reference to the subject property and structure, D1-D2 boundary, and FIRM elevations. The EHA boundary was located landward of the D1-D2 boundary because historic erosion on the order of -1 foot/year could erode the frontal dune, and short-term erosion could breach the dune crest. At the same time, a 2-ft rise in sea level would raise the existing A-zone and highest annual tide elevations on the subject property. The recommended developable envelope is shown. Topographic data from NOAA lidar (2004). See color plate in Appendix C. Image courtesy of Maine Geological Survey.

In the state of South Carolina, lidar data is used by the Department of Health and Environmental Control, Office of Ocean and Coastal Resource Management (OCRM), for determining the primary dune crest which determines setback regulations for development in the coastal zone. In the past, this important line was determined by either aerial photo interpretation or by traditional survey methods, both costing considerably more time and money, than to analyze quality lidar DEMs or contours derived from the data.

To update the state's setback lines in 1997, the lidar elevation points were processed into elevation contour lines. From these contours, the crest of the dune was delineated, and the setback line was established a minimum of 20 feet landward. It was estimated that one technician at a computer with the data could map an average of 10 miles of beach a day. That amounts to about 20 days of work per year, as compared to the 132 manpower days required using the GPS technology. Today, OCRM continues to use these beachfront jurisdictional lines, developed using lidar, and plans to conduct a remapping in 2007 using a similar approach.

Coastal Engineering

Nautical charting provides raw data for a broad assortment of coastal engineering applications. Shoreline dynamics and the movement of sand are central to many such uses. Areas of interest are sediment transport, sediment budgets, sand as a local resource, and the design, evaluation, and monitoring of structures such as breakwaters and jetties for shoreline stabilization and dredging. Other interests are mapping anchorage areas, support for harbor engineering and construction projects, port projects, pipelines, cables, and gas and oil production.

According to a FEMA study (FEMA, 1997b) that relied on study data from the U.S. Army Corps of Engineers, approximately 20,500 miles of the 84,240 miles of U.S. shoreline experience "significant" erosion, while 700 miles are subject to "critical" erosion. There are 260 coastal counties in the U.S. FEMA inventoried 26 of these counties (10%) in 1997, including GPS elevation surveys of 45,000 buildings within coastal high hazard zones (V-zones, subject to velocity wave action). Thousands of buildings are vulnerable to coastal erosion and/or velocity wave action from hurricane tidal surges. If other coastal counties are similar, then 450,000 buildings nationwide could be in V-zones. Projected erosion rates along the Gulf and Atlantic coasts are typically two feet per year, and one foot per year on the Pacific Coast. Elevation surveys are needed for all buildings in V-zones for multi-hazard mitigation.

Modeling and Mapping Coastal Inundation

Coastal inundation is the flooding of coastal lands by ocean waters. Severe inundation is an infrequent event and is normally of short duration; nevertheless, it can cause significant threat to life and damage to public and private property. Severe inundation can be caused by hurricanes, tsunamis, or large coastal storms such as nor'easters. Many areas within the coastal zone can be affected by a combination of coastal inundation and freshwater flooding during an event. The extent and behavior of such flooding is complex and depends upon the magnitude, variation and relative timing of freshwater inflows and coastal water levels. Identification of the level of coastal inundation is an essential starting point in the management of this hazard.

One of the most valuable parameters to coastal inundation modeling and mapping is a continuous bathymetric/topographic DEM of coastal regions. Computer models and GIS mapping utilize DEMs and simulated coastal water levels to determine the extent of coastal inundation as well as visualize the impacts of the flooding. High-resolution data sources such as lidar are extremely useful for providing accurate elevation data in upland, coastal, and intertidal areas and for defining the geographic boundary of flooding. The need for bathymetric lidar is particularly acute in the intertidal region, since there is generally a gap in conventionally obtained elevation data where collection systems cannot gain access.

Many computer models exist to model coastal inundation. Some models take the form of a structured grid (grid cells are the same size) where a DEM will naturally transfer easily, and some have unstructured grids (grids cells vary in size) where a DEM will have to be translated to the model grid. In either case, the DEM serves as the bottom boundary for the model both offshore and on land. Most coastal inundation models are 2D models that use the bottom boundary to calculate the forces of bottom friction that ultimately effect the propagation of the water towards the land. Bottom roughness and morphology affect the amount and morphology of this inundation propagation greatly and is considered to be equally important to coastal inundation modeling as atmospheric forcing. Wave effects on top of still water levels are also an important factor that many inundation models do not account for. Wave heights are directly related to bottom depth and morphology as well. The height of wave run-up on beaches depends upon many factors that include wave height and period, the slope, shape and permeability of the beach, the roughness of the foreshore area, and wave regularity. Many of these parameters are resolved in a high resolution DEM.

Appropriate grid size of a DEM must balance the resolution of the data needed for modeling, the file size best utilized by the model, and the grid size supported by the available data. A higher resolution DEM will resolve ground features that could potentially obstruct water flow across the land; however, these features

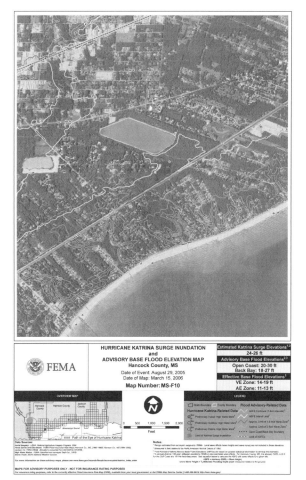

Figure 11.9 FEMA Coastal Flood Recovery Map of Waveland, MS. See color plate at Appendix C. Image courtesy of FEMA, State of Mississippi, and NOAA. See color plate in Appendix C.

tend to disappear in the gridding process, which reduces file size. Similarly for larger regions, a lower resolution DEM may be needed to model coastal inundation, where feature details are sacrificed for larger coverage.

The use of coastal DEMs is becoming an increasingly important part of coastal inundation modeling to better predict and prepare for coastal inundation events. Seamless integrated bathymetric and topographic DEMs are even more valuable to modelers for treating the offshore and onshore as one continuous surface. Because topography is generally referenced to an ellipsoidal or orthometric datum and bathymetry is generally referenced to a tidal datum, tools have been created to convert among the different datums. One of these tools is VDATUM which can convert all bathymetry and topography to a common reference, and, in this way, bathymetry outside of the intertidal area can be incorporated into the DEM with the high-resolution nearshore bathymetric and coastal topographic elevation data.

The 2005 hurricane season illustrated the devastating hazards of coastal inundation, with Hurricane Katrina causing a higher storm surge on the Northern Gulf Coast than Hurricane Camille (1969), the benchmark storm for that region for over 30 years. To quickly show the inundation footprint of Katrina, FEMA let contracts for the rapid collection of high water marks and mapping of the coastal inundation that occurred. The maps, called Coastal Flood Recovery Maps also displayed advisory base flood elevations and were intended to help state and local officials, as well as homeowners, to identify existing and increased flood hazards caused by Hurricane Katrina and other storms that have struck this region in the last 25 years, and to use this information during recovery and redevelopment to avoid future flood damages. The creation of the maps was possible in such a short amount of time due to the availability of lidar derived DEMs for the three Mississippi coastal counties. High water mark elevations were mapped using the high resolution DEMs, allowing for the most accurate portrayal of storm surge effects from Katrina as possible in a short amount of time. The maps were distributed via the FEMA website. Figure 11.9 is an example of a Coastal Flood Recovery Map for Waveland, MS.

TRANSPORTATION APPLICATIONS

Land Transportation and Safety

Highway design and construction requires high accuracy land surveys, normally equivalent to contours with 1' or 6" contour intervals. However, no land survey project is more dangerous than surveying next to speeding traffic. Warning signs to drive slowly often go unheeded, and serious accidents result. For this reason, low altitude photogrammetric or lidar surveys have become the norm for generating high accuracy topographic maps and DEMs on which highway and inter-change construction plans are based.

During highway construction, it has long been standard practice to perform construction stake-out operations to guide the operators of earth-moving equipment. As reported by (Long, 1998), Computer-Aided Earthmoving Systems (CAES) can now integrate differential GPS (DGPS) with real-time-kinematic (RTK) positioning and control of construction vehicles. Construction vehicles are equipped with DGPS receivers, linked to a GIS with DTMs updated "on-the-fly" as earth-moving machines make their cuts and fills. As each vehicle's onboard computer radios GPS-based position information back to a dispatch computer, the dispatcher monitors the location and status (full or empty, heading, and velocity) of each vehicle in the fleet, monitors where trucks are waiting to be loaded, and redirects them for maximum efficiency. Using the in-cab display, the earthmoving equipment operator views the design grade with cut or fill requirements. Using a moving cut/fill isopach map as a guide, the operator can minimize push distances and increase efficiency. After the CAES machine has started its cut, the heading and a long section is displayed on the monitor, providing the operator with a graphical display of the current topography in relation to the design surface. As the operator makes the cuts, the onboard processor updates the current DTM in real time. This on-the-fly updating enables the operator to assess excavation progress for each individual pass and maximize productivity by receiving immediate feedback. All of these features have combined to produce a dramatic increase in the amount of useful work that construction and mining machines can accomplish each day.

Whereas this example is not representative of the mining and earth moving industry as a whole, it demonstrates how DTM models are expected to be used in the future as managers continually seek more innovative and cost effective ways to performs redundant tasks.

Air Navigation and Safety

DEMs/DSMs support air navigation and safety in two principal ways:
- Terrain avoidance during enroute flight operations
- Airspace analysis for runway, take off and landing operations

The Federal Aviation Administration (FAA) has long been working on development of the Wide Area Augmentation System (WAAS) and/or the Local Area Augmentation System (LAAS) to use GPS technology for safe control of aircraft and airspace. The FAA also sees the future in other GPS guidance systems such as Project Capstone where aircraft are being equipped with Capstone satellite based guidance systems to overcome the hazards of flying in severe weather in dangerous areas lacking modern navigational aids. The system determines a plane's exact location by GPS and broadcasts it to controllers and other planes with the same equipment. The pilot uses a DSM that changes colors depending on the plane's altitude relative to the terrain. Black means the plane is at least 2,000 feet above the ground. Green, yellow and red indicate lower levels. "Anything that's red, you're dead," says a newspaper article. A plane's position, altitude, identity and other information is data linked to control centers and towers, even when the plane is in areas with no radar coverage. An FAA study indicates that these features have improved safety significantly.

Airport runways are normally surveyed with a very high level of accuracy, and airports are designed for safety. The same is true for flight paths used for take-offs and landings. DSMs are ideal for digital airspace obstruction analysis, which includes modeling the mathematical airspace surfaces defined by FAA FAR Part 77 that depicts airspaces surrounding and emanating from airports. These include (1) approach and departure surfaces, (2) transitional zones, (3) primary zones, and (4) horizontal surfaces above the airport. These surfaces must be free of trees, towers and other obstructions. See Figures 11.10 and 11.11.

Figure 11.10 Airspace obstruction model. Image courtesy of EarthData International. See color plate in Appendix C.

Figure 11.11 Topographic lidar collected by NOAA for utilization in detecting airborne obstructions. Image courtesy of NOAA. See color plate in Appendix C.

DSMs are ideal for terrain avoidance systems and for airspace obstruction analysis. DSMs from photogrammetric automated image correlation and IFSAR are perfectly acceptable for this purpose, although lidar will perform these tasks with higher accuracy. Also, see (Parrish et al., 2005) for an excellent article on the use of airborne lidar for detection of airport obstructions.

Marine Navigation and Safety

The safety and efficiency of shipping depends on the collection of accurate hydrographic data and the creation of accurate nautical charts. For the coastlines of the U.S. and all of its possessions, this responsibility is shared by NOAA's National Ocean Service (NOS) Office of Coast Survey (OCS) and the U.S. Army Corps of Engineers. Accuracy standards are set by the International Hydrographic Organization (IHO) in Monaco. Accurate, reliable, and up-to-date nautical chart information is more important today than at any time in the past. As margins of safety are challenged, consequences loom greater as cargo capacities are pushed to the limit. To meet this challenge, more current and precise information is required. New electronic navigation systems can meet the demands for greater protection of life, property and the environment, and significantly improve the efficiency of maritime commerce. Any action to improve marine navigation will also improve safety and efficiency. Free and safe passage of freight will benefit the local and national economy. On the other hand, a major accident within the marine industry due to navigation errors relative to the surveyed channel has the potential for disastrous consequences, with loss of life and loss of economic benefits. Tragedies such as the Exxon *Valdez* call for improved marine navigation systems based on bathymetric modeling of shipping channels and their surrounds.

Traditional paper charts are moving into the realm of "print on demand" (POD) (Hubbard, 2001). As paper charts in use became outdated, it is the responsibility of the mariner to obtain updated ancillary information. Using cutting-edge technology, NOAA now updates many charts daily, and they're printed only when the chart agent places an order. NOAA's Coast Survey, in partnership with OceanGrafix, LLC, is test marketing official nautical charts continually updated by NOAA to the latest Notice to Mariners and to all Critical Safety Information known to Coast Survey in advance of publication. The new charts show the latest discoveries like channel changes and other hazards, so sailing is safer. OceanGrafix prints charts to order for sale to mariners through a retail network. These charts have brighter colors and higher contrast for better readability in various light conditions, and are water and abrasion resistant. They have operational information such as tide tables, bridge clearance and point of contact, communication links for the commercial mariner, and educational and safety information for the recreational boater. Charts customized to the mariner's needs and a subscription service of charts and electronic information are anticipated in the future.

The era of Electronic Nautical Charts (ENCs), Electronic Chart Display and Information Systems (ECDIS), and Electronic Chart Systems (ECS) is here. ENCs and ECS are the greatest advancement in maritime safety since the introduction of radar to ships. An ENC is a vector-based digital file containing marine features suitable for marine navigation — a database of chart features. The structure and format of an ENC is defined by the IHO S57 standard, which means that the ENC is in a non-proprietary, publicly available format. ENCs and Raster Nautical Charts (RNCs) will eventually replace paper charts for vessels using electronic navigation. The RNCs and ENCs, which are produced by NOAA collaboratively with the private sector, will serve as the official charts that may be carried in place of paper charts. This "official" status applies to the regulated vessels for which chart carriage is mandatory. NOAA will continue to produce paper charts for those users who do not choose to use electronic navigation. The ENC is intended for use in ECDIS as well as in the more generic ECS. ENCs will also provide fully integrated vector base maps for use in geographic information systems (GIS) that are used for coastal management or other purposes. When nautical charts are in digital format, they can also be draped over a high resolution topo/bathy DEM as shown at Figure 11.12.

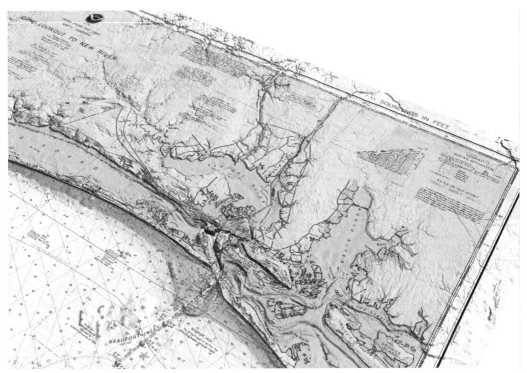

Figure 11.12 NOAA Nautical charts draped over a high resolution topo/bathy DEM.

Electronic chart systems (ECS) encompass any electronic system that uses digital chart data. The chart data can be vector or raster, and no specific format is currently defined, although many ECS can use ENC data. Standards for ECS are being developed by the Radio Technical Commission for Maritime Services (RTCM) (www.rtcm.org). ECDIS systems are certified to meet a suite of international standards: IHO (www.iho.shom.fr) Transfer Standard for Digital Hydrographic Data S- 57; IHO Specifications for Chart Content and Display aspects of ECDIS S- 52; International Maritime Organization (IMO) (www.imo.org) Resolution A.817 (19) Performance Standards for ECDIS; and International Electrotechnical Commission (IEC) (www.iec.ch) 61174: ECDIS – Operational and performance requirements, methods of testing and required test results. An ECDIS must use "official" ENC data to meet all of these standards and may use "official" raster data where ENC data is not yet available.

An ENC contains information about the location of each chart feature, as well as attribution information such as color, shape, depth, and so forth. This information is used by navigation system software to draw a display that resembles a nautical chart, but has greatly enhanced functionality. A raster chart, by contrast, is a facsimile of a paper chart, that is, a picture of a chart displayed on a computer screen. It is a file of information that can be thought of as pixels on the computer screen. The raster file tells the computer what color to draw at each pixel. Thus, the computer "knows" what color is there, but cannot distinguish a black pixel that is part of a sounding from a black pixel that is part of a dangerous wreck symbol. The ENC stores what the actual feature is, its latitude and longitude, and descriptive information. Incorporating digital chart data with a continuous GPS signal for automated vessel positioning enhances safety of navigation. A navigation system using an ENC would "know" that the dangerous wreck is a dangerous wreck, as well as how much water is over the wreck. A navigation system using an ENC can use this information to check planned routes to see if they cross or pass too near dangers, sound alarms if a vessel's projected course will carry it close to dangerous features, and inform the mariner about various warnings and regulations that relate to areas that the vessel is transiting.

Many marine mishaps are due to human error. Vector chart data with proper software applications will enhance safe navigation and provide the mariner with advance electronic warnings of unforeseen dangers. Further, the mariner can control the display of ENC data and remove features from the display that are not important to the safety of the vessel and declutter the screen. Users can selectively display only the information desired while the computer can continue to process all the information for safety of navigation. This allows important features to be more easily viewed.

Marine navigation, route planning, and GIS applications are just some of the uses for the data as a background display. The U.S. Coast Guard (USCG) already uses ENC in several Vessel Traffic Systems (VTS) to monitor ship movements in rivers, harbors, and bays in the U.S. Because ENC is a vector product, categories of data may be individually selected or queried. Because of this data flexibility, ENC is a powerful database supporting various marine and GIS applications. More information on these topics can be found at http://chartmaker.ncd.noaa.gov.

Hydrographic charting and other bathymetric requirements are normally satisfied by one or more of the sonar technologies described in Chapter 9, or by airborne lidar bathymetry described in Chapter 8. Nautical surveying and charting, which includes shoreline mapping, are very time consuming and expensive. Traditional approaches are being taxed to their technical and financial limits. New approaches in data collection and processing are badly needed and beginning to be adopted. Multibeam swath sonar is improving data quality and quantity. Airborne lidar bathymetry is beginning to take some of the load off waterborne vessels in shallow water where the latter may not be safe, practical, or cost effective to operate (see Chapter 8). Many charts are out of date due to environmental changes in shoreline and channels that occur far more rapidly than the survey and chart update rate. Shoaling in navigation channels must be constantly monitored and remedied by dredging. Dredging contractors are paid on the basis of measurements of removed materials.

The U.S. Army Corps of Engineers relies upon accurate bathymetric information to determine where dredging needs to be performed in order to open shipping lanes into ports and harbors and to clear routes for barge traffic on our nation's inland waterways. GPS controls the location of dredges, and GPS-controlled sonar vessels and bathymetric lidar aircraft map the underwater surface prior to dredging operations. Sonar is used to ensure that the correct locations were dredged and to compute the volume of dredged materials. When dredged materials are deposited on land, topographic lidar is common for computing the volume for use in determining payments due.

Shorelines are moving. There are many different legal definitions of shoreline. Bathymetric charts in the U.S. use mean lower low water (MLLW), while land maps use mean high water (MHW). Projects are currently underway to resolve the resulting datum mismatches. The development of DEMs of the land elevation to a single datum as an interim product, independent of the water surface, is a critical step in the resolution of this problem and the production of consistent products for a variety of customers. Furthermore, the boundaries of sovereign nations and their exclusive economic zones (EEZ) are based on bathymetric surveys. Such survey results can have enormous monetary impact.

Most of the port facilities in the U.S. are affected by tidal conditions that make navigation with large container ships difficult and hazardous. The ships need to be aware of under-keel clearance (relative to the channel bottom) and overhead clearance of the ship's superstructure (relative to bridges). Because timing of arrival and departure is critical in all shipping operations, it is important to have reliable elevation information (bathymetry) on a real-time basis for the height of water and bottom of navigation channels. Accurate bathymetry can minimize the use of ballast with ships, an operation where water is used to lower the ship to draw more water so the ship fits under bridges. This operation is not only time consuming, but it is also very expensive. Accurate bathymetry can also limit dependency on tidal conditions; excessive waiting for the right conditions to occur can cause unnecessary delay. Finally, accurate bathymetry is needed during docking operations because adequate clearance is needed for the operation of the crane for loading or unloading containers.

NOS has proven that kinematic GPS (KGPS) with on-the-fly (OTF) ambiguity resolution can provide real-time measurements of a vessel's settlement, squat, trim, roll, pitch, and heading (Huff et al., 1998; Zilkosi et al., 2000). Furthermore KGPS/OTF can provide the position of a vessel's keel in real-time to within 10 centimeters (4 inches) relative to the bottom of the shipping channel. This clearance is critical. Ships that only barely touch the channel bottom are stopped for several days for mandatory inspections. Depending on cargo, every additional inch of draft can be worth tens of thousands of dollars to shippers per voyage, so shippers are tempted to load their ships to the maximum. Ports with shallow channels lose business to competing ports with deeper channels. Ports with up-to-date bathymetric/hydrographic survey data gain business from ports with outdated data.

The DEM environment can serve as an aid in navigating both surface and subsurface vessels (either ROV's or AUV's) as well as a means to integrate a much larger range of data types. Figure 11.13 is an example where orthophotos, navigational charts and a DEM of multibeam bathymetry from Sydney Harbor in Australia have been merged into a single DEM presentation. The feature on the bottom right of the figure is the excavation and backfill for the Sydney Harbor tunnel.

The combination of multiple data sets in a quantitative, georeferenced DEM environment provides the navigator with much more detailed information about the operational area than a standard chart. At the same time, the navigator can be presented with a full 3D perspective view of the position of his vessel with respect to either historical data or, as real-time underkeel clearance systems are developed, with respect to the actual determination of underkeel clearance.

Figure 11.13 Integration of an orthophoto, nautical chart, and multibeam data from Sydney Harbor, Australia. Copyright © 2000 IEEE. See color plate in Appendix C.

UNDERWATER APPLICATIONS

Resource Management

Nautical charts and associated DEMs are also used for assessment and management of coral reefs and other critical environmental resources such as coastal wetlands and ecologically sensitive areas. The combination of multispectral data with bathymetry is a particularly powerful tool which lends itself to DEM representations. Because of the declining health of many coral reefs, this topic has been raised to one of national importance.

Seafloor Morphology

Seafloor morphology is the study of the form and structure of the seafloor, i.e., the physical geography of the seafloor. As demonstrated in the prior section pertaining to marine navigation and safety, complex hydrographic data sets can be represented by a DEM in a natural and intuitive manner. A DEM allows the integration of multiple components or data sets. The integration can be accomplished without compromising the quantitative nature of an individual data set, provided that each of the data sets is properly georeferenced. Artificial sun-illumination and shading of DEM's can be used to form natural looking and easily interpretable, yet quantative underwater scenes. Color can be used to represent depth or other parameters, like acoustic backscatter or sediment properties that may be draped over a DEM.

Using a multibeam sonar data set collected in San Francisco Bay, Figure 11.14 demonstrates a DEM of that underwater environment using color-coding, artificial sun-illumination, and shading. Figure 11.15 is a close-up view of a subset of the DEM presented in Figure 11.14. It is important to note that while such displays offer a natural and detailed view of seafloor morphology, they are also fully quantitative. All points are georeferenced and can be interrogated in the 3D scene for position, depth and any other attribute. Figure 11.15 demonstrates how quantitative information might be extracted from a properly georeferenced DEM. Superimposed on Figure 11.15 are two localized cross-sections of the DEM that show the shape and scale of the bed forms. Two-meter amplitude sand waves and 10-20 centimeter amplitude sand ripples are both discernable in the respective DEM cross-sections.

Figure 11.14 Underwater DEM of San Francisco Bay combined with a USGS DEM of surrounding land areas. Copyright © 2000 IEEE. See color plate in Appendix C.

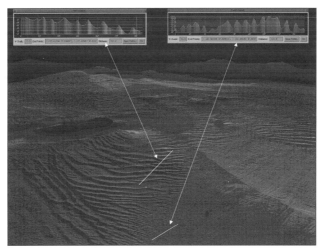

Figure 11.15 Zoom in to a subset of Figure 11.14 showing bed forms of two different scales. Copyright © 2000 IEEE. See color plate in Appendix C.

The quantitative exploration of seafloor morphology and backscatter data in a DEM environment is an extremely useful technique for understanding geologic processes. Figure 11.16 presents the results of a survey conducted off Atlantic City, N.J., where the DEM rendering of a 95-kHz multibeam sonar data set revealed a remarkable array of massive iceberg scours. Such features most likely would have not been recognized in a conventional depth contour presentation. The large scours are 20 m deep and 100 m across. The Head of Tom's Canyon is on the left edge of the image. The shelf break is about 150 m deep. The image represents approximately 30 km distance across the foreground.

Figure 11.16 Color-coded DEM rendering of large iceberg scours off Atlantic City, N.J. Copyright © 2000 IEEE. See color plate in Appendix C.

The planning and deployment of submarine cables and pipelines involves a massive investment of resources as well as huge risks. Fiber-optic cables are now typically plowed into the seafloor at water depths as great as 1500 meters. This creates severe demands for a detailed understanding of seafloor slopes and material types. Pipeline planners have other constraints, with concerns about slopes, spans and substrate stability, all of which require a detailed understanding of the nature of the seafloor on the prospective route. The DEM environment provides a means for the cable and pipeline route planner to integrate the various data sets collected in support of the deployment (e.g., bathymetry, backscatter, video, and even seismic data) into an intuitive and easily interpretable form. Figure 11.17 illustrates the planning route for the Sable Island gas pipeline. The acoustic backscatter (ABS) color code is: Yellow=high ABS, which implies rocks; and Blue=low ABS, which implies sand and/or silt.

Figure 11.17 Acoustic backscatter (ABS) draped on DEM rendering of multibeam bathymetry. Data courtesy of Mobil Oil Co. Copyright © 2000 IEEE. See color plate in Appendix C.

Underwater Archeology

Many important archeology sites are either inherently underwater, or are presently underwater due to rising sea levels. The overlying water makes the task of inspection, monitoring, and conservation of those sites significantly more difficult, particularly as depth increases. Fortunately, it is possible to use high-resolution bathymetric instruments to rapidly acquire information about such marine archeological sites that can be rendered into a DEM.

A DEM provides a basic map of the area of interest, and it also provides 3-D spatial information that is useful for optimizing the bottom time of divers that might be employed in direct inspection of the sites. An example of this application of an underwater DEM is provided by the Scapa Flow Marine Archeology Project (ScapaMAP), which seeks to document the German Imperial Navy ships that were scuttled in Scapa Flow, Scotland on 21 June 1919. Scapa Flow is near the island of Cava in the Orkney Islands of northern Scotland. ScapaMAP was designed to provide basic information on the wrecks in their current condition and to pave the way for further monitoring and sustainable management.

Figure 11.18 presents a color-coded DEM of sonar data taken on the SMS Brummer, a Bremse class light cruiser (4,400 tons, 461 ft. long). The DEM shows where salvage work was performed on the aft section of the hull to remove the valuable non-ferrous materials from the engine room. This DEM also shows significant portions of the hull, forward of the forward superstructure, have collapsed, which, due to the ship resting on its starboard side, has exposed the sub-decks as vertical surfaces.

An underwater DEM of sonar data may also be used to investigate the past history of wrecks that are now long gone. Figure 11.19 shows the remains of the scuttle site of the SMS Bayern, one of a pair of Baden class battleships, at 28,075 tons the heaviest in the German Imperial Navy. The SMS Bayern turned upside down as she flooded, sinking her superstructure into the soft mud of the area. An early salvage attempt using compressed air to raise her failed due to over-pressurization of the hull. This caused the hulk to rise too rapidly, which resulted in tearing out the four main-armament turrets. These turrets can clearly be seen in this color code by depth DEM. The SMS Bayern subsequently sank in the second marked depression and was finally recovered in 1933. The DEM is sufficiently detailed to see the remains of the detached 15" gun barrels and the turning gear used to steer the turrets.

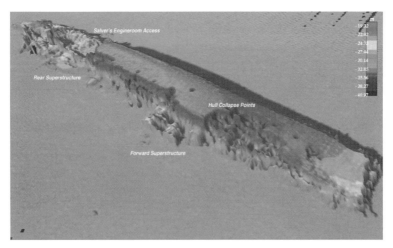

Figure 11.18 DEM of the SMS *Brummer*, resting at 30-meter depth in Scapa Flow. Image courtesy of the Center for Coastal and Ocean Mapping, University of New Hampshire. See color plate in Appendix C.

Figure 11.19 DEM of the Scapa Flow scuttle site of the SMS *Bayern*. Image courtesy of the Center for Coastal and Ocean Mapping, University of New Hampshire. See color plate in Appendix C.

One significant advantage of having a DEM of an archeological site is that the DEM can be used to guide future archeological dives that may be conducted on the site. The visibility in the Scapa Flow area is typically on the order of a few meters and, due to a combination of depth and water temperature, the diver bottom-time is limited to approximately 30 minutes. Under these circumstances, a DEM of the wrecks can provide divers with critical information that may significantly improve the efficiency of the dive work. From the ScapaMAP example, it is clear that DEMs have significant application to marine archeological work.

OTHER TECHNICAL APPLICATIONS

Water Supply and Quality

Everyone knows that a sustained supply of safe drinking water is mandatory worldwide, but few stop to realize the importance of elevation data for wellhead protection, water supply and quality, flood protection, and management of natural systems that support hydrological and ecological functions.

As indicated in EPA, 1989, the 1986 Amendments to the Safe Drinking Water Act (SDWA) established a Wellhead Protection Program (WHP) to protect ground waters that supply wells and well fields that contribute drinking water to public water supply systems serving 50% of all Americans and 95% of rural America. The wellhead protection area (WHPA) is "the surface and subsurface area surrounding a water well, or well field, supplying a public water system, through which contaminants are reasonably likely to move toward and reach such water well or well field." To comply with the SDWA, each State's WHP must: (1) delineate the WHPA for each wellhead, (2) identify sources of contaminants within each WHPA, (3) develop management approaches to protect the water supply within WHPAs from such contaminants, (4) develop contingency plans for each public water supply system to respond to well or well field contamination, and (5) site new wells properly to maximize yield and minimize potential contamination. Without high-resolution, high-accuracy DEMs, compliance with this mandate is essentially impossible. The Southwest Florida Water Management District takes their mission seriously and pays many thousands of dollars per square mile to obtain 1-foot contour data for this purpose.

Stormwater Management

Of all utility system managers, stormwater managers have the greatest need for DEMs for efficient hydrologic and hydraulic (H&H) modeling of watersheds, streams, and channels. Hydrologic models predict volumetric concentrations of water from peak rainfall events, and hydraulic models compute where those waters will go and how flood waters will back-up behind undersized culverts and bridges. Diverse computer models are used for stormwater management.

Subsidence Monitoring

Land subsidence, the loss of surface elevation due to removal of subsurface support, occurs in nearly every state in the United States. Subsidence is one of the most diverse forms of ground failure, ranging from small or local collapses to broad regional lowering of the earth's surface. The major causes of subsidence include: (1) dewatering of peat or organic soils, (2) dissolution in limestone aquifers, (3) first-time wetting of moisture deficient low density soils (known as hydro-compaction), (4) the natural compaction of soil, liquefaction, and crustal deformation, and (5) subterranean mining and withdrawal of fluids (petroleum, geothermal, and ground water).

Figure 11.20 demonstrates the magnitude of the problem in the San Joaquin Valley in California. The sign near the top of the electric pole shows the position of the land surface in 1925; the sign in the middle of the pole shows the elevation in 1955; and the sign on the ground shows the elevation of the ground in 1977 when this amateur photo was taken. Subsidence has continued during the past quarter century. This entire valley has subsided for many miles in all directions.

Figure 11.20 Subsidence in California's San Joaquin Valley. Image courtesy of National Geodetic Survey.

During a recent five year period of drought, the California Department of Water Resources estimated the state's aquifers were being over-drafted at the rate of 10 million acre-feet per year. Unfortunately, the results of over-drafting of aquifers has led to many problems caused by land subsidence, including:

- Changes in elevation and gradient of stream channels, drains, and other water transporting facilities
- Damage to civil engineering structures – weirs, storm drains, sanitary sewers, roads, railroads, canals, levees, and bridges
- Structural damage to private and public buildings
- Failure of well casings from forces generated by compaction of fine-grained materials in aquifer systems
- In some coastal areas, subsidence has resulted in tidal encroachment onto lowlands

The National Research Council (NRC, 1991) conservatively estimated the annual subsidence costs due to increased flooding and structural damage to be in excess of $125 million. These estimates do not include loss of property value due to condemnation, and they do not consider increased farm operating costs (re-grading of land, replacement of pipelines, replacement of damaged wells) in subsiding areas. The NRC estimates annual subsidence costs may be about $400 million nationally, including over $180 million per year for the San Joaquin Valley, California, over $30 million per year for Santa Clara County, California, over $30 million per year for the Houston-Galveston, Texas area, $30 million per year for New Orleans, Louisiana, and $10 million per year the State of Florida. The Louisiana coast line is undergoing constant coastal change, and it is subsiding at an alarming rate – as much as 1.5" per year is some areas. Combined with the predicted sea level rise of 1" every 30 months, millions of people now living in south Louisiana will see this land area and population living at and below sea level by the end of the current century.

Disaster Preparedness and Response

Surveying and mapping, both above and below the water surface, are being used increasingly for coastal wave and storm surge modeling and storm damage assessment. In the 1990's, FEMA embarked on a full-scale effort to help build safer communities. FEMA's goals included increased public awareness of hazards and loss reduction (mitigation) measures, reducing the risk of loss of life and property, and protecting our nation's communities and the economy from all types of natural and technological hazards. Two FEMA reports are referenced.

The first report (FEMA, 1997a) indicated that the overall costs of disasters to the United States has grown significantly over the last decade; the average annual losses have increased to $13 billion. The good news, however, is that *mitigation works*, and many things can be done to reduce the impact of future disasters. During Hurricane Opal in Florida in 1995, none of the 576 major habitable structures located seaward of the Coastal Construction Control Line (CCCL), and permitted by the State under current standards, sustained substantial damage. By contrast, 768 of the 1,366 pre-existing major habitable structures seaward of the CCCL sustained substantial damage.

A second report (FEMA, 1997b) identified and assessed risks for various types of natural and technological hazards. Many of those risks, especially flood, coastal erosion, and hurricane tidal surges, are elevation based. Even wildfire damage models are based on DTM and DSM elevations because fire fuel is estimated by subtracting the DTM elevations from the DSM elevations, and wildfires spread faster in steeper terrain. Thus, improved elevation data in computer models leads to improved risk identification and mitigation.

Floodplain Management

According to *A Common Sense Strategy* (June 2001) published by the Association of State Floodplain Managers (ASFPM), the average annual flood losses in the 1980's were $3.3 billion, and the average annual flood losses in the 1990's were $5.6 billion. This is a very dangerous trend that has continued unimpeded into the 21st century. FEMA estimates that over 9,000,000 households and $390 billion in property are at risk from flooding. Flood risks continue to worsen as trees are cut down and land is covered with concrete and asphalt, resulting in more rain water that previously would have soaked into the ground or stored in natural holding areas, flowing into floodplains. Another cause of increased flood risk is fill placed within floodplains to accommodate new construction. When obsolete flood studies are replaced by newer studies, it is common for base flood elevations (BFEs) to increase by several feet. Because a house doesn't move, it's risk of flooding increases continually because of the adverse impact of other development.

A third FEMA report (FEMA, 1997c) indicates that only one-third to one-half of U.S. floodplains are studied by *detailed* methods which compute the BFEs. Instead, over half use *approximate* methods in which BFEs are not computed. Furthermore, over 2,700 flood prone communities are <u>un</u>studied. These studies have been used to justify FEMA's current Map Modernization Program to address these issues.

High accuracy DEMs are needed to: (1) establish accurate flood risk criteria, (2) automate the hydrologic and hydraulic (H&H) analyses needed to rapidly and cost-effectively produce accurate and complete flood hazard information for the entire nation, (3) cost effectively support implementation of FEMA's Map Modernization Plan, and (4) yield the full benefits of proactive floodplain management.

Most current management approaches for reducing flood losses allow for construction to occur without considering the adverse impacts on other properties within the watershed. This has contributed to steadily rising flood losses and is increasing the potential for future flood damage. ASFPM supports a No Adverse Impact (NAI) approach to floodplain management which assumes that the harm caused by construction on neighboring properties and communities can no longer be ignored. Figure 11.21 demonstrates the effects of fill in one portion of a floodplain impacting other buildings in the floodplain previously unaffected by floods. Not just construction within the floodplain, but construction anywhere in the watershed can increase the flood risk to other properties. This risk includes increases in flood levels, flood velocity, erosion and sedimentation.

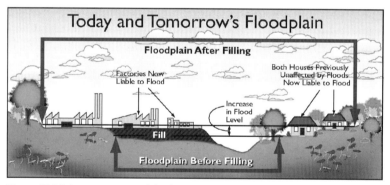

Figure 11.21 Image courtesy of the Association of State Floodplain Managers (ASFPM). If large areas of the floodplain are filled, then there will be an increase in the land area needed to store flood waters. This means other homes or businesses may be impacted. See color plate in Appendix C.

Mitigation refers to activities that lessen the potential for future flood damages. Examples include elevating structures above the predicted flood level, enhancing the natural flood storage of a floodplain with retention basins, mapping flood hazard areas based on future developed conditions, or updating floodplain ordinances to reflect the most recent flood data. Accurate digital elevation data are key to NAI and other proactive floodplain management initiatives. ASFPM's web site is www.floods.org. Information on NAI can be obtained from the web site or by e-mailing asfpm@floods.org.

Seismic Monitoring

Along seismic fault zones, including sites of volcanic and tectonic unrest, there is a need for high-resolution, high-accuracy DEMs collected in advance of earthquakes and volcanoes in order to establish a baseline for comparison with post-disaster conditions. Such DEMs are critical both for monitoring the on-going movement of the earth in areas of high seismic activity, as well as locating and assessing damage following major events. The City of Los Angeles, for example, had many problems and a great deal of uncertainty in evaluating locations of subsurface damage to utilities following the Northridge Earthquake of 1994. Major vertical change is a direct indication of subsurface damage. Being able to quickly monitor change is key to emergency response. Many of these problems had their root causes in the fact that there were not only different vertical datums within the Los Angeles basin, but that a great many of the vertical reference points (bench marks) the engineers and scientists were relying on had themselves become doubtful as a result of seismic activity and subsidence (discussed above).

Geological Applications

Digital elevation models have a variety of uses in geology, geomorphology, geophysics, and related fields. Typical applications include:

- Generation of shaded relief images with variable illumination angles, topographic contour maps, and other derivative products to support mapping of land forms and geologic hazards such as landslides and faults.
- Empirical and process-based geologic hazard modeling based on topographic variables such as slope angle, curvature, soil shear strength, and pore water pressure.
- Surface water or rainfall/runoff modeling.
- Generation of topographic profiles for use in groundwater modeling, slope stability, or earthquake hazard studies.

Derivative maps depicting variables such as slope angle, residual topography, and various measures of topographic roughness can be particularly useful for identifying landforms when layered over shaded relief images and covered with topographic contours. See Figure 11.22.

The level of DEM detail required for geoscientific applications depends on the scale of the problem. The Global 30 Arc-Second Elevation Dataset (GTOPO30) may be adequate for continental scale studies, whereas 1 or 3 arc second Shuttle Radar Topography Mission (SRTM) DEMs may be adequate for studies of sub-continental scale features such as individual mountain ranges or sedimentary basins. Detailed mapping at the 7.5' quadrangle scale is best undertaken using data equivalent to USGS

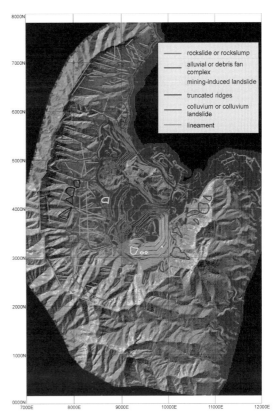

Figure 11.22 Terrain hazard and slope angle maps draped over a shaded relief image of the Louise caldera, Lihir Island, Papua New Guinea. The oval-shaped volcanic caldera collapsed catastrophically about 200,000 years ago and now contains a significant gold deposit. The shaded relief and slope angle maps were based on a 2 m lidar DEM produced for landslide hazard mapping under dense jungle cover surrounding the open pit mine in the center of the caldera. Image courtesy of William C. Haneberg. See color plate in Appendix C.

National Elevation Dataset (NED) 10 m DEMs or better, and high resolution 2 to 5 m lidar DEMs are becoming increasingly important tools for detailed mapping as prices decrease. IFSAR DEMs with 5 m postings are now becoming commercially available within the United States and Europe, and will likely become cost-effective geoscientific tools for intermediate or quadrangle scale mapping.

The magnitude and spatial variability of DEM elevation errors can be an important consideration in quantitative geoscientific applications. Comparison of DEMs with GPS ground measurements has shown that 10 to 30 m DEMs can yield slope angle measurements with standard deviations of $\pm3°$ to $\pm5°$, whereas lidar DEMs can yield slope angle standard of $\pm2°$ to $\pm3°$. Slope angle uncertainties of this magnitude can have significant effects on the reliability of DEM-based slope stability models.

Differential IFSAR, which uses radar images obtained at different times to produce millimeter scale estimates of elevation change, has proven to be especially valuable for monitoring surface deformation arising as a consequence of geologic processes. It has been used to map movement related to groundwater overdraft, earthquakes, landslides, and the movement of magma beneath volcanoes over periods ranging from months to years.

USGS and the Bureau of Land Management (BLM) have collaborated on an interdisciplinary effort to address science questions associated with land management and water quality for a study area of western Colorado underlain by Mancos Shale, a widespread unit which is a suspected prime contributor of salts and selenium to the upper Colorado River watershed. General research efforts include better understanding of spatial variations in geomorphology, vegetation, geology, soil type, soil chemistry, and mineralogy, and physical and chemical processes responsible for these variations. Salt, sediment, and selenium loading of the Upper Colorado River is a specific concern and focal point of this project. The Gunnison and Uncompahgre River basins, which encompass the study area, provide a majority of the salt, sediment, and selenium to the Colorado River. These waters flow naturally, and are piped to a wide region of the southwest United States and California. The presence of salts alone, as alkaline water, requires approximately $330 million dollars per year (as of this writing) to desalinate the water and repair the damage caused to public and private utilities. Project team members hope the results from this study will enable scientists and land managers to be predictive at both the scale of the study site and the Mancos Shale landscapes of the west.

One primary task of this project is the modeling and visualization of the landscape of the project area. A particularly important goal within this task is the quantification of high resolution slope and aspect areas from the best-available elevation data. Slope and aspect are critical factors that influence runoff, sedimentation, soil chemistry, and vegetation. Early work used standard 10-meter USGS DEM data downloaded from the National Elevation Dataset (NED) site (http://seamless.usgs.gov) and 2-meter DEM data synthesized from USGS topographic contour lines, but the desired slope and aspect information derived from both this 10- and 2-meter data was inadequate because of the low horizontal (spatial) resolution. One-meter bare-earth lidar was collected over the study area to rectify this problem, and the resulting slope and aspect information derived from the lidar greatly improved the geomorphologic modeling. Figure 11.23 shows the representative sizes of 30-, 10-, 2-, and 1-meter elevation (and, thus, slope) grid cells on a typical area within the study site. Note that the larger the cell footprint, the more attenuation, or smoothing, of the true surface that will occur in the elevation model. Figure 11.24 shows a comparison of the 10-, 2-, and 1-meter hillshaded elevation and derived slope datasets.

Preliminary results of the study should be available through USGS publication outlets by late 2006.

Figure 11.23 Varying grid-cell footprints superimposed on typical Mancos Shale terrain. Image courtesy of USGS. See color plate in Appendix C.

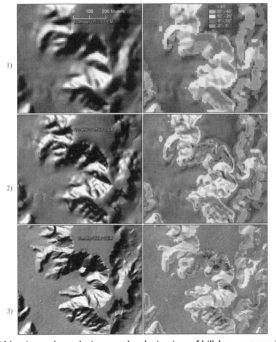

Figure 11.24 Effect of DEM horizontal resolution on the derivation of hillslope categories. 1a and 1b) 10-meter USGS DEM and associated slope categories. 2a and 2b) 2-meter DEM made from USGS 1:24,000-scale contours and associated slope categories. 3a and 3b) 1-meter bare-earth lidar DEM and associated slope categories. Images courtesy of USGS. See color plate in Appendix C.

MILITARY APPLICATIONS

In the U.S. Department of Defense (DoD), DEMs are called Digital Terrain Elevation Data (DTED), and most DTED datasets are produced by the National Geospatial-Intelligence Agency (NGA) or cooperating agencies from other countries with which NGA has mapping agreements. Typical DTED military applications include the following:

- Intervisibility (line-of-sight) for optimal positioning of communications, command, control and intelligence (C^{3}I) and weapon systems
- Cover and concealment planning, i.e., using the terrain to best advantage so that enemy ground forces cannot see friendly forces and engage them with direct line-of-sight weapons

- Cross country movement analyses, using DTED as one of several factors in determining the ease or difficulty in off-road movement of military vehicles
- Near shore bathymetry as needed for amphibious landings and logistics-over-the-shore support
- Terrain contour matching for guidance of cruise missiles
- Terrain avoidance for military aircraft
- Battlefield "fly-throughs" and simulation for mission planning and rehearsal

Many DoD R&D projects of past decades, involving different levels of DTED, have had direct benefits to the civilian community. Many of the GIS technologies in use today had their foundations in DoD. Furthermore, digital photogrammetry, IFSAR, topographic lidar, airborne lidar bathymetry, and sonar all had roots in DoD. GPS technology alone, on which all modern DEM technologies are dependent to some degree, is totally a result of DoD funding and ingenuity in using satellite technology to enable many of the DEM applications that follow. GPS technology became so indispensable to the civilian world that civilian applications came to overshadow many of the military applications for which GPS was originally funded.

COMMERCIAL APPLICATIONS

In two previous sections, many of the transportation and engineering applications are commercial, but with a public safety focus:

- How DEMs from photogrammetry or lidar are used for efficient highway and interchange design and construction, avoiding the safety hazards to land surveyors
- How real-time bathymetric data can increase marine navigation and safety (and profitability)
- How real-time terrain avoidance systems use DEMs for safety (and profitability)
- How high accuracy DEMs are needed for water supply and quality and for stormwater management
- How subsidence can be economically devastating to a community in many different ways, and how DEMs map the magnitude of the subsidence
- How buildings should be constructed so that they are not disaster-prone, or add to the hazards of others in floodplains and coastal high hazard areas

The following commercial applications for DEMs are less focused on public safety, and are more focused on entrepreneurial considerations. Many additional commercial applications undoubtedly exist and are just waiting to be documented.

Precision Farming

As reported in NGS, 1998, the agriculture community is undergoing a technological revolution as a result of its use of GIS and GPS technologies. The U.S. Department of Transportation, 1998, documents the benefits of these technologies to precision farming, because farmers are major users of the Nationwide Differential GPS (NDGPS) network. Using DEMs in conjunction with georeferenced (location-stamped) information regarding tillage, seeds planted, weeds, insect and disease infestations, cultivation and irrigation, farmers have been able to go from managing their farms by the acre to doing so by the square foot.

Precision farming enables farmers to implement best management practices (BMPs) through the careful control of the quantity of water, fertilizer and pesticides placed on different areas of land, depending upon soil type and condition, slope, and other factors. DEMs have special relevance because slopes determine the direction in which runoff will flow, and runoff could adversely impact unintended areas. For these reasons, the agriculture industry needs good vertical and horizontal control and accurate DEMs.

In recent years, the application of DGPS and DEM technologies has had the added benefit of reducing the quantity of herbicides, insecticides, and fertilizer. This has led to a decrease of the adverse environmental impact of these products. Additionally, the more effective use of insecticides, herbicides, and fertilizer has led to the decreased use of these products and increases in farm productivity, and has a direct impact on water quality and soil conservation. The reduction in the cost to produce foodstuffs will be carried to the consumer in lower costs for higher quality and safer food.

Recreation

Lidar DEMs have been acquired of the Grand Canyon, Yellowstone National Park, ski resorts (for snow grooming purposes), national forests, state parks, and beaches (both lakeside and ocean-front). Beach replenishment projects are often based on lidar surveys that show the location and volume of sand that needs to be added. Such projects often have dual benefits to help preserve the environment while enhancing the recreational value of the terrain. Often multiple data sets are acquired for change detection purposes. DEMs obviously have broad appeal to a variety of users in diverse industries.

Real Estate, Banking, Mortgage, and Insurance Industries

Real estate agents who list properties for sale need to know the flood risk of their listings, and the banking/mortgage/insurance industries need to know the flood risk of buildings they will be mortgaging or insuring. Flood risk determinations are important for many commercial applications, and not just to individual homeowners.

Many instances have been found where builders construct new homes below elevations authorized on building permits. This commonly occurs when an area shown to be used for unfinished storage or parking on building permits ends up being converted into unauthorized walk-out basements, or when lowest floor elevations are assigned to the main floor rather than to the basement floor – especially walk-out basements. These are typical "buyer beware" situations where neither the homeowner nor the mortgage or insurance representatives have any reason to suspect that anything is wrong. Many cases have been found where new buildings have been constructed with lowest floor elevations below the base flood elevation, in spite of building codes to the contrary. As documented in (FEMA, 2005), the flood insurance industry is attempting to develop an e-rating system to automatically identify flood risks, and lidar technology offers significant potential because of its ability to blanket the terrain with a high density mass points, as explained in Chapter 7. For these reasons, the real estate, banking, mortgage, and insurance industries need computer models that accurately depict flood risks for individual buildings, based on the elevations of the lowest adjacent grades that surround buildings in or near floodplains. For this purpose, the GPS Elevation Certificates, described below, have significant importance.

INDIVIDUAL APPLICATIONS

Sometimes a DEM user turns out to be an individual homeowner who uses the information from others who performed the computer modeling of the terrain. The best example of this is with an Elevation Certificate used to determine the flood risk of a house that someone wants to buy with a Federally guaranteed mortgage. Before approving the mortgage, Federal law requires that a determination be made as to whether or not the building requires flood insurance. An entire *map determination industry* exists, based on determinations of where the house is located horizontally with respect to the Special Flood Hazard Area (SFHA) boundaries shown on FEMA's FIRMs or DFIRMs. If the house is a pre-FIRM structure (meaning it was built before the publication of an effective FIRM for that area) located within the SFHA, the owner can acquire flood insurance at subsided rates, regardless of the building's lowest floor elevation (LFE) or lowest adjacent grade (LAG). If the house is a post-FIRM structure, the community should have required an Elevation Certificate to prove that the LFE as built is higher than the base flood elevation (BFE) for that location — to demonstrate that the new building shouldn't be flooded by the 100-year (1% annual chance) flood. Many communities also require "freeboards" one or more feet above the BFE, or they consider future conditions that continuously worsen flood risks. (*Freeboard* means a factor of safety usually expressed in feet above a flood level for purposes of floodplain management. Freeboard tends to compensate for the many unknown factors that could contribute to predicted flood elevations.) It is possible for a pre-FIRM home within a SFHA to be exempt from mandatory flood insurance purchase requirements if an Elevation Certificate proves that it too was built with a LAG that is higher than the BFE. Conventional Elevation Certificates (FEMA Form 81-31) can be produced with traditional survey procedures that are non-digital and don't require computers.

The advent of GIS and GPS technologies, however, changed the flood risk determination process into one that does include digital elevation data used for computer modeling of flood risks for individual homeowners. This is best exemplified with the GPS Elevation Certificate (see example at Figure 11.25). Such GPS Elevation Certificates are mass-produced by communities with proactive floodplain management programs, because knowledge of three factors enable accurate estimates of damages expected from standard predictable flood events, i.e., 10-, 50-, 100-, and 500-year floods. Those three factors are: (1) LFE and LAG elevations compared with upstream and downstream BFEs, (2) building "footprint" area, and (3) pre-flood replacement value. Thus flood damages to individual buildings, and to the community as a whole, can be accurately estimated (predicted) so that proactive steps can be taken in advance to mitigate future flood losses to a flood prone community.

GPS Elevation Certificates normally show all information on a conventional FEMA Elevation

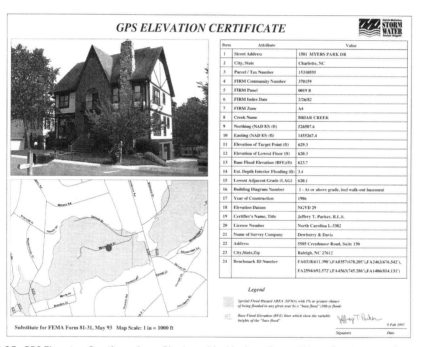

Figure 11.25 GPS Elevation Certificate from Charlotte Mecklenburg Storm Water Services; certificate prepared by Dewberry. See color plate in Appendix C.

Certificate, plus the background map. The center of the map shows the location of the building relative to the surrounding street network. The blue area shows the SFHA (100-year floodplain), with the floodway and 500-year floodplain shown with different shades of blue, where applicable. The red lines show the nearest upstream and downstream BFE elevations for comparison with the building's LAG and LFE. Rigorous GPS survey procedures are used, relative to survey monuments in the National Spatial Reference System (NSRS), to ensure network accuracy of all elevations and to ensure accurate registration to the background map or digital orthophotos to which the survey data would be linked in the community GIS.

Such GIS information is used proactively to determine who really needs flood insurance; to identify candidates for elevation or structure acquisition projects; to perform benefit-cost analyses for elevation/acquisition; to perform benefit-cost analyses to determine whether costs can be justified to improve bridges and culverts that currently are undersized for carrying 100-year flood flows and therefore cause flood elevations to increase upstream of the structure; for emergency warning/response; for mitigation planning; and for flood control projects (levees, floodwalls). Finally, when floods actually occur, it is only necessary to survey the actual flood elevations at selected locations (e.g., 14th Street bridge, 9th Street bridge, and 2nd Street bridge) to model the actual flood elevations in the community which, when compared with known LFE's of individual buildings, enable accurate damage estimates to be made immediately so that relief can be expedited. Not only does this enable accurate estimates of flood damages to individual buildings, without having to wait for individual post-flood surveys to be performed, but it accurately estimates flood damages to the community as a whole.

Charlotte-Mecklenburg County, NC, was the first community to acquire GPS Elevation Certificates for all flood prone buildings, and they quickly recovered the total costs involved by numerous benefits of proactive floodplain management. Charlotte-Mecklenburg now make their GPS Elevation Certificates available on a storm water services web site available to all. See www.stormwaterservices.com.

The example GPS Elevation Certificate at Figure 11.22 shows several interesting features. First, with the lowest floor elevation (LFE) 3.4 feet below the BFE, this new house was probably renovated at some point in possible violation of local building codes if the lowest level includes utilities (furnace, air conditioning unit, hot water heater) or habitable space; 43 other expensive, new homes in this area also had LFE's below their BFEs because of walk-out basements or drive-in garages at the lowest level. Second, this certificate shows five different BFEs varying in elevation from 626 feet to 621 moving downstream, over a distance of approximately 4,000 feet. Third, at the culvert two blocks east of this house, the BFE is two feet higher immediately up-stream of the culvert (626'), compared with immediately downstream of the culvert (624'), because the culvert is undersized for carrying the 100-year stream flow, thus acting as a dam to worsen the flooding by 2 feet for upstream buildings. Such information is vital for benefit-cost analyses to determine whether it is cost-effective to replace the culvert with a larger one. That's what "proactive floodplain management" is all about.

Wherever such GPS Elevation Certificates have been mass produced by communities or by FEMA (normally in post-disaster scenarios), homeowners have begged to receive copies of those certificates for various purposes to avoid the typical higher costs for contracting separately for individual Elevation Certificates. Furthermore, according to FIA, 1994, for flood insurance, an elevation difference of one foot can mean the difference between $1,160 and $450 in annual premiums for $100,000 coverage. Do homeowner needs for accurate Elevation Certificates make them DEM users? Yes, and they often don't even own a computer.

SUMMARY

Before this book was ever published, ASPRS recognized that the "DEM world" is growing so fast that it's almost unconceivable today what DEMs will be used for tomorrow.

In this section, DEM users have been defined as extremely diverse, to include military personnel, pilots, marine navigators, underwater archeologists, real estate agents, bankers and mortgage lenders, insurance salesmen, emergency response managers, floodplain managers, community managers and planners, seismic engineers, transportation engineers, infrastructure managers (especially those responsible for water supply and quality), civil and structural engineers, storm water managers, telecommunications system planners, construction engineers, precision farmers, foresters, recreation and environmental managers, and individual homeowners.

They either use or benefit from DEMs in someone's computer that models the terrain (both above and below water) to make a DEM-related assessment or decision. Like the homeowner who isn't sure if he/she really needs to purchase flood insurance or not, many may not recognize themselves as DEM users. Furthermore, in our colleges and universities, there are thousands of students performing research, using DEMs for new applications. Each day, USGS' web site receives thousands of "hits" from people inquiring about the availability of DEMs. We may not know just what DEM users look like, or what they need the DEMs for, but like the *Field of Dreams* movie, if we build DEMs, the users will come for the data. Once high-accuracy DEMs are available, many will wonder how they ever survived without them. Similarly, if we develop "The National Map" as described above, or the National Elevation Dataset (NED) described in Chapter 4, using all the new technologies now at our disposal, we will be amazed at the number of users.

Lastly, the sample DEMs on the DVD enclosed with this manual are intended to help users understand DEM technologies and applications, with actual hands-on datasets, so solutions can continue to be developed to solve the problems of mankind.

AUTHOR BIOGRAPHIES

Dave Maune is a senior Project Manager for mapping and GPS/GIS services at Dewberry in Fairfax, VA. He manages major Dewberry contracts with USGS, NOAA, USDA and other agencies that require the production of DEMs from cartographic source materials, lidar, IFSAR, and/or photogrammetry. He provides DEM consulting services to FEMA and to FEMA's contractors and mapping partners, and he served as FEMA's representative on the Technical Subcommittee of the National Digital Elevation Program (NDEP). He is also a consultant to individual states, counties, and local communities needing help in defining their needs for digital elevation data and in performing independent DEM accuracy assessments. He was the principal author of the National Geodetic Survey's (NGS) *National Height Modernization Study Report to Congress*, (NGS, 1998) and editor of the DEM chapter in ASPRS' *Digital Photogrammetry: An Addendum to the Manual of Photogrammetry*. Maune earned his MS and PhD degrees in Geodetic Science and Photogrammetry from the Ohio State University in 1970 and 1973 respectively. He is a retired Colonel in the U.S. Army Corps of Engineers, having retired as Director of the U.S. Army Topographic Engineering Center (TEC) at Fort Belvoir, VA. He previously served as Director, Defense Mapping School (DMS), and Inspector General, Defense Mapping Agency (DMA) — now the National Geospatial-Intelligence Agency (NGA). He is an ASPRS Fellow.

ACKNOWLEDGEMENTS

The author wishes to acknowledge the significant contributions of NOAA, especially the Coastal Services Center and the National Geodetic Survey's Remote Sensing Division, both of which contributed explanations and images for the Coastal Mapping Applications section of this chapter. The Coastal Services Center in turn expressed appreciation for input received from the Maine Geological Survey and the South Carolina Office of Ocean and Coastal Resource Management. Two former long-term NOAA employees, Lloyd Huff and Gary Guenther, contributed explanations and images for the Marine Navigation and Safety and Underwater Applications sections in the first edition of this manual, with content updated in this second edition; their biographies can be found in Chapters 8 and 9 for which they served as principal authors. The author wishes to acknowledge the contributions from William C. Haneberg and John J. Kosevich who contributed explanations and images for the Geological Applications section of this chapter. Other major portions of this chapter were drawn from (NGS, 1998), prepared by Dewberry for NGS; much information from that report is included in this chapter with permission of the NGS Director.

REFERENCES

EPA, 1989. Wellhead protection programs: Tools for local governments, U.S. Environmental Protection Agency, April 1989, *EPA/440/6-89-002*, Washington, DC., pg. 3.

EPA, 1997. Global warming, The probability of sea level rise, U.S. Environmental Protection Agency, *EPA Report No. 230-R-95-008*, Washington, DC.

FAA, 1996. Standards for aeronautical surveys and related products, Federal Aviation Administration, September 1, 1996, *FAA No. 405*, Washington, DC., pp. 3.1-3.10.

FEMA, 1997a. *Report on Costs and Benefits of Natural Hazard Mitigation*, Federal Emergency Management Agency, Washington, DC., pp. 1 and 33.

FEMA, 1997b. *MULTI HAZARD, Identification and Risk Assessment, A Cornerstone of the National Mitigation Strategy*, Federal Emergency Management Agency, Washington, DC., p.i.

FEMA, 1997c. *Modernizing FEMA's Flood Hazard Mapping Program, A Progress Report*, Federal Emergency Management Agency, Washington, DC., pp. 11 and 19.

FEMA, 2005. *Evaluation of Alternatives in Obtaining Structural Elevation Data*, Federal Emergency Management Agency, Washington, DC.

FIA, 1994. *Flood Insurance Manual*, Federal Insurance Administration, 1994 Edition, Revised October 1, 1997, p. "Rate 4."

Hubbard, R., 2001. Print on demand, *Ocean Navigator, No. 111*, January/February, pp. 74-79.

Long, James, 1998. Black Thunder's roar: Mining for solutions with RTK GPS," *GPS World*, pp. 23-28.

Huff, L. C., Gallagher, B. J., and Snead, E.C., 1998. On-the-fly GPS for determination of vertical ship motions, *Proc. MTS Ocean Community Conference '98*, November 16-19, Baltimore MD, Volume 2, 785-791.

Mayer, L. A., et al., 2000. Interactive 3-D visualization: A tool for seafloor navigation, exploration and engineering, *Proceedings IEEE/MTS Oceans 2000*, Vol 2; pp 913-920.

NGS, 1998. *National Height Modernization Study Report to Congress*, National Geodetic Survey.

NRC, 1991. *Mitigating Losses from Land Subsidence in the United States*, National Research Council, Washington, DC., National Academy Press.

Parrish, C.E., G.H. Tuell, W.E. Carter, and R.L. Shrestha, 2005. Configuring an airborne laser scanner for detecting airport obstructions, *Photogrammetric Engineering & Remote Sensing*, 71(1).

Shrestha, R.L., and B. Carter, 1998. Instant evaluation of beach storm damage using airborne laser terrain mapping, *EOM,* March, pp. 42-44.

U.S. Department of Transportation, 1998. *Nationwide Differential GPS Report*, Washington, DC., March, p. 64.

Zilkoski, D.B., Yorczyk, R.A., Gallagher, B.J., Huff, L.C., and Martin, D.M., 2000. NOAA proposes real-time GPS applications to position ships, *Proc. PACON 2000 (Recent Advances in Marine Science and Technology)*, Ninth Pacific Congress on Marine Science and Technology, June 5-9, Honolulu, HI, pp.155-166.

Chapter 12

DEM Quality Assessment

Timothy A. Blak

GOALS AND DEFINITIONS

This chapter has three basic goals:

1. To explain procedures for quantitative assessment of bare-earth DTMs to ensure conformance with topographic data accuracy requirements specified by users, including the Federal Emergency Management Agency (FEMA), and to explain accuracy testing and reporting procedures recommended by the Federal Geographic Data Committee (FGDC), National Digital Elevation Program (NDEP) and American Society for Photogrammetry and Remote Sensing (ASPRS).
2. To explain procedures for qualitative assessment of bare-earth DTMs to ensure topographic products are usable for their intended purposes.
3. To explain NOAA's procedures for qualitative assessment of Multibeam sonar DTMs to ensure bathymetric and hydrographic products are usable for their intended purposes.

Quality Assurance (QA) – Steps taken: (1) to ensure the end client receives the quality products it pays for, consistent with the Scope of Work, and/or (2) to ensure an organization's Quality Program works effectively. Quality Programs include quality control procedures for specific products as well as overall Quality Plans that typically mandate an organization's communication procedures, document and data control procedures, quality audit procedures, and training programs necessary for delivery of quality products and services.

Quality Control (QC) – Steps taken by data producers to ensure delivery of products that satisfy standards, guidelines and specifications identified in the Scope of Work. These steps typically include production flow charts with built-in procedures to ensure quality at each step of the work flow, in-process quality reviews, and/or final quality inspections prior to delivery of products to a client.

Independent QA/QC – Steps taken by a QA/QC specialty firm, hired by the client (e.g., government or data producer) to independently validate the effectiveness of the data producer's quality processes.

DEM Quality Assessment – Steps taken to test and report the accuracy of a digital elevation dataset and evaluate its usability. This includes quantitative assessment of data accuracy as well as qualitative assessment of data usability. It is not only possible, but common, for digital elevation datasets to pass vertical accuracy testing requirements and still fail other quality factors that adversely impact the usability of the elevation data.

QUANTITATIVE ASSESSMENT OF DIGITAL TOPOGRAPHIC DATA

Chapter 3 documents the guidelines and specifications relevant to the quantitative accuracy assessment of digital elevation data, presented in chronological sequence for their dates of publication. Highlights from Chapter 3 are summarized below. Unless specified to the contrary, much of the Accuracy Assessment portion of this chapter was extracted from (NDEP, 2004), drafted by the editor of this manual; these NDEP guidelines, in turn, were developed largely from content and recommendations contained in the 1st edition of this manual (ASPRS, 2001).

National Map Accuracy Standard (NMAS)

The NMAS (Bureau of the Budget, 1947) is relevant today only for (paper) maps published with a specific contour interval. The NMAS tests and reports the vertical accuracy of contours at the 90 percent confidence level whereby 90% of elevation test points should be accurate within one-half the published contour interval.

National Standard for Spatial Data Accuracy (NSSDA)

The NSSDA (FGDC, 1998) is relevant to all forms of digital elevation data. The NSSDA tests and reports the vertical accuracy of digital elevation data at the 95 percent confidence level, but accuracy thresholds are defined by user requirements (see Chapter 13, DEM User Requirements).

The NSSDA specifies that accuracy should be reported at the 95 percent confidence level for data tested by an independent source of higher accuracy for horizontal and/or vertical accuracy as:

Tested __ (meters, feet) horizontal accuracy at 95 percent confidence level
Tested __ (meters, feet) vertical accuracy at 95 percent confidence level

Accuracy$_r$ (= RMSE$_r$ x 1.7308) defines the horizontal (radial) accuracy at the 95 percent confidence level, and Accuracy$_z$ (= RMSE$_z$ x 1.9600) defines the vertical accuracy at the 95 percent confidence level. RMSE statistics are valid only when errors follow a normal (bell curve) distribution. An assumption of normal error distribution is erroneous for lidar datasets (and possibly for other datasets as well) where topographic elevations are complicated by uncertainty in the classification of vegetation from the bare-earth terrain. Errors in classification of vegetation are non-random and non-normal. Also, lidar elevations on asphalt often have systematic errors due to laser absorption.

The NSSDA further states that an alternative "compiled to meet" statement should be used when the guidelines for testing by an independent source of higher accuracy cannot be followed and an alternative means is used to evaluate accuracy. Accuracy should be reported at the 95 percent confidence level for data produced according to procedures that have been consistently demonstrated to achieve particular horizontal and/or vertical accuracy values as:

Compiled to meet __ (meters, feet) horizontal accuracy at 95 percent confidence level
Compiled to meet __ (meters, feet) vertical accuracy at 95 percent confidence level

FEMA Guidelines and Specifications

(FEMA, 2003) establishes accuracy thresholds by requiring digital elevation data to have accuracies equivalent to 2-foot contours in floodplains that are essentially flat (the majority of floodplains) or equivalent to 4-foot contours for floodplains that are hilly to mountainous, but leaving it up to Project Engineers to tailor project requirements to local needs and funds available. (FEMA, 2003) essentially follows NSSDA procedures explained in Chapter 3.

(FEMA, 2003) became the lidar industry's *de facto* standard by encouraging the use of selected breaklines; by providing specific guidance for selection/location of QA/QC checkpoints; and by requiring that 20 or more checkpoints be used for accuracy testing in each of the major land cover categories representative of the floodplain being modeled with the lidar data. FEMA requires a minimum of three land cover categories (60 checkpoints) but typically uses 100 checkpoints, i.e., 20 each for five common land cover categories:

- Open terrain
- Weeds and crops
- Scrub and bushes
- Forested
- Built-up areas

The land cover categories will vary by geographic location and could be different than those listed here.

National Digital Elevation Program (NDEP) Guidelines

(NDEP, 2004) expanded upon the User Requirements Menu and arguments presented in the first edition of this *DEM Users Manual* (ASPRS, 2001) that elevation errors in vegetated terrain are typically high with non-normal error distribution, and elevation errors on black asphalt are typically low with non-normal error distribution. These land cover categories are subject to "outliers" that unfairly skew RMSE calculations. This means that four of the five major land cover categories used by FEMA may have errors that do not follow a normal error distribution. The NDEP accepted the recommendations from the editor of (ASPRS, 2001) that the 95th percentile errors should be used in areas where elevation errors may potentially not follow a normal distribution, and that the RMSE methodology be used only in open terrain where errors should follow a normal error distribution.

The NDEP mandates the use of Fundamental Vertical Accuracy (FVA) in open terrain, and provides for the optional use of Supplemental Vertical Accuracy (SVA) in other individual land cover categories and Consolidated Vertical Accuracy (CVA) in all land cover categories combined. FVA is calculated at the 95 percent confidence level as a function of $RMSE_z$. SVA and CVA are calculated at the 95th percentile, where 95% of elevation errors have elevation errors equal to or less than the 95th percentile.

Fundamental Vertical Accuracy Test

Using check points in open terrain only:

1. Compute the vertical $RMSE_z = sqrt[\sum (z_{data\ i} - z_{check\ i})^2/n]$ (See explanations for Computing Errors, below).
2. Compute $Accuracy_z = 1.9600 * RMSE_z$ = vertical accuracy at 95 percent confidence level.
3. Report FVA as "**Tested _____ (meters, feet) fundamental vertical accuracy at 95 percent confidence level in open terrain using $RMSE_z$ x 1.9600.**"

Supplemental Vertical Accuracy Tests

When testing ground cover categories or combinations of categories excluding open terrain:

1. Compute 95th percentile error (described above) for each category (or combination of categories).
2. Report SVA as "**Tested _____ (meters, feet) supplemental vertical accuracy at 95th percentile in (specify land cover category or categories)**"
3. In the metadata, document the errors larger than the 95th percentile. For a small number of errors above the 95th percentile, report x/y coordinates and z-error for each QC check point error larger than the 95th percentile. For a large number of errors above the 95th percentile, report only the quantity and range of values.

Consolidated Vertical Accuracy Test

When 40 or more checkpoints are consolidated for two or more of the major land cover categories, representing both the open terrain and other land cover categories, a consolidated vertical accuracy assessment may be reported as follows:

1. Compute 95th percentile error (described above) for open terrain and other categories combined.
2. Report CVA as "**Tested _____ (meters, feet) consolidated vertical accuracy at 95th percentile in: open terrain, (specify all other categories tested)**"

3. In the metadata, document the errors larger than the 95th percentile. For a small number of errors above the 95th percentile, report x/y coordinates and z-error for each QC check point error larger than the 95th percentile. For a large number of errors above the 95th percentile, report only the quantity and range of values.

If the FVA accuracy test fails to meet the prescribed accuracy, there is a problem with the control, collection system, or processing system or the achievable accuracy of the production system has been overstated. If a systematic problem can be identified with any of these systems, it should be corrected, if possible, and the data should be retested.

If the SVA or CVA tests fail to meet accuracy targets, there may be a systematic problem with post-processing procedures used to classify the bare-earth datasets. These procedures may need to be changed, data reprocessed and retested.

Untested Vertical Accuracy

Use the 'compiled to meet' statement below when the above guidelines for testing by an independent source of higher accuracy cannot be followed and an alternative means is used to evaluate accuracy. This is particularly relevant for photogrammetry where production procedures are mature and "compiled to meet" statistics are reliable. Report accuracy at the 95 percent confidence level for data produced according to procedures that have been demonstrated to produce data with particular vertical accuracy values as:

Report FVA as: **Compiled to meet ___ (meters, feet) fundamental vertical accuracy at 95 percent confidence level in open terrain.** An FVA "compiled to meet" accuracy statement is mandatory for all untested elevation datasets

Report SVA as: **Compiled to meet ____ (meters, feet) supplemental vertical accuracy at 95th percentile in (specify land cover category or categories).** An SVA accuracy statement is optional.

Report CVA as: **Compiled to meet ___ (meters, feet) consolidated vertical accuracy at 95th percentile in: open terrain, (list all other relevant categories).** A CVA accuracy statement is optional.

Horizontal Accuracy

The NDEP does not require independent testing of horizontal accuracy for elevation products. When the lack of distinct surface features makes horizontal accuracy testing of mass points, TINs, or DEMs difficult or impossible, the data producer should specify horizontal accuracy using the following statement:

Compiled to meet ___ (meters, feet) horizontal accuracy at 95 percent confidence level

AMERICAN SOCIETY FOR PHOTOGRAMMETRY AND REMOTE SENSING (ASPRS) LIDAR GUIDELINES

(ASPRS, 2004) endorses the procedures in (NDEP, 2004) and provides additional guidelines, including the presumption that FVA is assumed to be the relevant standard if only a single (unspecified) accuracy is stated. For example, if a client says that the elevation dataset should have a vertical RMSE of 15-cm, ASPRS assumes the client means that FVA must be equal to 29.4 cm (0.96-ft) at the 95 percent confidence level ($RMSE_z$ x 1.9600). For other distinctions, see Chapter 3.

QA/QC Checkpoints

(FEMA, 2003), (NDEP, 2004) and (ASPRS, 2004) all have the same requirement concerning the location and survey of QA/QC checkpoints, conforming with checkpoint requirements in the 1st edition of this manual (ASPRS, 2001).

Checkpoints should be selected on flat terrain, or on uniformly sloping terrain for x-meters in all directions from each checkpoint, where "x" is the nominal spacing of the DEM or mass points evaluated. Whereas flat terrain is preferable, this is not always possible. Whenever possible, terrain slope should not be steeper than a 20 percent grade because horizontal errors will unduly influence the vertical RMSE calculations. For example, an allowable 1-meter horizontal error in a DEM could cause an apparent unallowable vertical error of 20 cm in the DEM. Furthermore, checkpoints should never be selected near severe breaks in slope (such as bridge abutments or edges of roads) where subsequent interpolation might be performed with inappropriate TIN or DEM points on the wrong sides of the breaklines.

Checkpoint surveys should be performed relative to National Spatial Reference System (NSRS) monuments of high vertical accuracy, preferably using the very same NSRS monuments used as GPS base stations for airborne GPS control of the mapping aircraft. This negates the potential that elevation differences might be attributed to inconsistent survey control.

GPS survey guidelines in (NOAA, 1997) are recommended to extend control from the selected NSRS monuments into the project area, using the National Geodetic Survey's latest geoid model to convert from ellipsoid heights to orthometric heights. GPS real-time-kinematic (RTK) procedures are acceptable as long as temporary benchmarks within the project area are surveyed twice with distinctly different satellite geometry to overcome the possibility of GPS multipath error. Subsequent to GPS surveys to extend control into the project area, conventional third-order surveys can be used to extend control to checkpoints that are typically located within forested areas or "urban canyons" where GPS signals would be blocked. QA/QC surveys should be such that the checkpoint accuracy is at least three times more accurate than the dataset being evaluated. For example, if a DEM is supposed to have a vertical $RMSE_z$ of 18.5-cm, equivalent to the accuracy required of 2-foot contours, then the checkpoints should be surveyed with procedures that would yield vertical $RMSE_z$ of 6 cm or better.

In all methods of accuracy testing and reporting, there is a presumption that the checkpoint surveys are error free and that discrepancies are attributable to the remote sensing technology assumed to have lower accuracy. This is especially true when the checkpoint surveys are performed with technology and procedures that should yield accuracies at least three times greater than the expected accuracy of the remote sensing data being tested. However, checkpoint surveys are not always error free, and care must be taken to ensure that all survey errors and blunders are identified. When discrepancies do appear, resurveying questionable checkpoints themselves, or asking for the original checkpoint survey data to be reviewed are ways to challenge the accuracy, or inaccuracy, of the checkpoints. Because of potential challenges to the surveyed checkpoints, it is recommended that each checkpoint be marked with a recoverable item, such as a 60d nail and an adjoining flagged stake, to assist in recovery of the checkpoints for resurveys.

Interpolation of Digital Elevation Datasets

Once checkpoints are collected and checked for blunders, elevations corresponding to each checkpoint must be derived from each dataset to be tested. Exact procedures for obtaining these elevations will vary depending on the elevation data model and on software tools available for the test.

Whereas checkpoints may be considered to be well-defined and recoverable, mass points, TIN/DEM points, and contours are not horizontally well-defined. Because digital elevation data do not contain well-defined points, it is nearly impossible to test exactly the same points as in a DEM or TIN dataset. Therefore, it is usually necessary to interpolate an elevation from the surface model at the horizontal (x, y) location of each checkpoint. Points interpolated from a distance on large TIN triangles typically (unfairly) indicate larger error than when interpolated from near-by points on small TIN triangles. Although a raw lidar dataset may have dense point spacing (and small TIN triangles), the classification of vegetation to obtain a bare-earth dataset removes many mass points, resulting in potentially large TIN triangles for which QA/QC checkpoint coordinates are interpolated from greater distances, subject to greater error.

When mass points are specified as a deliverable, a TIN derived from the mass points provides a surface from which elevations can be directly interpolated at the horizontal location of each checkpoint. A number of commercial GIS packages have commands (such as ArcInfo TINSPOT) that perform this interpolation automatically for a list of checkpoints.

When a gridded DEM is specified as a deliverable, it must be tested to ensure it meets required accuracies even when a TIN (tested to meet accuracy) is used as the DEM source. This is because generalization or smoothing processes employed during DEM interpolation may degrade the elevation surface. Some technologies such as IFSAR and image correlation directly produce a gridded elevation model. If a gridded DEM is to be tested, surface elevations at the checkpoint locations can be interpolated using 4-neighbor bilinear interpolation such as that used in the ArcInfo Latticespot command.

Contours may be directly collected from stereoscopic source by a compiler or may be derived from a TIN or DEM. The contours should be tested when specified as a deliverable whether they were directly compiled or derived from another data model, even if the source model meets required accuracies. This is because the accuracy of any derived product can be degraded by interpolation, generalization, or smoothing.

Contour tests can be performed two ways. One method consists of plotting checkpoint locations in relationship with surrounding contours and mentally interpolating an elevation for that checkpoint from surrounding contours. Another method requires the contours to be converted to a TIN, from which elevations can be automatically interpreted with software. The TIN method is somewhat risky because TINing software cannot apply the rationale that may be required of the human during interpolation. Therefore, the TINing process may introduce additional error into the interpolated elevations. However, if the TIN test meets accuracy, one can be fairly confident that the contours meet accuracy. If the TIN accuracy fails, it may be necessary to perform the mental interpolation and retest.

Computing Errors

The "difference" or error for each checkpoint is computed by subtracting the surveyed elevation of the checkpoint from the dataset elevation interpolated at the x/y coordinate of the checkpoint. Thus, if the difference or error is a positive number, the evaluated dataset elevation is higher than true ground in the vicinity of the checkpoint, and if the difference is a negative number, the evaluated dataset elevation is lower than the true ground elevation.

For check point$_i$, the vertical error$_i$ $= (z_{data\ i} - z_{check\ i})$,
Where:

- $z_{data\ i}$ is the vertical coordinate of the ith check point in the dataset
- $z_{check\ i}$ is the vertical coordinate of the ith check point in the independent source of higher accuracy
- i is an integer from 1 to n; n = the number of points being checked

Random Errors, Systematic Errors, and Blunders

The "errors" measured in accuracy calculations, in theory, pertain only to random errors, produced by irregular causes whose effects upon individual observations are governed by no known law that connects them with circumstances and so cannot be corrected by use of standardized adjustments. Random errors typically follow a normal distribution.

Systematic errors follow some fixed pattern and are introduced by data collection procedures and systems. Systematic errors may occur as vertical elevation shifts across a portion or all of a dataset. These can be identified through spatial analysis of error magnitude and direction or by analyzing the mean error for the dataset. Systematic errors may also be identified as large deviations from the true elevations caused by misinterpretations of terrain surfaces due to trees, buildings, and shadows, fictitious ridges, tops, benches, and striations. A systematic error is predictable in theory and is, therefore, not random. Where possible, systematic errors should be identified and eliminated from a set of observations prior to accuracy calculations.

A blunder is an error of major proportion, normally identified and removed during editing or QC processing. A potential blunder may be identified as any error greater than three times the standard deviation (3 sigma) of the error. Errors greater than 3 sigma should be analyzed to determine the source of the blunder and to ensure that the blunder is not indicative of some unacceptable source of systematic error. Checkpoints with large error should not simply be thrown out of the test sample without investigation; they may actually be representative of some error characteristic remaining in the elevation surface and should be addressed in the metadata.

It is generally accepted that errors in open terrain, whether from photogrammetry, IFSAR or lidar, represent random errors in the sensor system, whereas errors in vegetated areas may include systematic errors. For example, systematic inability to penetrate dense vegetation, and/or systematic deficiencies in procedures used to generate bare-earth elevation datasets. A single large error (outlier) in a forested area, for example, can totally skew RMSE calculations of a large population of checkpoints that otherwise satisfy the accuracy criteria. Such examples were documented in detail in Chapter 12 of (ASPRS, 2001) and led directly to the (NDEP, 2004) and (ASPRS, 2004) endorsement of FVA, SVA and CVA procedures documented above, where the 95th percentile is used for land cover categories other than open terrain.

For SVA and CVA accuracy tests, the 95th percentile method should be employed to determine accuracy. The 95th percentile method may be used regardless of whether or not the errors follow a normal distribution and whether or not errors qualify as outliers. Computed by a simple spreadsheet command, a "percentile" is the interpolated absolute value in a dataset of errors dividing the distribution of the individual errors in the dataset into one hundred groups of equal frequency. The 95th percentile indicates that 95 percent of the errors in the dataset will have absolute values of equal or lesser value and 5 percent of the errors will be of larger value. With this method, $Accuracy_z$ is directly equated to the 95th percentile, where 95 percent of the errors have absolute values that are equal to or smaller than the specified amount.

Accuracy Assessment Summary

Providers of digital elevation data use a variety of methods to control the accuracy of their products. Photogrammetrists use survey control points and aerotriangulation to control and evaluate the accuracy of their data. IFSAR and lidar providers may collect hundreds of static or kinematic control points for internal quality control and to adjust their datasets to these control points. To the degree that such control points are used in a fashion similar to control for aerotriangulation, for which the IFSAR or lidar datasets are adjusted to better fit such control points, then the data providers may use the "compiled to meet" accuracy statements listed above. With mature technologies such as photogrammetry, users generally accept "compiled to meet" accuracy statements without independent accuracy testing. However, with developing technologies such as IFSAR or lidar, users often require independent accuracy tests for which accuracy reporting is more complex, especially when errors include "outliers" or do not follow a normal distribution as required for the use of RMSE in accuracy assessments. Because of these complexities, the NDEP mandates the "truth in advertising" approach, described above, that reports vertical accuracies in open terrain separately from other land cover categories, and that documents the size of the errors larger than the 95th percentile in the metadata.

Example Vertical Accuracy Assessment Report

Tables 12.1 through 12.4 and Figures 12.1 through 12.4 were extracted from a lidar Accuracy Assessment Report, prepared by the author's firm, for a *real-world* dataset required to be suitable for generation of 2-foot contours. Such Tables and Figures are used by the author to help identify systematic errors that depart from random, normal error distributions.

Table 12.1 shows the accuracy criteria specified by the client. The first two rows (in white) identify $RMSE_z$ and $Accuracy_z$ criteria that would be desirable if errors follow a normal error distribution (bell shaped distribution, with mean of zero), consistent with NSSDA assumptions (FGDC, 1998); when accuracy statistics are computed, any large departures from the stated Measures of Acceptability could indicate that errors do not follow a normal error distribution. The next three rows (in grey) identify FVA, SVA and CVA criteria for this contract, consistent with (NDEP, 2004); the FVA uses $RMSE_z$ to compute $Accuracy_z$ and assumes a normal error distribution only in open terrain, whereas the SVA and CVA do not assume that errors in vegetated areas and asphalt follow a normal error distribution and they use the 95th percentile to compute $Accuracy_z$.

Table 12.1 DTM Acceptance Criteria from the Quality Plan. Courtesy of Dewberry.

Quantitative Criteria	Measure of Acceptability
$RMSE_z$ = NSSDA vertical accuracy statistic at 68% confidence level	0.60 ft for all land cover categories combined
$Accuracy_z$ = NSSDA vertical accuracy statistic at the 95% confidence level	1.19 ft ($RMSE_z$ x 1.9600) for all land cover categories combined
Fundamental Vertical Accuracy (FVA) in open terrain only = 95% confidence level	1.19 ft ($RMSE_z$ x 1.9600) for open terrain only
Supplemental Vertical Accuracy (SVA) in individual land cover categories = 95% confidence level	1.19 ft (based on 95th percentile per category; this is a target value only, not mandatory)
Consolidated Vertical Accuracy (CVA) in all land cover categories combined = 95% confidence level	1.19 ft (based on combined 95th percentile)

Table 12.2 summarizes the tested vertical accuracy by FVA, CVA and SVA methods. The surveyors that surveyed the QA/QC checkpoints were unable to identify 20 dispersed checkpoints in each of the five land cover categories that satisfied point location criteria, but statistics for the 91 points surveyed were sufficient to demonstrate that the dataset passed the mandatory FVA and CVA, and even each of the SVA target criteria.

Table 12.2 FVA, CVA and SVA at 95% Confidence Level. Courtesy of Dewberry.

Land Cover Category	# of Points	FVA — Fundamental Vertical Accuracy Spec = 1.19 (ft)	CVA — Consolidated Vertical Accuracy Spec = 1.19 (ft)	SVA — Supplemental Vertical Accuracy Target = 1.19 (ft)
Total Combined	91		0.76 ft	
Open Terrain	22	0.72 ft		0.59 ft
Weeds/Crops	17			0.58 ft
Scrub	14			1.03 ft
Forest	18			0.54 ft
Built Up	20			0.78 ft

Table 12.3 identifies the 5% of CVA outliers larger than the 95th percentile, as required by (NDEP, 2004). Whereas 5% of the checkpoint errors were allowed to be larger than 1.19 ft, none in fact were larger in this dataset. The two outliers in scrub, both with negative errors, indicate errors perhaps caused by one of the following possibilities: (1) the lidar elevations at those locations were actually too low for unexplained reasons, (2) the terrain undulated in the area, did not have uniform slope in the vicinity of those checkpoints, and interpolation was unreliable, or (3) the scrub (and dense vegetation up to 6 ft tall) were very dense in the vicinity of those two checkpoints and lidar mass points rarely reached the ground; when filtering the lidar mass points as part of the vegetation-removal process, the remaining mass points were far apart, leaving large TIN triangles for interpolation over long distances. Dewberry has learned that reason (3) is a primary reason for outliers in vegetated areas. Tests have consistently shown that apparent discrepancies are small when QA/QC checkpoints are located within 1-meter for one or more lidar mass points following vegetation removal (small TIN triangle on which interpolation is performed from near-by points), whereas apparent discrepancies get progressively larger when QA/QC checkpoints are located at greater distances from lidar mass points following vegetation removal (large TIN triangle on which elevations are interpolated from distant mass points).

Table 12.4 provides statistics consistent with Section A.8.6.3 of (FEMA, 2003). These statistics help identify data departures from normal error distributions by land cover category. For example, if the skew is greater than 0.5, this shows a departure from a normal error distribution (specifically scrub for this example dataset). The degree to which the mean and median depart from zero also show that the normal distribution *bell curve* will not be centered at zero.

Table 12.3 5% CVA Outliers Larger than 95th Percentile. Courtesy of Dewberry.

Land Cover Category	Elev. Diff (ft)	Five points had errors larger than the
Open Terrain	0.77	95th percentile error. However, there
Scrub	-1.19	were no errors larger than the CVA
Scrub	-0.95	standard (1.19 ft) which permits up to 5%
Built Up	0.78	of the checkpoints, normally 5 of 100, to
Built Up	0.85	be larger than 1.19 ft.

Table 12.4 Descriptive Statistics by Land Cover Category. Courtesy of Dewberry.

Land Cover Category	RMSE$_z$ (ft)	Mean (ft)	Median (ft)	Skew	Std Dev (ft)	# of Points	Min (ft)	Max (ft)
Consolidated	0.41	0.16	0.21	-0.88	0.38	91	-1.19	0.85
Open Terrain	0.37	0.21	0.20	-0.17	0.31	22	-0.48	0.77
Weeds/Crops	0.35	0.07	0.14	-0.32	0.36	17	-0.56	0.66
Scrub	0.49	-0.13	0.09	-1.21	0.49	14	-1.19	0.33
Forest	0.31	0.10	0.14	-0.65	0.31	18	-0.60	0.52
Built Up	0.51	0.44	0.48	-0.27	0.27	20	-0.07	0.85

Figure 12.1 shows SVA values by land cover category, compared with the 95th percentile target value of 1.19 ft. The ordinate values depict the following land cover categories from left to right: (1) open terrain, (2) weeds and crops, (3) scrub, (4) forests, and (5) built-up. The abscissa values show the five individual SVA 95th percentile values all below the 1.19 ft target value depicted by the dark horizontal line above the shaded bars.

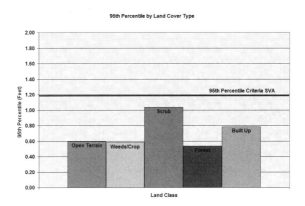

Figure 12.1 SVA Values by Land Cover. Courtesy of Dewberry.

Figure 12.2 shows the RMSE$_z$ values by the same land cover categories, compared with the RMSE$_z$ target value of 0.60-ft required to be equivalent to 2-ft contours if errors are normally distributed. Again the abscissa values show the five individual RMSE$_z$ values all below the 0.60 ft target value depicted by the dark horizontal line above the shaded bars. The differences between Figures 12.1 and 12.2 are minor because there were no major outliers that caused the errors to depart significantly from a normal error distribution. In other lidar projects, the author has seen numerous examples where the abscissa values in Figure 12.2 were above its dark horizontal line (failing its RMSE$_z$ target) whereas the abscissa values in Figure 12.1 were below its dark horizontal line (passing its 95th percentile target); this occurs when there are large outliers for which error values are squared in the RMSE$_z$ calculations, causing a disproportionately large RMSE$_z$ statistic.

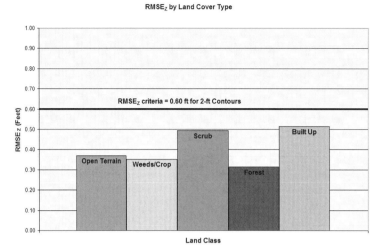

Figure 12.2 RMSE$_z$ Values by Land Cover. Courtesy of Dewberry.

Figure 12.3 illustrates the magnitude of the differences between the QA/QC checkpoints and lidar data by specific land cover category and sorted from lowest to highest in each category. The ordinate shows the sorted data checkpoints by land cover categories with different graph symbols, and the abscissa shows the actual size of the errors compared with the two dark horizontal lines that depict the highest and lowest values between which 95% of the errors should fall. Whereas 95% of the checkpoints should be accurate within ±1.19 ft as shown in Figure 12.3, all 100% of the checkpoints in this example met this criterion. Overall, Figure 12.3 shows a small positive bias (+0.14 ft) to the lidar data, as shown by the discrepancies in Open Terrain that vary between -0.48 ft and +0.77 ft. If the bare-earth elevations in Open Terrain followed a normal error distribution exactly, the mean would be zero, the maximum discrepancy would be approximately +0.62 ft and the minimum discrepancy would be approximately – 0.62 ft. However, it is extremely rare to see a lidar bare-earth dataset that is totally "normal." See the color plate at Appendix C where this Figure is more discernable.

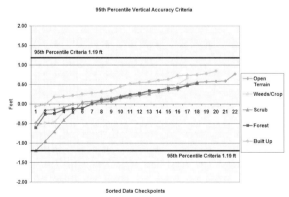

Figure 12.3 Error Distribution by Land Cover. Courtesy of Dewberry. See color plate in Appendix C.

Figure 12.4 illustrates a histogram of the associated elevation discrepancies between the QA/QC checkpoints and elevations interpolated from the lidar TIN. The frequency (abscissa value) shows the number of discrepancies within each 0.2-ft band of elevation differences (ordinate values). For example, the first band (between -1.2 ft and -1.0 ft) shows the single largest negative error (-1.19 ft) in weeds and crops discussed above; the eight band (between +0.2 ft and +0.4 ft) shows the greatest frequency with 23 errors of that order of magnitude; the eleventh band (between +0.80 and +1.0) shows the single largest positive error (+0.85 ft) in built-up area. Both

Tables 12.3 and 12.4 list the actual maximum and minimum errors and land cover categories in which they occur. Although the discrepancies vary between a low of -1.19 ft and a high of +0.85 ft in this example, the histogram shows that the majority of the discrepancies are skewed on the positive side of what would be a "bell curve" with mean of zero if the data were exactly normally distributed. This histogram is closer to "normal" than most of the hundreds of datasets evaluated by the author to date.

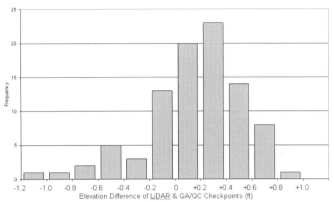

Figure 12.4 Histogram of Discrepancies. Courtesy of Dewberry.

QUALITATIVE ASSESSMENT OF DIGITAL TOPOGRAPHIC DATA

Mapping standards today address the quality of data by quantitative methods only. If the data are tested and found to be within the desired accuracy standard, then the data is typically accepted. Now with the proliferation of lidar, new issues arise due to the vast amount of mass points that are measured. Unlike photogrammetry where point spacing can be five meters or more and supplemented by breaklines, lidar point spacing can be less than 1 meter. The end result is that millions of elevation points are measured to a level of accuracy previously unseen for elevation technologies, and vegetated areas are measured that would be nearly impossible to survey cost effectively by other means. The downside is that, with millions of points, the dataset is statistically bound to have some errors both in the measurement process and in the classification of data to produce a bare-earth DTM. In previous years the process of classifying data was known as "vegetation removal process," but in reality elevated points in vegetation are not removed, they are reclassified to other, non-terrain categories.

As previously stated, quantitative analysis addresses the quality of the data based on absolute accuracy by comparing the surface product with an independent data source of higher accuracy. This accuracy is directly tied to the comparison of the discreet measurement of the survey checkpoints and that of the interpolated value within the three closest lidar points that constitute the plane connected by the vertices of a three-dimensional triangular face of the TIN or from a raster cell of a DEM. Therefore, the end result is that only a small sample of the lidar data is actually tested. However, there is an increased level of confidence with lidar data due to the relative accuracy. This relative accuracy is based on the commonality of how lidar data is derived. Since the GPS is the first initial source of position of the platform, many lidar measurements are based on this position. For example, the GPS is measured once every second, and a position is derived; the sensor may then fire over 100,000 pulses per second. Therefore there is a correlation of the position every one second to thousands of lidar pulses. Of course, many factors are then added to the measurement such as platform velocity, orientation, scan angle, pulse length etc. The end result is that the relative accuracy from one point to the next adjacent point within the scan is typically very good. Once the absolute and relative accuracy has been ascertained, the next stage is to address the cleanliness of the data for a bare-earth DTM. Cleanliness is defined as the correct classification of lidar data points that are representative of a bare-earth surface.

By using survey checkpoints to compare the data, the absolute accuracy is verified, but this also allows analysts to understand if the vegetation removal process was performed correctly at those particular locations. From the quantitative assessment, if the lidar operated correctly in open terrain areas, then it most likely operated correctly in vegetated areas also. This does not mean that the bare-earth was measured, but that the elevations surveyed are most likely accurate (including elevations of treetops, rooftops, etc.). In the event that the lidar pulse filtered through the vegetation and was able to measure the true surface (as well as measurements on the surrounding vegetation) then the level of accuracy of the vegetation removal process can be tested as a by-product.

To fully address the data for overall quality and suitability for their intended product, the level of cleanliness is paramount and a qualitative assessment should be performed. The qualitative assessment utilizes an interpretive and statistical based methodology to assess the quality of the data for a bare-earth terrain model. This process looks for anomalies in the data and also identifies areas where man-made structures or vegetation points may not have been classified correctly to produce a bare-earth model.

Macro Level Assessments

All examples shown are for illustration purposes and do not constitute a final delivered product to the end clients. No one company, entity or area is identified or implied, and some data has been manipulated for visualization purposes only.

DTMs and DEMs are based on one of two data types: vector and raster. Vector data models use coordinate geometry to represent geographic phenomena with points, lines, and polygons. In the case of elevation data, typically it is in the form of 3-D points (X, Y, Z coordinates) but 3-D lines representing breaklines are also used. Vector data is best for representing discrete features or measurements. DTM vector data allows the reviewer or user to view the exact laser measurement, or photogrammetric derived measurement of the surface at a precise location. The advantage is there is little to no interpolation based at these locations, but the disadvantage is there may be many millions of points to review which could be cumbersome. However over the last few years, newer software packages have been introduced that allow users to view millions of points in a 2-D or 3-D environment. Even with this ability to view millions of points, this does not ensure that all anomalies within the data can be identified as the viewing scale will dictate what can be visualized on screen.

DEMs on the other hand are typically raster datasets comprised of a simple matrix of rows and columns using grid cells where each cell represents an elevation value. Cell values are usually interpolated from vector data such as lidar, photogrammetry or IFSAR, and raster datasets are ideal for representing continuous surfaces. The advantage of raster datasets is the ability to perform statistical and spatial analysis as well as creating pseudo images, such as shaded relief images, to aid in visualizing the data. The disadvantage of raster datasets is the inherent spatial inaccuracies based on the interpolated data and the grid cell size. The grid cell size must be optimally balanced to represent the geographic phenomena. Additionally when viewing raster DEMs in a 2-D environment, sometimes it is difficult to visually identify small anomalies without further processing or visualizations (see Figure 12.16 and Figure 12.17, later in this chapter, illustrating this point).

With both data types, visualization is a key component to reviewing data for qualitative purposes. However it may not be practical to review 100% of the data for extremely large datasets. Limiting factors can be hardware (computing power and storage), software, and allocation of resources (time). Therefore these factors will dictate how a review is accomplished, but the end goal is to ensure that the data meets the desired requirements for the intended product. If only a percentage of the data can be assessed, it is still possible to perform simple automated tasks to verify components of the entire dataset. Tools to calculate descriptive statistics can provide a benefit with minimal human intervention.

Table 12.5 illustrates sample statistics derived from a lidar dataset. Within this table two issues are of potential interest; tile 350 has significantly fewer points than neighboring tiles, and tile 355 has a minimum elevation of -68.13 meters and a slightly higher standard deviation than comparable tiles. (In this case, standard deviation pertains to the range of elevations on each tile and has nothing to do with the accuracy of those elevations.) This straight forward table can help identify potential issues and direct the user to problematic areas. It should be noted that even though tile 350 has fewer points, this could be realistic as the area may have a large lake or could be on a boundary that did not require a full tile. The table is only meant to help guide the users to identify potential errors. This can also be shown graphically within the context of GIS.

Table 12.5. Sample statistics of a tiled lidar dataset illustrating the number of records for each tile as well as statistics, including the minimum, maximum, mean, and standard deviation for the range of elevation values.

Number of records, minimum, maximum, mean, standard deviation for range of elevations.					
Tile	NOR	Min (m)	Max (m)	Mean (m)	Std Dev (m)
350	353573	450.36	731.47	612.22	74.28
351	1167596	566.70	724.03	648.45	30.43
352	1523940	494.11	672.07	579.98	36.19
353	1363267	380.34	632.02	522.40	59.62
354	1496145	290.80	638.08	534.90	81.06
355	1935885	-68.13	548.79	292.69	111.15
356	1501918	290.51	539.30	397.40	63.32

Number of Records per Tile

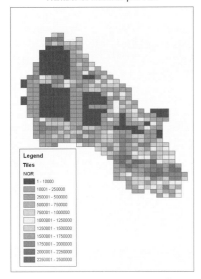

Figure 12.5 Illustrates a county tile scheme color coded by the number of records (lidar points) per tile. Areas of low records could potentially indicate issues. See color plate in Appendix C.

Figure 12.5 illustrates a tile scheme classified by color based on the number of records (NOR) per tile. This figure easily identifies many tiles that had insufficient data points and three tiles appear to be missing. Further investigation would be warranted.

From the descriptive statistics, no visualization of the actual data has occurred, but the user can isolate areas of concern for further review. In the event that not all data can be visually reviewed, strategic sample sets can be identified which may include areas that are important to the user. For example, those reviewing elevation data for flood studies may want to concentrate their effort in the floodplain. In any event the data should be evaluated in the areas of greatest interest, but also in other strategic locations to verify the data's integrity was maintained throughout the whole of the dataset. To satisfy FEMA requirements as outlined at the beginning of this chapter, different land cover representative of the floodplain should be verified through a visualization process. Other areas of potential error with lidar is at the beginning of flight lines as the GPS and IMU may have not "settled in" yet which potentially can have higher residuals yielding either noisy data or erroneous height measurements due to inaccurate aircraft position and orientation. Typically, lidar acquisition flights account for this, and lidar systems are usually on line ensuring the lidar system is firing well before the actual start of the flight line to ensure aircraft stability and diode temperature. However, this is a potential weak area. If possible, identify the flight pattern over the project area and choose locations near the beginnings and ends of flight lines for qualitative assessments. Most lidar missions fly parallel flight lines in opposite directions to ensure data overlap, lidar penetration, and to maintain relative accuracy between flight lines. Also if the project area is flown in blocks, it would be prudent to verify flights in the overlap between these blocks where the potential to have elevation shifts between the data is higher. Theoretically if the data has been processed correctly, and QC measures were employed, data in overlap areas should fit relatively well. Some lidar vendors also remove areas of overlap with a seam line and adjoin adjacent areas together (see Figure 12.6). By reviewing the scan pattern the user can test the relative accuracy between these two areas to ensure continuity. Similar to overlap, if an area has data holidays and the missing data is re-flown, it will be processed and integrated back into the main dataset. Again potential for error exists that the elevations can sometimes have a bias as can be seen in Figure 12.7.

Figure 12.7 illustrates a tile that consists of three flight lines flown on two different missions. Flight line 1 and 2 were flown in an east/west direction but did not contain any overlap which created a data holiday. A second flight mission was employed and flight line 3 was acquired, processed and integrated back into the main DTM. Since Flight line 3 was lower than line 1 and 2, the classification process identified areas in the direct overlap as low points and not added to the bare-earth ground DTM but maintained the data between flight lines 1 and 2. Clearly there is bias between these two datasets that needs to be resolved.

Figure 12.6 Illustrates two scan lines that are joined by a seam line and the overlap has been removed.

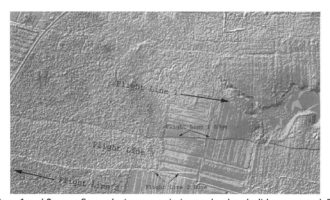

Figure 12.7 Flight lines 1 and 2 were flown during one mission and a data holiday occurred. The area of missing data (Flight Line 3) was then re-flown on a second mission, processed, and integrated into the main DTM. Clearly an elevation bias can be seen between the two datasets. See color plate in Appendix C.

By selecting strategic locations to verify data, there is a greater possibility that errors in the data, or at least in the areas of greatest concern, may be identified and subsequently resolved. However with newer, more powerful software, it is now possible to view many millions of lidar points at once. If available, this type of software will allow the user to review the data at a "project" level. Figure 12.8 illustrates over 85 million bare-earth mass points. The black areas show where there are no points either from the water features, or where the data has been classified as vegetation or man-made structure, plus one area of missing data that, after careful analysis, turned out to be a data holiday located near the eastern boundary of the area of interest.

To find void areas and data holidays more easily, it may be beneficial to calculate the density of each tile of the project area. Figure 12.9 illustrates a raster model with areas of no return classified in bright red. This type of image allows the user to verify if the void areas are legitimate, e.g., for bodies of water or heavily vegetated areas where points are reclassified as vegetation rather than bare-earth. Figure 12.10 illustrates a more detailed view of a lidar dataset that classifies the data based on the number of lidar points per raster cell. This type of image not only identifies areas of no returns but also illustrates flight line scan width and the overlap between flight lines.

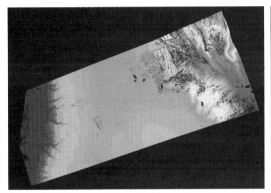

Figure 12.8 Project-wide point cloud data of over 85 million bare-earth ground points. Some void areas, shown in black in the interior of the project area, are due to water bodies, classification of vegetation and man-made objects, as well as one data holiday on the far right side of the image. See color plate in Appendix C.

Figure 12.9 Combined DEM and shaded relief classified by density. Areas of bright red indicate few to no points. See color plate in Appendix C.

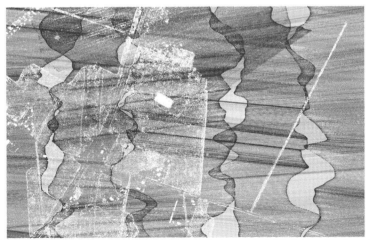

Figure 12.10 Illustrates a tile based on the number of lidar points per pixel. It is interesting to note the areas in the lighter shade of blue that exhibit only one pass of the lidar with no overlap, and also the concentration of data points at the end of the scan lines in the darkest blue. This dataset was acquired on a very windy day. See color plate in Appendix C.

Micro Level Assessment

Upon reviewing the data on a project wide macro level, there are many ways and processes to review the data on a micro level to assess whether the data fulfills the client's requirements. As previously stated, vector and raster formats have both advantages and disadvantages. Ideally both types of models yield different views and allows the users flexibility to visualize the data.

As discussed in Chapter 14, the production flow of post processed lidar data will be dictated by the user and the available tools to them. In most cases at this stage the lidar is in vector format with each lidar measurement having a 3-dimensional coordinate either in ASCII or binary which has been classified as a minimum to ground or non-ground features. This allows the data to be converted and viewed in many ways including creating pseudo imagery as well as by-products such as slope or contour maps. Within a vector environment, analysts know that looking at a macro level is feasible although it does require specialized software and hardware configurations. However to find smaller anomalies the data will have to be reviewed on a micro level and in most cases on a tile by tile basis.

The power of vector data, especially in LAS format, is the ability to view the full point cloud data or bare-earth ground points as measured by the lidar system. Using CAD, GIS or a specialized software package, the user can display data based on its x/y location. This allows the user to review the scan patterns to help identify issues or anomalies with the data. Taking this one step further, the user then can color code the data based on elevation as can be seen in Figure 12.11. This allows the user to get a different perspective of the data by using color to represent the height source. Using a color scheme with primary colors stretched from blue to red allows the user to review the variance of elevations within each tile quite easily and intuitively. For Figure 12.11 it appears no anomalies are present and the data looks to be of good quality. The next phase would be to view the data in true 3-D as illustrated in Figure 12.12. Most software packages that can view 3-D allow the user to manipulate the data to be able to view it from many perspectives. This approach allows the user to view the scan patterns, identify overlap areas, identify void

Figure 12.11 2-D view of vector lidar points color coded by elevation. See color plate in Appendix C.

Figure 12.12 3-D view of Figure 12.11. High points (spikes) on this DTM are not visible. See color plate in Appendix C.

areas, view the elevations based on color and use the color patterns to assess the data, and finally the ability to review the data in its true 3-D perspective. This approach works well when the user is looking at thousands of points but it may not find finite anomalies. For example, Figure 12.13 illustrates the same tile but in a pseudo 3-D image. This approach uses a hybrid raster/vector model which in essence combines a raster DEM/shaded relief draped over a TIN. Since a TIN creates triangles from each vector, the two high points are easily identifiable in 3-D. The advantage here is that by reviewing only the points not all anomalies can easily be identified. Using a combination of techniques yields different perspectives to help in quality assessment.

Figure 12.13 illustrates a large anomaly not easily visible in Figures 12.11 and 12.12. Figure 12.14 illustrates a vector 2-D perspective with lidar points color coded by elevation. Within this image two different scan lines are apparent; however, there is a bias in elevations between them. It is interesting to note that the classification process classified the points on one of the lines within the overlap areas as non-ground, but also classified legitimate points along the edge of the adjacent line as not ground because of the height discrepancy of approximately 0.5 meters. Through this classification process a small gap is created between the scan lines. To find this issue in a vector environment the user would have to be zoomed in quite far to see this, but by using a 3-D raster/ shaded relief, as seen in Figure 12.15, an elevation shift can be noted between flight lines. In this scenario using a shaded relief in a 3-D environment is superior to the vector approach.

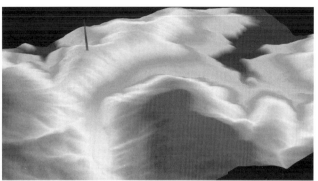

Figure 12.13 The hybrid vector/raster model of the same data shown in Figures 12.11 and 12.12. See color plate in Appendix C.

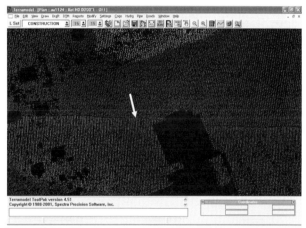

Figure 12.14 This is a vector model, illustrating two adjoining lidar flight lines color coded by elevation. Note the black east west gap of data between the two flight lines (see white arrow). This is a result of one flight line being higher than the other and the vegetation classification process identifying the points at the edge of one line and classifying them as non-ground. See color plate in Appendix C.

Shaded relief images combined with DEMs are an extremely effective tool for identifying anomalies and artifacts that are incorrectly classified as bare-earth. The use of shaded relief images, commonly referred to as *hillshades*, is a technique that calculates the illumination value of each cell based on a hypothetical light source. The result is a pseudo 3-D rendering of the terrain.

Figure 12.15 Because this is a 3-D vector rendered TIN, it can be oriented to provide a 3-D perspective of Figure 12.14. The elevation offset between the two flight lines is now easily identifiable. See color plate in Appendix C.

By varying the azimuth and angle of the light source, different perspectives of the surface can be observed and some anomalies which may not be as apparent in one perspective are more easily identified in another perspective. Figure 12.16 illustrates a raster DEM stretched with a grey scale color scheme. Upon first review of this dataset no major anomalies can be identified. However by converting this DEM to a shaded relief image (Figure 12.17), it is apparent that there are two lidar scan line issues where one scan line is higher than the adjacent terrain. To further enhance the effect, a color stretched DEM is overlaid on top of the shaded relief with transparency so that the shaded relief is illuminated through the DEM Figure 12.18.

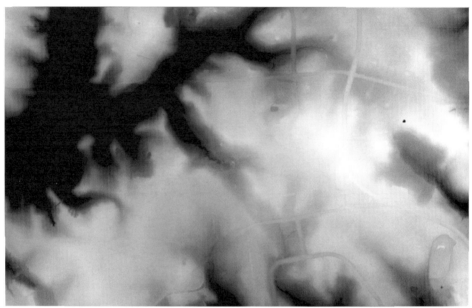

Figure 12.16 A raster DEM using a color stretched grey palette. No major anomalies are apparent.

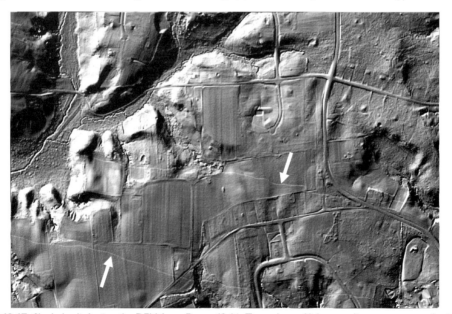

Figure 12.17 Shaded relief using the DEM from Figure 12.16. Two edges of lidar scan lines are now easily visible in the middle of the image and the south west field in the lower portion of the image which indicates an abnormal elevation change (see white arrows).

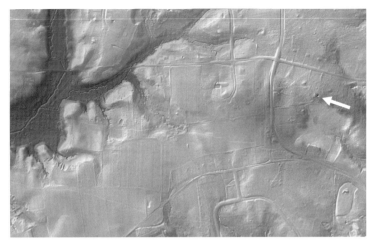

Figure 12.18 Combined DEM with shaded relief image. By using color to illustrate elevation, and transparency to feature the shaded relief, anomalies in the data can be easily identified. This dataset not only contains a scan line issue but it also may contain a spurious sink (elevations in blue, see white arrow) in the north east corner of the image where the elevation is considerable lower than the surrounding terrain including the stream channel below it. See color plate in Appendix C.

Figure 12.19 demonstrates how combined shaded relief images and DEMs are useful in identifying many types of anomalies or misclassifications of the bare-earth terrain. The image on the left illustrates a mismatch between adjacent flight lines where one line has a systematic bias in the data. Additionally this tile was classified as bare-earth terrain but it is apparent that vegetation is present and has been misclassified. The figure on the right illustrates a processing error by the lidar vendor where an antenna offset was not applied when processing the lidar data. The offset was exactly 2 meters.

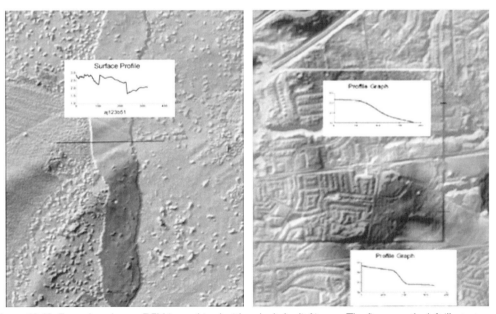

Figure 12.19 Examples where a DEM is combined with a shaded relief image. The figure on the left illustrates a scan line with high elevations that was merged with adjacent scan lines which had the correct elevations. This tile also was initially classified as bare-earth terrain but it is clear that vegetation still exists within this tile. The figure on the right illustrates a processing error by the vendor where an antenna offset was not applied when reducing the data. See color plate in Appendix C.

Classification Issues

When classifying data to bare-earth terrain, a balance must be maintained between retaining legitimate elevations and the classification of bare-earth terrain features. At times, geographic phenomenon emulates man-made features or man-made features become part of the bare-earth terrain such as a dam. With both of these scenarios, the classification algorithm may need refinement during lidar post-processing to ensure the features that represent the ground are defined. For example, a crop field in which the lidar could not penetrate may be identified as non-ground points as it is perceived similar to a wall or building. Figure 12.20 illustrates a dense crop field that was classified as the ground but is approximately 1 meter above the ground. Additionally the area to the south-east of the image is a forest where most of the forest has been classified correctly except for where it adjoins the crop field (as seen in bright red). This forest area appears "noisy" but further investigation with ground truthing shows that the forest indeed is quite undulating with high and low points as can be seen in the right portion of Figure 12.20. Figure 12.21 illustrates man-made features that may be important to a DEM because it contains a dam. Here the vegetation and man-made features have been removed but the dam structure has been maintained.

Figure 12.20 The DEM/ shaded relief image clearly shows a crop field that was misclassified due to poor lidar penetration. The classification process also classified most of the forest correctly (noisy area to the right) but remnants of the forest is still evident on the SE corner of the crop field. The image on the right is a ground truth photograph of the forest area that illustrates the roughness of the forest floor as indicated by the DEM and proving that the "noise" is real and should be retained in the DEM. See color plate in Appendix C.

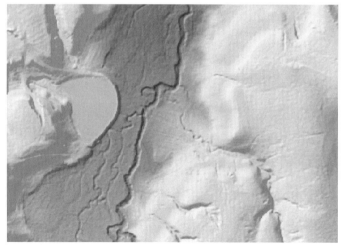

Figure 12.21 Good example of the classification process that maintains a balance between the classification of bare-earth and man-made features. See color plate in Appendix C.

When a DEM appears to be noisy, many geospatial data providers utilize more aggressing procedures to smooth their data. Figure 12.22 shows an area where a drainage canal of uniform cross-section dimensions appears totally different to either side of the dashed red line. The area to the southwest of the line appears noisy, but the drainage canal retains its correct dimensions; whereas the area north and east of the dashed line smoothed the DEM overall, but also changed the drainage canal so it is much wider and shallower. Because the cross section area of the drainage canal is important for hydraulic modeling of the floodplain, the area to the right of this line would be considered over-smoothed, and this processing algorithm should not be used.

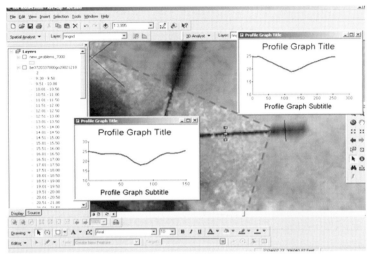

Figure 12.22 The area above and to the right of the red line is over-smoothed, losing the true dimensions of the man-made drainage canal that has the same actual dimensions on both sides of the red line. See color plate in Appendix C.

For projects where the processing is performed by many individuals, or through automatic image correlation, different levels of interpretation for the classification process can occur. Figure 12.23a illustrates two areas with different processing parameters. In Area A, the surface appears noisy but shows good channel definition for the stream corridor. However Area B which is smoother shows the stream as a levee. Figure 12.23b shows essentially the same thing in color. Figure 12.23c is the orthophoto of the same area illustrating that the terrain in A and B should be similar as well as the stream channel.

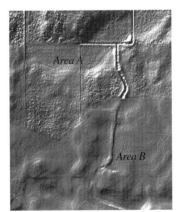

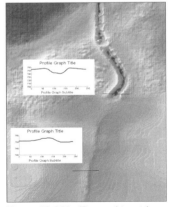

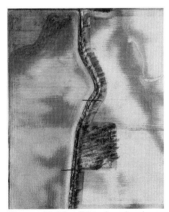

Figure 12.23a Areas A and B show two levels of processing from photogrammetric automated image correlation.

Figure 12.23b Zoomed in with profiles. While more noisy, Area A preserves the narrow drainage canal; Area B appears like a levee.

See color plates in Appendix C.

Figure 12.23c Digital orthophoto of the same area shows the drainage canal has same dimensions in both areas.

Summary

For the creation and verification of DTMs and DEMs, many automated techniques are employed. Even though automation is advantageous for many reasons, it is not 100% effective to find all anomalies in datasets. Quality assurance does not start or end with the final product. Each step in the creation of an elevation dataset needs to have quality control built into the process. As the technology improves, fewer errors will occur. However until that time, visualization will play a key role in assessing quality for elevation products.

QUALITY ASSESSMENT OF DIGITAL HYDROGRAPHIC DATA

The following is quoted from Section 5.5, Quality Control, of NOAA's March 2003 edition of "NOS Hydrographic Surveys Specifications and Deliverables (NOAA, 2003). It is interesting to see that crosslines and sun-illuminated DTM images are used by NOAA for quality control of sonar data, similar to procedures used for quality control of lidar DTMs.

Multibeam Sonar Calibration

Prior to commencing survey operations, the hydrographer shall conduct a system accuracy test to quantify the accuracy, precision, and alignment of the Multibeam system. Testing shall include determination of residual biases in roll, pitch, heading, and navigation timing error. These values will be used to correct the initial alignment and calibrate the Multibeam system. System accuracy testing should be conducted in an area similar in bottom profile and composition to the survey area, and during relatively calm seas to limit excessive motions and ensure suitable bottom detection. In addition, system accuracy tests should be conducted in depths equivalent to the deepest depths in the survey area. Static transducer draft, settlement and squat corrections, sound velocity corrections, and tide corrections shall be determined and applied to the data prior to bias determination.

The order in which these biases are determined may affect the accurate calibration of the Multibeam system. The hydrographer should determine the biases in the following order: navigation timing error, pitch, roll, heading. Variations from this order, or simultaneous determination of all values, must be explained and justified.

Pitch and navigation timing error biases should be determined from two or more pairs of reciprocal lines 500-1000 m long, over a 10° - 20° smooth slope, perpendicular to the depth curves. The lines should be run at different speeds, varied by up to 5 knots, for the purpose of delineating the along track profiles when accessing time delay. Navigation timing error bias could also be determined from running lines over a distinct feature (i.e., shoal) on the bottom, as long as the feature is pinged by the vertical (nadir) beam.

Roll bias should be determined from one or more pairs of reciprocal lines 500-1000 m in length over a flat bottom. Lines should be run at a speed which will ensure significant forward overlap.

Heading bias should be determined from two or more adjacent pairs of reciprocal survey lines, made on each side of a submerged object or feature (i.e., shoal), in relatively shallow water. Features with sharp edges should be avoided. Adjacent swaths should overlap by 10-20 percent while covering the shoal. Lines should be run at a speed which will ensure significant forward overlap.

Once calibration data have been processed and final system biases determined, the new corrections shall be used in a performance check to ensure that the new system biases are adequate. The hydrographer shall discuss procedures and results in the Data Reduction section of the project Data Acquisition and Processing Report. Copies of all system alignment, accuracy, calibration reports, and performance checks shall be included in the Data Acquisition and Processing Report.

System accuracy testing shall be repeated whenever changes (e.g., sensor failure, replacement, re-installations, re-configurations, or upgrade; software changes which could potentially affect data quality) are made to the system's baseline configuration, or whenever assessment of the data indicates that system accuracies do not meet the requirements in [Section 5.2 of (NOAA, 2003)].

Positioning System Confidence Checks

Confidence checks of the primary positioning system shall be conducted and recorded in the survey records at least once every week when USCG (U.S. Coast Guard) differential correctors are used as the primary positioning system, and once daily when non-USCG differential correctors are used. A successful confidence check shall compare positions from the primary system to simultaneously observed check positions from a separate, independent system with a positional accuracy better than 10 meters. The inverse distance shall not exceed 10 meters. If correctors for the primary positioning system are obtained from a non-USCG differential system, then the check system must use correctors from a reference station different from the primary system's. If correctors are obtained from a USCG differential station, the check system may use the same correctors as the primary system. The confidence checks shall be an integral part of the daily survey data record. Copies of positioning system confidence checks shall be included in section I of "Separates to be Included with the Survey Data" [see 8.1.3 of (NOAA, 2003)]

Crosslines

General

The regular system of sounding lines shall be supplemented by a series of crosslines for verifying and evaluating the accuracy and reliability of surveyed depths and plotted locations. Crosslines shall be run across all planned sounding lines at angles of 45° to 90°. The preferred area in which to run crosslines is in an area of gently sloping bottom.

Single Beam

The lineal nautical miles of crosslines for single-beam surveys shall be at least 8 percent of the lineal nautical miles of all planned sounding lines.

The hydrographer shall make a general evaluation of the single beam crossline to mainscheme agreement, and discuss the results in Section B of the Descriptive Report. If the magnitude of the discrepancy varies widely over the survey, the hydrographer shall make a quantitative evaluation of the disagreements area by area.

Multibeam

The lineal nautical miles of crosslines for Multibeam surveys shall be at least 5 percent of the lineal nautical miles of all planned sounding lines.

Comparisons shall be made between mainscheme lines and crosslines at 1% of all crossings (or 25 crossings, whichever is greater) distributed throughout the data both spatially and temporally. At these crossings the nadir or near-nadir depths of mainscheme lines shall be compared to each of the nearest unsmoothed soundings obtained from the crosslines. The hydrographer shall perform a separate statistical analysis as a function of beam number for each of the mainscheme/crossline intersections used for comparison. Include a statement about the results in Section B of the Descriptive Report, and include a summary plot of each crossing in Separate V, Crossline Comparisons.

Multibeam Sun-Illuminated Digital Terrain Model (DTM) Images

Regardless of the Multibeam coverage techniques used [see Section 5.3, Coverage in (NOAA, 2003)], the hydrographer shall create two sun-illuminated DTM images. These sun-illuminated DTM images are the preferred method for detection of depth artifacts associated with errors in bottom detection algorithms, vessel motion compensation, navigation timing, water level correctors and false bottom detections.

Each image shall depict data illuminated from orthogonal directions, using a light source with an elevation no greater than 45 degrees. At a minimum, an 8 bit color depth shall be used for compilation of the sun-illuminated images. The two sun-illuminated images shall be created from fully corrected data that meet accuracy and resolution specifications [see Section 5, Depth Soundings, of (NOAA, 2003)] are cleaned of all anomalous soundings, and serve as the source for smooth sheet soundings. Data shall be binned, line by line, using shoal biased filtering at a bin size not to exceed 5 meters + 5 percent of the depth.

The submitted digital image file shall be in a standard geo-referenced image format.

AUTHOR BIOGRAPHY

Timothy Blak is a Project Manager, geodesist, lidar manager, and DTM QA/QC manager for Dewberry where he has performed independent QA/QC of hundreds of countywide lidar and photogrammetric DTMs. He has worked in the mapping industry since 1987. He graduated from the Geographical Information Systems program at Algonquin College, Ottawa Canada while specializing in remote sensing applications. His career has focused on geodesy, particularly with GPS applications, Airborne GPS and lidar. He also serves as a lidar system "trouble-shooter," working with lidar firms to solve technical problems.

ACKNOWLEDGEMENTS

The author gratefully acknowledges the assistance provided by David Maune in compiling information for this chapter.

REFERENCES

ASPRS, 2001. *Digital Elevation Model Technologies and Applications: The DEM Users Manual,* (David Maune, editor), American Society for Photogrammetry and Remote Sensing (ASPRS), Bethesda, MD.

ASPRS, 2004. ASPRS guidelines, vertical accuracy reporting for lidar data, American Society for Photogrammetry and Remote Sensing (ASPRS), May 24, 2004, URL: http://www.asprs.org/society/committees/lidar/downloads/Vertical_Accuracy_Reporting_for_Lidar_Data.pdf.

Bureau of the Budget, 1947. *National Map Accuracy Standards (NMAS)*, Office of Management and Budget, Washington, DC.

FEMA, 2003. Appendix A, Guidance for aerial mapping and surveying, in *Guidelines and Specifications for Flood Hazard Mapping Partners*, Federal Emergency Management Agency (FEMA), April 2003, URL: http://www.fema.gov/plan/prevent/fhm/gs_main.shtm.

FGDC, 1998. Geospatial positioning accuracy standards, Part 3: National standard for spatial data accuracy (NSSDA), Federal Geographic Data Committee (FGDC), URL: http://www.fgdc.gov/standards/standards_publications.

NDEP, 2004. Guidelines for digital elevation data, Version 1.0, National Digital Elevation Program (NDEP), May 10, 2004, URL: http://www.ndep.gov/NDEP_Elevation_Guidelines_Ver1_10May2004.pdf.

NOAA, 1997. Technical memorandum NOS NGS-58, Guidelines for establishing GPS-derived ellipsoid heights (Standards: 2 cm and 5 cm), version 4.3, National Geodetic Survey, Silver Spring, MD.

NOAA, 2003. NOS hydrographic surveys specifications and deliverables, March 2003, URL: http://nauticalcharts.noaa.gov/hsd/specs/specs.htm.

Chapter 13

DEM User Requirements

David F. Maune

CHANGING REQUIREMENTS

Topographic Maps

For most of the past century, when compiling paper topographic maps for interpretation by humans, the choices were relatively simple. Specify the horizontal map scale, specify the contour interval, and specify the planimetric features to be shown and the symbology to be used. Until the mid-1980's, Americans mostly used the NAD 27 horizontal datum and the NGVD 29 vertical datum. The selection of the contour interval was really the only choice that specified the vertical accuracy of a topographic map to be produced or the manner in which the topography would be depicted. Since paper topographic maps with contours were devised for human interpretation, humans were trained to understand what the contours meant or they learned to understand the meaning of contours intuitively. Humans generally cling to their understanding of topographic contours.

Whereas contour generation may sound like a simple process, in fact it requires a great deal of labor intensive work by photogrammetrists and cartographers applying "cartographic license" to make topographic maps aesthetically pleasing and understandable by humans, and it's expensive to produce them with the very small contour intervals required by many.

Cost is a major reason why we haven't already mapped the entire United States with 1' or 2' contours, the interval that many users say they need in areas of relatively flat terrain. Additionally, 7.5-minute quadrangles, printed at a scale of 1:24,000 (1"=2,000'), would be too cluttered and unreadable with 1' or 2' contours depicted at that scale. The contour lines would be too close together, and they would coalesce into globs of contour lines that could not be distinguished. Local communities, however, can and do contract for topographic maps with 1' or 2' contours, but they are typically printed with scales of 1"=100' or 1"=200'. Such maps are expensive, but the costs are coming down as lidar technology matures. Furthermore, the cost of IFSAR is so reasonable that we could soon have 10' contours of the entire U.S.

Smooth contour lines can still be produced with the new digital technologies when required for human interpretation, but users must recognize that contours are considerably more expensive than DEMs, and the extra expense of generating nice looking contours is essentially wasted if the primary purpose is to have computers model and analyze the topography. Contour lines are primarily for human interpretation and understanding of elevations. Computers do better with the less expensive TINs or DEMs.

Digital Elevation Data

With digital elevation data, users suddenly have many more choices to make in defining their requirements.

The five technologies showcased in this manual (photogrammetry, IFSAR, topographic lidar, airborne lidar bathymetry, and sonar) all utilize digital technologies, not just to reduce the costs of producing topographic data, but also to improve the accuracy and utility of the data for automated interpretation and analysis by computers and their diverse computer models. That's essentially why we use the term "Digital Elevation Models" – because digital elevation data are usable for *computer modeling* of the terrain, either the terrain's bare earth surface (Digital Terrain Models – DTMs), the terrain's top reflective surface (Digital Surface Models – DSMs), or the bathymetric surface beneath the water's surface elevations.

In deciding what information the computer needs to receive in order to interpret and analyze the DEM automatically, there are many choices to make. The goal of this chapter is to clarify and simplify this decision-making process through the use of the DEM User Requirements Menu (described below) from which users may select their choices and/or tailor them into standard requirements for their organizations. What is a standard requirement for one organization may not be standard for another organization. By popular demand, this chapter will also provide an example Scope of Work (SOW) for a lidar dataset that satisfies requirements of FEMA's Appendix A [FEMA, 2003], as well as a second SOW for an enhanced lidar dataset, more demanding than required by FEMA.

Accuracy and Cost Comparisons

Some choices have little if any impact on costs, whereas other choices may significantly increase project costs if those choices are not well thought out.

The 1st edition of this DEM Users Manual compared USGS costs for acquiring DEMs from photogrammetry, IFSAR and lidar over large project areas of multiple 7.5-minute quadrangles, and it compared the relative costs of photogrammetry and lidar for 2' and 5' contours, for projects with variable areas. Whereas relative costs are essentially the same today, those graphs from the 1st edition are not repeated in this 2nd edition because absolute costs are changing (downward) rapidly as a result of automated processing, compared with considerable manual processing only five years ago. The advantages and disadvantages of these technologies are explained in Chapters 5, 6, 7 and 8. Highlights are as follows:

- Photogrammetry can generate bare-earth data at all accuracy levels and for all size projects. It remains a dominant technology for mid accuracy elevations, i.e., equivalent to 5-ft or 10-ft contours; but photogrammetry is losing market share to lidar for elevation data equivalent to 1-ft and 2-ft contours, and to IFSAR for 10-ft and higher contour intervals. Photogrammetry remains the technology of choice for small mapping projects, for generation of breaklines, and when aesthetically pleasing "cartographic contours" are required.

- IFSAR is best for DSMs, but it also produces DTMs and ortho-rectified radar imagery. It is the least cost option for elevation datasets, recognizing that the typical vertical $RMSE_z$ of 0.5 meters makes IFSAR elevations comparable to 10-ft contours when vegetation and manmade structures are removed. New IFSAR data is not acquired for small project areas, but existing IFSAR data is purchased at low cost with restricted data rights. IFSAR datasets are typically licensed differently than other datasets where data rights are often unrestricted. Normally, entire states are flown, and Intermap Technologies is producing nationwide coverage with its NextMAP USA initiative.

- Lidar is cost-competitive for projects where high accuracies are required. As indicated above, photogrammetry is still better for generation of breaklines and aesthetically pleasing contours, but lidar contours can be aesthetically pleasing when lidar mass points are enhanced with photogrammetric breaklines. Lidar costs have decreased significantly in recent years because of major improvements in automated lidar data processing. Lidar datasets in the $100 to $200 per square mile cost range are generally produced by automated processes, whereas lidar datasets in the $400 to $500 per square mile cost range receive considerable manual editing. Some lidar projects, though, are so technically complex that they cost thousands of dollars per square mile.

Some factors are common to all technologies and will impact the cost per square mile of any airborne data acquisition project:

- Projects that require higher elevation accuracy will be more expensive than projects that can accept lesser accuracy.
- The shape of a project area has a direct bearing on costs. Rectangular areas are the least expensive, and flight plans are simpler if flightlines are north-south or east-west. Irregularly-shaped areas are more expensive. Aircraft acquiring data of meandering streams normally fly larger rectangular blocks that include the meanders.
- Areas with flight restrictions near airfields or military installations are more expensive.
- Projects that can be flown at higher altitude, and/or with wider point spacing, will be less expensive than low altitude projects with narrower point spacing.
- Projects covering terrain that is generally flat can be mapped less expensively than projects covering mountainous terrain, partly because higher sidelap is required between adjoining flightlines and because more flightlines will be needed.
- The deployment distance, number of flightlines, turns, and elevation changes all have a direct bearing on costs.
- The availability of accurate and stable GPS base stations, and the Positional Dilution of Precision (PDOP) of available satellites has a bearing on project costs.
- The density of the vegetation has a bearing on any technology's ability to identify and remove that vegetation for bare-earth processing. It is more difficult, and costly, to remove vegetation so dense that few, if any, ground points are recorded.

DEM USER REQUIREMENTS MENU

In deciding the specifications for an organization's acquisition of DEMs, it ultimately comes down to making choices. Some of these choices impact costs, whereas other choices do not. For this reason, the author is presenting an updated version of his "menu" of choices (Table 13.1), with explanations to help users understand the various options and, where possible, their cost implications. This "User Requirements Menu" is also included, digitally, on the DVD that comes with this manual. The remainder of this chapter is designed to help users understand their choices.

Much of this chapter was extracted from (NDEP, 2004), drafted by this author, which in turn drew heavily upon the 1st edition of this *DEM Users Manual*. The secondary purpose of this chapter is (by popular demand) to provide an example Statement of Work for a lidar dataset that satisfies (FEMA, 2003) requirements because a large percentage of Federal, state and county lidar contracts specify that lidar data must satisfy FEMA's Appendix A which has become a *de facto* industry standard.

Each organization must establish its own requirements for digital elevation data. There is no "one size fits all." This menu establishes a methodical yet flexible process for determining data requirements, minimizing the risk of oversight and misunderstanding between data providers and users. Menu options are explained in the following sections. It is recommended that users establish default values for their various menu options in order to tailor a content standard for their needs.

Table 13.1 User Requirements Menu.

Project Area Name of Project Area if applicable: _____	

Project Boundary: ☐ Rectangular   ☐ Non-Rectangular   ☐ Project Extent Shapefile provided
Over-edge buffer width outside Shapefile area: _____

General Surface Description

Elevation Surface (choose one or more)   **Elevation Type** (choose one)
☐ Digital surface model (first/top reflective surface)   ☐ Orthometric height
☐ Digital terrain model (bare earth)   ☐ Ellipsoid height
☐ Bathymetric surface   ☐ Other _____
☐ Mixed surface   ☐ Point cloud

Data Model Types (choose one or more) * Designate either feet or meters
☐ Mass Points   ☐ Grid (post spacing = ___ feet/meters) *   ☐ Contour Lines
☐ Breaklines   ☐ Grid (post spacing = ___ arc-seconds)   ☐ Cross Sections
☐ TIN (average point spacing = ___ feet/meters) *   ☐ Other, e.g. concurrent imagery

Source (choose one)
☐ Cartographic ☐ Photographic ☐ IFSAR   ☐ Lidar   ☐ Sonar
If multi-return system, choose one or more: ☐ First return   ☐ Last return   ☐ All returns

Vertical Accuracy - General (See Table 13.2, choose one, or more with explanation)   ☐ Other
☐ 1' contour equivalent (Accuracy$_z$ = 0.60 ft)   ☐ 5' contour equivalent (Accuracy$_z$ = 2.98 ft)
☐ 2' contour equivalent (Accuracy$_z$ = 1.19 ft)   ☐ 10' contour equivalent (Accuracy$z$ = 5.96 ft)
☐ 4' contour equivalent (Accuracy$_z$ = 2.38 ft)   ☐ 20' contour equivalent (Accuracy$_z$ = 11.92 ft)

Vertical Accuracy - Specific (choose one or more; FVA is mandatory, SVA and CVA are optional)
☐ Fundamental Vertical Accuracy$_z$ = ___ (ft or cm) at 95% confidence level in open terrain = RMSE$_z$ x 1.9600
☐ Supplemental Vertical Accuracy$_z$ = ___ (ft or cm) = 95th percentile in other specified land cover categories
☐ Consolidated Vertical Accuracy$_z$ = ___ (ft or cm) = 95th percentile in all land cover categories combined

Horizontal Accuracy (See Table 13.3; choose one)   Accuracy$_r$ = RMSE$_r$ x 1.7308
☐ Accuracy$_r$ = ___ feet or meters*   *Designate either feet or meters

Accuracy Reporting (choose one vertical and one horizontal at the 95 percent confidence level)
☐ Tested ___ (meters/ft) vertical accuracy or   ☐ Compiled to meet ___ (meters/ft) vertical accuracy
☐ Tested ___ (meters/ft) horizontal accuracy or ☐ Compiled to meet ___ (meters/ft) horizontal accuracy

Surface Treatment Factors (optional – explain with separate text)   ☐ Vegetation
☐ Hydro-enforcement   ☐ Hydro-conditioning   ☐ Buildings
☐ No data areas (Voids)   ☐ Suspect areas   ☐ Artifacts

Horizontal Datum (choose one)   **Vertical Datum** (choose one)   **Geoid Model** (choose one)
☐ NAD 83 (default)   ☐ NAVD 88 (default) ☐ MSL   ☐ GEOID03 (default)
☐ WGS 84   ☐ MLLW   ☐ Other _____   ☐ Other _____

Coordinate System (choose one)   ☐ UTM zone _____   ☐ State Plane zone _____
☐ Geographic   ☐ Local   ☐ Other

Units Note: Choose one vertical (V) and one horizontal (H) units; V and H units may differ
☐ Elevations to ___ decimal places   ☐ U.S. Survey Feet   ☐ Meters
☐ Northings/Eastings to ___ decimal places   ☐ U.S. Survey Feet   ☐ Meters
☐ Decimal degrees to ___ decimal places   or   ☐ DDDMMSS to ___ decimal places

Data Format (See Table 13.4 and explanations. Specify desired format(s) for each product type)
Vector data _____ Format(s)_____
Mass points and TINs _____ Format(s)_____
Gridded DEMs _____ Format(s)_____

File Size/Tile Size   (Maximum file size, if applicable) _____ Mb / Gb / Other _____
Tile Size, if applicable ☐ ____ ft x ____ ft   ☐ ____ meters x ____ meters   ☐ Other

Metadata Compliant with FGDC's "Content Standards for Digital Geospatial Metadata"

Delivery Schedule Date(s) when deliverables are to be submitted by the Producer to the Customer

Project Area

What is the area to be mapped? In defining the Scope of Work, this is the first question to be answered. The project's extent must be clearly specified, preferably by providing a Shape file to the data producer defining the project area. Project boundaries may be rectangular, but normally they follow non-rectangular boundaries that define a watershed, a county, or a reservation, for example, for which project areas have names. Indicate if the data producer is to obtain the project extent from another source. If a buffer area surrounding the defined extent is desirable (for example, to ensure that a watershed is completely covered, or to have a buffer into surrounding counties) the width of the buffer should be specified.

General Surface Description

The second section of the User Requirements Menu refers to the Elevation Surface description. Check the appropriate box for the elevation surface needed. These surfaces are explained in detail at Chapter 1:

- Digital Surface Model (DSM): The top surface or first reflective surface including tree tops and roof tops.
- Digital Terrain Model (DTM): The bare-earth terrain or last reflective surface after removal of vegetation and manmade structures. This is also called the topographic surface.
- Bathymetric surface: The submerged surface of underwater terrain.
- Mixed surface: A hybrid of two of more surface types, explained under Surface Treatments.
- Point cloud: All returns from a multi-return dataset such as lidar that may collect multiple z-values for each x/y coordinate, e.g., DSM and DTM z-values for the same x/y coordinate.

The next section of the User Requirements Menu refers to the Elevation Type description. Check the appropriate box. These surfaces are explained in detail at Chapter 2:

- Orthometric heights: Equivalent to surveyed elevations above a geodetic vertical datum such as NAVD88 or NGVD29. Orthometric heights are traditionally obtained from conventional differential leveling where survey instruments are leveled to the local direction of gravity.
- Ellipsoid heights: From ground or airborne GPS surveys, including lidar and IFSAR sensors that typically collect ellipsoid heights above a mathematical ellipsoid such as GRS80. Ellipsoid heights are converted to orthometric heights by using the latest geoid model.
- Other: The most common "other" elevation type is bathymetric depth of water, expressed as positive numbers downward below the tidal datum. Minus signs are not depicted on bathymetric contours or soundings unless they are above Mean Lower Low Water (MLLW).

Data Model Types

Table 13.1 lists the most common data models discussed in Chapter 1. Users should select one or more of the following:

- Mass points are obtained from photogrammetric auto-correlation, as well as IFSAR, lidar and sonar. "Raw" mass points are post-processed to provide georeferenced coordinates of the desired surface (e.g., top reflective surface, bare-earth surface, bathymetric surface).
- Breaklines define the seam between two surfaces with different slopes. They are critical for accurate modeling of the 3-D topography when it is important to show the location of surface edges or the discontinuity of surfaces. There are many different kinds of breaklines. When breaklines are required, users must specify those breaklines to be included, e.g., stream centerlines, drainage ditches, tops and bottoms of stream banks, ridge lines, road crowns, levees, bulkheads, seawalls, retaining walls, road/highway embankments, and/or selected manmade features that constrict or control the flow of water (e.g., curb lines).
- TINs are used for many computer applications because they are formed from mass points and breaklines with topology so that the computer understands the relationship between each TIN triangle and its neighboring triangles.

- Gridded DEMs are the simplest data models widely used for general computer modeling of the topography or features thereon. DEMs are not mapped directly but are interpolated from TINs or from mass points and breaklines. The various interpolation procedures are explained in Chapter 1.
- Contour lines are needed primarily when the data will be used for human interpretation of elevation data. Contours have little value for computer modeling of the terrain.
- Cross sections (or transections) are used for special applications to show a string of elevations along a designated line from point A to point B. Cross sections are used for a broad variety of engineering applications, as well as for quality control of digital elevation data.

When selecting the average TIN point spacing or the DEM post spacing, users should recognize that TINs by definition are irregularly spaced, and their average point spacing is typically denser than the DEM post spacing because a larger number of TIN points is needed to interpolate DEM elevations at pre-calculated x/y coordinates for DEM elevation posts.

All of these data models may pertain to any or all of the three principal surfaces: (a) the top reflective surface (e.g., treetops, rooftops, towers, etc.), (b) the bare-earth terrain (normally void of vegetation and man-made structures), and (c) the below-water bathymetric surface.

The density at which elevations are sampled during collection by a lidar or IFSAR system is referred to as the ground-sample distance (GSD), point spacing, or post spacing. The average point spacing of irregularly spaced mass points (from lidar for example) or of uniformly spaced grid points is referred to as the horizontal resolution of the elevation model. The data density at which an elevation product is captured and modeled will determine how well terrain features are represented and how accurately the dataset represents the terrain. The specified horizontal resolution should be chosen carefully, however, because it can have a significant effect on production cost and on data handling efficiency.

The GSD specified for a collection system should be less than the minimum size of terrain features to be detected. Likewise, the horizontal spacing for the final product(s) should be chosen to most efficiently represent the size and frequency of terrain features to be modeled. For example, characterizing rough or dissected terrain may require collection at a 1-meter GSD while gentle relief may warrant collection at a 10-meter GSD. Widely varying terrain may require capture at a fine resolution but may be modeled at a variable resolution using a TIN. The TIN model can retain a high point density over rough terrain but sample to a low point density over gentle terrain.

When deriving a DEM from mass points or TINs, the mass points are normally collected at a higher GSD than the final resolution specified for the DEM. This approach provides multiple surrounding points for interpolation of DEM elevation posts. For example, to derive a DEM with uniform post spacing of 5 meters, it is common for lidar dataset mass points to have average post spacings of approximately 3 meters, a denser dataset from which some points will be removed as a result of post-processing which eliminates points on manmade structures or dense vegetation.

The vertical accuracy of mass points, TINs or DEMs is a function of the horizontal resolution of the digital topographic data. There are no established rules that directly correlate the horizontal resolution of digital elevation data with vertical accuracy, but there is general agreement that TINs/DEMs equivalent to 1-foot contours should have narrower post spacing than TINs/DEMs equivalent to 2-foot contours, for example. Cartographers typically associate DEM post spacing with contour intervals as follows:

- DEMs equivalent to 1 foot contours should have a vertical RMSEz of 9.25-cm (0.30 ft) with post spacings of 1 meter
- DEMs equivalent to 2 foot contours should have a vertical RMSEz of 18.5-cm (0.61 ft) with post spacings of 2 meters
- DEMs equivalent to 5 foot contours should have a vertical RMSEz of 46.3-cm (1.52 ft) with post spacings of 5 meters

- DEMs equivalent to 10 foot contours should have a vertical RMSEz of 92.7-cm (3.04 ft) with post spacings of 10 meters
- DEMs equivalent to 20 foot contours should have a vertical RMSEz of 185.3-cm (6.08 ft) with post spacings of 20 meters

From these correlations, it can be seen that it normally makes little sense to generate a DEM with a vertical accuracy equivalent to 1-foot contours if the DEM post spacing is 10 meters. However, there may be exceptions if the DEM is supplemented with breaklines. Normally, when breaklines are generated by alternative means to supplement the DEM data, then the average DEM post spacing may be relaxed. For example, for the equivalent of 2-foot contours, FEMA considers a 2-meter DEM post spacing to be appropriate if there are no supplemental breaklines, but 5-meter post spacings are adequate if breaklines along shorelines, and at the tops and bottoms of stream banks, for example, are available for use in the hydraulic modeling of floodplains. For some applications, such as the capture of airfield obstructions that may be less than a foot wide, lidar point spacing may be very narrow, with spot sizes large enough to capture 100% of the surface area.

Gridded DEMs have uniform post spacing depicted as Δx and Δy in Figure 1.1c (Chapter 1). When data are required in UTM coordinates, the post spacing is typically specified in terms of meters, typically between 1m and 10m. When data are required in State Plane coordinates, the post spacing is typically specified in terms of U.S. Survey Feet, typically between 5 ft and 20 ft. As explained in Chapter 4, DEMs from the National Elevation Dataset are provided with arc-second post spacing, i.e., from 1 arc-second to 1/9th arc-second.

Contour intervals are reasonably well understood by users. Contours are used for human visualization of the topography. In southern Florida, 1 ft contours are standard because there is so little variation in elevations; in the Rocky Mountains, 50 ft contours are common. Contour intervals are selected, depending on the variation between highest and lowest elevations in the area being mapped. Although contours are not used for computer modeling of topography, it is common to specify the accuracy of mass points, TINs or DEMs in terms of their equivalent contour intervals. This will be explained in greater detail below, and in Table 13.2.

For most users, there is no need to specify a requirement for cross sections. Cross sections typically map the x/y/z coordinates of a line between point A (zero station) and point B (terminal station). In Chapter 1, cross sections are used to show the effects of various methods of interpolation. In Chapter 12, cross sections are used as a tool for quality control of DEMs. For other applications, cross sections are used for volumetric computation of stockpiles, for defining the slope and shape of terrain, levees, road embankments, etc. For hydraulic modeling of floodplains, FEMA requires several forms of cross sections:

- Ground-surveyed cross sections of floodplains and stream channels, upstream and downstream of major bridges for example, surveyed across the floodplain from the left overbank to the right overbank, including stream invert elevations (underwater), especially at the deepest point of the stream. These are used to define floodplain and stream channel geometry above and below the water surface.
- Aerial-surveyed cross sections to define floodplain and stream channel geometry above the water surface only. Cross sections are easily "cut" across TIN surfaces from photogrammetry, IFSAR and lidar.

Among the model types listed in Table 13.1, "Other" typically refers to digital orthophotos or other imagery registered to the elevation data, e.g., digital panchromatic or color imagery, multispectral or hyper-spectral imagery, lidar intensity imagery, or ortho-rectified radar imagery that complements IFSAR elevation data.

Source

Cartographic source materials are used when no alternative source materials are available or viable. Cartographic sources include contours, drainage and transportation features from topographic maps such as USGS 7.5-minute quadrangles. Contour lines may be digitized in vector format to establish line strings of x/y coordinates with z-values for specified contours. Gridded DEMs may then be produced by interpolating at regular intervals between these attributed coordinate strings. TIN points may be interpolated at locations that optimally represent significant changes in slope. Similarly, shorelines of rivers, lakes and other hydrographic features may be digitized in vector format to establish 2-D (x/y) breaklines between the water surface and slope of the ground leading down to the water. Additional breaklines may be digitized for small stream centerlines, drainage ditches, and similar hydrographic features. Such breaklines, when combined with contour lines, are used to establish the direction of flow of rivers and streams. When known river elevations upstream and downstream are applied to 2-D breaklines, they can be converted into 3-D breaklines that gradually decrease from the known upstream elevation to the known downstream elevation. All such breaklines, whether 2-D or 3-D, may be "burned" into DEMs as a form of hydro-enforcement. Lastly, roads, railroads and bridges may also be digitized in vector format to establish breaklines that can be used to improve the accuracy of a DEM. A road may have a "soft breakline" along the crown, causing water to flow off the road into drainage ditches with "hard breaklines" on either side of the road. Bridges (and concrete box culverts) need to be carefully digitized to either delete elevations along the tops of the bridges, or to cut through the bridges with a breaklines to show that water passes under them. If an elevation is retained along the top of a bridge, a bare-earth surface DEM would erroneously appear to be dammed by the bridge and water would not be able to flow under it. Therefore, when producing bare-earth surface DEMs, bridges require a form of hydro-enforcement.

Aerial photography has long provided a common source for production of digital elevation data equivalent to any contour interval, with accuracy dependent primarily upon the flying height at which aerial photography is acquired. See Chapter 5 for stereo photogrammetric procedures used. Photogrammetric DEMs are best produced from photography acquired during deciduous leaf-off months (typically November through March). DEMs can also be produced from satellite imagery, but the accuracy is greatly reduced from that achievable with aerial photography.

IFSAR is a common source for broad area production of digital elevation data equivalent to 10-foot contours. See Chapter 6 for details. Because it is the least expensive option for broad area coverage, IFSAR is ideal for nationwide coverage with a uniform dataset that could, some day, replace portions of the National Elevation Dataset. Contrary to aerial and satellite photography, IFSAR sensors operate both day and night, and they penetrate cloud cover, allowing areas to be mapped that are regularly covered with clouds and haze.

Topographic lidar has become the dominant source for production of digital elevation data equivalent to 2-foot contours, and it is challenging photogrammetry for dominance in the market for 1-foot contours. See Chapter 7 for details. When selecting topographic lidar as the source, it is important to specify whether the first return is to be collected for a DSM, last return is to be collected for a DTM, or all returns are to be collected for analysis of multiple responses. Similarly, bathymetric lidar has become a dominant source for production of shoreline topography and near-shore bathymetry. See Chapter 8 for details. Both topographic and bathymetric lidar systems operate day and night, but they do not penetrate cloud cover as does IFSAR.

Sonar is the source for most bathymetric and hydrographic surveys other than near-shore bathymetry where airborne lidar bathymetry has advantages. See Chapter 9 for sonar details.

Vertical Accuracy

Vertical accuracy is the principal criterion in specifying the quality of digital elevation data, and vertical accuracy requirements ought to depend upon the intended user applications (see Chapter 11). There are five principal applications where high vertical accuracy is normally required of digital elevation datasets: (1) for marine navigation and safety, (2) for stormwater and floodplain management in flat terrain, (3) for management of wetlands and other ecologically sensitive flat areas, (4) for infrastructure management of dense urban areas where planimetric maps are typically required at 1 inch = 100 feet and larger scales, and (5) for special engineering applications where elevation data of the highest accuracy are required. Whereas there is a tendency to specify the highest accuracy achievable for many other applications, users must recognize that lesser standards may suffice, especially when faced with the increased costs for higher accuracy elevation data.

It is important to specify the vertical accuracy expected for all final products being delivered. For example, when contours or gridded DEMs are specified as deliverables from photogrammetric or lidar-generated mass points, a TIN may first be produced from which a DEM or contours are derived. If done properly, error introduced converting the TIN into a DEM or contours should be minimal; however, some degree of error will be introduced. Accuracy should not be specified and tested for the TIN with the expectation that derivatives will meet the same accuracy. Derivatives may exhibit greater error, especially when generalization or surface smoothing has been applied to the final product. Specifying accuracy of the final product(s) requires the data producer to ensure that error is kept within necessary limits during all production steps.

(NDEP, 2004) recommends that users attempt to assess vertical accuracy requirements in terms of potential harm that could be done to the public health and safety in the event that the digital elevation data fail to satisfy the specified vertical accuracy. Many states have regulations that require digital elevation data to be produced by licensed individuals to protect the public from any harm that an incompetent data producer may cause. Licensing of remote sensing professionals is generally linked to experience in proving that products are delivered in accordance with the various standards explained in detail in Chapter 3. User understanding of the basic principles of these Standards will be helpful for understanding the following guidance for determining vertical and horizontal accuracy requirements.

For users to understand the discussion that follows, it is necessary that they understand the various accuracy standards described in Chapter 3, especially (Bureau of the Budget, 1947), (FGDC, 1998), (NDEP, 2004) and (ASPRS, 2004) guidelines. The first two references define vertical accuracy in a general sense, based on contour intervals and the traditional assumption that vertical errors follow a normal error distribution, an assumption that is generally true for photogrammetrically-compiled contours. The latter two references recognize that lidar bare-earth elevation accuracies (and probably IFSAR as well) often differ in vegetative land cover categories where vertical errors may not follow a normal error distribution, as described in detail, with examples, in the first edition of this *DEM Users Manual*. (NDEP, 2004) and (ASPRS, 2004) both define the differences between Fundamental Vertical Accuracy (FVA), Supplemental Vertical Accuracy (SVA), and Consolidated Vertical Accuracy (CVA).

The traditional National Map Accuracy Standard (NMAS) (Bureau of the Budget, 1947) defines vertical accuracy at the 90% confidence level in terms of the published map's contour interval; the NMAS remains valid today only for paper maps. The National Standard for Spatial Data Accuracy (NSSDA) (FGDC, 1998) defines vertical accuracy at the 95% confidence level (Accuracy$_z$) in terms of feet or meters at ground scale; the NSSDA is relevant for all forms of digital elevation data but may overstate the vertical errors from lidar when errors are not normal. The National Digital Elevation Program (NDEP, 2004) and American Society for Photogrammetry and Remote Sensing (ASPRS, 2004) both subdivide Accuracy$_z$ into FVA (mandatory) and SVA and CVA (optional) for accuracy testing purposes, depending on whether Accuracy$_z$ is to be evaluated solely in open terrain (as with the mandatory FVA) or whether other individual or multiple land cover categories are to be evaluated (as optional with the SVA and CVA). (FEMA requires separate testing in major land cover categories representative of the floodplain being modeled.) Because the NSSDA does not address the suitability of data for any particular product, map scale, contour interval, or other application, no error thresholds are established by the NSSDA standard. However, it is often helpful to use familiar NMAS thresholds for determining reasonable NSSDA accuracy requirements for various types of terrain and relief.

The Accuracy$_z$ values shown in Table 13.2 are NSSDA equivalents to the NMAS error thresholds for common contour intervals. Values from the right column of this Table define general vertical accuracy requirements for the User Requirements Menu, Table 13.1.

Table 13.2 Comparison of NMAS/NSSDA Vertical Accuracy.

NMAS Equivalent Contour Interval	NMAS VMAS 90 percent confidence level	NSSDA RMSE$_z$	NSSDA Accuracy$_z$, 95 percent confidence level
1 ft	0.5 ft	0.30 ft or 9.25 cm	0.60 ft or 18.2 cm
2 ft	1.0 ft	0.61 ft or 18.5 cm	1.19 ft or 36.3 cm
4 ft	2.0 ft	1.22 ft or 37.0 cm	2.38 ft or 72.6 cm
5 ft	2.5 ft	1.52 ft or 46.3 cm	2.98 ft or 90.8 cm
10 ft	5.0 ft	3.04 ft or 92.7 cm	5.96 ft or 181.6 cm
20 ft	10.0 ft	6.08 ft or 185.3 cm	11.92 ft or 363.2 cm

In completing the User Requirements Menu (Table 13.1), the required vertical accuracy should be specified in terms of Accuracy$_z$, which may be uniquely derived for a particular application or extracted from the right column of Table 13.2 above. For example, if digital elevation data are required equivalent to 2-foot contours, then Accuracy$_z$ of 1.19 feet should be specified as the general accuracy requirement.

The NDEP and ASPRS both recommend specific vertical accuracy requirements, i.e., FVA (mandatory), CVA (optional) and SVA (also optional). Testing of elevation data over various ground cover categories has revealed that magnitude and distribution of errors often vary between different land cover types. For NDEP and ASPRS purposes, the dataset's FVA (accuracy required over open terrain) must be specified because the FVA determines the accuracy of the basic data, void of any complications from vegetation. If specific accuracy is to be met within other ground cover categories, SVAs should be stated for individual land cover categories, or CVA should be stated for multiple categories combined if the bare-earth DTM must satisfy specific accuracy test criteria also in vegetated areas. It is acceptable to specify a different vertical accuracy in one SVA category (e.g., forested areas) than in another SVA category (e.g., built-up area) where accuracy requirements may differ. Supplemental accuracy requirements should be explained in attached documentation.

SVA and CVA standards should never be more demanding than FVA standards. They may all be the same or they may be varied, such as shown with the following examples:
- FVA and CVA = 1.19 ft (exact equivalence to 2-ft contours)
- FVA = 1.19 ft; CVA = 1.5 ft; SVA = 2.0 ft in forests only (FVA is equivalent to 2-ft contours in open terrain, but CVA and SVA have lesser accuracy in vegetated terrain)
- FVA = 1.00 ft; CVA = 1.19 ft (equivalence to 2-ft contours in all land cover categories, plus FVA is more strict than required for 2-ft contours in open terrain)

Horizontal Accuracy

Horizontal accuracy of elevation data is largely controlled by the vertical accuracy requirement. If a very high vertical accuracy is required, then it will be essential for the data producer to maintain a very high horizontal accuracy. This is because horizontal errors in elevation data normally (but not always) contribute significantly to the error detected in vertical accuracy tests.

Horizontal error is more difficult than vertical error to assess in elevation products. This is because the land surface often lacks distinct (well defined) topographic features necessary for such tests or because the resolution of the elevation data is too coarse for precisely locating distinct surface features. For these reasons, (NDEP, 2004) does not require horizontal accuracy testing of elevation products; instead, the NDEP requires data producers to report the expected horizontal accuracy of elevation products as determined from system studies or other methods. Lidar data, for example, typically has a horizontal (radial) $RMSE_r$ of 50-70 cm which equates to $Accuracy_r$ comparable to maps compiled at a scale of 1" = 100' (see Table 13.3). This table also shows the horizontal accuracy of USGS' standard digital orthophoto quarter quads (DOQQs, 1"=1000') and 7.5-minute topographic quadrangles (1"=2000') as a basis for comparison. State, county and community maps are more likely to be at scales of 1"=100', 1"=200' or 1"=400'.

With the NSSDA, the $RMSE_r$ is defined in terms of feet or meters at ground scale, rather than in terms of the published map's scale. No error thresholds are established for horizontal accuracy by NSSDA. As a general guide, $Accuracy_r$ values shown in Table 13.3 are the NSSDA equivalents to horizontal error thresholds established by NMAS for common map scales.

Table 13.3 is primarily relevant to photogrammetric data for which both planimetric and elevation data are compiled and for which the mapped features are visible on the imagery. However, it is also important to specify some minimum expectation of horizontal accuracy for elevation data acquired through non-photogrammetric means. A horizontal accuracy specification requires the data producer to ensure that an appropriate technology and horizontal control structure is applied during the collection and processing of the elevation data.

Table 13.3 Comparison of NMAS/NSSDA Horizontal Accuracy.

NMAS Map Scale	NMAS CMAS 90% confidence level	NSSDA $RMSE_r$	NSSDA $Accuracy_r$, 95% confidence level
1" = 100' or 1:1,200	3.33 ft	2.20 ft or 67.0 cm	3.80 ft or 1.159m (typical for lidar)
1" = 200' or 1:2,400	6.67 ft	4.39 ft or 1.339 m	7.60 ft or 2.318m
1" = 400' or 1:4,800	13.33 ft	8.79 ft or 2.678 m	15.21 ft or 4.635m
1" = 500' or 1:6,000	16.67 ft	10.98 ft or 3.348 m	19.01 ft or 5.794m
1" = 1000' or 1:12,000 (standard DOQQs)	33.33 ft	21.97 ft or 6.695 m	38.02 ft or 11.588m
1" = 2000' or 1:24,000 * (standard 7.5' quads)	40.00 ft	26.36 ft or 8.035 m	45.62 ft or 13.906m

* The 1:24,000- and 1:25,000-scales of USGS 7.5-minute quadrangles are smaller than 1:20,000; therefore, the NMAS horizontal accuracy test for well-defined test points is based on 1/50 inch, rather than 1/30 inch for maps with scales larger than 1:20,000.

In completing the User Requirements Menu (Table 13.1), the required horizontal accuracy should be specified in terms of Accuracy$_r$ which may be uniquely derived for a particular application or extracted from the right column of Table 13.3 above.

Accuracy Reporting

Whether tested by the data producer or by a different firm that specializes in independent QA/QC, the NSSDA (FGDC, 1998) specifies that vertical and horizontal accuracy should be reported at the 95 percent confidence level for data tested by an independent source of higher accuracy as:

Tested __ (meters, feet) vertical accuracy at 95 percent confidence level

Tested __ (meters, feet) horizontal accuracy at 95 percent confidence level

The "independent source of higher accuracy" should be at least three times more accurate that the dataset being evaluated; typically GPS surveys accurate to 5-cm at the 95 percent confidence level are used as the source of higher accuracy.

The NSSDA further states that an alternative "compiled to meet" statement should be used when the guidelines for testing by an independent source of higher accuracy cannot be followed and an alternative means is used to evaluate accuracy. Accuracy should be reported at the 95 percent confidence level for data produced according to procedures that have been consistently demonstrated to achieve accuracy values as:

Compiled to meet __ (meters, feet) vertical accuracy at 95 percent confidence level

Compiled to meet __ (meters, feet) horizontal accuracy at 95 percent confidence level

The "compiled to meet" statement should be used by data producers when no independent test results are available or can be practicably obtained. For example, vertical accuracy may be impossible to test against an independent source of higher accuracy in very remote or rugged terrain. Note: The horizontal accuracy of elevation datasets is usually impossible to test because horizontal (planimetric) features are normally not well defined in elevation datasets.

It is important to note that the NSSDA test for vertical accuracy is valid only if errors for the dataset follow a normal or Gaussian distribution, i.e., one defined by a bell-shaped curve. (NSSDA modifications for testing and reporting accuracy of non-normal error distributions have been recommended to the FGDC by the NDEP.) Whereas horizontal and vertical errors in open terrain typically have a normal distribution, vertical errors do not typically follow a normal distribution in other land cover categories, especially in dense vegetation where active and passive sensors are unable to detect the ground. For this reason, additional NDEP and ASPRS guidelines have been developed for reporting the vertical accuracy of digital elevation data in land cover categories other than open terrain, e.g., forested areas, scrub, wheat or corn fields, tall weeds, mangrove, sawgrass, and urban terrain.

The NSSDA further specifies: "If data of varying accuracies can be identified separately in a dataset, compute and report separate accuracy values." This is directly relevant to the variable FVA, CVA and SVA criteria recommended by the NDEP and ASPRS and also accommodates the (FEMA, 2003) requirement that the accuracy of lidar bare-earth datasets be evaluated separately in three or more land cover categories representative of floodplains being modeled with the DEM dataset:

- **FVA** may be reported as either (1) "Tested ____ (meters, feet) Fundamental Vertical Accuracy at 95 percent confidence level in open terrain using RMSE$_z$ x 1.9600" or (2) "Compiled to meet ____ (meters, feet) Fundamental Vertical Accuracy at 95 percent confidence level in open terrain."
- **SVA** may be reported as either: (1) "Tested ___ (meters, feet) Supplemental Vertical Accuracy at 95th percentile in (specify land cover category or categories)" or (2) "Compiled to meet ____ (meters, feet) Supplemental Vertical Accuracy at 95th percentile in (specify land cover category or categories)." There is one SVA for each category tested.

- **CVA** may be reported as either: (1) "Tested ___ (meters, feet) Consolidated Vertical Accuracy at 95th percentile in open terrain plus (specify all other categories tested)" or (2) "Compiled to meet ____ (meters, feet) Consolidated Vertical Accuracy at 95th percentile in all land cover categories." When the dataset's accuracy is tested, the metadata should document the errors larger than the 95th percentile. For a small number of errors above the 95th percentile, x/y coordinates and z-errors are normally reported for each QC check point error larger than the 95th percentile. For a large number of errors above the 95th percentile, report only the quantity and range of values.

Surface Treatment Factors

The General Surface Descriptions, described above, define only broad categorizations of elevation surface characteristics. Merely specifying a "top reflective surface" or "bare earth" elevation surface does not sufficiently define how all terrain features are to be represented in the final surface. For example, specifying a bare-earth surface usually implies that elevations on buildings and vegetation should be reclassified but it does not necessarily imply that overpasses and bridges should be reclassified as not part of a DTM.

The intended application of an elevation model typically dictates the particular terrain features to be represented and how those features are to be depicted. Conventions for depicting various features have changed over time. Because of the increasing variety of applications for elevation models, the trend is moving away from strict standardization of how features should be depicted and is moving toward customization for the primary data application.

> **The user's Statement of Work should always provide explicit instructions for representation of the features discussed below or any other terrain feature that might require special treatment. Data producers should document special feature treatments in the metadata.**

Vegetation

For generation of bare-earth DTMs, vegetation is normally reclassified by automated processes, but these processes have limitations, especially when the vegetation is so dense that no remote sensing technology can see and measure the ground on which the vegetation is growing. FEMA's experience with mangrove and sawgrass indicates that such vegetation normally grows on terrain that is very flat, that even lidar cannot penetrate to the ground, and it is better to reclassify lidar points in known mangrove or sawgrass stands and then interpolate from surrounding points to estimate the ground elevations in such stands. Others have similar experiences with corn and wheat, but the terrain may not necessarily be flat and it is more risky to interpolate from surrounding areas.

Lidar first and last return elevations normally differ in soft vegetation, and some users want to not just delete points on vegetation, but to save them in a separate file for vegetation analyses or forestry applications, for example.

Regardless of the rationale, users should at least consider whether there is any need for special treatment of vegetation so the data provider can be informed and options assessed on what is practical and what is impractical.

Hydrologic Enforcement

Hydro-enforcement is defined in Appendix B, Definitions, as the "processing of mapped water bodies so that lakes and reservoirs are level and so that streams flow downhill." Hydro-enforcement is further explained in Chapter 1, including example Figures 1.21 through 1.24. Hydro-enforcement is required when remote sensing systems capture man-made structures as well as natural irregularities in the terrain, including shorelines that appear to undulate up and down. There are different forms of hydro-enforcement that may include any or all of the following: leveling of ponds, lakes and reservoirs that ought to be flat instead of undulating; rivers and streams that ought to depict the downward flow of water instead of undulating up and down; and manmade structures that erroneously appear to impede the flow of water, i.e., bridges and overpasses. Each of these topics is further explained in the following sections.

- Water Bodies. Water body areas are naturally occurring areas of constant elevation, provided that currents and other physical forces do not significantly alter the water surface. With the NGVD29 vertical datum, now obsolete, oceans, bays, or estuaries at mean sea level were traditionally assigned an elevation value of zero; but the current NAVD88 vertical datum accounts for the fact that mean sea level in one location may have an elevation above zero, but elsewhere mean sea level may have an elevation below zero. There are different elevations for mean sea level along coastlines because of variations in ocean topography, currents, and winds. Nevertheless, ponds, lakes and reservoirs are assumed to be level – assigned their known or estimated elevations. Their shorelines may be treated as breaklines with constant elevation. The horizontal position and shape of water body shorelines is normally determined from digital orthophotos or other georeferenced image source.

- Rivers and Streams. Mapped rivers and streams do not have level surfaces. They have variable elevations to depict the downward flow of water. These features are generally wide enough that both shorelines can be represented in the elevation model. The horizontal position and shape of the double shorelines is normally determined from digital orthophotos or other georeferenced image source. These shorelines are also treated as breaklines in one of several ways. (1) When contour lines exist, polygons can be established, bounded by the dual shorelines and upstream and downstream crossing contours, with a uniform elevation assigned to the entire polygon to match that of the lower crossing contour. This is a simple approach but causes the drainage polygons to be "stair-stepped" according to the contour interval. (2) When contour lines exist, the crossing contours can be used to establish the elevations at discrete points along the breaklines that delineate the double shorelines. Elevations are then linearly interpolated for each shoreline vertex between the discrete points. These shoreline breaklines are now 3-D breaklines in which the elevation gradually decreases from the upstream contour elevation to the downstream contour elevation. This is the preferred form of hydro-enforcement for rivers and streams. (3) When contour lines do not exist, the horizontal position and shape of the double shorelines may still be determined from digital orthophotos or other georeferenced image source. Then, alternative methods may be used to estimate water elevations at various locations along the stream for creating sloping 3-D shorelines. With lidar, for example, there are normally some pulses that reflect off of water ripples. When there are a dozen or more returns in water areas that depict consistent elevations, these values may be used to estimate the water elevation at those locations. Alternatively, the lowest elevations along stream banks at selected intervals or locations can be used for the same purpose, and then interpolated to depict continuously sloping shorelines as 3-D breaklines.

- Bridges and Overpasses. Because most aerial and satellite sensors detect the first (top) reflective surface (even with lidar last return), bridge and overpass top surfaces are represented in the original source data. For hydro-enforcement, it is standard procedure to cut 3-D breaklines through bridges and overpasses, assigning breakline elevations to merge with the upstream and downstream shoreline breaklines. The mass point elevations on bridge and overpass decks are reclassified and placed in a separate bridge/overpass file.

Hydrologic Conditioning

Hydro-conditioning is also explained in Chapter 1. This term is defined in Appendix B, Definitions, as the "processing of a DEM or TIN so that the flow of water is continuous across the entire terrain surface, including the removal of all spurious sinks or pits. The only sinks that are retained are the real ones on the landscape." Whereas "hydro-enforcement" is relevant to drainage features that are generally mapped, "hydro-conditioning" is relevant to the entire land surface and is done so that water flow is continuous across the surface, whether that flow is in a stream channel or not. A common example is for the small corrugated metal culverts that drain water from one side of a road to the other. An accurate DEM or TIN would normally show a sink or pit surrounding the water entrance to each culvert. Other sinkholes and depressions occur naturally in the terrain. Such sinks (pits or depressions) could be either *filled* or *drained*. With GIS software, it is very easy to fill such sinks by raising the elevation of sink points to equal that of the lowest surrounding point of higher elevation. However, storm drain modeling and other applications require that sinks be drained, and this is an expensive option that normally requires the manual insertion of 3-D breaklines to drain the sinks logically to other locations of lower elevation, similar to the way that 3-D breaklines are used to reclassify bridges and overpasses that appear to dam the flow of water. To create such 3-D breaklines, it is best if the location of culverts is maintained in a community GIS database, along with invert elevations of culvert inlets and outlets.

Buildings

For most applications, a bare earth DEM means that elevation points on buildings (and trees) are reclassified, basements are neglected, and the terrain where the building exists is smoothed and interpolated from ground elevations surrounding the buildings. However, for hydraulic modeling of floodplains, elevations (and footprints) of buildings may be retained to show that buildings occupy spaces where floodwaters flow and they also impede the natural flow of flood waters. If buildings are to be reclassified for generation of a bare-earth DTM, no further explanation is needed. However, if buildings are to be placed in a separate file, this needs to be clearly articulated to the data producer in the Statement of Work.

No-Data Areas (Voids)

Whether intentional or unintentional, No-Data Areas (Voids) are literally areas with no elevation data. NDEP (2004) recommends that specific information be provided by the data producer that differentiates whether the lack of data is intentional or unintentional. Some indication must be provided outside of the data model (for example in the project metadata or as a polygon) that describes where these void areas are located in the elevation deliverable.

Examples of intentional No-Data Areas would be areas outside the project area for which DEM tiles may be incomplete, large bodies of water on DEM tiles that are deliberately not collected to lower production costs, or areas of sensitive information such as military bases. For bare-earth processing, many elevation points are intentionally reclassified in order to identify points that impinged on the tops of manmade structures or failed to penetrate dense vegetation; such voids are common in all lidar and IFSAR bare-earth datasets and do not require polygon delineations.

Unintentional No-Data Areas include areas where lidar pulses are absorbed by water or hot asphalt and provide no returns; or where high winds, pilot or navigation errors cause gaps between adjoining strips.

For both intentional and unintentional No-Data Areas (typically one acre and larger) a unique value, such as –32768, may be used to flag the areas.

Because of confusion over the use of the term "data voids," many prefer to refer to "data holidays" — defined as areas of missing coverage, caused by missing or unresolvable data, data edits, or incorrectly positioned flightlines, normally identified for further investigation or reflying, including an unintentionally unsurveyed part of a region that was to have been completely surveyed.

Suspect Areas

NDEP (2004) defines Suspect Areas as areas of elevations for which there is a relatively low degree of confidence. They are areas where the producer questions whether the elevations compiled or sensed represent the bare earth, e.g., lidar last return data of dense mangrove or sawgrass where experience or evidence indicates the lidar did not penetrate to the ground beneath. This is similar to the conventional use of dashed contour lines when the photogramme-trist cannot see the bare earth in stereo for forested areas and can only estimate where contours appear to go. When digital elevation data are suspect, some indication must be provided outside of the data model (for example in the project metadata or as a polygon) that describes where these areas are in the elevation deliverable.

Artifacts

An important quality factor for a DEM is its "cleanness" from artifacts. Artifacts are detectable surface remnants of buildings, trees, towers, telephone poles or other elevated features in a bare-earth elevation model. They may also be detectable artificial anomalies that are introduced to a surface model via system-specific collection or processing techniques (for example, corn-row effects of profile collection, star and ramp effects from multidirectional contour interpolation, edge-join offsets, or detectable triangular facets caused when vegetation canopies are weeded from lidar data.). The majority of artifacts are normally removed by automated post-processing. However, the final cleaning of the last 10 percent of the artifacts may take 90 percent of the post-processing budget. Because of costs, users sometimes accept a moderate amount of artifacts, whereas others find artifacts totally unacceptable. Cleanness can be specified as a percentage of the total area. However, quantifying and testing to an acceptable threshold of artifacts is a difficult, subjective, and time-consuming process. Because artifacts are so difficult to quantify, it is best if the user discusses with the data provider the types of artifacts, which artifacts are acceptable (if any), and which artifacts are unacceptable and must be eliminated.

Horizontal Datum

The North American Datum of 1983 (NAD 83) is the official horizontal datum of the United States and should be the default horizontal datum for all geospatial datasets of the United States. NAD 83 is based on the Geodetic Reference System of 1980 (GRS 80) ellipsoid. When NAD 83 was first introduced, it was intended to be nearly identical to the World Geodetic System 1984 (WGS 84). However, recent evidence suggests that NAD 83 is nongeocentric by about 2.25 meters, while the latest version of WGS 84 is geocentric to a few centimeters. The official horizontal datum over the United States for military applications uses the WGS 84 ellipsoid.

Vertical Datum

As explained in Chapter 2, the North American Vertical Datum of 1988 (NAVD 88) is the official National Vertical Datum of the United States and should be the default vertical datum for all topographic elevation datasets of the United States. Whereas Mean Lower Low Water (MLLW) is commonly used for bathymetric data, Chapter 2 explains the various other tidal datums that might be used for bathymetric and hydrographic surveys.

Geoid Model

Chapter 2 explained the differences between orthometric heights, ellipsoid heights, and geoid heights. To accurately convert ellipsoid heights from GPS surveys into traditional orthometric heights, it is necessary to apply geoid height corrections as depicted in the latest geoid model of the area of interest. The National Geodetic Survey (NGS) updates the geoid model nominally every three years, e.g., GEOID93, GEOID96, GEOID99, and GEOID03. It is important that the latest geoid model be used for all surveys that involve GPS, including airborne GPS surveys from lidar and IFSAR, and it is also important that the metadata for any digital elevation dataset include the geoid model that was used. Now that GEOID03 is available, it is important to know whether GEOID03, GEOID99, or GEOID96 corrections were applied to an existing dataset to improve the accuracy of an old survey. It is also critical to remember that overlapping geoid models (such as GEOID03 for the USA and GSD95 for Canada) generally disagree with one another, causing step-functions in any DEM that crosses the border. The military uses the WGS 84 geoid for all applications globally. Therefore, this system has no discontinuities at country borders or boundaries.

Coordinate System

Regardless of the data model selected, users must specify whether they want horizontal coordinates specified in terms of UTM coordinates, State Plane coordinates, or geographic coordinates:

- UTM coordinates are normally used for large areas that cross state boundaries. They are normally the standard for Federal mapping projects.
- State Plane coordinates are normally standard for state, county and local community mapping projects. This is so because the smaller State Plane zones better fit the ellipsoid on which mapping calculations are performed, meaning the distortions are minimized in mapping the spherical earth onto a mapping surface (plane, cylinder, or cone). Furthermore, State Plane scale factor errors are normally small enough that local surveyors can utilize plane surveying instead of geodetic surveying (see Appendix B for definitions).
- Geographic coordinates are represented in terms of the latitude and longitude of each data point. With DEMs, geographic coordinates have fewer edge-join problems than either UTM or State Plane coordinates when it becomes necessary to merge adjoining tiles, and geographic coordinates may be preferred for large, seamless DEM databases such as the National Elevation Dataset. See Chapter 4 for additional details.
- Although not encouraged, some communities have local coordinate systems for a variety of reasons.

Units

Both vertical and horizontal units need to be specified realistically. It makes no sense to specify a higher number of decimal places than achievable from the technology or of value to the user. Excess decimal places can increase file sizes needlessly, but too few decimal places causes DEMs to have the plateau effect demonstrated at Figure 13.1.

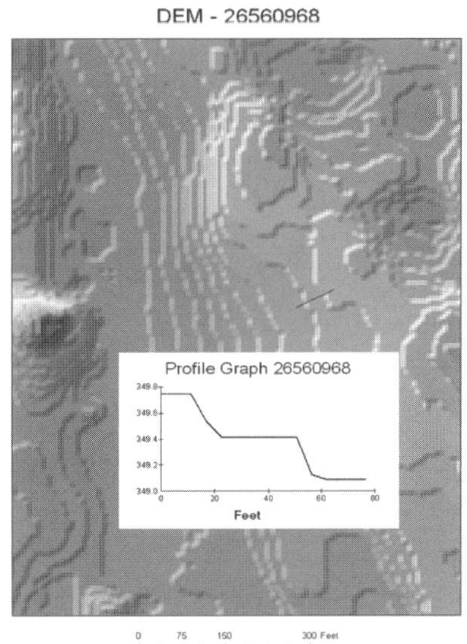

Vertical units are specified either as feet to __ decimal places, or meters to __ decimal places. It is not unusual to mix meters with feet. UTM or State Plane meters for horizontal coordinates are often accompanied by elevations expressed in U.S. survey feet because of nationwide reluctance to convert elevation data to metric units.

Horizontal units are normally specified in one of four ways: (1) feet to __ decimal places; U.S. Survey Feet are assumed unless International Feet are specifically indicated, (2) meters to __ decimal places, (3) decimal degrees to __ decimal places, or (4) degrees, minutes and seconds (DDDMMSS) to __ decimal places for the seconds. One degree of arc at the Equator represents approximately 69.4 miles or 367,000 feet on the ground; therefore decimal degrees to seven decimal places would indicate horizontal location to the nearest 0.367 feet or 4.4 inches. One second of arc at the Equator represents approximately 101.85 ft on the ground; therefore DDDMMSS to two decimal places would indicate horizontal location to the nearest 1.02 ft.

DEM - 26560968

Profile Graph 26560968

Figure 13.1 Elevations appear as plateaus when too few decimal places are used, as is common with DTMs used for rectification of digital orthophotos. See color plate in Appendix C.

Data Format

Users need to specify their desired formats for vector data, mass points, TINs, and uniformly-gridded DEMs. Table 13.4 lists common alternatives, but this list is not all-inclusive.

Table 13.4 Common Data Formats.

Vector Data	Mass Points and TINs	Gridded DEMs
.DGN	ASCII x/y/z	ASCII x/y/z
.DLG	ASCII w/attribute data	.BIL
.DWG	BIN	.BIP
.DXF	.LAS	.DEM (USGS standard)
.E00	TIN (ArcInfo Export	DTED
.MIF/.MID	File)	ESRI Float Grid
.SHP	Other _____	ESRI Integer Grid
SDTS		GeoTiff
VPF		.IMG
Other _____		.RLE
		Other _____

Vector Data

Digital contours and breaklines are vector datasets that are typically produced in any of the following file formats: .DGN, .DO (DLG Optional), .DWG, .DXF, .E00, .MIF/.MID, .SHP, SDTS, or VPF. Other vector file formats may be specified if required.

- DGN: MicroStation Design file, internal proprietary drawing data base format.
- DLG: Digital Line Graph (DLG) file format for vector data (USGS and FEMA).
- DWG: AutoCAD native file format; internal proprietary drawing data base format.
- DXF: Autodesk Drawing eXchange Format, ASCII or binary file format used to transfer data between CAD and GIS.
- E00: Arc/Info Export (Interchange) file of either binary coverages or grids.
- MIF/MID: MapInfo data interchange format; contains vector drawings and tables (data bases).
- SHP: ESRI Shape file, a collection of files (at a minimum, *.shp, *.shx and *.dbf) used by ArcGIS and ArcView for vector data and attributes.
- SDTS: Spatial Data Transfer Standard, ASCII or binary file format designed to handle earth-referenced spatial data between dissimilar computer systems.
- VPF: Vector Product Format, a binary vector format used by NGA.
- Other vector file format specified by the user.

Mass Points and TINs

Mass points are typically produced as ASCII x/y/z files, ASCII files with additional attribute data, LAS, or BIN format. They may be converted and stored in a TIN format, but TIN files are much larger than the mass point files from which they are derived because the TIN structure has to accommodate the topological data structure that exists between each TIN triangle and its adjoining neighboring triangles. For this reason, users often store the x/y/z point data files in ASCII format, and then reconstruct TINs when needed.

- ASCII x/y/z: American Standard Code for Information Interchange (ASCII), predominant character set encoding of computers.
- ASCII x/y/z with Attributes: In addition to x/y/z coordinates, additional attributes may be provided such as acquisition dates, sensor make/model (when different sensors are used on a project), or lidar intensity values for example.
- BIN: Binary encoding of ASCII data.
- .LAS: Binary file format that maintains information specific to lidar data; public file format for the interchange of lidar data between vendors and customers.
- TIN Arc/Info Export file format.
- Other file formats used by different GIS software programs and preferred by the user.

Uniformly-Spaced (Gridded) DEMs

Grid elevations are typically produced in any of the following file formats: ASCII x/y/z, .BIL, .BIP, .DEM (USGS standard), DTED (NGA standard), ESRI Float Grid, ESRI Integer Grid, GeoTIFF, or .RLE. Other grid elevation formats may be specified if required.

- BIL: Band Interleaved by Line format, treats each line of pixels as separate units and then stores by lines.
- BIP: Band Interleaved by Pixel format, treats pixels as separate storage units
- BSQ: Band Sequential format, all data for a single band (in this case DEM) are written to one file.
- DEM: a standard format used by USGS to record elevation data; cell values reflect elevation data and not pixel brightness.
- DTED: a standard format used by NGA to record elevation data. See Appendix B for an expanded definition of different DTED levels defined in terms of post spacing.
- ESRI Float Grid: 32 bit floating point raster grids for ESRI products.
- ESRI Integer Grid: 16 bit integer format.
- GeoTiff: Georeferenced Tagged Image File Format, one of the most widely supported file formats for storing bit-mapped images; can be used with TWF (tagged world file) for georeferencing.
- .IMG: ERDAS Imagine hierarchal file format for raster data.
- RLE: Run Length Encoding is a band sequential format that stores the cell value and the number of times it occurs along a given raster line.
- Other file formats used by different GIS software programs and preferred by the user.

File Size/Tile Size

For small projects, the entire project extent may fit well into one manageable file. For large projects, the project area must be broken into multiple files to make the datasets manageable. File boundaries may be rectangular – based on consistent intervals of feet, meters, or degrees – or nonrectangular – based on a string of x/y coordinates that define an irregular project area.

The size of the data file will have an impact on how the user will be able to manage and manipulate the product. A range of acceptable file sizes should be specified by the user if that is a factor that over-rides all other considerations. Factors to consider include: desktop computing power and capacity, storage/transfer media capacities, file transfer rates, and file display, manipulation, and maintenance efficiency. File sizes are typically limited to 1 gigabyte (Gb).

In many cases, users choose to limit files by "tile" size, such as 5000 ft x 5000 ft, 1000 meters x 1000 meters, or by 3.75-minute quarter-quad tiles. Depending on the horizontal resolution of data within these "tiles," the file sizes will vary.

Metadata

FGDC-compliant metadata should be mandatory for all digital elevation datasets. Requirements are defined in the FGDC Content Standards for Digital Geospatial Metadata (FGDC-STD-001-1998). Metadata describes the digital dataset, its lineage, production processes, file formats, positional accuracy, and other information needed to understand the dataset and use it correctly.

Delivery Schedule

The Statement of Work always includes the delivery schedule for which various deliverables must be provided to the client.

BASIC LIDAR STATEMENT OF WORK (SOW)

Example 1: Basic Lidar with no Breaklines

The following provides an example lidar project SOW, for lidar data with accuracy equivalent to 2-foot contours, designed to satisfy basic FEMA Appendix A requirements (FEMA, 2003) of an imaginary Flood County, North Carolina, considered to have relatively normal, flat floodplains. North Carolina's State Plane coordinates are metric. Note: Section A.4.3 of Appendix A states: "…if Mapping Partners are producing DFIRM work maps in flat terrain with digital topographic data equivalent to 2-foot contours, 2-meter post spacing may be appropriate if no supplemental breaklines are provided, but 5-meter post spacing is appropriate if supplemental breaklines are provided" and "… the horizontal resolution of [raw lidar] mass points normally is narrower than the DEM resolution." This example was chosen with no breaklines. The accuracy testing methodology in this SOW assumes that FEMA concurs with the FVA, SVA and CVA test criteria endorsed by the NDEP and ASPRS, and will incorporate these newer criteria in the next update to Appendix A. This Example 1 SOW is included, digitally, on the DVD included with this manual.

Overview

This Statement of Work (SOW) was developed by the Flood County GIS Coordinator to collect and deliver digital elevation data of the County to support FEMA Flood Insurance Studies and other County departments. The project area is defined by the attached Shapefile of the County, including a 100m buffer into adjoining counties. The entire project area, including buffers, is 1525 Km^2. As part of the County's Cooperating Technical Partner (CTP) agreement with FEMA, the data must satisfy requirements of Appendix A, *Guidance for Aerial Mapping and Surveying*, to FEMA's "Guidelines and Specifications for Flood Hazard Mapping Partners."

Technical Requirements

The Contractor shall collect lidar multiple-return mass points of the project area, with 1.5-meter nominal point spacing, and will deliver a Digital Terrain Model (DTM) of the bare-earth terrain consisting of variably-spaced mass points and a gridded DEM with 2-meter post spacing. The vertical accuracy of the DTM shall be equivalent to 2-ft contours, i.e., vertical accuracy of 1.19-ft or better at the 95 percent confidence level ($RMSE_z = 0.60$ ft). The elevation data shall be compiled so as to yield horizontal accuracy of 3.0 ft or better at the 95 percent confidence level.

The lidar last-return mass points will be filtered to remove vegetation, man-made structures, and artifacts that do not represent the bare-earth terrain.

Lidar data from different flight lines shall be consistent across flight lines, i.e., there is no significant vertical offset between adjacent flight lines. Lidar data holidays will be avoided.

Independent Accuracy Assessment

To ensure satisfaction of FEMA requirements, the County intends to perform independent accuracy assessment of the DTM, consistent with FEMA guidelines, in five major land cover categories: (1) open terrain, (2) weeds and crops, (3) scrub and bushes, (4) forested, and (5) built-up areas. Testing for "open terrain" will be performed using QA/QC checkpoints on dirt, sand, rock, and/or short vegetation up to 6-inches tall. Testing for "weeds & crops" will be performed in weeds and crops up to 3-ft tall. Testing for "scrub & bushes" will be performed in scrub, bushes and other vegetation up to 6-ft tall. Testing for "forests" will be performed in forests and/or orchards with trees taller than 6-ft. Testing for "built-up areas" will be performed on concrete or asphalt surfaces.

Consistent with 2-ft contours in open terrain only, the Fundamental Vertical Accuracy (FVA) must be 1.19 ft or less in open terrain based on $RMSE_z$ x 1.9600; and the Consolidated Vertical Accuracy (CVA) must be 1.19 ft or less, based on the 95th percentile errors in all land cover categories combined. Supplemental Vertical Accuracy (SVA) target values are 1.19 ft or less based on the 95th percentile errors in each of the five land cover categories, but some individual SVA values may be higher than 1.19 ft so long as other SVA values are low enough to reduce the combined CVA value to 1.19 ft or less to satisfy FEMA requirements.

Metadata

As a minimum, the project metadata records shall detail all flight lines, flight dates and times, datums, projections, processing steps, field records, and positional accuracy.

The Vertical Positional Accuracy should state the County's "tested values" for FVA and CVA as follows: "Tested ___ ft Fundamental Vertical Accuracy at 95 percent confidence level in open terrain using $RMSE_z$ x 1.9600" and "Tested ___ ft Consolidated Vertical Accuracy at 95th percentile in all land cover categories combined."

The Horizontal Positional Accuracy should state the Contractor's "compiled to" value as follows: "Compiled to meet 3.0 ft horizontal accuracy at 95% confidence level."

The metadata records shall conform to the Content Standards for Digital Geospatial Metadata (FGDC-STD-001-1998) as published on May 1, 2000 by the FGDC, or to any format that supersedes it as determined by the FGDC.

Deliverables

1. Bare-earth lidar mass points in ASCII x/y/z/intensity format. Elevation data shall be NAVD88 orthometric heights, meters to three decimal places; orthometric heights will be computed using the latest geoid model (GEOID03) conversion from ellipsoid heights. Horizontal coordinates shall be in the North Carolina State Plane Coordinate System, Zone 3200, NAD83, meters to two decimal places.
2. Gridded DEM with 2 meter post spacing, ESRI Float Grid format
3. FGDC-compliant metadata for all deliverables (project wide), meeting specifications defined above, containing sufficient detail to ensure all data products can be fully understood for future use and for posterity.
4. All datasets will be delivered on tiles, 1000m x 1000m, with the tile grid index based on even 1000m grid lines for the North Carolina State Plane Coordinate System. Data delivery shall be by external hard drive supporting USB 2.0 standards. The hard drive will not be returned by the County. Delivered elevation data shall become the property of the County and will be shared with the public. The Contractor shall also retain the ability to use and distribute the data.

Delivery Schedule

All deliverables will be submitted to the County GIS Coordinator not later than MM/DD/YY.

ENHANCED LIDAR STATEMENT OF WORK (SOW)

> **Example 2: Enhanced Lidar with 3D Breaklines**
> The following provides an example lidar project SOW for enhanced data, designed to satisfy FEMA Appendix A requirements (FEMA, 2003) <u>plus</u> additional more-demanding requirements of an imaginary Mangrove County, Florida Water Management District. Measurement units for the Florida State Plane Coordinate System are U.S. Survey Feet. Whereas most floodplains are essentially flat, this imaginary county is extremely flat. *Those SOW requirements in excess of "standard" FEMA requirements for flat floodplains are stated in italics*. These exceptions are included to demonstrate flexibility in meeting local requirements where, in the case of Mangrove County, the terrain is so flat that there is a need for higher-accuracy DTM and 3D breaklines, and where it is known that lidar cannot penetrate through dense mangrove to map the terrain beneath. Users must recognize that this SOW for Example 2 will cost considerably more than the basic SOW for Example 1. This Example 2 SOW is also included, digitally, on the DVD included with this manual.

Overview

This Statement of Work (SOW) was developed by the Mangrove County Water Management District to collect and deliver high-resolution, high-accuracy digital elevation data of the County to support local Coastal Zone Managers, Flood Plain Managers, Storm Water Managers, the state Department of Natural Resources, and other decision-makers. The project area is defined by the attached Shapefile of the County, including a 500 ft buffer into adjoining counties. The entire project area, including buffers, is approximately 610 square miles. As part of the County's Cooperating Technical Partner (CTP) agreement with FEMA, the data must satisfy requirements of Appendix A, *Guidance for Aerial Mapping and Surveying*, to FEMA's "Guidelines and Specifications for Flood Hazard Mapping Partners."

Technical Requirements

The Contractor shall collect lidar multiple-return mass points of the project area, with *3-foot* nominal point spacing, and will deliver *multiple-return classified mass point data in LAS format; 3D breaklines*; and a gridded DEM with *5-ft post spacing*. The vertical accuracy of the DTM shall be equivalent to *1-ft contours in open terrain* and 2-ft contours in vegetated areas. *In addition to the measured elevation value, the intensity value for each return shall be included and, at a minimum, returns shall be classified as water, bare-ground or not bare-ground according to the ASPRS LAS format classification table. The point data type used in LAS format shall include the GPS time, and the headers shall include the date of collection.* The elevation data shall be compiled so as to yield horizontal accuracy of 3.0 ft or better at the 95 percent confidence level.

Breaklines (3D) will be generated for all shorelines (streams >20 ft wide) or centerlines (<20 ft wide), top and bottom of stream banks, bulkheads, and edge-of-pavement for paved roads. Breaklines may be generated either by lidargrammetry – using lidar intensity images, or by photogrammetry – using digital imagery and photogrammetric data available from the County's GIS Coordinator, John Doe. Mr. Doe can be contacted for information at (123) 456-7890. Mr. Doe will also provide the Contractor with a Shapefile showing the perimeter of mangrove stands in the County. Recognizing that lidar will not penetrate dense mangrove, the GIS Coordinator recommends that all lidar returns in mangrove stands be classified as "not bare-ground" so that elevations in mangrove stands will be interpolated from surrounding terrain areas.

The DTM will be hydro-enforced by leveling of lake shorelines; by utilization of 3D breaklines on river shorelines (>20 ft wide) or centerlines (<20 ft wide) to enforce downward flow of water; and by reclassifying bridges to "not bare-ground". Once the DTM is accepted, the Contractor will provide a uniformly gridded DEM with 5-ft post spacing.

Lidar data from different flight lines shall be consistent across flight lines, i.e., there is no significant vertical offset between adjacent flight lines. Lidar data holidays will be avoided.

Independent Quality Assessment

Both quantitative (accuracy) and qualitative (usability) quality assessments will be performed. To ensure satisfaction of FEMA requirements, the County intends to perform independent accuracy assessment of the DTM, consistent with FEMA guidelines, in five major land cover categories: (1) open terrain, (2) weeds and crops, (3) scrub and bushes, (4) forested, and (5) built-up areas. Testing for "open terrain" will be performed using QA/QC checkpoints on dirt, sand, rock, and/or short vegetation up to 6-inches tall. Testing for "weeds & crops" will be performed in weeds and crops up to 3-ft tall. Testing for "scrub & bushes" will be performed in scrub, bushes and other vegetation up to 6-ft tall. Testing for "forests" will be performed in forests and/or orchards with trees taller than 6-ft. Testing for "built-up areas" will be performed on concrete or asphalt surfaces.

Consistent with 1-ft contours in open terrain only, the Fundamental Vertical Accuracy (FVA) must be 0.60 ft or less in open terrain based on $RMSE_z$ x 1.9600. Consistent with 2-ft contours, the Consolidated Vertical Accuracy (CVA) must be 1.19 ft or less, based on the 95th percentile errors in all land cover categories combined. Supplemental Vertical Accuracy (SVA) target values are 1.19 ft or less based on the 95th percentile errors in each of the five land cover categories, but some individual SVA values may be higher than 1.19 ft so long as other SVA values are low enough to reduce the combined CVA value to 1.19 ft or less to satisfy FEMA requirements.

The County or its independent QA/QC subcontractor will also perform a qualitative assessment of the DTM to assess usability, identify systematic errors and uncleaned artifacts.

No rigorous, independent horizontal accuracy assessments will be performed, but paint stripes on asphalt, if visible on the intensity images, will be spot checked for horizontal accuracy.

Metadata

As a minimum, the project metadata records shall detail all flight lines, flight dates and times, datums, projections, processing steps, field records, and positional accuracy.

The Vertical Positional Accuracy should state the County's "tested values" for FVA and CVA as follows: "Tested ___ ft Fundamental Vertical Accuracy at 95 percent confidence level in open terrain using $RMSE_z$ x 1.9600" and "Tested ___ ft Consolidated Vertical Accuracy at 95th percentile in all land cover categories combined."

The Horizontal Positional Accuracy should state the Contractor's "compiled to" value as follows: "Compiled to meet 3.0 ft horizontal accuracy at 95% confidence level."

The metadata records shall conform to the Content Standards for Digital Geospatial Metadata (FGDC-STD-001-1998) as published on May 1, 2000 by the FGDC, or to any format that supersedes it as determined by the FGDC.

Deliverables

1. *Multiple-return classified mass point data in LAS format meeting specifications described above.*
2. Elevation data shall be NAVD88 orthometric heights, U.S. Survey Feet to two decimal places; orthometric heights will be computed using the latest geoid model (GEOID03) conversion from ellipsoid heights. Horizontal coordinates shall be in the Florida State Plane Coordinate System, Zone 0901, NAD83, in U.S. Survey Feet to two decimal places.
3. *3D breaklines, .DGN format, in six files: (1) level shorelines for lakes, (2) non-level shore lines for streams, (3) breaklines through bridges, (4) tops/bottoms of stream banks, (5) bulkheads, and (6) road edge-of-pavement. A vector format other than .DGN may be recommended by the contractor for decision by the County.*
4. Gridded DEM with 5-ft post spacing, ESRI Float Grid format.

5. FGDC-compliant metadata for all deliverables (project wide), meeting specifications defined above, containing sufficient detail to ensure all data products can be fully understood for future use and for posterity.

6. All datasets will be delivered on tiles, 5000' x 5000', with the tile grid index based on even 5000' grid lines for the Florida State Plane Coordinate System. Data delivery shall be by external hard drive supporting USB 2.0 standards. The hard drive will not be returned by the County. Delivered elevation data shall become the property of the County and will be shared with the public. The Contractor shall also retain the ability to use and distribute the data.

Delivery Schedule

All deliverables will be submitted to the County GIS Coordinator not later than MM/DD/YY.

SUMMARY

Documenting DEM user requirements can be very complex. It is common for users to overstate or misunderstand their accuracy requirements, and then be unable to afford the cost. It is common for users to be confused by the different ways in which vertical and horizontal accuracy are specified. It is also common for users to be confused by the myriad of data models, datums, coordinate systems, digital data formats, and complex ways of assessing data quality. Don't be dismayed. You are not alone. This chapter, and in fact this entire DEM Users Manual, was designed to demystify these issues so that users now have a single menu to look at to help them understand their choices, and an example to follow if they require lidar data that satisfies FEMA requirements. If you still don't understand the issues, be sure to obtain clarification before you sign a contract for production of digital elevation data. It's best to get your answers in writing, and it's best to evaluate sample data sets in advance to ensure that you know what to expect. Only when the user knows what to expect, and the data provider knows what the user expects, will the client be happy. Happy clients lead to repeat business as the user's data needs updating in the future.

All geospatial data providers want their clients to be satisfied with their products. This chapter is designed to facilitate communications between user and provider so that there are no misunderstandings.

AUTHOR BIOGRAPHY

David Maune is a geodesist, ASPRS Certified Photogrammetrist, and Project Manager for Geographic Information Services at Dewberry in Fairfax, Virginia. He manages Dewberry's DEM production contracts with USGS, NOAA and USDA, and he manages Dewberry's contracts for independent QA/QC of statewide DEMs produced by others for North Carolina, Virginia, Maryland, Indiana, and hundreds of individual counties nationwide to ensure conformance with FEMA requirements (FEMA, 2003). As FEMA's representative on the Technical Subcommittee of the National Digital Elevation Program (NDEP), he drafted the NDEP *Guidelines for Digital Elevation Data* (NDEP, 2004), based on the first edition of this manual, and those guidelines became a major component of the *ASPRS Guidelines, Vertical Accuracy Reporting for Lidar Data* (ASPRS, 2004). He is the principal author of the National Geodetic Survey (NGS) "National Height Modernization Study, Report to Congress" on modernization of the National Height System in the U.S. He has over 40 years of experience in the geospatial profession, including 30 years with the U.S. Army Corps of Engineers where he served as Director, U.S. Army Topographic Engineering Center (TEC); Director, Defense Mapping School (DMS); and Inspector General, Defense Mapping Agency (DMA) — now the National Geospatial-Intelligence Agency (NGA). He teaches workshops for FEMA and ASPRS on DEM accuracy assessments. He earned his BS in Mechanical Engineering in 1961 from the University of Missouri, Rolla, and in 1970 and 1973 he received his MS and PhD degrees in geodetic science and photogrammetry from The Ohio State University.

ACKNOWLEDGEMENTS

The author gratefully acknowledges the assistance provided by Timothy Blak (Dewberry), as well as Eric Constance (USGS, Rolla, Missouri) who provided input for the User Requirements chapter in the first edition of this manual..

REFERENCES

ASPRS, 2004. ASPRS guidelines, vertical accuracy reporting for lidar data, American Society for Photogrammetry and Remote Sensing (ASPRS), May 24, 2004, URL: http://www.asprs.org/society/committees/lidar/downloads/Vertical_Accuracy_Reporting_for_Lidar_Data.pdf.

Bureau of the Budget, 1947. *National Map Accuracy Standards (NMAS)*, Office of Management and Budget, Washington, DC.

FEMA, 2003. Appendix A, Guidance for aerial mapping and surveying, in *Guidelines and Specifications for Flood Hazard Mapping Partners*, Federal Emergency Management Agency (FEMA), April 2003, URL: http://www.fema.gov/plan/prevent/fhm/gs_main.shtm.

FGDC, 1998. Geospatial positioning accuracy standards, Part 3: National standard for spatial data accuracy (NSSDA), Federal Geographic Data Committee (FGDC), URL: http://www.fgdc.gov/standards/standards_publications.

NDEP, 2004. Guidelines for digital elevation data, Version 1.0, National Digital Elevation Program (NDEP), May 10, 2004, URL: http://www.ndep.gov/NDEP_Elevation_Guidelines_Ver1_10May2004.pdf.

Chapter 14

Lidar Processing and Software

Mark E. Romano

TECHNOLOGY OVERVIEW

Lidar software is a rapidly evolving technology that is a significant part of the data collection, production workflow, and analysis for users wanting to efficiently manage and utilize the feature rich data generated from today's advanced lidar systems. Many existing software applications can ingest elevation data, but were not designed to handle the voluminous amount of data generated by the technology. In its native (raw) format, lidar datasets store additional information beyond straightforward elevation (x,y,z) data models, including intensity, flight-line, timestamp and other data fields that cannot be fully utilized by many familiar software applications. Understanding the level of usability for various project requirements should be carefully considered. Post-process data users may have significant issues to contend with regarding QA, data manageability, practical data reduction, and reformatting, without appropriate applications to manage its true potential. Users are encouraged to evaluate applications that are designed with this specific purpose in mind.

Premise

The premise of this chapter is to increase familiarity for creating and using DEM products utilizing lidar data in its native (.las) binary format as the primary input data source. Currently two versions of this format exist that are recognized by ASPRS, i.e., ASPRS Lidar Data Exchange Format Standard Version 1.0, released May 9, 2003, and version 1.1, released March 7, 2005. The initial versions encompassed primarily elevation only data. A new version (2.0), currently under investigation, will begin to address other types of ancillary data, most significantly multi-dimensional arrays to encompass the fusion of other raster and vector data to further exploit intelligent processing of the feature rich 3D reflective surface models generated by lidar technology. Once augmented and/or integrated (fused) with other types of ancillary data sources such as ground survey, photogrammetric, sonar, radar, ground based lidar, multi-spectral, hyper-spectral and others, lidar will realize its original paradigm shift from traditionally generated topography to the far reaches of efficient and automated extraction of planimetric databases, high resolution 3D visualization of fused data sources (raster and vector), and high-level correlated analysis between multi-sensor platforms.

Data accuracy, precision, and end use should always dictate the level of appropriate data processing and output data reduction and formatting. These constraints and standards are well described within this manual, especially for more traditional topographic, vector, and raster data deliverables and should be carefully considered when choosing the quality requirements and specifications for final products. Cost is always an important factor in considering the amount of processing that is affordable, practical, and necessary when evaluating data that have dramatically changed the rules that could previously be applied utilizing traditional photogrammetric techniques. While analogies can be made to traditional map scale and accuracies for final DEM products, it can appear ambiguous to directly correlate and quantify the aspects of this uniquely different data source. To that end this chapter will attempt to demystify the process flow utilized to produce accurate lidar DEMs today and look forward to where the industry will progress after applying research in the commercial, academic, and government sectors to significantly exploit the reflective surface model capabilities of this data source.

Developmental History

Since the onset of the first laser ranging systems, lidar has the ability to produce voluminous data sets. Early profilers to modern day high pulse rate scanning systems continue to increase demands on existing CAD and GIS software applications. These software applications are a good analogy for the "right tool for the wrong job." CAD and GIS applications were not intended for the requirements of the higher-fidelity data produced with today's airborne lidar sensors. While these applications are excellent resources for engineering and Geographic Information Systems (GIS) in the downstream process, there is an important distinction to make when evaluating the level of data processing and usability required for management of this data source in a timely, cost effective manner.

Early in the commercialization of airborne lidar processing technology, it was a common goal to reduce data to a ground base or topographic model only because available software and usability were minimal for the large data sets. Primary end users wanted a reduced mass point (often grid) surface model product to generate topography in existing CAD and/or GIS environments. Much of the data had to be reduced or removed, limiting the higher fidelity of terrain that can be produced in order to facilitate its use. However, as the first images of lidar reflective surface models were revealed, it was certain that much of the data were under-utilized. The only problem was, no one knew how or what could be effectively derived from it, nor to what accuracy.

No public standards or guidelines existed for quality assurance or formats until the FEMA lidar guidelines were published in 1999 and improved with the current guidelines (FEMA, 2003). Subsequently, ASPRS formed a Lidar Committee to define a lidar binary data exchange format standard; the LAS standard (.las 1.0) was first published in 2003 and improved with the current .las 1.1 (ASPRS, 2005). Both of these guidelines and standards are being widely adopted throughout the industry.

In the past several years, lidar software applications have emerged globally in the commercial, government, and academic environments. Other digital remote sensing platforms (e.g., multi-spectral and hyper-spectral) and instruments are rapidly approaching the commercial environment and are becoming main-stream as well. Fusion of these rapidly evolving technologies will significantly advance the exploitation of these feature rich data sources with far more advanced applications as a necessary result.

LIDAR SOFTWARE REQUIREMENTS AND PROCESS FLOW

The most modern lidar sensors have the capability to generate extremely accurate and high-fidelity reflective surface models, including Digital Surface Models (DSMs) then, after post-processing and breaklines, Digital Terrain Models (DTMs). These lidar sensors continue to evolve, increasing collection efficiency of continually higher-resolution Ground Sample Distance (GSD), further exacerbating demands on processing platforms. Terabytes of project data are not uncommon with today's high pulse rate systems. Per the existing .las 1.1 standard a single lidar point record reserves 28 bytes per point in memory to store all data fields, making efficient application development and data reduction key project components.

Users of lidar software can be separated into several categories within the process/work flow in order of:
- Data Collection (Level I processing)
- Raw Data Calibration and QA (Level II processing)
- Data Production of Classified Data (Level III processing)
- High-Level Analysis of Discrete Features (Level IV processing)
- CAD/GIS Post-Processed Data (Users)

Data Collection (Level I Processing)

Lidar data collection has specific requirements to evaluate field data. In contrast to film production workflows, digital sensors (lidar and other imagers alike) present unique challenges with respect to data management and quality assurance on a near real-time basis. For many years film was processed after field collection, sometimes weeks-months prior to entering the digital production workflow as scanned photos. Today's lidar and other digital sensor data collection allow for field data to be evaluated prior to leaving project locations, ensuring that data coverage and quality are present. This is truly a digital end-to-end process. However, this requires organized timely logistics and critical investment in processing infrastructure to be successful. Typically data are processed onsite or sent to processing support centers for quick evaluation and feedback to field teams. The steps for near real-time evaluations of field data include:

1. Airborne and ground base station GPS processing (sensor position) – vendor specific
2. Processing of inertial data (sensor orientation) – vendor specific
3. Processing of lidar (creation of elevation data/raw lidar) – vendor specific
4. Project coverage verification
5. Review of data against GPS field calibration control
6. Canopy penetration

Raw Lidar Processing

Commercial lidar hardware vendors typically provide software for GPS, inertial, and raw processing, which includes sensor models specific to sensor dynamics, flight planning, eye safety, altitude vs. accuracy, and other flight logistic parameters for project data collection design, and post-processing to the raw (.las) data format. This chapter will not attempt to cover specific hardware processing software as it is both proprietary and sensor vintage specific. Operational parameters should be designed by lidar operators knowledgeable of the specific hardware being utilized, mapping or other accuracy specifications, and final project deliverables meeting customer requirements.

Since steps 1-3 are hardware "vendor specific" they will not be covered in this chapter. Once the data have been processed to the raw or unclassified point cloud state, they can then be processed in the .las binary format.

Project Coverage Verification

Typically, coverage verification is a combination of statistical and visual review. The .las format contains a flight-line field record, which is useful for verifying coverage breaks in the data collection. Post-processed lidar point clouds are reviewed for data gaps visually. Figure 14.1 illustrates lidar data colored by flight-line. Note the hole (holiday) in the data coverage indicating a re-flight is necessary at this location.

The data review team will scan visually down the sidelap of all adjacent flight lines to verify there are no gaps in

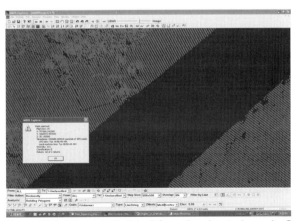

Figure 14.1 Lidar data "holiday." See color plate in Appendix C.

the terrain model. Since the .las record contains the flight-line number, timestamp and geo-coordinates, the area of concern is quickly identified by retrieving the information of points within. Additionally, each flight-line is displayed with a unique color to highly contrast which line is offset. A competent .las viewer should allow the user to load flight lines in their entirety to efficiently evaluate field coverage. Areas with insufficient coverage are provided (typically e-mailed) to the onsite field crew as re-flight or patch flight lines via GPS waypoints in the aircraft flight management system for additional data collection. The unique flight line field in the .las format allows the user to determine which lines are being reviewed without the need for an index map typical of analog data such as film. This significant benefit is the result of having a software application that can take advantage of this unique data field, ensuring timely completeness of project data collection.

Review of Data against GPS Field Calibration Control

Typical lidar collections consist of pre/post-calibration flights. Most collections include the use of higher accuracy control network (GPS or other high-accuracy survey) that are flown over at the beginning and end of each flight mission (a.k.a. lift). Lidar data are verified visually and/or statistically against the known control to verify that the appropriate information for post calibration and meeting predetermined specifications can be achieved. The control used may be a combination of a runway or other close to base station survey and/or overall project wide control for statistical analysis of final surface accuracy. Keeping rover GPS baselines short is an important aspect to maintain a quantifiable error magnitude. Figure 14.2 illustrates a cross-section of a GPS control point vs. lidar point cloud data. On the left (cross section view) the GPS control point (white) is shown intersecting the ground point data (brown) with canopy points (green). On the right (orthographic view) the depth and length of points encompassed by the cross-section are visualized on the TIN backdrop.

Figure 14.3 illustrates a statistical report of distributed high order GPS control compared to the derived lidar TIN model. Several map and data specification statistics are computed with resultant pass/fail criteria, and the individual magnitudes of their residual error are recorded. Data at this process stage may not fully meet final accuracy specifications; however it is a good indicator of initial data integrity, ensuring successful down-stream processing of robust calibration procedures.

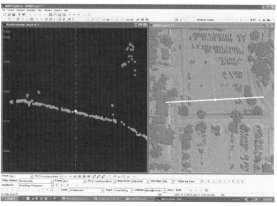

Figure 14.2 Lidar cross-section and orthographic view. See color plate in Appendix C.

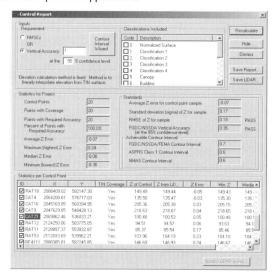

Figure 14.3 Statistical analysis of control compared with the lidar TIN.

Canopy Penetration

Evaluating canopy penetration of the data collection is perhaps one of the most important factors of the quality assurance process early on. Many projects are planned for what may be deemed the appropriate flight system parameters, only to fall short. With early detection of poor canopy penetration, the flight parameters can be re-adjusted to facilitate the collection of an appropriate density of ground points (densification) for the final DEM. When using a lidar viewer for this purpose, it is important to have the capability to cross section data points and display the result obliquely (side view). Additionally, vertical exaggeration control of oblique and cross section depth view is important as tall canopy height and/or steep terrain may require that the viewing scale be reduced to encompass all the data in the vertical axis. Figures 14.4a and 14.4b illustrate examples of insufficient and sufficient vegetation penetration. For this illustration points were pre-classified with automated filter algorithms to facilitate better contrast of ground points (brown) and canopy points (green) Note: Data gaps in ground model points under canopy points in the cross sectional view in Figure 14.4a. Conversely good penetration of the canopy exists in Figure 14.4b cross sectional view. The right view of both figures represent the orthographic view (top down). Note that Figures 14.4a and 14.4b represent the significant improvement achieved for the ground model utilizing improved filtering processing techniques used on the very same raw lidar datasets. Improving the number of points on the ground is an iterative post process. Filters are "tuned" so that maximum point density is achieved for the data collected.

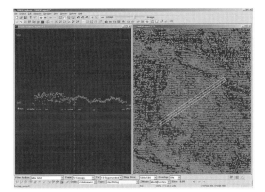

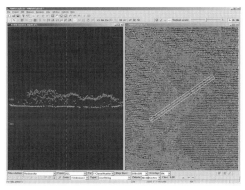

Figure 14.4a Insufficient canopy penetration. See color plate in Appendix C.

Figure 14.4b Sufficient canopy penetration. See color plate in Appendix C.

Project specifications for lidar, while often dictating GSD, may overlook other important operational parameters. This is typically driven by technical/cost constraints or inexperience with a specific canopy type cover. In this situation the client can often be alerted to the potential risks associated with poor ground penetration (canopy penetration) and provided with options to improve the data collection. This may often increase the cost of the data collection but is never-theless worthy of early detection in the field collection evaluation.

Typically higher altitudes with narrow scan field of view will alleviate this issue in most canopy environments unless it is a completely closed canopy. Completely closed canopy typically have no light penetrating, thus nothing grows under it. The number of ground points are a key factor downstream for highly automated algorithmic approaches to be successful in differentiating ground (bare earth) points from the canopy model, and providing adequate point density for the downstream modeling process. Additionally, it greatly reduces the amount of time and expense of the post filter editing process and provides for higher overall surface accuracy, potentially outweighing the additional collection cost.

Raw Lidar Data Calibration and QC (Level II Processing)

Once collected, a lidar dataset consists of multiple data strips (flight lines) that require calibration in a two- phase process consisting of relative and absolute accuracy adjustment. Software applications vary in techniques from completely manual to automated adjustments. Modern lidar systems have greatly reduced calibration requirements with improved system accuracies. These systems benefit from higher precision and accuracies with regard to improvements in inertial measurement systems, scanner position measurement (encoders), improved signal-to-noise ratios (SNRs), high accuracy airborne GPS, and roll compensation. Regardless, the actual mission data from these technologies needs to be quantified in the calibration and QA processes.

Relative Accuracy Calibration and Assessment

Relative accuracy assessment is a key first step when producing precise lidar datasets. Once processed, the raw data typically have both dynamic and systematic biases that require calibration to provide a seamless DSM. It is not likely that data, when initially processed, are robustly calibrated nor will they maximize the potential accuracy that can be derived from particular flight missions. Whether manual or automated techniques are employed, flight line data strips should be assessed on a project wide basis to ensure the DSM has high relative and absolute accuracies far upstream of any filtering (classification) of raw point cloud data. While evolving hardware technology continues to improve lidar's applicability toward larger map scale accuracies, it is a well accepted and necessary practice to calibrate data for these more demanding accuracies. Many factors contribute to biases and limitations in these dynamic systems, which post-processing software must address. These factors include:

- **Scanner Acceleration** – This can affect a condition known as encoder windup, which requires specific algorithmic (mechanical torsion) correction based on accelerations within the mechanical scanner assembly.
- **GPS Lever Arms** – If a new aircraft installation has been performed, the relationship of the GPS antenna, as it relates to the IMU and scanner position relationships, must be properly calibrated.
- **Boresight Calibration** – The relationship of the IMU to the laser beam optical train must be precisely calculated at specific project operational altitudes. The resulting angular offsets for pitch, roll, and yaw must then be applied to the post-processor for proper projection of the data when translating data from earth center (ellipsoid) to earth fixed (geoid) vertical systems and horizontal (often planer) coordinate systems.
- **SNR** – Mission Signal-to-Noise Ratios are affected by laser pulse width and shape, reflectivity of the target, maximum scan angle (ellipsoidal illumination footprint), and altitude of the aircraft (distance to target). Small vertical biases are typical in saturation and should be accounted for in the total calibration.
- **Extended GPS Baselines** – GPS errors can be on the order of 1-2 ppm, which can translate to 20 cm/100km. This must be accounted for by limiting baseline length for projects demanding large-scale mapping or calibration for larger map scales will be impossible, imparted as a floating error that cannot be systematically within an acceptable error band.
- **Other Systematic Startup Biases**

While all of the factors may appear seemingly complex in nature, they are measurable, quantifiable, and can be precisely modeled to greatly improve the DSM. Various software techniques have been applied to this problem, some of which are semi-automated. The first step is to take all the processed project area data and quantify systematic offsets on a mission to mission basis.

While this process is somewhat empirical and iterative in nature, it is somewhat analogous to the photogrammetric aerial triangulation (AT) process with imagery where many iterative and significant bundle adjustments are made to improve the overall residual errors in the exterior orientation file in order to achieve consistent accuracy overall, typically to the 90-95th percentile for error residuals for all flight line – flight line strips combined (total project area of interest — AOI). The result of this process is the relative accuracy adjustment, calibration or final boresight as it is often referred to in the lidar industry. However, there is one important distinction between these two processes. The lidar calibration does not require numerous ground control points to be measured to correlate; rather data are adjusted to each other, relying on the repeatability of the high accuracy airborne GPS and inertial instrumentation. Over time these instruments have improved dramatically, providing quantifiable large scale map accuracies.

At this stage the DSM within itself only is robustly calibrated, but may still lack appropriate absolute accuracy. Control in this case is used primarily for final x,y,z bias adjustment and its resultant error statistics for the absolute adjustment process step. In fact, if there is no control network or particular point of origin for a given project, the data could enter the filter workflow at this stage. Additionally, post-absolute adjustment can occur at any time downstream if required.

Evaluating Results

One software method for assessing the result of the relative calibration is often achieved by color contrasting the individual data (flight strips) and profiling (intersecting) the resultant generated TIN surface models independently, verifying (measuring) appropriate horizontal and vertical calibration has been achieved. Figures 14.5a and 14.5b illustrate profiles of the same data (geographic extent) clearly showing the contrast in relative alignment (accuracy) of pre/post-calibrated datasets. In the bottom view data points are colored independently by flight line with the profile (white line) intersection is displayed. Top view colors correspond to the same flight strips' colors and are a result of the TIN intersection. Note the offset in the pre-calibrated profile in Figure 14.5a.

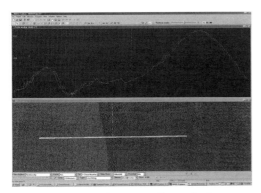 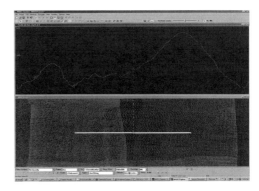

Figure14.5a Pre-calibration profile method. See color plate in Appendix C.

Figure 14.5b Post-calibration profile method. See color plate in Appendix C.

Another software utility allows the user to treat each flight line strip again as an independent surface model and compare its relative accuracy to adjacent flight lines in an interleaved topographic display. When utilizing this technique the user reviews contours in the flight overlap area, containing well defined hard surface or natural slopes, which contrasts any horizontal or vertical errors on a more global (broader trending) scale vs. the previous individual profile segment technique in order to indicate any directional biases.

Figure 14.6a illustrates poor calibration on a natural slope. Note the contour offset (separation), particularly on the left steep most terrain running southeast, when comparing the corresponding red and blue 5 ft index contours generated independently from each flight strip TIN indicating a bias. Figure 14.6b compares the same flight strips after robust calibration, to the 1 ft topographic specification, has been performed. ASPRS specifications dictate that the data be aligned to ≤ 1/3 the contour interval or 0.33 ft evidenced by convergence of the Red and Blue index contours generated by the independent surface models. These types of errors typically require small adjustments to the inertial (orientation file) pitch, roll, and yaw axes of rotation. This error is measured, then re-processed to correct the bias(s). The major factor for an efficient

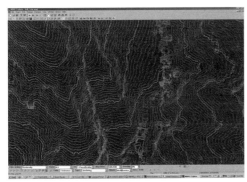 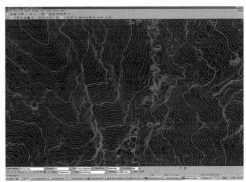

Figures 14.6a Pre-calibrated contour method. See color plate in Appendix C.

Figure 14.6b Post-calibrated contour method. See color plate in Appendix C.

process is to be able to review all the data to assure that error is not compounding due to a stack-up of error(s), which can occur if data are treated piecemeal.

It is common to employ both methods to fully realize the potential accuracy of any dataset. Both software utilities have unique merit, in contrast; the profile method is a more discrete measurement (fine tuning) while the contour method is employed to rapidly evaluate overall trends (coarse) globally.

Absolute Accuracy Assessment, Adjustment, and Final Reporting

Well distributed unobscured ground control check points can now be used to assess the lidar DSM for absolute accuracy as it relates to the final project coordinate datum and projection systems. While these points are important in the final (absolute) accuracy assessment, it is important to note that they do not play a key role in the relative data calibration.

At this stage project-wide control is compared to the calibrated lidar surface TIN. Any remaining horizontal and/or vertical biases in the data are adjusted to obtain a best fit to project control and provide the user with appropriate error statistics quantifying the final absolute accuracy of the total project dataset. This step is accomplished by adjusting the total lidar data block to obtain an average error of zero with respect to project control network. At this stage data should meet the accuracy specifications for the project and be submitted as a certified report to the client, similar to a traditional photogrammetric AT report showing that the supporting residuals are within the appropriate error band. Figures 14.7a and 14.7b illustrate the results of this analysis post and final absolute calibration.

The average Z error has been adjusted to near zero (-0.03 ft). Twenty project area control points were used in this example for a 1 foot (±0.5 ft) vertical accuracy goal at the 95% confidence level. The largest Z error was 0.11 ft, sufficient to produce supporting mass points for ASPRS Class I one foot topographic generation. Important note: For this assessment, only un-obscured control networks should be utilized as it is a critical step. This assessment is not attempting to test filtering results at this stage, but rather to best assess the data accuracy prior to entering the classification and hydro enforcement processes. Testing the accuracy of the classified data should also be accomplished. This is typically done by comparing known control to the lidar data within a variety of land use and land cover types. A well-documented ground truth study was recently performed in Tallahassee, Florida.

Data Production of Classified Data Models (Level III Processing)

Users of lidar data often request data deliverables consisting of ground model data only. It is noteworthy that data in the .las format are never deleted during lidar production processing. Point data are merely re-classified to other classifications, and are reserved should additional data processing be required later in the project lifecycle or for a different end user application. Specifying all point data be delivered in the .las format allows the user to employ other aspects of the data that may be important now or in the future. An analogy for photogrammetrists is to specify deliverables such as film, scans, diapositives, control, and other important project ancillary data that may be useful for another application.

Ground Model DTM

Once data are calibrated, project deliverables will dictate the level of filtering (classification) required for lidar point cloud data. The most basic of these is to filter the data into ground (bare earth) and non-ground (everything above ground) classifications in order to create topographic and other engineering level DEMs. This process step requires that raw point cloud data be further statistically analyzed.

Should canopy or other DSM analysis be required for another application, it is highly dependent on deriving a high quality DTM with which to compute accurate results. This topic is discussed more thoroughly later in this chapter.

Lidar data are somewhat analogous to the elevation data generated from softcopy correlation processes. That is to say that they are randomly placed in nature. After correlation, softcopy

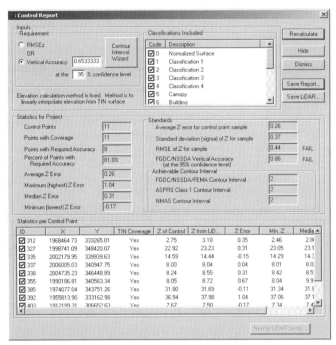

Figure 14.7a Prior to adjustment of calibration.

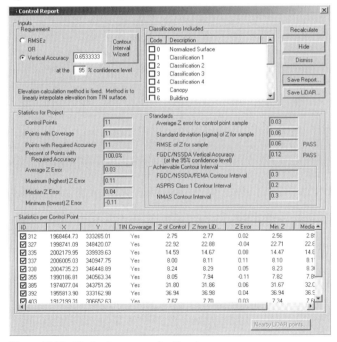

Figure 14.7b Final adjustment of calibration.

elevation data must also be filtered and edited to model the bare earth points for DTM generation. Lidar filtering applications can operate on any elevation data and can therefore be considered as part of the modern digital workflow for users considering shifting to a consistent automated process where many data types are being utilized. Conversely, lidar yields a much higher ground point resolution, due to its incident angle (minimal off nadir) of trajectory, than photogrammetric stereo pairs captured from a super-wide angle lens system. Lidar also yields a more robust statistical success ratio, particularly in vegetation rich environments.

Various proprietary techniques are employed to filter (classify) point clouds in order to obtain a high level of DTM accuracy and points on the ground. A successfully designed filter process flow will typically yield a 90-95% accurate DTM. The success of automated processing is highly dependent on the lidar acquisition strategy, terrain, canopy, and urban cover. The overall morphology of the scene will directly impact the amount of automated vs. manual editing required for obtaining a high quality DTM. The remaining 5-10% typically require some level of manual intervention (point/TIN editing) in order to meet large-scale (e.g., 1"=200') accuracy requirements. As always, the map scale or statistical specification will dictate the appropriate level of editing necessary. For production level processing, filter parameters are custom tailored and must run sequentially in an iterative batch processing environment. Users at this level require training, and a learning curve is typical in order to become proficient. Keep in mind this stage of the process does not always require softcopy (stereo) techniques in the modern lidar workflow.

Figures 14.8a and 14.8b illustrate the results of a fully automated processed dataset.

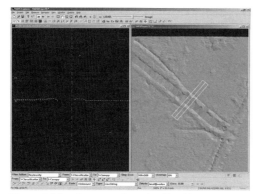 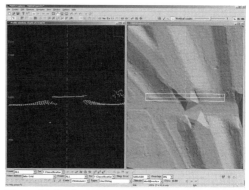

Figure 14.8a Automated results: Road berm. See color plate in Appendix C.

Figure 14.8b Automated results: Bridge. See color plate in Appendix C.

Note that there are still anomalies (spikes) in the TIN that must be edited by a trained terrain analyst to obtain required DTM accuracy. An overly aggressive filter routine will remove valid ground points, while one that is not aggressive enough will entail more surface editing (a labor intensive process). Note the road berm in Figure 14.8a has been too aggressively filtered. In this case the editor will correct the model by reclassifying the berm points (green) back into the ground model (brown). In Figure 14.8b the bridge has been un-aggressively filtered and will require the editor to reclassify the remaining ground points (brown) on the top of the bridge to the canopy points (green) classification in order to remove the bridge from the DTM.

As illustrated, no filter is perfect and will require some level of surface editing; it's achieving the appropriate balance of automated vs. manual processing that will dictate the best mix. These examples contrast over/under aggressive filter workflow, but when running a specific filter routine (sequence), if the overall success is minimizing the result in both directions, it is most likely the best overall process or point of diminishing returns has been reached. Also, see Chapter 12 for examples of over-smoothing that address this same issue.

Surface Editing

The final surface edit process is one of the most critical steps with regard to final DTM accuracy. For many years the only way to edit remaining errors was in existing softcopy platforms and/or CAD environments. While this was often an accurate technique given appropriate photo scales, it left much to be desired with respect to elevation file size limitations (efficiencies) and the necessity to load stereo image pairs to review elevation data. Today the process is typically accomplished directly within the .las data workflow. Editing tools are simple to use; however they do require a professional that understands the characteristics of terrain and how to best represent discrete changes in a DTM. Data can be visualized and edited in a variety of ways with useful ancillary image and vector data layer backdrops. Useful viewing/editing utilities include: point clouds, TINs, image-vector overlays, vertical exaggeration, elevation color/gradient color cycling, intensity (grayscale), contour overlays, transparency layer control, and many other combinations thereof as needed and/or required.

Software tools allow for editing in the orthographic and cross section (oblique) views with a variety of simple paintbrush and smart-line drawing tools designed to rapidly select and re-classify point cloud data.

In Figure 14.9a, a horizontal line is drawn and the points above are selected and re-classified to a user selectable class. In Figure 14.9b, a horizontal line is drawn and the points below are re-classified to a user selectable class. In Figure 14.9c, a vertical broom (line) is used to select points below and is re-classified to a user selectable class. In Figure 14.9d, a paintbrush tool is used to select (paint) points and are re-classified to a user selectable class. In all instances the user has complete control of the "from/to" classes that are to be affected by each operation. For production workflows, numerous hot keys are typically utilized for the most common operations to facilitate rapid editing techniques. This environment is easy to learn and is an appropriate entry level step for production personnel to become familiar with the lidar workflow process.

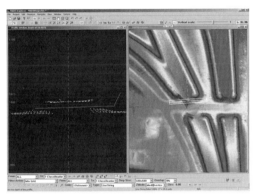

Figure 14.9a Re-class above line. See color plate in Appendix C.

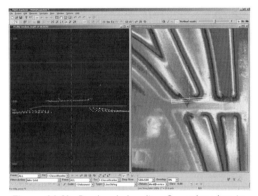

Figure 14.9b Re-class below line. See color plate in Appendix C.

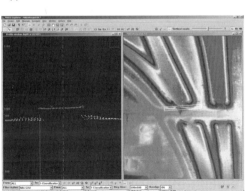

Figure 14.9c Re-class below vertical broom. See color plate in Appendix C.

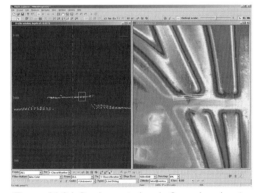

Figure 14.9d Re-class paintbrush. See color plate in Appendix C.

Hydrologic Enforcement

Hydrologic enforcement of single and double drains, lakes, and other hard and soft breaklines are still an integral part of the final DTM deliverable. While the lidar surface is an excellent model of terrain, appropriate connectivity of hydro features are still necessary for users to obtain accurate flow model analysis and topographically (cartographically) correct results. The higher density of lidar data has dramatically reduced the number of breaklines necessary to produce an accurate hydro model when compared to a traditionally compiled DTM; however *lidar data alone are analogous to mass points* and therefore do not completely replace the necessity for breaklines. Project specifications should be very clear as to the location and quantity of breaklines to be added that support the end user application.

Breakline Strategies to Create the DTM

Users familiar with heads up digitizing of planimetric features from 2D (raster/image) data sources are thoroughly familiar with the drawbacks of radial displacement and its associated (inherent) horizontal error. The typical orthophoto is rectified to the ground surface elevation leaving features above ground with significant radial (horizontal) displacement as the compiler moves away from most nadir (image center) collection. Conversely, compiling with lidar data, a 2D environment is completely feasible because the point data are already in their true vertical and horizontal positions; in fact resolution is the primary limitation, which is analogous to film scale utilizing softcopy techniques. The physical rules are the same, but the source data are already 3D, thus eliminating the need for optical measurement in a vertically exaggerated perspective. This is truly beginning to alleviate the need for stereo compilation for large maps and continues to evolve as a result of improved lidar system accuracies and higher data resolutions.

Lidar returns on water are neither consistent nor accurate for large scale applications and should not be included in the DTM. This is especially significant for users who intend to use the data for flow model analysis. Appropriate scope covering the use of breaklines should be an integral part of project specifications. While this process can add significant cost to a project, it is often one of the most overlooked scope requirements for many lidar projects. Specifying the minimum length and breadth of drains and minimum area of water bodies to be compiled will ensure that users get what is expected. Remember again *lidar data alone are analogous to mass points* and do not replace breaklines.

Breaklines are generally collected by two methods. 1) compiled photogrammetrically (stereo) and post-combined with the lidar DTM, and 2) compiled directly from the lidar DTM. Because this chapter's intent is to address lidar software only, the second method will be addressed here. In the lidar workflow environment, drains are compiled in 2D with tools that allow the user to evaluate the TIN model directly for flow direction and position. Utilizing an accurate orthophoto backdrop is also useful when available to assist in evaluating the location of drains and at-ground elevation manmade infrastructure.

Single Drain 3D Polylines (Streams & Ditches)

Employing this technique, the user evaluates the horizontal drain position by maximizing the elevation contrast. This is a combination of a scale appropriate elevation color cycles (color shading) from TIN and/or points, and project contour scale to indicate the flow direction.

Note: This is somewhat analogous to acquiring film scale necessary for appropriate vertical perception in stereo, but is uniquely different as it is accomplished in a 2D drawing environment with highly accurate results.

As with any method, an experienced user terrain analyst will maximize the contrast of available data at a level appropriate to effectively edit elevation data and minimize cost. When creating a single drain brealine, the software tool must only allow the breakline to connect points of the next lowest elevation in the direction of flow, ensuring that only point elevations in the bottom (lowest elevation) of the drain are connected and flow downhill, generating a 3D breakline. This is an especially useful technique where vegetation data are present in the drain feature. Once the drain is compiled with this technique in 2D, a specified buffer distance of points about the breakline are removed (re-classified) from the ground model. This buffering technique is also used in traditional softcopy breakline compilation as well, to ensure that the TIN is not stressed and a clean (cartographically correct) contour elevation break is achieved. This process produces an accurate 3D single drain polyline as a result of 2D compilation and is real-time (immediate compiler feedback) enforced in generation of the TIN and resulting contours.

Figures 14.10a and 14.10b illustrate pre/post hydro enforcement respectively. Note how the channel has been improved and connected for appropriate directional flow. Lidar will often leave residual (damming) effects in channels, specifically in heavy vegetation environments typical of many hydro features. The removal of potential damming effects is critical to obtain flow connectivity for subsequent hydrographic and hydraulic modeling and analyses.

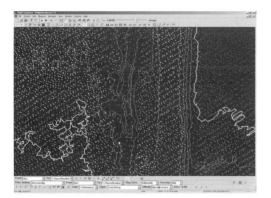

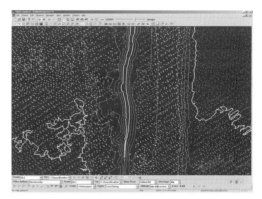

Figure 14.10a Raw ground point model. See color plate in Appendix C.

Figure 14.10b Single drain enforcement. See color plate in Appendix C.

Double Drain 3D Polylines (Rivers and other Large Channels)

Double drains are essentially the same as single drains except that: 1) breaklines are compiled on both sides (embankments) of a wider channel, e.g., wider than 20 ft.; 2) all lidar points are removed between the embankments to ensure no roughness or damming of the channel occurs within the channel flow model; and 3) an outside channel buffer is implemented. This process produces accurate 3D double drain polylines as a result of 2D compilation and is enforced in generation of the TIN and resulting contours as illustrated in Figure 14.11.

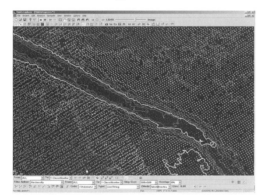

Figure 14.11a Pre-hydro-enforced ground model. See color plate in Appendix C.

Figure 14.11b Hydro-enforced model. See color plate in Appendix C.

Note how this technique improves cartographic correctness of the channel flow with respect to equivalent contour elevations perpendicular to channel direction.

Water Body 3D Polygons (Ponds & Lakes)

Ponds and lakes must have a single closed elevation polygon surrounding the entire edge of the feature embankment. In this case the user: 1) begins the breakline at the lowest lake elevation obtainable to show the low water mark; 2) implements a Z lock for the remainder of the elevations along the shoreline breakline; 3) removes lidar points from the interior to ensure contours do not flow across the water body; and 4) implements a buffer at the polygon exterior to again ensure a cartographically correct interpolation of contours." Figures 14.12a and 14.12b illustrate the use of this technique and the resultant pre-post surface models.

The high water mark may also be specified in the scope of the project; however appropriate scale photography is necessary to correctly (horizontally) interpret and compile the line. Simultaneously captured lidar and imagery data are the most advantageous source data for this task as water body elevations are consistent; however this is not always practical with all but the most modern integrated (lidar/imaging) sensors. This process automatically deletes interior points and buffers the exterior polygon surface interface, generating a 3D polygon and enforces the TIN as illustrated in Figure 14.12b.

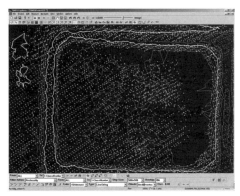 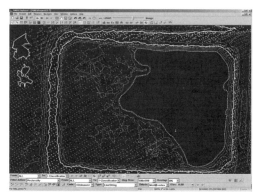

Figure 14.12a Lake pre-compilation. See color plate in Appendix C.

Figure 14.12b Lake post-compilation. See color plate in Appendix C.

Other Breaklines and Methods

Other hard/soft breaklines and connected drains such as culverts may be obtained utilizing these techniques in order to enforce the lidar DTM. Once completed, the final DTM can be used for downstream hydro-analysis, topographic generation, and other engineering level design analyses. As aforementioned, stereo compiled breaklines are often integrated with lidar data sets, and intensity (grayscale) images can also be used, but often lack sufficient resolution – the tradeoff being a potentially expensive data collection approach. Softcopy photogrammetry is typically required when breaklines are required on features such as culverts.

Interpolation of Contour Data

Interpolation of contours is the technique used to produce a more cartographically correct (aesthetically pleasing) output for map production. While some degradation of the surface integrity may occur, it is often the choice of topographic end-users. Early on, many lidar DEM users were not pleased with the aesthetics of lidar terrain generated topographic map products. This is primarily due to the higher data density and the resultant number of TIN vertices that are generated. Traditionally compiled maps, even at the largest scales, had orders of magnitude fewer TIN surface points and resultant contour vertices. In order to alleviate this with lidar, final surface data are typically gridded and a minimal level of normalization (smoothing) is applied, e.g., employing IDW, Gaussian, krigging, or other method, to produce a topographic surface that is more similar to traditionally compiled surface models produced from lower mass point resolutions and a higher level of breakline supplementation in order to model terrain. These procedures are discussed in detail in Chapter 1. Lidar data are by nature higher resolution and yield contours that are often referred to as aesthetically noisy (jagged) due to a much higher level of TINs generated.

While both techniques are accurate, existing trends seem to indicate that the traditional (smoother) output is still preferred possibly for clarity, especially in flat terrain where contours can wander with a larger than previously obtainable horizontal displacement. Most if not all of these techniques have been successfully employed and are valid if correct parameter weights are understood for appropriate mapping scales and post user disciplines.

Note: Much debate over which method is the best may be biased more by industry specific preference when considering topographic deliverables. For example, IDW or Gaussian techniques are a popular choice within the hydro-modeling community while krigging is often applied to many forestry post-user data applications. This is not to suggest that a particular method should be employed, but only to understand that this is an interpolation method often utilized and worthy of consideration, depending on end-user specifications and requirements.

The gridded model used in this process should always be approximately 2x (over-sampled) the average density of the raw (random collected) data to ensure that key elevations are not excluded in the generation of the topography, if rigorous surface integrity are to be maintained. The basis for the 2x factor will be explained further in this chapter. Since the grid model is 2x denser than the original dataset to maintain the accuracy of the contour, over- sampling the lidar will maintain the x/y location of the contour, where if the grid is under-sampled, the contour location can vary in x/y, depending on grid size. However, this over-sampled grid is extremely cumbersome due to its enormous volume (increased file size) and is typically not recommended as a DEM deliverable for most post-user analysis.

Example: A 2x over-sampling of a 10 ft average GSD lidar dataset has to be considered in 2 dimensions, thus increasing file size a total factor of approximately four. Most post-user applications would suffer dramatically when attempting to efficiently utilize the data, an important consideration in the post-analysis of data.

Figures 14.13a and 14.13c represents a hydro-enforced lidar DTM. This model benefits from smaller file size for terrain analysis, but may not be appropriate for some topographic user representations. Conversely in Figures 14.13b and 14.13d, the model benefits from a more cartographically correct topographic representation but was generated from an interpolated (grid) Gaussian smoothed model DEM with a file size of approximately 4x.

Figure 14.13a Lake pre-compilation. See color plate in Appendix C.

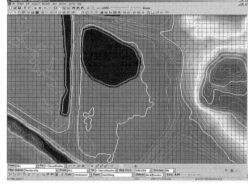

Figure 14.13b Lake post-compilation. See color plate in Appendix C.

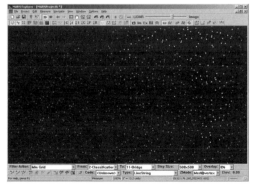

Figure 14.13c Closer look at the random key point spacing (Average 6 ft spacing). See color plate in Appendix C.

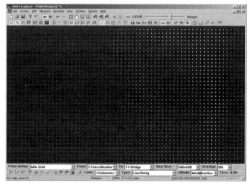

Figure 14.13d Closer look at the 1m grid spacing (Grid 2 ft spacing) which provides a higher level of contour accuracy based on sampling theory (Nyquist). See color plate in Appendix C.

In the final quality inspection of the DEM, regardless of methodology, the DEMs should meet the specified project accuracy. NSSDA procedures are routinely used for DEM accuracy assessment, as documented in Chapter 12.

TAKING LIDAR BEYOND TOPOGRAPHY

High-Level Analysis of Discrete Features (Level IV Processing)

DTM generation utilizing lidar has been "mainstream" since the late 1990's. Over the past decade newer sensors and processing techniques have successfully supplanted traditional methods, for all but the largest map scales, in an efficient and cost effective manner. The focus has shifted in recent years to utilize the data from the remainder of the reflective surface model. The ability to effectively use this information in extraction of specific vegetation and manmade features is the topic of much debate and research. This is truly the next "Holy Grail" for many scientists wanting to effectively exploit the feature-rich above ground data.

Planimetric Extraction of Manmade Features

To date, planimetric compilation (vector mapping) of above ground features (i.e., buildings, etc.) is primarily performed in the softcopy or analytical photogrammetric environments for large scale map requirements and can be a highly labor intensive and costly endeavor. Two primary factors are improving the practical ability to exploit this information from lidar data:

1. Improved sensor accuracy
2. Significantly improved data resolution

Because of the above improvements in lidar collection, automatic feature extraction will be a focus of software companies.

Sensor Accuracy

Accuracy of modern lidar systems has improved primarily as a result of higher accuracy inertial sensor technology. Early sensors could position a lidar elevation in the range of ±1-meter absolute at a distance of 1000 meters above ground. Newer sensors employing the latest inertial technology can position an elevation in the range of ±30 centimeters absolute at a distance of 3000 meters above ground and higher.

This is extremely encouraging for use of lidar data to potentially supplant the traditional stereo compilation process for feature extraction at certain scales. Flying higher above ground allows for greater mapping coverage of an area, but the GSD will decrease and the accuracy of the building and other planimetrics will not be defined as well for accurate representation with today's sensors. With future technology the pulse rate is increasing, thus allowing the possibility to accurately capture some planimetric features from lidar data.

Greater Resolution

The second factor, and just as important, is the data resolution (density). In order to resolve features in the traditional stereo environment, the film scale and post-scan resolution dictate the accuracy supported from the compilation process. Analogous to an aerial image flown lower to be able to clearly interpret objects, improved lidar accuracy and sample density are increasing the true *resolving power* of the data. Until recent years, lidar had lacked sufficient cost effective resolution to accurately resolve these features. Today's modern sensors, with pulse rates exceeding 150 Khz, are increasing this resolution to image-like quality, yielding sufficient edge detection capability for extraction directly from the entire (ground or canopy) DSM. Sub-meter data resolutions will become mainstream and cost effective over the next 3-5 years. Figure 14.14 illustrates the practicality for resolving high-accuracy planimetric data left to right 0.5m, 1m, and 3m sample densities respectively.

Early users of this technology include electric power industry users where line mapping has been accomplished with helicopter based platforms and low altitude flights, mapping wires and

Figure 14.14 Resolving power with 0.5m, 1m, and 3m ground sample distances (GSD).

towers to engineering level (larger map scale) standards. This has not been implemented universally for large urban projects primarily due to large data volumes, cost constraints of data collection, and sensor accuracy limitations. With the next paradigm, newer sensors will overcome the collection cost, but higher-efficiency processes will be necessary to overcome increasing data volumes.

What GSD is Needed?

This question is best answered with a review of the traditional (photogrammetric) process requirements and a simple statistical theorem – depending on the smallest feature to be resolved and the horizontal accuracy requirement. The Nyquist theorem is a common method to predetermine necessary data resolution.

Nyquist's theorem states that, if one samples a complex waveform uniformly at a rate just over twice the highest frequency component sine wave contained within, the conglomeration of samples thus obtained contain sufficient information to reconstruct the waveform. This same theorem also applies to feature recognition applications.

In laymen's terms, to detect an object that is 10 feet on a side, that object should be sampled at slightly more than a 5 ft GSD to guarantee that the feature is detected. To resolve the edges in sufficient detail for planimetric capture, the resolution will have to be much greater.

Reversing this theorem, lidar resolution of 1-foot GSD would guarantee that the edge would be resolved to approximately ±1 ft or 2ft (absolute) accuracy. Lidar sensors can achieve this type of data resolution now with appropriate project design and meet large scale mapping specifications. To meet the 1"=100' ASPRS scale would dictate that a 1-foot GSD should be sufficient to directly extract features from the data.

Although early in the technology curve, this is theoretically sound and proven. The drawbacks for early implementers beyond practical/collectable data resolution have been similar to topographic representation with regard to their cartographically correct (aesthetic) representation, again a result of the numerous vertices generated from a higher-fidelity DSM.

Previously, buildings were compiled in stereo to produce 2D vector maps of building footprints (foundation outlines) or with 3D attributes including gutter height, vertical obstruction height, or single elevation polygons, typically at gutter height elevation, as it was not practical to obtain all but the most basic (generalized) building outlines. This is primarily due to the labor/cost intensiveness of the process.

Manual or Automated Processing?

Highly promising work has already been accomplished in the commercial, academic, and government environments to automatically classify lidar data. The automated process requires several steps to achieve high yielding results. In truth, the best data is most likely a combination of both processes. The basic steps to extract building features require the following:

1. Sufficient supporting (collected) data resolution
2. Classification of robust ground points (separation of canopy)
3. Classification of consistent above ground surface planes
4. Anomalous point cleanup
5. Manual compilation or automated polygon analysis for vector based output

Assuming that step 1 has the supporting data resolution, step 2 must be robustly performed. Ground data typically contain much of the planar data in a lidar DSM (example roads are planar features). In step 3, significant planer algorithms with user variable parameters must be applied to canopy (above ground) point data in order to re-classify (separate) manmade above-ground-level feature points. Figure 14.15 illustrates the result of automated routines applied to canopy data to extract only above-ground planar features from the data. Shown are ground points (brown), planar features (blue), and remaining canopy points (green) in cross sectional and orthographic perspectives left to right.

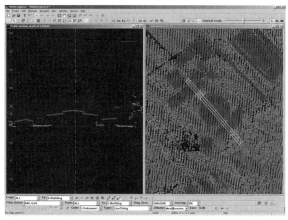

Figure 14.15 Automated building point classification. See color plate in Appendix C.

Note: Automated routines are significantly dependent on the complexity of the morphology within a given scene. Terrain, building density and separation, and vegetation cover all play important roles in the yield percentage of the automated building point classification process. Consider also that traditional stereo compilation techniques suffer from similar obstacles. *If you can't see it you can't map it.* So it is worthy to keep this in perspective as one considers this technology evolution.

In step 4 the remaining canopy points will generally require cleanup employing aforementioned manual editing techniques.

Step 5 requires either manual compilation or automated polygon analysis for vector based output.

Manual Extraction

To manually compile a building feature, for example, the user can draw the feature in 2D from the point cloud or TIN backdrop to obtain the horizontal position of the planimetric feature. Then elevations are obtained from the Z-values where the planimetric feature line or polygon intersects the TIN. Color shading by elevation and/or lidar intensity yields contrast to the feature for the compiler without the use of imagery. Figures 14.16a, 14.16b and 14.16c illustrate the use of this technique and the resulting 3D planimetric feature obtained.

Automated Extraction

In recent years, significant research has been performed on lidar point clouds (Figure 14.17) to yield automated feature extraction of vegetation and man-made features (Figure 14.18).

Figures 14.17 through 14.24 and Table 14.1 all come from a study prepared by Dewberry for FEMA (FEMA, 2005) to extract buildings from lidar data and determine flood risks to those buildings based on their elevation. Automated feature extraction was performed by Computational Consulting Services, LLC.

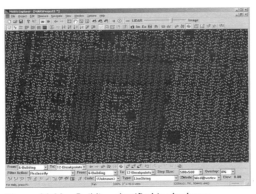

Figure 14.16a Building classified in the laser.

Figure 14.17 Lidar raw data point cloud. See color plate in Appendix C.

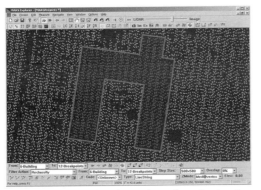

Figure 14.16b Building foot print collected using the classified laser data.

Figure 14.18 Automated extraction of vegetation and planimetric features. See color plate in Appendix C.

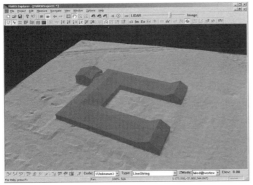

Figure 14.16c 3D view of the extracted building with the ground solution from the classified laser data.

Table 14.1 provides a top-level summary of the lidar operating parameters and their effect on data measurements and extraction results.

Figure 14.19 shows examples of automated building extractions.

Table 14.1 Lidar Data Parameters.

Lidar Data Parameters	Effect on Derived Information
Distance measurements from lidar (dynamic range and receiver response)	Determines accuracy of terrain and building elevation calculations
Number of measurements per unit area and distance between those measurements(laser repetition rate, scan angle and other system design settings)	Influences ability to extract object details and resolve closely spaced objects
Measurement of multiple reflections (returns) from single light pulse(receiver and electronics design)	Provide ability to filter objects such as foliage that obscure buildings and terrain
Intensity measurements(receiver and electronics design)	Allows determination of general material types for reflecting objects
Laser-light footprint or spot size on reflecting object/surface(system optics)	Influences ability to extract object details and resolve closely spaced objects

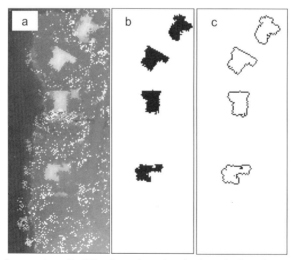

Figure 14.19 Automated extraction of building footprints, showing jagged edges that result. Such "footprints" could be used to intersect the bare-earth DTM to automatically determine lowest adjacent grades (LAG) of these buildings, compared with base flood elevations (BFEs), to determine their need for flood insurance. This method has also been used to detect blunders in conventionally-surveyed Elevation Certificates where LAGs varied significantly from lidar data.

The selection of pixel size (influenced by data density) plays a critical role in feature extraction, DTM generation, and resolving and discriminating objects on the ground. Figure 14.20 illustrates the affect of pixel size on the ability to extract buildings. Panel "a" shows a plot of Z_maximal and Panel "b" shows a plot of Z_minimal. Panel "c" is a pixel map of the extracted buildings. Note that buildings extracted using Z_minimal from the last returns are smaller than the actual buildings by up to one pixel on each side of the buildings. As a result, the processing of lidar data with a large pixel (16 ft) can result in small buildings (< 36 ft in width) being omitted. In addition, some building features are filtered as noise.

Figure 14.21 shows complications when buildings are surrounded by trees with dense foliage where lidar pulses do not penetrate to the ground. Figure 14.22 shows complications when no lidar returns are received from tar or asphalt roofs. Hot asphalt highways also have similar problems, one reason why highways are better mapped using lidar data collected at night.

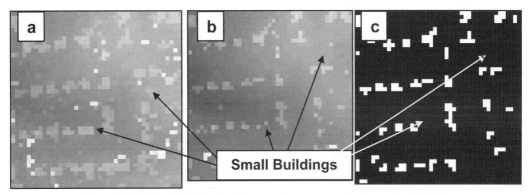

Figure 14.20 Small buildings lost in extraction process using large pixels (16 ft).

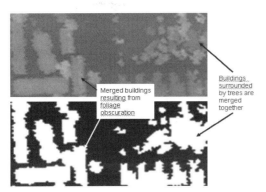

Figure 14.21 Automated extraction of buildings is complicated by surrounding trees with dense foliage, resulting in unintended merger of outlines.

Figure 14.22 Hot tar and asphalt often absorbs lidar pulses, yielding no returns, as shown with these dark roofs (i.e., tar or asphalt).

Figures 14.23 and 14.24 show successful extraction of features, including thousands of buildings (Figure 14.23) and even electrical power transmission lines (Figure 14.24) for which the change in concatenation of power lines is measured with changing voltage being carried.

Other firms are engaged in automated feature extraction of roads, bridges, and forests, for example. Many such projects have been publicized by ASPRS in various volumes of *Photogrammetric Engineering and Remote Sensing* (PE&RS).

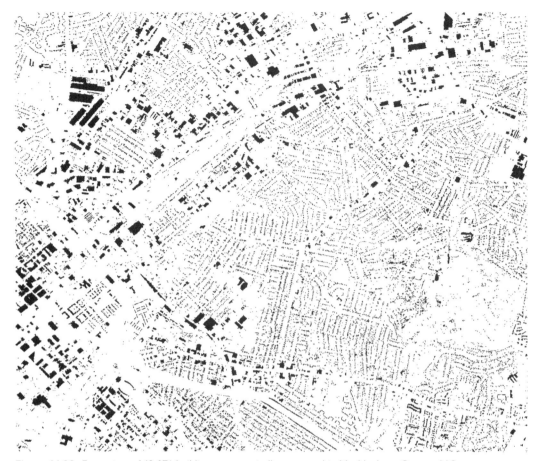

Figure 14.23 Footprints of 13,076 buildings automatically extracted in Mecklenburg County, NC.

Figure 14.24 Detection of power lines from lidar last returns indicates very sensitive lidar equipment was used in Beaufort County, SC.

CAD/GIS POST-PROCESS USERS

Understandably, not all lidar data users are at the production end of the spectrum; however if users want to make the most of this data source it is worthwhile considering what options are available. For example if deliverables consist primarily of topographic, planimetric, and orthophoto deliverables, there may be no need to consider utilizing a true lidar software solution. An organization's unique requirements should be considered with a few key questions:

1. Can all users within my organization use the data in their delivered formats?
2. Is there potential for additional analysis of canopy data?
3. Is there a hydro model component to post-data use?
4. Are there file size constraints to in-house applications?
5. Will data be warehoused or served via inter/intranet portals?
6. Will data parsing or re-formatting be necessary?
7. Is there a QA/QC acceptance workflow in place?

If users have never dealt with lidar data, they may be in for a big surprise. For the educated user, the answers to these questions are probably understood. Many users have learned difficult and expensive lessons early on without options to take advantage of the more compact format storage and subsequent process efficiencies that can be obtained today working with applications that can deal with the binary (.las) data. Most commonly ASCII deliverables are requested without knowledge of the ensuing data volumes significantly impacting timely cost effective solutions. It is well worth investigating lidar application options that are developed specifically for this purpose.

THE FUTURE IS NOW FOR LIDAR SOFTWARE

Lidar processing software is one of the most exciting and rapidly evolving areas within the modern mapping disciplines. With a wide range of end users wanting to exploit more information from this feature rich data set, advancements in software capabilities will grow exponentially in the coming years. The most exciting aspects of these new software capabilities are: 1) taking advantage of higher pulse rates, multiple returns, intensity images; 2) making the native .las lidar format fully functional in mainstream GIS and CAD software; 3) automated planimetric feature extraction due to high fidelity feature definition from high ground sample distance, and, 4) fusing lidar with other geospatial and remotely sensed (i.e. hyperspectral imagery) data so that scientific analysis can be possible. As software companies begin to answer the demands from a variety of public, commercial and military users the geospatial community will soon be able to enjoy the robust capabilities of lidar data in the very near future.

AUTHOR BIOGRAPHY

Mark Romano is the Director of GeoSpatial Solutions Technology at Merrick & Company. He has 26 years of experience in electro-mechanical and electro-optical systems development including over 16 years in the aerospace industry. He has played a significant role in the development of Merrick's lidar software: MARS® (Merrick Advanced Remote Sensing Software), Digital Airborne Camera systems (DACS™), and associated lidar technology integration. Prior to joining Merrick, he led the engineering, systems integration, calibration, and operational activities associated with the EnerQuest Remote Airborne Mapping System (RAMS) lidar sensor. Additionally, he was instrumental in the development, management, and marketing of the EagleScan Digital Airborne Topographic Imaging System (DATIS) lidar system. He has a BS degree in Electrical Engineering from Keene State College.

ACKNOWLEDGMENTS

Appreciation is expressed to Brian Raber, of Merrick & Co., who provided input and reviewed this chapter.

REFERENCES

ASPRS, 2005. Lidar data exchange format standard, Version 1.1, March 7, 2005.

FEMA, 2003. Appendix A, Guidance for aerial mapping and surveying, in *Guidelines and Specifications for Flood Hazard Mapping Partners*, Federal Emergency Management Agency (FEMA), April 2003, URL: http://www.fema.gov/plan/prevent/fhm/gs_main.shtm.

FEMA, 2005. Evaluation of alternatives in obtaining structural elevation data, Federal Emergency Management Agency, January, 2005.

Hartsfield, Lee and Brian Raber, 2005. "Ground Truthing Lidar Data, TLC's Lidar Landbase." *Geospatial Solutions*, 15(4): 22-28.

Romano, Mark E., 2004. "Innovation in Lidar Processing Technology." *Photogrammetric Engineering and Remote Sensing*, 70(11): 1201-1206.

Sample Elevation Datasets

Craig L. Lees

INTRODUCTION

The purpose of this chapter is to enable readers to work with sample datasets for visualization, exploration and analysis of elevation models. It is helpful if readers understand the basic concepts and typical DEM applications explained in the prior chapters. With a basic understanding of different elevation datasets, readers should be ready to put the book aside, turn on their computers and get some hands-on experience.

This chapter describes data included in a PC-formatted DVD included with this *DEM Users Manual*. In order to read these data, users need a Windows-based PC equipped with a DVD reader. Place the DVD in the drive and access the disc contents using Windows Explorer. Users must have read/write access to certain files in order to view them. If an error is encountered when attempting to open a file, copy the folder where the file resides to a drive with read/write access and then open it from the new location. Three types of digital data are offered on the DVD in three folders: (1) text, (2) software and (3) sample data. The text includes an electronic version of this chapter, along with the User Requirements Menu and Statements of Work (SOW) described in Chapter 13. The software is provided to allow users to view and explore the sample data, and it must be properly installed before users can view the electronic data (unless users already have existing software installed). The sample data are included to provide users an opportunity to visualize and analyze a variety of types and formats of elevation datasets and associated products. This sample data section is the most important and interesting part of the DVD contents. The following sections detail the DVD content.

TEXT

This folder contains an electronic copy of this chapter, named Chapter_15.pdf, included for reference while users are exploring the DVD. In addition, the three files referenced in Chapter 13 are provided in Microsoft Word format. These files are as follows:

- Basic_Lidar_SOW.doc. This is an example statement of work for an imaginary Flood County, NC. This SOW is relevant for a typical community or county needing lidar data that satisfies basic requirements in the Department of Homeland Security, Federal Emergency Management Agency (FEMA), Appendix A (see Chapter 3 for details).
- Enhanced_Lidar_SOW.doc. This is an example statement of work for an imaginary Mangrove County, FL Water Management District. This SOW is enhanced in that it is intended to not only satisfy basic FEMA requirements but also additional, more-demanding requirements of this imaginary water management district.
- User_Requirements_Menu.doc. This form facilitates the selection of typical alternatives facing the DEM procurement authority. It is an electronic version of Table 13.1; if desired, unlock the form by clicking the unlock button on the Microsoft Word forms toolbar.

SOFTWARE

A key aspect of working with DEMs is the selection of a software application to view or analyze the model. When selecting the DEM software application, there are a multitude of considerations including cost, performance, format and functionality. Users interested in investigating various software alternatives are encouraged to explore other resources; two websites are offered as a starting point for this research:

1. The US Army Corps of Engineers, Topographic Engineering Center, hosts a website that includes a survey of over 500 terrain visualization software applications. An overview of each application, and details on how to obtain additional information, is provided and updated periodically. The website is available at http://www.tec.army.mil/TD/tvd/survey/ survey_toc.html.

2. The Virtual Terrain Project (VTP) focuses on tools to construct and interact with 3D digital models and the website offers a free download of their VTP open-source terrain visualization software. Under the heading of "Other Terrain Software" (scroll down to the lower-right portion of the home page), several links provide summary reviews of a wide variety of commercial, non-commercial and government/academic software applications. The website is available at www.vterrain.org.

An entire book could be dedicated to the exploration of the various DEM user software applications. It is beyond the scope of this chapter to provide a software evaluation. Instead, this text will focus on DEM data types, typical applications and analysis using selected software programs. The provided software applications were selected mostly because they are free, relatively simple to use and allow (at a minimum) viewing of the included data formats. Users are not required to install the provided software if appropriate software is already loaded.

The included software applications are Leica Cyclone, FARO Scout LT, Global Mapper, MARS FreeView and Trimble RealWorks Viewer. Installation instructions are described below. Global Mapper is included because it has an impressive number of supported formats, such as bmp, jpg, tif, shp, ASCII text, las, and ESRI grids. Almost every file included on the DVD can be opened and viewed with Global Mapper. However, 3D viewing is not possible with the included, unlicensed (free) version of Global Mapper. Therefore, MARS FreeView is included because it will allow 3D viewing. However, all data must first be in las format (a data converter for formats like ASCII text is provided) and the number of supported formats is significantly less than Global Mapper. Leica Cyclone, FARO Scout LT and Trimble RealWorks Viewer are included exclusively to view the terrestrial laser scanning datasets in the Sample_Data\Laser_Scan folder.

Remove the DVD from the sleeve in the back of this *DEM Users Manual* and place it in a PC-DVD reader. Ensure the PC meets the minimum system requirements before attempting to install. Users must have sufficient PC privileges (typically, administrator privileges) to install the software. Follow the instructions below to install one or more applications or skip ahead to the Sample Data section if appropriate DEM software is already loaded.

Leica Cyclone

Minimum System Requirements:
- Compatible Operating Systems:
  - Windows 2000 (SP2 or higher)
  - Windows XP (SP1 or higher)
- 512 MB of RAM
- 1 GB of hard drive space
- SVGA or OpenGL accelerated graphics card

Installation Instructions:
- Double-click the file named Cyclone.exe in the Software folder. This will launch the installation wizard. Follow the instructions to install the software on a PC, accepting all defaults until you reach the Setup Type screen.
- Select "Cyclone: Customized Installation" and click Next.
- Review and select (click the check box) the components that you want to install and clear (click the check box) the components that you do not want to install. Some components "plug into" other applications such as AutoCAD or SmartPlant; users will need to have

these other applications already installed in order for these components to properly install. Click on the component to see a brief description of each component. At a minimum, select the first three options (components starting with "Cyclone"). See Figure 15.1 for a sample of this step. Click Next to continue.
- Accept the remaining defaults and complete the installation process.

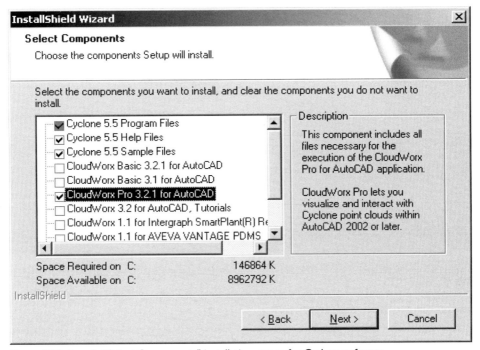

Figure 15.1 Sample "Select Components" installation screen for Cyclone software.

Initial Setup:
- Once the installation is complete, launch Cyclone by clicking on Start>Programs>Leica HDS Cyclone 5.5>Cyclone
- Review the license agreement and, if you accept the terms, click Agree
- This opens the Cyclone Viewer Navigator. Click Configure>Databases…
- This opens a new dialogue. At the top, select the server from the drop-down list that does not say "(unshared)" at the end. Click the add button.
- This opens a new dialogue. Give the database a descriptive name, such as "Church". Browse to your database file by clicking the "…" button. For this example, browse to Sample_Data\Laser_Scan\Leica and select Church.imp. Click Ok. (To add other databases, enter a different name and browse to the associated imp file).
- Click Close at the bottom of the configure databases dialogue and return to the Cyclone Viewer Navigator.
- Continue clicking "+" to drill down to ModelSpaces>Church 1 View 1 and double-click to launch this view. See Figure 15.2 for an example.
- The view will open in a new window. Explore the view. To pan, click the left or right mouse button and move the mouse. To zoom, click both mouse buttons simultaneously and move the mouse.

These brief instructions are provided to help users get up and running quickly. Cyclone is provided for viewing the imp files in the Sample_Data\Laser_Scan\Leica folder. Additional help for using Cyclone is available by clicking Start>Programs>Leica HDS Cyclone 5.5>Cyclone 5.5 User's Manual or Cyclone On-line Help. The user's manual is installed by default at C:\Program Files\Leica Geosystems\Cyclone\Cyclone 5.5.pdf. Note that this free version of the software has

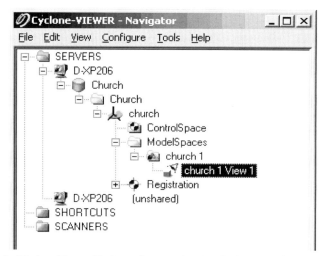

Figure 15.2 Sample "Cyclone Viewer Navigator" screen showing the location of the 3D model for viewing.

limited functionality. A license must be purchased in order to access full functionality of the software; questions and limited-duration demonstration license requests may be directed to support@lgshds.com. Additional information is available from Leica Geosystems HDS, LLC at www.leica.com.

FARO Scout LT

Minimum System Requirements:
- Compatible Operating Systems:
  - Windows 2000
  - Windows XP
- 512 MB of RAM
- 20 MB of hard drive space
- OpenGL graphics card
- 2-button mouse plus scroll wheel

Installation Instructions:
- Double-click the file named FARO_Scout_LT.exe in the Software folder. This will launch the installation wizard.
- Follow the instructions to install the software on a PC, accepting all defaults.

The program will launch automatically; browse to Sample_Data\Laser_Scan\FARO and select a file to open and view. Select Help>Contents from the FARO Scout LT menu to access the help files. Additional information is available from FARO Technologies Inc. at www.faro.com.

Global Mapper

Minimum System Requirements:
- Compatible Operating Systems:
  - Windows 95/98/NT
  - Windows 2000
  - Windows ME
  - Windows XP
- 32 MB of RAM
- 20 MB of hard drive space

Installation Instructions:
- Double-click the file named Global_Mapper.exe in the Software folder. This will launch the installation wizard.
- Follow the instructions to install the software on a PC, accepting all defaults.

For help on using the software, double-click the file named Help_Main.html in the Software\Global_Mapper_Help folder on the DVD and launch the offline user's manual. Note that this free version of the software has limited functionality and a reminder will display each time the program is launched. A license must be purchased in order to access full functionality of the software. Additional information is available from Global Mapper Software LLC at www.globalmapper.com.

MARS FreeView

Minimum system requirements:
- Compatible Operating Systems:
  - Windows 2000
  - Windows XP
- 512 MB RAM
- 200 MB available hard disk space

Installation Instructions:
- Double-click on the file named MarsFreeView.exe in the Software folder. This will launch the installation wizard.
- Follow the instructions to install the software on a PC, accepting all defaults.

For help on using the software, double-click the file named MARSExplorer.exe in the folder where MARS is installed and launch the software. Click on "Help" on the menu bar then select "Help Topics" to access the help files. From the left pane, with the "Contents" tab active, select "MARS Functionality" and "Setup". Follow the instructions to locate and explore the sample project data included with the software. Data must be in las format to view; a data converter for formats like ASCII text is provided with the Project>Import function. Note that this free version of the software has limited functionality. A license must be purchased in order to access full functionality of the software. Additional information is available from Merrick & Company at www.merrick.com/MARS.

Trimble RealWorks Viewer

Minimum System Requirements:
- Compatible Operating Systems:
  - Windows 2000
  - Windows XP Professional
  - Windows NT
- 2GHz processor
- 1 GB of RAM
- 40 MB of hard drive space
- 128MB NVIDIA, ATI or equivalent graphics card
- 3-button mouse with scroll wheel

Installation Instructions:
- Double-click the file named RealWorks_Viewer.exe in the Software folder. This will launch the installation wizard.
- Follow the instructions to install the software on a PC, accepting all defaults.

The program and help file will launch automatically; browse to Sample_Data\Laser_Scan\Trimble and select the Union_Station.rwp file to open and view. Additional information is available from Trimble at www.trimble.com.

SAMPLE DATA

This section of the DVD is divided into several folders each containing sample elevation data or related products in a variety of formats, as described in the following subsections. The purpose is to allow users the opportunity to view and explore various elevation products and geographic areas from a number of data providers using different acquisition technologies. These data are intended to support previous chapters, as presented in Table 15.1. The included data can be accessed using the various software applications provided, except for the avi and wmv video clips. Most DVD hardware comes with a software application capable of viewing avi and wmv files; users who do not have an avi or wmv player installed are encouraged to search the internet, download and install an appropriate player in order to view the video clip files.

Table 15.1 Matrix of Section Titles, Chapters and DVD Folders.

Sample Data Section Title	Chapter: Title or Topic	Sample Data Folder/Subfolder
3D Model	11: DEM User Applications	3D_Model_Harris_Pictometry
Bathymetric Lidar	8: Airborne Lidar Bathymetry	Bathymetric_Fugro_Pelagos
IFSAR	6: Interferometric Synthetic Aperture Radar	IFSAR_Intermap
Laser Scan: FARO	7: Terrestrial Laser Scan	Laser_Scan\FARO
Laser Scan: I-SiTE	7: Terrestrial Laser Scan	Laser_Scan\I-SiTE
Laser Scan: Leica	7: Terrestrial Laser Scan	Laser_Scan\Leica
Laser Scan: Trimble	7: Terrestrial Laser Scan	Laser_Scan\Trimble
Lidar: Airborne 1	7: Topographic Lidar	Lidar\Airborne1
Lidar: Dewberry	12: DEM Quality Assessment 7: Topographic Lidar	Lidar\Dewberry\Delaware Lidar\Dewberry\Grand_Canyon
Lidar: Riegl	7: Terrestrial Laser Scan, Topographic Lidar	Lidar\Riegl
National Elevation Dataset	4: National Digital Elevation Program	NED_USGS
Photogrammetry	5: Photogrammetry	Photogrammetry_Pinnacle
Sonar	9: Sonar	Sonar_NOAA

In addition to the data described in this section, some software on the DVD includes sample datasets. For instance, a sample terrestrial laser scan dataset is included (installed with Cyclone by default) at C:\Program Files\Leica Geosystems\Cyclone\Databases\Samples\Plant.imp. This sample dataset is viewable using Cyclone and not discussed further in this section. In addition, sample elevation data are also included with the MARS FreeView software application, but not described in this section. Refer to the Software section for instructions on how to install Cyclone and MARS and access the sample datasets.

3D Model

This folder contains a video clip (Detroit.avi) of the Detroit, Michigan area and was provided by Harris Corporation (www.harris.com) and Pictometry International Corporation (www.pictometry.com). The video clip supports the "virtual city" information presented in Chapter 11. Please email Tom Kubancik at tom.kubancik@harris.com for additional information regarding this video clip.

At the Sample_Data\3D_Model_Harris_Pictometry folder, double-click on the Detroit.avi file to launch the video. The clip shows a fly-through of a 3D model of a portion of the City of Detroit with sample pop-up advertisements; the hyperlinks and phone numbers are for demonstration only.

The video was created using Harris' RealSite plug-in to their Multi-Image Exploitation Tool (MET) using imagery provided by Pictometry. Once the imagery is captured, the data are processed to create the 3D model and fly-through simulation. MET enables the semi-automated generation of 3D building polygons from overlapping images. An operator outlines the building or building feature footprint in one image and the RealSite software associates that footprint with the building in a second image. Building or feature heights are calculated based on the sensor models captured in MET and building polygons are generated. The software automatically textures the sides of the buildings using the actual imagery, not artificial or typical textures.

Highly-accurate 3D models can be generated using these techniques and have numerous potential applications beyond the commercial advertising application simulated in the Detroit video. For example, the technology could enhance emergency response for homeland security and law enforcement officials. It could also be used by city planners and the architectural/engineering community in the planning and design phases of major projects. The technology also has useful applications for training and visual simulation.

Bathymetric Lidar

This folder contains a sample bathymetric dataset from the Lake Ontario, Canada area prepared by Fugro Pelagos (www.fugro.com). These data support the information presented in Chapter 8. Please email Fugro Pelagos at fugropelagos@fugro.com for additional information regarding these data. Table 15.2 presents a description of the contents of the Sample_Data\Bathymetric_Fugro_Pelagos folder.

Table 15.2 Contents and Description of the Sample_Data\Bathymetric_Fugro_Pelagos Folder.

File or Folder Name	Description
Data_Voids.jpg	A graphical image documenting the location and corresponding explanation of why some data gaps exist in the included sample bathymetric data set
info	Folder required by the ESRI Grid format. Users should avoid directly accessing, moving or renaming this folder or its contents.
shoals_1000t	SHOALS_1000T.txt converted to ESRI Grid format. A collection of files stored in a subfolder; users should avoid directly accessing, moving or renaming this folder or its contents.

SHOALS_1000T.txt	ASCII text of a bathymetric lidar survey from an area in Pickering, Canada east of Toronto.
	• Projection: WGS84/UTM 17N meters
	• Vertical Datum:WGS84 ellipsoid heights in meters
	• Lidar System: SHOALS-1000T
	• Sounding Density: 4 meter postings
	• Data Format:
	  ▪ ASCII text as space-separated values: easting, northing and elevation
	  ▪ No header row

This sample dataset was acquired by Fugro Pelagos using the SHOALS-1000T airborne hydrographic lidar system manufactured by Optech Incorporated (www.optech.ca). The system combines a 1-kHz bathymetric laser, a 10-kHz topographic laser and a high-resolution RGB camera. The area is used regularly for system calibration and was flown at a height of 400-meters at 126 knots with a swath width of 215 meters. The data were post processed using kinematic GPS and meets International Hydrographic Organization Order 1 accuracy standards for position and depth.

Several areas in the sample dataset have null values or data gaps resulting from various natural phenomena or complications with data capture such as surf, turbidity and water depth. These areas are shown and explained in the Data_Voids.jpg file, included as Figure 15.3.

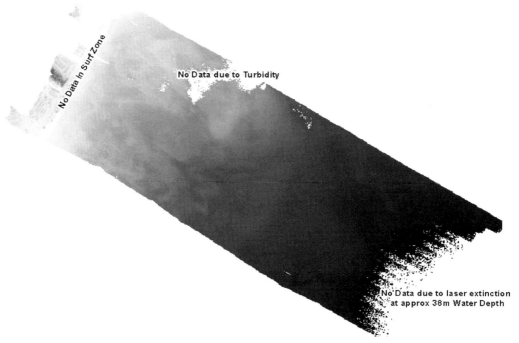

Figure 15.3 Grayscale version of the Data_Voids.jpg image included in the Sample_Data\ Bathymetric_Fugro_ Pelagos folder. Graphic shows the Shoals_1000T elevation model, annotated to show areas where and why data capture is affected by site conditions. Flight line is in a northwest-southeast direction. Image provided courtesy of Fugro Pelagos.

IFSAR

This folder contains an ortho-rectified radar image (ORI) and a DEM of the Morrison, Colorado area prepared by Intermap Technologies, Inc (www.intermap.com). These data support the information presented in Chapter 6. The ORI was collected in 2002 using Star3i, Intermap Technologies' X-band IFSAR system. Please email Marc Wride at mwride@intermaptechnologies.com for additional information regarding these data. Table 15.3 presents a description of the contents of the Sample_Data\IFSAR_Intermap folder.

Table 15.3 Contents and Description of the Sample_Data\IFSAR_Intermap Folder.

File or Folder Name	Description
info	Folder required by the ESRI Grid format. Users should avoid directly accessing, moving or renaming this folder or its contents.
MorrisonDEM.asc	DEM created by editing a digital surface model, in ASCII grid format with 5-meter post spacing and a 1-meter $RMSE_z$ vertical accuracy
MorrisonMetadata.txt	Federal Geographic Data Committee-compliant metadata for the dataset in ASCII text format
MorrisonOri.jgw	World file used to geospatially register the associated MorrisonOri.jpg
MorrisonOri.jpg	Ortho-rectified radar image at 1.25-meter pixel size. A low-resolution version of this image is shown as Figure 15.4.
MorrisonOri.prj	Text file describing the projection and datum for the MorrisonOri.jpg
Morrisonrast	MorrisonDEM.asc converted to ESRI Grid format. A collection of files stored in a subfolder; users should avoid directly accessing, moving or renaming this folder or its contents.

Figure 15.4 IFSAR-derived HillShaded image of the Morrison, Colorado area. This image is also included in the Sample_Data\IFSAR_Intermap folder on the DVD as MorrisonOri.jpg. Image provided courtesy of Intermap Technologies, Inc.

Laser Scan: FARO

This folder contains a selection of terrestrial laser scanning data provided by FARO Technologies Inc. (www.faro.com). These data support the information presented in Chapter 7 and can only be viewed using the FARO Scout LT software application. Please email Dr. Bernd-Dietmar Becker at Bernd.Becker@faroeurope.com for additional information regarding these data. Table 15.4 presents a description of the contents of the Sample_Data\Laser_Scan\FARO folder.

Table 15.4 Contents and Description of the Sample_Data\Laser_Scan\FARO Folder.

File or Folder Name	Description
Church1.fls	Data file showing the laser scan results from the survey of the interior of a church in Pongau, Austria. Scan was taken in 2005 and includes 2 million points. Church2.fls shows the interior of this same room with the laser scanner in a different position.
Church2.fls	Data file showing the laser scan results from the survey of the interior of a church in Pongau, Austria. Scan was taken in 2005 and includes 2 million points. A screenshot from this dataset is presented as Figure 15.5. Church1.fls shows the interior of this same room with the laser scanner in a different position.
Factory.fws	FARO Scout LT project file showing the laser scan results from the survey of the interior of an oil pipe equipment workshop in Scotland. Scan was taken in 2005 and includes 2 million points.
scans	Subfolder containing files which support the Factory.fws dataset. Users should only access this folder's contents through the FARO Scout LT application by double-clicking on the Factory.fws file after software installation.

Figure 15.5 Screen capture of the Church2.fls dataset included in the Sample_Data\Laser_Scan\FARO Folder viewed using FARO Scout LT software. Every pixel represents a survey point captured by the laser scanning system and has a 3D coordinate. Source data and viewing software provided courtesy of FARO Technologies Inc.

Laser Scan: I-SiTE

This folder contains two video clips derived from terrestrial laser scanning data and provided by I-SiTE Pty Limited (www.isite3d.com), a division of Maptek. These data support the information presented in Chapter 7. Please email John Dolan at John.Dolan@Maptek.com for additional information regarding these data. Table 15.5 presents a description of the contents of the Sample_Data\Laser_Scan\I-SiTE folder.

Table 15.5 Contents and Description of the Sample_Data\Laser_Scan\I-SiTE Folder.

File Name	Description
Building_Intensity.avi	Video clip showing a fly-through of a laser scan dataset showing the exterior of a building and the parking area. Some of the points include the intensity of the laser return. The survey area is the Spar Point Research LLC office building in Danvers, Massachusetts and was captured using the I-SiTE 4400 laser scanning system.
Building_Texture.avi	Video clip showing a fly-through of a laser scan dataset showing the exterior of a building and the parking area. The survey area is the Spar Point Research LLC office building in Danvers, Massachusetts and was captured using the I-SiTE 4400 laser scanning system.

Laser Scan: Leica

This folder contains a selection of terrestrial laser scanning data provided by Leica Geosystems HDS, LLC (www.leica.com). These data support the information presented in Chapter 7 and can only be viewed using the Cyclone software application; refer to the Software section for Cyclone quick start instructions. Please email Leica at support@lgshds.com for additional information regarding these data. Table 15.6 presents a description of the contents of the Sample_Data\Laser_Scan\Leica folder.

Table 15.6 Contents and Description of the Sample_Data\Laser_Scan\Leica Folder.

File or Folder Name	Description
Boiler_Room.imp	Cyclone database file of a laser scan dataset collected from interior of the boiler room at Leica Geosystems HDS group headquarters in San Ramon, California. This dataset contains a raster image view (click on the Images folder in Cyclone viewer), as well as a model space view of the vector (point) data.
Church.imp	Cyclone database file of a laser scan dataset collected of the exterior of the Saint Peter and Paul Church on Washington Square, San Francisco, California. A screenshot from this dataset is presented as Figure 15.6.
Interchange.imp	Cyclone database file of a laser scan dataset collected of the I-30 and I-45 freeway interchange in Dallas, Texas.
eventlog	Folder with subfolders containing log files to support the imp files. Users should avoid directly accessing, moving or renaming this folder or its contents.
recovery	Folder with subfolders containing recovery files to support the imp files. Users should avoid directly accessing, moving or renaming this folder or its contents.

Figure 15.6 Screen capture of the Church.imp dataset included in the Sample_Data\Laser_Scan folder viewed using Cyclone software. Every pixel represents a survey point captured by the laser scanning system and has a 3D coordinate. Source data and viewing software provided courtesy of Leica Geosystems HDS, LLC.

Laser Scan: Trimble

This folder contains a terrestrial laser scanning dataset provided by Trimble Navigation Limited (www.trimble.com). These data support the information presented in Chapter 7 and can only be viewed using the RealWorks Viewer software application. Please email laserscanning@trimble.com for additional information regarding these data. Table 15.7 presents a description of the contents of the Sample_Data\Laser_Scan\Trimble folder.

Table 15.7 Contents and Description of the Sample_Data\Laser_Scan\Trimble Folder.

File or Folder Name	Description
Union_Station.rwp	RealWorks Viewer project file showing the laser scan results from the survey of the exterior of the Union Station train station in Denver, Colorado. Data were captured in October 2005 using a Trimble GX scanner. A screenshot from this dataset is presented as Figure 15.7.
Union_Station.rwi	Subfolder containing files which support the Union_Station.rwp dataset. Users should only access this folder's contents through the RealWorks Viewer application by double-clicking on the Union_Station.rwp file after software installation.

Figure 15.7 3D perspective view of the Union_Station dataset included in the Sample_Data\Laser_Scan\ Trimble folder exported from the RealWorks Viewer software. Every pixel represents a survey point captured by the laser scanning system and has a 3D coordinate. Source data and viewing software provided courtesy of Trimble Navigation Limited.

Lidar: Airborne 1

This folder contains a variety of lidar data and derived images compiled from data provided by the Airborne 1 Corporation (www.airborne1.com). These data support the information presented in Chapter 7. Please email Todd Stennett at info@airborne1.com for additional information regarding these data. Table 15.8 presents a description of the contents of the Sample_Data\Lidar\Airborne1 folder.

Table 15.8 Organization and Contents of Sample_Data\Lidar\Airborne1 Folder.

Folder Name	Folder Contents	Format; Extension
Hoover_Dam	Lidar data and derived images of the Hoover Dam on the Nevada/Arizona border. An image from this dataset is presented as Figure 15.8.	ASCII text and bitmap image; txt and bmp
Landfill	Lidar data and a derived image of a landfill in Orange County, California	ASCII text and tagged image; xyz and tif
Misc_Images	Lidar-derived images from various locations and settings or applications	Tagged image; tif
Powerline_Images	Lidar-derived images of three electrical power transmission line corridors	Tagged and bitmap images; tif and bmp

Figure 15.8 Lidar-derived image of the Hoover Dam. This image is also included in the Sample_Data\Lidar\ Airborne1\Hoover_Dam folder on the DVD as Ground.bmp. Image provided courtesy of Airborne 1 Corporation.

The Hoover_Dam and Landfill folders include lidar point-cloud data suitable for creation of DEMs, as well as associated lidar-derived images. The following presents details of the lidar data contained within these two folders.

Hoover Dam
- Flight Date: October 2004
- Projection: UTM 11
- Lidar System: Optech ALTM 2025
- Accuracy: Data suitable for 1-foot contours (18-centimeter vertical accuracy at 95% confidence level)
- Data Format:
  - ASCII text as space-separated values with the following columns: easting, northing, elevation and intensity. (Intensity was formatted using a special code that users should ignore; customer preference has resulted in the limited usability of the data in this column)
  - No header row
- Data types:
  - Ground.txt – bare-earth returns only
  - Veg.txt – all returns

Landfill
- Flight Date: June 2002
- Projection: UTM Zone 11
- Lidar System: Optech ALTM 2025
- Accuracy: Data suitable for 1-foot contours (18-centimeter vertical accuracy at 95% confidence level)
- Data Format:
  - ASCII text (lidar.xyz) as space-separated values with the following columns: easting, northing and elevation
  - No header row

The Misc_Images and Powerline_Images folders contain various lidar-derived images colored and rendered using a variety of techniques. These images are interesting to zoom and explore, illustrating how various industries and organizations use lidar to portray their business processes visually. Each file name gives an indication of the geographical location or how the image is colored (i.e., by elevation or lidar return intensity).

Lidar: Dewberry

This folder contains a variety of lidar data and associated products compiled or prepared by Dewberry (www.dewberry.com). It is divided into two subfolders, Delaware and Grand_Canyon, each of which is described below. These data support the information presented in Chapter 12 and 7, respectively. Please email Craig Lees at clees@dewberry.com for additional information regarding these data.

Delaware

This subfolder includes a lidar dataset from a portion of the East Branch Delaware River watershed in and around Delaware County, New York. This section provides more detail than others, reflecting the author's professional experience in working with these particular data. The dataset was created as part of a quality assurance review accomplished by Dewberry in 2005 using ESRI's (www.esri.com) ArcGIS software. The dataset is provided courtesy of FEMA (www.fema.gov) which contracted Terrapoint (www.terrapoint.com) to acquire the data. Terrapoint flew the lidar mission in the Spring of 2005. An explanation of the data included in each subfolder is provided in Table 15.9.

Table 15.9 Organization and Contents of Sample_Data\Lidar\Dewberry\Delaware Folder.

Folder Name	Folder Contents	Format; Extension
HS	HillShade GIS data created from the TinGrid and stored in subfolders. A collection of files stored in subfolders; users should avoid directly accessing, moving or renaming these folders or their contents.	ESRI Grid; adf, aux, xml*
IMG	Graphical images created from various views of the lidar dataset. See Table 15.12 for a description of the contents of this folder.	Compressed image; jpg
Lidar_Points	Lidar point data (post-processed bare-earth) in a comma-separated text format with a header row (x,y,z,i) where "x" and "y" represent point co-ordinates, "z" is elevation and "i" is the intensity of the lidar return.	ASCII text; txt, xml*
MXD	Project document which defines the GIS data view	ESRI ArcMap versions 9.1 and 8.3 Documents; mxd, xml*
SHP	Shapefile GIS data, 2D point feature created from the lidar point data	ESRI shapefile; shp, shx, dbf, sbn, sbx, prj, xml*
TG	TinGrid GIS data created from the TIN and stored in subfolders. A collection of files stored in subfolders; users should avoid directly accessing, moving or renaming these folders or their contents.	ESRI Grid; adf, aux, xml*
TIN	Triangular Irregular Network GIS data created from shapefile points and stored in subfolders	ESRI TIN; adf, xml*
*Note: Most folders include metadata in xml format named filename.xml or metadata.xml that is best viewed using an FGDC-compliant metadata viewer such as ArcCatalog.		

Users should note that this dataset is provided for illustrative purposes only to support this *DEM Users Manual* and is included as a complement to the theory and process described in Chapters 7 and 12. Users now have an opportunity to examine the various datasets. However, the data should not be used for business applications (modeling, planning, surveying, remote sensing, etc.) because the values within the dataset may not represent current real-world conditions.

The following sections summarize the steps taken to create and analyze the various data "products;" users should refer to ESRI help files to learn how to accomplish these steps using ArcGIS. In addition, some terminology used in this section is specific to ESRI, the most important of which is the term "TinGrid" which is a raster that stores elevation data and is also known as a DEM. Finally, there are references to lidar points; these are bare-earth last-return lidar mass points in ASCII text format that have been post-processed by Terrapoint, the data acquisition vendor.

Dewberry is an ESRI Business Partner and has developed a lidar data quality review workflow using ArcGIS software. The design of the folder structure and data included supports the performance of lidar data quality reviews using ESRI's ArcGIS. Although non-ESRI users may still access portions of the included data using other software products (such as Global Mapper), some of it is only useful in an ESRI environment. To fully explore the included data, contact ESRI for a demonstration copy of ArcGIS. Also, shapefiles are included in this chapter instead of the preferred geodatabase feature class format, in an effort to make these data accessible to non-ESRI users. All files except those in the IMG folder include metadata that can be viewed using ArcCatalog by selecting the file in the left-hand pane and clicking on the Metadata tab in the right-hand pane.

Data Inventory and Product Creation

A good place to start when performing a quality assurance review is to create an inventory of the lidar data. Because lidar datasets typically include millions of points divided into thousands of individual files, maintaining a data inventory is a helpful management tool. An inventory should include basic details about each file such as the name, date created or last modified and size (kilobytes); users might also consider other data relevant to a specific business process. An excellent complement to this basic information is file content statistics. Calculations such as the number of records and the minimum and maximum values for x, y and z within each file can yield significant insight. For example, if a negative value in the z column (elevation) was discovered and the study area was of a mountainous area well above the elevation datum, an error might be suspected and further investigation appropriate.

To illustrate this point, a sample inventory template is provided. It is in database format (dbf) and may be viewed with programs including ArcGIS, Microsoft Excel or Access. Open the file named inventry.dbf (file name intentionally limited to eight characters) in the Sample_Data\Lidar\Dewberry\Delaware folder for a summary of the lidar text files within the Sample_Data\Lidar\Dewberry\Delaware\Lidar_Points folder. The data fields included in this file are explained in Table 15.10.

Table 15.10 Field Names and Description for Sample_Data\Lidar\Dewberry\Delaware\inventry.dbf.

Field Name	Contents
ID	Unique identifier for each file
FILE_NAME	Name of the file including extension
BYTES	Size of the file (in kilobytes)
DATE	File date (date created/modified)
XMIN	The lowest value in the first column (x) of the file
XMAX	The highest value in the first column (x) of the file
YMIN	The lowest value in the second column (y) of the file
YMAX	The highest value in the second column (y) of the file
ZMIN	The lowest value in the third column (elevation) of the file
ZMAX	The highest value in the third column (elevation) of the file
NUM	The total number of records (excluding the header row) in the file

Once an inventory has been created, the next step is to convert the lidar point data into a variety of formats (or "products") useful for performing quality assurance reviews in an ESRI environment. Refer to ESRI help files and on-line resources to determine the software licenses, extensions and commands necessary to replicate each step. The overall workflow is diagrammed in Figure 15.9.

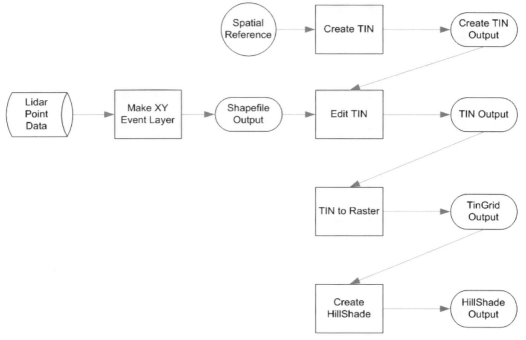

Figure 15.9 Workflow chart illustrating the process for creating various data products from the lidar point data. Chart provided courtesy of Dewberry.

Four core products are created (each named "output" in Figure 15.9) from the lidar point data: shapefile, TIN, TinGrid and HillShade. Each of these reveal unique and important aspects of the lidar data and may be important to a quality review process. The first step is to convert the point data to an XY Event Layer and exporting that layer as a point shapefile. The next step is to create a TIN from the shapefile. Using ArcGIS' ArcToolbox, this is actually a two step process: first an empty TIN "shell" is created and second it is "filled" or populated with point data from the shapefile and TIN faces (slope and aspect) are computed. Finally, a TinGrid is created from the TIN and a HillShade is created from the TinGrid.

Checkpoints and Visualization
A key part of performing a quality assessment review of lidar data includes the comparison of the lidar dataset to conventionally-surveyed data called "checkpoints." These checkpoints are acquired using high-order survey techniques to achieve centimeter-level accuracy and are, for the purposes of lidar quality review, considered to be "correct." Theoretically, a statistical comparison of these checkpoints to points captured using lidar will indicate the accuracy of the lidar dataset. Refer to Chapter 12 for a detailed discussion of this concept.

Checkpoints are selected by field surveyors from flat areas away from breaklines and do not necessarily represent a clearly-defined feature on the ground. Points are selected to ensure a reasonable distribution across the project area within the major land cover categories encountered (in this example, Open Terrain, Weeds/Crops, Scrub, Forest and Built Up/Urban). To illustrate this, a shapefile named Checkpoint.shp is provided in the Sample_Data\Lidar\Dewberry\Delaware\SHP folder; the attributes of these checkpoints are listed and described in Table 15.11. These sample points have been used for comparison with the lidar-derived TIN; the results (TIN elevation minus checkpoint elevation) are included in the "DeltaZ" field.

Table 15.11 Field Names and Description for Checkpoint.shp.

Field Name	Description
OBJECTID	Internal feature number
Shape	Feature geometry
PT_ID	A unique name/identifier for each survey checkpoint; used to link back to original survey data if needed
E	Easting (x) coordinate value for the checkpoint
N	Northing (y) coordinate value for the checkpoint
Z	Surveyed elevation of the checkpoint in feet (NAVD88)
Land_Cover	A code and description of the land cover at the survey location
TINz	Elevation in feet of the survey point as extracted from the TIN created from the lidar data
ClosestID1	The ObjectID of the lidar point closest to the checkpoint
ClosestID2	The ObjectID of the lidar point second closest to the checkpoint
ClosestID3	The ObjectID of the lidar point third closest to the checkpoint
Dist1	The straight line distance (in feet) between ClosestID1 and the checkpoint
Dist2	The straight line distance (in feet) between ClosestID2 and the checkpoint
Dist3	The straight line distance (in feet) between ClosestID3 and the checkpoint
DeltaZ	Simple mathematic calculation (TINz-Z) indicating the difference between the lidar elevation (TINz) and surveyed checkpoint elevation (Z)
Rename	The name of the lidar tile where the checkpoint exists, based on its spatial location per the Lidar_Tile_Index.shp shapefile in the Sample_Data\Lidar\ Dewberry\Delaware\SHP folder

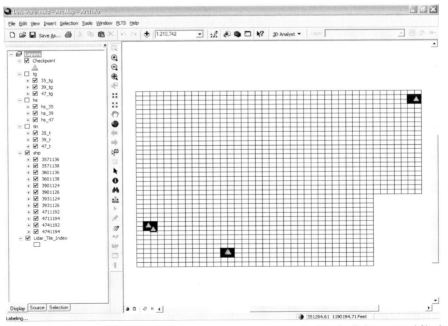

Figure 15.10 Screen capture of ArcMap displaying the feature classes involved in the Delaware.mxd file. Image provided courtesy of Dewberry.

Readers with access to ArcGIS software (version 9 or 9.1) should launch the Delaware.mxd file stored in the MXD folder to easily view the included sample data (see Figure 15.10). ArcGIS version 8.3 users should open the Delaware_v8.mxd file. Once ArcMap has opened, update the path to each data layer as necessary; refer to Table 15.9 for a list of folders where data are stored. Data within the map document are grouped by type, and are named and organized geographically according to the Lidar_Tile_Index shapefile. The 12 shapefiles created from the lidar points were consolidated into three separate blocks (based on adjacency) when converting to TINs, TinGrids and HillShades. Each block was named with a two-digit code based on the first two digits of the first file name for the lidar point data. Users may explore this dataset by zooming to various locations and comparing the output/products using ArcMap's identify tool.

Lidar Graphics

The graphical images in the IMG folder were created based on a lidar dataset covering a portion of the East Branch Delaware River in New York. The contents of this folder are described in Table 15.12. Using ArcGIS, bare earth mass points were converted to a point feature class which was used to build a TIN. A TinGrid was created from the TIN and a HillShade raster was created from the TinGrid. A blue to red color ramp (indicating low to high elevations, respectively) was applied to the TinGrid and set at 50% transparency on top of the HillShade. The HillShade raster was set using a grey color ramp simulating shadows created based on a specified azimuth and altitude for the sun. Using ArcGIS and ArcScene, various views were set and the images exported to jpg format with different resolution settings.

Table 15.12 Contents and Description of the Sample_Data\Lidar\Dewberry\Delaware\IMG Folder.

File Name	Description
HillShade.jpg	The HillShade raster of the river (also Figure 15.11)
River.jpg	A 2D view of a several mile stretch of the river. Created at a high resolution, the image is suitable for close examination. Search the image to explore details of the river morphology and note how structures (buildings and bridges) have been removed from the full point cloud to produce the bare earth model.
River_3D.jpg	A 3D perspective view of River.jpg
River_Detail_3D.jpg	A close-up view of River_3D.jpg from the opposite (of River_3D.jpg) angle
TG_HS.jpg	The TinGrid overlaid (at 50% transparency) on the HillShade
TinGrid.jpg	The TinGrid raster of the river
Watershed_3D.jpg	A 3D perspective view of a 900-square-mile watershed
Watershed_Detail_3D.jpg	A close-up view of Watershed_3D.jpg

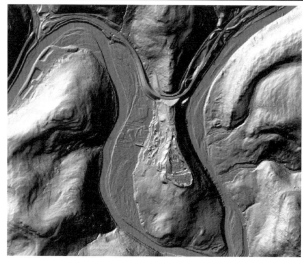

Figure 15.11 HillShade view of a portion of the East Branch Delaware River, also included in the Sample_Data\ Lidar\Dewberry\ Delaware\IMG folder on the DVD as HillShade.jpg. Image provided courtesy of Dewberry.

Chapter 15

Grand Canyon

This subfolder contains lidar point data and an associated image from a short reach of the Grand Canyon in Arizona. These data are provided courtesy of the US Geological Survey (www.usgs.gov) and the Grand Canyon Monitoring and Research Center (www.gcmrc.gov) and were flown by Airborne 1 as subcontractor to Dewberry in May 2005. Table 15.13 presents a description of the contents of the Sample_Data\Lidar\Dewberry\Grand_Canyon folder.

Table 15.13 Contents of Sample_Data\Lidar\Dewberry\Grand_Canyon Folder.

File Name	File Description
Grand_Canyon_3D.tif	A 3D perspective view of the lidar points. A grayscale version of this image is shown as Figure 15.12.
Grand_Canyon_Sample.mprj	MARS project file for easy access to the Lidar_Ground_Points.las file. If MARS FreeView is installed, simply double-click this file to launch the program and display the lidar data.
Lidar_Ground_Points.las	A copy of Lidar_Ground_Points.xyz in ASPRS' binary lidar data exchange format
Lidar_Ground_Points.xyz	ASCII text of a lidar survey from a short reach of the Grand Canyon and Colorado River. • Projection: Arizona State Plane Zone 202 • Lidar System: Optech ALTM 2050 • Accuracy: Data suitable for 1-foot contours (18-centimeter vertical accuracy at 95% confidence level) • Data Format: 　▪ ASCII text as comma-separated values: easting, northing and elevation 　▪ No header row

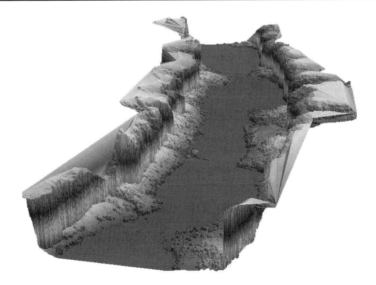

Figure 15.12 3D perspective of the Grand Canyon lidar point dataset. A color version of this image is included in the Sample_Data\Lidar\Dewberry\Grand_Canyon folder on the DVD as Grand_Canyon_3D.tif. Image provided courtesy of Dewberry.

Lidar: Riegl

This folder contains two video clips, one captured using terrestrial lidar and the other using airborne lidar, provided by Riegl USA, Inc. (www.rieglusa.com). These data support the information presented in Chapter 7. Please email Riegl at info@rieglusa.com for additional information regarding these data. Table 15.14 presents a description of the contents of the Sample_Data\Lidar\Riegl folder.

Table 15.14 Contents and Description of the Sample_Data\Lidar\Riegl Folder.

File Name	Description
Salzburg.wmv	Video clip showing a fly-through of a terrestrial lidar laser scan dataset in Windows Media audio/video format. This dataset was captured using Riegl's LMS-Z420 laser scanner, coupled with a Nikon D100 digital camera. Using Riscan Pro software, the data point data and imagery were integrated, post-processed and the fly-through created. The data were overlaid on an orthophotograph and georeferenced; the castle shown "floating" in the background is up on a hill. Windows Media Player version 8 or higher or a program capable of playing this format is required to display the video (software is not included on the DVD).
Schoendt.avi	Video clip showing a fly-through of an airborne lidar dataset of Vienna, Austria. This dataset was captured using Riegl's LMS-Q560, a full-wave form laser scanner. The data were processed using Riegl's Airborne Software suite. The video shows the same area from various perspectives, while moving though a variety of rendering alternatives such as intensity, classification, TIN and elevation.

National Elevation Dataset

This folder contains sample DEMs from the National Elevation Dataset (NED) provided by the US Geological Survey (http://seamless.usgs.gov). These data support the information presented in Chapter 4. Refer to the Data_Descriptions.pdf and NED_Data_Dictionary.pdf files in the Sample_Data\NED_USGS folder for an additional explanation of the data provided. Please email Dean Gesch at gesch@usgs.gov for more information regarding these data. Table 15.15 presents a description of the contents of the Sample_Data\NED_USGS folder.

Table 15.15 Organization and Contents of Sample_Data\NED_USGS Folder.

Folder Name	Folder Contents	Format
Louisiana	1-, 1/3- and 1/9-arc second elevation data and shaded relief images, textual and spatial metadata for an area in southern Louisiana	ESRI Grid, Shapefile, HTML and Geotiff
Montana	1- and 1/3-arc second elevation data and shaded relief images, textual and spatial metadata for an area in western Montana. A portion of the 1/3-arc second data is shown in Figure 15.13.	ESRI Grid, Shapefile, HTML and Geotiff
West_Virginia	1-, 1/3- and 1/9-arc second elevation data and shaded relief images, textual and spatial metadata for an area in southern West Virginia	ESRI Grid, Shapefile, HTML and Geotiff
Note: Each folder contains a subfolder named "info" required by the ESRI Grid format. Users should avoid directly accessing, moving or renaming these folders or their contents.		

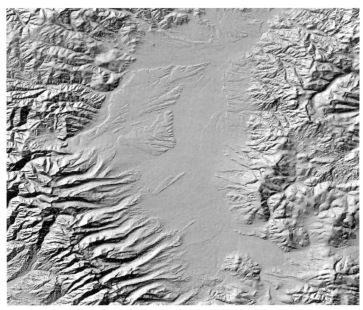

Figure 15.13 HillShade view of a portion of the data included in the Sample_Data\USGS_NED\Montana folder. Image provided courtesy of US Geological Survey.

Photogrammetry

This folder contains photogrammetric data and derived products from the City of Greeley, Colorado acquired or created in the Spring of 2005. These data support the information presented in Chapter 5 and were provided by Pinnacle Mapping Technologies, Inc. (www.pinnaclemapping.com). Please email Brian Mayfield at bmayfield@pinnaclemapping.com for additional information regarding these data. Table 15.16 presents a description of the contents of the Sample_Data\Photogrammetry_Pinnacle folder.

Table 15.16 Contents and Description of the Sample_Data\Photogrammetry_Pinnacle Folder.

File Name	Description
breakline.shp (et. al.)*	Shapefile (polyline ZM) containing breaklines
contour.shp (et. al.)*	Shapefile (polyline ZM) containing topographic contours
mass_point.shp (et. al.)*	Shapefile (point ZM) containing mass points
obscured_area.shp (et. al.)*	Shapefile (polygon ZM) showing obscured areas in the orthophotograph
Ortho_025_ft.tfw	World file used to geospatially register the associated Ortho_025_ft.tif image
Ortho_025_ft.tif	Full-color orthophotograph of the sample area. All other files in this directory were derived from this image. Each pixel represents 3-inches on the ground.
Sample_1foot_contours.dgn	Topographic contours of the project area in CAD format
Sample_1foot_dtm.dgn	Digital terrain model of the project area in CAD format
spot_elevation.shp (et. al.)*	Shapefile (point ZM) containing spot elevations of the project area
*Note: Shapefiles are a collection of several files (seven, in this instance) with the same file name but different extensions containing GIS data.	

These data were created based on aerial photography flown using a Leica RC30 Aerial Camera System. The film was scanned and a stereoscopic surface was captured using traditional photo-grammetric methods. The final product was used to support both orthorectification of a 1"=50'-scale color orthophoto with a 0.25' (3-inch) ground pixel resolution and to model 1' contours. The breaklines define hard surface features, such as edges of roads and ponds, as well as soft features like road crowns. Mass points have been added manually by the photogrammetrist in flat, open areas to supplement the breaklines and help define the contours. The mass points and breaklines are used to create a TIN which is used to produce contours. A grayscale 3D perspective view of a portion of these data are presented in Figure 15.14.

Figure 15.14 Grayscale 3D-perspective view of topographic contours and Ortho_025_ft.tif draped over a HillShade and elevation model. Because a bare-earth model is used, buildings in the background appear flat. Source data provided courtesy of Pinnacle Mapping Technologies, Inc.

Sonar

This folder contains multi-beam and side scan sonar data from a hydrographic surveying mission (#H11028) conducted on the Chesapeake Bay, Virginia in 2001-2002. These data support the information presented in Chapter 9. They were downloaded from the National Oceanic & Atmospheric Administration's National Ocean Survey website, http://map.ngdc.noaa.gov/website/mgg/-nos_hydro. Please email hydro.info@noaa.gov for additional information regarding these data. Table 15.17 presents a description of the contents of the Sample_Data \Sonar_NOAA folder.

Table 15.17 Contents and Description of the Sample_Data\Sonar_NOAA Folder.

File Name	Description
H11028_1m.txt	Gridded point data (soundings) from the survey using a 1-meter point spacing. ASCII text format, space delimited, no header, xyz (three additional columns are included for a future product enhancement and should be ignored). Horizontal datum is UTM zone 18 N, NAD 83, meters. Vertical datum is depth in meters below Mean Lower Low Water.
H11028_50m.txt	Gridded point data (depth soundings) from the survey using 50-meter point spacing. ASCII text format, space delimited, no header, xyz (three additional columns are included for a future product enhancement and should be ignored). Horizontal datum is UTM zone 18 N, NAD 83, meters. Vertical datum is depth in meters below Mean Lower Low Water.
Project_Area.shp (et. al.)	Shapefile polygon of the project extent. Note that shapefiles are a collection of several files (seven, in this instance) with the same file name but different extensions.
Report.pdf	Descriptive report of the sonar survey
Sidescan.tfw	World file used to geospatially register the associated Sidescan.tif image
Sidescan.tif	Sidescan sonar mosaic image from the full survey results at 1-meter postings. A portion of this image is presented as Figure 15.15.
Smooth_Sheet.tif	Graphic image of the smooth sheet produced from the survey. The smooth sheet is the final, neatly drafted, accurate plot of the survey. It is the traditional method for documenting hazards to navigation and sonar survey results.
Survey_Results.tfw	World file used to geospatially register the associated Survey_Results.tif image
Survey_Results.tif	Full-color image created from the full survey results at 1-meter postings

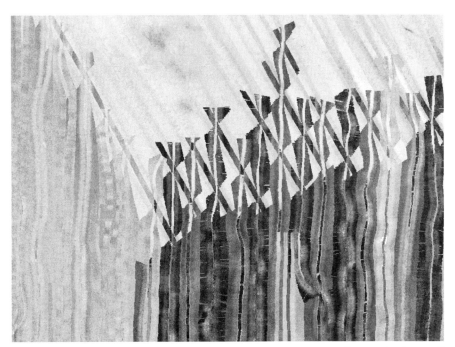

Figure 15.15 Close-up view of a portion of the Sidescan.tif image included on the DVD in the Sample_Data\ Sonar_NOAA folder. Image indicates the path of the boat and overlapping scan areas. Source data provided courtesy of the National Oceanic & Atmospheric Administration.

AUTHOR BIOGRAPHY

Craig L. Lees is a Project Manager with the Geographic Information Services Division at Dewberry in Fairfax, Virginia. He works on a variety of lidar, enterprise GIS, utility mapping, business process reengineering and database design projects. Since joining Dewberry in 1994, he has worked on environmental compliance management and flood insurance mapping projects. He received his BA in Geology from Bucknell University in 1993.

ACKNOWLEDGEMENTS

The author would like to thank his wife, Jaime Lees, for her love, support and editorial expertise. In addition, special recognition goes to Tim Blak who has taught the author everything he knows about lidar and DEMs; without Tim's expertise and tutelage, this chapter would not have been possible. Finally, the author would like to express sincere appreciation to Dave Maune for the unique opportunity to prepare this chapter and the associated DVD. Dave's selfless contributions to the industry and tireless efforts are an inspiration to us all.

The author would also like to acknowledge the firms and agencies who generously contributed software and sample data. They are leaders in the industry and their willingness to support this effort is a benefit to DEM users everywhere. Their websites and specific software or data contributions are referenced at the appropriate place in the foregoing text and an alphabetic summary follows.

- Airborne 1 Corporation
- Department of Homeland Security, Federal Emergency Management Agency
- Dewberry
- FARO Technologies Inc.
- Fugro Pelagos
- Global Mapper Software LLC
- Grand Canyon Monitoring and Research Center
- Harris Corporation
- I-SiTE Pty Limited
- Intermap Technologies, Inc
- Leica Geosystems HDS, LLC
- Merrick & Company
- National Oceanic & Atmospheric Administration
- Pictometry
- Pinnacle Mapping Technologies, Inc.
- Riegl USA, Inc.
- Terrapoint
- Trimble Navigation Limited
- US Geological Survey

Appendix A

Acronyms

AAA	American Automobile Association
AAGS	American Association for Geodetic Surveying
ABGPS	Airborne GPS
ABS	Acoustic Backscatter
ACSM	American Congress on Surveying and Mapping
AGL	Above Ground Level
AINS	Aided Inertial Navigation System
ALB	Airborne Lidar Bathymetry
ALH	Airborne Lidar Hydrography
ALS	Airborne Laser Scanning
ALTM	Airborne Laser Terrain Mapper (or Mapping)
AM	Amplitude Modulation
AMT	Above Mean Terrain
ANSI	American National Standards Institute
AOL	Airborne Oceanographic Lidar
APD	Avalanche Photodiode
ARC	Automatic Radar Controller
ASCII	American Standard Code for Information Interchange
ASFPM	Association of State Floodplain Managers
ASL	Above Sea Level
ASPRS	American Society for Photogrammetry and Remote Sensing
ATC	Air Traffic Control
ATM	Airborne Topographic Mapper
AUV	Autonomous Underwater Vehicle
BAG	Bathymetric Attributed Grid
BATS	Bathymetric And Topographic Survey
BFE	Base Flood Elevation
BIL	Band Interleaved by Line (File Format)

BIN	Binary
BIP	Band Interleaved by Pixel (File Format)
BIT	Built-In Test
BLM	Bureau of Land Management
BMP	Best Management Practice
BSQ	Band Sequential (File Format)
C^3I	Communications, Command, Control, and Intelligence
C/A	Coarse/Acquisition
CAD	Computer-Aided Design
CADD	Computer-Aided Design and Drafting
CAES	Computer-Aided Earthmoving System
CASI	Compact Airborne Spectrographic Imager
CCCL	Coastal Construction Control Line
CCD	Charge Coupled Device
CCRS	Canada Centre for Remote Sensing
CE	Circular Error
CEP	Circular Error Probable
CHARTS	Compact Hydrographic Airborne Rapid Total Survey
CHS	Canadian Hydrographic Service
CI	Contour Interval
CMAS	Circular Map Accuracy Standard
CO-OPS	Center for Operational Oceanographic Products and Services
CORPSCON	Corps Conversion
CORS	Continuously Operating Reference Station
COTS	Commercial Off-the-Shelf
CRAB	Coastal Research Amphibious Buggy
CSDGM	Content Standard for Digital Geospatial Metadata
CTOG	Contour To Grid
CW	Continuous Wave
DARPA	Defense Advanced Research Projects Agency
DAS	Data Acquisition System
DAT	DEM Analysis Tool

DCM	Direction Cosine Matrix
DDDMMSS	Degrees, Minutes, and Seconds
DED	Digital Elevation Data
DEM	Digital Elevation Model
DES	DEM Edit System
DFIRM	Digital Flood Insurance Rate Map
DG	Direct Georeferencing
DGN	MicroStation Design (File Format)
DGPS	Differential GPS
DHQ	Diurnal High Water Inequality
DLG	Digital Line Graph
DLQ	Diurnal Low Water Inequality
DLT	Digital Linear Tape
DO	DLG Optional (file format)
DoD	Department of Defense
DOQ	Digital Orthophoto Quad or Digital Orthophoto Quarter-Quad
DOQQ	Digital Orthophoto Quarter-Quad
DPI	Dots per Inch
DRG	Digital Raster Graphic
DSM	Digital Surface Model
DTED	Digital Terrain Elevation Data
DTG	Dry Tuned Rotor Gyro
DTHM	Digital Tree Height Model
DTL	Diurnal Tide Level
DTM	Digital Terrain Model
DVD	Digital Video Disk
DVS	DEM Verification System
DWG	AutoCAD Drawing (File Format)
DXF	Drawing Exchange (File Format)
E00	ArcInfo Export (File Format)
ECDIS	Electronic Chart Display and Information System
ECEF	Earth-Centered-Earth-Fixed

ECS	Electronic Chart System
ED	Existence Doubtful
EDME	Electronic Distance Measuring Equipment
EDNA	Elevation Derivatives for National Applications
EEC	European Economic Community
EEZ	Exclusive Economic Zone
EGI	Embedded GPS-Inertial
EGM	Earth Gravitational Model
EHA	Erosion Hazard Area
ENC	Electronic Nautical Chart
EPA	Environmental Protection Agency
ERDC	U.S. Army Engineer Research and Development Center
ERIM	Environmental Research Institute of Michigan
ESRI	Environmental Systems Research Institute
EU	European Union
EVS	Effective Vertical Spacing
FAA	Federal Aviation Administration
FAR	Federal Acquisition Regulation
FDC	Frequency-to-Distance Conversion
FEMA	Federal Emergency Management Agency
FGCC	Federal Geodetic Control Committee
FGCS	FGDC's Federal Geodetic Control Subcommittee
FGDC	Federal Geographic Data Committee
FIRM	Flood Insurance Rate Map
FM	Frequency Modulation
FMS	Flight Management System
FOG	Fiber Optic Gyro
FOV	Field of View
FTP	File Transfer Protocol
FWD	Full Waveform Digitizing
FWHM	Full Width at Half Maximum
GB	Gigabyte

GDOP	Geometric Dilution of Position
GeoTIFF	Georeferenced Tagged Image File Format
GHz	Gigahertz
GIS	Geographic Information System
GLONASS	Global Navigation Satellite System
GLORIA	Geological Long Range Inclined Asdic
GMT	Greenwich Mean Time
GNSS	Global Navigation Satellite System
GOTS	Government Off-the-Shelf
GPRA	Government Performance and Results Act
GPS	Global Positioning System
GSD	Ground Sample Distance
Gt	Great Diurnal Range
HARN	High Accuracy Reference Network
H&H	Hydrologic and Hydraulic
IAG	International Association of Geodesy
IDW	Inverse Distance Weighted
IEC	International Electrotechnical Commission
IFOV	Instantaneous Field of View
IFSAR	Interferometric Synthetic Aperture Radar (also InSAR)
IFSARE	IFSAR-Elevation
IGLD	International Great Lakes Datum
IGS	International GNSS Service
IHO	International Hydrographic Organization
IMO	International Maritime Organization
IMU	Inertial Measurement Unit (also IRU)
INS	Inertial Navigation System (also INU)
InSAR	Interferometric Synthetic Aperture Radar (also IFSAR)
INU	Inertial Navigation Unit (also INS)
ION	Institute of Navigation
IOS	Institute of Oceanographic Sciences

IPP	Interpulse Period
IR	Infrared
IRU	Inertial Reference Unit (also IMU)
ISAR	Interferometric Synthetic Aperture Radar (also IFSAR)
ISO	International Standards Organization
ISPRS	International Society for Photogrammetry and Remote Sensing
ITRF	International Earth Rotation Service Terrestrial Reference Frame
IV & V	Independent Validation and Verification
JALBTCX	Joint Airborne Lidar Bathymetry Technical Center of Expertise
JPL	Jet Propulsion Laboratory
JPSD-PO	Joint Precision Strike Demonstration Project Office
KAR	Kinematic Ambiguity Resolution (also see OTF)
KGPS	Kinematic GPS
KHz	Kilohertz
KW	Kilowatts
L1	Level 1 frequency of GPS satellites
L2	Level 2 frequency of GPS satellites
L3	Level 3 frequency of GPS satellites
L5	Level 5 frequency of Block IIF GPS satellites
LAAS	Local Area Augmentation System
LADAR	LAser Detection And Ranging
LADS	Laser Airborne Depth Sounder
LAG	Lowest Adjacent Grade
LAPF	Laser Altimeter Processing Facility
LARSEN	Laser Airborne Remote SENsor
LASER	Light Amplification by Stimulated Emission of Radiation
LAT	Lowest Astronomical Tide
LBMS	Laser-Baseline Measurement System
LCD	Liquid Crystal Display
LFE	Lowest Floor Elevation

LIDAR	LIght Detection And Ranging
LIF	Laser Induced Fluorescence
LINZ	Land Information New Zealand
LIS	Land Information System
LLR	Lunar Laser Ranging
LMSL	Local Mean Sea Level
LRF	Laser Rangefinder
LVIS	Laser Vegetation Imaging Sensor
MASER	Microwave Amplification by Stimulated Emission of Radiation
MB	Megabytes
MEIS	Multi-spectral Electro-optic Imaging Sensor
MGS	Maine Geological Survey
MHHW	Mean Higher High Water
MHW	Mean High Water
MHz	Megahertz
MIF/MID	MapInfo File (format)
MIT	Massachusetts Institute of Technology
MLLW	Mean Lower Low Water
MLW	Mean Low Water
MMP	Modular Mission Payload
MRR	Measurement Residual Ratio
MRS	Microwave Ranging System
MSE	Mean of the Squared Errors
MSL	Mean Sea Level
MTL	Mean Tide Level
NAD 27	North American Datum of 1927 (horizontal datum)
NAD 83	North American Datum of 1983 (horizontal datum)
NADCON	North American Datum Conversion
NAI	No Adverse Impact
NAPP	National Aerial Photography Program
NASA	National Aeronautics and Space Administration

NAVD 88	North American Vertical Datum of 1988
NAVOCEANO	Naval Oceanographic Office
NAVSTAR	Navigation Signal Timing and Ranging
NBA	No Bottom At
NCITS	National Committee for Information Technology Standards
NCS	Navigation Computer System
NDCDB	National Digital Cartographic Data Base
NDEP	National Digital Elevation Program
NDGPS	Nationwide Differential GPS
NED	National Elevation Dataset
NEOS	National Earth Orientation Service
NFIP	National Flood Insurance Program
NGA	National Geospatial-Intelligence Agency
NGS	National Geodetic Survey
NGVD 29	National Geodetic Vertical Datum of 1929
NHAP	National High-Altitude Photography
NIMA	National Imagery and Mapping Agency
NIR	Near Infrared
NMAS	National Map Accuracy Standard
NMD	National Mapping Division (USGS)
NMP	National Mapping Program
NOAA	National Oceanic and Atmospheric Administration
NOS	National Ocean Service
NP	Navigation Processor
NRC	National Research Council
NRCS	Natural Resources Conservation Service
NSDI	National Spatial Data Infrastructure
NSGIS	National States Geographic Information Council
NSRS	National Spatial Reference System
NSSDA	National Standard for Spatial Data Accuracy
NTBMS	National Tidal Bench Mark System
NTDE	National Tidal Datum Epoch
NTM	National Technical Means

NWLON	National Water Level Observation Network
O&M	Operations and Maintenance
OC	Order/Class Code
OCS	Office of Coast Survey
OEM	Original Equipment Manufacturer
OGC	Open GIS Consortium
OIM	Orthorectified Image Mosaic
OLOPS	Off-Line Orthophoto Production System
OTF	On-the-fly (GPS ambiguity resolution), also see KAR
OTS	Off-the-shelf
PA	Position Approximate
PD	Position Doubtful
PDOP	Position Dilution of Precision
PGPS	P-code GPS
PMT	Photomultiplier Tube
PNEOS	Preliminary National Earth Orientation Service
POD	Print on Demand
POS	Position and Orientation System
POS/AV	Position and Orientation System for Airborne Vehicles
POS/LV	Position and Orientation System for Land Vehicles
POS/MV	Position and Orientation System for Marine Vessels
POS/TG	Position and Orientation System for Railroad Track Geometry
PPM	Parts Per Million
PPP	Precise Point Positioning
PRF	Pulse Repetition Frequency
PRR	Pulse Repetition Rate
PSP	Pseudo Stereo Pair
QA	Quality Assurance
QC	Quality Control

QA/QC	Quality Assurance/Quality Control
R&D	Research & Development
RAN	Royal Australian Navy
RASCAL	RAster SCanning Airborne Laser
RFI	Radio Frequency Interference
RLE	Run Length Encoded
RLG	Ring Laser Gyro
RMS	Root-Mean-Square
RMSE	Root-Mean-Square Error
$RMSE_r$	Radial RMSE (horizontal, as function of $RMSE_x$ and $RMSE_y$)
$RMSE_x$	RMSE in the x dimension (Easting or longitude)
$RMSE_y$	RMSE in the y dimension (Northing or latitude)
$RMSE_z$	RMSE in the z dimension (Elevation)
RNC	Raster Nautical Chart
ROV	Remotely-Operated Vehicle
RPH	Roll-Pitch-Heave
RPI	Repeat Pass Interferometry
RSS	Root Sum Squaring
RTCM	Radio Technical Commission for Maritime Services
RTK	Real Time Kinematic
RTKGPS	Real Time Kinematic Global Positioning System
SA	Selective Availability
SAR	Synthetic Aperture Radar
SASS	Sonar Array Sounding System
SAT	Single Antenna Transmit
SBCD	(FGDC's) Subcommittee on Base Cartographic Data
SBES	Single-Beam Echosounder
SD	Sounding Doubtful
SDDS	Seamless Data Distribution System
SDTS	Spatial Data Transfer Standard
SDWA	Safe Drinking Water Act

SE	Squared Errors
SFHA	Special Flood Hazard Area
SHOALS	Scanning Hydrographic Operational Airborne Lidar Survey
SHP	ArcView Shape (File Format)
SIO	Scripps Institution of Oceanography (MIT)
SIR	Space Imaging Radar
SLA	Shuttle Laser Altimeter
SLICER	Scanning Lidar Imager of Canopies by Echo Recovery
SLR	Satellite Laser Ranging
SONAR	Sound Navigation and Ranging
SPCS	State Plane Coordinate System
SPI	Single Pass Interferometry
SRTM	Shuttle Radar Topography Mission
SST	Sea Surface Topography
SVGA	Super Video Graphic Array
SWMB	Shallow-Water Multibeam

TDOP	Time Dilution of Position
TEC	U.S. Army Topographic Engineering Center
TEC	Total Electron Count
THED	Terrain Height Error Data
TIFF	Tagged Image File Format
TIN	Triangulated Irregular Network
TLS	Terrestrial Laser Scanning
TOF	Time-of-Flight
TPE	Total Propagated Error
TVF	Tagged Vector File
TWF	Tagged World File

UAV	Unmanned Aerial Vehicle
USACE	U.S. Army Corps of Engineers
USCG	U.S. Coast Guard
USD	U.S. Dollar

USFS	U.S. Forest Service
USGS	U.S. Geological Survey
UTC	Universal Time, Coordinated, the same as Greenwich Mean Time
UTM	Universal Transverse Mercator
UUV	Unmanned Underwater Vehicle
UV	Ultraviolet
VERTCON	Vertical Conversion
VG	Vertical Gyro
VHF	Very High Frequency
VLBI	Very Long Baseline Interferometry
VMAS	Vertical Map Accuracy Standard
VPF	Vector Product Format
VPS	Vertical Point Spacing
VRS	Virtual Reference Station
VTS	Vessel Traffic System
VTUAV	Vertical takeoff and landing Tactical UAV
WAAS	Wide Area Augmentation System
WADGPS	Wide Area Differential GPS
WGS 84	World Geodetic System of 1984
WHP	Wellhead Protection
WHPA	Wellhead Protection Area
WRELADS	Weapons Research Establishment LADS
2-D	Two Dimensional
3-D	Three Dimensional

Definitions

Accelerometer – A device that measures the total specific force with respect to an inertial reference comprising gravity plus acceleration.

Acoustic Wave – See Sound Wave.

Accuracy – The closeness of an estimated value (e.g., measured or computed) to a standard or accepted (true) value of a particular quantity. Note: With the exception of Continuously Operating Reference Stations (CORS), assumed to be known with zero errors relative to established datums, the true locations of 3-D spatial coordinates of other points are not known, but only estimated. Therefore, the accuracy of other coordinate information is unknown and can only be estimated.

- **Absolute Accuracy** – The value expressed in feet or meters that reports the uncertainty in vertical or horizontal positions due to systematic and random errors in measurements in the location of any point on a geospatial dataset relative to the defined vertical or horizontal datum at the 95 percent confidence level. The absolute vertical accuracy is normally different than the absolute horizontal accuracy.

- **Accuracy$_r$** – The NSSDA reporting standard in the horizontal component that equals the radius of a circle of uncertainty, such that the true or theoretical horizontal location of the point falls within that circle 95-percent of the time. Accuracy$_r$ = 1.7308 x RMSE$_r$.

- **Accuracy$_z$** – The NSSDA reporting standard in the vertical component that equals the linear uncertainty value, such that the true or theoretical vertical location of the point falls within that linear uncertainty value 95-percent of the time. Accuracy$_z$ = 1.9600 x RMSE$_z$.

- **Horizontal Accuracy** – The positional accuracy of a dataset with respect to a horizontal datum. The horizontal accuracy reporting standard (Accuracy$_r$) is defined above.

- **Local Accuracy** – A value that represents the uncertainty in the coordinates of a control point relative to the coordinates of other directly-connected, adjacent control points at the 95-percent confidence level. The reported local accuracy is an approximate average of the individual local accuracy values between this control point and other observed control points used to establish the coordinates of the control point.

- **Network Accuracy** – A value that represents the uncertainty in the coordinates of a control point with respect to the geodetic datum at the 95-percent confidence level. For National Spatial Reference System (NSRS) network accuracy classification in the U.S., the datum is considered to be best expressed by the geodetic values at the CORS supported by the National Geodetic Survey (NGS). By this definition, the local and network accuracy values at CORS sites are considered to be infinitesimal, i.e., to approach zero.

- **Positional Accuracy** – The accuracy of the position of features, including horizontal and/or vertical positions.

- **Relative Accuracy** – The value expressed in feet or meters that reports the uncertainty in vertical or horizontal positions due to random errors in measurements in the location of any confidence level. Relative accuracy may also be referred to as point-to-point accuracy. The general measure of relative accuracy is an evaluation of the random errors (systematic errors and blunders removed) in determining the positional orientation (e.g., distance, azimuth) of one point or feature with respect to another.

- **Vertical Accuracy** – The measure of the positional accuracy of a dataset with respect to a specified vertical datum. The vertical accuracy reporting standard (Accuracy$_z$) is defined above.

Adjustment – The process of changing the values of a given set of quantities so that results calculated using the changed set will be better than those calculated using the original set. The concept of "better" is vague. The most common interpretation is that the sum of the squares of differences between results obtained by measurement and results obtained by calculation shall be a minimum. With this criterion, the method of least squares is the required process.

Aerial Triangulation (Aerotriangulation) – The process of measuring a number of points on overlapping images and/or ground control points to determine the most probable values of exterior orientation elements of aerial photographs. The output of this process includes ground space coordinates for all points measured on at least two images.

Affine Transformation – Linear transformation plus a translation. Affine transformation can be decomposed into rotational, scale, skew and translation components and for most sensors small errors are well modeled by these terms.

Aliasing – The difference between the values of constants in a mathematical model and the value the constants would have if the model were improved by adding more terms or denser data.

Altimetry – The science of measuring height or *altitudes* of different objects.

Ambiguity Resolution – Combining the phase data from two or more GPS receivers so that, after eliminating all other significant errors, the unknown number of integer wavelengths can be determined for signals coming from GPS satellites. Redundant L1 and L2 phase observations from two or more receivers, each tracking five or more satellites, provide the information for rapid unambiguous resolution. Once the ambiguities are resolved, the corrected phases for each observed satellite become precise ranges that allow the computation of the baseline vector(s) between the receivers with a typical accuracy of 2-10 centimeters.

Analog Photogrammetry – Stereo photogrammetric procedures that utilize direct viewing of film imagery in analog stereoplotters that optically and/or mechanically replicate, at reduced scale, the physical geometry that existed when stereo photography was acquired. Analog stereoplotters are less accurate than analytical stereoplotters, and they are ill-suited for DEM production.

Analytical Photogrammetry – Stereo photogrammetric procedures that utilize direct viewing of film imagery in analytical stereoplotters that mathematically replicate, at reduced scale, the physical geometry that existed when stereo photography was acquired. Analytical stereoplotters can also mathematically apply camera calibration (interior orientation) parameters, and correct for atmospheric refraction and earth curvature.

Arc Second (Arc-Second or Second of Arc) – 1/60th of a minute of arc, or 1/3600th of a degree.

Artifacts – Detectable surface remnants of buildings, trees, towers, telephone poles or other elevated features in a bare-earth elevation model. Also, detectable artificial anomalies that are introduced to a surface model via system specific collection or processing techniques (e.g., corn-row effects of profile collection, star and ramp effects from multidirectional contour interpolation, or detectable triangular facets caused when vegetation canopies are weeded from lidar data. See Figure 7.20. Orthophotos and other geospatial datasets also have blemishes referred to as artifacts.

Aspect – The slope direction or steepest downslope across a surface, normally measured clockwise in degrees from due north. The value of each location in an aspect dataset indicates the direction the surface slope faces. See Figure 1.31.

Atmospheric Refraction – The bending of light rays as they pass through the atmosphere.

Attitude – The position of a body defined by the angles between the axes of the coordinate system of the body and the axes of an external coordinate system. In photogrammetry, the attitude is the angular orientation of a camera (roll, pitch, yaw), or of the photograph taken with that camera, with respect to some external reference system. With lidar and IFSAR, the attitude is normally defined as the roll, pitch and heading of the instrument at the instant an active pulse is emitted from the sensor.

Bald Earth – See Bare-earth.

Bare-Earth – Digital elevation data of the terrain, free from vegetation, buildings and other man-made structures. Elevations of the ground.

Base Flood – A flood that has a one-percent chance of being equaled or exceeded in any given year. Often called the 100-year flood.

Base Flood Elevation (BFE) – An elevation that has a one-percent chance of being equaled or exceeded in any given year by a base flood.

Base Station – A survey station with known coordinates from which all unknown differentially measured positions are derived.

Bathymetric Chart – A topographic chart of the bed of a body of water. Generally, bathymetric charts show depths by contour lines and gradient tints. Regional bathymetric surveys are conducted to determine the location and orientation of depth contours in water depths and areas where safety of surface navigation is not a major concern. This type of surveying might be accomplished with an interferometric sonar, a vertical beam echo sounder, or a multibeam sonar. Software used for bathymetric surveying is attuned to production of a digital elevation model, or bathymetric surface, from cleaned or smoothed soundings.

Bathymetric Surface – The underwater terrain model.

Bathymetry – The measurement and study of water depths. Traditionally bathymetry has been expressed with contours and hydrography with spot depths. Bathymetry may not meet hydrographic standards, as it may not show all of the bottom characteristics important to the mariner who is navigating. Bathymetric contours depicted on nautical charts may be displaced cartographically to accommodate sounding data which need to be displayed. NOAA's hydrographic depths and bathymetric contours represented on a nautical chart are all related to the national chart datum of MLLW. These depths are expressed as positive numbers below the chart datum. Minus signs are not depicted on nautical charts unless above MLLW, meaning the point is above water when the water level is at MLLW or below.

Bench Mark (Benchmark or BM) – A relatively permanent, natural or artificial, material object bearing a marked point whose elevation above or below an adopted vertical datum is known.

- **Permanent Bench Mark** – A bench mark as nearly permanent in character as is practicable. The National Spatial Reference System classifies bench marks in terms of their "stability," with *Stability A* being the most stable, and *Stability D* being of questionable stability.

- **Temporary Bench Mark** – A bench mark established to hold, temporarily, the end of a completed section of a line of levels and to serve as a starting point from which the next section is run. Spikes and screws in poles, bolts on bridges, and chiseled marks on masonry are typically used as temporary bench marks (TBMs).

- **Tidal Bench Mark** – A bench mark whose elevation has been determined with respect to mean sea level at a nearby tide gauge. The tidal bench mark is used as reference for that tide gauge.

Blunder – An error of major proportion, normally identified and removed during interactive editing.

Boresight – Calibration of a sensor system equipped with an IMU to determine the accurate orientation (roll, pitch, heading) of active sensor pulses (IFSAR, lidar, sonar) or the optical axis of a film camera or a digital imaging system.

Breakline – A linear feature that describes a change in the smoothness or continuity of a surface. The two most common forms of breaklines are as follows:

- A *soft breakline* ensures that known z-values along a linear feature are maintained (e.g., elevations along a pipeline, road centerline or drainage ditch), and ensures that linear features and polygon edges are maintained in a TIN surface model, by enforcing the breaklines as TIN edges. They are generally synonymous with 3-D breaklines because they are depicted with series of x/y/z coordinates. Somewhat rounded ridges or the trough of a drain may be collected using soft breaklines.

- A *hard breakline* defines interruptions in surface smoothness, e.g., to define streams, shorelines, dams, ridges, building footprints, and other locations with abrupt surface changes. Although some hard breaklines are 3-D breaklines, they are often depicted as 2-D breaklines because features such as shorelines and building footprints are normally depicted with series of x/y coordinates only, often digitized from digital orthophotos that include no elevation data.   See dotted shorelines and stream centerline in Figure 1.1a.

C-Factor – An empirical measure of the inherent contouring accuracy of a photogrammetric plotter and its operator.

Calibration – The process of identifying and correcting for systematic errors in hardware, software, or procedures. Determining the systematic errors in a measuring device by comparing its measurements with the markings or measurements of a device which is considered correct. Airborne sensors can be calibrated geometrically and/or radiometrically.

- **Camera Calibration** – The geometric calibration of a conventional film mapping camera includes the determination of the following quantities: (a) the calibrated focal length, (b) the location of the principal point with respect to the fiducial marks, (c) the location of the point of symmetry, (d) the distortion effective in the focal plane of the camera and referred to the particular calibrated focal length, (e) the resolution of the lens system, (f) the degree of flatness of the focal plane, (g) the opening and closing cycle of the shutter as a function of time, and (h) the locations of fiducial marks – all of which help to ensure that μm measurements made on aerial film will translate correctly into accurate ground coordinates via photogrammetric calculations. Depending on camera design, digital cameras have different forms of geometric calibration and also include radiometric calibration, e.g., spectral response of CCD sensors over the spectral range of the sensor, and determination of the pixel-to-pixel uniformity.

- **Lidar System Calibration** – Factory calibration includes both radiometric and geometric calibration unique to each manufacturer's hardware, and tuned to meet the performance specifications for the model being calibrated; factory recalibration is normally performed every 24 months. The "lever-arm" calibration determines the sensor-to-GPS-antenna offset vector (lever arm) components relative to the antenna phase center; the offset vector components are redetermined each time the sensor or aircraft GPS antenna is moved or repositioned in any way. Field calibration is normally performed for each project, or even daily, to determine corrections to the roll, pitch, and scale calibration parameters.

Cartesian Coordinates – Coordinate values of two types:

- **2-D Cartesian Coordinates** – A pair of numbers (x/y coordinates) that locate a point by its distance from two intersecting, normally perpendicular lines in the same plane. Each distance is measured along a parallel to the other line. UTM and State Plane coordinates are examples of 2-D Cartesian coordinates.

- **3-D Cartesian Coordinates** – A triad of numbers (x/y/z coordinates) that locate a point by its distance from three fixed planes that intersect one another at right angles. However, except for unique applications, 3-D Cartesian coordinates with z-coordinates are rarely used. Instead, z-values are more popularly understood as heights or elevations above a curved surface defined by the vertical datum, ellipsoid, or geoid. Thus, when 3-D coordinates are mentioned, the term normally pertains to x/y coordinates and z-values.

Cartography – The science and art of making maps and charts. It is customary to distinguish between maps in general and maps used for navigation; the latter are generally called *charts*.

Charts – Maps used for nautical or aeronautical navigation.

Check Point (Checkpoint) – One of the surveyed points in the sample used to estimate the positional accuracy of the data set against an independent source of higher accuracy.

Cleanness – A subjective term to describe the degree to which artifacts have been removed from a DEM or TIN.

Collimation – The process of bringing the optical elements of an optical system into proper relation with each other. Adjusting the fiducial marks in a camera so that they locate the principal point.

Compilation – The production of a new or revised map or chart, or portions thereof, from existing maps, aerial photographs, surveys, new data and other sources. The process is called *stereocompilation* if stereoscopic plotting instruments (stereo plotters) are used.

Confidence Level – The probability that errors are within a range of given values.

Consolidated Vertical Accuracy (CVA) – The result of a test of the accuracy of 40 or more checkpoints (z-values) consolidated for two or more of the major land cover categories, representing both the open terrain and other land cover categories. Computed using a nonparametric testing method (95th percentile) explained in Chapter 3, a consolidated vertical accuracy is always accompanied by a fundamental vertical accuracy.

Contours – Lines of equal elevation on a surface. An imaginary line on the ground, all points of which are at the same elevation above or below a specified reference surface (vertical datum). See Figure 1.20.

Contour Interval – The difference in elevation (z-values) between two adjacent contours.

Control – The coordinates of a control station. The geometric data associated with a collection of control stations, such as coordinates, distances, angles, or directions between control stations. The data associated with a set of control stations and used as the basis for detailed surveys. Generally synonymous with *geodetic control*.

Control Network – Geodetic control together with the measured or adjusted values of the distances, angles, directions, or heights used in determining the coordinates of the control.

Control Point – Stationary point with accurately surveyed horizontal (x/y), vertical (z), or horizontal and vertical (x/y/z) coordinates. When used for aerotriangulation, control points are either chosen as photo-identifiable points or are "paneled" prior to flying.

Control Station – A point on the ground whose horizontal or vertical location is used as a basis for obtaining the location of other points.

Control Tide Stations – Primary water level stations, located with open ocean exposure or within the mouth of a bay or estuary, that have operated for 19 or more years, are expected to continue to operate in the future, and are used to obtain a continuous record of the water levels in a locality. They are sited to provide datum control for national applications.

Coordinates – A set of N numbers designating the location of a point in N-dimensional space. Horizontal coordinates are 2-dimensional coordinates, normally expressed as x/y coordinates, Eastings and Northings, or Longitude and Latitude (geographic coordinates). A vertical coordinate may be 1-dimensional, i.e., the vertical distance of a point above or below a reference surface (vertical datum) such as the elevation of a bench mark without known x/y coordinates. However, most vertical coordinates are specified as 3-dimensional coordinates, i.e., x/y coordinates and z-values.

Correlation – The extent to which one randomly varying quantity can be expressed as a function of another, or to which both quantities can be expressed as function of a third, nonrandom quantity. See also Image Correlation. With IFSAR, interferometric correlation is a measure of the similarity of the signal received at the two antennae.

Data Format – The specific arrangement of data in a file, including records, data types, and data labels. For example, floating point numbers as x/y pairs with one set per record.

Data Model – The conceptual view of what information is to be represented. For example, the surface of the earth can be represented as a grid of posts of varying heights (i.e., raster data model), or as lines of equal elevation (i.e., vector data model).

Datum – Any quantity or set of such quantities that may serve as a basis for calculation of other quantities. See Table 2.3 for a listing of 26 different vertical datums included in NGS' Vertical Datum Transformation Tool (Vdatum).

- **Diurnal Tide Level (DTL)** – A tidal datum which is the average of Mean Higher High Water and Mean Lower Low Water.

- **Geodetic Datum** – A set of constants specifying the coordinate system used for geodetic control, i.e., for calculating coordinates of points on the Earth. At least eight constants are needed to form a complete datum: three to specify the location of the origin of the coordinate system, three to specify the orientation of the coordinate system, and two to specify the dimensions of the reference ellipsoid. (Before geocentric geodetic datums became possible, it was customary to define a geodetic datum by five quantities: the latitude and longitude of an initial point, the azimuth of a line from this point, and the two parameters of a reference ellipsoid. In addition, specification of the components of the deflection of the vertical at the initial point, or the condition that the minor axis of the ellipsoid be parallel to the Earth's axis of rotation provided two more quantities. The datum was still not complete because the origin of the coordinate system remained free to shift in one dimension. This meaning does not conform to modern usage.)

- **Horizontal Datum** – A geodetic datum specifying the coordinate system in which horizontal control points are located. The North American Datum of 1983 (NAD 83) is the official horizontal datum in the U.S.

- **Hydrographic Datum** – A datum for depths (soundings), depth contours, and elevations of foreshore and offshore features. Also called *chart datum*.

- **Local Datum** – A datum defining a coordinate system that is used only over a region of very limited extent.

- **Low Water Datum** – An approximation to mean low water that has been adopted as a standard tidal datum for a specific region although it may differ slightly from a later determination.

- **Lower Low Water Datum** – An approximation to mean lower low water adopted as a tidal datum for a limited area and retained for an indefinite period. It is used primarily for river and harbor engineering, e.g., Columbia River lower low water datum.

- **Mean Higher High Water (MHHW)** – A tidal datum computed as the arithmetic mean of the higher high water heights of the tide observed over a specific 19-year Metonic cycle denoted as the NTDE. Only the higher high water of each pair of high waters of a tidal day is included in the mean. For stations with shorter series, a comparison of simultaneous observations is made with a primary control tide station in order to derive the equivalent of the 19-year value.

- **Mean High Water (MHW)** – A tidal datum computed as the arithmetic mean of the high water heights observed over a specific 19-year Metonic cycle. For stations with shorter series, a comparison of simultaneous observations is made with a primary control tide station in order to derive the equivalent of the 19-year value.

- **Mean Lower Low Water (MLLW)** – A tidal datum computed as the arithmetic mean of the lower low water heights of the tide observed over a specific 19-year Metonic cycle. Only the lower low water of each pair of low waters of a tidal day is included in the mean. For stations with shorter series, a comparison of simultaneous observations is made with a primary control tide station in order to derive the equivalent of the 19-year value. MLLW is the chart datum used in the U.S.

- **Mean Low Water (MLW)** – A tidal datum computed as the arithmetic mean of the low water heights observed over a specific 19-year Metonic cycle. For stations with shorter series, a comparison of simultaneous observations is made with a primary control tide station in order to derive the equivalent of the 19-year value.

- **Mean Sea Level (MSL)** – A tidal datum computed as the arithmetic mean of hourly heights observed over a specific 19-year Metonic cycle. Shorter series are specified in the name, e.g., monthly mean sea level or yearly mean sea level.

- **Mean Tide Level (MTL)** – A tidal datum which is the average of Mean High Water and Mean Low Water.

- **Sea Level Datum** – An equipotential surface passing through a specified point at mean sea level which is used as a reference for elevations.

- **Tidal Datum** – A surface with a designed elevation from which heights or depths are reckoned, defined by a certain phase of the tide. A tidal datum is local, usually valid only for a restricted area about the tide gauge used in defining the datum.

- **Vertical Datum** — A set of constants defining a height (elevation) system. It is defined by a set of constants, a coordinate system, and points that have been consistently determined by observations, corrections, and computations. The North American Vertical Datum of 1988 (NAVD 88) is the official vertical datum in the U.S.

Decorrelation (IFSAR) – A measure of the dissimilarity of the signal received at the two antennae caused by geometry, thermal noise and other factors (see Figure 6.16).

Deflection of the Vertical – The angle at a point on the surface of the Earth (from the geoid) between the vertical at that point, and the line through the point which is normal to the given reference ellipsoid. See Figure 2.12.

Delaunay Triangulation – A mesh of contiguous, non-overlapping, triangles established from a set of points in the plane such that each triangle's circumscribing circle is empty, containing no point from the set in its interior.

Diapositive – A positive photograph on a transparent medium. A positive film transparency as opposed to a positive paper print which is not transparent.

Differential Leveling – Survey procedures used to measure the elevation differences between two or more points, to extend vertical control, and to monitor the stability of water level measurement gauges. The quality of leveling is a function of the procedures used, the sensitivity of the leveling instruments, the precision and accuracy of the leveling rod, the attention given by surveyors, and the refinement of the computations.

Digital Correlation – Image correlation performed automatically through the use of digital imagery and digital (softcopy) photogrammetry. DEMs produced through automatic digital correlation are normally edited manually, especially when bare-earth DTMs or contours are required instead of DSMs.

Digital Elevation Model (DEM) – See three different definitions below:

- A popular acronym, as in the title of this book, used as a generic term for digital topographic and/or bathymetric data in all its various forms. Unless specifically referenced as a Digital Surface Model (DSM), the generic DEM normally implies x/y coordinates and z-values of the bare-earth terrain, void of vegetation and manmade features.

- As used by the U.S. Geological Survey (USGS), a DEM is the digital cartographic representation of the elevation of the land at regularly spaced intervals in x and y directions, using z-values referenced to a common vertical datum. As described in Chapter 4 of this manual, there are several different standard USGS DEMs archived in the National Elevation Dataset (NED) based on 1-arc-second, 1/3-arc-second, and 1/9-arc-second grid spacing.

- As typically used in the U.S. and elsewhere, a DEM has bare-earth z-values at regularly spaced intervals in x and y, where Δx and Δy (see Figure 1.1c) are normally measured in feet or meters to even units; however, grid spacing, datum, coordinate systems, data formats, and other characteristics may vary widely.

Digital Line Graph (DLG) – Geospatial data, digitized as node, line and area features, using hundreds of different attribute codes to define basic cartographic data categories such as hypsography (contours), hydrography, transportation, manmade features, vegetation, boundaries, survey control, etc. USGS digitizes 11 categories of cartographic features on its topographic quadrangles at various scales and archives DLGs in the NDCDB. FEMA digitizes 4 categories of cartographic features on flood hazard maps for the National Flood Insurance Program. Data collection in all major mapping programs is typically directed toward producing topologically structured Level-3 DLG data, referred to as DLG-3. Other government and private sector organizations collect and produce geospatial data sets in DLG-3 format in order to facilitate the interchange and use of DLG data in a standard format compatible with diverse GIS software programs.

Digital Orthophoto – A digital photograph prepared from a perspective photograph by digitally removing displacements of points caused by tilt, relief, and perspective. A "true digital orthophoto" is defined as one in which the sides of vertical features are not visible, as though looking straight down on each natural and man-made feature from infinity; this feature is especially desired in urban areas with skyscrapers and tall buildings, the sides of which are normally photographed with aerial photography.

Digital Photogrammetry – See Softcopy Photogrammetry.

Digital Surface Model (DSM) – Similar to DEMs or DTMs, except that they depict the elevations of the top surfaces of buildings, trees, towers, and other features elevated above the bare earth. DSMs are especially relevant for telecommunications management, air safety, forest management, and 3-D modeling and simulation.

Digital Terrain Elevation Data (DTED) – A uniform matrix of terrain elevation values produced by the National Geospatial-Intelligence Agency (NGA). It provides basic quantitative data for military systems that require terrain elevation, slope, and gross surface roughness information. Data density depends on the level produced.

- DTED0 post spacing is 30 arc seconds (approximately 1,000 meters), corresponding to small-scale hardcopy products.

- DTED1 post spacing is three arc seconds (approximately 100 meters), corresponding to medium-scale hardcopy products.

- DTED2 post spacing is one arc second (approximately 30 meters), corresponding to large-scale hardcopy products.

- DTED3 post spacing is one-third arc second (approximately 10 meters)

- Specifications for high-resolution DTED levels 4 (3 m) and 5 (1 m) are being developed.

Digital Terrain Model (DTM) – See two different definitions below:

- In some countries, DTMs are synonymous with DEMs, representing the bare-earth terrain with uniformly-spaced z-values

- As used herein, DTMs may be similar to DEMs, but they may also incorporate the elevation of significant topographic features on the land and mass points and breaklines that are irregularly spaced to better characterize the true shape of the bare-earth terrain. The net result of DTMs is that the distinctive terrain features are more clearly defined and precisely located, and contours generated from DTMs more closely approximate the real shape of the terrain. Such DTMs are normally more expensive and time consuming to produce than uniformly spaced DEMs because breaklines are ill suited for automated collection. DTMs are technically superior to standard DEMs for many applications.

Diode – Specialized electronic equipment with two electrodes that conduct one energy (electric) and convert to another form (light).

Direct Georeferencing – The direct measurement of Exterior Orientation parameters, i.e., position (x/y/z coordinates) and attitude (roll/pitch/heading) at the instant an aerial photograph is taken, to aid or replace aerial triangulation. The term is also applicable to the position and orientation of airborne lidar or IFSAR sensors.

Direction of Gravity – The direction, toward the Earth's center, indicated by a plumb line. Gravity is a force and therefore has both magnitude and direction. The direction of gravity is independent of any coordinate system, but its components may be described with respect to two mutually perpendicular planes through the local normal, one being that of the local meridian. Both components are given in terms of the *deflection of the vertical* from those planes.

Diurnal High Water Inequality (DHQ) – The difference between Mean Higher High Water and Mean High Water.

Diurnal Low Water Inequality (DLQ) – The difference between Mean Low Water and Mean Lower Low Water.

Dual Frequency – A high performance GPS receiver for precision applications that tracks the L1 C/A pseudoranges and carrier phase, and either tracks L2 pseudoranges and carrier phase or computes derived L2 pseudoranges and carrier phase using the known cross correlation between the L1 and L2 code modulations.

Drainage-Enforced – See Hydro-Enforced.

Drape – The superimposition of 2-D features over a 3-D surface, normally for viewing of all features in 3-D perspective, for 3-D fly-throughs or walk-throughs in virtual reality.

Easting – The grid coordinate of a point eastward (positive) or westward (negative) from a reference meridian. The grid coordinate eastward (positive) or westward (negative) from the central (zero) meridian (the line of zero eastings or the y-axis) on a gridded map. The central meridian is frequently replaced by another called the false meridian, sufficiently far to the west of the central meridian so that all eastings on the map are then positive with respect to the false meridian. A *false easting* is the constant value added to all eastings so that only positive values of easting are recorded.

Echogram – The graphic record produced by an echo sounder and showing, as a function of time, the strength of the echo signal and the time taken for the echo to return.

Echo Sounder – An instrument for determining the depth of water by measuring the time of travel of a sound pulse from the surface of a body of water to the bottom and back. An echo sounder consist of an oscillator for generating pulses, a hydrophone for detecting the echo, a clock for timing the pulses, and a recorder for converting the time of travel to a depth and plotting that depth on a continuous chart.

Echo Sounding – Determining the distance from the surface of water to the bottom by measuring the time interval required for sound waves to go from a sound generator to the bottom and back again. The principal source of error in echo sounding is uncorrected refraction; another source is schools of fish that reflect sound back before it reaches the bottom.

Effective Vertical Spacing – The vertical point spacing minus the vertical footprint diameter.

Electromagnetic Spectrum – The complete range of wavelengths of electromagnetic radiation, beginning with the longest radio waves and extending through visible light all the way to the extremely short gamma rays.

Elevation – The distance measured upward along a plumb line between a point and the geoid. The elevation of a point is normally the same as its orthometric height, defined as "H" in the equation: $H = h - N$.

Elevation Certificate – A form on which the lowest floor elevation, lowest adjacent grade, and highest adjacent grade of a building are certified relative to the base flood elevation for the location of the building. Other descriptive information is also provided to help identify the flood risk to the building surveyed.

Elevation Post – The vertical component of a DEM lattice mesh point, having height above the vertical datum equal to the z-value of its mesh point.

Elevation Post Spacing – The constant sampling interval in x and y directions of a DEM lattice or grid. The horizontal resolution of a DEM.

Ellipsoid – A closed surface whose planar sections are either ellipses or circles. The Earth's ellipsoid is a biaxial ellipsoid of revolution, defined by an ellipse with major axis "a" and its minor axis "b", obtained by rotating the ellipse about its minor (shorter) axis.

Ellipsoid Height – See Height.

Ensonify – See Insonify.

Ephemeris – A tabulation of the locations and related data for a celestial body, including Earth-orbiting satellites, for given epochs (dates) at uniform intervals of time.

- **Broadcast Ephemeris** – The ephemeris broadcast from a satellite, from which Earth-fixed satellite positions can be computed.

- **Precise Ephemeris** – The ephemeris of a satellite computed by adjustment of observations obtained from a worldwide tracking network in order to obtain maximum accuracy.

Epoch – A particular instant of time from which an event or a series of events is calculated. A starting point in time to which events are referred.

Equator, Geodetic – The circle of the reference ellipsoid midway between its poles of rotation. The geodetic Equator is the line on which geodetic latitude is 0° and from which geodetic latitudes are reckoned, north and south, to 90° at either pole.

Equipotential Surface – A surface with the same gravity potential at every point. An equipotential surface is also referred to as a level surface. The force of gravity is everywhere perpendicular to this surface. The surface of a body of still water is an equipotential surface.

Error – The difference between the observed value of a quantity and the theoretical or defined value of that quantity. In the computation of root-mean-square errors (RMSE), x-, y- and z-errors are the differences in x- or y-coordinates or z-values between a sample dataset and a dataset of higher accuracy for the same sample points.

- **Random Error** – An error, produced by irregular causes whose effects upon individual observations are governed by no known law that connects them with circumstances and so cannot be corrected by use of standardized adjustments.

- **Systematic Error** – An error whose algebraic sign and, to some extent, magnitude bears a fixed relation to some condition or set of conditions. Systematic errors follow some fixed pattern and are introduced by data collection procedures and systems. Systematic error artifacts include vertical elevation shifts, misinterpretations of terrain surfaces due to trees, buildings, and shadows, fictitious ridges, tops, benches, and striations. A systematic error is, in theory at least, predictable, and therefore is not random; such errors are regular, and so can be determined *a priori*. They are generally eliminated from a set of observations prior to RMSE calculations and before applying the method of least squares to eliminate or reduce random errors.

Euler Angle – One of a sequence of three angles (rotations) specifying the orientation of one (three-dimensional) coordinate system with respect to another, in which the first and third rotations are about the same axis, and the second is about a different axis. For example, let the system whose axes are x, y, z be rotated into the system with axis X, Y, Z. A sequence of Euler angles is given by a rotation about z yielding x', y', z; then a rotation about x' yielding x', y", Z; finally a rotation about Z, yielding X, Y, Z. Used with inertial measurement units (IMUs).

Exterior Orientation – The position and attitude of an imaging system with respect to a ground coordinate system. The six parameters that define the position (x/y/z coordinates) and attitude (roll, pitch and heading) of a remote sensing system, relative to a ground coordinate reference frame, at the instant that a pulse is emitted from an active sensor (e.g., IFSAR, lidar or sonar) or an image is acquired by a passive sensor (e.g., exposure station of an aerial photograph). With digital imaging systems, the exposure station differs with each image line; therefore, the exterior orientation elements vary over time and are often modeled as a non-linear function requiring some measure of time tied to the image lines, ABGPS and IMU data. Also see Direct Georeferencing.

Fathom – A measure of water depth equal to exactly 6 feet.

Feathering – Adjusting the relative weighting of the different data sets over a specified distance to smoothly transition from one data set or combination of data sets to another.

Field of View – The angular extent of the portion of object space surveyed by an aerial camera or lidar sensor, measured in degrees.

First Return – The first significant measurable portion of a return lidar pulse.

Flood Insurance Rate Map (FIRM) – An official map of a community on which FEMA has delineated both the flood hazard areas and the risk premium zones applicable to the community.

Flood Mitigation – Activities that lessen the potential for future flood damages.

Floodplain – The low lying area along a river, stream, or coast that is subject to flooding. Any land area susceptible to being inundated by water from any source.

Floodway – The channel and portion of the adjoining area required to discharge the base flood without increasing flood heights more than one foot.

Fly-Through – A terrain visualization technique, used in computer simulations, in which the 3-D perspective view of the terrain continuously changes relative to the location of the viewer who appears to be moving as though flying over the terrain in an aircraft. The terrain models used for fly-throughs may be overlaid with digital imagery, simulated clouds or smoke, or added or enhanced virtual features to depict landmarks or objects of unique importance to a specific fly-through. See Figure 1.28 and example fly-throughs on the enclosed DVD.

Focal Length – The distance between the rear node of a lens (or the vertex of a mirror) and the point at which the image of an infinitely distant object comes into critical focus.

Footprint – Different definitions in geospatial community, depending on usage:

- **Footprint (General Usage)** – The beam size or surface area measured by a single beam from an active sensor such as IFSAR, lidar or sonar.

- **Lidar Horizontal Footprint** – The area illuminated by a laser beam on the face of a horizontal surface, typically based on the full width at half maximum (FWHM) points of the beam, or alternative criteria such as $1/e$ or $1/e^2$ of the maximum irradiance or amplitude. These different definitions are used because a lidar beam diverges/spreads, does not have a constant spatial energy distribution, and decays similar to a Gaussian distribution away from the center of a beam.

- **Lidar Vertical Footprint** – The area illuminated by a laser pulse (beam) on the face of a vertical surface, based on the FWHM points of the beam. This term is only used when the lidar sensor is tilted into a forward-looking position so that consecutive scan lines "walk up" a vertical surface.

- **Building Footprint** – The outline of a building, normally as viewed orthogonally from above.

Foreshortening – IFSAR relief displacement towards the direction of the radar, opposite to that of optical imagery where relief displacement is away from the direction of the camera.

Fundamental Vertical Accuracy (FVA) – The value by which vertical accuracy can be equitably assessed and compared among datasets. The fundamental vertical accuracy of a dataset, defined in Chapter 3, must be determined with checkpoints located only in open terrain where there is a very high probability that the sensor will have detected the ground surface. It is obtained utilizing standard tests for RMSE, where $FVA = Accuracy_z = RMSE_z \times 1.9600$.

Geocentric – Referred to the center of the Earth. The exact meaning of "center" must usually be inferred from the context. The following kinds of center are in common use: (a) the center of an ellipsoid representing the Earth's shape or figure, as in "geocentric longitude"; (b) the Earth's center of mass, as in "geocentric orbit"; (c) the point at which the Earth's axis of rotation intersects the plane of the celestial Equator.

Geodesy – The science that determines the size and shape of the Earth, locates positions on the Earth, and determines the Earth's gravity field.

Geodetic Survey – A survey that takes into account the size and shape of the Earth, as distinguished from a plane survey in which the surface of the Earth is considered a plane.

Geographic Information System (GIS) – A system of spatially referenced information, including computer programs that acquire, store, manipulate, analyze, and display spatial data.

Geoid – That equipotential (level) surface of the earth's gravity field which, on average, coincides with mean sea level in the open undisturbed ocean. In practical terms, the geoid is the imaginary surface where the oceans would seek mean sea level if allowed to continue into all land areas so as to encircle the earth. The geoid undulates up and down with local variations in the mass and density of the earth. The local direction of gravity is always perpendicular to the geoid. See Figures 2.11 and 2.12.

Geoid Height – See Height.

Geodetic Height – See Height.

Geomorphology – The study of the physical features of the Earth, the arrangement and form of the Earth's crust and of the relation between the physical features and geological structures beneath.

Geop – A geopotential surface that approximates the Earth's potentials of gravitation. The geoid is a specific geop, selected to pass through the average sea surface for the Earth.

Geopotential Number – The geopotential number (C) of a bench mark is the difference in potential measured from the reference geopotential surface to the equipotential surface passing through the survey mark. It is the amount of work required to raise a unit mass of 1 kg against gravity through the orthometric height to the mark. Geopotential differences are differences in potential which indicate hydraulic head, i.e., the direction water flows.

Geospatial Data — Information that identifies the geographic location and characteristics of natural or constructed features and boundaries of earth. This information may be derived from, among other things, remote sensing, mapping, and surveying technologies. *Geospatial data is* generally considered to be synonymous with *spatial data*; however, the former is always associated with geographic or cartesian coordinates linked to a horizontal or vertical datum, whereas the latter (e.g., generic architectural house plans) may include dimensions and other spatial data not linked to any physical location.

Gravity – The force which is the resultant of gravitation, the force exerted by the mass of the Earth, and the centrifugal force, caused by the rotation of the Earth. The acceleration is a function of the body's location but is independent of the mass, shape, size, or other properties of the body. The term gravity is used for both the force and the acceleration and for both the vector and its magnitude. Thus the word may have any one of several different meanings. At the Equator and close to the surface, the acceleration of gravity (g) is approximately 978.03 cm/s^2; at the poles, it is approximately 983.22 cm/s^2. The quantity "1 cm/s^2" is called the *gal*.

Great Diurnal Range (Gt) – The difference between Mean Higher High Water and Mean Lower Low Water.

Grid – A rectangular array of cells, each of which stores an elevation value for the centroid of the cell, that forms the basic structure of the most common and uniformly-spaced DEMs. The resolution of the grid (the width and height of the cells) determines the precision of the grid representation. See Figure 1.7.

Grid Post – See Elevation Post.

Ground Sample Distance (GSD) – The size of a pixel projected to the ground surface, reported as linear units/pixel, such as 1 meter/pixel or 1 foot/pixel. Actual or nominal distance in ground measurements between ground elevation samples. Different from horizontal post spacing in that *horizontal post spacing* describes the ground-distance interval of a uniform elevation grid, whereas *ground sample distance* describes the spacing on the ground of the source data. For example, the ground distance between data points collected by a lidar system, although variable, will yield some nominal *ground sample distance*. A gridded data model produced by resampling the lidar data may be incremented on a different, user-selected *horizontal post spacing*.

Ground Truth – Verification of a situation, without errors introduced by sensors or human perception and judgement.

Gyro – A device that measures angular rate or angle increments with respect to an inertial reference.

Hardcopy Photogrammetry – Stereo photogrammetric procedures that utilize direct viewing of film imagery in analog or analytical stereoplotters.

Heading – The azimuth of the longitudinal axis of a vehicle; the "straight-ahead" direction. True heading is the vehicle azimuth with respect to true North; magnetic heading is the azimuth with respect to the magnetic North pole.

Height – The distance, measured along a perpendicular, between a point and a reference surface, e.g., the height of an airplane above the ground surface. The distance, measured upwards along a plumb line (line of force), between a point and a reference surface of constant geopotential. *Elevation* is preferred if the reference surface is the geoid. Height systems are called by different names depending on the geopotential number (C) and gravity (G) selected. When G is computed using the Helmert height reduction formula, which is what was used in NAVD 88, the heights are called Helmert orthometric heights. When G is computed using the International formula for normal gravity, the heights are called normal orthometric heights. When G is equal to normal gravity at 45 degrees latitude, the heights are called normal dynamic heights, which is what was used in IGLD 85.

- **Dynamic Height** – The value, assigned to a point, determined by dividing the geopotential number for that point by the value of gravity on the reference ellipsoid at 45° latitude, as calculated from a standard gravity formula. Dynamic heights are geopotential numbers scaled by a constant, using normal gravity at 45 degrees latitude equal to 980.6199 gals. Points that have the same geopotential number will have the same dynamic height. The primary users of dynamic heights use the heights for measuring water-level heights and/or height differences on large bodies of water, i.e., the Great Lakes, because they are interested in knowing the hydraulic head.

- **Ellipsoid Height** – The height above or below the reference ellipsoid, i.e., the distance between a point on the Earth's surface and the ellipsoidal surface, as measured along the normal (perpendicular) to the ellipsoid at the point and taken positive upward from the ellipsoid. Defined as "h" in the equation: $h = H + N$. See Figure 2.11. Same as ellipsoidal height and geodetic height.

- **Geoid Height** – The difference between an ellipsoid height and an orthometric height. Defined as "N" in the equation: $N = h — H$. See Figure 2.11. Same as geoidal height.

- **Helmert Orthometric Height** – An approximate value $H_N{}^H$ found for the elevation of a point P_N by dividing the *geopotential number* W_N at that point by an approximation $(g_N{}^H)$ to the average value of gravity along the vertical between P_N and the geoid. The value $g_N{}^H$ is calculated from the measured value g_N of gravity at P_N and two forms of gravity corrections, i.e., the Bouguer and free-air gravity corrections. The difference between adjusted Helmert orthometric heights is computed using geopotential differences based on observed gravity.

- **Orthometric Height (Elevation)** – The height above the geoid as measured along the plumbline between the geoid and a point on the Earth's surface, taken positive upward from the geoid. Defined as "H" in the equation: $H = h - N$. See Figure 2.11. The difference between adjusted orthometric heights is computed using a normal gravity formula. The orthometric height (H) and the geopotential number (C) are related through the following equation: $C = G \times H$, where G is the gravity value estimated for a particular system.

Hillshade – A function used to create an illuminated representation of the surface, using a hypothetical light source, to enhance terrain visualization effects. See Figure 1.29.

Histogram – A graphic representation of a frequency or relative frequency distribution consisting of vertical rectangles whose widths correspond to a definite range of frequencies and whose heights correspond to the number of frequencies occurring within the range. See Figure 12.4.

Holiday – An area of missing coverage, caused by missing or unresolvable data, data edits, or incorrectly positioned flightlines, normally identified for further investigation or reflying. An unintentionally unsurveyed part of a region that was to have been completely surveyed.

Horizontal Accuracy – Positional accuracy of a dataset with respect to a horizontal datum. According to the NSSDA, horizontal accuracy at the 95% confidence level is defined as "Accuracy$_r$."

Horizontal Error – Magnitude of the displacement of a feature's recorded horizontal position in a dataset from its true or more accurate position, as measured radially according to the NMAS and NSSDA standards, or as measured separately, for x and y, according to NSSDA and ASPRS 1990 standards. Horizontal errors comprise the errors that are squared in the computation of horizontal root-mean-square errors (RMSEs), whether RMSE$_x$, RMSE$_y$, or RMSE$_r$. Note: RMSE$_r$ = square root of $[\text{RMSE}_x{}^2 + \text{RMSE}_y{}^2]$.

Horizontal Post Spacing – The ground distance interval between grid posts in a uniformly gridded data model. It is important to note that features of a size equal to, or even greater than the post spacing, may not be detected or explicitly represented in a gridded model. For gridded elevation data, the horizontal post spacing may be referenced as the cell size, the grid spacing, the posting interval, or the ground sample distance.

Hydraulic Modeling – The use of digital elevation data, rainfall runoff data from hydrologic models, surface roughness data, and information on hydraulic structures (e.g., bridges, culverts, dams, weirs, sewers) to predict flood levels and manage water resources. Hydraulic models are based on computations involving liquids under pressure, and there are many other definitions of hydraulic modeling that have nothing to do with terrain elevations, e.g., modeling of hydraulic lines in aircraft and automobiles.

Hydrographic Survey – A survey conducted to determine the configuration of the bottom of water bodies and to identify and locate all features, natural and man-made, that may affect navigation. Hydrographic surveys are conducted for the purpose of safety of navigation and require very accurate bathymetry and the detection of all hazards to surface navigation like wrecks and obstructions. This type of surveying is most often conducted with a multibeam sonar and/or a sweep sonar, which might be augmented with towed side scan sonar to ensure full coverage of the seabed. Hydrographic surveys may include the delineation of the submerged contours of channels, banks and shoals, and the collection of bottom specimens and samples of water. Also included are consideration of tides and currents, and information on temperature and salinity of the water and their effects on the accurate measurement of depths by echo sounding.

Hydrography – That branch of applied science which deals with the measurement and description of the physical features of the navigable portion of the Earth's surface and adjoining coastal areas, with special reference to their use for the purpose of navigation. Hydrography also includes the collection of other oceanography, geodesy and geologic data (e.g., bottom classification) in conjunction with the depth data, and it may be used for other coastal engineering purposes (e.g., maintenance dredging, construction) in addition to nautical charting.

Hydrologic Modeling – The computer modeling of rainfall and the effects of land cover, soil conditions, and terrain slope to estimate rainfall runoff in streams and lakes. Digital elevation data are used as part of hydrologic modeling.

Hydrologically-Conditioned (Hydro-Conditioned) – Processing of a DEM or TIN so that the flow of water is continuous across the entire terrain surface, including the removal of all spurious sinks or pits. The only sinks that are retained are the real ones on the landscape. Whereas "hydrologically-enforced" is relevant to drainage features that are generally mapped, "hydrologically-conditioned" is relevant to the entire land surface and is done so that water flow is continuous across the surface, whether that flow is in a stream channel or not. The purpose for continuous flow is so that relationships/links among basins/catchments can be known for large areas. This term is specifically used when describing EDNA (see Chapter 4), the dataset of NED derivatives made specifically for hydrologic modeling applications.

Hydrologically-Enforced (Hydro-Enforced) – Processing of mapped water bodies so that lakes and reservoirs are level and so that streams flow downhill. For example, a DEM, TIN or topographic contour dataset with elevations removed from the tops of selected drainage structures (bridges and culverts) so as to depict the terrain under those structures. Hydro-enforcement enables hydrologic and hydraulic (H&H) models to depict water flowing under these structures, rather than appearing in the computer model to be dammed by them because of road deck elevations higher than the water levels. Hydro-enforced TINs also utilize breaklines along shorelines and stream centerlines, for example, where these breaklines form the edges of TIN triangles along the alignment of drainage features. Shore breaklines for streams would be 3-D breaklines with elevations that decrease as the stream flows downstream; however, shore breaklines for lakes or reservoirs would have the same elevation for the entire shoreline if the water surface is known or assumed to be level throughout. See Figures 1.21 through 1.24. See also the definition for "hydrologically-conditioned" which has a slightly different meaning.

Hydrology – The scientific study of the waters of the Earth, especially with relation to the effects of precipitation and evaporation upon the occurrence and character of water in streams, lakes, and on or below the land surfaces.

Hypsography – The description of elevations or heights of land surfaces with reference to a specified surface (usually the geoid). The configuration of land or underwater surfaces with respect to a horizontal and vertical datum. Hypsography includes topographic and bathymetric contours, spot heights, mass points, breaklines, and all forms of generic DEM data, except DSMs that depict surfaces above the ground.

Image Correlation – Directly comparing hardcopy or softcopy images, or patches of pixels on conjugate digital images, or indirectly comparing information derived from the stereo images, to determine that points on stereo images (viewed from different perspectives) represent the same points on the imaged surface. Automated image correlation is a computerized technique to match the similarities of pixels in one digital image with comparable pixels in its digital stereo image in order to automate or semi-automate photogrammetric compilation. Automated image correlation provides an efficient method for generating DEMs photogrammetrically, but automated correlation normally results in DSMs instead of DEMs because such correlation generates elevations of rooftops, treetops and other surface features as imaged on the stereo photographs.

Image Resolution – The size of the smallest feature that can be resolved or interpreted in an image. Often confused with ground sample distance (GSD). With digital imagery, the GSD is the size of the ground footprint of a pixel and is reported as linear units/pixel, such as 1 meter/pixel, 1 foot/pixel, etc. The interpretive image resolution is normally superior to the GSD; for example, it is common to interpret highway paint stripes only 4"-6" wide on digital imagery with a GSD of 1 meter.

Independent Source of Higher Accuracy – Data acquired independently of procedures to generate the dataset that is used to test the positional accuracy of a dataset. The independent source of higher accuracy shall be of the highest accuracy feasible and practicable to evaluate the accuracy of a dataset.

Infrared – The portion of the invisible spectrum consisting of electromagnetic radiation with wavelengths in the range from 750 nanometers to 1 millimeter.

Insonify (Ensonify) – To expose an area, or portion of seabed, to sonar energy. Seabed that has been covered by imaging sonar, provided acceptable backscatter and interpretable sonar data, is said to have been insonified. Ping rates (numbers of output pulses per second) are often referred to as "insonification rates."

Interferometer – An instrument which measures differences between the phases of two different electromagnetic signals originating from a common source, but which have traversed different paths. The phase differences are measured by combining the two signals. The amplitude of the combined signal is a function of the phase difference between the two signals. The phenomenon of fluctuations in the amplitude of the combined signals in response to phase changes in the input signals if sometimes referred to as interference.

Interferometric Synthetic Aperture Radar (IFSAR) – An airborne or spaceborne interferometer radar system, flown aboard rotary or fixed wing aircraft or space-based platform, that is used to acquire 3-dimensional coordinates of terrain and terrain features that are both manmade and naturally occurring. IFSAR systems form synthetic aperture images of terrain surfaces from two spatially separated antennae over an imaged swath that may be located to the left, right or both sides of the imaging platform.

Interior Orientation – Definition of the elements of the image and how they relate to the optical system used to acquire them, e.g., the camera's focal length, location of the "principal point" on the image, and any known distortions induced by the optics and film.

Interpolation – As used in this manual, interpolation is the estimation of z-values at a point with x/y coordinates, based on the known z-values of surrounding points. There are many different forms of interpolation:

- **ANUDEM** – A variation of spline interpolation optimized for the creation of hydrologically correct (hydro-enforced) terrain models.

- **Inverse Distance Weighted Interpolation** – A method for interpolating the elevations of new points by using a linearly weighted combination of values from nearby points, where the weight is a function of inverse distance. See Figure 1.9.

- **Kriging** – A method for interpolating the elevations of new points by using geostatistical techniques that weight the surrounding measured values to derive a prediction for each location. However, the weights are based not only on the distance between the measured points and the prediction location but also on the strength of the overall correlation among the measured points. With kriging, the data are used to define the spatial correlation model to determine the weights for neighboring samples that are used to fit a surface to the points. See Figures 1.18 and 1.19.

- **Natural Neighbor Interpolation** – A method for interpolating the elevations of new points by using an area based weighting scheme to interpolate heights. See Figures 1.11 through 1.14.

- **Spline** – A method for interpolating the elevations of new points by using a mathematical formula to create a surface that minimizes the overall surface curvatures, resulting in a smooth surface that passes through the input points. See Figures 1.15 and 1.16.

Intervisibility – The identification of all points that are visible from a designated input point (see triangle in Figure 1.32). Generally synonymous with "viewshed" and "line-of-sight."

Kalman Filter – A recursive minimum variance estimation technique that uses statistical models to weight each new measurement relative to past information and estimate quantities of interest having statistical characteristics. It can be thought of as a recursive least squares adjustment.

Kriging – See Interpolation.

L1 – Level 1 frequency of 1575.42 MHz, one of the radio frequencies transmitted by GPS satellites. This frequency carries the C/A code, P-code, and the navigation message.

L2 – Level 2 frequency of 1227.6 MHz, one of the radio frequencies transmitted by GPS satellites. This frequency carries only the P-code.

L3 – Level 3 frequency of 1381.04 MHz of GPS satellites.

L5 – Level 5 frequency of 1176.45 MHz, an additional frequency used on new "Block IIF" satellites, intended for civilian applications in air traffic control.

Last Return – The last significant measurable portion of a return lidar pulse.

Latitude, Geodetic – The angle that the normal to the ellipsoid at a point makes with the equatorial plane (the geodetic Equator) of the ellipsoid. Geodetic latitudes depend on the chosen geodetic datum, which determines the orientation and dimensions at the ellipsoid.

Lattice – A 3-D surface representation method created by a rectangular array of points spaced at a constant sampling interval in x and y directions relative to a common origin. A lattice differs from a grid in that it represents the value of the surface only at the lattice "mesh points" or "elevation posts" of the lattice, rather than the elevation of the cell area surrounding the centroid of a grid cell. See Figure 1.8a.

Layover – A limiting case of foreshortening where points arranged with increasing ground coordinates appear reversed in the radar imagery, precluding the determination of elevation in layover regions. Geometrically this happens when the slope of the terrain is greater than the angle the incident radiation makes with respect to vertical.

Lead Line – A long chain or line with a lead weight attached at one end. The line is used to measure water depths (usually up to 10 fathoms) by survey parties not equipped with electronic depth-measuring equipment. It also can be used to check such equipment.

Least Squares Adjustment – An adjustment satisfying the condition that the sum of the squares of the differences between the given and changed quantities be a minimum.

Leveling – The process of finding differences of elevation.

- **Differential Leveling** – Determining the difference in elevation between two points by the sum of incremental vertical displacements of a graduated leveling rod.

- **Spirit Leveling** – Leveling with a leveling instrument that depends of a spirit level for making its line of sight horizontal. A spirit level uses a closed glass container filled with a fluid with free space so that a bubble of air rises to the top to indicate when the instrument is level.

- **Trigonometric Leveling** – Determining differences of elevation by observing vertical angles between points. Either the horizontal distance between the points must be known or the straight-line distance must be measured.

Lever Arm – A relative position vector of one sensor with respect to another in a direct georeferencing system. For example, with aerial mapping cameras, there are lever arms between the inertial center of the IMU and the phase center of the GPS antenna, both with respect to the camera perspective center within the lens of the camera. Lidar sensors also have similar lever arm vectors.

Lidar – An instrument that measures distance to a reflecting object by emitting timed pulses of light and measuring the time between emission and reception of reflected pulses. The measured time interval is converted to distance.

Line-of-Sight – See Intervisibility.

Local Accuracy – See Accuracy.

Longitude, Geodetic – The angle between the plane of the local geodetic meridian and the plane of an arbitrarily chosen, geodetic meridian, normally the prime meridian in Greenwich, England. A geodetic longitude may be measured by the angle, at one of the poles of the ellipsoid, between the local and geodetic meridian, or by the arc of the ellipsoid's Equator intercepted by these meridians. In recording a geodetic location, it is essential that the geodetic datum on which it is based also be stated.

Lunation – The interval of time between two successive conjunctions (new moons) or oppositions (full moons) of the Moon. A lunar month.

Map – A representation, usually on a plane surface and at an established scale, of the physical features (natural, artificial, or both) or a part or the whole of the Earth's surface. Features are identified by means of signs and symbols, and geographical orientation is indicated.

- **Planimetric Map** – A map that shows only the horizontal positions of the features represented. It does not show relief (elevations) in measurable form.

- **Topographic Map** – A map showing the horizontal and vertical locations of natural and artificial features. It is distinguished from a planimetric map by the presence of numbered contour lines or comparable symbols to indicate elevations of mountains, valleys, and plains; in the case of hydrographic charts, symbols and numbers are used to show depths in bodies of water.

Map Manuscript – The original drawing of a map as compiled or constructed from ground surveys, photogrammetry, etc.

Map Projection – A function relating 3-D coordinates of points on a curved surface (usually an ellipsoid or sphere) to 2-D coordinates of points on a plane map.

Mark – A dot, the intersection of a pair of crossed lines, or any other physical point corresponding to a point in a survey. It is the physical point to which distances, elevations, heights or other coordinates refer.

Mass Points – Irregularly spaced points, each with x/y location coordinates and z-value, typically (but not always) used to form a TIN. When generated manually, mass points are ideally chosen to depict the most significant variations in the slope or aspect of TIN triangles. See Figures 1.1a and 1.1b. However, when generated automatically, e.g., by lidar or IFSAR scanners, mass point spacing and pattern depend upon the characteristics of the technologies used to acquire the data.

Mean (Arithmetic Mean) – The average of all numbers in a dataset.

Mean Range – The difference between Mean High Water and Mean Low Water.

Mean Sea Level – The average location of the interface between ocean and atmosphere, over a period of time sufficiently long so that all random and periodic variations of short duration average to zero. The U.S. National Ocean Service has set 19 years as the period suitable for measurement of mean sea level at tide gauges.

Median – The value in a dataset at which there are as many larger numbers as there are smaller numbers.

Meridian – A north-south line from which differences of longitude and azimuths are reckoned. At the International Meridian Conference held in Washington D.C. in 1884, the adoption of the Greenwich Meridian as the *prime meridian* for the Earth was approved by the representatives of 22 governments, including the U.S.

Mesh Points – The regularly spaced points in a lattice. Mesh points are located at a constant interval in x and y directions relative to a common origin, and contain the z-values for the surface at each location. Often referred to as elevation posts or grid posts in USGS DEMs and other regularly spaced elevation data sets.

Metonic Cycle – A period of 6940 days (approximately 19 years) devised by the Athenian astronomer Meton (c. 450 B.C.) for obtaining a period in which new and full moon would recur on the same day of the year.

Micron – One-millionth of a meter. One micrometer.

Mode – The value at which the greatest number of values is concentrated in a dataset. In a histogram, the mode is the value or range of values which has the highest abscissa value at the peak of the histogram.

Model – The copy of a physical object such as the Earth, normally at reduced scale.

- **Mathematical Model** – The mathematical reconstruction of a physical object such as the Earth, normally for computer display and analyses.

- **Photogrammetric Model** – The visual or optical image produced by optically combining light transmitted through a stereoscopic pair of photographs. A stereoscopic model is not a material object but an image or pair of images that give the same visual effect as would a material model.

Morphology – The form and structure of a surface. In TINs, the morphology of a surface is defined by mass points and breaklines used to build the TIN. Breaklines are very significant in defining surface morphology. In lattices, the morphology of a surface cannot be directly represented in the model by linear features (e.g., breaklines) and must be implied from the mesh point z-values.

Mosaicking – The process whereby multiple images and/or DEMs are merged into a single image and/or DEM with a common datum, map projection and data format.

Multipath – Reflected signals that traverse different longer paths than the direct line-of-sight signal before arriving at the receiving device.

Multipath Error – Errors in GPS positioning caused by signals reflected off of fixed surfaces or refracted by foliage, both causing signals with multiple path lengths to impinge on the GPS antenna.

National Elevation Dataset – A single, nationwide seamless elevation database with product areas defined by the customers, available in several product format options. It includes the "best available" data that meet a common standard. It is one of the seven framework data themes within the NSDI. Standard datasets have 1-arc-second, 1/3-arc-second, and 1/9-are-second post spacing and typically comprise the best available, multi-resolution dataset.

National Tidal Datum Epoch (NTDE) – A specific 19-year period (closest full year to the 18.6-year nodal cycle of the moon) used to average out local meteorological effects on sea level and to compute tidal datums.

Natural Neighbor Interpolation – See Interpolation.

Nautical Chart – A chart specifically designed to meet the requirements of marine navigation, showing depths of water, nature of bottom, elevations, configuration and characteristics of coast, dangers, and aids to navigation.

Neap Tide – A tide that occurs approximately midway between the times of the new and full moon. The neap tidal range is usually 10 to 30 percent less than the mean tidal range.

Network Accuracy – See Accuracy

No Bottom At – Historically, depths apparently deeper than the maximum length of a lead line. Now, used to describe areas that have been "cleared" of hazards to an assumed lidar extinction depth, or areas that may be surveyed by sonar without fear of danger to the vessel.

Nodes – The beginning and ending location of a vector or arc, topologically linked to all vectors or arcs that meet at the node. When specifically applied to elevation data, nodes represent the corner points of each triangle in a TIN. A triangle node is topologically linked to all triangles that meet at that node. See Figure 1.3.

Normal – A straight line perpendicular to a surface or to another line. Also, the condition of being perpendicular to a surface or line. In geodesy, a *normal* is a straight line perpendicular to the surface of a particular ellipsoid.

Northing – A linear distance, in the coordinate system of a map grid, northwards from the east-west line through the origin or false origin. A *false northing* is a value assigned the east-west line through the origin on a map grid to avoid the inconvenience of negative northings at some points.

Outlier – An error larger than justified by a dataset of errors having a normal distribution, often assumed to be errors larger than three times the standard deviation, i.e., "3-sigma" which is equivalent to the 99.75% confidence level for a normal distribution.

Orientation – The rotation or set of rotations needed to make the axes of one rectangular Cartesian coordinate system parallel to the axes of another.

Orthometric Height – See Height.

Orthophoto – A photograph prepared from a perspective photograph by removing displacements of points caused by tilt, relief, and perspective.

Orthophoto DEMs – Digital Elevation Models used to correct relief displacement in the production of digital orthophotos.

Panel Points – Ground control points used for aerotriangulation and designed to present clearly visible points that can be accurately measured on aerial photographs. They may be removable plastic or wooden panels, for example, or painted over the reference point, normally as "X", "V" or "T" symbols, and surveyed at the center of the intersecting lines of these symbols. The symbols are sized to be accurately measured based on the image scale.

Parallax – The apparent displacement of the position of an object with respect to a reference system, because of a shift in the location of the observer. Because photogrammetry is based on the imaging of the terrain from two different perspectives, parallax is key to the determination of 3-D measurements from stereo photography.

Parallel – A line which has the same latitude at every point.

Pass Points – Image points that appear in the overlap area of photos in the same strip of aerial photography, normally measured at the center, left center edge, and right center edge of each image along the direction of flight so as to "pass" control from one photograph to the next in a single flight line. Pass points typically fall within the triple-overlap areas when the aerial photography has a forward overlap of at least 60%, meaning that some points on the ground appear on three consecutive aerial photographs, adding strength to the aerotriangulation process.

P-Code – Precision Code (or Private Code) in relationship with the usage of GPS for military applications. It has a 10.23 MHz rate, a period of 7 days and is the principal navigation ranging code.

Peak – A point around which all slopes are negative.

Percentile – As used in this manual, a percentile is any of the values in a dataset of errors dividing the distribution of the individual errors in the dataset into one hundred groups of equal frequency. Any of those groups can specify a specific percentile, e.g., the 95th percentile. The 95th percentile indicates that 95% of the errors will be of equal or lesser value and 5% of the errors will be of larger value.

Photogrammetry – The science of deducing the physical 3-dimensional measurements of objects from measurements on stereo photographs that photograph an area from two different perspectives.

Ping Rate – Number of sonar output pulses per second.

Pit – A point around which all slopes are positive. See puddle.

Pixel – A two-dimensional raster cell, normally used for computer display of imagery or coded feature data.

Planimetrics – Data about non topographic features on the Earth surface that are represented only by their horizontal position.

Pitch – The angular deviation from the horizontal of a craft about the horizontal axis normal to its direction of movement. The pitch is positive if it causes the craft's front end to rise. In photogrammetry, the term is applied to a rotation of the camera, or of the coordinate system of the photograph, about either the y-axis of the photograph's coordinate system or about the y-axis of the ground coordinate system.

Plumb Line – A line perpendicular to all equipotential surfaces of the Earth's gravity field that intersect with it. It is a line of force in the Earth's gravity field, and thus is curved rather than straight.

Position – The location of a point on the surface of the Earth, expressed in terms of one of several coordinate systems. Examples are geographic position (latitude, longitude and altitude), UTM northing, easting and height, or State Plane northing, easting and height.

Positional Dilution of Precision (PDOP) – An indicator of a GPS receiver's positional accuracy that can be derived from the geometry of the visible GPS satellites in relation to the GPS receiver. The approximate 3-D positional accuracy is approximated by the product of PDOP and the statistical pseudorange errors.

Precision – A statistical measure of the tendency of a set of random numbers to cluster about a number determined by the dataset. *Precision* relates to the quality of the method by which the measurements were made, and is distinguished from *accuracy* which relates to the quality of the result. The term "precision" not only applies to the fidelity with which required operations are performed, but, by custom, has been applied to methods and instruments employed in obtaining results of a high order of precision. Precision is exemplified by the number of decimal places to which a computation is carried and a result stated.

Principal Point – The intersection of the optical axis of the camera with the image and origin of an image coordinate system. Film cameras use imprinted "fiducial points" at the corners and sides of each image that define the orientation of the image coordinate system and a context for locating the principal point. Lens distortion is generally modeled as being both radial and tangential to the principal point.

Profile – The side view of a cross section of a terrain surface. In USGS DEMs, profiles are the basic building blocks of an elevation grid and are defined as one-dimensional arrays, i.e., arrays of n columns by 1 row, where n is the length of the profile.

Profilometer – A device to measure the vertical profiles of surfaces on earth.

Projection – A function relating points on one surface to points on another surface so that for every point on the first surface corresponds exactly to one point on the second surface. A map projection is a special case in requiring that one of the surfaces be a spheroid or ellipsoid and the other be a developable surface (normally a plane or a cylinder or cone that can be "cut" and flattened into a plane).

Pseudorange – A GPS receiver's computed pseudorange to each satellite is its estimate of the time of signal propagation from the satellite to the GPS antenna multiplied by the speed of light. The computed pseudoranges comprise the true ranges between the satellites and the GPS antenna plus several pseudorange errors, the most dominant being the receiver clock error.

Puddle – One or more DEM grid cells totally surrounded by cells of higher elevation.

Pulse Duration – Time, measured in nanoseconds, that the optical power of a laser pulse is at Full Width at Half Maximum (FWHM).

Pulse Energy – The total energy content of a laser pulse measured in micro joules (µJ).

Pulse Repetition Frequency – The number of emitted light pulses per second; also known as Pulse Repetition Rate. For example, a 50 kHz lidar system generates 50,000 pulses of laser energy in one second.

Quadrangle (Quad) – A map or plat of a rectangular or nearly rectangular area usually bounded by given meridians of longitude and parallels of latitude.

Quality Assurance (QA) – Steps taken: (1) to ensure the government receives the quality products it pays for and/or (2) to ensure an organization's Quality Program works effectively. Quality Programs include quality control procedures for specific products as well as overall Quality Plans that typically mandate an organization's communication procedures, document and data control procedures, quality audit procedures, and training programs necessary for delivery of quality products and services.

Quality Control (QC) – Steps taken by data producers to ensure delivery of products that satisfy standards, guidelines and specifications identified in the Scope of Work. These steps typically include production flow charts with built-in procedures to ensure quality at each step of the work flow, in-process quality reviews, and/or final quality inspections prior to delivery of products to a client.

Radar – An instrument for determining the distance and direction to an object by measuring the time needed for radio signals to travel from the instrument to the object and back, and by measuring the angle through which the instrument's antenna has traveled.

Radar, Synthetic-Aperture – A radar containing a moving or scanning antenna; the signals received are combined to produce a signal equivalent to that which would have been received by a larger, stationary antenna.

Random Error – See Error.

Range (IFSAR) – The distance in a direction perpendicular to the flight path (cross path direction) imaging the terrain below. Range or cross track resolution is achieved by finely gating the received echo in time.

Rangefinder – A device which uses laser energy for determining the distance from the device to an object.

Real Time Kinematic (RTK) – A method of utilizing carrier phase differential GPS with on-the-fly ambiguity resolution transmitted from a base station with known coordinates to a rover receiver via a radio link. This technique will compute a position in real time, relative to the base station within an accuracy of a few centimeters.

Rectification – The process of producing, from a tilted or oblique photograph, a photograph from which displacement caused by tilt has been removed. Ortho-rectification, in addition to correction of tilt displacement, also corrects for perspective and relief displacement.

Relative Accuracy – See Accuracy.

Relief – Topography. The deviation of a surface, or portions thereof, from some surface such as a reference ellipsoid.

Relief Displacement – The displacement of an image, outward from the center of an aerial photograph, caused by the elevation (relief) of features above an established base elevation.

Resolution – In the context of gridded elevation data, resolution is synonymous with the horizontal post spacing. Other definitions include:

- The size of the smallest feature that can be represented and detected in a surface or image.

- Sometimes used to state the number of points in x and y directions in a lattice, e.g., 1201 x 1201 mesh points in a USGS one-degree DEM.

Roll – The angular deviation from the horizontal of a craft about its longitudinal axis. In photogrammetry, the angular deviation of an aerial camera or coordinate system of a photograph about either the photograph's x-axis or about the x-axis of the ground coordinate system.

Root Mean Square Error (RMSE) – The square root of the average of the set of squared differences between dataset coordinate values and coordinate values from an independent source of higher accuracy for identical points. The vertical RMSE ($RMSE_z$), for example, is calculated as the square root of $\sum(Z_n - Z'_n)^2/N$, where:

- Z_n is the set of N z-values (elevations) being evaluated, normally interpolated (for TINs and DEMs) from dataset elevations of points surrounding the x/y coordinates of checkpoints

- Z'_n is the corresponding set of checkpoint elevations for the points being evaluated

- N is the number of checkpoints

- n is the identification number of each of the checkpoints from 1 through N.

Root Mean Square Error (RMSE), Limiting – The Limiting RMSE is the maximum permissible RMS error established by the ASPRS Accuracy Standards for Large-Scale Maps, 1990, for specified map classes, i.e., Class 1, Class 2, or Class 3 maps.

Selective Availability (S/A) – An intentional error imposed by the U.S. Department of Defense to limit the highest achievable autonomous (non-differential) GPS positioning accuracy to authorized military users. This was done by intentionally degrading the quality of the broadcast transmitted parameters in the C/A signal that are required to compute each satellite position and clock corrections. S/A limited the achievable autonomous positioning accuracy to 100 meters horizontal and 150 meters vertical. S/A was turned off on May 2, 2000 and, as a result, the autonomous positioning accuracy improved to 8 meters horizontal and 15 meters vertical.

Scale (Map) – A number, constant for a given map, which is representative of the ratios of small distances on the map to the corresponding actual distances. Map scale is normally presented as a fraction expressed as, for example, 1/50,000 or 1:50,000. Because 1/50,000[th] of something is smaller than 1:20,000[th] of something, a 1:50,000-scale maps is considered to be a smaller scale map than a 1:20,000-scale map.

Scale Factor – A number by which a distance obtained from a map by computation or measurement is multiplied to obtain the actual distance on the datum of the map.

Scan Period – The period of time, measured in nanoseconds, taken by a scanner to complete a scan pattern and return to its starting point.

Scan Rate – The number of times per second a scanning device samples its field of view, measured in Hz.

Sea Level – In general, the reference elevation of the surface of the sea from which elevations are measured. This term is used as a curtailed form of "mean sea level."

Secchi Depth – An intuitive water clarity measure that is the depth at which a standard black and white disc, deployed over the side of a boat, is no longer visible to the human eye.

Secondary Tide Stations – Water level stations, located within the mouth of a bay or estuary, that have operated for more than 1 year but less than 19 years, and have a planned finite lifetime. When reduced by comparison with simultaneous observations at a suitable control tide station, they provide accurate control in bays and estuaries where localized tidal effects are not realized at the nearest control station. They also provide data for the reduction of soundings in connection with hydrographic surveys.

Shadow – A dark area is a radar image where the radar beam cannot reach a portion of the terrain being imaged because it is occulted by other parts of the terrain or other objects in the scene. Shadowed regions have no useful interferometric signal and consequently no elevation values can be determined.

Shoreface — The narrow zone, seaward or lakeward from the shoreline at low water, that is permanently covered by water and over which the sands and gravel actively move with the action of the waves.

Shoreline – The boundary line between a body of water and the land, in particular, the boundary line between the water and the line marking the extent of *high water* or *mean high water.*

Sidelap – The overlap between adjoining swaths of lidar data or adjoining strips of aerial photography.

Signal-to-Noise Ratio – The quantitative ratio between the part of an event that is considered *signal* to the part that is considered *noise.*

Single Frequency – A GPS receiver that tracks only the C/A pseudoranges and carrier phases on the L1 carrier from each satellite.

Slope – The measure of change in elevation over distance, expressed either in degrees or as a percent. For example, a rise of 4 meters over a distance of 100 meters describes a 2.3° or 4% slope. The maximum rate of change in elevation, either from cell to cell in a gridded surface or of a triangle in a TIN. Every cell in a DEM or triangle in a TIN has a slope value; the lower the slope value, the flatter the terrain; the higher the slope value, the steeper the terrain. See Figure 1.30.

Softcopy Photogrammetry – Stereo photogrammetric procedures that utilize digital imagery in digital stereo photogrammetric workstations (DSPWs) — also called softcopy workstations — that have significant advantages compared with analytical stereoplotters. These advantages include: automatic digital image correlation, efficient production of DEMs and digital orthophotos, and superimposition of all types of geospatial data over digital imagery. For DEM generation, superimposition means that all elevation mass points, breaklines and contours can be reviewed in stereo against the actual ground form, and old 3-D data can be superimposed on new stereo models to see where DEMs, breaklines or contours need to be revised.

Sonar – An apparatus that detects the presence of, or determines the distance or direction of, an object underwater by receiving and interpreting sound from the object. The term is applied principally to an apparatus that itself generates the sound; the object then reflects or scatters the sound back to the apparatus.

Sounding – A measurement of depth in water — usually a measurement of the distance of the bottom below the boat or ship from which the measurement is taken. The usual method is to transmit a sonic pulse downwards and to measure the time required for the pulse to travel to the bottom and back. Since the path of the pulse is considerably bent by refraction and the pulse itself also penetrates some distance into the bottom, both factors must be accounted for in depth calculations. In shallow water, alternative techniques are used, to include airborne lidar bathymetry or weighted graduated plumb lines.

Sound Wave – Normally used interchangeably with "acoustic wave" for frequencies within the range of human hearing (sound) plus ultrasonic and sub-sonic frequencies that are respectively above and below the range of human hearing. Acoustic waves are based on vibrations of the actual material of the medium and are manifested as periodic variations of pressure in the medium.

Special Flood Hazard Area (SFHA) – The land area in the floodplain within a community subject to a 1 percent or greater change of flooding in any given year.

Spot Elevations – Elevation points collected at identifiable points, to leave behind a record of points that can be checked, or at local maxima or minima not represented by contour lines. Spot elevations are most typically collected for hill tops, dam spillway elevations, tops of selected bridge decks and road intersections, and bottoms of volcano craters and local sink holes. Also called spot heights.

Spring Tide – A tide that occurs at the time of the new and full moon when tides have their greatest amplitude. The times when highest and lowest waters are recorded.

Standard (1) – An agreed-upon procedure within a particular industry or profession, that is to be followed in producing a particular product or result.

Standard (2) – A number, or set of numbers, established within an industry, a science, or a technology, setting limits on precision or accuracy with which operations, measurements, or products are to be made.

Standard Deviation – A statistical term used to describe the general variability of a dataset or random process such as noise about its average or mean value.

State Plane Coordinate System – One of the plane rectangular coordinate systems, one for each State in the U.S., established by the U.S. Coast and Geodetic Survey in 1933 for use in defining locations of geodetic stations in terms of plane-rectangular Cartesian coordinates. Each State is mapped by a conformal map projection in one or more zones, over each of which is placed a rectangular grid. Zones of limited east-west extent and indefinite north-south extent are mapped by a *Transverse Mercator* map projection; zones of indefinite east-west extent and limited north-south extent are mapped by the *Lambert Conformal Conic* map projection with two standard parallels. Zone One of Alaska is on the *Oblique Mercator* map projection. The use of the projections assures that, for zones having a width of 250km, the greatest departure from exact scale (scale error) is 1 part in 10,000.

Stereo Comparator – A photogrammetric instrument that permits stereoscopic viewing of two photographs and measurement of the coordinates of corresponding points, the coordinates of one point and the stereoscopic parallax of its conjugate point on the other image.

Stereo Model – The surface area of elevation and feature models visible in 3-D by viewing the overlapping areas of stereo imagery in an analog, analytical or softcopy stereoplotter.

Stereoscopic Image – A three-dimensional impression given by viewing one of a pair of overlapping pictures of an object with the left eye and the other with the right eye, either simultaneously or in rapid succession.

Strip – A set of overlapping photographs that can be arranged in sequence so that, except for the last photograph, part of the object space shown in one photograph is also shown in the succeeding photograph. A set of overlapping photographs obtained sequentially from a moving aircraft or satellite.

Striping – A DEM anomaly caused by photogrammetric profiling where the floating mark is allowed to pass either above the ground or below the ground on a profiling pass.

Subsidence – The loss of land surface elevation due to removal of subsurface support.

Superimposition – See Softcopy Photogrammetry.

Supplemental Vertical Accuracy (SVA) – The result of a test of the accuracy of z-values over areas with ground cover categories or combinations of categories other than open terrain. Obtained utilizing the 95th percentile method explained in Chapter 3, a supplemental vertical accuracy is always accompanied by a fundamental vertical accuracy.

Surface – A 3-D geographic feature represented by computer models built from uniformly- or irregularly-spaced points with x/y coordinates and z-values.

Systematic Error – See Error.

Terrain Visualization – Viewing the terrain in 3-dimensions, normally from differing perspectives. See Figures 1.25, 1.26 and 1.27.

Three Dimensional (3-D) – Having horizontal (x/y) coordinates plus elevations (z-values)

Tidal Day – The time of rotation of the earth with respect to the moon. Its mean value is approximately equal to 24.84 hours.

Tide – The alternating rise and fall of the oceans with respect to the land, produced by differential variations in the gravitational attraction of the moon and sun. There are three types of tides: diurnal, semidiurnal, and mixed. A diurnal tide has one high tide and one low tide per tidal day. A semidiurnal tide has two high tides and two low tides each tidal day. A mixed tide is similar to a semidiurnal tide except that the two high tides and two low tides of each tidal day have marked differences in their heights. See Figure 1.34.

Tie Points – Image points that appear in the sidelap area of photos in overlapping strips of aerial photography, used to "tie" adjoining strips together. When the aerial photography is flown with 60% forward overlap, and when tie points are measured at the top and bottom corners of each image with adjoining strips, tie point images will appear on 4-6 images, adding extra strength to the aerotriangulation process.

Tide Gauge – A device for measuring the rise and fall and the current height of the tide. The simplest form is a graduated staff placed vertically in the water; the height of the water is read visually from markings on the staff. A more common version has a float with pointer attached to the staff; the float is free to move up and down the staff with the tide. Readings may be made visually, or may be recorded on paper or electronically.

Tilt Displacement – The displacement of features in an image caused by the roll and pitch of the aircraft at the instant a photograph is taken.

Topography – The form of the features of the actual surface of the Earth in a particular region considered collectively. Also called *relief.*

Topology – The spatial relationships which exist between adjacent digital objects. The digitization of node, point, line and area features so that computers are able to determine relationships that humans recognize logically when they determine what feature is connected to, adjacent to, or in close proximity to a point, line, area or surface; what feature intersects a line, area or surface; or what features are contained within an area or surface. See Figure 1.3.

Triangulated Irregular Network (TIN) – A set of adjacent, non-overlapping triangles computed from irregularly-spaced points with x/y coordinates and z-values. The TIN data structure is based on irregularly-spaced point, line, and polygon data interpreted as mass points and breaklines and stores the topological relationship between triangles and their adjacent neighbors. The TIN model may be preferable to a DEM when it is critical to preserve the precise location of narrow or small surface features, such as levees, ditch or stream centerlines, isolated peaks or pits in the data model. See Figure 1.2.

Two Dimensional (2-D) – Having horizontal (x/y) coordinates only, without elevations (z-values)

Undulation – A rise and fall with time, e.g., the undulation of the ocean's surface. A rise and fall with distance, e.g., the undulating hills of Oklahoma.

Undulation of the Geoid – The rise and fall of the geoid, sometimes used synonymously with *geoid height*. Used with the geoid separation.

Vegetation Removal – Correction of reflective surface elevations so as to depict the elevation of the bare-earth terrain beneath the vegetation. Elevations on vegetation are not actually removed; instead, they are reclassified as non-terrain feature points.

Veronoi (Thiessen) Polygon – A polygon that contains areas which are nearer to the point around which it is constructed than to any other point.

Vertical – The direction in which the force of gravity acts. Whereas the *vertical* is the perpendicular to an equipotential surface of gravity (e.g., the geoid), a *normal* is the perpendicular to a given ellipsoid.

Vertical Accuracy – See Accuracy.

Vertical Datum – See Datum.

Vertical Error – The displacement of a feature's recorded elevation in a dataset from its true or more accurate elevation.

Vertical Point Spacing – The vertical distance between laser points from consecutive scan lines when the lidar sensor is tilted into a forward-looking position and laser points "walk up" the face of vertical objects.

Viewshed – See Intervisibility.

Void – Portions of a digital elevation dataset where no elevation data are available. In USGS DEMs, each elevation post located within a void area is assigned a discrete false value representing the void. Treatment of void areas should be documented in the metadata file.

Voxel – A three-dimensional "cube" that serves as a counterpart to a traditional pixel, used for three-dimensional visualization of elevation data. A 3-D pixel. See Figure 1.8b.

Water – A synonym for tide, in the sense of the elevation of the surface of the hydrosphere at a particular longitude and latitude.

- **High Water** – The greatest elevation reached by a rising tide

- **Higher High Water** – The higher of the two high waters occurring on a particular tidal day.

- **Higher Low Water** – The higher of the two low waters occurring on a particular tidal day.

- **Low Water** – The least elevation reached by a falling tide.

- **Lower Low Water** – The lower of two low waters of any tidal day.

- **Lower High Water** – The lower of two high waters of any tidal day.

- **Mean High Water (MHW)** – The average elevation of all high waters recorded at a particular point or station over a considerable period of time, usually 19 years.

- **Mean Higher High Water (MIIIIW)** – The arithmetic average of the elevations of the higher high waters of a mixed tide over a specific 19-year period.

- **Mean Low Water (MLW)** – The average elevation of all low waters recorded at a particular point or station over a considerable period of time, usually 19 years.

- **Mean Lower Low Water (MLLW)** – The average elevation of all the lower low waters recorded over a 19-year period.

- **Mean Water Level** – The elevation determined by averaging the elevations of the surface of water at equal intervals of time (usually hourly) over a considerable period of time.

Weight – A factor by which a quantity is multiplied to increase or decrease the effect of that quantity on the results of an adjustment.

Well-Defined Point – A point that represents a feature for which the horizontal position is known to a high degree of accuracy and position with respect to the geodetic datum.

Wellhead Protection Area – The surface and subsurface area surrounding a water well, or well field, supplying a public water system, through which contaminants are reasonably likely to move toward and reach such water well or well field.

World Geodetic System (WGS) – A set of quantities, developed by the U.S. Department of Defense, for determining geometric and physical geodetic relationships on a global scale, based on a geocentric origin and a reference ellipsoid. The current WGS-84 is based on the Geodetic Reference System 1980 (GRS 80).

X-coordinate – The distance along the x-axis from the origin of a 2-D or 3-D Cartesian coordinate system. An x-coordinate is the first half (the easting) of UTM coordinates or the Easting of State Plane coordinates.

Yaw – The variation, or amount of variation, of the longitudinal axis of a craft from the direction in which the craft is moving, i.e., the difference between the direction in which a craft is pointed and the direction in which it is moving (when typically altered by winds).

Y-coordinate – The distance along the y-axis from the origin of a 2-D or 3-D Cartesian coordinate system. A y-coordinate is the second half (the northing) of UTM coordinates or the Northing of State Plane coordinates.

Z-coordinate – The distance along the z-axis from the origin of a 3-D Cartesian coordinate system. Note, this is not the same as the elevation or height above the vertical datum.

Z-units – The units of measure used for the z-values in a geographic dataset.

Z-values – The elevations of the 3-D surface above the vertical datum at designated x/y locations.

Appendix C

Color Plates

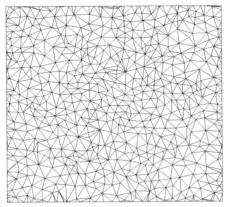

Figure 1.2a A geometric view of a TIN where the terrain sample points are connected into a set of non-overlapping triangles.

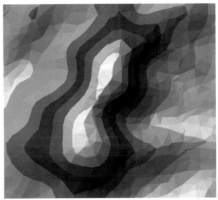

Figure 1.2b A surface view of a TIN where the triangles are hillshaded and colored by elevation.

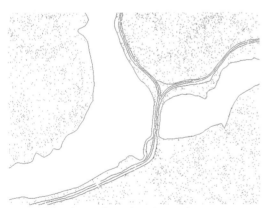

Figure 1.4a A set of sample points and breaklines collected to create a TIN.

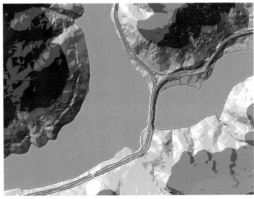

Figure 1.4b The resulting surface model.

565

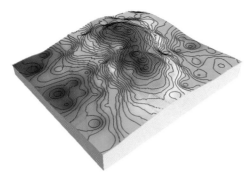

Figure 1.10b IDW interpolated surface.

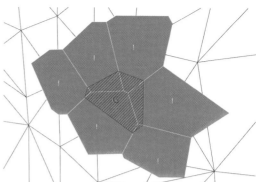

Figure 1.12 The weighting scheme used by natural neighbor interpolation. The point symbolized by a cross in the center is a query point requiring height estimation. The hatched polygon represents its voronoi region if it were to be inserted in the triangulation. The other solid fill polygons are the voronoi regions for the surrounding nodes in the triangulation. The weight of each node is based relative to the area of overlap between its voronoi region, the query point's region, and the areas of overlap for the other nodes. In this example, the natural neighbor to the southwest will be given the most weight.

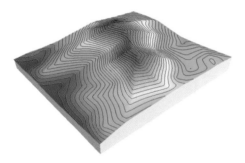

Figure 1.14a Natural neighbor linear interpolation.

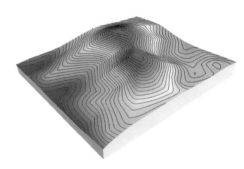

Figure 1.14b Natural neighbor interpolation with blended gradients.

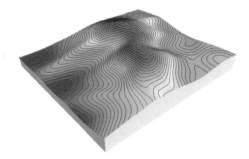

Figure 1.16 Spline interpolated surface.

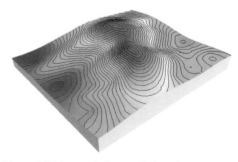

Figure 1.19 Interpolation result from kriging.

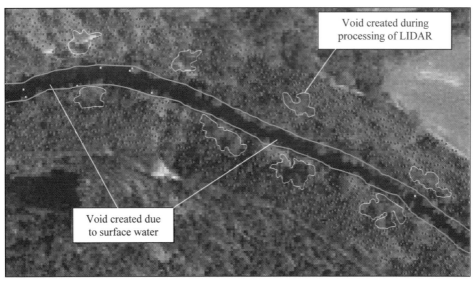

Figure 1.21 Post-processed bare-earth lidar mass points along a North Carolina stream.

Figure 1.22 Geometric view of a TIN, hillshaded by elevation, created without breaklines.

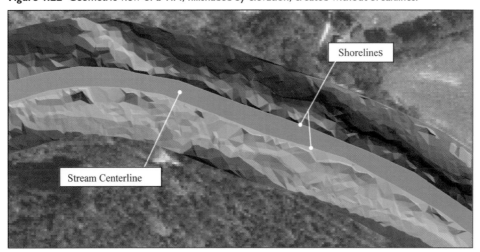

Figure 1.23 Geometric view of the same TIN, hillshaded by elevation, after breaklines are added.

Figure 1.24 The dots on this image show lidar "hits" on the ground. The contour lines were produced by auto-mated post-processing procedures, prior to manual clean-up. The bridge in the southeast corner shows contours crossing over the bridge, making the bridge appear as a dam in a hydraulic model. The bridge in the northwest corner shows contours that are almost hydro-enforced. To be fully hydro-enforced, a human analyst would "cut" a breakline through the bridge, with the breakline having an elevation at or slightly below the elevation of the water level; then, the contour lines on either side of the river would be separated by the breakline, and the hydraulic model would accommodate water passing beneath the bridge. Image provided as a courtesy by Dewberry.

Figure 1.27a Composite display between soils and hillshaded terrain model. The composite makes it easier for those familiar with the area to orient themselves and shows some correlation between soil type and terrain.

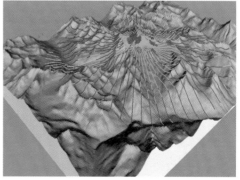

Figure 1.27b Multiple lines of sight generated radially around an individual observation point. Green portion of lines are visible, red are not. These are draped on a terrain model in perspective to increase information content.

Figure 1.28 LANDSAT Thematic Mapper satellite imagery draped on a terrain model. Sky, haze, and fog are added to provide a sense of realism.

Figure 1.29 Hillshade elevation model.

Figure 1.30 Slope calculated from an elevation model. Red is high slope, green is low slope.

Figure 1.31 Aspect calculation from elevation model.

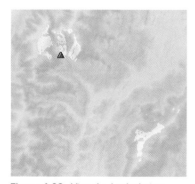

Figure 1.32 Viewshed calculation from an elevation model showing areas visible from the triangle.

Figure 1.33 Watersheds and stream networks delineated from an elevation model. Hillshading has been added to show the underlying terrain.

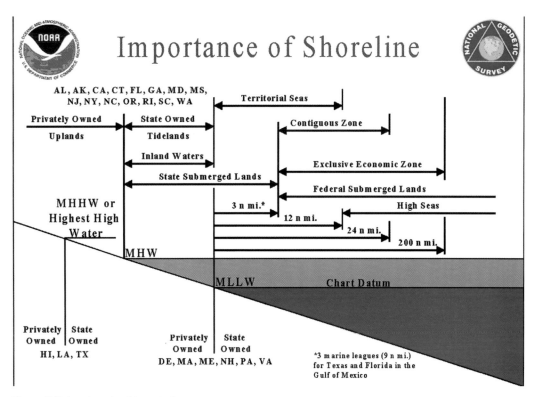

Figure 2.7 Local sea level boundaries.

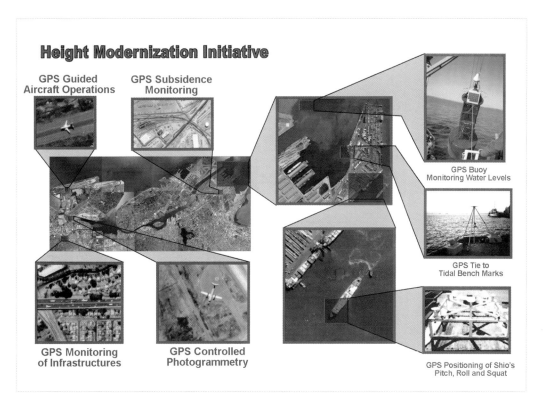

Figure 2.10 Pictorial representation of Height Modernization Initiative.

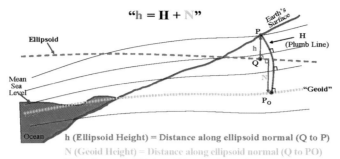

"h = H + N"

h (Ellipsoid Height) = Distance along ellipsoid normal (Q to P)

N (Geoid Height) = Distance along ellipsoid normal (Q to PO)

H (Orthometric Height) = Distance along plumb line (PO to P)

Figure 2.11 Relationships between ellipsoid, geoid, and orthometric heights.

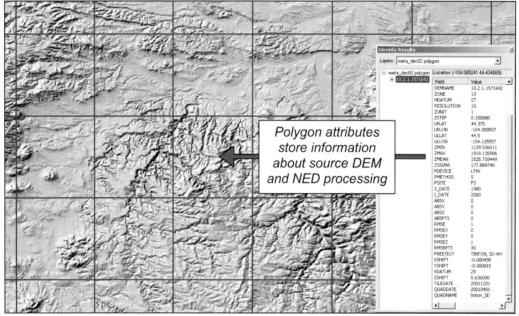

Figure 4.2 NED spatially referenced metadata layer.

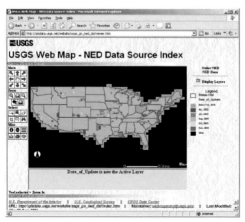

Figure 4.7 Data source index, available on the NED home page (http://ned.usgs.gov/), displays the most recently updated areas in the NED.

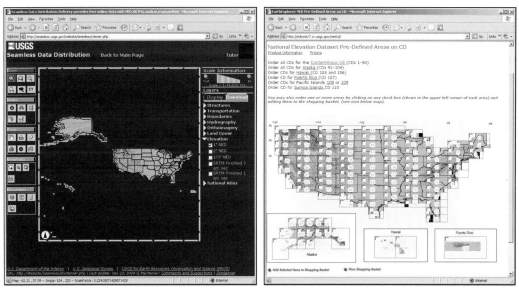

Figure 4.8 Web-based seamless data distribution system (http://seamless.usgs.gov/) for viewing and downloading of NED products (left). Large area coverage of NED products available on hard media (right).

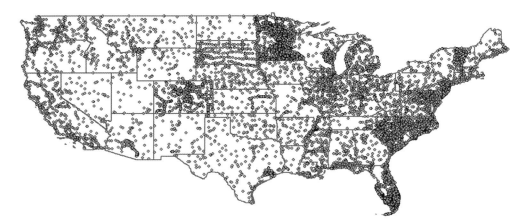

Figure 4.9 Reference control point data set used for accuracy assessment of the NED.

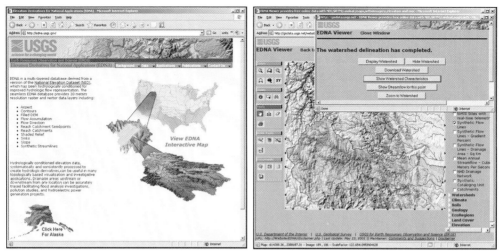

Figure 4.12 EDNA Web site (http://edna.usgs.gov/), on the left, and the Web-based interactive drainage basin delineation tool available on the EDNA data viewer, on the right.

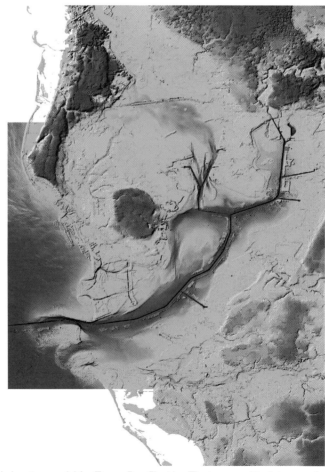

Figure 4.13 Merged elevation model for Tampa Bay, Florida. The topographic data came from the 1-arc-second NED layer and the bathymetric data came from NOAA's hydrographic survey database.

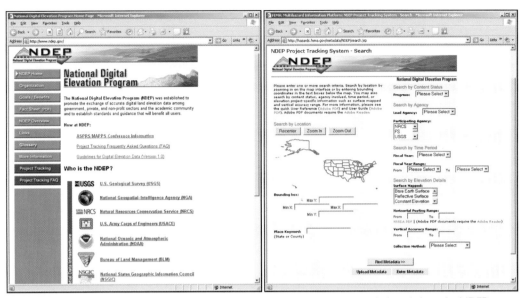

Figure 4.14 The NDEP Web site (http://www.ndep.gov/), shown on the left, includes a link to the NDEP project tracking system, shown on the right.

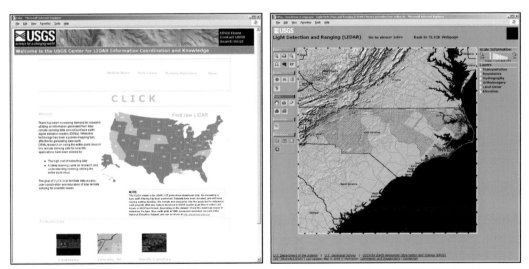

Figure 4.15 The USGS Center for LIDAR Information Coordination and Knowledge (CLICK) is a Web-based (http://lidar.cr.usgs.gov) virtual center that serves as a clearinghouse for lidar information exchange and point cloud data distribution.

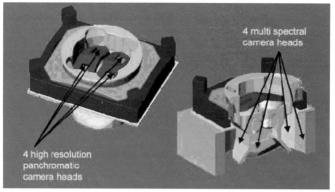

Figure 5.1 Optical configuration of the Z/I Imaging DMC camera.

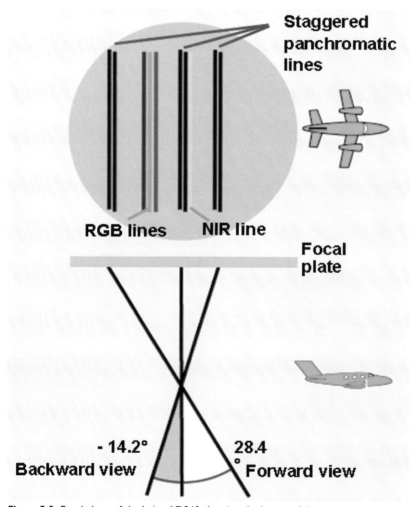

Figure 5.3 Focal plane of the Leica ADS40 showing the layout of the sensors.

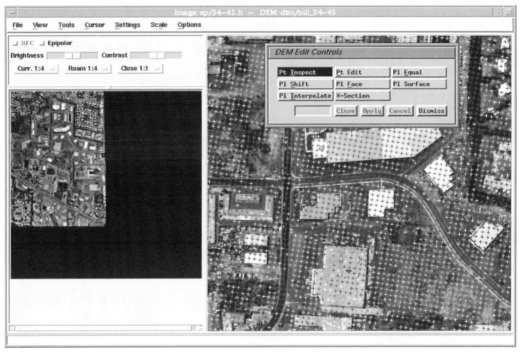

Figure 5.4 Review of automated terrain extraction by superimposing color-coded crosses to show post accuracies. Courtesy of Boeing.

Figure 5.5 Digital orthophoto showing bridge distorted by use of bare earth DTM only. Courtesy of Dewberry.

Figure 5.6 Digital orthophoto showing bridge corrected by use of DTM with breaklines. Courtesy of Dewberry.

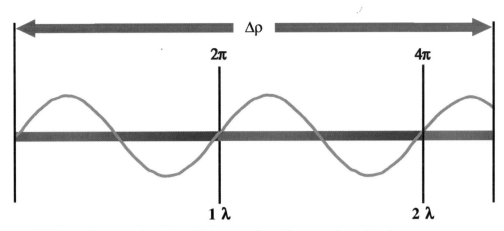

Figure 6.1 Figure illustrating the relationship between phase, distance and wavelength.

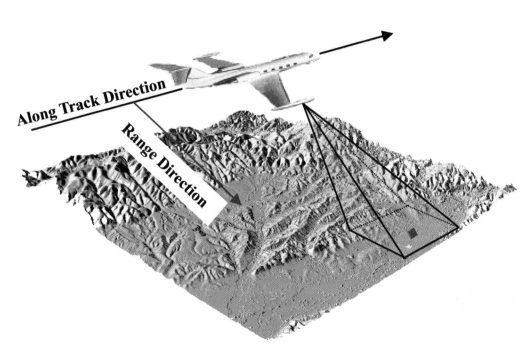

Figure 6.2 A typical SAR imaging geometry has a platform containing a radar instrument moving in the along track direction and imaging the terrain to one side of the flight path. The SAR transmits a series of pulses at regular intervals along track that simultaneously illuminates an area in the along track direction much greater than the desired azimuth resolution. By recording the returned echo from each pulse and using signal processing techniques to "synthesize" a larger antenna, fine resolution in azimuth is achieved. The blue square in the center of beam shows the size of a resolution element compared with the illuminated area from a single pulse indicated in green.

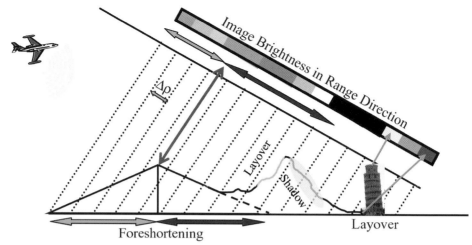

Figure 6.8 The three-dimensional world is collapsed to two dimensions in conventional SAR imaging. After image formation, the radar return is resolved into an image in range-azimuth coordinates. This figure shows a profile of the terrain at constant azimuth, with the radar flight track into the page.

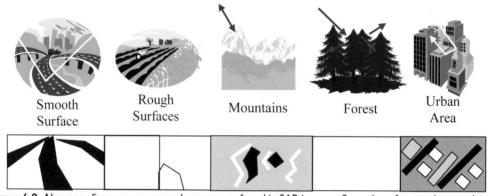

Figure 6.9 Above are five common ground cover types found in SAR imagery. Smooth surfaces such as roads or water tend to reflect energy away from the radar and appear dark in radar images. Rough surfaces, such as often found in fields and cropland, exhibit a type of checkerboard pattern of fields with the texture and brightness level varying with crop and field condition. Extremely bright lines running parallel to the look direction as a result of layover coupled with shadowed regions is typical of that found in mountainous regions. Forested areas generally appear relatively bright since the rough nature of the canopy at most wavelengths generates high levels of backscatter. Depending on the resolution of the SAR, urban areas can show individual buildings or groups of building and the associated roadways.

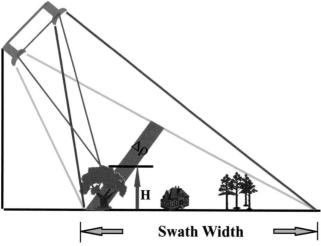

Figure 6.11 Interferometric SAR for topographic mapping uses two apertures separated by a "baseline" to image the surface. The phase difference between the apertures for each image point, along with the range and knowledge of the baseline, can be used to infer the precise shape of the imaging triangle (in red) to determine the topographic height of an object.

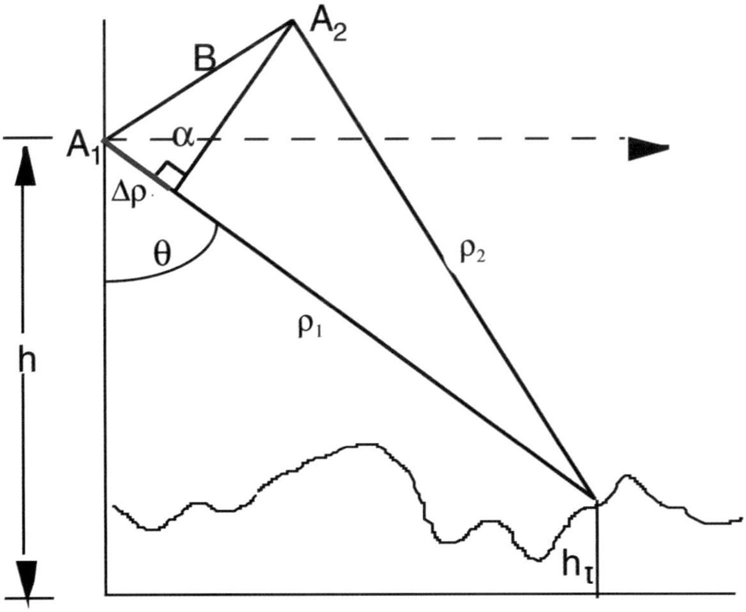

Figure 6.12 Simplified broadside looking (zero Doppler) radar interferometry geometry. The difference in range from the two observing antennas to the target is approximately equal to the projection of the baseline vector onto the line-of-sight vector shown in blue. This range difference can be related to a phase measurement using equation 6.1 and forms the primary interferometric observable.

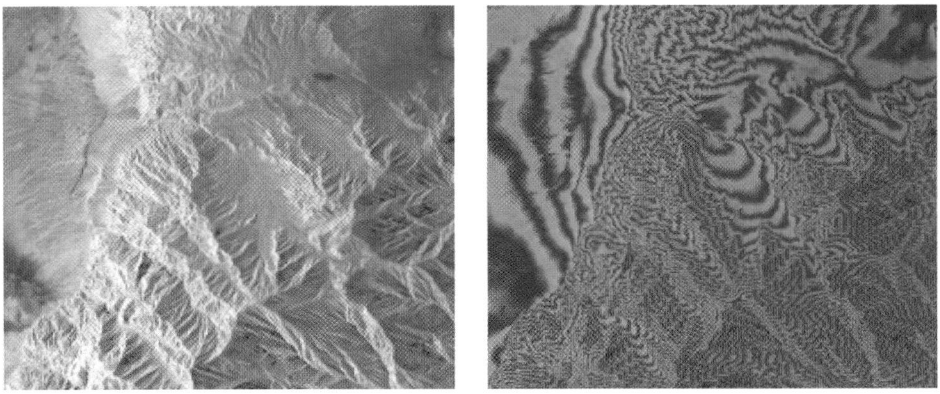

Figure 6.14 Interferometric phase and associated amplitude image of the Mojave Desert, CA, generated from repeat pass observations using the SIR-C radar.

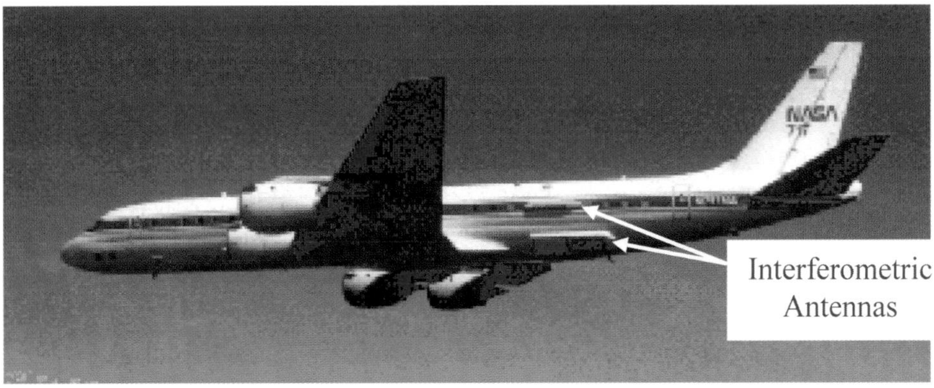

Figure 6.18 View of the NASA DC-8 in flight with the AIRSAR and TOPSAR antennas clearly visible where they are mounted on the fuselage.

Elevation in meters

0   600   1200

Scale in kilometers

0   10   20

N

Figure 6.20 Radar DEM of the Napa Valley. This view of Napa Valley, California and the surrounding area was created with data from NASA's Airborne Synthetic Aperture Radar while it was being flown in its topographic (TOPSAR) mode on a NASA DC-8 aircraft. The colors in the image represent topography, with blue areas representing the lowest elevations and white areas, the highest. Total relief in the image is approximately 1400 meters. The height information has been superimposed on a radar image of the area, which was collected simultaneously. The image is 70 by 90 kilometers with the Napa Valley the broad flat long area (green—blue) in the center left of the image. Lake Berryessa is the dark area in the center right of the image.

C-band   L-band   P-band

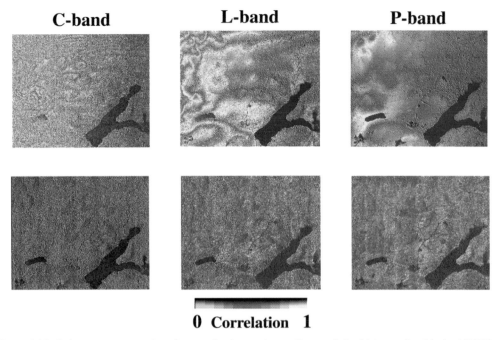

0 Correlation 1

Figure 6.22 Airborne repeat pass interferometric observations at Portage Lake, Maine made with the AIRSAR system. The top row shows the interferometric phases for C-, L- and P-bands. At bottom are the corresponding correlation maps. Conditions were windy when the data was collected and the branch movement resulted in greater decorrelation at shorter wavelengths.

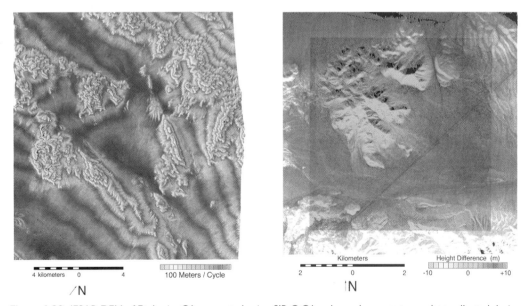

Figure 6.23 IFSAR DEM of Ft. Irwin, CA generated using SIR-C C-band one day repeat pass data collected during the October, 1994 flight of the instrument. The limiting source of error is most likely a result of changes in tropospheric water vapor between passes.

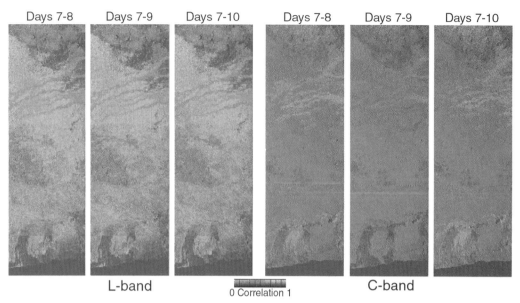

L-band   0 Correlation 1   C-band

Figure 6.24 Correlation maps produced for one, two and three day repeat pass intervals at C-band and L-band obtained during the second SIR-C mission.

Figure 6.25 The three images show the STAR-3i, TopoSAR and STAR-4 platforms respectively. TopoSAR is the only system with antennas not enclosed within a radome. Figure courtesy of Intermap Technologies Inc.

Figure 6.27 The image is a three-dimensional visualization of an area in northern Wales U.K. A color air-photo has been merged with the STAR-3i DSM and presented as a perspective view or 'hill-shade'. The air-photo was supplied by GetMapping plc. Figure courtesy of Intermap Technologies Inc.

Figure 6.28 TopoSAR quad-pol P-Band DTM of test area within King County, WA, USA. The river valley was relatively bare while the steeply sloped terrain and plateau region included dense mixed forest of 10-35 meters height. Comparisons with control points and lidar 'truth' indicated RMSE differences of about 1.5-2.5m RMSE in the heavily forested plateau region but with differences growing with slope to several meters RMSE in the strongly sloped zone. Figure courtesy of Intermap Technologies Inc.

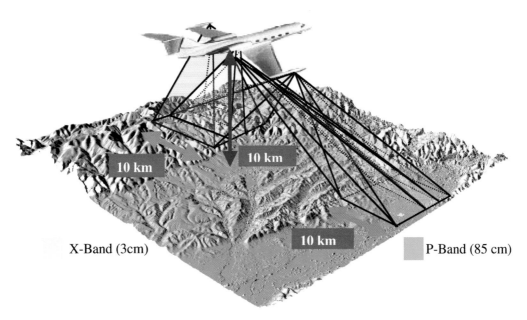

Figure 6.29 GeoSAR collects 10 km swaths simultaneously on both left and right sides of the aircraft at both X- and P-bands.

0   **Contour**   50

Figure 6.30 GeoSAR X-band (left) and P-band (right) DEM data collected at Monarch Grove, CA. Note the elevation contours of eucalyptus tree stand inside the orange box is clearly visible in the X-band data but barely detectable in the P-band data. The GeoSAR mapping system will use a combination of X-band and P-band data to generate bare surface elevation maps in vegetated regions.

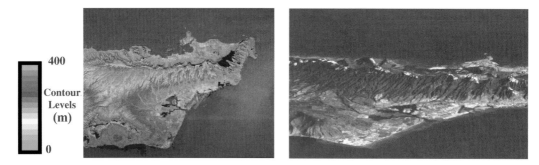

400

Contour
Levels
(m)

0

Figure 6.33 The left image of Oahu is a combination of radar backscatter with color contours overlain. Each color cycle, i.e. going from green to blue and back to green again represents 400 m of elevation change. Honolulu International Airport, Waikiki, and Diamond Head are clearly visible in the image. The right image is a perspective view using the SRTM generated topography with Landsat imagery overlaid.

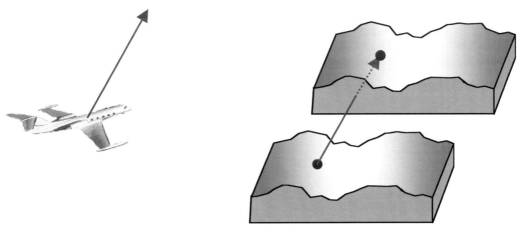

Figure 6.34 An error in platform position, indicated by the red vector in the figure, causes a translation error in the IFSAR DEM equal to the platform position error.

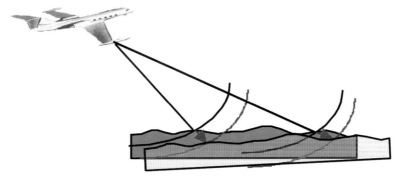

Figure 6.35 Range errors cause displacements along the line-of-sight. Points in the near range are displaced more vertically than horizontally whereas points in the far range are displaced more horizontally than vertically as illustrated above.

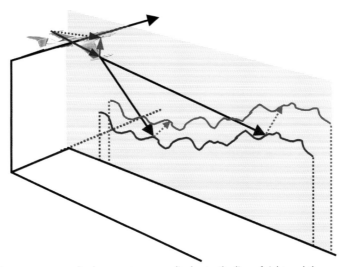

Figure 6.36 Baseline errors cause displacements perpendicular to the line-of-sight and the magnitude of the error is a function of cross track location. The correct baseline is the solid blue arrow on the aircraft, the red arrow is the baseline error (in this case mostly baseline orientation) and the dotted blue arrow is the incorrect baseline. The blue squiggly line represents topographic heights processed using the correct baseline and the red squiggly line the topographic heights with the incorrect baseline. The dotted red arrows point perpendicular to the line-of-sight from the correct to incorrect height.

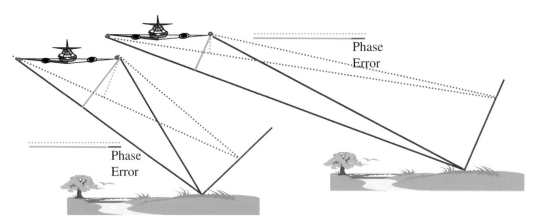

Figure 6.37 Phase errors viewed as differential range errors distort the interferometric observation triangle. The blue triangles represent the nominal interferometric observation triangles with the differential range indicated by the solid green lines. A phase error is introduced by changing the differential range by an amount equivalent to the length of the solid red line. The dotted red triangles show the resulting observation triangles. The position differences lie on a line perpendicular to the line-of-sight, the purple lines, and the amount of height error is range dependent as seen from the near range (left image) and far range (right image) examples.

Figure 6.38 Signal reflected from the aircraft, blue line, that is received at the same time as the direct signal return from the surface, red line, introduce a range varying phase error.

Range

Azimuth

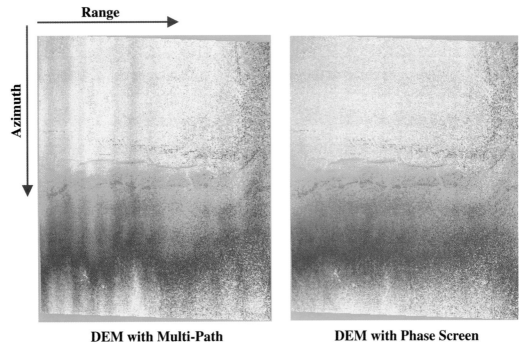

DEM with Multi-Path   **DEM with Phase Screen**

Figure 6.39 Topographic map of Mojave Dessert, CA created with and without using a phase screen. Note the cross track ripples 1-10 m in amplitude in the map without the phase screen characteristic of multipath.

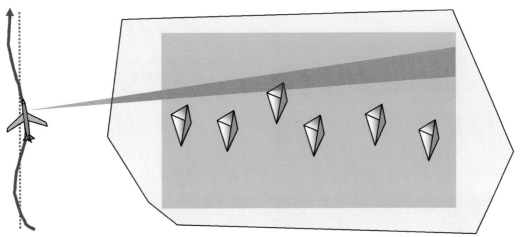

Figure 6.40 IFSAR calibration site is equipped with an array of corner reflectors deployed across the imaging swath of the radar (shown in green). A high accuracy DEM covering the range swath (shown in blue) may be co-located with the corner reflector array or at a different site. Multiple lines are flown at the corner reflector array, and the DEM location if different, in order to determine the calibration parameters.

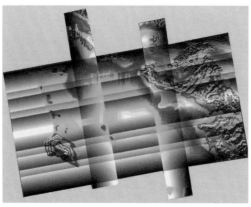

Figure 6.43 The left figure is a mosaic of image masks from 8 flight lines used in planning an Orange County data collection. Visible is the planned overlap of a quarter of a swath (3 km) between the 6 adjacent east-west flight lines and the 2 orthogonal flight lines used to maintain control. The right figure is a mosaic of the processed TOPSAR data from the Orange County collection. Each color cycle used to depict elevation contours represents 100 m of elevation change. Brightness in the image mask mosaic is derived from a shaded relief of the USGS DEM used to make the mask whereas in the TOPSAR mosaic it is the radar backscatter.

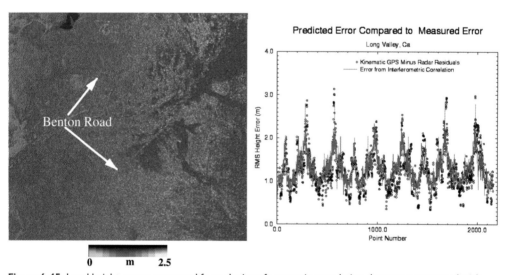

Figure 6.45 Local height errors computed from the interferometric correlation data were compared with kinematic GPS measurements by computing the "local" RMS height difference between the TOPSAR and GPS measured heights along Benton Road in LongValley, CA.

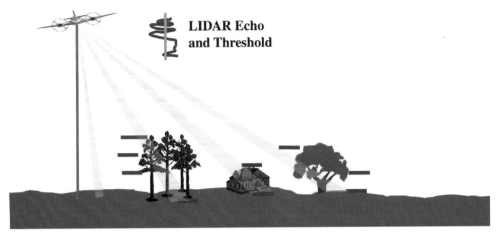

Figure 6.46 Lidar systems like IFSAR systems are active sensors that measure range. Liears use narrow scanning beams to localize their targets spatially. Some lidar system measure the height of multiple returns (denoted by blue bars next to object in scene) exceeding a specified threshold (sample echo in blue with threshold in green next to plane) thereby providing additional information about the vertical structure of objects in the scene.

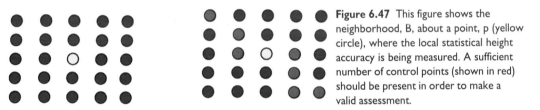

Figure 6.47 This figure shows the neighborhood, B, about a point, p (yellow circle), where the local statistical height accuracy is being measured. A sufficient number of control points (shown in red) should be present in order to make a valid assessment.

Figure 7.10 First return lidar data of Baltimore, MD. Note the ships at dock in the harbor at "3 o'clock." Courtesy of the Joint Precision Strike Demonstration Project Office (JPSD-PO), Rapid Terrain Visualization (RTV) Advanced Concept Technology Demonstration (ACTD), Fort Belvoir, Virginia.

First Return
Second Return
Third Return
Fourth Return

Figure 7.15 When viewed horizontally, we can see lidar "point clouds" in trees. Note that many of the first returns (yellow) reach the ground, whereas some of the 3rd returns (red) are still in the trees. Many pulses do not even receive 3rd and 4th returns, so their last returns may still be in the trees. From Stoker, et al. 2006.

Figure 7.18 Last return lidar data of Lakewood, CA prior to post-processing. The image to the right shows pixels (in black) where there were no lidar returns, presumably absorbed or not reflected by water in the ditches or ponds. Images courtesy of the U.S. Army Engineer Research and Development Center (ERDC), Topographic Engineering Center (TEC).

Figure 7.19 Last return lidar data of Lakewood, CA after post-processing. The left image now represents the bare-earth. The right image shows pixels where elevation points were moved due to reclassification of points on rooftops and dense vegetation. Images courtesy of U.S. Army Engineer Research and Development Center (ERDC), Topographic Engineering Center (TEC).

Figure 7.21 Example of digital elevation data used for urban modeling of San Francisco. Courtesy of Optech.

Bare earth LIDAR **Last return LIDAR** **IFSAR**

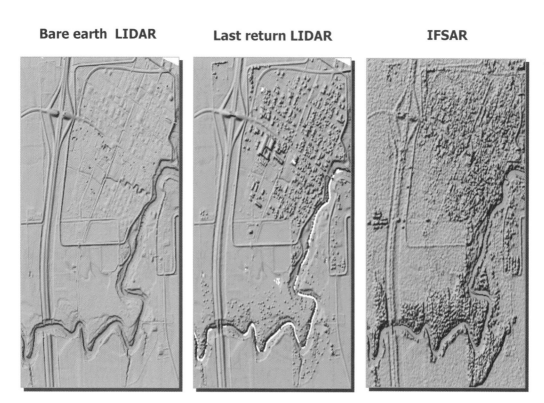

Figure 7.22 The left image shows the last-return lidar data after completion of post processing. The center image shows the last-return lidar data prior to post processing. The right image shows IFSAR data that includes the tree canopy. Lidar data and IFSAR datasets often complement each other. Figures courtesy of the U.S. Army Corps of Engineers.

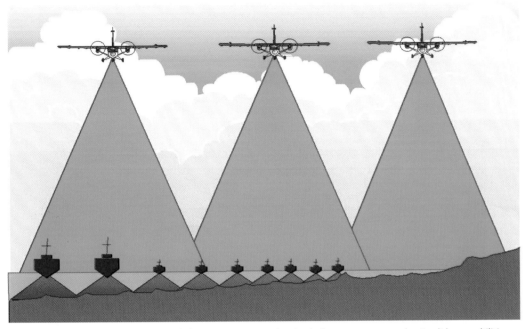

Figure 8.1 Depiction of lidar and multi-beam sonar operation in shallow water to empha-size lidar capabilities and efficiency.

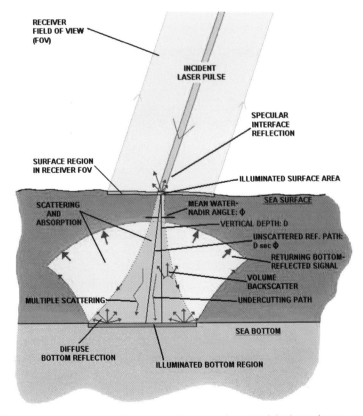

Figure 8.3 Schematic diagram of the effects of scattering on the green lidar beam (not to scale).

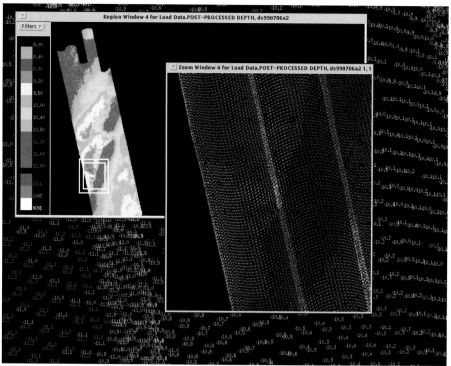

Figure 8.4 Example of region and zoom displays of overlapping swaths flown in opposite directions with semi-circular scan and nearly constant nadir angle.

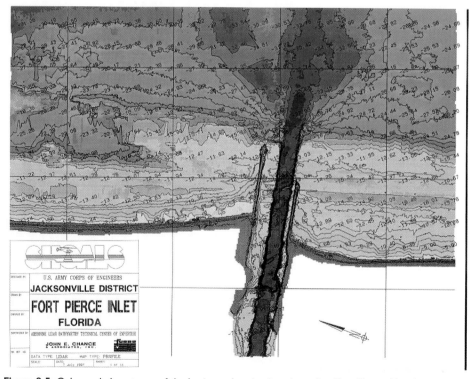

Figure 8.5 Color-coded contours of the Jetties and navigation channel at Fort Pierce, Florida.

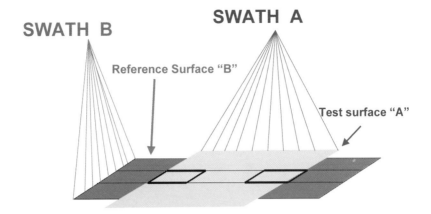

Comparison between two data set models:
- **Center beam portion of "B" assumed fixed Reference Surface**
- **Outer beam array portion of surface "A" tested**

Figure 9.16 System test using comparisons between surfaces.

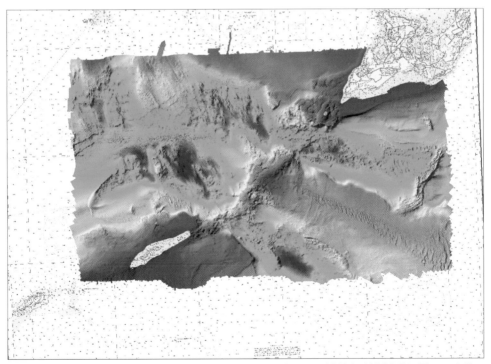

Figure 9.17 Digital Terrain Model on chart of Eastern Long Island Sound in 2003 by NOAA Ship Thomas Jefferson.

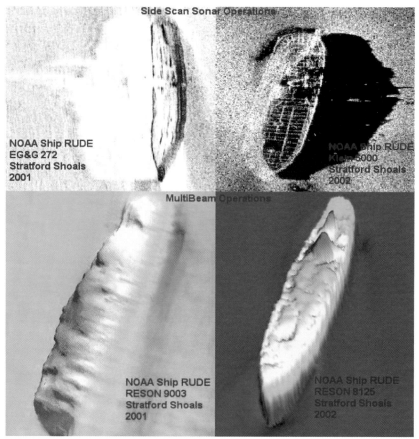

Figure 9.18 Examples of unfocused and focused.

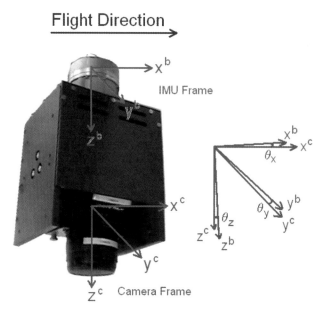

Figure 10.21 Boresight between camera and IMU frame of references.

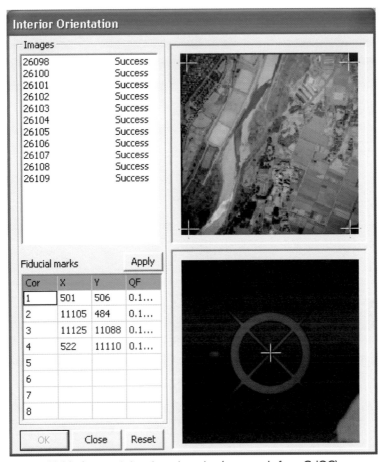

Figure 10.23 Automatic interior orientation (an example from CalQC).

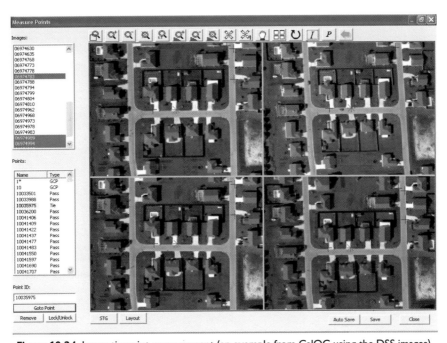

Figure 10.24 Image tie point measurement (an example from CalQC using the DSS images).

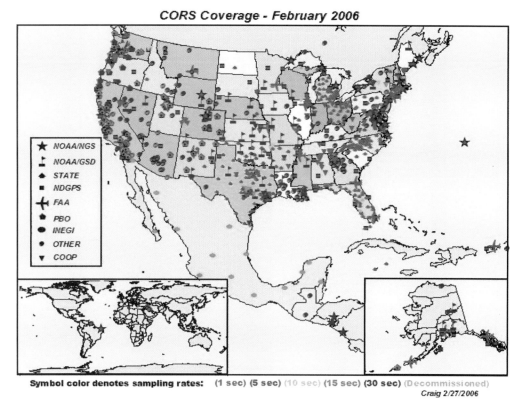

Figure 10.26 The U.S. CORS (courtesy of NOAA-NGS).

Figure 10.28 Greater Los Angeles continental shelf DEM generated with a multibeam sonar (courtesy U.S. Geological Survey).

DFIRM Components

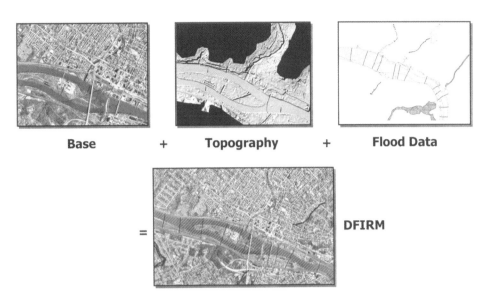

Figure 11.2 Components of a Digital Flood Insurance Rate Map (DFIRM). Images courtesy of FEMA.

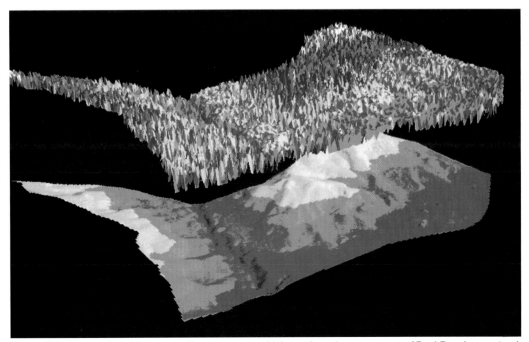

Figure 11.3 Bare-earth and first return (forest canopy top) lidar surfaces. Image courtesy of EarthData International.

Figure 11.4 The National Map prototype. Image courtesy of USGS.

Figure 11.5 Extraction of a Mean High Water (MHW) tidal datum from a lidar derived DEM on Mullet Key, Florida. Image courtesy of NOAA.

Figure 11.7 NOAA 2004 lidar draped over an aerial orthophoto showing the regulatory D1-D2 boundary, existing highest annual tide position (which defines the limits of a coastal wetland), and projected highest annual tide position after 2-ft of sea level rise. The transect A-A' shows topography across the site in Figure 11.8. Image courtesy of Maine Geological Survey.

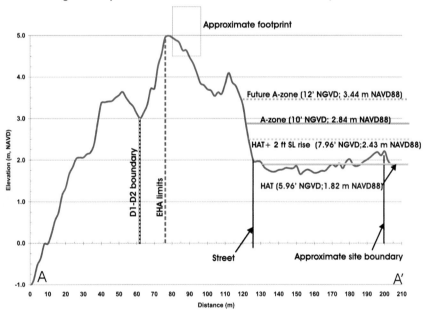

Figure 11.8 Topography along the transect A-A' shown in Figure 11.7 in reference to the subject property and structure, D1-D2 boundary, and FIRM elevations. The EHA boundary was located landward of the D1-D2 boundary because historic erosion on the order of -1 foot/year could erode the frontal dune, and short-term erosion could breach the dune crest. At the same time, a 2-ft rise in sea level would raise the existing A-zone and highest annual tide elevations on the subject property. The recommended developable envelope is shown. Topographic data from NOAA lidar (2004). Image courtesy of Maine Geological Survey.

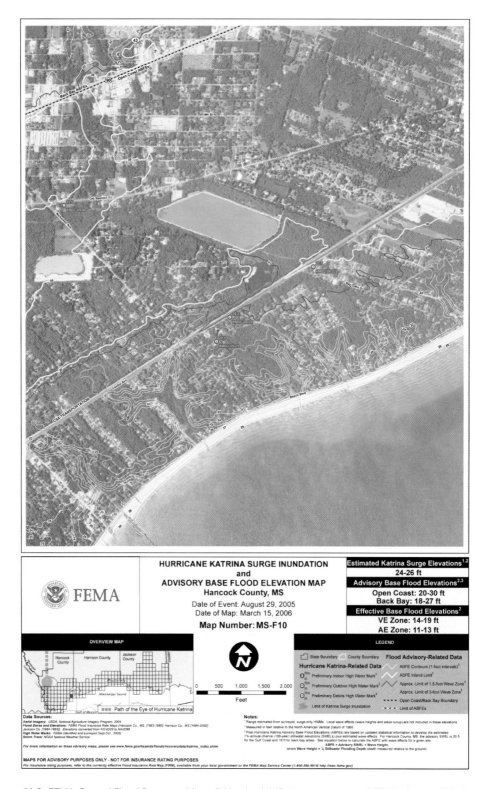

Figure 11.9 FEMA Coastal Flood Recovery Map of Waveland, MS. Image courtesy of FEMA, State of Mississippi, and NOAA.

Figure 11.10 Airspace obstruction model. Image courtesy of EarthData International.

Figure 11.11 Topographic lidar collected by NOAA for utilization in detecting airborne obstructions. Image courtesy of NOAA.

Figure 11.13 Integration of an orthophoto, nautical chart, and multibeam data from Sydney Harbor, Australia. Copyright © 2000 IEEE.

Figure 11.14 Underwater DEM of San Francisco Bay combined with a USGS DEM of surrounding land areas. Copyright © 2000 IEEE.

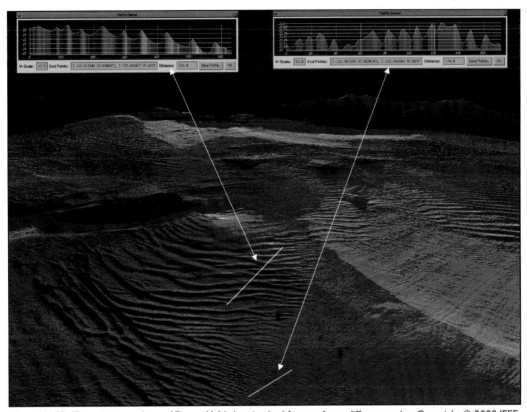

Figure 11.15 Zoom in to a subset of Figure 11.14 showing bed forms of two different scales. Copyright © 2000 IEEE.

Figure 11.16 Color-coded DEM rendering of large iceberg scours off Atlantic City, N.J. Copyright © 2000 IEEE.

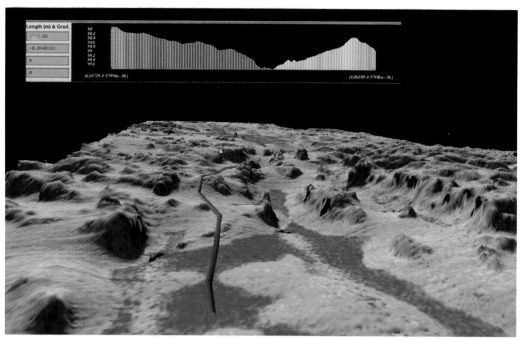

Figure 11.17 Acoustic backscatter (ABS) draped on DEM rendering of multibeam bathymetry. Data courtesy of Mobil Oil Co. Copyright © 2000 IEEE.

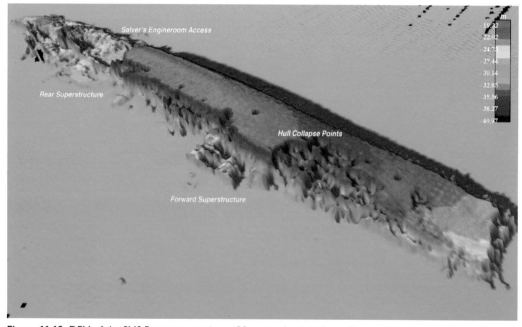

Figure 11.18 DEM of the SMS Brummer, resting at 30-meter depth in Scapa Flow. Image courtesy of the Center for Coastal and Ocean Mapping, University of New Hampshire.

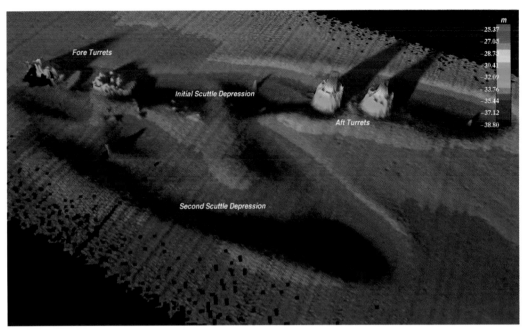

Figure 11.19 DEM of the Scapa Flow scuttle site of the SMS Bayern. Image courtesy of the Center for Coastal and Ocean Mapping, University of New Hampshire.

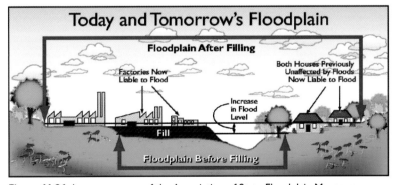

Figure 11.21 Image courtesy of the Association of State Floodplain Managers (ASFPM). If large areas of the floodplain are filled, then there will be an increase in the land area needed to store flood waters. This means other homes or businesses may be impacted.

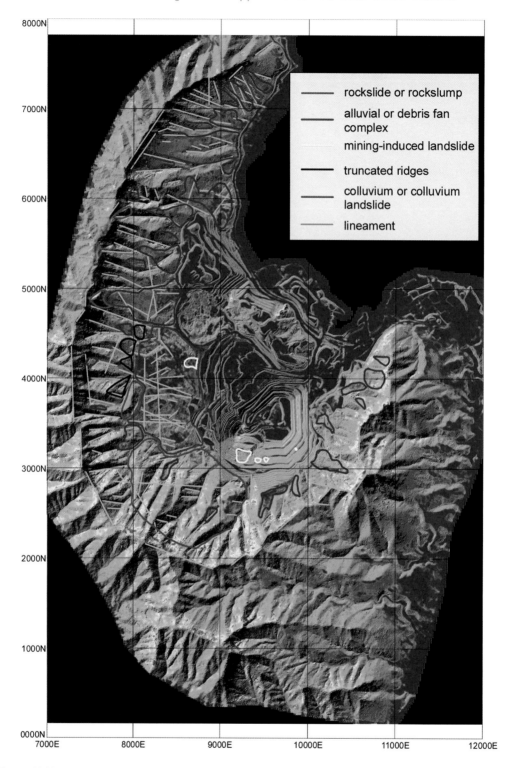

Figure 11.22 Terrain hazard and slope angle maps draped over a shaded relief image of the Louise caldera, Lihir Island, Papua New Guinea. The oval-shaped volcanic caldera collapsed catastrophically about 200,000 years ago and now contains a significant gold deposit. The shaded relief and slope angle maps were based on a 2 m lidar DEM produced for landslide hazard mapping under dense jungle cover surrounding the open pit mine in the center of the caldera. Image courtesy of William C. Haneberg.

Figure 11.23 Varying grid-cell footprints superimposed on typical Mancos Shale terrain. Image courtesy of USGS.

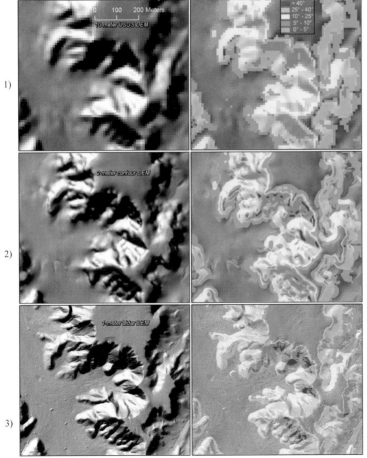

Figure 11.24 Effect of DEM horizontal resolution on the derivation of hillslope categories. 1a and 1b) 10-meter USGS DEM and associated slope categories. 2a and 2b) 2-meter DEM made from USGS 1:24,000-scale contours and associated slope categories. 3a and 3b) 1-meter bare-earth lidar DEM and associated slope categories. Images courtesy of USGS.

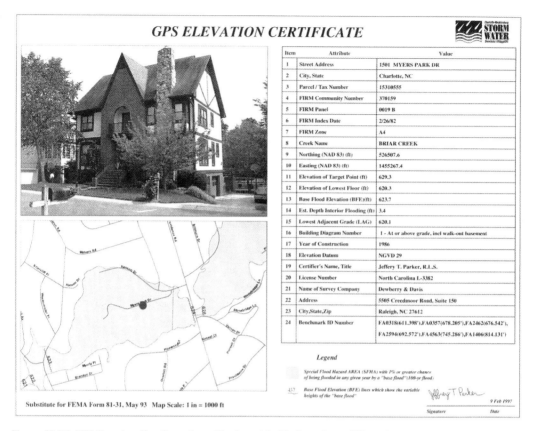

Figure 11.25 GPS Elevation Certificate from Charlotte Mecklenburg Storm Water Services; certificate prepared by Dewberry.

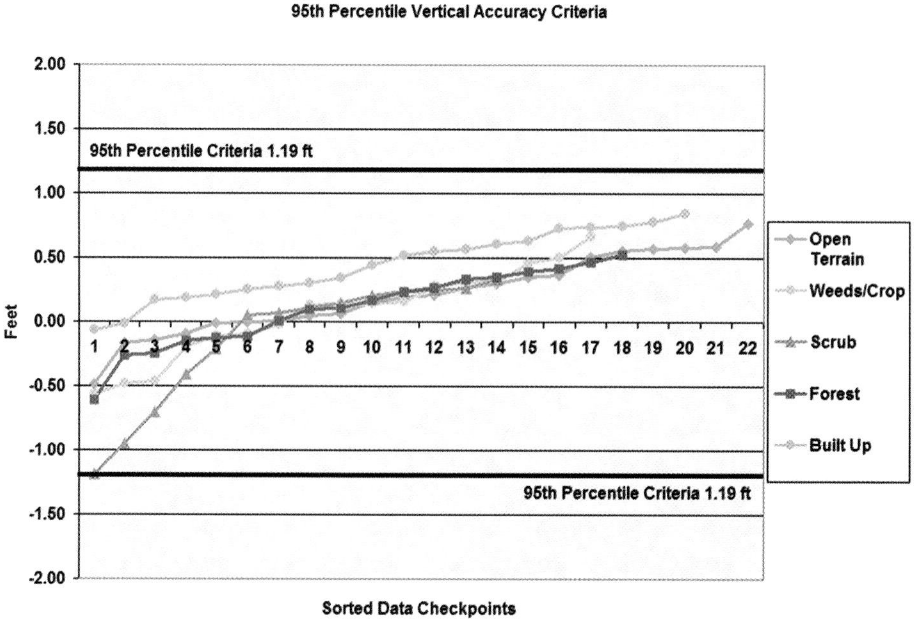

95th Percentile Vertical Accuracy Criteria

Figure 12.3 Error Distribution by Land Cover. Courtesy of Dewberry.

Number of Records per Tile

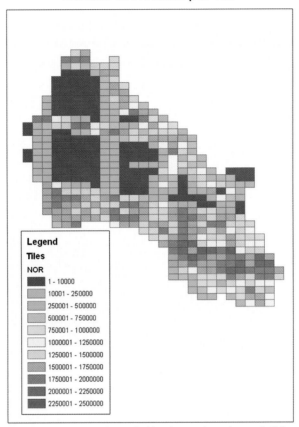

Legend
Tiles
NOR

	1 - 10000
	10001 - 250000
	250001 - 500000
	500001 - 750000
	750001 - 1000000
	1000001 - 1250000
	1250001 - 1500000
	1500001 - 1750000
	1750001 - 2000000
	2000001 - 2250000
	2250001 - 2500000

Figure 12.5 Illustrates a county tile scheme color coded by the number of records (lidar points) per tile. Areas of low records could potentially indicate issues.

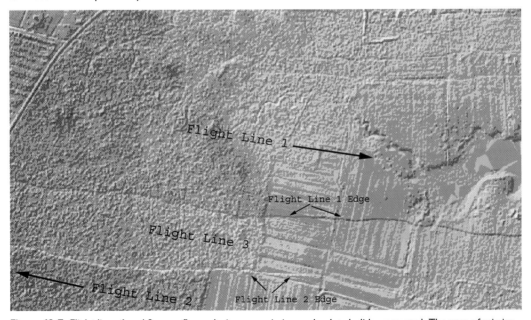

Figure 12.7 Flight lines 1 and 2 were flown during one mission and a data holiday occurred. The area of missing data (Flight Line 3) was then re-flown on a second mission, processed, and integrated into the main DTM. Cleary an elevation bias can be seen between the two datasets.

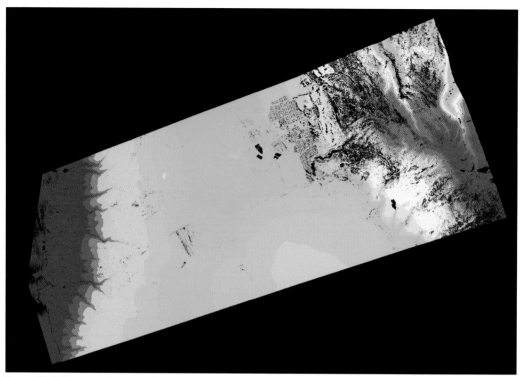

Figure 12.8 Project-wide point cloud data of over 85 million bare-earth ground points. Some void areas, shown in black in the interior of the project area, are due to water bodies, classification of vegetation and man-made objects, as well as one data holiday on the far right side of the image.

Figure 12.9 Combined DEM and shaded relief classified by density. Areas of bright red indicate few to no points.

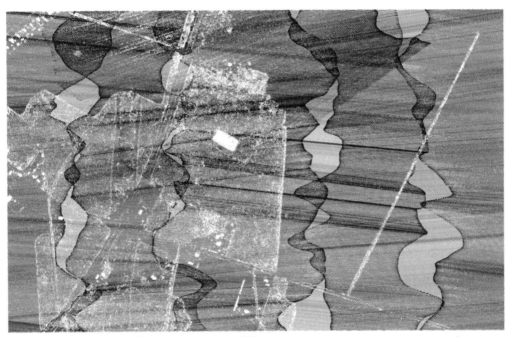

Figure 12.10 Illustrates a tile based on the number of lidar points per pixel. It is interesting to note the areas in the lighter shade of blue that exhibit only one pass of the lidar with no overlap, and also the concentration of data points at the end of the scan lines in the darkest blue. This dataset was acquired on a very windy day.

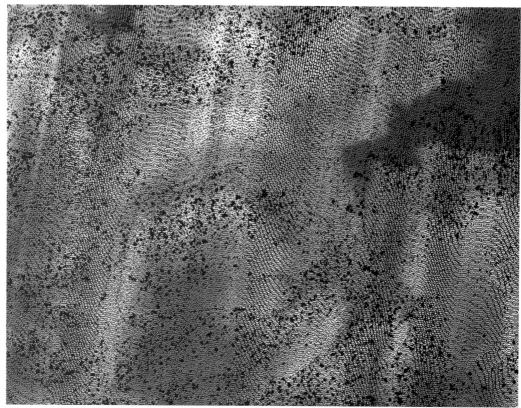

Figure 12.11 2-D view of vector lidar points color coded by elevation.

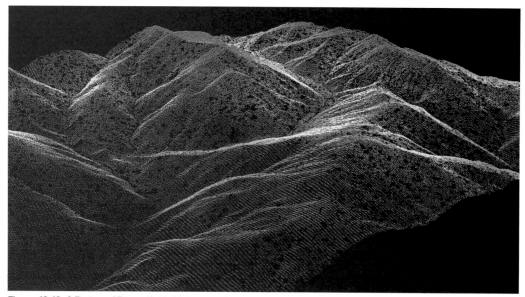

Figure 12.12 3-D view of Figure 12.11. High points (spikes) on this DTM are not visible.

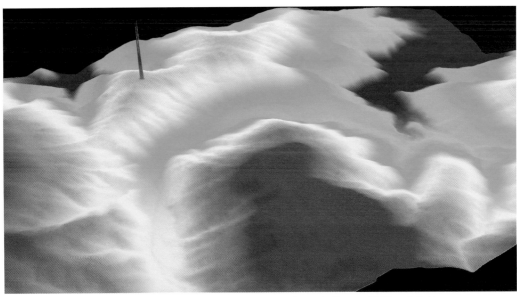

Figure 12.13 The hybrid vector/raster model of the same data shown in Figures 12.11 and 12.12.

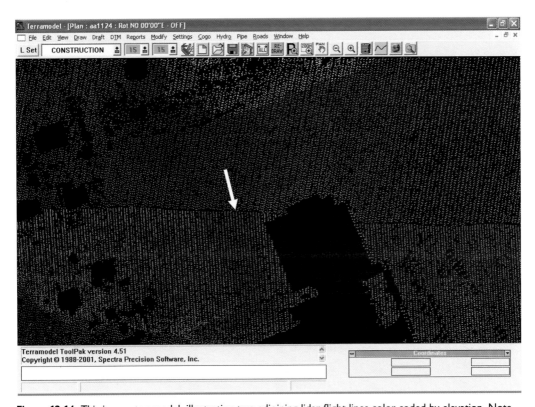

Figure 12.14 This is a vector model, illustrating two adjoining lidar flight lines color coded by elevation. Note the black east west gap of data between the two flight lines (see white arrow). This is a result of one flight line being higher than the other and the vegetation classification process identifying the points at the edge of one line and classifying them as non-ground.

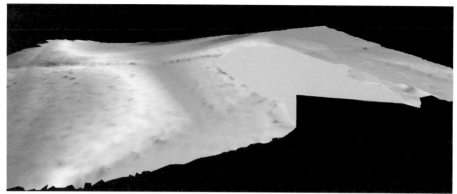

Figure 12.15 Because this is a 3-D vector rendered TIN, it can be oriented to provide a 3-D perspective of Figure 12.14. The elevation offset between the two flight lines is now easily identifiable.

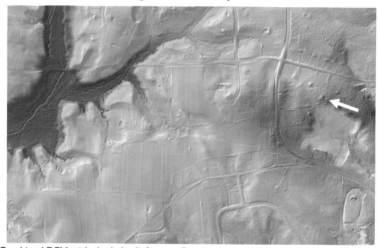

Figure 12.18 Combined DEM with shaded relief image. By using color to illustrate elevation, and transparency to feature the shaded relief, anomalies in the data can be easily identified. This dataset not only contains a scan line issue but it also may contain a spurious sink (elevations in blue, see white arrow) in the north east corner of the image where the elevation is considerable lower than the surrounding terrain including the stream channel below it.

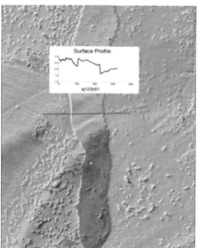
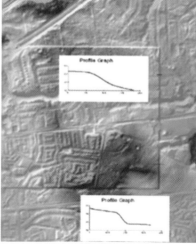

Figure 12.19 Examples where a DEM is combined with a shaded relief image. The figure on the left illustrates a scan line with high elevations that was merged with adjacent scan lines which had the correct elevations. This tile also was initially classified as bare-earth terrain but it is clear that vegetation still exists within this tile. The figure on the right illustrates a processing error by the vendor where an antenna offset was not applied when reducing the data.

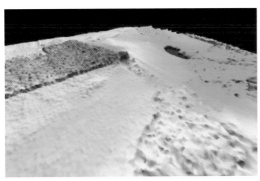 

Figure 12.20 The DEM/ shaded relief image clearly shows a crop field that was misclassified due to poor lidar penetration. The classification process also classified most of the forest correctly (noisy area to the right) but remnants of the forest is still evident on the SE corner of the crop field. The image on the right is a ground truth photograph of the forest area that illustrates the roughness of the forest floor as indicated by the DEM and proving that the "noise" is real and should be retained in the DEM.

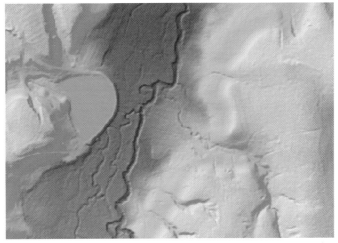

Figure 12.21 Good example of the classification process that maintains a balance between the classification of bare-earth and man-made features.

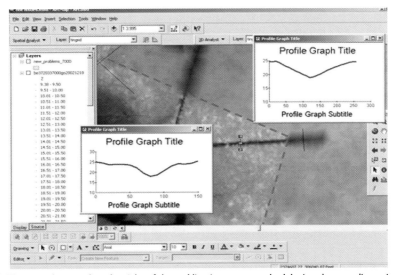

Figure 12.22 The area above and to the right of the red line is over-smoothed, losing the true dimensions of the man-made drainage canal that has the same actual dimensions on both sides of the red line.

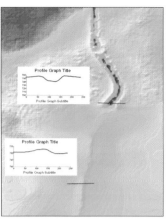

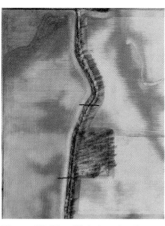

Figure 12.23a Areas A and B show two levels of processing from photogrammetric automated image correlation.

Figure 12.23b Zoomed in with profiles. While more noisy, Area A preserves the narrow drainage canal; Area B appears like a levee.

Figure 12.23c Digital orthophoto of the same area shows the drainage canal has same dimensions in both areas.

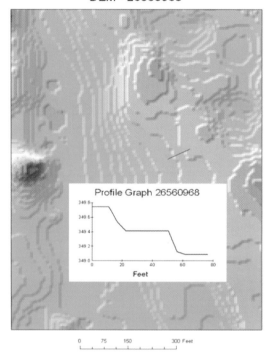

Figure 13.1 Elevations appear as plateaus when too few decimal places are used, as is common with DTMs used for rectification of digital orthophotos.

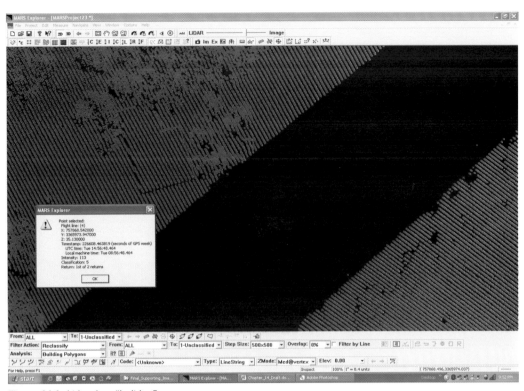

Figure 14.1 Lidar data "holiday."

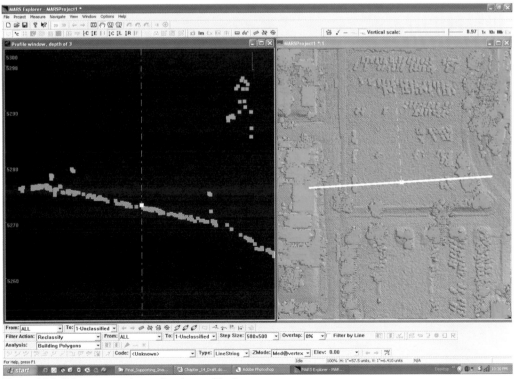

Figure 14.2 Lidar cross-section and orthographic view.

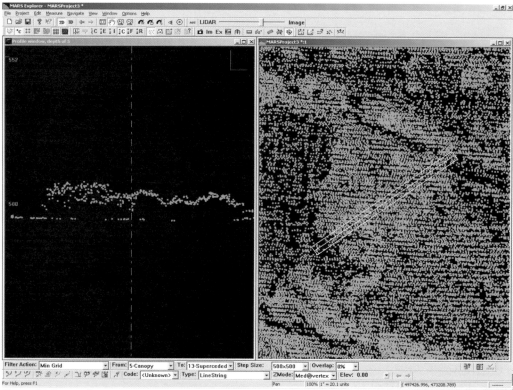

Figure 14.4a Insufficient canopy penetration.

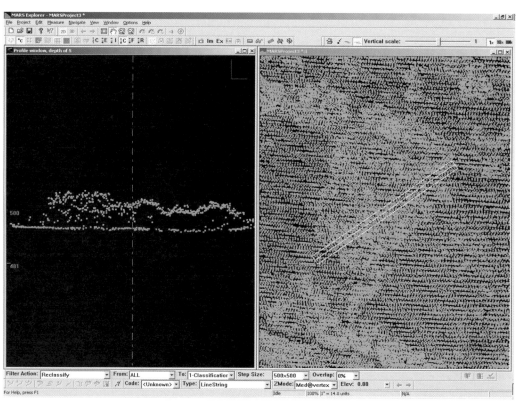

Figure 14.4b Sufficient canopy penetration.

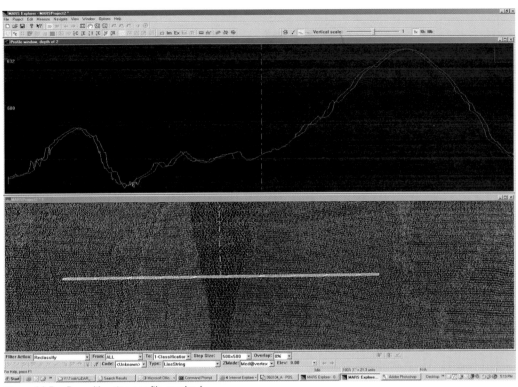

Figure14.5a Pre-calibration profile method.

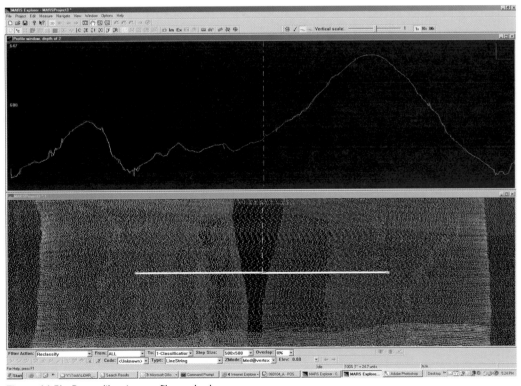

Figure 14.5b Post-calibration profile method.

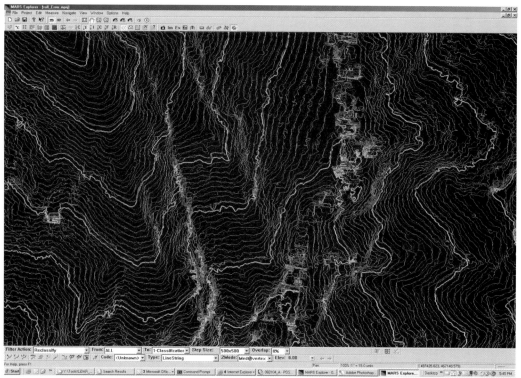

Figures 14.6a Pre-calibrated contour method.

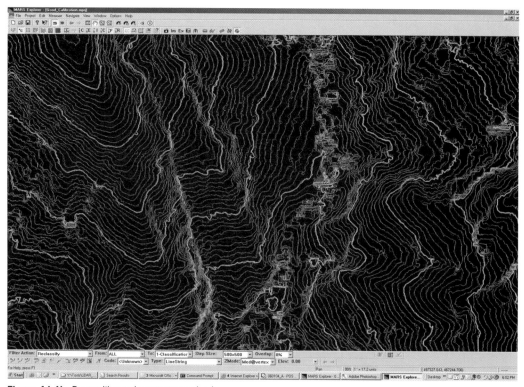

Figure 14.6b Post-calibrated contour method.

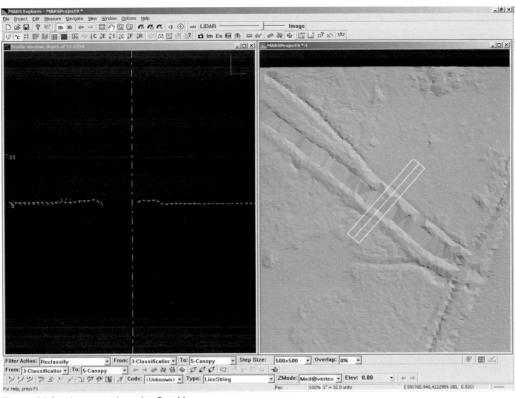

Figure 14.8a Automated results: Road berm.

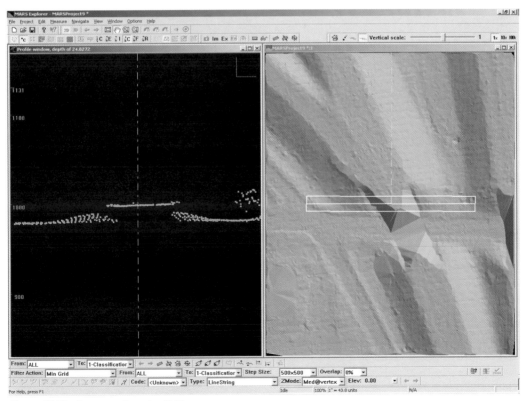

Figure 14.8b Automated results: Bridge.

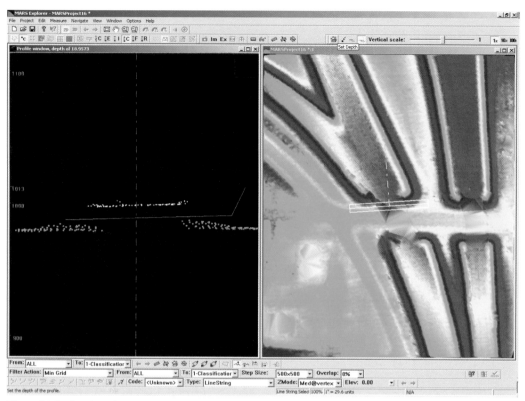

Figure 14.9a Re-class above line.

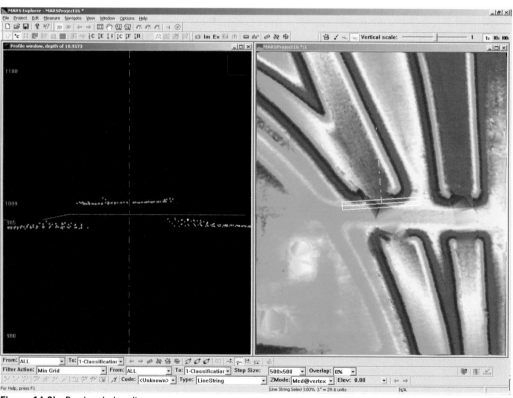

Figure 14.9b Re-class below line.

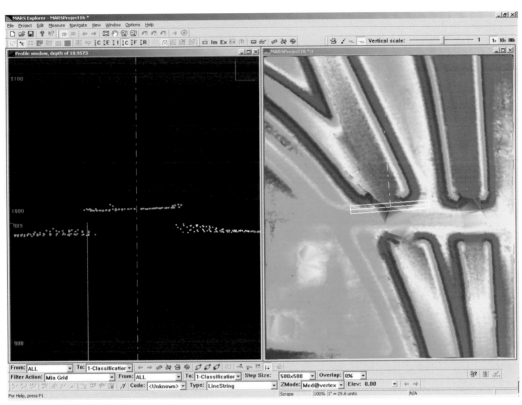

Figure 14.9c Re-class below vertical broom.

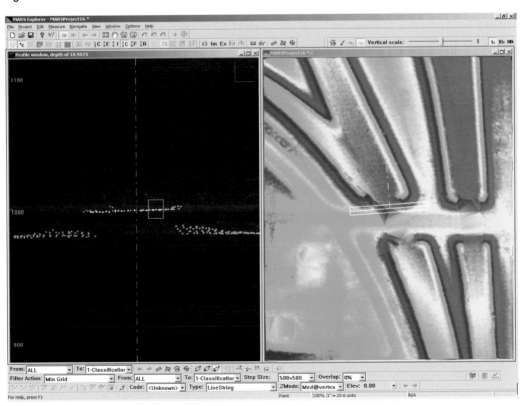

Figure 14.9d Re-class paintbrush.

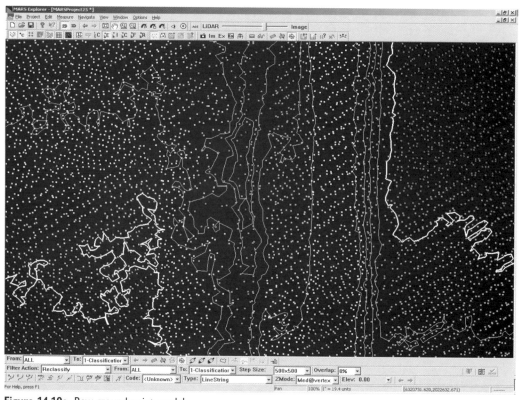

Figure 14.10a Raw ground point model.

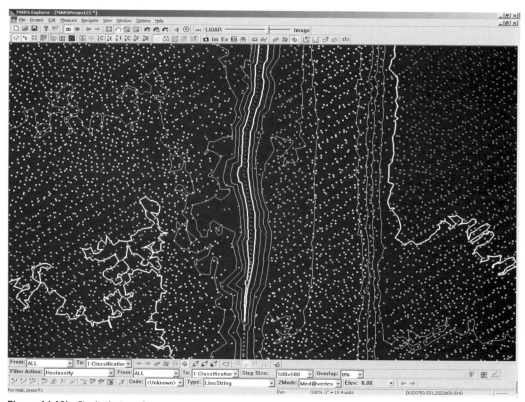

Figure 14.10b Single drain enforcement.

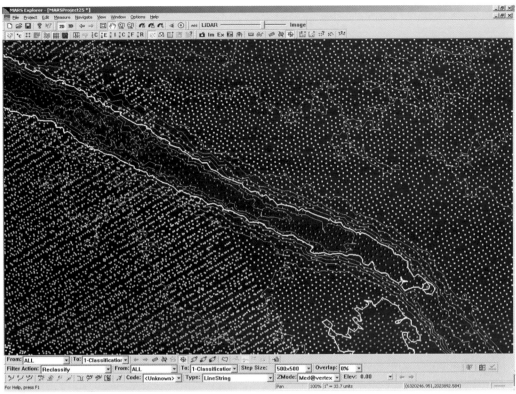

Figure 14.11a Pre-hydro-enforced ground model.

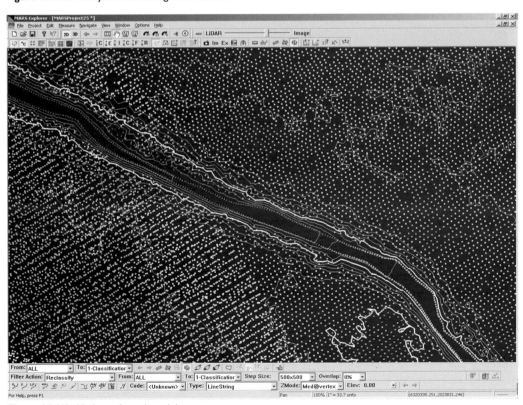

Figure 14.11b Hydro-enforced model.

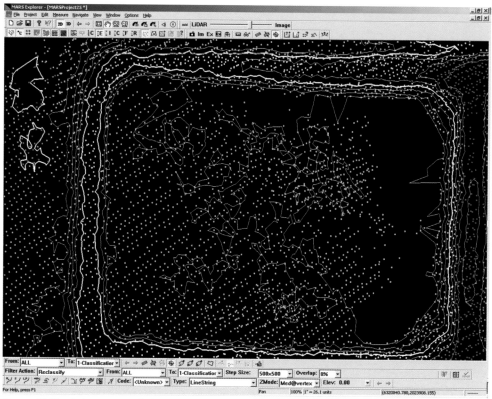

Figure 14.12a Lake pre-compilation.

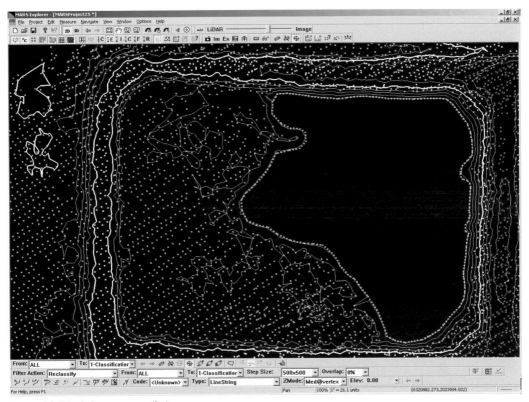

Figure 14.12b Lake post-compilation.

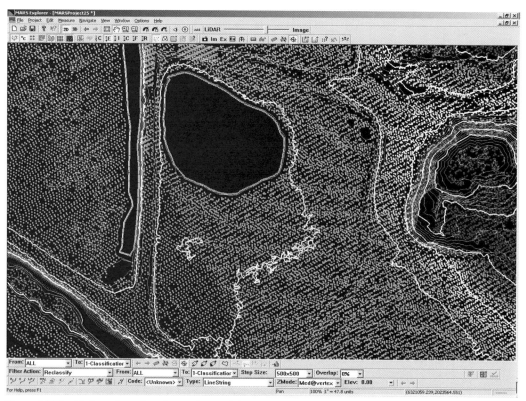

Figure 14.13a Hydro-enforced random point model.

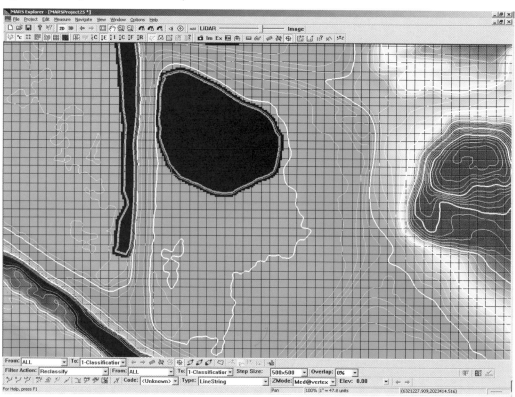

Figure 14.13b Hydro-enforced grid point model.

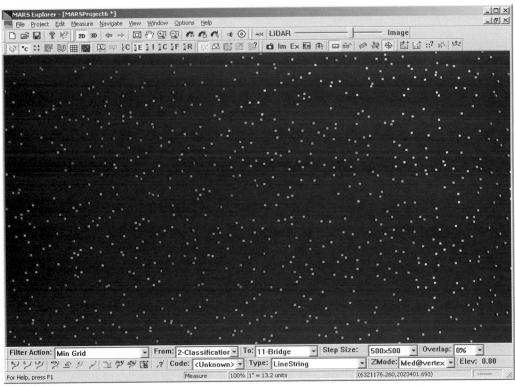

Figure 14.13c Closer Look at the random key point spacing (Average 6 ft spacing).

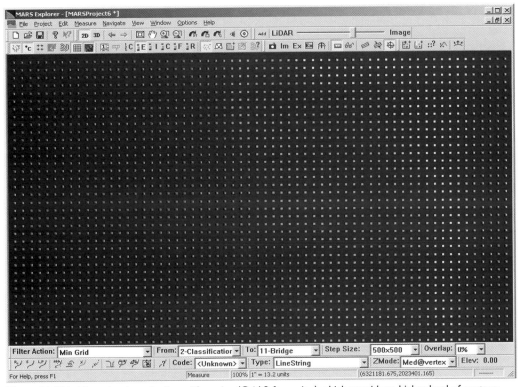

Figure 14.13d Closer Look at the 1m grid spacing (Grid 2 ft spacing) which provides a higher level of contour accuracy based on sampling theory (Nyquist).

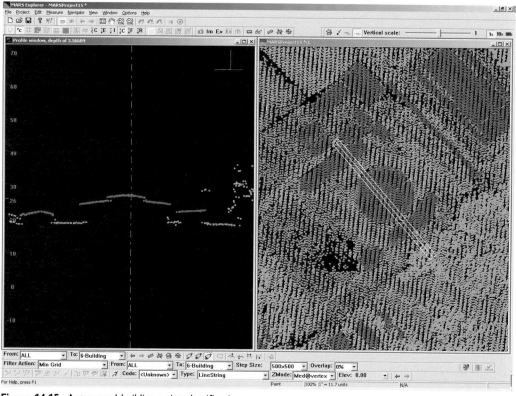

Figure 14.15 Automated building point classification.

Figure 14.17 Lidar raw data point cloud.

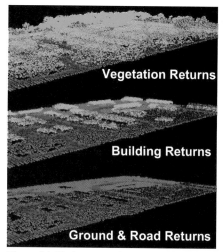

Figure 14.18 Automated extraction of vegetation and planimetric features.

Page references in *italic type* refer to figures or tables.

Index

A

3-D surface modeling. *See* three-dimensional surface modeling

ABGPS. *See* Global Positioning System (GPS), airborne

accuracy, 65, 535
    absolute, 68, 482, 535
    boresight calibration, 376, 480, 538
    error adjustment, 482
    extended GPS baselines, 480
    factors in, 480
    geodetic control survey standards, 66–68, *66, 67*
    geoid height corrections, 464
    geometric relative positioning standards, 66–68, *67*
    GPS lever arms, 480
    height error maps, 191, *191*
    of lidar data, 219, 480–482, *481, 483, 623, 624*
    local, 67, 68, 535
    network, 67, 68, 535
    order/class codes for GPS ellipsoid height differences, 66, *67*
    precision vs., 65–66
    random errors, 430
    relative, 68, 535
    scanner acceleration, 480
    of sensors, 490
    signal-to-noise ratio, 479, 480, 560
    systematic errors, 430
    test reports, 75, 460–461
    See also errors; horizontal accuracy; interpolation accuracy; vertical accuracy

accuracy standards
    for hydrographic surveys, 260
    Intermap DTM elevations, *170*
    for large-scale maps, 3, 68, 71–72, 457, 458
    for sonar, 322
    for three-dimensional surveys, 66, *67*
    for vertical control surveys, 66–68, *66*
    See also mapping standards; *specific standards by name*

acoustic waves, 321, 322–323, 561

acronyms, 523–534

aerial photography, 456
    boresight calibration, 377, *378, 379,* 538, *598, 599*
    direct georeferencing and, 374–376, *374, 375*

aerial surveys, specifications, 70–71

AeroSensing GmbH, 168

aerotriangulation, 124–127, 536

AeS-1 IFSAR system (now TopoSAR), 168, *169,* 171, *584*

affine transformations, 188

agriculture, precision farming, 418–419

airborne bathymetric lidar, sample dataset, 505–506, *505*

airborne digital systems, 121–122, *121, 122, 576*
    calibration, 135

airborne direct georeferencing systems. *See* direct georeferencing systems

Airborne I Corporation, laser scanning sample dataset, 510–511, *510*

airborne IFSAR, shoreline mapping, 290

airborne laser scanning, 200, 201, 204, 211
    accelerometers, 212
    flight altitude, 211
    GPS in, 211
    inertial measurement technology in, 211–212
    weather conditions and, 211
    See also laser-based remote sensing systems; laser scanning techniques

airborne lidar bathymetry, 204, 253, 342
    accuracy, horizontal, 267–268
    accuracy, vertical, 266–267
    added products for, 305–306
    advantages, 257
    aircraft positioning, 293–295
    air/water interface, 260
    applications, 255–257, 284–286, 290–291
    beam scattering in water, 262, *263, 595*
    bottom reflectivity and, 305
    bottom return, 261–262, *261*
    calibration procedures, 291–293
    CHARTS, 275, 307, 308
    for coastal mapping, 256
    comparison with similar technologies, 284–291
    costs, 253, 279, 281–283, *283*
    coverage rate, 265–266
    data post-processing, 297–300
    data visualization and spatial editing, 299
    deliverables, 299–300
    development, driving factors in, 302
    digital imagery with, 307
    drawbacks, 260
    EAARL, 259, 275–277
    future technology, 301–308
    geodetic datum adjustments, 262
    GPS use in positioning aircraft, 293–295
    green return waveforms, 261–262, *261*
    ground-based processing, 304–305
    Hawk Eye systems, 258, 259, 277–278, 307
    history, 256, 258–259, 277–278
    hyperspectral scanners with, 307–308
    infrared beams, 261, 262

Page references in *italic type* refer to figures or tables.

Index

Page references in *italic type* refer to figures or tables.

Index

Page references in *italic type* refer to figures or tables.

Index

Page references in *italic type* refer to figures or tables.

Index

Page references in *italic type* refer to figures or tables.

Index

Page references in *italic type* refer to figures or tables.

Index

Page references in *italic type* refer to figures or tables.

Index

Page references in *italic type* refer to figures or tables.

Index

Page references in *italic type* refer to figures or tables.

Index

Page references in *italic type* refer to figures or tables.

Index